BUSINESS ENVIRONMENT

Business Environment

[For B.Com./M.Com., and other Management Courses of All Universities]

By

Ved Prakash

ANMOL PUBLICATIONS PVT. LTD.

NEW DELHI - 110 002 (INDIA)

ANMOL PUBLICATIONS PVT. LTD.
4374/4B, Ansari Road, Daryaganj
New Delhi - 110 002
Ph.: 23261597, 23278000
Visit us at: www.anmolpublications.com

Business Environment

First Published, 2005

ISBN 81-261-2186-6

PRINTED IN INDIA

Published by J.L. Kumar for Anmol Publications Pvt. Ltd., New Delhi - 110 002 and Printed at Mehra Offset Press, Delhi.

Contents

	Preface	*vii*
1.	Business Environment and Scanning	1
2.	Economic Systems and Business Environment	27
3.	Economic Reforms and Liberalisation	56
4.	Socio-Cultural Environment	102
5.	Political Environment	140
6.	Legal Environment in India	171
7.	Technology Environment in India	220
8.	India's Fiscal and Monetary Policies	241
9.	Industrial Growth and Policy	266
10.	Foreign Trade Policies	292
11.	Development Banking in India	328
12.	Exim Policy	346
13.	Business Theory	365
14.	Global E-Business	399
15.	Liberalisation and Foreign Investment	419
16.	Tariff and Non-Tariff	458
17.	Global Competitiveness	481
18.	Financial Integration	517
19.	Globalisation and Investment	562
20.	Globalisation with Social Responsibility	591
21.	Multinational Corporation and Foreign Collaboration	616
22.	International Economic Institutions	636

Preface

Business Environment as a paper is being taught at the graduate and post graduate level in B.Com., M.Com. and other Management courses syllabus in almost all the Indian Universities and Institutions. The various courses conducted by management institutions at the Central and State level too have been considered in respect of their syllabus, course contents and requirements. Thus the material presented here would be of interest as well as great use to the students of B.Com., M.Com. and other Management Courses. This book will provide complete knowledge of economic, socio-cultural, political, legal, technology, foreign trade policies, globalisation, financial integration, tariff and non-tariff and Industrial growth and policy of Business Environment.

The major topics dealt in this book are—Business Environment and Scanning; Economic Systems and Business Environment; Economic Reforms and Liberalisation; Socio-Cultural Environment; Political Environment; Legal Environment in India; Technology Environment in India; India's Fiscal and Monetary Policies; Industrial Growth and Policy; Foreign Trade Policies; Development Banking in India; Exim Policy; Business Theory; Global E-Business; Liberalisation and Foreign Investment; Tariff and Non-Tariff; Global Competitiveness; Financial Integration; Globalisation and Investment; Globalisation with Social Responsibility; Multinational Corporation and Foreign Collaboration; International Economic Institutions.

Ved Prakash

1

Business Environment and Scanning

BUSINESS ENVIRONMENT

Business is an economic act which is carried out by an ogrnanisation to achieve some targets related to production, profit, diversification, technological upgradation, expansion etc. Each bussiness requires some kinds of resources for the fulfilment of the targets. The fulfilment of targets of a business depends not only on its resources but also on the business environment. Environment by definition is something external to an individual or an organisation and it is beyond the control of an individual or an organisation. Therefore, in strict sense, Business environment refers to all external factors which have a direct or indirect bearing on the activities of business. In other words, business environments may be defined as the set of external factors such as the economic factors, socio-cultural factors, government and legal factors, demographic factors, geophysical factors, which are uncontrolable in nature and affects the business decisions of a firm or company.

Business environment may be classified on different criteria, such as time, space, forces and and factors. Based on time, we may talk of post, present and future environment of business. Based on the relevance of economc or non-economic factors, we may specify economic and non-economic environment of business. Similarly business environment may be classified as internal environment and external environment. In the opinion of experts, environment of business can be sub-divided into macro environment and macro environment.

MEANING OF BUSINESS

Generally Business refers to those activities which are related to the buying and selling of goods. Modern business covers activities related to both production and distribution. A firm or company normally carries a number of activities connected with production, trade, transport, finance, banking, insurance, advertising and certain other activities related to industry and commerce. All these activities are normally motivated by profits. In case, any of these activities is carried out by some organisation for purpose other than profit seeking, it cannot be justifiably considered as business. Further, business includes only those efforts on the part of manufactures, traders and other agencies which comply with legal requirements. This implies that any activity connected with production, trading, financing, advertising etc. must be excluded from business if it is violative of the laws of the country. Thus any activity carried out by an organisation for seeking profit can be called business if it does not violate the laws of the country.

Over the years business has undergone radical changes and thus modern business is quite different in comparison to yesteryears business. The main characteristics of the modern business are the following:

1. The size of modern business is very large in most of the developed countries. In India, its size is low. Indian companies in terms of market capitalisation, sales etc. are not impressive in comparison to developed countries. For example, there is only one Indian company in world's 500 largest companies *i.e.* Indian Oil, a public sector undertaking.
2. Another feature of modern business is its oligopolistic nature. In this type of market, any change in the price, sales or in the quality of the product by one firm evoke retaliation from other firms in the same line of business. In oligopolistic markets, usually the same firm produces different qualities to sell them to different groups at different prices.

3. Now a days modern business firms do not confine their production activities to a single commodity. These firms go for diversification of the production.
4. Till recently, even big companies had confined their business to domestic markets. Now companies which matter have expanded their revenue and assets base across countries and engage in cross-border flow of capital, goods and know-how.
5. In modern business life, modern technology and its upgradation play an important role. If business houses ignore technological changes for whatever reasons, they may lose in competitiveness and be pushed out of the market.
6. 'Change' is the basic mantra of modern business. The business follows the strategy of making changes in product quality, design or packaging speedily so that the demand for the product can be increased over a period of time.
7. Since the beginning of1991-92, the role of the government has dimnished with the dismantling controls over modern business in India. It is widely accepted that controls affects modern business adversely.

Internal Environment. Internal environment may be defined as the set of value system, goals and objectives, management structure, relationship among the various constituents, physical assets, technological capabilities and human, financial and marketing resources.

Business is normally undertaken for profit maximisation. In the traditional theory of business firm, profit maximisation has been assumed to be the sole objective of the firm. Since short run profit maximisation does not necessarily result in profit maximisation in the long run, some experts assert that rational firms attempt to maximise longrun profit. Managerial theories of firm, however state that sales revenue maximisation and the balanced rate of growth maximisation rather than profit maximisation are the real goals of modern business firms. In the behavioural theory of the firm, it is asserted that a firm seek to satisfied, that is to affair a satisfactory overall performance in terms of set aspiration goals, rather than maximise profits, production, sales or some other magnitude.

These divergent approaches with regard to goals of a modern firm are based on empirical evidences. From the one things that clearly averages is that in modern times all firms do not pursue a single goal. There are often major differences in the goals and objectives of the various firms which, in turn leads to differences in their overall interval environment and also in priorities, policies and direction of development.

Apart from differences in goals and objectives, other factors like availability of physical resources, management of the firm, production technology, R & D work, distribution logistics also influence the companys internal environment. For example the nature of management also influence the internal environment significantly. A corporate enterprise may be professionally managed or family controlled. On its board of Directors there may be dynamic entrepreneurs capable of taking quick decisions or the Board of Directors may be dominated by persons with conservative or bureaucratic outlook. Nominess of financial institutions having large holdings in companies may or may not have decisive say in decision making. Thus this factor also influence the company's internal environment.

External Environment. External environment of business consists of institutions, organisations and forces operating outside the company. In other words, any institution or institutions and forces individually or collectively influence the company, is called external environment. The external environment of business may be classified into micro environment and macro environment. The micro environment refers to such players whose decisions and actions have a direct bearing on the company. Since modern business has two aspects namely production and selling of goods, therefore micro environment affects both aspects of the business. Workers unions, customers, market intermediaries, competitors and public influence production and or salling of goods, constitutes micro environment. Macro environment, on the other hand, comprise larger societal and physical forces which affect the company and also the players in the company's micro environment.

Micro Environment. The micro environment consists of the factors, having direct bearing on the performance of the company. It includes such players like suppliers, markeing intermediaries, competitors, customers and the public whose decisions and actions affect the working of the firm of company. These players are more intimately linked with the company than the macro factors. The micro factors need not necessarily affect all the firms in a particular industry in the same way. Some of the micro factors may be particular to a firm and may affect significantly than their micro factors.

Macro Environment. Macro environment of a company refers to all those economic and non-economic factors which exercise their influence on the business activity in general and thus determine opportunities that a company may have to promote its business. Macro environment can be classified into economic environment and non-economic environment. Since business in basically an economic activity, economic environment of business national and global is of strategic importance. In the economic environment of the country, country's economic system, macroeconomic scenario, phase of businesscycle through which the economy is passing, organisation of the financial system and economic policies of the government are most important elements.

Business is also get influenced non-economic environment. Political system, ideology of the government, legal framework, social system, cultural values, demographic factors, level of technological development and natural and physical environment of the country constitution non-economic environment of business. In fact, all these non-economic elements are of great relevance to present day business.

The role of macro environment which includes economic and non-economic environment both, from the point of view of the business may be both positive and negative. This implies that the larger forces in the company's environment do not always provide wider space for business operations. They often put restraints on the business activities of the firm.

Factors Influencing Micro Environment

From the point of view of a company's business operations micro environment has great relevance usually the factors of micro environment do not affect all the companies in an industry in the same way. Their decisions and actions *vis-a-vis* individual company differ in accordance with the size, capability and stateges of each company. For example, a competitor does not mind starting price on if the rival company is small but he will be reluctant to do so if the rival firm is large and capable of retaliating. Sometimes micro environment of the various firms in an industry is almost the same but their response may be different. The main factors constituting micro environment are the following.

Customers. A business exists only because of its customers. The major task of a business is to create and sustain customers. A company may have different categories of consumers. For example, the customers of tyre company may include of individual automobile owners, automobile manufactors, public sector transport undertakings and other transport operators.

Depending on a single customer is often too riscky because it may place the company in a poor bargaining position, apart from the risks of losing business consequent to the winding up of business by the customers or due to the customer's switching over to the competitors of the company. The choice of the customer segments should be made by considering a number of factors including the relative profitability, dependability, stability of demand, growth prospects and twe extent of the competition.

2. Suppliers. An important force in the micro environment of a company is the suppliers, *i.e.*, those who supply the inpus like raw materials and components to the company. The importance of reliable source of supply to the smooth functioning of the bsuiness is obvious. Uncertainty regarding the supply or other supply constraints often compel companies to maintain high inventories causing cost increases. It has been pointed out that factories in India maintain indigenous stocks of 3-4 months and imported stocks of 9 months as against an average of a few hours to two weeks in Japan.

It is very risky to depend on a single supplier because a strike, lock out or any other production problem with that supplier may seriously affect the company. Similarly, a change in the attitude or behaviour of the supplier may also affect the company. Hence, multiple sources of supply often help reduce such risk.

Because of the sensitivity of the supply, many companies give high importance to vendor development. Vertical integration, where feasible, helps to solve the supply problems.

3. Marketing Intermediaries. The immediate environment of a company may consist of a number of marketing intermediaries which are "firms that aid the company in promoting, selling and distribution its goods to final buyers".

Marketing intermediaries are vital links between the company and the final consumers. A dislocation or disturbance of this link, or a wrong choice of the link, may cost the company very heavily, retail chemists and druggists in India once decided to boycott products of a leading company on some issue such as poor retail margin. This move for collective boycott was, however, objected to by the MRTP Commission; but for this the company would, perhaps, have been in trouble.

The marketing intermediaries include middlemen such as agents and merchants who "help the company find customers or close sales with them", physical distribution firms which "assist the company in stocking and moving goods from their origin to their destination" such as warehouses and transportation firms; marketing service agencies which "assist the company in targeting and promoting its prodcuts to the right markets" such as advertising agencies, marketing research firms, media firms and consulting firms; and financial intermediaries which finance marketing activities and insure business risks.

4. Competitors. A firm's competitors include not only the other firms which market the same or similar products but also all those who compete for the discretionary income of the consumers. For example, the competition for a company's washing machine may come not only from other washing machines manufactures but also from cooking ranges, two-wheelers, refrigerators, stereo sets and so on and from firms offering savings and investment schemes like banks, Unit Trust of India, companies accepting public deposits or issuing shares or debentures etc. This competition among these products may be described as *desire competition* as the primary task here is to influence the basic desire of the consumer. Such desire competition is generally very high in countries characterised by limited disposable incomes and many unsatisfied desires.

If the consumer decides to spend his discretionary income on recreation (or recreation cum education) he will still be confronted with a number of alternatives to choose form like washing machine, stereo, two-in-one, three-in- one etc. The competition among such alternatives which satisfy a particular category of desire is called *generic competition.*

If the consumer decides to go in for a washing machine, the next question is which form of the washing machine - semi automatic or fully automatic etc. In other words, there is a *product form competition.* Finally the consumer encounters the *brand competition i.e.*, the competition between the different brands of the same product form.

An implication of these different demands is that a marketer should strive to create primary and selective demand for his products.

5. Public. "A public is any group that has an actual or potential interest in or impact on an organisation's ability to achieve its interests". Media public, citizens action publics and local publics are some examples. Growth of consumer publics is as important development affecting business.

Some companies are seriously affected by such publics. For example, one of the leading companies in India was frequently under attack by the media public, particularly by a leading daily which was allegedly bent on bringing down the share prices of the company by tranishing its image. Many companies are also affected by local publics. Environmental pollution is an isssue often taken up by a number of local publics.

It is wrong to think that all publics are threats to business. Some publics, are an opportunity for the business. For example, the media public may be used to disseminate useful information.

Factors Affecting Macro Environment

The macro environment consits of the larger societal forces that affect all the sectors in the Company's macro environment—namely, the demographic, economic, natural, technological, political and cultural forces. These environmental factors are beyond the control of a firm, its success will depend to a very large extent on its adaptability to the environment, *i.e.* its ability to properly design and adjust the internal variables to take advantage of the opportunities and to combat the threats in the environment.

From the point of view of analysis macro environment is broadly classified between economic and non-economic environment. There we shall analyse both economic and non-economic macro environment of business.

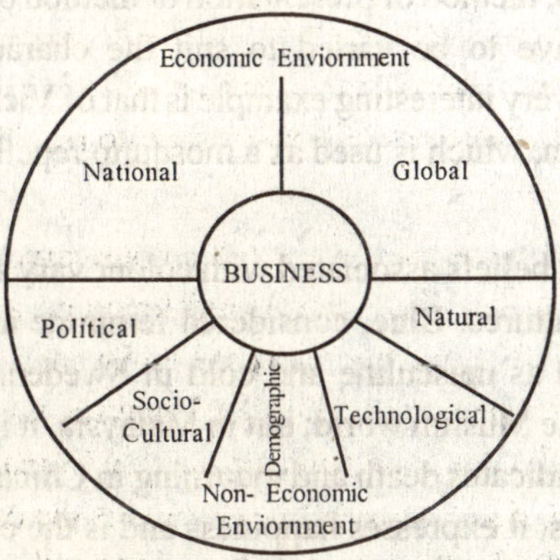

Fig. Macro Environment of Business

(A) Non-Economic Environment of Business. Business is an economic activity. It is nonetheless influenced by its non-economic environment. The non-economic environment of business can be broadly classified as socio-cultural, natural, demographic, physical and technological, political and government.

1. Socio-cultural Environment. The buying and consumption habits of the people, their language, beliefs and values, customs and traditions, tastes and preferences, education etc. are the constituents of socio-economic environment.

The socio-cultural fabric is an important environmental factor that should be analysed while formulating business strategies. The cost of ignoring the customs, traditions, taboos, tastes and preferences, etc., of a people could be very high.

For a business to be successful, its strategy should be the one that is appropriate in the socio-cultural environment. The marketing mix will have to be so designed as best to suit the environmental characteristics of the market. Nestle, a Swiss multinational company, today brews more than forty varieties of instant coffee different national tasts.

Even when people of different cultures use the same basic product, the mode of consumption, conditions of use, purpose of use or the perceptions of the product attributes may vary so much so that the product attributes, method of presentation or method of promoting the product may have to be varied to suit the characteristics of different markets. A very interesting example is that of Vicks Vaporub, the popular pain balm, which is used as a mosquito repellant in some of the tropical areas.

The values and beliefs associated with colour vary significantly between different cultures. Blue, considered feminine and warm in Holland, is regarded as masculine and cold in Sweden. Green is a favourite colour in the Muslim world; but in Malaysia, it is associated with illness. White indicates death and mourning in China and Korea; but in some countries, it expresses happiness and is the colour of the wedding dress of the bride. Red is a popular colour in the communist countries; but many African countries have a national distaste for red colour. There are also a number of demographic factors, such as the age and sex composition of population, family size, habitat, religion, etc., which influence the business. While dealing with the social environment, we must also consider the social environment of the business which encompasses its social responsibility and the alertness or vigilance of the consumers and of society at large.

2. Natural Environment. Geographical and ecological factors, such as natural resource endowments, weather and climate conditions, topographical factors, locational aspects in the global context, port facilities, etc., are all relevant to business.

Differences in geographical conditions between markets may sometimes call for changes in the marketing mix. Geographical and ecological factors also influence the location of certain industries. Climatic and weather conditions affect the location of certain industries like the cotton textile industry. Topographical factors may affect the demand pattern. For example, in hilly areas with a difficult terrain, jeeps may be in greater demand than cars.

3. Demographic Environment. Demographic factors like the size, growth rate, age composition, sex composition, etc. of the population, family size, economic stratification of the population, educational levels, language, caste, religion etc. are all factors which are relevant to business.

Demographic factors such as size of the population, population growth rate, age composition, life expectancy, family size, spatial dispersal, occupational status, employment pattern etc. affect the demand for goods and services. Markets with growing population and income are growth markets. But the decline in the birth rates in countries like the United States have affected the demand for baby products. *Johnsons and Johnson* have overcome this problem by repositioning their products like baby shampoo and baby soap, promoting them also to the adult segment, particularly to the females. A rapidly increasing population also indicates a growing demand for many products. The population growth rate, is an important environment factor which affects business. Cheap labour and a growing market have encouraged many multinational corporations to invest in developing countries.

The occupational and spatial mobilities of population have implications for business if labour is easily mobile between different occupations and regions, its supply will be relatively smooth, and this will affect the wage rate.

If labour is highly heterogeneous in respect of language, caste and religion, ethnicity, etc., personnel management is likely to become a more complex task. The heterogeneous population with its varied tastes, preferences, beliefs, temperaments, etc. gives rise to differing demand patterns and calls for different marketing strategies.

4. Physical and Technological Environment. Physical Factors, such as geographical factors, weather and climatic conditions may call for modification in the product, etc., to suit the environment because these environment factors are uncontrolable. For example, Esso adapted its gasoline formulations to suit the weather conditions prevailing in different markets.

Business prospects depend also on the availability of certain physical facilities. Some products, like many consumer durables, have certain use facility characteristics. The demand for refrigerators and other electrical appliances is affected by the extent of electrification and the reliability of power supply.

Technological developments may increase the demand for some existing products. For example, voltage stabilisers help increase the sale of electrical appliances in markets characterised by frequent voltage fluctuations in power supply. However, the introduction of T.*Vs.* Fridges etc. with in-built voltage stabiliser adversely affects the demand for voltage stabiliers.

The television has added a new dimension to product promotion. The advent of TV and VCP/VCR has, however, adversely affected the cinema theatres.

5. Political and Government Environment. Political and government environment has close relationship with the economic system and economic policy. For example, the communist countries had a centrally planned economic system. In most countries, apart from those laws that control investment and related matters, there are a number of laws that regulate the conduct of the business. These laws cover such matters as standards of product, packaging, promotion etc.

In many countries, with a view to protecting consumer interests, regulations have become stronger. Regulations to protect the purity of the environment and preserve the ecological balance have assumed great important in many countries.

Certain changes in government policies such as the industrial policy, fiscal policy, tariff policy etc. may have profound impact on business. Some policy developments create opportunities as well as threats, in other words, a development which brightens the prospects of some enterprises may pose a threat to some others. For example, the industrial policy liberalisations in India, particularly around the mid-eighties have opened up new opportunties and threats. They have provided a log of opportunties to a large number of enterprises to diversify and to make their product mix better. But they have also given rise to serious threat to many existing products by way of increased competition; many seller's markets have given way to buyer's markets. Even products which were seldom advertised have come to be promoted very heavily. This battle for the market have provided a splended opportunity for the advertising industry. Advertising billing have been increasing substantially.

Many countries today have laws to regulate competition in the public interest. Elimination of unfair competition and dilution of monopoly power are the important objectives of these regulations. In India, the monopolistic undertakings, dominant undertakings and large industrial houses are subject to a number of regulations which prevent the concentration of economic power to the common detriment. The MRTP Act also controls monopolistic, restrictive and unfair trade practices which are prejudicial to public interest. Such regulations brighten the prospects of small and new firms. They also increase the scope of some of existing firms to venture into new areas of business. The special privileges available to the small scale sector have also contributed to the phenomenal success of the Nirma.

(B) Economic Environment. Economic environment of business is of strategic importance. In economic environment global and national environments are included.

1. Global or International Environment. The global or international environment is very important from the point of view of certian categories of business. It is particularly important for industries directly depending on import competing industries. For example, a recession in foreign markets, or the adoption of protectionist policies by foreign nations, may create difficulties for industries depending on exports. On the other hand, a boom in the export market or a relaxation of the protectionist policies may help the export-oriented industries. A liberalisation of imports may help some industries which use imported items, but may adversely affect import-competing industries.

In has been observed that major international developments have their spread effects on domestic business. Oil price hikes have seriously affected a number of economies. These hikes have increased the cost of production and the prices of certain products, such as fertilisers, synthetic fibres, etc. The high oil price has led to an increase in the demand for automobile models that economise energy consumption, the demand for natural fibers increased because of the oil crisis. The oil crisis led to a reorientation of the Government of India's energy policy. Such developments affect the demand, consumption and investment pattern.

A good export market enables a firm to develop a more profitable product mix and to consolidate its position in the domestic market. Many companies now plan production capacities and investment taking into account also the foreign markets. Export marketing facilitates the attainment of optimum capacity utilisation; a company may be able to mitigate the effects of domestic recession by exporting. This will lead to adverse developments in foreign exchange recession by exporting. However, a company which depends on the export market to a considerable extent has also to face the impact of adverse developments in foreign markets.

Economic conditions, economic policies and the economic systems are the important external factors that constitute the national environment of business in a country.

2. National Environment. The economic conditions of a country—for example, the nature of the economy, the stage of development of the economy, economic resources, the level of income, the distribution of income and assets, etc.—are among the very important determinants of business strategies.

In countries where is investment and income are steadily and rapidly rising, business prospects are generally bright, and further investments are encouraged. There are a number of economists and businessmen who feel that the developed countries are no longer worthwhile propositions for investment because these economies have reached more or less saturation levels in certain respects.

In a development country, the low income may be the reason for the very low demand for a product. The sale of a product for which the demand is income-elastic naturally increases with an increase in income. But a firm is unable to increase the purchasing power of the people to generate a higher demand for its product. Hence, it may have to reduce the price of the product to increase the sales. The reduction in the cost of production may have to be effected to facilitate price reduction. It may even the necessary to invent or develop a new low-cost product to suit the low income market. Thus, **colgate** designed a simple, hand-driven, inexpensive ($ 10) washing machine for low-income buyers in less developed countries. Similarly, the National Cash Register Company took an innovative step backward by developing a crank-operated cash register that would sell at half the cost of a modern cash register and this was well received in a number of developing countries.

In developed economies, replacement demand accounts for a considerable part of the total demand for many consumer durables whereas the replacement demand is negligible in the developing economies.

The economic policy of the government, needless to say, has a very great impact on business, some types or categories of business are favourably affected by government policy, some adversely affected, while it is neutral in respect of others. For example, a restrictive import policy, or a policy of protecting the home industries, may greatly help the import-competing industries, while a liberalisation of the import policy may create difficulties for such industries. The monetary and fiscal policies, by the incentives and disincentives they offer and by their neutrality, also effect the business in different ways.

Similarly, an industry that falls within the priority sector in terms of the government policy may get a number of as incentives and other positive support from the government, whereas those industries which are regarded as inessential may have the odds against them.

In India, the government's concern about the concentration of economic power restricted the role of the large industrial houses and foreign concerns to the core sector, the heavy investment sector, the export sector and backward regions.

INTER-RELATIONSHIP BETWEEN ECONOMIC AND NON-ECONOMIC ENVIRONMENT

The economic environment of business exercise a strong influence on the non-economic environment of business. Similarly non-economic environment influences the economic environment significantly. The economic environment is thus both exogerous and endogenous, it is determined as well as determining. In other words economic environment and non-economic environment affect or interact each other. Let us consider a few specific intersections. These are:

1. **Sociological Environment and Economic Environment.** The sociological environment affects and gets affected by economic environment of business. The social attitude influences how many people get attracted to private business. In business gets a social sanction as a respectable profession, the occupational structure of a country will reflect a sizeable category of professional managers. On the other hand, if more and more of active labour force joint

professional management service, the social attitude towards business and its management also changes. As we know social movements largely determined the economic system. If the workers cultivate the attitude of confrontation rather than cooperation with management, a repressive economic system may be needed to cope with industrial disorder. On the other hand, if the attainment of rapid economic growth is the aspiration, the labour productivity revolution must be brought about and for that payment may be based on productivity of labour rather than profitability of the business. To operate on the productivity-based wages is to operate on the system of incentives and attitudes of labour. The attainment of a specific economic objective is thus conditioned by a specific social attitude and discipline.

2. **Educational-Cultural Environment and Economic Environment.** These are also interrelated. The stage of economic development is a decisive factor for the available system of education; only a relatively high income country can afford to impart costly higher education in science and technology. The sysem of education on the other hand, may be responsible for a given economic environment; the emphasis on liberal arts, education and the lack of vocational training courses may be held responsible for the economic problem of unemployment in many countries. At the corporate level, the interdependence between educational and economic environmental factors may at time work out to be a vicious circle. For example, a low profit-making business concern may not find resurces to finance training or executive development programme. As a result, there may be skill deformation among its staff-managerial inefficiency may cause low business efficiency as measured in terms of profitability of the business.

3. **Historical Environment and Social Environment.** These are also interdependent. The present environment of business can be treated as a legacy of past environment. Every

business has a history, every history has a lesson. As such, the present is a reflection to the past, and the present can also be handled in terms of the experience of the past. A number of examples may be quoted. The economic environment of a country today is partly constitued in terms of the available structure of industry in that country. The past history is a record of events—storehouse of lessons which can provide guidelines for present economic policy decisions. The achievements of the Five-Year Plans of Reforms Programme in the past may provide direction to the formulation and implementation of the present Five-Year Planned programmes of an economy. And the present performance of a plan will make the course of history of planning. This suggests that the environments factors are interrelated on the the time scale.

4. **Political-Legal Environment and Economic Environment.** These too affect each other. In a situation of political stability business enterprises happened to grow better, businessmen venture to shoulder more economic risks. But if there is political instability, business uncertainties multiply and, therefore, individuals may not like to step in business ventures. In the same way, the ideology of the ruling party influences the economic system. The government which believes in socialism (Swadeshi) as a strategy and nationalisation of enterprises (closed door to Videshi multinationals) as a tactic may remove the private business sector and kill the business incentives to expand its scale of operations. On the other hand, sometimes a series of political legislations may be necessary to cope with the economic environment. To fight economic crisis and industrial recession, streamlining of administration and simplification of procedural matters may be evoked.

5. **Physical Environment and Economic Environment.** These are inter-related too. The environment considerations limit the expansion activities of a business firm. On the other hand the size of plant, the scale of output, the

organisation or firms, the structure and location or industries may lie at the root of either environmental improvement or environmental decay. Thus, the social responsibility of business to-day is to take care of the environmental impact of its economic and technological activities. To the extent this social responsibility is not discharged, laws relating to the business and industry will increasingly turn out to be laws relating to the physical environment of business. The point remains that the physical environment as a factor is assuming so much significance day to day that it may be trated as critical element within the economic environment of business, rather than outside.

ENVIRONMENTAL SCANNING

It is the process by which managers and promoters of firms and companies tries to monitor the economic changes, governmental change, suppliers attitude and changes in the market to decide about new options, opportunities and threats if any. In very simple words environmental analysis relates of identification and analysing environmental influences individually and collectively to face the future effects upon the society and business. In environmental scanning, the main emphasis is on finding out the sources of new opportunities or threats. Environmental scanning or analysis is useful for evaluating the present strategy, new norms for future strategic decisions.

Every business fortune is influenced by non-economic change apart from economic changes. Among non-economic changes, social changes and political changes influence business strategy and planning significantly. If a firm or company does not keep an eye on economic, political and social changes occurring in the country then it will affect the business fortunes adversely. Here we can give the example of textile industry. In textile industry, except Reliance, no other industry is making remarkable progress and profitability. The reason is that Reliance took advantage of market needs and formulated strategies so that products are related to market needs. On the other hand, the management philosophy, practice, procedures, products and technology of other textile mills were out of line with change in environment. Hence, these textile mills suffered from sickness and lesser profitability.

Thus the management must be altert to new opportunities arising out of new product so that it can expand the business and earn high profits.

Requirement for Environment Scanning

The objective of most of the business managements is to earn more profit. Environment scanning helps every management in attaining more profits and growth and at the same time helps in minimisation of future threats. The future of an organisation is related with the environment in which the business is running. The growth and innovations and philosophy of change should be viewed with environmental effects. A fast changing business needs close study of facts: What are the probable threats to company. Some of the future events can be predicted by systematic scanning and follow up of environmental effects. The environmental scanning comprises information processing of social, economical, political, technological, product and changed market conditions.

The Research work on desirability of environmental analysis has revealed that there is high degree positive correlation between environmental analysis and success of corporates. The related areas which are needed for growth due to environmental analysis needs the following considerations:

(A) Firms growing by mergers and thus increasing the complexity of environment.

(B) Firms which had to face competition, Government regulations and healthy environment.

(C) Firms which are facing environment problems and headed by risk and uncertainty.

The study revealed that corporations succeeded with little or no extra efforts at environment appraisal. The following are such firms:

(i) Firms with slow effect of Environment changes and having risk prone management.

(ii) Firms with a desire of Innovation of new product.

(iii) Dominant firms with moderate risk-prone management.

It is a considered opinion that increasing knowledge of the strategists in environment scanning there is a positive gain to the firm.

FEATURES OF ENVIRONMENTAL ANALYSIS

Changing environment, the process of environmental analysis is very well comparable with the functions of radar. If a boat is sailing on a "sea of uncertainty", there are two essential requirements for a successful voyage. There has to be a star to steer the ship. Secondly, there must be radar to signal the existence of rocks, reefs and clear water in the uncharted sea. Thus in a business firm operating in an uncertain environment must have a vision (a giding star) and a system of environmental analysis (the radar). From this analogy, it is possible to derive three important characteristics of the process of environmental analysis.

1. The analysis of environment must be a continuous process rather than being an intermittent scanning system. Like the radar, it must operate continuously in order to keep the speed of development.
2. Environmental analysis is an exploratory process. While the monitoring aspect of the system is concerned with present developments, a large part of the process seeks to explore the unknown terrain, the dimensions of possible futures, what could happen, not necessarily what will happen.
3. Environmental analysis is an exercise that it must comprise a total view of the environment rather than viewing trends piecemeal. A radar covers 360 degrees of the horizon, not just a segment, although it can focus on a particular segment if need be. The corporate radar must scan the whole circumference of its environment in order to minimise the change of surprises and maximise its utility as an early warning system.

Which aspect of the environment should be management of any Organisation be concerned with? The factors that can influence future events and the sheer weight and volume or primary data be studied covering all major aspects.

Each company to set for itself the boundaries of the relevant environment and examine those variables which are critical to its own activities. This does not mean that firm engaged in manufacturing and selling products for the domestic market should monitor only the national environment, or an export firm should ignore the demestic product market conditions. For example, Reliance Textile Industries Ltd. initially focused on importing nylon yarn and polyster filaments for manufacturing fabrics primarily for the export market. The company deliberately chose not to expand its activities in the domestic market at that stage as it had identified that the market which was dominated by established leaders was not ripe for high-priced-quality products. It was in 1977 that the management realised potentiality of the internal market and decided to expand their operations on a large scale having the benefit of accumulated experience of supplying high-quality fabrics in the more competitive markets abroad.

Environmental factors are economic, political, social, legal/ regulatory and technological—may be of general specific relevance to enterprises. Further, each enterprise may perceive the relevant environment in the light of its own interest and set of circumstances which affect its functioning. Distinction may be made three orders of environment indicators to decide upon the question of relevance. Thus, depending on the nature of environment factors to be considered, management may distinguish between:

(i) Indicators relevant to individual enterprises, *e.g.*, for a company manufacturing agricultural pumpsets for irrigation—the progress of rural electrification; for a transport company—planned investment in the expansion of railway tracks and haulage capacity road construction, costs fuel and user needs for additional freight capacity.

(ii) Indicators which affect all business enterprises at the national level. These indicators may be easy to identify but difficult to measure, *e.g.*, attitude of political parties towards private enterprise as reflected in election manifestos, foreign economic relations, possibilities of armed conflicts, encounters, cold war and hostilities with neighbouring countries. etc.

(iii) Indicators relating to particular industry sectors, *e.g.*, for garment industry in India—the import-export policy of the Government of India, import restrictions in the United States and Western European countries, reservation of industries for the small-scale sector, delicensing of specific industries, and the like. These indicators may be relatively easier to measure though not so easy to identify.

Thus business environment may be defined as the set of external factors such as; economic factors, Geo-physical factors Government and Legal factors which are uncontrollable in nature and affects the business decisions.

Process of Environment Scanning

The study or scanning process is not difficult but not so easy as to which areas be covered and which should be left out.

Researches conducted in the late 60s and 70s being revealed that the process of environmental analysis has been far from being systematic except with regard to information relating to current developments. Oral information from personal sources dominated the,total input of information. Written and documentary information was much less frequently used by strategists. When written information were used they tended to be general information sources. Formal forecasting, if at all used, was viewed with great scepticism. Very little use was made of written studies, research reports, and meetings for environment search. Notwithstanding the above findings of research studies in the sixties and seventies and, perhaps because of these findings combined with the research findings on the beneficial effects of systematic analysis and diagnosis of external conditions the critical importance of developing as effective system of information gathering and information evaluation has been increasingly recognised over time by large enterprises.

Essentially, environmental scanning requires information inputs which can be derived from different sources:

1. **Industrial Informations.** Industrial espionage (spying) could also be a source of information about actual and potential competitors based on contacts with the employees, suppliers or customers of the competitors. Judging by survey data and expenses incurred on systems to protect trade secrets and industrial processes, it has been observed that industrial espionage and spying have been increasing in the United States. There is very little evidence in this respect about Indian industries.
2. **Verbal Informations.** Verbal information from such sources as the audio-visual media (radio and television); conversation among employees, managers, supervisors and subordinates; customer; distributors of the company's products (wholesalers, dealers, retailers); suppliers; competitors and their employees, financial executives in banks; stock brokers; consultants; government employees.
3. **Written Informations.** Written and documentary information from news papers, trade journals, industry newsletters, reports, documented clipping services;
4. **Management Informations.** Information made available through the management information system which is specially designated to served the needs of strategic planners.

Forecasting and reports based on forecasts regarding changes in economic, social and financial conditions available from governmental agencies and other specified consultancy service organisations.

Important Publications. A number of publications in India provide valuable information and forecasts relating to environmental conditions:

1. *The State of the Nation Report* (Annual) *Quarterly Survey of Industries*; and *Economic Scene* (monthly) published by the Tata Economic Consultancy Services.

2. *Business Intelligence and Data* published by the Centre for Monitoring Indian Economy.
3. *Indian Trade* Journal (Weekly) published by the Directorate General of Commercial Intelligence and Statistics, Calcutta.
4. *Economic Trends* (fortnightly) published by the Federation of Indian Chamber of Commerce and Industry, New Delhi.
5. *Economic Survey* published annually by the Ministry of Finance (Economic Division), Govt. of India.
6. Decennial Census Reports, Govt. of India.
7. Reserve Bank of India Bulletins (monthly) and annual Reports on Currency and Finance.
8. *Guidelines to Industries* in two volumes published by the Union Ministry of Industries.
9. *Five year* plans and mid-term survey reports on planned development published by the Planning Commission.
10. ICCI Portfolio Studies (Annual).
11. *Economic Times* (Bombay, New Delhi), *Financial Express* (New Delhi), and Business Standard (Calcutta, New Delhi)—dailies.
12. *Business Indian* (fortnightly), Bombay.

    Business World (fortnightly), Calcutta.

    Capital (fortnightly), Calcutta

    Commerce (Weekly), Bombay.
13. *Yojana trends* (fortnightly) published by the Planning Commission.
14. *Foreign Trade* (monthly) published by the Indian Institute of Foreign Trade, New Delhi.

    The following publications relating to international business provide economic, trade and financial data;
15. Bombay Stock Exchange Directory.

1. **United Nations Publications**

   World Economic Survey (Annual)

   Economic Survey of Latin America (Annual)

   Commodity Trade Statistics (Quarterly and Annual)

   Statistical Year Book (Annual)

   International Financial Statistics (Monthly)

   Economic Survey of Asia and the Far East (Annual)

   Year Book of International Trade Statistics

   Economic Bulletins for Europe, Latin America and Africa (Biannuals)

2. Annual Report on Exchange Restrictions published by the International Monetary Fund.
3. Indian Export serivce Bulletins (Weekly) published by the Trade Fair Authority of India.
4. Overseas Business published by United States Department of Commerce.
5. Monthly Statistics of the Foreign Trade of India in two volumes published by the Department of Commercial Intelligence and Statistics.
6. Fortnightly, monthly and quarterly Bulletins/Newsletters/ Journals published by the Export Promotion Councils for different products.

❒

2

Economic Systems and Business Environment

CAPITALIST ECONOMIC SYSTEM

Economic system of country provides its broadest economic environment. In a capitalist economic system activities of a business firm are by and large market determined. Nearly all economic activities are carried out by private sector. The scope for private sector to operate is wide in capitalism in comparison into any other economic system.

According to G.D.H. Cole, capitalism is that profit-oriented system which is characterized by private ownership of objects of labour, instruments of labour and means of labour. Production is mainly carried out with the help of labour sercies rendered by the working class in returns for wages and the class of capitalists has the right to whatever output is produced within the system.

Cole's definition of capitalism is scientific. It clearly underlines the fact that of the private ownership of the means of production the implication of which is that the capitalist economic system offers ample scope for private business.

FEATURES OF THE CAPITALIST SYSTEM

It is the oldest type of economic system. Presently a large number of countries notably the U.S.A. Japan, Germany, France, the U.K., Itally etc. have the capitalist economic system. The main features of a capitalist economy and the following:

1. **Economic Sovereignty.** In a capitalist economy, producers are free to use their capital in the production of any

commodity. Workers are free to acquire any type of skills and choose any occupation. Similarly, consumers are free to purchase any commodity and in any amount they like. These freedoms are also referred to as producers sovereignty' and consumer sovereignty in the capitalist system.

2. **Right of Private Property.** In a capitalist economy every individual has the right to hold and use of property and the means of production such as farms, factories, mines, transport etc. After the death of the owner, his property is inherited by his legal heirs. In this way the right of property perpetutates in the economy.

3. **Private Ownership of Means of Production.** Under Capitalism the means of production such as farms, factories, mines, transport, etc., are owned by private individuals or firms and they use these means of production for their private benefit.

4. **Labour Power as a Commodity.** An important feature of the capitalist system is that under it the labour power of man becomes a commodity and can be bought and sold just like any other commodity. In a capitalist economy the majority of the people own only one thing *viz.*, their capacity to work or their labour power. Whatever the nature of the economy, man has always possessed his labour power. Labour power just like any other commodity commands a price which is equivalent to the cost of those commodites which are essential for the maintenance of the labourers and their family members.

5. **Production for the Market.** One main features of capitalist economy is that under capitalism business firms produce mainly with the aim of selling the output in the market.

   The producers forms follow division to undertake the production of different commodities. The development of the factory system renders the division of labour even more complex. As long as the tools required in the process of production were possessed by everybody it was normal practice for all to produce just everything which they needed. It is only when the means of production get concentrated in a few hands that the capitalist system based on commodity production starts emerging.

6. **Price Mechanism.** The working of a capitalist economy is regulated by the functioning of price mechanism. The decisions of producers to produce particular commodities depend on price, demand and costs of production of different commodities. Producers produce such commodities that are priced high, and engage such factors of production that are priced low and contribute relatively more to output. Households purchasers are also influenced by prices of different commodities. Households prefer to buy more of such commodities that are priced low and yield greater amount of statisfaction. Thus price mechanism helps prodcuers and consumers to take decisions about production and consumption.

7. **Exploitaion of Labour.** Workers are exploited under capitalism. Very often due to the freedom granted to the workers at a formal level, many people are wrongly given to believe that the workers by bargaining in the free market are able to get a fair price in return for their labour power. But this is not true, according to Marx, businessmen exploit workers and pay less wages than the goods produce by them.

8. **Growing Wealth of the Capitalist.** In a capitalist economy the wealth of the capitalist class increases in a sustained manner. Under capitalism to earn more profit, generally every firm makes the utmost effort to eliminate every often firm. A firm which losses out in the competition leave the market and its share is captured by sucessful firm. In this way only a handful of firms manage to survice in every industry and with them large wealth is concentrated. Another

may by which wealth is accumulated is the exploitation of workers.

9. **Class Contradiction.** The capitalist system rests fundamentally on class distinctions. As capitalism develops, the society gets divided into two mutually hostile classes. On the one hand are the handful of capitalists with whom wealth as well as power is concentrated. In spite of the enormous power vested in the capitalist class it cannot do without the class of workers. Machines are not self-operative. Therefore the labour power is indispensable for the survival of the capitalists. The workers who through their hard labour create immense wealth themselves remain poor and exploited throughout their lives, while the capitalists by laying a claim to the entire output become richer over time. The class of interests of capitalists and workers takes the form of class conflict. Since the power is with the capitalists they are offered all possible help in their supperssion of workers by the government agencies like the police.

10. **Emergence of the Working class.** The working class in capitalism is totally dependent on the capitalist for its livelihood. The freedom enjoyed by the working class in only at a formal level. Under capitalism the increasing use of machinery leads to widespread unemployment and an increase in the rate of exploitation of workers which implies a decline in the share of workers in the national income over time.

WORKING OF A CAPITALIST ECONOMY

In a capitalist economy neither an individual nor any institution takes decisions in a planned manner concerning its day-to-day functioning. However, the people of capitalist countries know that in spite of all this the producers generlly produce those commodities which they effectively demand in the market. Besides this the producers find it necessary to demand their services on the rendering of which they obtain their income. It is only by spending this income that the poeple can buy goods and services of their choice.

In a free market economy the behaviour of all individuals including causumers and producers both develop the system of price mechanism. This system not only solve the central problems of a economy but also helps in reaching the state of equilibrium. This can be understood with the help of the following figure.

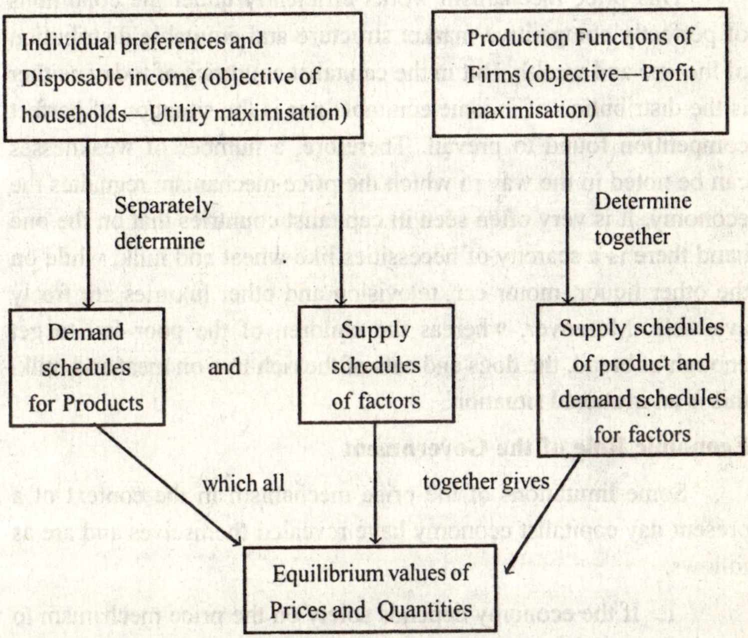

Fig. Working of Price Mechanism

It is clear from the diagram that the preferences of the people with regard to consumption goods and their income which they wish to spend on them will together determine the demand for various goods in the market. The production function or alternatively the quantity and proportion in which labour, capital, land and other factors are used in the productive process determine the supply of products in the market. It is these conditions of demand and supply in the commodity market which determine the prices of all products which enter it. In the various factor markets the wage rate, rent, etc., are determined in more or less the same manner.

Very often the economists of capitalist countries claim that it is through the working of this price mechanism that the free enterprise economy takes decisions regarding the three central problems *viz.*, what to produce, how to produce and for whom to produce in favour of maximum social welfare.

This price mechanism works efficiently under the conditions of perfectly competitive market structure and equitable distribution of income and wealth. But in the capitalist countries of today neither is the distribution of income equitable nor is the situation of perfect competition found to prevail. Therefore, a number of weaknesses can be noted in the way in which the price mechanism regualtes the economy. It is very often seen in capitalist countries that on the one hand there is a scarcity of necessities like wheat and milk, while on the other liquor, motor car, television and other luxuries are freely available. Moreover, whereas the children of the poor fail to get enough of bread, the dogs and cats of the rich live on meat and milk. this is an irrational situation.

Economic Role of the Government

Some limitations of the price mechanism in the context of a present day capitalist economy have revealed themselves and are as follows:

1. If the economy depends solely on the price mechanism to solve its central problems, then given the income and wealth inequalities there is a possibility that a large number of people die of starvation while a handul possess the good things of life very much in excess of what is required by them. Thus, in a Welfare State the government finds it necessary to curb such inhuman traits in the working of the price mechanism.
2. The growth of monopoly firms in the market has put an end to the consumer's sovereignty. J. K. Galbraith asserts that the giant corporations by spending huge amounts of

money on advertisement campaigns distort the demand pattern of consumers. This implies that very often people in response to sales promotion drives launched by producers of non-essentials switch over their demand from basic necessities to luxuries. Thus, the ability of the gaint corporations to influence the pattern of demand which emanates from the market deters the production of right commodities in the market. Given such circumstances, intervention by the government becomes invitable.

3. Generally the price mechanism due to the individualistic orientation of human behaviour cannot adequately provide for education, medical facilities and other social services. If in any society in addition to the above mentioned services, the level of production of such other services of immense national importance, like transportation, communications, water and electricity, is also to be determined by the price mechanism alone, then it is likely to result in a very short supply of each one of them. Therefore, it becomes imperative for the government to participate directly in the production of these services. In the Third World countries like India the regulation of the economy in the past by the price mechanism has been very defective, so much so that the development of steel, heavy engineering, chemical and other basic industries has suffered considerably.

MEANING OF SOCIALISM

Socialism was in fashion till the breakup of U.S.S.R. Though its popularity has declined sharply, still it is approved by most of the economists, social reformers, politicians etc. Socialism is used by different persons in a different way. Socialism is a economic system where private sector does not have any kind of control over production and distribution and all major economic activities including production distribution and consumption are controlled by the state or state-established agencies.

There is no universal definition of socialism. The concept of socialism has conceived in different ways by different thinkers.

Thererfore it become necessary on our part to study a few important definitions of socialism. According to Paul M. Sweegy, "Socialism is a complete social system which differ from capitalism not only in the absence of private ownership of the means of production but also in its basic structure and mode of functioning."

According to Prof. H.D. Dicknson, "Socialism is an economic organisation of society in which the material means of production are owned by the whole community and operated by organs representative of and responsible to the community according to a general economic plan, all members of the community being entitled to benefit from the results of such socialised planned production on the basis of equal rights."

There are numerous definitions given by various economists, politicians and socialists. They differ in terminology but the following features are common in all the definitions.

FEATURES OF SOCIALISM

1. **State Ownership.** In socialist economy, there is a social or state ownership of the means of production. Because of social ownership, there is no profit motive to produce goods and services. The production is guided by social and other economic motives.
2. **Equality of opportunity.** Every individual should have equal opportunity to rise in life whether he is born in the poor family or the rich one. One must get equal opportunity to get education and training so that he should enter occupation of his choice. Under socialism steps are taken to ensure that every child whatever his birth and whatsoever his parental background is provided sufficient opportunities to develop fully his latent talents and potentialities. Health services and free education upto a certain standard and or level sould be made for all.
3. **Equality of Income.** In socialist economy there is perfect equality of income but each person is paid according to work, performance and needs. Thus, the gulf between the rich and the poor is minimum.

4. **Social Welfare Motive.** An important features of socialism is that it is the motive of social welfare rather than private profit which guides production. Under capitalism, luxury goods are produced for their rich as they ensure greater profits while poor go even without necessaries as their production does not bring adequate profits to the producers. Under capitalism profit motive is the driving force of the economy. But under socialism the welfare of the society as a whole is the driving force fall economic activities. The place of impersonal forces of market which work under capitalism (Price mechanism) is taken by a central authority or the Planning commission which takes decisions about all important issues.
5. **Economic Planning.** Economic planning has been most closely associated with socialism. Effective planning cannot be adopted under capitalism because under capitalism means of production are owned and controlled by private individuals and production of goods and allocation of resources are directed by price mechanism. Planning ensures rapid economic development along desired. It granautees efficient and optimum allocating of resources in under developed countries where the level of national income and wealth is very low.
6. **Classless Society.** Socialism believes in a classless society. The existence of caste system is country to the concept of socialism. In a socialist state every body irrespective of his caste, class need and religion is provided with equal opportunity in all fit fields of life. A truly socialist state is a secular state. The two main classes of labour and capitalist no longer exist under socialism. Zamindars and capitalists are not allowed to remain under socialism because ownership of private property is strictly restricted every body is rewarded according to his work, and merit. Thus class struggle which is the chief feature of capitalism comes to an end under socialism.

The capitalist manufacturing industries being more developed, can easily be nationalised soon after the revolution. Similarly, the Government may also take over the core sectors such as electricity generation, construction, railways and other transportation.

In agriculture, farming is sought to be carried out on State cooperative farms. Important agricultural inputs like modern implements, seeds, fertilisers and cattle are owned by the State or cooperative societies. Therefore, even in the field of agriculture private ownership of the means of production is abolished and it is for this reason that no one individual can use the means of production owned by cooperatives to exploit other individuals.

In a socialist society farmers, mill workers and the people working in offices are given the right to own privately some amount of property, the ceiling for which is stipulated by the State. Private property which is generally in the form of land is allowed to be used for production of those goods which are required for the personal consumption of the family. In China and the other socialist countries, people apart from growing vegetables and fruits on this on this land also use it for poultry farming and animal husbandry. In order to alleviate the problem posed by the limited housing space, people are sometimes granted permission to construct a house strictly for their own use. Thus, one thing which should be noted is that some means production which individuals can retain for themselves cannot be used for the production of commodities, that is, goods and services which are produced with the intention of sale.

Though, under a socialist set-up the means of production get socialised yet, the consumption goods earned by the workers through their labour become the personal possessions of these people. The incomes earned by the people, their savings, some residential accommodation, furniture and various other consumption goods constitute their personal possessions. Labour is the sole source of personal wealth under socialism and the government under this system does not allow transformation of this wealth into capital which could later on be used as a means of exploitation.

Role of Planning. Planning under socialism plays exactly the same role as is played by the price mechanism in a capitalist economy. The Planning Commission, in other words, is required to solve the basic central problems of what to produce, how to produce and for whom to produce. In order to do this the Planning Commission has to, on the one hand, make an estimate of the entire economic, human and natural resources at its command, while on the other it has to determine the requirements of the nation for various goods and services. To put it more clearly, the Commission has to decide upon the various commodities which the economy should produce with the available resources. There can be many different ways of achieving the output targets. The Planning Commission in a socialist country takes into consideration the social welfare aspect and the development related goals of the nation while choosing the technique of production to be used. The price mechanism in a capitalist economy operates in such a way that production takes place only to meet the demands of all those people who have considerable amount of disposable income. Under this system not much attention is generally paid to the production of those commodities which belong to the poor man's basket. In a socialist economy, however, income inequalities are drastically reduced so that everyone has an adequate amount of disposable income. While determining the pattern and size of output the Planning Commission has to see to it that its decisions in this regard are such that they ensure the availability of commodities for all in the market.

Economists view socialist planning as equivalent to planning for economic development. Therefore, every economic plan of the nation which determines its economy's pace and pattern of development should necessarily incorporate two elements: First, the way in which national income is to be distributed between consumption and accumulation, and secondly, the manner in which investment is to be allocated among the different sectors of the economy.

Role of Prices in a Socialist Economy

Prices play a secondary role in the working of a socialist economy. However, it would be wrong to jump to the conclusion from this that they have no useful task to perform in the economy.

They perform the following two functions in a socialist economy. In the first place it is the prices of consumer goods which determine the distribution of these goods amongst the people. Secondly, prices are essential for carrying out rational economic calculations for the nation. In a socialist economy, therefore, two types of prices can be seen to prevail. In case of those goods and services for which a market exists, *viz.*, consumer goods, the equilibrium prices or the market prices are determined at a point at which the demand for each one of them is matched by their respective supplies. On the other hands, for producer goods in the absence of a market, accounting prices are used. These prices are set by the Planning Commission on the basis of historically given prices and thus are not arbitrarily determined. If the price for any producer good happens to be set too high, then at the end of current time period a surplus of it will result. This is because a price higher than what is necessary will compel the State enterprises to unduly economise on that particular producer good. On the other hand, if too low a price is set, then a deficit of the producer good in question will arise. If the Planning Commission is faced with the former situation of a surplus ensuing for some prodcuer good at the end of the planning period, it will raise the price of the resource in question. In this way through a procees of trial and error the right accounting prices can be arrived at. These accounting prices of means of production and the market prices of consumer goods are used for the purpose of economic calculation in the planning process of the country.

MIXED ECONOMY

A mixed economy represents a mixture of features of the two types of economies capitalism and socialism. Under this form of economic system, the ownership of means of production is partly in the hands of privae individuals and partly owned by the society. The public authority usually own public utility sevices like supply of water and electricity, roadways and railways, shipping and air services, hospitals, schools and colleges, defence industries. As regards the distribution the Governmenis tries to remove disparities and inequalities in the income distribution by various measures such as taxes and their levies and through public expenditure.

According to Samuelson, a mixed economy is characterised by the existence of both public and private institutions excercising economic controls. In this economy price mechanism and partial planning both plays an important role. Indian is perhaps the best example of such an economy and can legitimately be called a mixed economy.

FEATURES OF MIXED ECONOMY

1. Coexistence of the Private and Public Sectors. The concept of mixed economy presupposes the existence of two or three sectors. In the Public or state sector the entire system of production and distribution is managed, owned, controlled and financed by the state itself. Private individuals are not permitted to undertake any economic activity in this sphere. The public sector performs three functions:

(i) it is to provide/create social heads;

(ii) it has to create industrial climate; and

(iii) it has to create a sound industrial base in the economy.

2. Price Mechanism and Government Control and Regulation Work Together. A mixed economy contains the goods features of both socialism and capitalism. Every possible effort is made to make the best possible use of available economic resources. The price mechanism and the profit motive and all kinds of freedoms result in the efficient allocation and utilisation of the available resources. As a result shortages and surpluses are easily avoided and business fluctuations are eliminated.

3. Ecoomic Freedom and Control. In mixed economy freedom of expenditure, production, occupation, investment, to hold property and have property by inheritance are present. But these freedoms are not granted to people in unlimited way. These freedoms are not given at the expense of the public welfare. These freedoms are restricted or controlled by the state in the public interest.

4. Economic Welfare. The system is adopted to overcome the evils of capitalism. Exploitation of the poor by the rich is one of the chief evils of capitalism. The conflict between the labourers and the capitalists is avoided. The state posses labour laws and fixes minimum wages, working hours etc. and provides social security benefits.

5. Economic Planning and General Balance, Economic Planning is an Important Feature of a Mixed Economy. It derives all the benefits of planned socialist economy. It maintains a general balance between the public sector and the private sector. The two sectors are not rivals of each other; they cooperate with each other.

CRITICAL APPRAISAL OF THE WORKING OF MIXED ECONOMIES

A mixed economy despite the fact that it has overcome certain weaknesses of the *laissez faire* economy is exposed to various criticism. We shall examine these criticisms in the following discussion:

1. Less Firm Framework of the Mixed Economy and its Vulnerability to Political Manoeuverings. No doubt in all mixed economies both public and private sectors co-exist, yet the role that they play may not be the same in all the countries. In the same country the relative importance of these sectors may change over time. The exact form which a mixed economy assumes in a country at some point of time depends partly on economic expediency and partly on the correlation of political forces. Often political factor is far more dominant and causes an unwarranted change in the form of a mixed economy. This can be easily understood by examining India's case. In this country after Independence the need for evolving a mixed economy had arisen from the overall backwardness of the economy and the inability of the capitalist class to undertake the task of diversified industrial development. The political forces at that juncture also favoured creation of a large public sector which played a strategic role in the country's economic development. Now the correlation of political forces has undergone some change. The growing strength of the big business class and the emergence of powerful traders and large farmers' lobbies are combining to make determined attempts to undermine the importance of the public sector in the Indian economy. The regulatory system is being gradually dismantled and role of planning is beings reduced. All these developments are important and are a pointer to imminent changes in the form of the mixed economy in this country. In other less developed countries where democratic traditions are less firmly rooted, changes in government through violent coups often drastically change the complexion of the mixed economy.

2. Concentration of Economic Power. Transformation of a capitalist economy into a mixed economy in underdeveloped economies is often motivated by the objective of economic growth which over time results in growth of monopolies and concentration of economic power. Development of infrastructure and the setting up of heavy industries by the State induces development in the organised private corporate sector. In this sector the law of capitalist development operates as a consequence of which big corporations record much faster growth and over time show a tendency to control substantial proportions of the supplies of different industrial products. In this attempts in this direction they are helped not only by the economies of scale but often also by the licensing policy of the government and their capital raising abilities *vis-a-vis* small producers in the unorganised sector. India's case firmly lends support to the contention that in a mixed economy, on account of the in-built system, development process results in the concentration of economic power. It may be noted that in 1963-64 there were only two monopoly houses—Tata and Birla—having total assets exceeding Rs. 200 crore each. In 1997-98 there were 10 business houses having assets worth Rs. 14,852 crore or more each.

3. Bureaucratic Inefficiency and Corruption. In a number of developing countries though a large public sector has been created, no serious attempts have been made to develop efficient managerial cadre to run public enterprises. Interestingly in most of the developing countries after they got independence colonialist administrative machinery was retained and, for managing the affairs of public sector economic units, managerial cadre was drawn from this sources. The inefficiency in public sector enterprises emanates partly from this fact. Another factor that may also be mentioned is that even now "bureaucrats carry out their duties in formal structures that are reminscent of the pre-Independence imperialist administration. Rules, regulations, procedures, control mechanisms and basic management practices have essentially remained unchanged." over the years. Obviously this kind of administrative system can neither ensure efficiency in the completion of development projects nor activate high standards of productivity when actual production is carried out.

Introduction of discretion and administrative controls in a mixed economy created conditions for widespread corrpution. It has been observed in a number of mixed economies that corruption impedes the process of decision-making and execution at various levels. Corrpt officials explit the position of public responsibility for private gain by using the threat of obstruction and delay. At the macro level influence of corruption gets reflected in the low rates of economic growth. Corruption may also introduce an element of irrationality in planning and may influence the course of development in a way that distortions develop in the plain itself.

4. Built-in-tendency to Slide Back. Now a days in India the policy of drifting away from economic planning is being pursued. The public sector is criticised for its poor performance and by implication privatisation is advocated for the improvement of the performance of the economy. But this is not correct. However, once in a mixed economy a new capitalised classs grows, often proposed up by the public sector and physical controls, it starts exercising pressures for dismantling the regulating sturcture. This results in a emergence of pure capitalism in which state shows little concern for the poor.

5. Denial of Social Justice. The mixed economy framework generally tends to favour relatively rich on account of their strong economic position. The deprived in the social system expect the government to counte this tendency by regulating the activities in the private sector and through direct participation in extensive areas of economic activities. However, in a class society that is to be found in all the countries having a mixed economy, the government has neither the ability nor the required will to prevent the tendency of the concentration of economic power.

GLOBAL ENVIRONMENT

The business environment has changed radically world over during the 1990s. Economic and political changes have surprised both business analysts and business practioners. Presently there is so much uncertainty that even the most competent corporate executives are not feeling confident about their business strategies. Now we shall analyse the impact of global and national economic environment on business and trade in India.

Presently for the Indian business the global scenaniro is not very encouraging. The global environment can be discussed under the headings of the unipolar world globalisation, economic crises in East and South-East Asia, the wash of Japan, Underdelopment of Russia and East Europe, global recession, regional economic groupings, protectionism and multinational corporations.

1. The Unipolar World. The collapse of Eastern Europe and U.S.S.R. marked the end of a bi-polar world. With the demise of socialism in these countries the USA established its supremacy over the world economy. Though Japan is a second largest economy but it is in no position to challenge the political and economic moves of the USA. The West European countries such as Germany, France, Italy and the U.K. could match the USA collectively but not individually. The USA now behaves like a big brother and punish all those countries which dare to take independent policy decisions. Recently the nuclear tests by India in 1998 invited the wrath of the USA and it slapped sanctions on our country. The USA has recently threatened South Korea of a trade unless it agrees to import more American cars. This type of environment is not congengial to including India.

On Jan 1, 1999 the European Economic and monetary Unions launched a single european currency '*euro*'. With the euro's launch coinciding with the weakening of major Asain currencies including the Japanese yen and Chinese yuan, the dollar and euro are likely to dominate world economy as reserve and key currencies. This trend may spell doom spell doom for developing economies including India by triggering off competitive devaluation and increasing debt burden. IMF Managing Director however, believes that the world is moving towards a multipolar world in monetary field. However, in immidate future this does not seem to be the possibility.

2. Globalisation. Broadly globalisation implies simply the expansion of economic activites across political boundaries of the nation, states. The word has been used in two ways. When the term globalisation is used in a positive sense it implies a process of integration in the world economy. When the world gloabalisation is used in a normative sense, it prescribes a stretegy of economic development involving a rapid integration with the world economy. In whatever manner one defines globalisation, its fundamental attribute is the increasing degree of openness in a large number of countries. The three important of this process are International Trade, International investment, and International Finance. The openness is not conflined to these aspects only. It often extends to flows of technology, information and services across national boundaries. But it must be recognised that these movements are far more restricted than trade flows, investment flows and financial flows. It is probably this reason why most people consider trade, investment and finance as the core of globalisation.

Rapid globalisation over the past two and a half decades has made profound changes in the world economy. A study of the Top 200 global corporations has revealed that these colossal corporations, most of them larger than many national economies, now control around 28 per cent of the world's economic activity. Their combined sales at $ 7.1 billion surpass the combined economies of 182 countries. The study noted that presently there are 191 countries and if we substract the GDP of the big nine economies—the USA, Japan, Germany, France, Italy, the UK, China, Brazil and Canada, the combined GDP of the other 182 countries is $ 6.9 billion. Moreover, over half of the sales of the Top 200 corporations is in just five economic sectors, *viz.,* trading, automobiles, banking, electronics and retailing. There is also a growing concentration of a few firms in each of these sectors. In automobilies the top five firms account for almost 60 per cent of the global sales. The top five firms also have over 30 per cent of the global sales in personal computers, steel, oil, airlines, aerospace, chemicals and media. Finally, 186 of the Top 200 corportations are headquartered in seven countries, *viz.*, Japan, the USA. Germany, France, the UK, the Netherlands and Switzerland. Brazil and South Korea are the only developing countries to join the group of the Top 200 global corporations.

3. Economic Crisis in East and South-East Asia. For about two decades since the mid-1970s certain economies of East and South-East Asia Malasia, South Korea, Indonesia, etc., registered high rates of economic growth. Since these economies are basically markt economies, the IMF—World Bank functionaries aggressively marketed their model to other developing countries. In India, since we had registered only a modest rate of growth until 1990, we developed a great fancy for these economies. In fact, by adopting the liberalisation policy and pursuing greater opennes in the matters of trade flows, investment flows and finance flows we had hoped to repeat the performance of thse economies. When the Indian government was contemplating along these lines, the 'miracle' economies of Asia almost collapsed in 1997-90. The crisis engulfing these economies of was as harsh as unexpected.

The Asian crisis is relevant to India business in two ways—first, it may have some impact on the Indian economy and second, it may influence the policy makers in this country and they might opt for a reversal of the liberalisation process. Bhalla and Nachane are of the view that there are three likely channels through which India can catch East and South-East Asian economic meltdown contagion. These are as follows:

(1) the direct and indirect impact on India's exports due to the downturn in the Asian economies and the spread of the contagion to other markets for Indian goods;

(2) the imapct on the inflow of foreign capital; and

(3) the impact of contractionary domestic policies initiated in response to the crisis.

Presently there is a sharp decline in the world demand and prices for such products as electronics, semi-conductors and petrochemicals. Hence, chances of recovery are dim in East and South-East Asian economies. India should thus be cautius about fast spreading contagion.

4. The Crash of Japan. Performance of the Japanese economy was simply spectacular during the 1960s and 1970s. However, it considerably slowed down during the 1980s and its GDP growth rate was as low as 1.4 per cent per annum between 1990 and 1997. Never since the Great Depression of the 1930s a developed country has been cought in an economic crisis of the dimension Japan faces presently. It is interesting to observe that Japan continues to amass a large trade surplus, as against the unprecedented US deficit on external account. These phenomena, however, do not strengthen the yen and cause the slide of the dollar as certain analysts surmised. According to Frederic F. Claimont, "Far more crucial is the capital account of the balance of payments. Here Japan is in the deepest of quagmires with the return on yen assets woefully uncompetitive on international capital markets, and becoming more so daily. The public debt in Japan stand at 127 per cent of GDP and the non-performing loans of the banking system hovering around $ 1.6 trillion hence loans that will never be repaid.

There are also serious problems of growing unemployment, falling real wages and wholesale prices, and slump in housing construction. *The Financial Times* describing the situation wrote, "This is an economy from which confidence is being drained by the minute." This is reflected in the daily outflow of dollars from Japan. The real source of Japan's current difficulties lies in the major economic crises in the East and South-East Asian countries. This has cut down demand for Japanese exports in these countries drastically and the value of assets held by Japanese investors has fallen sharply. From the point of view of the India business, malaise in the Japanese economy is of great relevance as Japan accounts for about 6 per cent of exports from this country.

5. Underdevelopment of Russia and East Europe. Ever since the East Europe and Russia abandoned socialism and opted for capitalism, the economies of these countries have been caught in deep crisis. The reform measures adopted in these countries have failed miserably and the GDP has been falling at the rate of 10 per cent per annum or even more.

Now it is well known that the IMF and the World Bank had designed the package of reforms for Russia and East Europe. They are still calling the shots without realising that their short sighted policies designed from extremely narrow economic standpoint of industrialised countries do not serve anybody's interest. It has to be understood that an impoverished Russia or East Europe will not provide large markets for the goods produced in the Western countries. This fact is as much relevent for the Indian business which until the 1980s had large exports to these countries. Inability of Russia and East Europe to import from the West in a big way at a time when economies in Asia are caught in deep crisis in helping to accentuate the recession in the developed countries of the West. This phenomenon obviously will have adverse effects on the demand for the Indian exports as well.

6. Global Recession. Free markets and the IMF-World Bank experts did not think till recently that their activities would inevitably push the world economy towards recesion. But what was not suspected has happened. The world is now in the grip of recession.

At present two-fifths of the global economy is already in the grip of recession; and another two-fifths is on the brink. Leaving aside a few hardcore free marketers now everyone else seems to the convinced that there is a great likelihood of the repeat of the Great Depression of the 1930s. So far India and China have not caught economic melt-down contagion but the rates of growth have certainly declined. How long these countries will remain insulated from global recession will depend on the economic policies of these countries.

7. Regional Economic Groupings. Developed countries had become aware of their interdependence even before World War II, but after the War when reconstruction began in West Europe they realised the need for having a permanent system whereby it could be possible for them to cooperate with each other. As a result, organisations like OECD (Organisation for Economic Cooperation and Development), EU (European Union) and EFTA (European Free Trade Association) came into existence. The European Union (EU) was organised as a customs union.

The following regional groupings of the less developed countries have come ito existence over the years:

1. The Latin American Free Trade Association (LAFTA) formed in 1960 and consisting of eleven Latin American countries—Argentina, Bolivia, Brazil, Chile, Colombia, Ecuador, Mexico, Paraguay, Peru, Uruguay and Venezuela. It was later replaced by the Latin American Integration Association under Montevideo Treaty of 1980.
2. The Central American Common Market (CACM), comprising Costa Race El Salvador, Guatemala, Honduras and Nicaragua was formed in 1960. CACM functioned like a customs union.
3. The Caribbean Free Tade Area (CARIFTA) formed in 1968 and consisting of twelve Caribbean nations. In July 1973 this free trade area was converted into a full-fledged Caribbean community.
4. The Central African Customs Union (CACEU) formed in 1964 and comprising Cameroon, Central African Republic, Congo and Gabon.
5. The Andean Group was forme in 1969 consisting of Bolivia, Chile, Ecuador, Colombia and Peru. It operated in a more liberal trading atmosphere.
6. MEROSUR came into existene on January 1, 1995. This is a major free trade agreement originally signed by Argentina, Brazil, Paraguay and Uruguay. Chile and Bolivia joined it more recently.
7. Economic Community of West African States (ECOWAS) was formed in 1975 consisting of fifteen West African countries.

These regional groupings have bestowed benefits on business firms of the member countries in a number of ways. Yet their achievements are rather limited. This is due to the fact that the regional spirit has yet to grow. Most of the participating countries are guided by narrow national interests and nurture a feeling of suspicion towards other member countries. It is partly due to the fact that Western industrialised countries constantly try to sabotage such efforts at economic cooperation by giving military aid to some member countries of these regional groupings. It is this kind of sabotaging by the industrialised countries that the concept of Asian Common Market (ACM) could never become a reality though most countries of the region accept the advantage of creating such a common market. The Association of South East Asian Nations (ASEAN) founded in 1967 is the oldest grouping in East Asia. It comprises Brunei, Indonesia, Malaysia, the Philippines, Singapore and Thailand. This arrangement started as a preferential trade zone but new initiatives are afoot to convert the block into a free trade zone.

8. Protectionism. Since the mid 1970s the industrialised countries of the West have been increasingly resorting to protection. The success of Japanese exports and then of exports from the newly industrialising countries produced pressure on the USA and the West European countries for pursuing the protectionist policy. The older industrialised countries want to avoid competition from newly industrialising countries in their domestic markets and thus create non-tarriff barriers (NTBs). During the past two decades trade in textiles, leather goods, footwear, steel, ship-building, cars and consumer electronics has been subjected to blantant protectionism by the western countries.

Tariffs are now low and thus not used for protection. The main instrument of protection during the past two decades has been the non-tariff barrier (NTB). It violates widely accepted principles of non-discrimination and transparency in trade. Recently European Union has imposed anti-dumping duties on Indian export of stainless steel products while the EU countries continue to heavily subsidies their steel industry. This is obviously a case of blatant protectionism. It amply clarifies that it is not easy for the business firms of the developing countries like India and Pakistan to penetrate the markets in development countries.

9. Multinational Corporations. At present the global economy is dominated by 40,000 corporations. The activities of these enterprises cross national boundaries. These firms operate in overseas markets through some 2,50,000 foreign affiliates. According to the letest estimates of the Washington based Institute for Policy Studies (IPS) the top 100 of these global firms account for a growing share of the world's economic activity. Illustrating the growing economic clout of the global gaints the IPS report states that out of the 100 largest economies in the world, 51 are corporations; only 49 are countries. Wal-Mart the number 12 corporation is bigger than 161 countries including Greece, Poland and Israel, Mitsubishi is larger than the fourth most populous nation on earth, Indonesia, Toyata is bigger than Norway, General Motors is bigger than Denmark and Ford is bigger than Portugal.

The giant corporations with massive resources at their command, in the face of falling demand are engaged in ruthless competition with relatively smaller companies. Peter F. Drucker has rightly pointed out that medium and small businesses also operate in the world economy and they are not always visible. These firms in the prosperity phase of the business cycle grow and generate substantial revenues. However, with the onslaught of global recession their existence is threatened. In this period no goal setting, no vision and no strategy will help these small corporate enterprise in their growth pursuit.

The National Scenario

The national scenario at present is not as much encouraging as it was a few years ago. The country nevertheless lacks political stability. It seems that for some time the country can hope to get only coalition governments at the Centre which means that economic policies may not have a clear cut long-term perspective. The coalition governments which are likely to last for sort periods may follow adhocist economic policies. However, there is not much dispute on liberalisation and globalisation.

1. Liberalisation. In response to the economic crisis of 1991 the government embarked on a wide ranging reform of the policy regime. Prior to 1991 the Indian economy was a highly regulated economy. In July 1991 a beginning was made to dismantle controls which had over time become a major obstacle to industrial growth. Policy changes made to unshackle the economy from controls and to orient it towards the free market are known as the liberalisation measures. These measures are related to *(a)* the industrial sector, *(b)* the trade region, *(c)* foreign investment and technology, *(d)* the public sector, and *(e)* the financial sector.

In the industrial sector, barriers to entry for new firms and limits on growth in the size of existing firms have been removed. Industrial licensing has been abolished for most of the industries irrespective of the levels of investment. The MRTP Act has been amended to remove the threshold limit of one billion rupees on the assets of large business houses. The prior approval from the government is no longer required for capacity creation, amalgamation, merger or acquisitions on the part of such companies.

The abolition of controls in the sphere of investment decisions was necessary and desirable. However, deregulation by itself does not reduce the degree of monopoly. It may also fail to increase the degree of competition among the firms. Some recent developments in India suggest that mergers acquisitions or takeovers by firms in the industrial sector have enabled the enlarged corporate enterprises to capture larger market share. There are so many examples which one can cite, but some cases are worth noting: the merger of Brooke Bond Lipton with Hindustan Lever, acquistion of Goa Electrical by Crompton Greaves, the merger of Parle with Coca Cola and the merger of Ponds India with Hindustan Lever. In these cases either the established competition has been eliminated or potential competition has been pre-empted.

The policy regime for foreign investment and foreign technology has been liberalised at a rapid pace. The government now wants to enlarge non-debt-creating inflows. Hence, prior approval for foreign investment is not the rule. It may be required in excepted cases. The liberal access to imports of technology aims at facilitating technology upgradation which is a necessary condition for increasing international competitiveness in industry.

The trade policy reforms have eliminated quantitative restrictions on imports and exports. Further, there has been a substantial reduction in tariffs on imports alongwith abolition of subsidies on exports. The exchange rate changes have led to a sizable depreciation of the rupee. It is hoped that the exposure of domestic firms to international competition in this manner will compel them to become more efficient. In this relatively open environment domestic firms will have to upgrade technology, reduce cost and improve the quality of products. The assumption of the trade policy reform introduced in the country is that internationally competitive good products can always be exported. In practice, this may not always be true export surplus. Some countries in any case must have matching import surplus. This implies that it is not easy for Indian firms to raise exports unless certain countries choose to cooperate with them.

Till recently the commericial banking system and the domestic capital market were over-regulated and under-governed. Over the past few years an attempt has been made to improve the health of the financial sector through deregulation. With the reductions in the statutory liquidity ratio and the cash reserve ratio resources received by the banks in the form of deposits are not pre-empted by the government but are made available to the private sector. Interest rates in the domestic capital market have been deregulated. Now prior government approval regarding the size and price of equity issues in the primary capital market is not required. Market forces are now expected to discipline the capital market. The Securities and Exchanges Board of India, however, establishes rules and regulations to government the stock market and intermediaries.

As a result of liberalisation the activties of the public sector have been reduced. Now the focus of public sector is only on those sectors which are strategic and high-technology or constitute an integral part of the infrastructure. Chronically sick public enterprises are being referred to the Board of Industrial and Financial

fundamentals of the economy were strong enough to sustain this. The RBI had projected a growth rate of 6.5 per cent in its annual report as well. However, speaking at a function organised by FICCI and confederation of Asia Pacific Chambers of Commerce and Industry (CACCI) Jalan had hoped that growth would touch 6.0 per cent in India. He was confident that the industrial downswing in some sectors was being matched by a good performance in others.

The optimism of the RBI Governor about the country's growth prospects was not shared by many. The Federation of Indian Chambers of Commerce and Industry (FICCI) conducted a survey of 342 corporates. The survey revealed that 68 per cent respondents felt that the economic slowdown would continue at least for six months to a year. The Asian meltdown and slowdown in international trade are the causes of India's slowdown with 63 per cent of the respondents, while 58 per cent felt that the shrinkage in world trade also contributed a lot to recessionary situation in Indian industry. Hence, both research organisations and the associations of commerce and industry did not expect an early recovery.

The CSO's quick estimates for 1998-99 however indicate that GDP registered a growth of 6.8 per cent against the RBI's projected growth of 6.5 per cent. This shows how consistent were the RBI's growth projections for 1998-99 with the reality. Now the CSO's advance estimates for 1999-2000 are available. They indicate GDP growth of 5.9 per cent. Growth of GDP from manufacturing is expected to almost double to 7.0 per cent in 1999-2000 from 3.6 per cent in 1998-99. In the light of these facts now it is claimed that the country's economy is firmly on the road to recovery. Most economists are, however, not so certain about the economy's prospects.

❑

3

Economic Reforms and Liberalisation

THE ORIGIN OF ECONOMIC CRISIS

In early 1991, a major economic crisis surfaced in India. It was the worst crisis that India had experienced since Independence. Increasing fiscal deficit adverse balance of payments position, high rate of inflation and Gulf crisis in late 1990 led to the economic crisis. Let discuss these factor in detail.

1. The Fiscal Imbalance. When a country faces budgeting deficit, revenue deficit, monetised deficit and/or gross difical deficit for a long period of time, is called fiscal imbalance. The steep rise in non-development expenditure was the main cause for rise in governmental expenditure. If the government revenue does not match with the increased expenditure, government fill this gap through, market borrwings, small savings, provident funds, external borrowings etc. The conventional measures of fiscal imbalance do not reflect this. In contrast, the concept of gross fiscal deficit is a complete measure of fiscal inbalance. It equals the excess of total government expenditure over revenue and grants. The gross fiscal deficit rose from 4.1 percent in 1975 to 8.4 percent in 1990-91. Since the fiscal deficit had to be met by recourse to borrowings, the internal debt of the government increased rapidly. This naturally made burden of servicing the debt overones. Interest payments which were 10 percent of total Central Government expenditure in 1980-81, rose to 20 percent total Central Government Expenditure in 1990-91. It was equivalent to 36.4 percent of the total revenue collections of the

Central Government. This was an unsustainable situation. The danger of the government falling into debt-trap was real.

2. Adverse Balance of Payments Situation. The balance of payment situation was very serious. The deficit in current account was continuously rising. It increased from $2.1 billion in 1980-81 to $9.7 billion in 1990-91. As a consequence of this govt. had to resort to external borrowings. The continuance increase in external borrowing led to an increase in debt service burdem from 15 percent of export earnings in 1980-81 to 30 percent of expert earnings in 1990-91. This put strains to the breaking point in 1991 due to Gulf crisis. The balance of payments position was on the brink of disaster and the level of foreign exchange reserves dropped to levels which were not sufficient to finance imports of even ten days in the month of June, 1991. The country's balance of payments position was extremely vulnerable and to avert the default, of the Government used stocks of gold to obtain foreign exchange, took emergency bilateral assistance from donor countries and borrowed under special facilities from the IMF. All these pushed the country into a recessionary situation.

3. Increasing Inflationary Pressures. The price situation was not alarming in the later half of the 1980s as the average rate of inflation was 6.7 percent annum. However, the rate of inflation rose to 10.3 percent perannum in 1990-91. During this inflationary situations, the prices of food rose sharply in spite of three good monsoons in a row. The abnormal increase in food prices was mainly due to the excessive growth of money supply. This liquidity overchange, in conjunction with real disproportionalities and underlying supply demand inbalances was bound to fuel inflation.

The counter the economic crisis government introduced economic reforms to deal with demand side and supply side management.

ECONOMIC REFORMS

In response to the crisis situation the government introduced economic policy reforms which consisted to two distinct strands-macro-economic stabilisation and structural reforms. While stabilisation deals with demand management, structural reforms deal with sectoral adjustments designed to tackle the problems on the supply side of the economy.

Under macroeconomic stabilisation (*i.e.,* demand management) government tried:

(i) tc control inflation;

(ii) to adjust fiscal inbalance and

(iii) to adjust balance of payment situation.

On the other hand, under structural reforms (*i.e.,* supply side management) the govenrment introduced:

(i) trade and capital flows reforms

(ii) industrial deregulation

(iii) disinvestment and public enterprise reforms

(iv) financial sector reforms

(v) reforms in agriculture sector, human resource sector etc.

A. MACROECONOMIC STABILISATION

Macroeconomic stabilisation or stabilisation involves returning to low and stable inflation and a sustainable fiscal and balance of payments position. Stabilisation in necessary to overcome a crisis but it assumes a special importance if structural reforms are also introduced together with stabilisation. This is because structural reforms often add to macroeconomic pressures. Under the stabilisation programme, government took the following steps:

1. Control of Inflation. The rate of inflation in 1990-91 was well above 10 per cent annum. This could be brought down on the one hand by introducing fiscal and monetary discipline in the economy and on the other by improving output and supply position. It seems that the government's achievements are modest on both the fronts.

During the period from 1990 to 2000, government followed liberal monetary policy in one and strict monetary policy in another year. In the year 1991-92 money supply and wholesale price index increased by 20.6 percent and 13.7 percent respectively. In 1992-93, satisfactory growth in agriculture and industrial production along with control money supply it increased by 7.6 percent) brought down the rate of inflation to 7.6 percent and further came down to around 1.5 percent in 2000-01. This was mainly the result of slower monetary growth.

A low trend rate of inflation in Indian context requires firm control of the rate of monetary expansion. Joshi and Little argued that if the controlled expansion of money supply is accompanied by a high rate of fiscal deficit, real interest rates are driven up and private investment is squeezed. If high rates of private investment are necessary for rapid growth, this in effect means that low inflation becomes incompatible with high growth.

2. Fiscal Adjustment. Fiscal adjustment is necessary for dealing with the twin problems of high domestic inflation and large deficits in the balance of payments. Fiscal deficit of the government (Centre, State and Union Territories together) was less than 7 per cent of GDP at the beginning of the 1970s. It, however, rose to about 11 per cent of GDP in 1990-91. The factor which contributed most to the growing fiscal deficit was sharp deterioration of the balance on revenue account. The government having recognised that such high levels of fiscal deficits, both overall and on revenue account were not sustainable, committed itself to a policy of fiscal adjustment. The Central government initiated a programme of fiscal adjustment under which its fiscal deficit which was around 8.3 per cent of GDP in 1990-91, was reduced to 5.9 per cent in 1991-92 and further to 5.7 per cent in 1992-93. The fiscal deficit once again rose to a higher level because. States never committed themselves to any fiscal adjustment programme. Indulging in populism they are neither inclined to curtail nonplan revenue expenditure, nor willing to optimise resources mobilisation through tax and non-tax sources.

In India, the fiscal imbalance has been caused mainly by imprudent increase in public expenditure. The government expenditure which was about 19 per cent of GDP in 1970-71 rose sharply to 37 per cent of GDP in 1990-91. Therefore, if fiscal imbalance is to be corrected, it is necessary to reduce the government expenditure to aroud 25 per cent of GDP. However, in 1997-98, the government expenditure constituted about 28.8 per cent of GDP. To curtail if further, the government should reduce particularly the consumption expenditure mainly of defence expenditure and administrative expenditure, subsidy payments and interest payments. Although for the purpose of fiscal adjustments containment of the government expenditure should receive overriding priority, some efforts at additional resource mobilisation through tax and non-tax sources may also be necessary in the short-run. In India, since built-in revenue elasticity with respect to GDP is around unity, almost all the increase in revenue has to be obtained from additional revenue mobilisation efforts. The Planning Commission has stated, "The required additional revenues may have to be generated by a judicious mixture of broadening the tax base, rationalising the tax rates and through non-tax sources." An area where there is considerable scope for revenue mobilisation is public services. User charges on publicly provided utilities such as irrigation, electricity, water, road transport and higher education are much below their cost of provision. The government can justifiably raise user charges on public utilities like electricity, irrigation, transportation and water. The government, however, does not seem to be serious about additional resource mobilisation through raising the recovery rates on public utility services. It has also failed to cut down its consmption expenditures and subsidy payments. Its interest payments continue to increase as there is no serious attempt to liquidate substantial part of the existing stock of internal debt. Having failed in adopting hard corrective measures, the government has opted for some soft options such as reduction in capital expenditure and social services in real terms. A fall in capital expenditure by government is generally expected to cause an overall decline in the rate of capital formation, while the containment of expenditure on social services adversely affect the human well-being.

3. Balance of Payments Adjustment. At present balance of payments situation is not as precarious as it was in 1990-91. The level of foreign exchange reserves has risen from a meagre $ 2.2

billion in March 1991 to $ 60.0 billion on Aug. 10, 2002. This accumulation of foreign exchange reserves suggests that the Indian economy has moved to a somewhat stable and sustainable balance of payments position in the last eight years. The current account deficit was 3.3 per cent of GDP in 1990-91 but fell to 0.4 per cent in 1991-92 mainly due to import compression which in trun adversely affected the overall performance of the economy. The government adopted a policy of import liberalisation considering a relatively comfortable foreign exchange reserves position. An impressive growth of export reduced the trade deficit bringing down the current account deficit to 0.4 per cent of GDP.

In later years a higher import growth and lower export growth widned the trade deficit. The current account deficit was 1.0 per cent of GDP in 1989-99 and 1999-2000.

Policies relevant to the balance of payments which were adopted during the past seven years were guided but both stabilisation and structural reform considerations. In India's case, the balance of payments problems arose largely from inadequate coverage of import by export earnings. In the beginning of the 1980s, this coverage ratio was only 52.4 per and led to a massive trade deficit. There was some improvement in it during the 1980s and in 1990-91 export earnings accounted for about 66.2 per cent of the value of imports. Hence there is need to boost the export growth rate.

According to experts, export will have to grow at around 14 per cent in value (9 per cent in volume) to achieve a sustainable balance of payments position. However, for rapid export growth the real exchange rate is critically important because export competitiveness largely depends on it. According to Joshi and Little, "The correct policy assignment in India is to target the exchange rate on export competitiveness." Joshi and Little further argue that an appropriate exhcange rate policy is necessary but not sufficient to promote exports. It will have to be accompanied by fiscal consolidation, trade reform, infrastructure development and incentives for private investment in export capacity.

B. STRUCTURAL REFORMS

The major structural reforms and the following:

1. Trade and Capital Flows Reforms. Since July 1991, the government has introduced a series of reforms in the trade sector which will help integration of the Indian economy better with the rest of the world. Among these reform measures, devaluation of rupee in July 1991 and subsequently its depreciation against the currencies of the leading industrialised countries, introduction of the convertibility of the rupee first on trade account and then for the entire current account transactions, liberalistion of import regime, substantial reduction in customs tariff rates, decanalisation of many items of trade and wide ranging measures to give a thrust to exports are important. The details of the steps taken are following:

(i) The system of fixed exchange rates was abandoned by India in September 1975 and since then the system of managed exchange rate float has been in operation. However, due to higher rate of inflation in India as compared to that in the developed countries, the real effective exchange rate of rupee did not fall as much as the nominal effective exchange rate of rupee. Hence, as already written earlier, the government formally devalued rupee by around 22 per cent in July 1991 to restore India's international competitiveness. This was followed by a liberalisation of the foreign trade through dismantling of some physical controls. Not only the import procedures were simplified but a significant number of items were shifted outside the purview of import licensing. The partial convertibility of rupee was also introduced. The 1993-94 Budget introduced full convertibility of rupee on trade account and thus the dual exchange rate system was replaced by a unified exchange rate system. Since the rupee exhibited good strength after the announcement of full convertibility of the rupee for the entire current account transactions was introduced in August 1994 alongwith some relaxation of exchange control.

(ii) As a first step towards a gradual reduction in the tarrif, the 1991-92 Budget had reduced the peak rate of import duty from more than 300 per cent to 150 per cent. The process of lowering the customs tariff rate was carried further in subsequent Budgets. The Budget reduced the peak rate of import duty to 30 per cent in 2002-03.

(iii) Earlier a large number of export and imports used to be canalised throgh public sector agencies. During the past six years a large number of export and import items have been decanalised. However, 8 items including petroleum products, fertilisers, foodgrains and edible oils remain canalised. Decanalisation of imports and exports as it has been done in recent years is an important step towards opening of more area of the external sector to the private sector.

(iv) Over the past few years not only substantial import duty cuts have been made in the case of machine tools, steel ores and concentrates, leather industry, electronics and telecommunications sectors, but the prevailing system of imports duties has also been considerably rationalised with the purpose of establishing a party in prices of goods produced domestically and internationally.

(v) As a part of structural reforms the government has taken various export promotion measures. A part from the systems of Eximscrips and liberalised exchange rate mechanism which were short lived, the government adopted a variety of export promotion measures under the Exim Policies (1922-97 and 2002-07). The important measures introduced were–establishment of Export Oriented Units for promoting exports from the agricultural and allied sectors, simplification of Export Promotion Capital Goods Scheme, introduction of Export Promotion Capital Goods scheme for the services sector, adoption of a more rational and convenient criterion for recognition of export houses/traditing houses/star trading houses, broadening of areas of activity in Export Processing

Zones, duty free import for exports under advance licensing scheme, and creation of an exporters' grievance cell in the Ministry of Commerce to facilitate action on problems being faced by exporters.

(vi) The government has also liberalised capital flows in the form of foreign direct investment as a part of the package of external sector reforms. Important measures in this direction are *(i)* automatic approval of foreign equity participation upto 51 per cent in 48 industries and automatic approval upto 50 per cent foreign equity in 3 industries related to mining; *(ii)* approval of foreign equity participation upto 51 percent in service areas; *(iii)* delinking technology transfer from equity investment to import flexibility in the choice of technology; *(iv)* automatic clearance for import of capital goods in cases where foreign exchange flows through foreign equity; and *(v)* amending Foreign Exchange and Regulation Act (FERA) to place FERA companies on par with Indian companies for all operational pruposes. Now FERA has been replaced by Foreign Exchange Management Act (FEMA). These liberalisation measures in respect of foreign investment though highly acclaimed in the official circles, have exposed the industrial activity to extensive control of multinational corporations (MNCs). According to Dalip Swamy, the possible onslaught of MNCs in coming years will lead to increasing use of capital intensive technology and the consequent displacement of labour.

2. Industrial Deregulation. Historically, India's dometic economic activities have been subject to a wide array of physical controls. In the industrial sector, such controls took various forms: industrial licensing which regulated entry and expansion; reservation of a large number of industries for the public sector as well as small scale sector; time consuming procedures required for the exit of industrial units; and price and distribution controls on various industrial products. Isher J. Ahluwalia blamed the industrial licensing system and bureaucratic controls for the industrial stagnation during the second half of the sixties and the seventies. L.K. Jha recognised the positive role of regulatory appratus in a planned economy, but nonetheless argued that the industrial licensing machinery over the years had become a major obstacle to industrial development. The long time taken by the industrial licensing authorities to give clearance to the various proposals made it impossible for any project of importance to be completed within the scheduled time period. The industrial licensing authorities often took exception to the attempts of the industrial units to produce more than licensed capacity. Thus the objective of maximisation of ouput from a given licensed capacity got undermined.

Limit on the size of the companies which was earlier enforced under the monopoly and Restrictive Trade Practices Act has now been scrapped. This will allow industrial units to grow to optimum size and enjoy the benefits of economies of scale. The anti-monopoly legislation until this relaxation was made, had prevented many firms from growing to optimum size and thus achieve higher efficiency levels. The industrial location policy has been both simplified and liberalised. The phased manufacturing programme under which domestic manufactures were required to increase the domestic input-content of their products in a specified period has also been abolished under the new indsutrial policy.

In recent years, it has been increasingly realised that the regulatory device has led to widespread inefficiency in the industrial sector. The government had, therefore, been relaxing some of these controls even before it committed itself to structural reforms in 1991. The thrust of the new industrial policy announced in July 1991 is on deregulation of the industrial economy in a substantial manner and opening up a large number of industries to the private sector. The requirement of industrial licensing has been abolished for all but 6 product categories. These are alcohol, cigarettes, hazardous chemicals, industrial explosives, durgs and pharmaceuticals (excepting bulk drugs), electronics aerospace and defence equipment. In another significant step the number of industries reserved for the public sector has been reduced from 17 to 4.

3. Public Sector Reforms and Disinvestment. The public sector has failed to generate sufficient internal resources for its further expansion and, as a result, has now become a major constraint on economic growth. Under structural reforms the government has decided to give greater managerial autonomy to public enterprises to enable them to work efficiently. In addition to this, two other key elements of the government's strategy for public enterprises reforms are the promotion of increased private sector competition in areas where social considerations are not paramount and partial disinvestment of equity in selected enterprises. The government has taken concrete steps for encouraging private entry into sectors previously dominated by the public sector. Disinvestment in the form of transfer of a part of the ownership of State owned enterprises to the public is another form of privatisation undertaken by the government.

It is often argued that there are strong reasons for disinvestment in public sector undertakings. R.K. Mishra *et al* point out that disinvestment of shareholdings enables public sector undertakings in acquiring their corporate identity whereby they can "keep pace with the market dynamism flowing from quick business reflexex resulting from their being distanced away from the government." Further, disinvestment permits public enterprises to develop their own financing plans reducing thereby their dependence on the government. In any case, the government has undertaken disinvestment of shareholdings on a modest scale during the past seven years.

4. Financial Sector Reforms. The government, set up a Committee on Financial System (CFS) under the chairmanship of M. Narasimham, to examine the country's financial system and its various components and to make recommendations in respect of the following:

1. For improving the efficiency and effectiveness of the financial system, with special reference to economy of operations, accountability and profitability.
2. For infusing greater competition into the financial system so as to enable the banks and other financial institutions to

respond more effectively to the credit needs of the economy.

3. For ensuring appropriate and effective supervision over the various entities in the financial sector, in particlar the commercial banks and term lending institutions.

The Committee was also required to review the existing legislative framework and to suggest necessary amendments for implementing the recommendations.

The report of the Narasimham Committee on Financial System (submitted in December 1991) has now become the basis for financial sector reforms in this country.

The CFS has among other things, recommended *(a)* establishment of a four tier hierarchy of the banking structure with 3 or 4 large banks including State Bank of India at the top and rural banks at the bottom mainly engaged in financing agriculture and related activities; *(b)* assigning supervisory functions over banks and financial institutions to a separate quasi autonomous body sponsored by the Reserve Bank of India; *(c)* phased achievement of 8 per capital adequacy ratio as recommended by the Basle Committee; *(d)* abolition of branch licencing policy; *(e)* phased reduction in statutory liquidity ratio starting from 1991-92; *(f)* deregulation of interest rates which are related to the bank rate on the basis of guidelines provided by the Chakravarty Committee; *(g)* competition among financial institutions which will adopt a syndicating or participating approach rather than a consortium approach; *(h)* retention by the Industrial Development Bank of India of only its refinancing role and delegation of its direct lending activity to a separate corporate body; *(i)* prudential guidelines should govern the functioning of financial institutions; *(j)* proper classification of assets and full disclosure and transparency of accounts of banks and other financial institutions; and *(k)* setting up of a separate institution by the Government of India to be known as Asset Reconstruction Fund with the pupose of taking over a portion of the loan portfolio of banks which has become bad and doubtful and whose recovery is not easy due to slow legal process.

The report of the CFS was placed before the Parliament in December 1991, and since then it has become the basis for introducing reform in the banking sector. The major reform measures undertaken during the past few years are as follows:

1. The government has over the past eight years brought down both statutory liquidity ratio and cash reserve ratio in a phased manner. The effective statutory liquidity ratio has been lowered down to 25 per cent. The cash reserve ratio which is the only effective instrument of monetary control in India is being no longer depended upon to combat inflation. It has thus been brought down to 10 per cent.
2. The earlier formats of the balance sheet and profit and loss account did not reflect the true financial position of the banks. Hence, they have been revised and made effective from the bank accounting year 1991-92.
3. The RBI has introduced new prudential norms in respect of income recognition, classification of assets, provisioning of bad debts and capital adequacy. The minimum capital standards have been prescribed in accordance with the Basle Committee norms under which banks are required to maintain unimpaired capital funds equivalent to 8 per cent of the aggregated of the risk weighted assets.
4. Commercial banks attaining capital adequacy norms and prudential accounting standards have been given freedom to set up new branches without the approval of the Reserve Bank of India. Banks can now also rationalise their existing branch network by relocating branches, opening of specialised branches, setting up controlling offices etc.
5. The Central Government provided budgetary support of Rs. 17,346 crore for recapitalisation of public sector banks till 1996-97. This, however, was not sufficient for achievement of norms by all banks. Hence banks had to raise had to raise debt and equity resources from the public. By the end of March 1997, only two public sector

banks could not achieve the prescribed 8 per cent capital to risk weighted assets ratio.

6. The RBI has announced guidelines for setting up banks in the private sector. These banks should be financially viable and should avoid concentration of credit and crossholdings with industrial groups. Further, they will have to observe priority sector lending targets as applicable to other banks. Ten banks have already started functioning and, "in principle approvals" have also been given to three other proposals for setting up new local area private sector banks one each in Andhra Pradesh, Karnataka and Maharastra.

7. Number of interest rates slabs on banks advances were reduced from about 20 in 1989-90 to 2 in the financial year 1994-95. This attempt to unify interest rate structure aims at reducing the degree of cross-subsidy in the banking system.

8. The supervisory system of the RBI is being strengthened with the establishment of a new Board for Financial Supervision under the chairmanship of Deputy Governor of the RBI. The Board will ensure implementation of the regulations with respect to credit management, asset classification, income recognition, provisioning, capital adequacy and treasury operations.

9. Agreements between the RBI and public sector banks have been made to improve the management and the quality of the performance of the latter. This includes management information system and the internal audit and control mechanisms.

10. Recovery of debts due to banks and other financial institutions in the past has been unsatisfactory. Hence, an Act was passed in 1993 under which Special Recovery Tribunals have been set up to facilitate quicker recover of loan arrears.

11. The guidelines for determning the maximum permissible bank finance have been made more flexible. Banks will

now have greater freedom in determining the working capital needs of the borrowers and responding to local requirements in an appropriate manner.

Following the recommendations of the Narasimhan Committee on Financial System (CFS) the above reform measures were undertaken. The government appointed the Committee on Banking Sector Reforms (CBSR) under the chairmanship of M. Narasimham. The Committee (CBSR) submitted its report in April 1998. Its major recommendations are as follows:

1. Strong banks should be merged and relatively weak and unviable ones should be closed.
2. The Committee recommended new and higher norms for capital adequacy. It suggested that the minimum capital to risk assets ratio be increased to 10 per cent from its earlier level of 8 per cent.
3. Legal framework is not adeqaute for credit recovery. It should be strengthened.
4. The country should have two or three banks with international orientation, eight to ten national banks and a large number of local banks. The third-tier banks should remain confined to smaller geographical regions. The first and the second tier banks shall take care of the needs of the corporate sector.
5. There should be rationalisation of branches and staff.
6. Bank board should be depoliticised under the RBI supervision.
7. Budgetary support for recapitalisation is not viable and should thus be abandoned.
8. Net non-performing assets for all banks be brought down to below 5 per cent by the year 2000 and to 3 per cent by 2002.
9. The polcy of licensing new private banks may be continued.

10. Foreign banks may be allowed to set up subsidiaries or joint ventures in India. Such subsidiaries or joint ventures should be treated on par with other private baks and subject to the same conditions with regard to branches and directed credit as these banks.
11. There has to be an integrated system of regulation and supervision to regulate and supervise the activities of banks, financial institutions and non-bank finance companies. The agency for this purpose be renamed as the Board for Financial Regulation and Supervision (BFRS).

AN APPRAISAL OF ECONOMIC REFORMS

Since July 1991 the government has undertaken both stabilisation programmes and structural reforms as two components of the economic reforms package.

In the real sectors, the structural reforms have started showing some results. In 1991-92 there was near stagnation. However, during the period of the Eighth Plan, the industrial production rose at the rate of 8.4 per cent per annum. Since 1990-91 there was a steep fall in both savings and investment rates for three years. However, both savings and investment rates showed an upturn in 1994-95 which could not be sustained in later years. These gains from structural reforms notwithstanding, the economic reforms have been subjected to various criticism which are following:

1. Absence of a Broader Development Strategy. The focus of both macroeconomic stabilisation and structural reforms is to create a competitive environment in industry in which entrepreneurial decision-making will depend entirely on the market forces. The government's new industrial policy therefore lacks a well defined strategy. The case of industrialisation in South Korea is quite revealing. The government in this country steadfastly pursued a policy of heavy and chemical industrialisation despite the still opposition from the IMF and the World Bank. Judged against the experiences of these countries, the interventionist strategy of the government in this country can be criticised only for lack of dynamism. On the basis of our experience in the past it is patently wrong to conclude that a well articulated industrial strategy and heavy State intervention have no positive role to play in accelerating industrial growth.

2. Hasty Pace of Reforms. The rapid pace of reforms has been determined by the controversial goal to globalise the Indian economy quickly. This has led to rapid deterioration in the quality of industrial structure. *EPW* Research Foundation points out, "A sharp reduction in industrial growth, reduction in the growth of capital goods' industries, a relative shift of exports away from manufactures, and arresting of the growth of industrial employment, have been some of the glaring effects of rapid reforms without providing for some breathing time and appropriate checks and balances for the Indian industry."

3. Wrong Sequencing of Reforms. As a result of wrong sequencing of reforms, serious distortions have surfaced in economic management. There are at least three examples of wrong sequencing of reforms. First, while for drastic reduction in fiscal deficit, revenue deficit and even budget deficit the prerequisites are decisive reduction of non-development expenditure and widening the tax base, the government has initiated fiscal correction programme with surrendering of revenue through substantial reductions in tax rates and compression of capital expenditure. Second, a more obvious case of inappropriate sequencing relates to compression of government's capital expenditure and contraction of public investment before ensuring that the private sector and the foreign investors will fill the gap. The third case of flawed sequencing is of liberalising imports of capital goods before adopting a strategy for technology advancement of the domestic capital goods sector. The latter was necessary for adopting outward oriented stratgy of economic growth.

4. Absence of Human Development Goals as an Integral Part of the Strategy. The stabilisation and structural reform programme in India is implemented against a background of incomplete structural transformation, widespread poverty, low level of human development and distorted pattern of expenditure on health and education oriented towards the relatively well off sections of the society. Given these dismal conditions and a low rate of economic growth, structural reforms must be undertaken with a human face. This requires that human development goals should be an integral part of the strategy of structual adjustment. Unfortunately in India no such attempt has been made.

5. Prerequisites of Reforms Ignored. The literature on stabilisation and structural reforms is full of evidence that the shocks of these policies are better absorbed and their consequences for the well-being of the masses are very much reduced if the society has already reached a certain minimal level of human development. South Korea, Malaysia, Thailand and Indonesia are the recent successful cases but in all these countries not only the socio-economic structure was far more egalitarian due to land reforms and such other measures but the human development indices like expectancy and literacy rates were at higher levels, while infant mortality was at a lower level before they embarked on significant structural reform programme. In contrast, the Indian situation is not at all encouraging from the point of view of human development and socio-economic structures.

Because of these reasons the economic reforms lack sustainbility led to low growth rate and recession in the economy.

ECONOMIC CRISIS : CONTEXT OF REFORMS

Indian economy faced a major economic crisis in 1990 which is known as macro economic imbalances. To start with, the Gulf war led to a sharp increase in oil prices. Foreign exchange reserves began to decline since September 1990; it declined from Rs. 5480 crore (31 Aug., 90) to R. 1,666 crore (10th Jan., 1991). During this period our Government took recources to the IMF for Credit Tranche (CT) Arrangement and also Compensatory and Contingency Financing Facility (CCFF). But the decline in foreign exchange reserves continued unabated.

The payments crisis (1990-91) was due not only to a decline in trade account, it was accompanied by other adverse developments on the capital account reflecting the loss of confidence in the Government's ability to manage the economic environment. Short-term credits began to dry up, as India's credit-rating started deteriorating to a low level. This imposed a severe strain on our balance of payments position. The drying up of commercial loans in 1990-91 was accompanied by a net ouflow of NRI deposits at the monthly average rate of $ 190 million during April-October 1991. The then payments crisis had become overwhelmingly a crisis of confidence of confidence in the Government's ability to manage the situation. A default on payments had become a serious possibility in June 1991, and this was for the first time in our history.

A default is essentially a failure to repay debt. Our public debt, both internal and external, had assumed such a massive proportion by then that it was but natural for everyone to think that Indian economy would collapse *under debt service burden*. This confidence reaction led to a breakdown in credit availability and in normal payments arrangements. Suppliers became reluctant to sell goods and services and insisted on advance payments through banks of their own country. This led to *trade disruption*, which in turn forced severe and prolonged import compression, and resulted in shortage, *industrial dislocation*, *severe/unemployment and higher inflation*-a series of crises in the Indian economy.

The new Government which assumed office in June 1991 had to act swiftly to deal with that deteriorating economic environment and bring our economy back from the brink of default. Therefore, an emergency action was taken in organising the *sale of gold* by our Government. The Government immediately leased 20 tonnes of gold out of its stock to the State Bank of India to enable it to sell gold abroad with an option to repurchase it at the end of six months. In addition, the Government allowed the Reserve Bank of India to ship 47 tonnes of gold to the Bank of England in July 1991 when the exchange rate of the rupee was also adjusted to bring it to a creditable level which could be defended. A massive *devaluation* of the rupee in successive bouts by a sum-total of about 20% against major currencies was aimed at improving the trade-and payments situation. It was expected that devaluation would make our exports cheaper and imports dearer, and thereby reverse the trend of growing trade deficits.

In the wake, of devaluatution, came the inflation. An *inflationary spriral* began in October 1990. The wholesale price index, on a point-to-point basis, showed a rapid increase in our annual inflation rate from 70% to about 17% during, October and August 1991. A number of demand-pull and cost-push factors together with a set of long-run structural factors and short-run shock factors-all factors together triggered the then inflation rate. The rate and structure of inflation adversely affected the terms of trade between agriculture and industry. In particular, the then prevailing inflation brought out clearly the damage done by fiscal imbalances.

Fiscal imbalances were reflected in growing budget deficits mainly because of escalating non-Plan expenditure in the face of sluggish revenue growth. Increasing budget deficit on the revenue account indicated danger signal. In fact, budget deficits, trade deficits and payments deficits-all became organisationaly linked to damage the state of our national economic. As the deficits in the budget were financed by money creation, the demand-pull inflation got engineered. And some of the cost-push factors like hike in administered price, poor performance of public sector, alarming size of subsidy got together to throw our fiscal economy totally out of gear.

It was evident that the Indian economy needed substantial reform if those crises were to be fully overcome. The new Government moved urgently to implement a programme of *macro-economic stabilization* through a number of structural reforms of trade, industry and public sector. The objective was to initiate a series of fiscal and financial reforms to ensure both efficiency and equity norms in managing our economy. Structural reforms were necessary to reverse various unhealthy economic trends and tendencies. Without engineering, initiating and then accelerating the pace of such reforms, our economy could not have been brought back on the rail and thereby signalled its engine-of-growth which came to a temporary halt, to proceed further and forward.

The major economic reforms undertaken are the following:

1. **Fiscal Policy Reforms.** When the volume of fiscal deficits assumed a huge proportion of Rs. 43,331 cr. in 1990-91, it

was decided to bring down the fiscal deficits from 8.4% of the GDP in 1990-91 to 6.5% in 1991-92 and further to 5% in 1992-93. To this end, a number of tax reforms were introduced in the Budget Proposals since 1991-92 in line with the Chelliah Committee Report. Also, some improvements in fiscal performance were made possible by the decision to abolish export subsidies of CCS, to increase fertilizer prices and to keep non-Plan expenditures (including defence expenditure) in check.

2. **Trade Policy Reforms.** New initiatives were taken in trade policy to create an environment to seize the opportunities of globalisation. Devaluation of our currency facilitated 18% exchange rate adjustment towards promoting exports and restricting imports. A few other measures were taken in 1991-92: import entitlement (introduction of Eximscrips), advance licensing system for exports, permission to import capital goods. Export and Trading Houses, 51% foreign equity in Trading Houses. Subsequently by way of new EXIM policy, a few more progressive steps have been taken, such as abolition of Eximscrips, partial and finally full convertibility of the rupee, abolition of foreign exchange travel tax, introduction of liberalised exchange rate management system (LERMS), pruning of negative list of imports etc.
3. **Industrial Policy Reforms.** Industrial policy reforms announced in July 1991 should be seen complementary to those undertaken in trade, financial and fiscal policies. The central elements of these reforms were: abolition of industrial licensing for all but 18 industries amendment of MRTP Act defining the asset limit to allow Indian firms to grow in size to compete globally, discontinuance of the phased manufacturing programme (PMP), privatisation except for 8 industries of strategic and security concerns, reservation of items for small units, public sector disinvestment, new guidelines for joint venutres, amendement of FERA to

facilitates the inflow of foreign capital, foreign technology and foreign enterprises; enhancement of the limit of foreign equity holding to 51% and more; deregulation, ôpen sky policy, liberalised industrial location and mineral policy, dispersion of industries, decentralisation, debureacratisation etc. These measures have been instrumental in assisting the trend towards economic liberalism and market-friendly approach.

4. **Public Sector Reforms.** The performance of public sector units deteriorated so sharp in 1990-91 that is was immediately felt that these units must work towards improvement in its profitability and productivity. These units must earn an adequate return on its own investment. The Public sector has become a public burden, they are to be subsidized such that they yield a higher net social return than before. The Government undertook a limited public disinvestment of a part of public sector equity to the public through public financial institutions and mutual funds in order to raise non-inflationary finance for development. It is argued that such policies of disinvestment will bring in greater public accountability. The Government specially amended the Sick Industrial Companies Act, in view of growing sickness and took ameliorative measures like BIFR. A National Renewal Fund has been set up to facilitate modernisation of industry and to provide a safety net to its workers. Our Government is also involved in the process of finalising a draft on the exit policy. All these measure taken together are expected to tone up the level of operational efficiency of our public enterprises.

5. **Financial Reforms.** The operation of both banking and non-banking sector has come in for criticism time and again since the days of nationalisation of banks. From time to time, a number of Committees have been set up, and some of their recommendations have also been accepted. Of late attention has been drawn towards specific structural

reforms of the financial sectors. For example, Late Prof. Sukhomoy Chakravarty, while commenting on the need for monetary reforms obseved that the RBI "has tremendous responsibility but not enough authority", as a result of which the non-banking organised sector as well as unorganised sector often remain outside the effective control of the RBI and, therefore, the instruments of monetary policy fail to perform their functions. Also, the Report of Narasimham Committee (1991 Dec.) has been considered. The Government initiated a set of measures, in line with the theme of liberalisation, to introduce structural reforms in the financial sector. It has been accepted that the financial markets should work on laissez faire principles applicable within a regulatory framework. The office of Controller of Capital Isses has been abolished. Among other measures introduced in 1991-92, we may note:

(a) enhancement of bank rate from 10% to 12%;

(b) additional CRR of 10% on incremental deposits of the scheduled commercial banks;

(c) withdrawal of finance facility;

(d) ceilings imposed on drawing power of big borrowers;

(e) easier terms for export credit,

(f) liberalised guidelines for commercial paper (CP) and certificates of deposits (CD);

(g) concessional housing loans etc. Also, a number of institutional developments has been ushered in the establishment of National Housing Bank (NH B), Money Market Mutual Funds (MMMFs), Discount & Finance House of India (DFHI), Credit Rationing Information Services in India Ltd. (CRISIL), Security & Exchange Board of India (SEBI).

Despite all these development in the capital market and the money market, the recent *security scam* has brought the banking and financial reforms to a grinding halt. The extent of corruption and incompetence right acros the financial sector has come as a shock. The Government has now enacted special legislation and has brought in the CBI to prosecute the guilty. The Joint Parliamentary Committee (JPC) is also on the job. Legal process will take its own time, but the agenda of financial reforms should not be suspended.

The critics have stated that the security scam, on the whole, is a price that the economy must pay for hectic liberalisation. It is the process of uncontrolled liberalisation, without any checks and balances, that allowed the scam to happen. This does not mean that the economic reforms must stop; rather, based on the lesson we have learnt, the reforms must continue within the framework of care and caution, rules and regulations. Economic reforms do stand at a critical stage now.

The Government is currently reviewing the pre-and post-reforms gains and pains so as to work out future strategy with regard to the size, structure and speed of these reforms. There is no two opinions that the reforms must continue, that the recommendations of various committees must be re-examined and adopted with or without modifications, wherever desirable and feasible. To understand the future course of economic reforms, a reference to the Reports of several Committees which stand as solid background, is, therefore, in order.

Consequences of Economic Reforms

The consequences of economic reforms can be of two types, short range and long range. The short term purpose of economic reforms was to set the economy at the right track. This objective has been achieved at a great extent. The foreign exchange reserves have increased manifold, the deficit in balance of payment has brought down to the lower level, foreign investment is picking up and moreover the reforms have increased the confidence of domestic, non-resident India and foreign investors. The short run impact of economic reforms is excellent.

The long run impact of these economic reforms is to increase the pace of development so that social welfare can be increase and India can be placed in the category of developed nations. Due to the scarcity of capital and non-availability of superior known how, the rate of growth has been quite low during the four decade of planned development. Indian has a big potential market. Natural resources, skill labourers and other key inputs are also available in plenty. By bringing foreign capital and techinical known how in India, growth rate can be increased. The economic reforms undertaken recently by government will encourage the growth rate in long run.

PUBLIC SECTOR AND ECONOMIC DEVELOPMENT

The public sector have a multitude of objectives set for them, *viz.* to help in the rapid economic growth and industrialisation, to promote redistribution of income and wealth, to create employment opportunities, to promote regional balanced development etc. The public sector is defened as passionately as it is attacked in India. However, the overwhelming view appears to be that, in the process of planned economic development, it must continue the assumption of more and more responsibilities. It is expected to ensure productivity, profitability and the fulfilment of a veriety of social objectives. Keeping in view the idea of modern welfare state and other aspects it may be worthwhile to focus briefly on certain other aspects which justify the existence and growth of public sector in India.

Firstly, as India has opted for a planned economy, the responsibility of national planning cannot be assumed by any person or authority other than the government. "The concept of a planned economy necessarily leads to the government, the state, participating in the acutal management and no merely the regulation of commerce and industry. This is so because the answers to the problems which arise cannot normally be found unless the government and government agencies have direct experience of managing and controlling such enterprises. In any case, it has been noticed that any country following the pattern of 'planned economy', necessarily moves towards active state participation in, and management of, numerous commercial and industrial undertakings.

Secondly, in spite of the existence of an industrial base and the availability of fairly large capital investment funds, it may be a mistake to presume that the existing state of affairs in the country is satisfactory. Moreover, whatever industrial base or capital investment fund is visible today, is a recent phenomenon. It is, indeed, a result of the strong infrastructural base provided by the government of free India. The situation would have been worse, had the state not intervened and allocated a major 'participative role' to itself.

Thirdly, for a welfare government committed to the objective of a socialist society, increasing participation by it in industrial enterprises is inevitable, irresistible and compulsive. If the objective of a socialist society is denied, there might still be some room for debate, but with the postulate of a socialist society, state participation follows inevitably.

Fourthly, the functions of the government, today, are not limited to the maintenance of law and order. They have expanded much beyond. In this context, revenue from tax collections cannot be solely depended upon for meeting the rapidly increasing requirements of the government. Direct participation in industry and commerce may help state to raise substantial funds to discharge its additional obligations.

Fifthly, the specific aim of social and economic justice, such as labour welfare, requires state to take the lead by introducing concepts like "workers' participation in industry" in state enterprises. Government may lead the private sector in this respect. "Let it not be thought, however, that when the state establishes an enterprise or when the state nationalises an industry, the millennium has arrived in employer-employee relationship far from it. And this has been one of the first lessons learnt after the entry of the public sector into trade and industry."

Finally, profits in public sector enterprises enrich the common pool which is available for redistribution and re-investment. The larger the pool of wealth that can be dealt with as a homogeneous whole, the more valuable it is. Unless government participiles in industry and commerce, the dividend it has to pay may take the form of a division of poverty, not a division of wealth.

At the time independence, the activities of public sector were confined to a few areas like irrigation, power, railways, ports, communications and some departmental undertakings. After independence, public sector expanded at a very rapid speed particular in the field of basic and heavy industries. The important point that arises is why were these industries selected for development in the public sector? According to R.K. Hazari the industrial programme of government was built on two hypothesis.

(i) Private investment in relatively simple goods would be promoted by shutting out imports as well as through excess capacity at home, with a consequent boost to profits; and

(ii) Public investment, being autonomous of profits, would take place in basic areas which had long gestation periods, low or no profits, a large foreign exchange component, complex technology and equally complex problems of coordination.

The logic of the first hypothesis was that private investment was in the nature of 'induced investment' and could be promoted by adopting a policy of protection against imported substitutes. The logic of the second hypothesis was that investment in low profit yielding and heavy investment requiring industries were in the nature of 'autonomous the investment' and could accordingly, be undertaken only by the State.

FORMS OF ORGANISATION OF PUBLIC SECTOR UNDERTAKINGS

There are four types of organisation of public sector undertakings—*(i)* departmental undertakings, *(ii)* public corporation, *(iii)* government company, and *(iv)* holding company.

(i) Departmental Undertakings. Departmental undertakings are run and managed by the concerned department of the government. Therefore this form of public enterprise is directly under the control of the government. These departmental undertakings are under the direct control of the concerned ministry. Example in India are Indian Railways, Ports and Telegraphs, atomic power projects, ordinance factories, security and currency presses, mint etc.

(ii) Public Corporation. It is a public body incorporated under a separate statute and is created by a special Act of Parliament or Legislature. Public corporations have their powers, duties and privileges and prescribes the pattern of management. Examples are LIC of India, UTI, ONGC, etc.

(iii) Government Company. A government compnay is established under the Companies Act, 1956 like any other company. According to the Companies Act, a government company is that in which not less than 51 per cent of the paid-up share capital is held by the Central and State Governments. Examples are State Trading Corporations, the General Insurance Corporation of India etc. In 1999, there were 1,240 companies in operation with a paid-up capital of Rs. 88,966 crore.

(iv) Holding Company. The Study Team on Public Sector Undertakings recommended that integral public authorities should be created for particular sectors of industry and entrusted with the task of the general development of the respective sectors including the running of undertakings in those sectors and the setting up of new projects. The idea of a holding company was first mooted in India in the context of iron and steel industry. Steel Authority of India Ltd. (SAIL) was established in 1973. Hindustan Steel Limited (HSL) which owned an managed the steel plants at Bhilai, Rourkela, Durgapur and Bokaro Steel Limited (BSL) which owned and managed the BSL became the wholly owned subsidaries of SAIL. The management of HSC is also under SAIL.

Suitable Form of Organisation. The Study Team made the following recommendations:

(a) In the case of those public sector undertakings which provide services to the entire community (like railways, P&T) departmental form of organisation is the most appropriate.

(b) In those field of activities wherein private sector units also operate, the preferred form of organisation is that of a government company.

(c) Public undertakings in the industrial and manufacturing field should be organised in the form of a public corporation, each covering a number of units operating in the same industry.

ROLE OF PUBLIC SECTOR IN INDIA

Public sector in India plays an important role in the development of the economy. Public sector has not only given a strong industrial base to the nation but it is providing precious foreign exchange to it. Public sector has played a definite positive role in the economy.

1. Capital Formation. The public sector has been playing an important role in encouraging investment since the common cement of planning in India. This is very clear from the table given below.

(In percentage)

Plan	*Public Sector*	*Private Sector*
I & IInd Plan	54	46
IIIrd Plan	60	40
Vth Plan	43.3	56.7
VIth Plan	47.8	52.2
VIIth Plan	45.7	54.3
VIIIth Plan	34.3	65.7
IXth Plan (envisaged)	33.0	67.0

This table reflects that relative importance of public sector in total investment is no declining but it is still very high. The public sector has played a key role by encouraging investment in the private sector. Moreover nationalised banks and other financial institutions have played an important role in collecting savings and mobilization of resources.

2. Development of Infrastructure. The primary condition of economic development in any underdeveloped country is that the infrastructure should develop at a rapid pace. India had inherited an undeveloped basic infrastructure from the colonial period. After Independence, the private sector neither showed any inclination to develop it nor did it have any resources to make this possible. This made the State's participation in industrialization essential since only the government could enforce a large-scale mobilization of capital, the coordination of industrial construction, and training of technicians. The government has not only improved the road, rail, air and sea transport system, it has also expanded them manifold. Thus the public sector has enabled the economy to develop a strong infrastructure for the future economic growth.

3. Strong Industrial Base. The share of the industrial sector in Gross Domestic Product at factor cost has increased slowly but steadily. According to the Old Series (at 1980-81 prices.). The share of the industrial sector in GDP at factor cost rose from 13.3 per cent in 1950-51 to 21.6 per cent in 1980-81 and 25.0 per cent in 2000-2001. On the other hand, the share of agriculture in GDP at factor cost declined from 59.2 per cent in 1950-51 to 41.8 per cent in 1980-81 and further to 26.6 per cent in 2000-2001. Not only this, the industrial base of the Indian economy is now much stronger than what it was in 1950-51. There has been significant growth in the defence industries and industries of strategic importance. The government has strengthened the industrial base considerably by placing due emphasis on the setting up of industries in the following fields—iron and steel, heavy engineering, coal, heavy electrical machinery, petroleum and natural gas, chemicals and drugs, fertilizers, etc. Because of their low profitability potential in the short run, these industries do not find favour with the private sector.

4. Removal of Regional Disparities. The government in India has sought to use its power of setting up of industries as a means of removing regional disparities in industries in Industrial development. In the pre-Independence period, most of the industrial progress of the country was limited in and around the port towns of Mumbai. Calcutta and Chennai. Other parts of the country legged far behind. After the initiation of the planning process in the country in

1951, the government has paid particular attention to the problem and has set up industries in a number of areas hitherto neglected by the private sector. Thus a major proportion of public sector investment has been directed towards backward States.

5. Economies of Scale. In the case of those industries where for technological reasons, the plants have to be large requiring huge investments, getting up of these industries in the public sector can prevent the concentration of económic and industrial power in private hands. It is a known fact that in the presence of significant economies of scale, the free market does not produce the best results. Accordingly, considerations of economic efficiency require some form of government regulation or public ownership. Countries like France and the United Kingdom have explicitly preferred public ownership in field of electric power, natural gas, telephone etc.

6. Check Over Concentration of Economic Power. In a capitalist economy where the public sector is practically non-existent or is of a very small size, economic power gets increasingly concentrated in a few hands and inequalities of income and wealth increase. Public sector can help in reducing inequalities and concentration of economic power in the economy in a number of ways. For instance *(i)* profits of the public sector can be used directly by the government on the welfare programmes of the poorer sections of community; *(ii)* public sector can adopt a discriminatory policy by supplying materials to small industrialists at low prices and big industrialists at high prices; *(iii)* public sector can give better wages to the lower staff as compared to the private sector and can also implement programmes of labour welfare, construction of colonies and townships for labourers, slum clearance, etc.; and *(iv)* public sector can orient production machinery towards the production of mass consumption goods.

7. Important Substitution and Export Promotion. The foreign exchange problem often emerges as a series constraint on the programmes of inudstrialization in a developing economy. Bharat Heavy Electricals Limited, Bharat Electronics Ltd., Hindustan Antibiotics Ltd., Indian Oil Corporation, Oil and Natural Gas

Commission, etc., in the public sector are of special importance from the point of view of import substitution. These units have saved lot of foreign exchange by producing import substitution product.

PERFORMANCE OF PUBLIC SECTOR

1. The Question of Profitability. If we look at the growth of public sector we find that during planning period (1960-61 to 1999) the number of companies and paid-up capital rose by 8.5 and 163 times respectively. This shows that public sector undertakings have wide capital base. It is often said that the performance of public sector undertakings is poor because they are not earning enough profit of the money invested in these public sector undertakings. Some economists argue that their performance should not be judged by the yardstick of the profit carried by them instead of profit, the yardstick should be the contribution made by these undertakings to the flow of goods and services or the total value of sales. Even if we look from the profitability point of view the performance of public sector has improved considerably. As is clear from the table gross profit of public sector.

Expansion and Performance of Public Sector Undertakings

	1980-81	*1990-91*	*1999-2000*
No. of Enterprises	*163*	*236*	*232*
		Rs. crore	
Capital employed	18,207	1,02,084	3,03,611
Turnover	28,635	1,18,676	3,89,310
Gross profit	1,418	11,102	42,422
Net Profit	–2,203	2,272	14,555

has increase considerably from Rs. 1,418 crore in 1980-81 Rs. 42,422 crore in 1999-2000 and net profit which was negative in 1980-81 turned to an impressive positive figure of Rs. 14,555 crore in 1999-2000. Thus it can be said that the performance of public sector has improved considerably. But if we look at the ratio of net profit of capital employed, we find that it is very low *i.e.,* 4.8 percent in 1999-2000. According to Bimal Jalan this low return on investment in the public sector enterprises large exent, responsible for the fiscal crisis of the Central Government.

2. Public Sector and Foreign Exchange Earnings. Enterprises in the public sector have helped the economy in earning substantial amount of foreign exchange and also in saving the foreign exchange and expenditure via their efforts at import substitution. Capital goods, industrial machinery, and other equipment which were totally imported three decades back are now being mostly manufactured in the country itself. This has saved valuable foreign exchange. As far as foreign exchange earnings are concered, the public sector has contributed in three ways: *(i)* through direct export of items produced in the public sector, *(ii)* through serivces rendered by the public sector undertaking, and *(iii)* through and marketing services of the undertaking through which exports are canalized. The public sector has been providing more than one-fifth of total export earnings.

3. Employment and Labour Welfare. As far as this criterion of the performance public sector has contributed to a significant extent in improving the overall employment situation in the country and has acted as a model employer by providing the workers with better wages and other facilities as compared to the private sector. The number of persons employed in the central public sector enterprises exceed 2 million. The average wage per worker in public sector enterprises is also higher than in the private sector. The public sector enterprises have also spent a considerable amount on the development of townships around them. These townships are provided with facilities like schools, hospitals, shopping complexes, etc. A substantial sum of money is spent annually on the maintenance and administration of these townships and social overheads. The employees of the public sector enterprises also enjoy medical amenities, subsidized canteen facilities, transport and educational facilities, etc.

4. The Question of Efficiency. Though there is no dispute regarding the role of the public sector undertakings in country's economic development, yet the feeling widely prevalent is that the rate of profit in these undertakings is either too low or is negative. Accordingly, they are inefficient.

However, it is not so easy to decade about the efficiency of the public sector undertakings. As noted by us earlier, the rate of profit might be a good criterion to judge the efficiency of a private sector enterprise but cannot be deemed so far a public sector enterprise. To judge the efficiency of a public sector undertaking, A.E. Khan and Hollis B. Chenery have recommended the criterion of social marginal productivity. According to Chenery, the utility of investment in any project should be judged by its impact on the national income, balance of payments and distribution of income. According to G.K. Shirokov, efficiency of a public enterprise should not be judged on the basis of profitability alone. The fact is that a higher proportion of the value produced by the public sector industries is realised outside this sector, and it is, therefore, very difficult to estimate the efficiency of public sector enterprises in terms of cost and profitability. Most of the critics of the public sector enterprises fail to take social costs and benefits into account and consider only net profits or losses. They are thus guilty of ignoring the right criteria for judging the performance of public sector enterprises.

PROBLEMS OF PUBLIC SECTOR ENTERPRISES

The most important criticism levied against the public sector has been that, in relation to the capital employed, the level of profits has been too low. Even the government has criticised the public sector enterprises on this count. For instance, the Eighths Five Year Plan notes that the public sector has been unable to generate adequate resources for sustaining the growth process. The following are main problems faced by public sector undertakings:

1. Delay in Completion. Many of the projects took a long time to be completed. Some of the projects have taken less or more years to go into production. The fact has led to many unfavourable consequences.

2. No Specific Purposes. In certain cases in specific purposes for which different enterprises have been set up have not been clearly indicated. Nor has there been any clear definition of financial and economic obligations. The government failed to evolve proper yardstick to evaluate the performance.

3. Heavy Overhead Expenditure. It has been observed that public sector enterprises tends to spend rather heavily on unnecessary and minor items.

4. Poor Manpower Planning. A widely published defect of the public enterprises is that recruitment of labour is in excess of actual requirements. Once workers have been recruited they could not be dispensed with. Poor manpower planning is clearly reflected in the poor and adequate arrangements for training and education of workers.

5. No Precise Targets. Public enterprises do not lay down precise targets of production to be achieved in a prescribe period. There is no proper assessment of capacities and the established capacities have been already used. Unless precise targets of production and prepared and every effort is made to realise them, public sector enterprises will definitely run into losses.

6. Labour Troubles. In many public enterprises serious troubles have occured continuously. Trade Union leader have almost wrecked some enterprises like the Steel Plant of Durgapur. Public enterprises have a special obligation to follow labour policies which are conducive to securing and keeping a competent and contented working force at reasonable cost.

7. Price Policy. A balanced and proper price policy is based on a policy of profit. There has been considerable confusion and difference of opinion in India on this question. It is asserted that government undertakings should not bother about getting proifts, they should give greater importance to provision of welfare to the community. Public sector enterprises in India have failed because their pricing policies are no rational.

8. Poor Return. The most important criticism is that public Undertakings have largely failed and that they have been continuing to exist because of large volume of financial assistance given by the government. Till recently the public enterprises were incurring net losses. The biggest culprits are the Steel Plants, Heavy Electricals, Heavy Engineering, etc.

9. Faulty Financial Control. It is argued that the poor performance of Public Undertakings is due to faulty financial control over public enterprises. In India fianncial control is exercised by the Parliament, the Finance Ministry and the Minister in charge of the undertaking. Parliamentary control over the operations and capital development plants of public enterprises tend to become quite rigid. Parliament does not restrict itself to a survey of overall position but goes into day to day working of the enterprises. The Audit of the Auditor General tends to be inhibitive of all initiatives by the enterprises.

10. Waste of Resources. There are two types of criticisms against public sector undertakings on the question of waste of resources. One complaint is that there is considerable wastage and shortage of rare and scarce raw materials because norms for their consumption have not been fixed. Another complaint is that most of public enterprises carry heavy and unbalanced inventories.

11. Inefficient Management. For efficiency in business and industrial enterpises, it is necessary that operational decisions are prompt. This necessaries a large measure of autonomy and flexibility of operations in government enterprises. The delegation of authority and elasticity in working are therefore needed in a high degree. But in practice executive centralisation and ministerial interference have played hovoc with the efficient working of public undertakings.

Thus, there are many efficiencies and shortcomings of public enterprises. Therefore, sometimes it is said the public sector in India has failed to deliver the goods. But it is not wholly true. All the defects that have been pointed out can be removed if the government follows a sound policy. Further with the gaining of experience many of the problems would be automatically removed. We hope that very soon, the public sector industries will become successful and profitable.

DIFFERENT ROLES OF GOVERNMENT IN THE ECONOMY

There are four important roles played by the the Government in an economy, namely:

(i) The regulatory role;

(ii) The promotional role;

(iii) The entrepreneurial role; and

(iv) The planning role.

1. The Regulatory Role. A large part of the economy of even the most non-centrally planned coutries is regulated by the Government.

First, Government may determine the conditions under which persons or associations may enter certain lines of business, as in the granting of a charter, a franchise, or a licence or permitting any 'person' to use any public facilities or resources.

Second, Government may regulate or assist in the conduct of economic ventures of many kinds once they are under way. This includes controls that merely lay down general standards and prohibitions, and those that interefere with matters that may be considered managerial.

Third, Government controls the relationships between the various segments of the economy, the purpose being to settle conflicts of interests or of legal rights and to prevent an undue concentration of economic power in one place. Examples are the prohibition of interlocking of directors among corporations, the abolition of certain kinds of holding companies, and the regulation of labour relations.

Fourth and Finally, public control may extend to the resutls of business operations, as in the limitaion of public-utility profits, ceiling on dividends and the imposition of excess profits tax on business generally.

Government regulation of the economy may be broadly divided into:

(i) Director control and

(ii) Indirect controls.

Director controls have assumed increasing signifiance in many developing countries, including India. Their justification are reasons that are economic, political and historical in nature; and in most countries, these reasons are often interwined with one another. Most economic reasons are based on a variety of market failures, including imperfections and high-risk aversion on the part of private entrepreneurs.

The indirect controls are usually exercised through various fiscal and monetary incentives and disincentives or penalties. Certain activities may be encouraged or discouraged through monetary and fiscal incentives and disincentives. For instance, a high import duty may discourage imports and fiscal and monetary incentives may encourage the development of export-oriented industries.

The direct administrative or physical controls are more drastic in their effect. They can be applied selectively from firm to firm and industry to industry, at the discretion of the state.

2. The Promotional Role. In developing countries, where the infrastructual facilities for development are inadequate and entrepreneurial activities are scarce, the promotional role of the Government assumes special significance. The state will have to assume direct responsibility to build up and strengthen the necessary development infrastructures, such as power, transport, finance, marketing, institutions for training and guidance and other promotional activities. The promotional role of the state also encompasses the provision of various fiscal, monetary and other incentives, including measures to cover certain risks, for the development of certain priority sectors and activities.

3. The Entrepreneurial Role. The growing importance of the entrepreneurial or participative role of the state is evident from the rapid expansion of the public sector in most countries. Marshall Dimock mentions the following reasons for the growth of public ownership in free societies.

(i) The growth of public ownership in a free society depends in part on a combination of belief systems plus practical necessity.

(ii) In a democracy the national emergency of war inevitably causes an expansion in state activity, including public ownership, because modern requirements of total war cause people to forsake their convictions concerning private responsibility and to concentrate on massed power. During such an emergency, Government and big business both tend to become bigger and more concentrated. When the war is over, it is possible to turn back towards competition and the private direction of economic affairs; but there seems always to be a residue of expanded Government responsibility.

(iii) When private undertakings become unprofitable but the need for their service continues, the Government may be prevailed upon to acquire and manage such non-profitable business concerns at a loss.

(iv) Major economic dislocating such as the depression of the 1930s, tend to stimulate state activity, again leaving a residue of public ownership that takes time and effort to dissipate, if it is ever finally accomplished.

(v) In the economic growth of a nation as in the early history of the United States and in the economic development of underdeveloped nations today, governments are called on to act as bankers, assisters, or owners of infant industries, and generally to expand their central concern for the economic, thus creating a considerable degree of public ownership at the outset.

4. The Planning Role. In developing countries, the state plays important role as a planner. The need for economic planning is very implied in the famous "scarcity definition" of economics. As Robbins points out in his "scarcity definition" the main business of the science of economics is the optimum allocation of scarce resources between competition ends.

The modern state is a custodian of the welfare of sociaty. The welfare government has the responsibility for fulfilling the aspiration of the people by bringing about all-round prosperity. The ends *i.e.*, the objectives to be achieved and the purposes to be saved, are many. In the pursuit of his task, the most important problem, especially in less developed countriės, is the scarcity of resources. The resources that are readily available are quite insufficient to meet all the ends. The resource constraints demand that some of the purpose should go unserved. This calls for the determination of the more urgent needs or national priorities and the optimal allocation of the available resources to subserve the common goods. And this is the principal objective of national planning.

The importance of planning in a less developed economy was often emphasised by Jawaharlal Nehru, the chief architect of Development Planning in under-developed countries like ours, which have to develop fairly rapidly, the time elements is important and the question is how to use our resources to the best advantage. If our resources are abundant, it will not matter how they are used. They will go into a common pool of development. But where one's resources are limited, one has to see that they are directed to the rights purposes so as to help to build up whatever one is aiming at.

ECONOMIC ROLES OF THE GOVERMENT OF INDIA

Indian economic is a mixed economy. It comprises by both private and public sector. In India, the Government is both regulator and promoter of private enterprise. The Government performs the following functions:

1. As Regulator
2. As Promoter
3. As Planner
4. Role of Public sector.

We shall now discuss these functions in detail

1. As Regulator. Overtime, India has created a plethora of economic legislation for regulating various aspect of economic behaviour. The objectives of most of the legislations are commendable as they try to fulfil a perceived economic or social need. However, as the reports of Monopolies Enquiry Commission (1966), the Industrial Licensing Policy Enquiry Committee (1969) and the Committee on Controls and Subsidies (1979) show, government regulation has failed in achieving the desired objectives.

The report of the Industrial Licensing Policy Enquiry Committee has noted that the licensing system and other industrial controls did not suscced in developing industries according to Plan priorities. Licensing rarely prevented growth of non-essential industries and also failed in ensuring the development of the more essential ones. The Industrial Licensing Policy Enquiry Committee Report identified 45 companies producing far in excess of the licesned capacities. In many cases the excess capacities created by the erring companies were later approved by the government. Influential industrialists often obtained licenses to pre-empt entry of competitors. Sudip Chaudhari states, "No legal or administrative action was taken against the violator though the licensing system was government by an Act of the Parliament. The case study on the alcoholic bevarages industry, regarded as non-essential by the government, reveals that most of the important companies not only produced more than the licensed capacities but continued to expand capacities despite the official ban. The gap between declared policies and actual practice here was so wide that the corporate studies group wondered whether any regulatory system existed in the country at all.

During the 1970s the government enlarged regulatory framework as it legislated the Monopoloies and Restrictive Trade Practices (MRTP) Act in 1970 to control large corporates and the Foreign Exchange Regulation Act (FERA) in 1974 to control foreign firms. The objectives of these regulatory legislations were laudable as they attempted to cover important social and economic needs. However, the enforcement was found to be difficult.

In the opinion of J.N. Bhagwati, Padma Desai, T.N. Srinivasan and Isher Judge Ahluwalia controls and regulations were a fundamental constraint on industrial growth. They also controls and regulations were a fundamental constraint on industrial growth. They also contended that disappointing industrial performance reflected simply poor productivity performance. And the low industrial productivity was the result of extensive bureaucratic controls over production, investment and trade.

2. Role of the Government as Promoter. The government has played a vital promotional role in the Indian economy. Like other governments in both developed and underdeveloped countries, the government in this country has actively developed infrastructure, especially means of transport, communication system and sources of energy. The government's direct involvement in agricultural development has enabled farmers to raise their production and thereby incomes. This has created extensive market in the rural areas for manufactures goods. Reservation of certain products for the small scale industries has promoted their development. The government's role as mobiliser of financial resources for the private sector by setting up development banks and other investment institutions has been particularly important in the absence of a developed capital market. Policy of protection to domestic industries until recently promoted industrial development. Lately since the government has adopted the strategy of export led growth, it has introduced various export promotion measures.

Agriculture at the time of Independence was extremely underdeveloped. The government introduced new technology, during the 1960s. This strategy did miracle in Punjab, Haryana and Western Uttar Pradesh. There was a spectacular rise in agricultural productivity and in big farmers' income. Over the years this strategy has been adopted in other regions as well and the result have been encouraging. The government's role in promoting industrial activity in the private sector has been both direct and indirect. Indirectly it facilitated industrial development by developing infrastructure and agriculture. Directly it promoted industrialisation by participating in the risk capital of certain private sector enterprises, by setting up institutions to train technical and managerial cadres and providing incentives for export production. The government's role as mobiliser of financial resources for the private sector is, however, most commendable. During the post Independence period, thanks to the initiative taken by the government, a number of financial in institutions were set up with the purpose of providing finance to private enterprises. These financial institutions can be divided into the following categories:

(i) **Specialised Financial Institutions.** Risk Capital and Technology Finance Corporation Ltd. (RCTC), TDICI Ltd. (formerly known as Technology Development and Information Company of India Ltd.) and Tourism Finance Corporation of India Ltd. (TFCI).

(ii) **All India Development Banks.** Industrial Development Bank of India (IDBI), Industrial Finance Corporation of India Ltd. (IFCI), Industrial Credit and Investment Corporation of India Ltd. (ICICI), Industrial Investment Bank of India (IIBI), and Small Industries Development Bank of India (SIDBI).

(iii) **State Level Financial Institutions.** State Financial Corporations (SFCs) and State Industrial Developmental Corporations (SIDCs).

(iv) **Investment Institutions.** Unit Trust of Inida (UTI), Life Insurance Corporation of India (LIC), General Insurance Corporation of India (GIC) and its subsidiaries.

Role of the government as promoter has been least controversial in this country. The only criticism that has been levelled against the government in this regard is that it has not done enough to promote private business. Infrastructure requires special attention and should be a priority area for investment. At present, the state of essential facilities is well below international standards. Regarding finance the common criticism is the public sector financial institutions charge high rates of interest on their lendings which lead to a cost disadvantage to firms which are particularly interested in operating at the global level. Finally, though government has done a lot to promote exports, yet the 'quality' of its policies has been poor as compared with policies pursued by successful exporters like Japan, Korea, Malaysia and China. Unlike India, their intervention was strategic and not detailed.

3. Role of the Government as Planner. Economic planning was adopted by the government economy. The government thus as a planner set up basic and capital goods, developed infrastructure, carried out agrarian reforms and created conditions for the growth of private business. It also promised social justice to the disadvantaged sections of the society.

Economic planning was adopted in India because it could compensate for 'market failure'. But the four and a half decades of development planning have shown that there can be 'government failure' as well. In this countries, the regulatory system caused economic losses due to misallocation of resources resulting from wrong investment decisions and diversion of resources to what economists call 'rent seeking'. C. Rangarajan thus argues that there can be both government failure and market failure, and that "critical issues is not so much the presence and absence of State intervention but the extent and quality of intervention." However, the issue could not be possed in this manner, in fifties or even sixties. In that period, India's primarily agrarian economy could not be exposed completely to the imperialistic designs of the western developed countries. Hence, economic planning had to orient itself towards self-reliance. This naturally forced India to follow the strategy of import-substitution based growth even if it meant slow growth. The stress on heavy industry development first was thus not wrong as perceived by some economists. This development policy nonetheless resulted in the growth of high cost industry which was not internationally competitive. Unfortunately plethora of controls and bureaucratic restrictions created a mess in the economy and provided scope for rent seeking activities.

Most economists in the country are of the opinion that the broad objectives of planning are still valid and in India's liberalised economy, with some changes in instrumentalities to achieve these goals, economic planning should play an important role. However, given the policies of the Indian government economic planning is likely to be sabotaged both at the programming and implementational level. There is now incontrovertible evidence of the government's casualness towards planning. The basic justification for planning is clearly stated in Narashimha Rao's foreward to the Eighth Five Year Plan : "The market can be expected to bring about an 'equilibrium' between 'demand'—backed by purchasing power—and 'Supply'.

4. Role of the Public Sector. The government plays its role as a producer through the public sector. In India, public enterprises have been producing goods what theoretically could have been produced by private enterprises as well. The government established a large number of enterprises over the two years to produce steel, sophisticated machine tools, heavy engineering goods, railway locomotives and so on. In 1999-2000, there were 232 Central government undertakings which employed capital amounting to Rs. 303411 crore. Their turnoever was as large as Rs. 3,89,310 crore. This reflects the absolute size of the public sector under the control of the Central government.

These days it has become a fashion to condemn puiblic sector. But the approach was more rational during the 1950s and 1960s. In those days the government was committed to the cause of distributive justice. Under the dynamic leadership of Jawahar Lal Nehru, the Prime Minister of the country, the public sector was conceived not as a commercial institution but as one useful for achieving social objectives of development. Hence, profitability was not the criterion to judge the performance of the public sector. This led to dilution of commercial principle causing enormous wastage and inefficiency in production. Lately the political leadership has often missued public enterpries for personal gains for extending patronage. The inefficiency in production in a number of enterprises thus created has now reached a point where productivity is so low that these enterprises are in no position to generate any reinvestible surplus. This has jeopardised the modernisation programme very seriously.

The government should now withdraw from direct production of goods and services except in the areas a basic and social infrastructure because the experience of public sector in India has confirmded Lange's worst apprehensions about the success of attempts to control and plan production and investment without removing private enterprise and private ownership of means of production. Lange stated even before the experiments in economic planning in the mixed economy framework had started, "the great economic power of corporations and banks being what it is, it would be they who would control the public planning authorities, rather than the reverse. The result would be planning for monopoly and restrictionism, the reverse of what was aimed at.

Government and Private Business

The policies of the Government affect private business both directly and indirectly. The Government provides infrastructure and basic amenities and this helps in the develoment of private sector. Similarly creation of financial institution helped in mobilsing resources for the development of private sector. The establishment of reported institutes like Indian Institute of Tecnology, Indian Institute of Management etc. has provided trained manpower to the private sector. The Government has announced and implemented various economic policies for the development of small scale industries and cottage industries. The Government has helped private sector in getting raw material from agriculture sector by boosting its growth. Moreover the Government has successfully created demand and provided input for the development of private sector at reasonable prices.

Thus it can be safely said that the Government has contributed a lot for the growth of private business in India.

❑

4

Socio-Cultural Environment

CONCEPT OF BUSINESS

The term business is used in different senses. In a functional sense, it is used to refer to the functions or activities of an organisation or individual. Sometimes it is used to refer to the enterprise or units rendering the business. Traditionally, the term business commonly refers to commercial activities aimed at making a profit or to organisations formed to make a profit. Indeed, in the past economic theory made a fundamental assumption that profit maximisation was the basic objective of every firm. The modern outlook, however, is different. For many organisations, profit maximisation in the short run is not the primary objective. For them, profit is only secondary. There are, moreover, many organisation, both private and public, which do not aim at profit from their business.

The old concepts of business, confining it to commerce and private profit, has undergone a radical change. Today, business is regarded as a social institution forming an integral part of the social system. As Davis and Blomstorm observe, business is "a social institution, performing a social mission and having a broad influence on the way people live and work together."

Thus, "viewed in a broad way, the term business typically refers to the development and processing of economic values in society. Normally, we used the term to apply to the private (non-government) portion of the economy whose primary purpose is to provide goods and services to customers at a price, but the lines of distinction are getting hazy as business and government overlap their functions in organisation such as the Communications, Satellite Corporation and the Tennessee Valley Authority. In addition, business is a term applied to economic and commercial activities of institutions having other purposes, such as the business office of an opera association."

The modern concept of business is thus, a very broad one. Business is viewed as a subsystem of the total social system. According to Davis and Blomstorm, "our modern view of society is an ecological one. Ecology is concerned with the mutual relations of human populations or systems with their environment. It is necessary to take this board view because the influence and involvement of business are extensive. Business cannot isolate itself from the rest of society. Today the whole society is a business' environment."

According to modern thinking, business is an integral part of the social system. It is a social organ to help accomplish the social goals. Its activities and attitudes are therefore, subject to public judgement, which may have far reaching implications. A business enterprise shall make profit only by accomplishing the socially accepted goals and by satisfying society.

CONCEPT OF CULTURE

There are very varying definitions of culture, "Culture in its broadest definition, refers to that part of total repertoire of human action which is socically as opposed to genetially transmitted." A very popular definitions is that of E.B. Tylor, "Culture or civilization is that complex whole which includes knowledge, belief, art, morals, law, customs and other capabilities and habits acquired by man as a member of society."

On the basis of various definition of culture, Francis Merill formulates the concept of culture as follows : culture he says:

(a) is the characteristically human product of soical interaction.

(b) provides socially acceptable patterns for meeting biological and social needs;

(c) is meaningful to human beings because of its symbolic quality;

(d) is learned by each person in the course of his development in a particular society;

(e) is cumulative, for it is handed down from generation to generation in a given society;

(f) is, therefore, a basic determinant of personality; and

(g) depends for its existence upon the continued functioning of society but is independent of any individual or group.

Culture consists of both material culture and non-material culture. Material culture involves man-made things (*e.g.*, automobiles, television, telephone, etc.) and man-made alterations in the environment. Non-material culture includes such factors as language, ideals, beliefs, values, music etc.

ELEMENTS OF CULTURE

Culture, the sum total of social behaviour, includes at least three elements, namely knowledge and beliefs, ideas and preferences.

Ideals. Ideals refer to the societal norms which define what is expected, customary, right or proper in a given situation. Norms are enforced by sanctions, *i.e.*, by rewarding the right behaviour and punishing the wrong behaviour.

Folkways and mores are important aspects of every culture. Folkways are norms of proper behaviour (like the proper way to greet a friend) that are informally enforced. But mores are norms of obligatory behaviour considered vital to the welfare of the group.

Knowledge and Beliefs. The knowledge and beliefs refere to a people's prevailing notions of reality. They include myths and metaphysical beliefs as well as scientific realities. As Rose remarks : "One of the features of culture in general that is of special sociological interest is the shared quality of a belief system. People who share a given culture tend to take a hostile attitude towards those within their midst who cannot, or will not, accept conventional definitions of fact."

Preferences. Preferenes refer to society's definition of those things in life which are attractive or unattractive as objects of desire. Preferences may differ between cultures. Interestingly enough, the judgement of the ideal or the proper do not always correspond to our judgements of the pleasant or enjoyable. An example in point is the temptations (not proper but desirable). All the things I really like to do are immoral, illegal, or fattening," said Alexander Woolcott.

Cultural characteristics are very important in the formulation of pragmatic business strategies. The cost of ignoring customs, traditions, taboos, tastes and preferences, etc., can be very high. For example, in Italy, a US company that set up a corn-processing of corn as "pig food". Similarly, Compbell Soup tried to sell its US tomato formulation to the British; but it discovered, after considerable losses, that the English prefer a more bitter taste. Is it, than, any wonder that the Nestle company should brew more than 40 varieties of instant coffee to satisfy different national tastes? The culture therefore helps in deciding about preferences.

ORGANISATION OF CULTURE

The term organisation of culture refers to the social structure and the integration of traits, complexes and patterns that make up the cultural system. That cultures are organised or integrated "does not mean that every single item of each culture is neatly and precisely integrated with everything else. It means rather that it is normal for the parts to be somewhat organised, and that culture traits receive their significance and meaning out of their relation to the rest of the culture."

The social structure---"the web of organised relationship among individuals and groups that defines their mutual rights and liabilities"—together with traits, complexes and patterns, reflects the organisation of a culture.

The economic system; the political administrative system; the educational system; religion; family; expressionistic, aesthetic and recreational institutions, etc. Such institutions have been established to meet society's common needs of a biological, sociological, psychological, economic, and political nature-the type and nature of institutions reflect the common goals, aspirations and the ways of achieving them, definition and regulation of roles, positions, inter-relationships, etc., of the individuals and sub-groups and groups and the overall organisation of the culture. Culture traits, complexes and patterns also help us to understand the organisation of a culture. A trait is a unit of observation.

Sometimes it is necessary to know the process and nature of the cultural environment for a successful formulation of business strategies. For example, while introducing new ideas, techniques, products; while segmenting the market; while formulating the product and promotion mix strategies; one should consider the extent to which different categories of consumers adapt to the new things or environment and the factors favouring and disfavouring adaptations (and also the general attitude of society to the new ideas and environment and their impact on different categories of consumers).

Transmission of Culture

A very important character of culture is its transmissive quality. The elements of culture are transmitted among the members of the culture, from one generation to the next and to the new members admitted into the culture. Some of the aspects of a culture may be transmitted to other cultures also. The transmissive quality of cultures makes its cumulative. Every generation inherits a stock of cultural elements, many of which have been accumulated over a long period of time. As time goes on, cultures accumulate more techniques, ideas, products and skills. It is also quite obvious that certain old elements are dropped as new ideas and traits are acquired.

Many cultural behaviours are handed down by one's parents teachers and other elders. The reference groups play an important role in handing down new traits and ideas. Some cultural behaviours are, however, "handed up" to the elders. It is not uncommon to come across elders imitating or adopting some of the new traits of the youngsters who are the trend-setters. Cultural transmission is not only downward and upward; a lot of transmission takes place among contemporaries, too *e.g.*, styles of dress; recreational fads; reading and learning habits; political, social and economic views. These are often transmitted among contemporaries. Cultural transmission, thus, takes place horizontally as well as vertically. One rather learns it. However, as cuber points out, "much of the learning process, both for the teacher and the learner, is quite unconscious, unintentional, or accidental; but it is learning and teaching nevertheless."

Transmission also facilitates cultural diffusion, *i.e.*, the spread of cultural elements from one areas to another. Cultural transmission and diffusion are easy in a culture with high educational levels and a well-organised communication system. An effective communication system and high educational levels facilitate socio-economic change through better cultural transmission and diffusion, for new ideas and innovations are easily and quickly transmitted, diffused and absorbed in such a culture. In the context of the generally low literacy rates in India, the government has realised the importance of the media, such as film, television and radio, in transmitting useful information, such as better agricultural practices and techniques, market information, the concept and importance of family planning, and so on.

Relationship Between Business and Culture. The nature and process of cultural transmission and diffusion in a society is important to business-making. For example, to formulate a promotional policy for a product, a service or an idea, it is important to identify the relevant element of transmission, to evaluate the relative effectiveness of alternative communication media, to identify the reference groups and the extent of their influence, to identify the channel of influence on the reference groups, and so on. People of different cultures use the same product, the mode of consumption, conditions of use, purpose of use or the perceptions of the product attributes may very so much so that the product attributtes, method of presentation or method of promoting the product may have to be varied to suit the characteristics of different consumers. An example of Vicks Vaporub, the popular pain balm, is used as a mosquito repellant in some parts of the world.

SOCIAL STRUCTURE

The social structure of Indian society is characterised by diversities but unity. India has been a country where numerous groups migrated from Asia and Europe during different time in past. But over the centuries, the culture of each groups had undergone enough changes and become the part of Indian society and culture.

The population of India is racially diverse, containing elements from six main racial types—the Negrito, the Proto-Australoid, the Mongoloid, the Mediterranean, the Western Brachycephals and the Nordic. The population of India is not only divided racially, the study of Indian society will prove that it is divided both horizontially and vertically. The caste system in Indian society is an important institution which constituted different layers of the society. Linguistically too Indian society is divided in many groups. Diversity is also seen in the patterns of rural as well urban settlements, community life, forms of land tenure and agricultural operations. All the great religions of the world are represented in this country. In kinship, marriage rites and customs, inheritance, and the general mode of living, there are striking differences between groups. Moreover, except the urban and rural population, there are many tribal groups, with different religions and rituals. Thus the study of Indian society, at a first glance, shows the mutual differences among different groups. Therefore, a thorough study is required to understand the binding forces in society and their origin.

India is a geo-political entity under one constitution. In fact the British rule of India helped it in beoming a single political entity in modern times. After independence, the Indian Government tried to maintain the unity and enforced a common law. Constitutional supremacy was established. India was declared a secular state. The Process of economic development ushered in by the Five Years Plans and the spread of egalitarian ideals have brought about, revolutionary changes in the Indian pattern of social life. Now we will discuss role of caste, kinship and religion in Indian society

Caste System. The first literary traces of caste system are to be found in Rig Veda. The Purusasukta hymn speaks of four classes—Brahmana. Rajanya, Vaisya and Sudra. These are referred as Chaturvarna. In the earlier literature Verna was applied to differentiate between Arya and Dasa—fair and dark respectively only. Later it developed in three and then in four varnas. The occupations of the first two varnas—Brahmana and Rajanya or Kshatriya are clearly stated to be priesthood and administrative and military duties respectively. But the duties of the Vaisya an Sudra are not very clear. The village headman was usually a Vaisya and Sudras were servants.

The post-vedic period sow the growth and consolidation of the power of Brahmins. This defined the duties and rights of each caste and its place in the hierarchy. In the Bhagavad Gita for instance, the caste system is sought to be justified on the basis of the ideas of Guba, Karma, and Dharma. Thus the institution of caste has existed in India for thousands of years. The essence of caste is the arrangement of hereditary groups in hierarchy. Brahmins are at the top and Harijans are at the bottom of the hierarchy.

In the Indian society caste system prevails not only among Hindus but also among Muslims, Sikhs and Christains, though all these religions preach equality of all. In Utter Pradesh, Muslims, who have a tradition of foreign ancestry (Iran, Arbia) are called Shurafa or Ashaf and are considered to be the highest. After them come converts from high caste Hindus and at the bottom are occupational castes such as weaver, Barber, Potter etc.

Among the Sikhs, there are broadly two groups—Sardara and Mazhabis, the former consisting of high castes and the latter of Sweepers. Sansi (Shepherd) converts to Sikhism rank even lower than Mazhabis.

Jews and Christians are not exception to this caste division. The Beni-Israel Jews, found principally in Bombay and considered higher in rank. They are divided into groups Gora and Kala. Gora are in higher rank than Kala. Caste division occur among Indian Christians—both Catholic and Protestant. The Syrian Christians of Kerala, the earliest converts of Christianity in India claim to have been recruited from Nambudri Brahmins and Nayars, hence they think themselves higher in the rank. Caste restrictions are rigidly observed among the Christians of the West Coast. A Catholic Brahmin from Maharashtra would marry only a Catholic Brahmin.

The caste conflict in Indian society is very common. It had given birth to the concept of untouchability. The higher caste groups refused to accept cooked food and water from the lower castes.

Inter caste marriages were also forbidden and punishable. The Brahminical writers continued their attempts to systemize and codify inter-caste relations in among Hindus.

The hereditary association of a caste with an occupation was a striking characteristic of Indian society till recent past. The cast was associated with an occupation and had a limited kind of monopoly over it. Generally the Kumhars were potters and Nais were barbers. But most castes also practised agriculture in the monsoon months in addition to their traditional occupation. Often the artisan and servicing castes had not an adequate income from their traditional occupations and they therefore work on land either as tenants or as casual labourers. Indeed, in the context of growing population and changes in tools and apparatus, the occupation aspect of the caste system have broken down.

In the Hindu society, occupations are classified into high and low, those practised by the high castes being regarded as high Manual labour is looked upon as low, and certain occupations like Swine-herding and butchery are considered to be polluting.

Among Muslims, only artisans castes such as the Teli, Darzi and Julaha are associated with traditional occupations. Priests tend to come more from the Syed and Shaikh castes. Among Sikhs, the traditional occupation is often practised along with agriculture. Jats were generally landowners, while the Mazhabis were agriculture labourers.

An individual in a caste society lives in a hierarchical world. It is not only the people, who are divided into higher and lower groups, but even the food, dress and ornaments, customs and manners are also divided. Elaborate rules govern the acceptance of cooked food and water from another caste. Pakka food, cooked with Ghee, butter may be accepted from the inferior castes, but not Kaccha food, which is cooked with water. It may be accepted normally only from equivalent or superior castes. In North India, hukka smoking offers an index of caste-status. Castes which may share, on occasions, a single hukka are equals.

The culture of each caste is to some extent peculiar to itself. There are differences in dress, speech, manners ritual and ways of life. The lower castes are barred, at least in theory, from taking over the customs and rituals of the higher castes. The concepts of pollution plays a crucial part in maintaining the required distance between different castes. There is a broad line between caste Hindus and Harijans in the matter of pollution. The village barber and washerman do not serve Harijans. They had to take water from a lower end of a river or canal than the high castes and they could not use the caste Hindu well. The breaking of pollution rules resulted in the higher castes becoming "impure", and the latter had to perform certain purificatory rites to regain normal status. Sometimes, the person breaking the rules used to be even thrown out of caste irrevocably.

The idea of pollution is present among the Sikhs, The Mazhabis had a well of their own everywhere. Their wedding parties were not accommodated in gurudwaras as they were regarded as "impure".

In the Indian society, which was very much based on village, the relationship between different caste groups was of a particular form. Most Indian villager do not have more than a few of the essential castes and hence people depend on neighbouring villages for certain services skills and goods. In rural India, with its largely subsistance and not fully monetized economy till recently, the relationship between the difference groups in a village takes a particular form. The essential artisans and service castes are paid annually in grain at harvest. In some parts of India they are provided with fine food, clothing fodder and some times residential site. Primarily and economic or ritual tie has tendency to spread to other fields and become a patron-client relationship. This relationship is generally stable and mostly inherited.

Caste was related to the exercise of differential rights in land. At the top were the castes who were either absentee or non-cultivating owner. Next come the cultivating tenants, and at the bottom of the hierarchy came the landless agriculture, meant that the stratification rase deep. This enabled the landowners to exploit the tenants as much as they could.

Indeed, the caste system in India has such a deep root in the society that it covers all the aspects of social life of an Indian. The Indian Government, after independence has introduced many socio-econmic and cultural reforms to erase the system. Provisions were envisaged in an constitution of India and laws were also made to wipe of out the caste division and its negative affects on the society, but it is still a burning issue. It is to be noted that its intensity is lesser in the urban areas and particularly in the metropolitan cities. But in the rural area, it is still a crucial problem which often disturbs peace and law and order conditions. Inspite of increasing literacy and social consciousness, caste differences and caste-hatred and the major social issues even today.

Kinship. The social institution of marriage ensures the children both of it a recognised and legally sanctioned position in society. A domestic group consisting of a man and his wife and unmarried children is called an elementary or nuclear family. Domestic groups which are bigger than the elementary family, and often include two or more elementary families, are termed joint or extended families. They may be patrilineal as in most parts of India, or matrilineal as among the Nayars of Kerala or the Khasis of Assam. Several joint families descended from the same ancestor and acting together on certain occasions form a lineage.

In several parts of the country people live in lineage groups. The members of the lineage lived under the same roof on in a group of neighbouring houses, held property together and ate together. Such a lineage formed a coparcenary, every member (male in the case of partrilineage and famale in the case of a matrilineage) have a share in the ancestral property. Among the poorer and uneducated folk in rural areas, the residential groups generally tend to be small, being confined to members, of the elementary family and one or two relatives. In this section of the population, the family group holds together during the father's lifetime, partition being usually after his death. Joint family system is mostly in practice among richer. Every joint family has a manager who takes decisions on behalf of all. Every male member has a vested interest in the ancestral property. A joint family splits up into constituent elementary families when partition occurs. Indeed joint and elementary families are parts of a single cyclical process.

The composition of a joint family depends upon the mode of descent and the pattern of residence general to a group. Decent may to partrilineal or matrilineal or cognatic, and residence may be virilocal (staying with husband) or uxorilocal (staying with wife) or neolocal (both moving to a new house). Virilocality is the general rule in India and this is not confined to Hindus only but extends to Muslims, Christians, Sikhs and Jains. The wife joins her husband soon after marriage and the latter generally lives with his own parents and brothers. It is only after, the death of the parents that the brothers separate from each other. Even this may not happen and the brothers may decide to stay together. Among the poorest groups and the lowest castes, the family breaks up soon after parents death. Among the westernized and urban sections, neolocality is most common. But the establishment of a new home does not mean the severance of ties with kin-groups of the husband and wife. Kinship connections are recognised on both the sides and a close relative of either side may live with the couple. In recent years spatial mobality has increased considerably and young men have jobs away from their natal towns. This means, in the urban areas, there are many families which are seemingly elementary.

While the composition of a household is usually determined by the particular principles of descent and the type of post-martial residence obtaining in a caste, the bilateral principal finds greater recognition than is commonly thought. A household may include not only patrilineal relatives such as two full brothers, their wives, their children and unmarried sisters, but also the brother or sister of a wife of one of them. In a matrilineal household, on the other hand, increasing recognition of the bilateral principle may result in the parents of either the husband or wife residing with the couple. Among the urban and educated sections of the population, the household consists of the husband, wife, their children and a relative of the husband or less frequently a relative of the wife. These households are justifiably considered as part of wider kinship groups elsewhere. In metropolitan cities, high rent act as a limiting factor on the size of the household.

In the traditional Hindus joint family the senior male is usually the head of the household. It is his duty to look after the property meet the expenses out of the income of the ancestral estate and clear the debts. The head of the house hold the manager of the joint familycorporation and as such he wielded much power and authority. Mostly power and privilege being concentrated in the hands of elders. The younger members in the family are required to show respect to the elder. Ideally, the children in a joint family are the children of all the male members of two parental generation, and discrimination by a parent in favour of his own children in rejected as reprehensible.

The relation between women members in a joint family in frequently one of conflict. The mother-in-law and daughter-in-law relationship is celebrated in folklone for its intensity of conflict. Relations between a woman and her husband's sisters and between here and her husband's brothers, wives are also conflict-ridden. The relation between a man and his parents-in-law is a formal one.

With the changing socio-economic conditions, the relationship is also changing, large traditions pattern of kin-groups, in rural at any rate had been confined to a few landowning higher castes. The new economic opportunities which came through the link-up the local economy with a much wider one, increased monetization, greater opportunities for trade and increased spatial mobility due to the building of roads and railways led to the emergence of smaller in groups. The present economic conditions and political developments operated against living in big joint families. Spread of education has developed a sense of individuality which is against the norms of joint family system, Residence away from the natal kin-group removed the stresses and strains to day-to-day living, while increased communications kept the links alive.

All Hindus are patrilineal, with the expected of the Nayars and Bants, and other castes on the West Coast and Khasis and Garos of

Assam. Muslims, excepting the Moplahs of North Malabar and Christians excepting Khasi converts, are patrilineal. All Jain Buddhist and Sikhs are patrilineal, Among the patrilineal groups some movable property is given to daughters, women did not inherit the immovable property In the matrilineal system of inheritance, a person inherits from his maternal uncle and not from his father. The Hindu succession Act and the Hindu Adoption and Maintenance Act, 1956, has made the husband legally responsible for the maintenance of his wife and children.

All Muslims excepting matrilineal Moplahs, are governed by the Shariat Act of 1937. Under Islamic Law, the mother, wife and daughter are the three famale heirs. The maximum share of the mother is one-third and the minimum one-sixth, depending on the existence or otherwise of other heirs. The share of the wife is one-fourth or one-eighth. The wife is also the owner of the Meher given to her at wedding. She is also entitled to be maintained by her husband, The daughter is a primary heir like the son. Her share fluctuates, depending upon the member of surviving children.

The Hindu succession Act of 1956, governs the inheritance of Hindus, Buddhists, Sikhs and Jains. It applies to both matrilineal as well as patrilieal groups. According to this Act, the property of a Hindu dying in state devolves on his sons, daughters, widow and mother. This Act included mother in the same category of heirs as the widow and children of the deadman. Thus the Act had introduced some changes in the traditional system and gave them legal sanction.

Religion. India has all the important religion of the world—Hinduism, Islam, Christianity, Zionism, Bhuddhism, etc. The census reports have revealed that Hindus are in majority. Among the minority religions groups, a few have fared better in the economic field and specially commerce. Some of the minority religious groups are well educated and well employed such as Christians and Parsis.

We shall now consider the role of religious groups in the social and political structure of India.

(i) Religion and Society. Though villages embracing multi-religious groups are not as common as multi-caste villages, they are not infrequent, such villages are not confined to any one part of India, but are found everywhere. There are villages with Hindu tenants and Muslim land lords and Hindu landlords and Muslim tenants. A few Hindu landowners had Muslim tenants and servants, while Muslim tenants. A few Hindu landowners had Muslim tenants and servants, while Muslim landowner had Hindu servants. The bulk of the Muslims were engaged in a variety of actvities—trading in several articles, including paddy and mangoes, tailoring, carpentary, smithy and butchery. Ownership of land, seemed to prevent a majority of the Hindus from becoming traders. In some regions Hindu and Muslim families are liked together by friendship and patron-client ties, Muslims often provide the goods needed in Hindu festivals. Muslims are invited to Hindu weddings when the members of a religion or sect dominate trade or commerce, the customers are drawn from serval religious groups. At the local level, economic-social ties are mained by different religious groups.

Some religious groups have played an important role in the economic department of the country. The small community of Parsis in Bombay is an example. Jains have also played important role in economic development of Bombay, Gujrat and Rajasthan as they are mostly traders and businessmen. The Syrian Charistians of Kerala played a pioneering role in banking and in growing plantation crops, such as tea, coffee and rubber.

(ii) Religion and Politics. The role played by religion in the political life of the country is similar to that the caste. In the thirties, the Muslim League first began to press its demand for an independent Muslim state to be called Pakistan. This led to the antagonizm between Hindus the Muslims. Even after creation of Pakistan. This led to the antagonizm between Hindus and Muslims. Even after creation of Pakistan, Muslim Leage remain active in Sourth as a political party.

The Akhil Bharat Hindu Mahasabha is another religious party, which aimed at promotion of Hindu Rastra. Vishwa Hindus Parisad and Janasanga were also very much guided by religious motives. Later, Janasangha was renamed as Bhartia Janta Party. This party is today the major opposition party which is guided by staurich Hindu nationalism.

Rastriya Swayam Sevak Sangha (R.S.S.) is another Hindu Organization which though claim to be an organization interested only in reviving Hindu religion and culture, it exhibited a para-military character with uniform, drill and training in the art of self-defence.

Sikh politics is closely connected with the control of the gurudwaras, which are in charge of the Siromani Gurudwara Prabhandhak Committee (S.G.P.C.). The Akali Dal, led by Master Tara Singh was long in control of SGPC. But the party is now divided in factions, and some of them are agitating for a separate Sikh dominated state.

The Christians have not formed any prominent political party. Their role is like caste role in politics. But the Anglo-Indians enjoy some concessions including reservation of seats in Parliament and in some of the states.

From the social viewpoint most of the religious groups belong to the minorities and they create problems in socio-political life of the country. The present environment of the Indian society is very much dominated by the caste and religious differences. It has dominated all the aspects of socio-political life of people. Inspite of the constitutional legal and political efforts of the Indian Government, the caste and religious differences among the Indian citizens could not be sorted out. The Indian Government could not enact any law which effects institutions of Muslims and Christians. Therefore, the difference continued and those were exploited by the politicians for the benefit of their own political organization.

In recent years, this problem has become very intense. The caste conflicts have become very common in rural areas. They control people's socio-political and economic activities particularly in rural areas and small towns. Metropolitan cities are least affected by it. Again, religious difference, has recently became an alarming problems, particularly after the fall of Babri structure in December 1992. Hindu-Muslim amnity has more or less vanished from society.

Communal riots has become a common phenomenon in all parts of India.

Caste and religious difference are not the only problems of the society today. The problem of the minority—representation and the benefits granted to them has also became an acute problem to be solved by the authorities. The stratified and multi-religious society is suffering from instability and feeling of insecurity among minorities. All these problems posed a challenge to the government and cause, in turn a political instability within the country.

SOCIAL AND POLITICAL ISSUES

As a political system of a country affects the socio-economic environment of the country, it is also affected by the socio-economic environment of the country. It does not work in isolation, rather there is a causal relationship between the political system and the socio-economic process-each affecting the other and in turn be affected by it.

Usually, the political system and the socio-economic process of a political not only complement and supplement each other; rather they work simultaneously and harmoniously. But in India this did not happened. After the 200 years of colonial rule, dawn of independence in 1947 and sudden introduction of democracy raised peoples' hopes and aspirations from the newly formed political system. Thus, the democratic political system was looked upon the change the static socio-political process in the country and ameliorate the lot of the common man. With no previous experience in the working of democracy in India, the newly imposed democratic set-up was a mixed blessing in dealing with the socio-economic process.

The contemporary social and political Issues Indian Society has been a traditional society—ridden with archaic considerations *e.g.*, caste, community race, language, region and with the deepest stress possible-religion. These characteristic features of the Indian society made specific demands from the new democratic polity and in turn influenced its course in the following years. Also, the policy of new policy vis-a-vis these traditional features was to modify or modernize them and not to completely and these.

1. Casteism. One of the specific feature of the traditional Indian society has been Casteism, which has existed in India for thousands of years. Caste system in Indian politics has come in for severe condemnation only in recent years due to its increasing politicisation and consequent parochial outlook of politics. The modern politics is certainly caste-ridden politics—candidates are chosen on caste considerations, caste issues are fanned to the extent of leading to violent conclusions in the society; the national interests get receded to the background; each political party vies with one another in seeking the reservations of advantages of some castes; political parties are constituted on caste-considerations; and the political patronage in distributed on caste-considerations. There is increasing domination of higher caste on the lower ones. However, the casteism in Indian politics over the years, has been suitably modernised not to stress upon the hereditary factor. The importance of a man in the new set-up has come in be determined by his socio-economic status and not heredity alone. The introduction of universal adult franchise in India, devoid of its caste, colour and creed nature, has politicised the lower castes and increased their political importance. The lower castes have taken the advantages offered to them in the Indian Constitution for their political, social and economic uplift. Many of them have come to hold important positions in the administrative set-up of the country.

2. Communalism. Another important feature of the traditional Indian society is its multi-religious character with due place to each religious community. The religions in India have generally not worked at cross-purposes and hence the multiplicity of religions has not posed a serious problem in the smooth functioning of the Indian polity. Religions, have generally taught us to be tolerant towards one another. But conditions have particularly changed in 1990s, when the religion became the tool of power-Carving by the political parties. One needs to distinguish between religion and communalism; while religion binds the people communalism is divisive in character. The problem of communalism was in fact the legacy of the British colonial rule which fanned antagonism between various religious communities in order to reap political advantages for itself. The problem of communalism whether in colonial days or in free India has assumed proportions only when the political power has tended to use religions for sectarian political interests. Thus, it is not religious but the political use of the religions which needs to be decried and condemned.

Political parties such as Hindus Mahasabha, Muslim League, Jamait-e-Islami, Akali Dal and Vishwa Hindu Parisad etc. have come to be formed on religious basis to work and fight for narrow religious demands. These religious groups and leaders have at times tasted the fruit of political power and hence when out of it, they fail to reconcile with the situation and adopt the extra-constitutional methods to acquire power. It would however be wrong to blame these religious groups alone since many national parties, at times, have joined hands with these religious groups of remain in political power. This unholy alliance of religion with politics, has created distortions in the polity. The problem of communalism, a serious canker eating into the vitals of India; can only be solved when the national political parties rise above their parochial vote-catching devices and are able to see directly into the fact of the communal monster with a purpose to quell its head.

3. Language Problem. India is a unique polity with people of difference languages inhabitating it. Besides 15 fully developed languages found in the Eighth Schedule, there are various dialects being spoken in the country. Also, English has continued to enjoy a special status in the country. After independence, since the ruling class was deeply entrenched in English should remain the official language alongwith Hindi. This posed many problems. It led to the rivalry between Hindi and English—It led to antagonism between the advocates of two different education-systems owing to increasing disparties. Also, the antagonism between Hindi and the other Indian languages grew. Many states in the southern part of India were against what they called the imposition of Hindi. The language problem has acquired new dimensions with the state reorganisation having been accepted on lingual basis with the creation of Andhra Pradesh in 1953, Gujarat and Maharashtra carved out of the erstwhile

Bombay state in 1960, and Haryana in 1966 etc. The language-based organisation of the states has also led to many secessionist movements in the country thus complicating the problem.

4. Illiteracy. Another important feature of Indian social system has been widespread illiteracy in the country. Despite government effects, the situation has remained stagnant over the years. A large part of the male and female population of rural India still remains illiterate. Despite provisions in Part IV of the Constitution *viz.* Directive Principles of State Policy, the free and compulsory education for children upto the age of 14 to a far cry. Thre is a constant problem of dropouts from the schools are the primary level. There are no equal opportunities for seeking education due to sharp class-differences in the country. Hence, there is a lop-sided development of education in the country. Only a few convent educated elites rule over the multitudes of people who could not afford public school education due to economic constraints.

The Government has taken up major steps recently and helping economically the adult education centres. The literacy drive of the Government and the Non-Government Organisation (NGOs) is gradually helping the people at least be become literate.

5. Economic Disparity and Poverty. In additional to socio-cultural problems of the Indian society, one cannot affort to ignore the appalling economic disparities in the Indian society, largely as the legacy of the colonial rule besides the colonial exploitation, even the policies of the rulers of independent India have not improved conditions considerably for the common man. Poverty even today continues to be an untackled problem despite tall claims by the ruling governments. It has grilled the common man of India over the years and even today almost half of the population in the country lives below the poverty line. Poverty is a universal phenomenon in India—it is present both in the rural and the urban parts of the country; and amongst the educated and the uneducated sections of the Indian population. Even a change in the ideology of the Indian State—from a mixed economy to socialist and then liberalization policy—has no helped in providing benefits to the poorer section of the society. However, on the whole, these economic measures by the Indian State has widened the gulf between the rich and the poor. These policies have led to concentration of wealth in fewer hands. There has been enormous increase in black money in the Indian economy by way of tax-evasion and unlimited appropriation of unaccounted money by some vested interests. There is an unholy alliance between the political and the economic elites- while the economic elites provide tons and tons of black money to the politicians to contest and win elections, the political elites in turn benefit their accomplice, the economic elites, through legislation of class policies. The hold of the economic-elites on the Indian political sytem has increased.

The populist measure of the Indian State cannot really solve the problem. There is need for real commitment on the part of the government and the bureaucracy to really benefit the poor and the downtrodden. There is need to check all kinds of corruption and nepotism including political corruption, to restore the confidence of he common man in the democratic institution.

The poverty in rural parts of Indian society need to be tacked with greater vigour and strength. One finds greater economic disparities and tensions amongst the rural folk. Consequently, the lower castes especially the Harijans are the targets of violent attack by the upper castes and are no better than bonded labourers. The democratic process in the country has increased the political consciousness of the rural masses who no longer feel shy to take recourse to forced violence in a bid to fight their exploitation by the rural haves.

It is not to deny that any social or political change in a polity without corresponding economic change is partial and lopsided. Nehru and the other leaders of independent India were hence keen to seek the corresponding economic freedom—freedom from want—through constitutional means, using the Constitution of India as an instrument of economic change besides social and political upliftment. It was with this aim in view that the policy of Mixed Economy was announced. The three main planks of the policies of Nehru era were: Democracy, Socialism and Secularism. Socialism was sought to be achieved within democratic framwork. It is not that only democratic socialism of Nehru era failed to benefit the common man, event he subsequent changes in the ideology of the state in the post-Nehru years failed to satisfy the aspersions of the common man.

6. Regionalism. There is growing regionalism in the country. Regionalism is as much an economic problem as social. At the root of the growth of regionalism lies the discriminatory policies of the British colonial rule and also of the rulers of new independent India. Consequently, some regions have enormously developed as compared to some others, due to the political patronage of the new set of rulers. The economic development of a region has been closely linked with the position of a political leader at the helm of national affairs. Hence, one finds enormous regional disparities even today. The Eastern and the Southern regions in India have remained comparatively less developed than the Western and the Northern regions.

It is not shocking to find the growth of regional parties in these less developed regions. The economic discontent of the people of the region is suitably exploited by these regional parties to capture political power; and once in power these regional parties fan the regional and communal instincts of their people to remain in the saddle of power. These regions generally complain of step-motherly treatment by the Central Government, raise parochial issue *e.g.* language, boundary and water disputes in order to enlarge the gulf with people of the neighbouring states, raise communal and regional issues at the time of elections.

It is undeniable that the Central Government does discriminate between "loyal" and "unloyal" states at the time of distributing the economic resources. The Central Government should become magnanimous in its approach by not economically punishing the non-Congress regional governments; through it alone the evil of regionalism would be checked.

7. Political Unstability and Corruption. Political unstability has become a major issue in Indian policy today. The Government in the Centre is now-a-days, mostly a minority government which is influenced by the many vested interest groups. Therefore, such a government could not take strong decisions and even if the decision are taken, such Government cannot implement those decisions. The frequent change of Government at the centre or the State has created a fluid situation.

The political instability has led to the corruption among the political leader and the bureaucrats. realising their short term in the power, mostly they try to accumulate more and more money and power. Under such a condition, masses also loose the moral strength. All these recent developments are posing new problem to the Indian society and polity.

8. Lack of United and Strong Opposition. In a democratic policy, opposition plays a very important role. It is called a "Shadow Government" as it influences the Governmental policies, and compel them to the moulded according to the need of masses. But since last few year, Indian polity lacked a strong opposition. Opposition is divided in multiple parties with their differences of opinion on different issues.

This is a major political problem for a democratic system. The party in power mostly is benefited due to this characteristics of Indian democracy.

The foregoing discussion would enable to understand the social and political issues in contemporary India. There is an unmistakable relation between the social and political issues and they cannot be separated in water-Light compartments. The nature of the polities is verymuch determined by the policies. The present issues like casteism, communalism, regionalism etc., are the off-springs of political decision, and only a political solution could check increasing intensity of the problems. The populist slogan are not enough to solve the problem.

The policy of the Government is not proving advamtageous to the common people. Consequently, the disgruntled common man at times is forced by the circumstances to keep the democratic means in abeyance and take his battle to the street. Hence, the phenomenon of violence is gaining momentum with the years passing because the common poor is being pushed to the position of his back with the wall. The socio-economic constent of the Indian polity would have to change drastically in favour of the poor if the democratic system in

India is to survive. There can be no hope for the survival of Indian polity as a strong and vibrant system if the mass of its population remains alienated with it due to its anti-people policies and practices.

SOCIAL RESPONSIBILITY

According to George Goyder: "Industry in the twentieth century can no longer be regarded as a private arrangement for enriching shareholders. It has become a joint enterprise in which workers, management, consumers, the locality, Government and trade union officials all play a part. If the system which we know by the name private enterpriseis to continue, some way must be found to embrace many interests which go to make up industry in a common purpose."

In 1978, while delivering the C.C. Desai Memorial Lecture, he reiterated his plea that if the corporation has to function effectively, it has to be accountable to the public at large. He sought to equate the suggestion of a responsible company with the trusteeship concept advocated by Gandhiji, the aim of which was to ensure that private property was used for the common good. The declaration issued by the international seminar on social responsibility of business held in Inida in 1965 also co-related the Gandhian concept of trusteeship with the social responsibility of business as "responsibility to customers, workers, shareholders and the community."

There has been a growing acceptance of the idea that business should be socially responsible. The business enterprise which makes use of the resources of society and depends on society for its functioning, should discharge its duties and responsibilities in enhancing the welfare of the society of which it is integral part. In its Report submitted to Government in August 1978 the High-Powered Expert Committee on Companies and MRTP Acts (Sachar Committee), observed that, "in the development of corporate ethics, we have reached a stage where the question of the social responsibility of business to the community can no longer be scoffed at or taken lightly". The Committee further points out that, "in the environment of modern economic development, the corporate sector no longer functions in isolation. If the plea of the companies that they are performing a social purpose in the development of the country is to be accepted, it can only be judged by the test of social responsiveness shown to the needs of the community by the companies. The company must behave and function as a responsible member of society, like any other individual. It cannot shun moral values, nor can it ignore actual compulsion. The real need is for some focus of acceptability on the part of the management which is not limited to shareholders alone. In modern times, the objective of business has to be the proper utilisation of resources for the benefit of others. A profit is still a necessary part of the total picture; but it is not the primary purpose. This implies that the claims of various interests will have to be balanced, not on the narrow ground of what is best for the shareholders alone but from the point of view of what is best for the community at large. The company must accept its obligation to be socially responsibile and to work for the larger benefit to the community."

NATURE OF SOCIAL RESPONSIBILITY OF BUSINESS

H.S. Singhania has classified the nature of the social responsibility of business into two categories:

1. The manner in which a business carries out its own business activity; and
2. The welfare activity that it takes upon itself as an additional function.

[A] Mode of Business Activity. It involves the acceptance of the fact that business is not merely a profit-making occupation but a social function which invovled certain duties, and requires that appropriate ethics are followed. Business must obey all the laws, even when they are disagreeable. It should produce the maximum goods of good quality. It should ensure smooth supplies at competitive prices. It should pay taxes and shun malpractices. It should pay a fair wage to employees and a reasonable dividend to shareholders. It should undertake a new investment and promote the dispersal of economic activity through ancillarisation and the setting up of inudstries in backward areas so as to spread enterprise and take employement to the doorsteps of labour. It shall pay a role in promoting social welfare activity, even directly.

[B] Welfare Activity.

1. Shareholder's Welfare. The responsibility of a company to its shareholders is a primary one as the shareholders have taken great risk in making investment in a business. To protect the interest of the shareholders and employees, "the primary business of a business is to stay in business." To safeguard the capital of the shareholders and to provide a reasonable dividend, The company has to strengthen and consolidate its position. It should develop and improve its business and build up its financial independence. It should earn a sufficient profit to provide dividend. It should be built up to declare a reasonable dividend during a lean period as well. If continuously suffers losses, it can not pay dividends. The value of its shares will fall and result is the erosion of the shareholders capital. Hence, a company shall earn sufficient profit to discharge its responsibilities to the shareholders. If it fails to cope with changes in a changing and dynamic world its position will be shaken, and the shareholders' interests will be affected. It should consolidate and improve by growth, innovation and diversification of its position and help strengthen the share prices.

The shareholders are interested in the protection of their investment and the return on it. The company should ensure that its public image is such that the shareholders can feel proud of their company. The shareholders also have certain reponsibilities which they have to discharge to protect their own interests. They shall offer whole-hearted support and co-operation in the positive efforts of the company. They shall also properly guide and control its policies and activities. They shall appreciate the responsibility of the business to other sections of society, the workers, consumers and the community.

2. Labour Welfare. The success of an organisation depends on the morale of the employees and their whole-hearted co-operation. Employee morale depends to a large extent on the discharge of the company's responsibilities to them and the employer-employee relationship. The committee which conducted the "social audit" of Tata Iron and Steel Company (TISCO) observed that "not only should the company carry out its various obligations to the employees as well as the larger community as a matter of principle, but this has also led to a higher degree of efficiency in TISCO works and an unparalleled performance in industrial peace and considerable team spirit and discipline which have all resulted in high productivity and utilisation of capacity". Thus, by discharging its responibilities to the employees, the business advances its own interests.

However, the expenditure on labour welfare, etc., should have relevance to the financial position of the company and the economic conditions of the nation. It should not exceed the socially and economically warranted limits. It should not cause undue burden on the consumers or the general public. It should not result in the formation of islands of affluence of comfort in the midst of property and suffering at the expense of society.

3. Consumer's Welfare. According to Peter Drucker, "there is only one valid definition of business purpose; to create a customer". He further observes; "The customer is the foundation of a business and keeps it in existence. He alone gives employment. To supply the wants and needs of a consumer, society entrusts wealth-producing resources to the business enterprise."

Customer satisfaction is the key to satisfying the organisational goals. Customers welfare includes the following:

(i) Improve the efficiency of the functioning of the business so as to *(a)* increase productivity and reduce prices, *(b)* improve quality, and *(c)* smother the distribution system to make goods easily available;

(ii) Research and development to improve quality and introduce better and new products;

(iii) Take up appropriate steps to remove the imperfections in the distribution system, including black marketing or profiteering by middlemen or anti-social elements;

(iv) Supplying goods at reasonable prices even when there is a seller's market;

(v) Providing the required after-sale services;

(vi) Ensuring that the product supplied has no adverse effect on the consumer;

(vii) Avoiding misleading the customers by improper advertisements or otherwise;

(viii) Providing suffficient information about the products, including their adverse effects, risks and care to be taken while using the products;

(ix) Providing an opportunity for being heard and to redress genuine grievances;

(x) Understanding customer need and to take necessary measures to satisfy these needs.

Consumerism is unorganised endeavour of the consumer to protect their rights. In India many businessmen pay scant attention to their responsibilities to consumers. To protect consumer rights and to make the business discharge its responsibilities to them, the consumers should build up a strong consumer movement.

4. Community Welfare. A business has a lot of responsibility to the community around its location and to the society at large. Community Welfare may include :

(i) Taking appropriate steps to prevent environmental pollution and to preserve the ecological balance;

(ii) Assisting in the overall development of the locality;

(iii) Rehabilitating the population dislocated by the operation of the business, if any;

(iv) Taking steps to conserve scarce resources and developing alternatives, wherever possible;

(v) Improving the efficiency of the business operation;

(vi) Promotion of ancillarisation and small-scale industries;

(vii) Making possible contribution to furthering social causes like the promotion of education and population control;

(vii) Contributing to research and development;

(ix) Development of backward areas;

(x) Contributing to the national effort to build up a better society.

SOCIAL RESPONSIBILITY OF BUSINESS IN INDIA

The Indian business sector presents a mixed picture about social responsibility. J.R.D. Tata who conducted the first social audit in India and perhaps in the world, believed that while Indian industry has done reasonably well on the side of production, of growth and of efficiency, however, judged by the size of the blackmarket, the volume of black money and the general corruption that pervades our economic life its record has often been poor.

Hoarding and blackmarketing-mercilessly gouge the unfortunate consumer. "Although it is the trader rather than the manufacturer who is mainly responsible for such diversion of goods and for the resulting heavy burden imposed on the consumer, the fact remains that, to that extent, corporate management of even of large Indian industries has, perhaps unavoidably, failed in the important obligation of ensuring that their goods reach the consumer at fair prices". The producer should realise that his responsibility does not end with producing goods and services. He should ensure that whatever is produced reaches the ultimate consumer in time and at reasonable prices.

Today a number of leading companies in India have shown recognition of the social responsibility of the corporate sector. They have been instrumental in setting up hundreds of institutions of public service like schools, colleges, management institutes, dispensaries, hospitals, technological institutes, research institutes (medical, scientific and technological), liberaries, dharamshalas, cultural institutions, institutes for the dumb, deaf and blind, museums and places of religious worship. Some of the leading enterprises have extended welfare measures like health and medical facilities to people of the surrounding villages. They have risen up to help the victims of droughts, floods, earthquakes and other natural calamities.

The problem of environmental pollution caused by industries is very serious. In India though some enterprises have take pollution abatement measures, many continue to the major offenders against the environment. Some of the public sector enterprises are notorious for their irresponsibility in this matter.

As have been rightly pointed out by J.R.D. Tata, high standards of behaviour and the discharge of social obligations should be demanded from all economic groups in the country whose actions have an impact on the public weal. This applies in particular to trade unions which have in recent years, acquired and often misused enormous economic powers. The millions of man-days of production lost in India every year owing to labour unrest and the violent form which such unrest has taken in many cases, indicate the need for a new approach to trade unionism and a recognition of its social obligations.

The participation of labour in management has been suggested as a remedy for many causes of industrial unrests. It should be ensured that the "collaboration" between labour and capital does not become instrumental in exploiting society. As long as labour gets its slice of the cake, it would support capital to a mass profit by exploiting society.

The social responsibility of business is usually advocated for the private sector, on the assumption that the public sector is socially quite responsible. But the public sector in India has yet to prove that it is more responsive to society than the private sector. In some cases the record of the public sector is more dismal than that of the private. As far as the pollution of the environment is concerned, the public sector is as guilty as the private. Many public sector enterprises in India has failed to discharge their primary responsibilities about increase in the productivity and production, efficiency in the provision of the service, etc. This is led to mounting losses of many public enterprises. The public sector should generate surpluses to finance fruther development programmes. The huge losses incurred by the India public sector are the inevitable outcome of inefficiency, irresponsibility and mismanagement at various levels. Their failure in discharging primary duties has made the plight of the common man worse than shortages, higher prices and more taxes. There is a very wide gap between the sweet expectations from the public distribution system designed to save the common man from the elutches of the "unscrupulous private sector" and the bitter experiences of the way the public distribution system functions. A social audit is needed in India more of the public sector than the private sector.

The Sachar Committee has suggested that companies in the public sector, which are very much a part of the total corporate sector and account for about 70 per cent of the total investment in the corporate sector, must reckon with the social costs and social benefits arising out of any given investment. Social cost-benefit analysis has been accepted as one of the prime considerations for making any investment in the public sector. It is natural to expect from the private corporate sector that, it will also show a similar consideration of social cost and social benefit. The accountability of the public sector is in the form of social accountability. Social responsibility of business is another name for social accountability. It is a mere extension of the principle of public disclosure to which the corporations must be subject.

CONSUMERISM

Consumerism is a social movement seeking to augment the rights and power of the buyers in relation to sellers. Harper and Allen Jr. defined consumerism as the dedication of those activities of both public and private organisations which are designed to protect individuals from practices that impinge upon thin rights as consumers. Consumerism, interpreted as a collective endeavour of the consumers to protect their interests, is a manifestation of the failure of the business, including that of the public sector, and the government to guarantee and ensure the legitimate rights of the consmers.

The effective consumer protection apart from the response from business and government depends upon the consumers. Consumers accept consumerism as a means of asserting and enjoying their rights. Consumerism should succeed in making the busienss and the government more responsive to the rights of the consumers.

Consumerism is a social forces to (i) make the busines more honest, efficient, responsive and responsible, and (ii) pressurise the government to adopt the necessary measures to protect consumer interests by guaranteeing their legitimate rights.

Peter F. Drucker, has pointed out that "consumerism is the shame of the total marketing concept, "implying that the concept is not widely implemented. Consumerism reflects not only the failure of the business to widely implement the marketing concept but also the need to give the busienss policies a social orientation so as to enhance long-run social welfare. As Philip Kotler observes, "Consumerism is a clarion call for a revised marketing concept." Hence, the original marketing concept has to be broadened to include the societal marketing concept.

UTILITY OF CONSUMERISM

Well-origanised and dynamic consumerism may be expected to produce the followig results:

(i) Consumerism will provide feedback for the business. It will enable the producers to understand consumer needs and wants. This will assist in the more effective implementation of the marketing concept or the societal marketing concept, depending upon the nature of consumerism.

(ii) Producers and sellers will not take the consumer for granted. When consumers are strong enough to protect their rights, the businessmen will be compelled to shun unfair trade practices.

(iii) Consumerism will make the government more responsive to consumer interests, prompt it to take necessary statutory measures, and make the required institutional arrangements to safeguard consumer rights.

(iv) Producers will be able to enlist the support of consumers to minimise the imperfections on the distribution front. Several times the supply position is made worse by hoarding and blackmarketing by traders. Further, many sellers have a tendency to charge a price which is higher than the actual by giving one or other reason. There is no reason why the consumer and producer should not co-operate to get rid of the unscrupulous traders.

PROBLEMS OF INDIAN CONSUMERS

The important problems being faced by the Indian Consumer are the following:

(i) Short supply of many goods and services, especially of essential items, is a very serious problem affecting the Indian consumer. This demand-supply imbalance has produced all the associated evils of profiteering, hoarding and blackmarketing, corruption, nepotism, irresponsiveness and arrogance towards consumers.

(ii) The Indian consumer is also the victim of lack of effective or workable competition. Effective competition depends upon the general availability of essential information; buyers cannot influence the behaviour of sellers unless alternatives are known. It requires the presence in the market of several sellers, each of them possessing the capacity to survive and grow, and the preservation of conditions which keep alive the threat of potential competition from others. Effective competition cannot be expected to obtain in Indian markets where sellers are so few in number, capital requirements so large, and the pressure of fixed charges so strong, that price warfare, or the threat of it, will lead almost inevitably to collusive understanding among the members of the trade. Therefore, we do not find effective competition in Indian markets.

(iii) It has been said that the legal process in India is comparatively time-consuming and cumbersome. This discourages the consumers from seeking the redressal of their grievance by means of the judicial process.

(iv) Many products with which consumers in advanced countries are quite familiar are still new to a very large segment of the Indian consumers. The unfamiliarity of the consumers with product features makes the sale of substandard, inferior or even defective products easier in India than in advanced countries.

(v) Due to low literacy levels and unsatisfactory information flows, the Indian consumers, by and large, are not conscious of all their rights. This encourages irresponsible and unscrupulous business attitudes and tactics.

(vi) Consumerism in India is not well organised and developed.

(vii) Though there are a number of laws to safeguard the interests of consumers, they are not effectively implemented and enforced to achieve the objectives.

(viii) Thought the public sector has been developed and expanded to serve the public interest by providing effective competition to the private sector, increasing production, improving distribution, etc., it has yet to produce benefits that are commensurate with the investment. It is an irony that though consumer welfare is an avowed objective of the public sector, in certain areas the poor performance of the public sector monopolies has made the plight of the consumer more miserable. Some of them are even charged with unfair trade practices. For instance, electricity consumers are compelled to pay service changs for the service they never or hardly receive. Such is the plight of the telephone consumers also.

The above factors call for effective State intervention and consumerism to ensure the rights of consumers.

GOVERNMENT MEASURES

The Government of India has taken a number of measures to protect consumer interests. The various government measures may be classified into

(i) growth and expansion of the public sector and

(ii) the statutory regulation of private business.

Growth and Expansion of Public Sector. There have been a significant growth and expansion of the public sector in India. One of the most important objectives of the public sector in the enhancement of consumer welfare by increasing production, improving efficiency in production and supply, making available goods and serives at fair prices, curbing private monopolies and reducing market imperfections, improving the distribution system, and so on.

To improve the public distribution system, the Government has developed the public distribution system to reduce the hardships of consumers, especially of the vulnerable sections, by making essential consumer goods available more equitably and at fair prices. There is, however, a common complaint that some of the items, especially the foodgrains supplied by the system, are of inferior quality.

Statutory Regulation. Government of India has armed itself with a number of statutory weapons to control the production, supply, distribution, price and quality or a large number of goods and services. It is empowered to regulate the terms and conditions of sale, the nature of trade and commerce, etc.

Important legislations in this respect includes the MRTP Act, Industries Development and Regulation Act, Essential Commodities Act, Prevention of Food Adulteration Act, Prevention of Blackmarketing and Maintenance of Supplies the Essential Commodities Act, Trade Marks and Merchandise Marks Act, Sale of Goods Act, Indian Patents and Designs Act, Agricultural Products Grading and Marketing act, Drugs Act and Drugs Control Act, Indian Standard Institute's Certificate Act. Standard Weights and Measures Act, Imports and Exports Control Act. Packaged Commodities Order, Prince and Stock Display Order, Consumer Protection Act etc. There are, thus, a good number of laws to protect consumer interests. But a common complaint is that these laws are not effectively implemented.

CONSUMERISM IN INDIA

It may be said that there is no consumerism worth the name in India. True, there have been occasional mass consumer demonstrations against market imperfections, mainly shortages and exorbitant prices.

But several of these demonstrations have been organised with vested political interests and consumer involvement and dedication have been formed in different parts of the country. But with the exception of a very few, they have yet to demonstrate their practical utility. Further, whatever little organsied consumer movement there is in India is almost confined to urban areas, leaving the large majority of the Indian consumers high and dry.

A well developed consumerism is essential for the protection of consumer rights. Consumerism has the following important roles to play:

1. Liaison with Government and Producers. The important role of consumer organisation is to maintain liaison with producers on the one hand and Government authorities on the other. As Government is the key factor in meeting most consumer needs in India, these factor in meeting most consumer needs in India, these organisations have to realise that they have a larger role in the direction, espectially in India.

2. Consumer Education. The consumer is given information about various consumer goods and services. This relates to prices, what the consumer can expect, standard trade practices, etc.

3. Product Rating. In order to guide the consumer in his choice of products, some of the agencies carry out tests and submit reports on them.

The consumerism in India has not developed as a social reaction against overselling by industry, as happened in the West. On the contrary, it has been more a reaction to the evil effects of shortages and inflation. Therefore, the industry in India has a unique opportunity to respond to consumerism in a positive manner as outlined below:

(i) Industry will have to invest increasingly in testing the safety of the products in use. It is far better to organise for this than to wait for nasty accidents which will make it all mandatory and exaggerated.

(ii) Dealing with consumer complaints satisfactority is yet another responsibility of the industry. Promptness, courtesy and generosity are expected by the consumer with a genuine complaint. Apart from the loss and irritation caused to the consumer, persistent complaints, even if small in number, are often a good indicator of necessary improvement.

(iii) Yet we cannot be complacent even with good marketing because it is not possible they may manufacturers, including large ones, will always ask all the questions that are relevant to the consumer, particularly with regard to product safety, comparative cost effectiveness, etc. Consumer movements tends to focus on such questions and may well be seen as an extension of the marketing role. Therefore industry should co-operate with consumer movements in terms of information on, and education in the products. Conversly, such information may also educate the consumer in the issues facing the producers, *viz.*, cost of capital, norms, of profitability, impact of Government policies, etc.

(iv) The marketing must be recognised and practised as something more than sales and distribution. It has to be considered as the Company's relationship with the consumer. In the wider context, it can be extended to become a part of the organisation's total responsibility to society. When we talk of the social responsibility of industry, one of its prime social responsibilities is to the consumer through the adoption of sound marketing methods.

(v) Another important role, of the industry is in relation to claims made on behalf of the products through advertising. Restraint is best exercised voluntarily than through legislation which will otherwise become inevitable. Advertising agencies and marketing managements have a very important role to play in this respect. By overplaying the claims, they will cut the very branch on which they are perched.

(vi) Lastly, if industry has to continue to cope with consumerism, it has to invest in R & D because consumer expectations and needs are constantly rising and the constraints on meeting them are changing. To cope with this effectively, industry has to find solution through R and D. It is when consumer needs exceed the industry's ability to meet them that consumerism tends to become menacing. With adequate anticipation by industry, such a situation need not arise.

The above facts indicate that co-operative efforts on the part of consumers, business and the Government are very necessary to protect the rights of the consumers. A well organised consumerism is needed to make the Government responsive and effective and the business responsible and obliging. To sincere and dynamic business enterprises, consumerism does not pose a threat but offer an opportunity.

❐

5

Political Environment

DEMOCRACY

Various definitions can be given to the term "Democracy". In the broader sense, it is a "government of the people, for the people and by the people". In the limited sense, it is synonymous with "self-rule" or decentralisation. In the limited sense, in the sense of decentralisation, democracy existed in the Ancient Indian polity—in the form of Sabha and Samiti in the Rig Vedic polity and in the form of Janpadas (Republics) in the 6th century B.C.—yet these cannot be regarded as good examples of a democratic process. Democracy as a concept had its origin in the Greek System. But the Western world had played a significant role in the development of the concept. Therefore, the concept "Democracy" is generally regarded as a Western concept. The Indian polity has also addressed itself to the Western ideal of democracy.

The British rule in India, being a colonial and an imperialist one was not expected to be democratic. Being an alien rule, it lacked responsibility to the people of India. Later, due to the benevolence of some Indian Viceroys, especially Lord Ripon, some kind of democratic process began but it was in the field of local self-government. With the spread of English education, the demand for a responsible government and the representative institutions increased in the country. Hence, the Council's Acts of 1861, 1892 and the act of 1909 were enacted by the British Parliament in this spirit. This however, could not satisfy the Indian. After the First World War, it was to what the Indians' desire for democratic institutions that the colonial rulers enacted the Acts of 1919 and 1935. While Dyarchy of Dual Government was introduced by the Act of 1919 by which some

Indians enjoyed the status of ministers for the first time, complete provincial autonomy was accorded to the Indians by the Act of 1935. It was in pursuance top this that the elections took place in 1937, and the National Congress succeeded in forming its governments in most of the Indian provinces. The World War II was also viewed by the national leaders in India as a fight between forces of fascism and democracy and these leaders were keen to make the impending Indian national as a bastion of democracy. Both Gandhi and Nehru were staunch supporters of democracy in the country though their conception of democracy differed vitally from each other.

The modern theory of democracy does not believe in a government of the people, for the people and by the people. P.Herring is right when he states: "When democracy is analysed, not in the language of its high prophets but in terms of its behaviour, we observe that it is a system and an attitude of mind that tolerates many elites in many groups jostling and struggling." Hence, the modern theory lays stress only on the existence of some democratic institutions and processes. Also, it believes in a kind of "eltist democracy"—the elites being political or the economic, in the form of representative of the people or the members of legislatures etc.

At the outset two unique features of democracy in the India be pointed out. Firstly, owing to pure colonial rule and the existence of a state and primitive social order in the country, democracy was not looked upon as merely the "management of political affairs." On the other hand, democracy was looked upon as an instrument of ushering in a socio-economic revolution in the country. Hence, the common man had high expectations from the working of the democratic process to transform and develop the semi-feudal Indian society at the dawn of Independence. Secondly, democracy in India was imposed from above—it was introduced without creating the necessary socio-economic conditions. Even in the best of democratic politics, the level of political participation had graduated slowly depending on the growth of the socio-economic level. The Indian case negated this correlation between the economic development and political participation.

Before discussing the nature of democracy in India, one has to look up the pages of the Constitution of India to find the frame-work of a democratic set-up in the coutnry. The following democratic elements are obviously present in the Government of India *viz.*, *(a)* the nature of the state being Sovereign Democratic Republic as explicity mentioned in the Prembel to the Constitution; *(b)* the form of Government to be Parliamentary democracy, the executive being responsible to the legislature; *(c)* a union cabinet with Prime Minister as its leader working on the principle of collective responsibility to the legislature; *(d)* a dual executive with President as the head of the state thus keeping a check on the head of the government, *(e)* an impressive list of Fundamental Rights for the people and also provision for safeguiding these rights through judiciary with the power of judicial review; *(f)* a framework of rights for the poor through Directive Principles of State Policy; *(g)* a federal set-up with divisions of powers between the Centre and the States; and *(h)* an electoral system whereby the common man is to be the ultimate authority to provide power and legitimacy to the government of the day.

Now we will briefly discuss the democratic process of the Indian Polity.

1. Nature of Franchise and the Voting Behaviour. Indian polity is the largest Democracy in the world. It has been specifically provided in the Indian Constitution that an adult (21 years or more) is entitled to vote, seek election and get elected, without any discrimination of caste, colour, creed, sex, property, education etc. It was perhaps the democratic overzeal of the Indian national leaders that universal adult franchise, with almost no reservation of any kind, was introucted in the country. In the British parliamentary democracy, adult franchise had been made universal in stages, spread over to hundred of years. The nature of franchise in independent India, with no earlier experience, has been both a blessing, and a course in the smooth functioning of the democratic process in the country. It has only reduced democracy in India as a "voting robot" because it is virtually impossible for an average Indian with average financial means to get elected to the legislature. This brings us to the question of election process which is both legally complicated and financially demanding. Violence has become an inevitable part of the election process. Also, the voting behaviour presents rather an unsatisfactory picture over the years. With a mass of electorate being illiterate, ignorant, caste-ridden and entrenched in communalism, these elections have become mockery. Elections are rigged, election results are sometimes manipulated and there are cases of violently booth-capturing or coerçing the helpless to vote for a particular individual or community. There have been large cases of misuses of governmental machinery during the elections and many a times the election results have been reversed by the law courts on such grounds. This has led to disillusionment among the voters and consequently the percentage of people (genuinely) exercising their right of franchise has been decreasing. As a result, instead of "majority" governments, often the "minority" governments are formed. Also, the voting behaviour in most of these elections has been landslide victories either for the ruling or the opposition parties, depending on the myths created by some charismatic national leaders. It is also regretting that often the bulk of the electorate votes on parochial and sectarian considerations, unworthy of a good democractic system.

2. Nature of the Party System and Role of the Opposition. It is said that the political parties are a *sine-qua-non* of a good democracy due to their role in a democratic polity *e.g.* choice of leaders, political education to the electorate, and maintaining contacts with the electorates at the grass root levels etc. Hence, no democratic polity can be imagined without the existence of political parties. However, it is the nature of the party system that determines whether or not the polity is a true democracy. Needless to add that the ideal bi-party system is only a far-cry in India and much remains to be achieved in this direction. One finds many political parties in India; but that does not make the party system in the country as "multi-party". Most of these parties are in fact small groups revolving around some individuals or some special vested interests. They are mostly active just before the elections and plead for sectarian and regional demands. Most of the "national" parties in India do not have any strong cadre base, or any grass-root organisation. The Indian party system even defines the classification of "one Party System" of the kind found in sociolist and communist polities. In India one finds a unique classification : One party Dominant System. It is a system in which one finds the long uninterrupted rule of one and the same political party for a long time without banning the existence of other political parties—a characteristic feature of one party system. Hence, the Indian National Congress, the dominant political party, which led the national movement has remained firmly in the saddle of power of years. It is Congress that ruled both in the Centre and the majority of the States from 1947 onward except two short intervals—1977-79 and 1989-90.

The One Party Dominance system has undergone a radical change in the recent years. The dominance of the One-Party Congress—has gradually eroded yielding important place to regional parties. One fields the enormous growth of regional parties, not only in terms of their numbers but also in terms of acquiring and wielding political power.

Telgu Desham is in power in Andhra Pradesh, Communist Party of India (Marxist) and other leftist parties are in power in Tripura and West Bengal, Janta Party is in Bihar Smajwadi Janta Party is in U.P. ADMK is powerful in Tamil Nadu. Bhartia Janta Party (BJP) is becoming major opponent part and it is in power in Rajasthan, Gujarat and Maharashtra.

This brings us to the questions of the role of the opposition parties. The importance of the opposition parties in a democracy cannot be denied since dissent is the essence of democracy and this dissent is generated, formulated and voiced by the opposition is a must. However, if one does not find strong opposition in India, the cause of the malady lies deeper. The opposition parties, owning to their parochial, sectarian and regional interests, refuse to come together. Even when the opposition parties get closer and form coalition governments, as they did in 1977 and 1989, they soon fall apart due to lack of ideological cohesiveness.

The poor, ignorant yet politically mature voters in India have given a fair change to the opposition parties to acquire political power and become strong wherever they have exhibited a genuine concern for opposition unity or people-oriented policies. It is hence a tribute to the Indian voter that one finds consistently non-Congress governments in some states where the opposition parties have generally followed pro-people policies. It is the opposition parties in India who failed to rise to the occasion and came up to the expectations of the masses.

It is also desirable that both the opposition and the ruling parties must observe certain norms of behaviour towards one another. While the ruling party should not always be over-bearing and opposed to democratic norms, the conduct of opposition should also be understanding.

3. Pressure and Interest Group. The pressure or the interest groups are inevitably present in the working of a democracy. They are called "interest" groups due to various class interests propagated by them; and are termed the "pressure" groups because they generally adopt the pressure-tactics to get their class-demands fulfilled. They generally take the form of a social, cultural, religious, educational organisation and informally involve themselves in the decision-making process. They generate and influence public opinion for their class-demands on the one hand, and lobby with decision makers to get them legitimized on the other. These is identity of interests between the interest groups and the decision-making personnel. They need each other because they perform complimentary and identical interests. The political decision-makers equally need the inerest groups, as they percolate down the influence to the common man, the vote bank.

Some of the important pressure groups found working in India are—Indian Chamber of Trade and Commercc, in the field of commerce, popular trade unions etc. AITUC, CITU, HMS, INTUC etc., for furthering trade-union interest; various student organisations *e.g.*, SFI, NSUI, ABVP, Yuva Morcha etc.; teacher's organisations like the INTEC, NDF, DTF etc. beside several religious social interested groups. These interest-groups act as informal political bodies endeavoring to further their own interest and as well help the political party or ideology they belong to. Thus they are an inseparable part of a democratic set up.

4. Mass Media. The mass media—newspaper, radio, television etc. is an important aspect to determine the functioning of a democratic polity. It is an acknowledged fact that the mass media is a effective instrument to form the image of a government. The radio and the television should not be monopolised by a democratic government. Similarly, the principle of the freedom of the press is held sacrosant in a democratic polity. The leaders in the national movement reacted strongly against the alien rule whenever it tried to imipose restrictions on the press.

It is common knowledge that the radio and the television in India are under the thumb of the ruling Government who has decried all attempts by the opposition to make these autonomous. Both these mediums have generally monitored and presented news in a manner suited to the ruling political party.

The principle of the freedom of the press has generally been agreed upon by all political parties in India. Hence, there is no pre-censorship of the press. The press in India has generally been free, except during the days of internal emergency in the country in the year 1975-77. However, the freedom of press should not be taken in absolute terms and as a negation of even reasonable restrictions since such a measurement would lead to the destabilisation of the polity. The freedom of the press hence has to be regulated—to help serve the national interests. This however, does not vest with the government the right, to discriminate between various newspapers as regards sanctioning of newsprint, government advertisement etc. It would among to indirect coercion of the press and check its independence and impartiality. Any coercive measure to gag the press must receive the opposition of all and sundry. A Press Bill in Bihar was staunchly opposed by all sections of the population since it tantamounted a to virtual "gagging" of the free press. The pressure of the public opinion was so great that Bihar Government was virtually forced to shelve the Bill. There is a strong case for maintaining and even increasing the freedom of the press to help it work responsibly and in national interest. The press in India is financially dependent upon the Government for cheap news-print and grant of governmental advertisements to supplement the cost of production and a government should not take undue advantage of this situation to impose draconian measures on the press.

Perspective of Democratic Polity in India

A democratic form of government is the order of the day of most of the third-world or developing country. Since the end of World War II, many countries who had gained independence were enchanted with the democratic system. Hence, these third-world countries of Asia, Africa and Latin America started as democratic politics, but it is regretting that the democratic process did not work smoothly in quite a few of these countries. It indicates that the desirable conditions for working of a democratic process were missing in these polities and hence they failed to sustain democracy for long. The resultant coups, military dictatorship or authoritarian regimes unleashed oppressive policies on the people. India, on the other hand, has shown enough maturity in its working of the democratic experiment. The rulers of many third-world politics have at times in fact paid rich compliments to the people and leaders of India for being able to hold and maintain democratic traditions. Notwith-standing the constraints in the smooth functioning of democracy in India, the Indian polity is still cited as an ideal case in the developing world.

That the plural Indian polity has been able to withstand the challenges of the time is a sufficient tribute to the otherwise illiterate, ignorant, caste-ridden and poor masses of India. Often India's democratic fate was characterized as full of gloom. It is to the credit of the uneducated electorate of India to have risen equal to the occasion and behave in the manner befitting the circumstances. It is now generally held that the Indian voter is shrewd and behaves responsibly. A glance at the eight General Elections in the country would substantiate the argument. While in the General Elections of 1952, 1957 and 1962 the electorate elected the national Congress to power for having successfully led the national movement and had promised to translate pro-people policies; the electrorate rejected the ruling Congress in eight Indian States and one unions territory in the

General Elections of 1967 and gave only a slender majority to the Congress in the Lok Sabha. It provided an opportunity to the oppositions parties to emerge as the alternative to the Congress. However, the coalition governments consisting of the opposition parties failed to emerge as one part. Later, when Mrs. Gandhi's government failed to deliver and goods—and she imposed internal emergency in the country, she was throroughly rejected in the next elections. The record of the electorate since 1947 onwards would prove that the Indian voters exhibited the fundamentals of political education and had elected the governments suited to the national interests at a time.

One of the redeeming features of democracy in India has been that the citizens, despite diverse religions, languages, cultural values, had submerged their regional or sectarian interests to the national ones when the situations had so demanded. They have stood the tests of time-1962, 1964-65 and 1971—when the unity and integrity of the country was at stakes owing to external aggressions. It would also go to the credit of the opposition parties that they had whole-heartedly supported the ruling governments in meeting these external challenges, thus subduing their political interests to national interests.

PROBLEMS OF DEMOCRATIC POLITY IN INDIA

As stated above, the working of the democracy in India, though largely successful, has not been without problems. Most of these problems have remained in the polity since the advent of independence; these problems have even assumed serious proportions at times. Casteism, for example, has been a perennial problem of the Indian democracy. Indian society is not only caste ridden but it traditional as well.

It is a blur on the democratic nature of the Indian Polity. The higher castes oppress the lower ones; they even treat them as social outcastes or untouchable. To overcome, it is free India, the Constitution provided certain safeguards for the scheduled castes and backward classes. It was necessary to elevate their social, economic and cultural position. The ruling governments, however, unfortunately developed vested interests and used them as vote-banks, thus instead to solving the problem, they continued with it. Hence, there has been politicisation of caste-system—the political parties have used them for their political advantages and the lower castes have also used national politics to advance their class interests. The contain casteism, a two-pronged attack be made: at the social level, the increasing modernization of the polity be done to gradually eclipse caste-influence, and at the government level, the political decision-makers should rise above parochial vote-bank considerations.

Another important problem of the democratic policy of India is communalism.

Communalism in India has a long history. It was earlier limited to Hindu-Muslim relations but has now extended its sphere to include the Hindu-Sikh relations, with political overtones. Communalism is a cancer which is eating the vitals of the society. The Hindu-Muslim communal riots, on the one hand, and the rise of Fundamentalism on the other are potential dangers to the smooth working of the Indian polity. The common mass of the Indians are religiously tolerant; but people are often utilised by the politicians to fan up religious frenzy.

Among the political problems of Indian democracy are Defection, LACK OF INTEGRITY and LOSS OF CREDIBILITY etc. Political defection takes place when an elected legislator leaves his party to join another. During the formative years of the working of Indian democracy there were many occasions when some important national leaders left Congress to form other parties on ideological considerations. But today, conditions have totally changed. The legislators became akin to a commodity ready to be bought and sold for purposes of making a new government or destroying the existing one. Some Chief Ministers had become so past-masters in the game of numbers that even if their party did not get the required majority to form the government, they could still perform the feat with the help of the "bought" legislators. The consequence is that public life has been so corrupt and unmoral that people lost all hopes of expecting integrity in it. The erosion of credibility in public life is great. Anti-defection law was enacted, but it became useless. In order to make the democracy in India a success and to achieve its designed objectives. It is imperative that the decision-making process must become above-board to be able to tackle corruption in public life and restore credibility of the system.

There is also need to tackle the problem of political corruption in India; the electoral politics or the game of number has become so important that a political party only cares to win an election without bothering for the means in doing so. The election process is so expensive that each political party depends on the unaccounted money of trade and commerce to contest and win the elections. Obviously, there are unholy alliances between the political parties and the interest groups especially the business groups. To tackle political corruption, the election-process be made less expensive as Election Commission has done recently, the indigenous institution of Lok Ayakut be made more effective. These measures can succeed only if there is a strong will on the part of the government of the day to contain and wipe out political corruption rather than generating and protecting it.

Religionalism and Lingualism are two other major problems of the working of democracy in India. Regionalism is generally looked upon as a political issue but it is in fact the consequence of a serious economic crisis prevailing in a region. It is the result of regional disparities prevailing over the years. The western part of India is more affluent as compared to the eastern part of the country; again the southern region is comparatively backward than the northern one. In fact, political considerations have governed the economic development of a region. Hence, the backward regions feel the necessity of voicing their grievances and agitating for greater economic concessions. At times, these demands assume ugly forms and proportions. If, however, the advocacy of regionalism poses to threaten the unity and integrity of the country, the same must be resisted and even contained. The ruling Government should, at the same time, try to redress the genuine economic grievances of the backwards regions and try to bridge the gap of regional imbalances especially in the economic sphere. The regional parties and groups should also adopt only constitutional methods for the redressal of their grievances and not to indulge in unwanted violence which threaten the integrity of the country.

The Central Government also should not try to make political capital out of this by supporting the violent regional struggle in a bid to embarass a opposition ruled government in a state. Such a step may destabilisc the polity. Ligualism means having a chauvinist view of one's language. Language is a vehicle and should be used as such for bringing closer the people in different parts of India. But use of Hindi in non-Hindi belt has become a problem. However, government and people are trying to adopt constitutional methods to find out a solution.

The absense of grass-root leadership is still another problem of democracy in India. It India one finds Charismas playing a vital role. The charismatic leadership is indicative of a traditional polity and the feudal values. The charismatic leadership gives rise to a multi-party system wherein an individual controls the entires political group.

DEMOCRACY IN INDIA

In a polity of limited economic resources and unequal competition, the social upheavals, are bound to take place. But the real revolutionary measures are called for the combat ever-increasing inflation, growing mass poverty, educated unemployment and the rising level of people below the poverty-line. If democracy in India has to survise, politico-economic measures would have to be taken by the ruling government in the true spirit of the welfare of the poor man. It is high time that the politicians in India indulge in a bit of intro-spection, rise above their parochial class-interests and do something significanct and and he crisis through which thc Indian democracy is passing at present.

FUNDAMENTAL RIGHTS

The Constitution of India attempts to transform the country into a modern welfare state. In thise sense, it is much more than an organisational document and amounts to a social document in as much as it clearly lays down the relationship of the individual with the state and society as well as the rights of minorities and backward classes. The Constitution declares India a Sovereign Democratic Republic and the Fundamental Rights provided in part III of the Constitution impart India the character of a political democracy. However, as is well known, the basic rights of the individual and political democracy are meaningless unless there is economic and social justice in society. That is why the Constitution aims at providing socio-economic justice alongwith political freedom, by incorporating in itself directives to the Governments in the form of Directive Principles of State Policy, as well as a provision for civil rights.

The makers of the Indian Constitution visulaised it as an instrument of socio-economic change. The Constitution of India was drafted at a time when the concept of welfare state had become quite current and, therefore, its framers had certain ideals and objectives before them. It was the time when political thinking has started favouring an increasing role of the state in social and economic development, and it was believed that such development could be achieved more rapidly by adopting state policies and guidelines based on certain cherished ideals and principles.

These ideals ensuring social and economic well-being of the people first found expression in a major way in the 1931 Karachi Resolution of the Indian National Congress, which said : "In order to end the exploitation of the masses, political freedom must include real economic freedom of the starving millions." These liberal ideas were sure to affect the making of the Constitution of India. And the Constitution of India provides for both the Fundamental Rights to safeguard the individuals' liberty and dignity, and the Directive Principles, to ensure social, economic and political justice to every member of the community. Therefore the makers of the Indian Constitution aimed at providing all the people of India social economic and political justice. The Constitution is to secure to them equality of status, equal opportunity and equality before the law. It provides for freedom of thought, expression, belief, faith and worship, vocation, association and action.

The Preamble highlights the basic ideals and the stupendous tasks, as well as the aspirations of the people, which the makers of the Constitution wanted to be fulfilled in view of the prevailing social and economic-conditions in the country. The two provisions in the Constitution—the Fundamental Rights and the Directive Principles of State policy—are meant to give a practical shape to the declared ideals and to suggest an approach to achieve them.

Fundamental Rights are the basic rights of the individual which protect him against the abuse of executive as well as the legisltative powers. These rights contained in Part III of the Constitution, ensure an effective guarantee against any anti-democratic action of the state. Dr. Ambedkar explained: "The object of the Fundmantal Rights is two-fold. First, that every citizen must be in a position to claim those rights. Secondly, they must be binding upon every authority—every authority which has got either the power to make laws or the power to have discretion vested in it." In fact the intention of the makers of the Constitution was that the Fundamental Rights should be binding on the Central and the state governments as well as on the other local authorities. The Constitution have elaborately enumerates the Fundamental Rights, and also have provided for an express prohibition against their infringement by the state. Article 12 of the Constitution have defined the term 'state as—

(a) the Government and Parliament of India;

(b) the Government and legislature of each of the states; and

(c) all local or other authorities within the territory of India or under the control of Government of India.

Fundamental Rights are protected by the state and any law which infringes on them or takes away any of them can be declared unconstitutional and void by the courts. The grounds on which freedom can be restricted, generally, are security of the state, public order, sovereignty and integrity of India, decency, morality, etc. The Fundamental Rights can be classified into seven types.

1. The Right to Equality. Article 14 provides for equality before law and equal protection by law. That means that all are equal before the law. However, if there is any 'reasonable' basis for 'classification', such classification would not be a violation of equality.

Article 15 prohibits discrimination against individuals on the grounds of religion, race, caste, sex or place of birth. But any special provision for woman and children, or for the advancements of socially and educationally backward classes, can be made by the state. Article 16 gives equality of opportunity in matters of public employment. Article 17 abolishes untouchability and declares the practice of untouchability as a punishable offence. Article 18 prohibits the state from conferring any title, except military or academic awards and disinctions, on its citizens.

2. Right to Particular Freedoms. The individual freedoms of civil liberties are the main basis of Fundamental Rights. Articles 19 to 22 mention these personal liberties in detail. The foremost among these are the six fundamental freedoms guaranteed to the citizens in Article 19(1). These are: freedom of speech and expression, freedom of assembly, freedom of association, freedom of movement, freedom of residence and settlement, and freedom of pression, occupation, trade and business. Besides these freedoms, there was one more freedom, the freedom to acquire, hold or dispose of property, which has been deleted by the the 44th Amendment of the Constitution later.

But the rights cannot be enjoyed, absolutely and hence some restrictions have been imposed on individual rights. The restrictions have been imposed for the benefit and the interest of the community at large and for the sovereignty and the integrity of the nation. There cannot be any such thing as absolute or uncontrolled liberty, wholly freed from restraint, for that would lead to anarchy and disorder. The enjoyment of rights is subject to such reasonable conditions as are essential for the safety of the country, peace, public order, morals and health of the community. These restrictions are provided for in the subsequent clauses (2) to (6) of Article 19 itself. For example, while the freedom of speech and expression is guaranteed, an individual cannot use this freedom to defame another, which constitutes an offence under the law. A law which may be made by the state on any of the specified grounds, such as public order, defamation and contempt of court, cannot be challenged as unconstitutional or inconsistent with the freedom of expression, except where the restrictions imposed by the law can be held "unreasonable" by the court. Article 19 gives a list of individual liberties and prescribes in the various clauses the restraints that may be placed upon them by law, so that they do not conflict with public welfare on general morality. It is, sometimes argued that it is easy for the state to curtail or put a restriction on these rights, classifying it as a 'reasonable restriction', and that this reduces the substance of these rights, notwithstanding the fact that the court has the authority to go into the reasonableness of the restriction on the rights.

Article 20 forbids retrospective criminal legislation and double punishment for the same offence, and protects the right of an accused person not to be a witness against himself. Article 21 declares that no person shall be deprived of his life a personal liberty except according to the procedure established by law. That means that the member of the Executive, who make the law in the Parliament, shall determine whether or not the right of an individual to personal liberty should be curtailed in the collective interest or in the interest of the security of the state itself in view of the exigencies of the situation. However, a law made by the state which seeks to deprive a person of his personal liberty must prescribe a procedure for such deprivation and it must not be arbitrary, unfair and unreasonable. Article 22 provides for certain safeguards against arbitrary arrest and detention. According to this article, no person, who is arrested, shall be detained in custody without being informed, as soon as possible, of the grounds for his arrest, he shall not be denied the right to consult and to be defended by a legal practitioner of his choice; and he shall be produced before the magistrate within twenty-four hours of his arrest and shall not remain in custody without the authority of the magistrate.

But clause (4) of Article 22 contains certain provisions which authorise the legislature to make laws for "preventive detention, "for reasons connected with the security of a state or the whole of India, maintenance of public order, or the maintenance of the supplies and services essential to the community or for reasons connected with defence and foreign affairs. Preventive detention means detention without trial, only on the basis of suspicion or apprehension.

It is often argued that preventive detention is not only against democracy, rule of law and principle on independent judiciary, but it is also oppressive and dangerous. The ruling party, with a majority in the Parliament, can use it to advance its own political interests. The classical example of a such a misuse is the detention of hundreds of persons uner the Preventive Detention Act and the enactment of such laws as the Maintenance of Internal Security Act, during the emergency in 1975. There are, of course, certain safeguards against the abuse of this power in Article 22 (4) to (7), but they are not very effective in protecting the detenues. The Janata Government passed the 44th Amendment to the Constitution and strengthened these safeguards in 1978. However, the Janata Government could not drop the preventive detention clause from the Constitution.

3. Right Against Exploitation. Article 23 makes a provision for the prohibition of immoral traffic in human beings and forced labour. In pre-independent India, the evil of begar or forced labour prevailed in many parts of the country and the landlords compelled their tenants to render free service. This practice become a punishable offence. Prohibition of immoral traffic in human beings includes not only the prohibition of slavery but also of the misuse of women, children and the crippled for immoral purposes. Article 24 prohibits employment of children of tender age in factories and hazardous employment.

4. Right to Freedom of Religion. India is a secular state and it has an impartial attitude to all religions. Articles 25-28 provide for the freedom of conscience and profession and practice and propagation of religion, subject to public order and morality and to the provision of Part III.

Thus Indian has accepted the doctrine of religious tolerance, will certain exceptions. Religious and cultural safeguards have been guaranteed to the minority communities in order to ensure them justice and freedom of thought, expression, belief, faith and worship. In addition, Articles 29 and 30 provide for cultural and educational rights. But it is an irony that, in spite of the fact that the word 'secular' was inserted in the Preamble of our constitution by the

42nd Amendment, 1976, to highlight this aspect of the Indian policy. But communalism is constantly growing.

5. Cultural and Educational Rights. The Indian Constitution declares that the State shall not impose upon it any culture other than the community's own culture. It is mentioned in Article 29(1). Article 30 further mentioned that such community shall have the right to establish and administer educational institutions of its choice and the state shall not discriminate against such an educational institution in granting aid.

The sum to total of the above provisions maket Indian State more secular than even the US Constitution. The term secular was inverted in the Preamble by the Constitutional amendment (42nd amendment) in 1976. But as we know, the aim of the makers of Constitution could not be achieved as the communal feelings in the country are gradually increasing.

6. Right to Property. It is the most controversial rights of the Indian Constitution, which has ceased to exist today. It had been amended several times before its dissolution. This right, derived from liberal philosophy, not only guaranteed the right to private ownership of property but also the right to acquire, enjoy and dispose of property, subject only to reasonable restrictions in the public interest. This right was irrelevant to the millions of landless and propertyless Indians. It was a highly conservative right, because the laws made to facilitate agrarian reforms, transformation of the feudal structrue and abolition of zamindar were declared unconstitutional on the basis of this right granted under Articles 31 and 19(1)(f). The Congress Government, which was committed to a socio-economic change, reducing economic inequalities and proper distribution of property, especially land and other means of production, resorted to successive constitutional amendments to reduce the scope of Article 31. This Article underwent serious changes as a result of amendments of the Constitution by the first, the fourth, the seventh, the Twenty-fifth and the 42nd Amendment Act. Eventually, it was the Janata Government which deleted the right to property altogether from the list of Fundamental Rights in Part III by the 44th Amendment Act, 1978.

7. Right to Constitutional Remedies. The Constitution also provides for a constitutional remedy or device for the realisation of Fundamental Rights as a right under Article 32. The Fundamental Rights in the Constitution are useless, unless there is the mean to make them effective. Reality of the existence of such rights is tested only in the courts. The Fundamental Rights guaranteed by the Constitution safeguard the individual not only against the executive but also against the executive but also against the legislature. Any act of the executive or of the legislature which takes away or abridges any of these rights shall be declared unconstitutional by the courts. In other words, the courts are empowered to act as the guardian of Fundamental Rights.

The Indian Constitution lays down the following provisions for the enforcement of the Fundamental Rights guaranteed by the Constitution.

(a) The Fundamental Rights are guarnteed by the Constitution not only against the action of the Executive but also against that of the legislature. Any act of the Executive or of the legislature which takes away or abridges any of these rights void and the courts are empowered to declare it a void (Article 13).

(b) Apart from the Power to treat a low as void as being in contravention of the provision of the Constitution guaranteeing the fundamental rights, the judiciary has been covered with the power to issue the writs such as habeas corpus, mandamus, prohibition etc., in order that it may enforce such rights against any authority in the state, at the instance of an individual whose right has been violated.

The power to issue these writs for the enforcement of the Fundamental Rights, is given by the Constitution to the Supreme Court and High Courts under Article 32 and 226.

(c) The rights so guarnteed shall not be suspended execpt during a proclamation of Emergency according to the Constitution (Article 359).

Though a fundamental right may be enforced by other proceedings such as a declaratory suit under the ordinary law or an application under Article 226 or by way of defence to legal proceeding brought aginst an individual, a proceeding under Article 32 is described by the Constitution as a "Constitutional remedy" for the enforcement of the Fundamental Rights included in Part III and the right to bring such proceeding before the Supreme Court is itself a fundamental right in Part III. Article 32 is thus the corner stone of the entire edifice set up by the Constitution.

The Supreme Court is constituted the protector and guarantor (Article 32(1) of fundamental rights, and it cannot refuse, to entertain applications seeking protection against infringement of such rights on technical grounds. Where, therefore, the infringement of a fundamental rights has been established, the Supreme Court cannot refuse relief under Article 32 on the ground—

(a) That the aggrieved person may have his remedy from some other court or under the ordinary law; or

(b) That disputed facts have to be investigated or evidence has to be taken before relief may be given to the petitioner; or

(c) That the petitioner has not asked for the proper writ application to his case. In such a case, the Supreme Court must grant him the proper writ and if necessary, modify it to suit the exigencies of the case. Moreover, not only is the remedy under Article 32 is immune from being overridden by legislation, but any law which renders migatory or illusory the Supreme Courts power to grant this remedy shall be void. This was illustrated in the leading case of Gopalan *vs.* State of Madras, where the Supreme Court invalidated Section 14 of the Preventive Detention Act 1950, as it originally stood. The Supreme Court struck down its provision on the ground that it contravened Article 32 by way of preventing the Supreme Court from effectivey exercising its power under this Article.

RESTRICTIONS ON FUNDAMENTAL RIGHTS

The Fundmental Rights could be restricted or limited by the following process:

(a) Parliament shall have the power of modify the application of the Fundamental Rights, to the members of the Armed Forces or Police Forces so as to ensure proper discharge of their duties and maintenance of discipoline among them (Article 34).

(b) When Martial law has been in force in any area, Parliament may by law indemnify any person in the service of the Union or a state for any act done by him in connection with the maintenance of order in such areas or valiadate any sentence passed or act done while martial law was inforce (Article 34).

Moreover the Fundamental Rights, as guaranteed by the Constitution could be suspended during a Proclamation of Emergency by the President under Article 352. In normal time too, Articles 31A-31D, as introduced by successive amendments, constitute exeptions to the application of Fundamental Rights, wholly or partially. Article 31D was later repealed by the 43rd Amendment Act and changes were introduced to Articles 31A to 31C which are exceptions to the Fundamental Rights as envisaged in 1949. Except this, with the 42nd Amendment Act in 1976, ten duties had been incorporated in Article 51A (Part IVA). Under this Article, it shall be the duty of every citizen of India—

(1) to abide the the Constitution and respect the National Flag, the National Anthem;

(2) to cherish and follow the noble ideals which inspired our national struggle for freedom;

(3) to defend the country;

(4) to protect the sovereignty, courtesy and integrity of India;

(5) to promote the spirit of common brotherhood amongst all the people of India;

(6) to preserve the rich heritage of our composite culture;

(7) to safeguard public property;

(8) to strive towards excellence in all spheres of individual, and collective activity;

(9) to protect and improve the natural environment;

(10) to develop the scientific temper and spirit of inquiry.

Of course, there is no provision in the Constitution for direct enforcement of these Duties nor for any section to prevent their violation. But it may be expected that in determining the Constitutionality of any law, if a court finds that it seeks to give effect to any of these duties, it may consider such law to be reasonable, in relation to Article 14 or 19, and thus save such law from unconstitutionality. It could also serve as a warning to recklers citizens against anti-social and anti-national activities.

Thus the Indian Constitution aimed at to establish, equality fraternity and social justice with the help of Fundamental Rights. It was incorporated in the Constitution to safeguard individual liberty and thus help the citizens in developing their own individuality.

DIRECTIVE PRINCIPLES

After the Second World War political thinking favours an expansion of the role of state in social and economic development, which can be achieved more easily if policies are framed on the basis of certain guidelines and objectives. The Directive Principles (Articles 36-51) suggest such guidelines and objectives and demand a positive action by the government that is to be a 'Welfare State' and not a mere 'Police State'. The Fundamental Rights, in their turn, prevent the state from infringing upon themselves. The two types of rights are in fact, complementary to each other and strengthen each other.

The commitment of the frames of the Constitution to the social revolution is reflected in the Fundamental Rights and the Directive Principles of State Policy enshrined in Part III and Part IV of the

Constitution respectively. These parts are the conscience of the Constitution. Dr. Ambedkar, Chairman of the Drafting Committee, explained : "While we have established political democracy, it is also the desire that we should lay down as our ideal economic democracy. We do not want merely to lay down a mechanism to enable people to come and capture power. The Constitution also wishes to lay down an ideal before those who would be forming the Government. That ideal is economic democracy." Thus, it is clear that the makers of the Constitution adopted the Fundamental Rights to safeguard individual freedom against encroachment from the state authority and included the Directive Principles of State Policy to ensure social, economic and political justice to every member of society. These two provisions reflect the hopes and aspiration of the people as well as image of society the framers of the Constitution wanted Indian to have. The Directive Principles are in the form of instructions to the government and Parliament to enact laws which would establish a social order based or justice, quality and liberty. These principles constitute a novel feature of our Constitution and suggest the political, social and economic programmes to implement for which the government should formulate its policies. They strive to provide freedom and justice to all.

Article 37 determines the degree of applicability and viability of the Directive Principles. The article reads : "The provisions contained in this part shall not be enforceable by any court, but the principles therein laid down are nevertheless fundamental in the governance of the country and it shall be the duty of the state of apply these principles in making laws." Therefore, if Fundamental Rights are 'negative injunctions' preventing the state from infringing upon and abridging them, the Directive Principles are like "positive directions" to the state the formulate its action. The former project political democracy, the latter try for the establishment of socio-economic democracy. But, while the Fundamental Rights can be enforced in a court of law, the Directive Principles are not enforceable in the courtsee and do not create any justiciable right in favour of the individual.

CONFLICT BETWEEN FUNDAMENTAL RIGHTS AND DIRECTIVE PRINCIPLES

The question of priority in case of a conflict between the two types of rights, may easily arise. Under Article 43, the state is required to secure a living wage to all workers, yet no worker can secure a living wage by moving a court of law. The courts cannot compel the government to carry out any Directive Principle. Thus, a law which contravenes a Fundamental Rights can be declared void by the appropriate court, but a law which is contrary to a Directive Principle cannot be held void. Article 32 of the Constitution guarantees the right to move the Supreme Court for the enforcement of Fundamental Rights if they are violated or abridged by an authority of the state, and Article 13(2) expressly lays down that the state shall not make any law which takes away or abridges any of the Fundamental Rights. The Directive Principles cannot override this categorical restriction imposed on the legislative power of the state. It means that the state would certainly implement the Directive principles, but while doing so, it must not make any law which takes away or abridges any of the Fundamental Rights. This is to say that the Directive Principles should conform to and run as subsidiary to the Fundamental Rights.

In case of a conflict between the Fundamental Rights and the Directive Principles, the former prevail over the latter. In Hanif Qureshi's case which was decided in 1958, there was a conflict between a Fundamental Right under Article 19(1)(g), the right to carry on a buthcer's business and the Directive Principles under Article 48, prohibiting the slaughter of specified animals. It was held in this case that the Directive Principles under Article 48, prohibiting the slaughter of specified animals. It was held in this case that the Directive Principles cannot override the categorical restriction imposed on the legislative power of the state; therefore, a harmonious interpretation must be placed upon the Constitution. It means that the state should certainly implement the Directive Principles but it must do so in such a way as not to take away or abridge the Fundamental Rights.

Thus by way of implementing the Directive in Article 45—to provide free and compulsory education to children—the state cannot override the Fundamental right, under Article 30(1), of minority communities to establish educational institutions of their own choice.

Though these Directives are not enforceable by the Courts end, if the Government of the day fails to carry out these objectives, no Court can make the Government ensure them, yet these principles have been declared to be "fundamental in the governance of the country and it shall be the duty of the State to apply these principles in making laws" (Article 37). The sanction behind them is, in fact, political.

Implementation of the Directives

The Governments of the Union and the State faced a lot of problems in implementing the Directive Principles of State Policy as it clashed with the Fundamental Right.

The difficulty in implementing the Directive Principles of economic importance was faced in the very first year of the enforcement of the Constitution. Several of the land reform laws were held invalid by the Supreme Court because they violated the Fundamental Right to property. The first case which came before the Supreme Court was State of Bihar *v.* Kameshwar Singh, in which the validity of Zamindari Abolition Act was questioned on the groupn that it violated theFundamental Right to property guaranted under Article 31. Finding that the provisions of Part III were coming in the way of implementing the Directive Principles for bringing in socio-economic changes for the benefit of the poor people and the backward classes, the government, which was committed to introducing social welfare legislation and agrarian reoforms. resorted to constitutional amendments under Article 368. The first Constitutional Amendment, 1951, affected the property right in Article 31 and made an attempt to remove the obstacles in the way of the implementation of Directive principles with an economic import. The validity of this amendment was upheld in the Shankari Prasad *v.* Union of India case. Subsequently, the Fourth and the Seventh Amendments to the Constitution further circumscribed the right to property. The court had held the view that the Fundamental Rights, though they were sacrosant and constituted limitations on the powers of the executive and the legislature, were not immutable and absolute in character and were subject to Parliament's power to amend the Constitution and article 368.

The question of the amendability of Fundamental Rights became a subject matter of great controversy after the historic decision of the Supreme Court in Golaknath's case in 1967. In Golaknath v. State of Punjab, a contrary view was taken by the Supreme Court by a majority of 6 : 5 that the Parliament had no power to amend the Fundamental Rights so as to take away or abridge them. The immediate consequence of the decision of the Supreme Court in Golaknath's case was that the Parliament had no power to amend either Article 31 or 31-A and 31-B, which, in turn, adversely affected the competence of Parliament to implement the Directive Principles of Part IV of the Constitution. This disabled the executive to achieve the constitutional goal of socio-economic justice. It was argued against the judgment that, if the Parliament would not be given power to amend the Constitution, it would be difficult to implement the directive principles and, consequently.

The decision of the Supreme Court preventing the Parliament from amending the Constitution so as to take away or abridge any of the Fundamental Rights in Part III, opened the floodgate of controversy and became a cause of confrontation between the executive and the judiciary. As a result of the decision, the government found itself helpless to purse its political policy and to implement the Directive under Article 39, which enjoins the state to direct its policy towards preventing the concentration of wealth and means of production in a few hands and utilizing the material resources of the community for the common good. The Fundamental Rights under Articles 14, 19 and 31 came in the way of the government's socio-economic programmes. But the controversy could be resolved only after the mid-term Lok Sabha polls in 1971, provided the Congress got the required majority to amend the Constitution.

The Congress won the 1971 election with an overwelming majority, and the Parliament passed the 24th Constitution Amendment Act and restored to the Parliament its power of making any changes in the Constitution, including Part III. The Parliament passed the 24th Amendment which amended Articles 368 and 13. Later, the 25th Amendment added a new article. Article 31C, which not only restricted the property right but also put the Directive Principles over and above the Fundamental Rights. Thus, the hindrance caused to the Government by the provisions of Part III in the discharge of its constitutional duty to provide socio-economic justice to the people, was sought to be removed by the Constitutional (Twenty-fourth) Amendment Act, 1971. The Act also provided for a mechanism for amending the Constitution and thus removed the hindrance that the Golaknath case had created. Article 31C made Article 14, 19 and 31 inapplicable to certain laws which aimed at implementing the Directive Principles enshrined in Article 39(b) and (c) *i.e.* The State shall directs its policy towards securing equitable distribution of the material resources of the community. These laws were kept beyond judicial scrutiny. It is worth here to quote Article 31C which reads "Notwithstanding anything contained in Article 13, no law giving effect to the policy of the State towards securing the principles specified in clause (b) and clause (c) of Article 39 shall be deemed to be void on the ground that it is inconsistent with, or takes away or abridges any of the rights conferred by Article 14, Article 19, or Article 31 and no law containing a declaration that it is for giving effect to such policy shall be called in question in any court on the ground that it does not give effect to such policy." The validity of these amendments, and 26th Amendment which abolished the privy Purses and the status of native rulers, and the 29th Amendment which added two Kerala Acts to Schedule nine, was challenged in the Kesavananda Bharati *v.* State of Kerala case.

In the Kesavananda case, the Supreme Court by a majority of 9 : 4 upheld the first part of Article 31C, but it declared the second part of the article (which provide that "no law containing a declaration that it is for giving effect to such policy shall be called in question in any court on the ground that it does not give effect to such policy") as invalid. Thus, the Supreme Court no longer put the right to property above social welfare and the creation of a just social order as envisaged in the Directive Principles. No doubt, Kesavnanda's case pro-pounded the theory that the basic structure of framework of the Constitution was beyond the amending power of Parliament. But property was not a part of the basic structure and that, if the right it was admitted that to property became an impediment to giving effect to the Directive Principles, the amending power extended to abridging or abrogating the property right because the Directive Principles were also fundamental in the governance of the country. Thus, the question regading the power of Parliament in Golaknath's case—was reopened for consideration in the Kesavananda's case and the validity of amendment to the Fundamental Rights was presumed to depend on whether or not it violated the basic structure or framework of the Constitution.

The problems still remained and hence the 42nd Amendment Act was adopted in 1976 According to this amendment the Directive Principles were put above the Fundamental Rights by amending Article 31C which now provides that 'no law giving effect to the policy of the State towards securing all or any of the Directive Principles laid down in Part IV shall be deemed to be void on the ground that it is inconsistent within, or takes away or abridges any of the right conferred by Articles 14, 19, and 31. Thus, instead of only Article 39(a) and (b), the whole of Part IV has been conceded to be of greater importance than the Fundamental Rights in Part III, by this amendment.

When the Janata Party Government came in power in March 1977, the Forty-fourth Amendment Act, 1978 was passed. Article 31 pertaining to the right to property was eliminated as a Fundamental Right and was made an ordinary right. Similarly, Article 19(1)(f), whch provided for the right to acquire, hold and dispose the property, was also deleted from the chapter on Fundamental Rights. This amendment has set at rest the controversy over the status of Fundamental Rights and the implementation of Directive Principles for removing economic disparities. The Government tried to remove the hazards to implement directive Principle—to minimise inequality in income status, facilities and opportunities, amongst individulas and groups Article 38(2).

This innocently-looking amendment is to be read along with the Janta elimination of the Fundamental Right to property. They paved the way for confiscatory taxation and for equalising salaries and wages for different vocations and different categories of work, which would usher in a socialistic society. The 44th Amendment abolished the right to property and thus payed the way for fuller implementation of the Directive Principles. As regards the implementation of Directive Principles after independence, it is not possible here to make a survey of the progress of such implementation with a view to achieving socio-economic justice and making India a welfare state. Nevertheless, the importance of Directive Principles for socio-economic changes can be suggested by referring to some cases of the implementation of these principles.

The Union Government particuarly worked for the implementation of directive in Article 39(b). The Planning Commission, in its first plan, recommended the abolition of Zaminders, Jagirdars and such other intermediaries so as to bring the tillers of the soil in direct relationship with the state and improve their condition. A large number of legislations have been passe to improve agriculture (Article 48) and industry. For instance, for the improvement of cottage and village industry many boards have been set up. Similarly, more facilities for education. Article 45 directs to provide free and compulsory primary education. The Government have provided facilities for health and efforts are being made to provide employment to the people and raise their standard of living (Article 47). Most of the states have taken positive steps to organise village panchayats and the powers of local self-government have been bestowed on them. (Article 40) Steps have also been taken by several states to provide free and compulsory education to children up to the age of 14. Medical facilities are also provided, particularly to the rural population to raise the health standard of the people. The Government of India launched its Community Development Project in 1952 with a view to providing better communication, housing, civil amenities, sanitation and education to the people.

For the establishment of economic democracy, such measures as nationalisation of banks, abolition of privy purses, nationalisation of insurance, etc., have been taken. Positive steps have been taken to improve the education and protect the economic interests of scheduled castes and scheduled tribes and other weaker sections of society.

Equal wages for equal work, abolition of bonded labour, food for work, and employment under the antyodaya programmes are all important steps which go to implement some of the Directive Principles. In fact, since independence, the policies of the government—especially its social, labour, agricultural and land-reform policies—have been shaped with the Directive principles in view. The industrial and taxation policies are also guided by these principles.

For the promotion of the cottage industries (Article 43), which is a state subject, the Central Government has established several Boards to help the State Governments in the matter of finance and marketing.

The foreign policy of India is based on Article 51 or the Directive which reads "The State shall endeavour to promote international peace and aminity. The country's policy of non-alignment," its contribution to the non-alignment movement, its principles of peaceful co-existence, and its faith in the Punch Sheel amply illustrate the government's deep concern for interenational peace and security.

DIRECTIVES COMPARED WITH FUNDAMENTAL RIGHTS

The Directives, differ from the Fundamental Right contained in Part III of the Constitution or the ordinary laws of the land in the following respects:

(i) While the Fundamental Rights constitute limitations upon state action, the Directive Principles are in the nature of instruments of instruction to the Government of the day to do certain things and to achieve certain ends by their actions.

(ii) The Directives, however, require to be implemented by legislation and so long as there is no law carrying out the policy laid down in a Directive, neither the State nor an individual can violate any existing law or legal right under or legal right under colour of following a Directive.

(iii) The Directives are not enforceable in the courts and do not create any justiciable rights in favour of the individuals.

In the final analysis, the Directive Principles envisage a just social order. But because of the absence of a legal sanction behind them, the state not being equipped with the necessary powers to implement them, and the judicial interpretations making them subsidiary to the Fundamental Rights, there have been tremendous hurdles in the way of implementing the Directive Principles and ushering in a just society. The achievements have not been very heartening and the the situation on the social and the economic fronts is still very gloomy. The expectation that the Constitution would usher in a great social and economic revolution, has not yet been fulfilled. The interests of the downtrodden and the weak have been thrown into the abeyance in the constitutional and political game, and the result is that effective measures to eradicate poverty, backwardness, and social and economic injustice are still awaited. In short, the Directives emphasise, in amplification of the Preamble, that the goal of the Indian policy is not laissey faire, but a 'welfare state' where the State has a positive duty to ensure to its citizens social and economic justice and dignity of the individual. It would serve as an 'Instrument of Instructions' upon all future governments, irrespective of their party creeds.

❐

6

Legal Environment in India

The Government of India uses a number of economic legislation to regulate various aspects of private business. Some of the main instruments of economic legislation and industrial (Developent and Regulation) Act, the monopolies and Restrictive Trade Practices (MRTP) Act, the Foreign Exchange Regulation Act (FERA) and the Imports and Exports (Controls). Now we shall discuss a few of them.

1. Industries (Development and Regulation) Act, 1995. To control and regulate the process of industrial development in the country, an Act was passed by the Parliament in October 1951 and came into force on May 8,1952. The objectives of this Act were: *(i)* the regulation of industrial investment and production according to plan priorities and tagets; *(ii)* protection of small enterpreneures; *(iii)* prevention of monopoly and concentration of economic power; and *(iv)* balanced regional development.

In the initial stage 37 industries were brought under the preview of the Act which was later extended to include 70 inudstries. The Government a number of changes in this Act from time to time. An important change came in 1960 when all enterprises with fixed capital of Rs. 10 lakh or less were exempled from licensing produce. The exemption limit was raised to Rs. 25 lakh in 1963 and to Rs. 1 crore in 1970. Later on the limit was raised from Rs. 1 crore to Rs. 3 crore and then to Rs. 5 crore. A major change came in 1988-89. Now there was no need to take licensing for installing a unit involing investment in fixed assets of Rs. 50 crore in backward areas and Rs. 15 crores in non-backward areas. The year 1991 saw a major change in industrial policy which abolished licensing policy for all but 18 industries. With the passage of time, most of these industries have also been delicensed. Licensing in compulsory only in case of 6 industries. These are alcohol, cigarettes, hazardous chemicals, electronics aerospace and defence equipment, drugs and pharamaceuticals (excepting bulk drug industry which has been delicensed and industrial explosives. In respect of delicensed industry, no approval is required from the government. An Industrial Enterpreneum Momorandum (IEM) to the Secretarait for Industrial Approval (SIA) which acknoweledges receipt. Thus inudstrial licensing has been abolished for all except a few industries.

2. The Monopolies and Restrictive Trade Practices (MRTP) Act. Under the MRTP Act, all firms with assets above Rs. 100 crore since 1985 were classified as MRTP firms. Such firms were permitted to enter selected industries only and this also on a case-by-case approval basis. In addition to control through industrial licencing, seperate approvals were required by such large forms for any investment proposals. The government felt that this was having a deleterious effect on many large firms in their plans for growth and diversification. The new industrial policy scrapped the thershold limit of assets in respect of MRTP and dominant undertakings. The MRTP Act has been accordingly amended. The new amended Act gives more emphasis to the prevention and control of monopolistic, restrictive and unfair trade practices so that consumer are adequately protected from such practices.

3. The Foreign Exchange Regulation Act (FERA). FERA was promulgated in 1973 and came into force on Jan 1,1974. According to the Section of 29 of this Act, all non-banking foreign branches and subsidiaries with foreign equity exceeding 40 per cent had to obtain permission to establish new undertakings, to pruchase shares in existing companies, or to acquire wholly or partly any other company. Guidelines for administering this section of FERA were announced in 1973 and later amended in 1976.

In line with the liberalisation measurs, the government announced major concessions to FERA companies in November 1991 and Jan 1992. On Jan 8, 1993, the government promulgated an ordinance to amend FERA with immediate effect. The ordinance removed a large number of restrictions on companies with more than 40 per cent non-resident equity, removed FERA controls on Indian ·forms setting up joint ventures abroad and allowed Indians to hold immovable property abroad, subject to certain conditions. The removal of restrictions made FERA redundant and FERA companies were at per with Indian companies. The Union Budget, 1998-99 advocated repealing FERA and replacing it with FEMA. The Government adopted FEMA in 1999. Under FEMA, the emphasis is on 'management' rather than 'regulation.'

MRTP ACT

The Monopolies Inquiry commission had submitted its report and recommendations in the form of a draft bill in 1965. With this draft as the basis, the Monopolies and Restrictive Trader Practices Bill was presented to Rajya Sabha in August 1967. It was passed by Parliament in December 1969. The objectives of the legislation are:

(i) to ensure than the functioning of the economic system does not result in concentration of economic power to the common detriment; and

(ii) to control such monopolies and rsestrictive trade practices as are injurious to the public welfare. For counteracting the adverse effects of concentration of economic power, the Act seeks to invest the Central Government with wide powers, *inter alia*, to investigation and control mergers as well as expansion.

A regards monopolies and restrictive trade pratices, the Act seeks to establish a permanent statutory commission to be called as the Monopolies and restrictive trade practices commission. (MRTPC) which will consist of not less than two and not more than nine members including the Chairman. It will perform two main functions; investigation and control of monopolies and all restrictive trade practice. It will also be available for advice on matter relating to concentration of economic power. In relation to monopolistic pratice, the Commission will have only advisory status with no powers of enforcement. In relation to restrictive trade practices its status will be that of judicial court with powers of enforcement. In matters pertaining to concentration of economic power (expansion of existing undertakings, setting up of new undertakings, and mergers), powers of investigation and enforcement shall vest with Government which will decide whether or not to refer a particular case to MRTPC for advice which, again, will not be binding on Government.

The Moncpolies and Restrictive Trade Practices Act provides for the appointment of two officials, the Director of Investigation and the Registrar of Restrictive Trade Practices who will assist the Commission in its work. The function of the Director of Investigation is to carry out preliminary investigations into the complaints of restrictive practice with a view to etablishing their veracity and importance. The Registrar will mainly look after the registration of restrictive trade agreements.

On August 2, 1970, Government set up a three-man, Monopolies Commission to prevent concentration of economic power, for the control of monopolies and for prohibiting monopolistic and restrictive trade practices by controlling the activities of dominant or large undertakings as defined under the Act. The Act defines a dominant undertaking as one which, either by itself or along with inter-connected undertakings, controls not less than one-third of items of production, supply or distribution of a commodity or provides or otherwise controls not less than one-third of any services rendered in India. The Act also defines a monopolistic undertaking as any dominant undertaking which by itself, or together with not more than two other independent undertakings, supplies or distributes or otherwise controls not less than one-half of total goods or services.

APPRAISAL OF LEGISLATION

Both within Parliament and outside, the provisions of this 'verbose piece of legislation' have been subject to criticism and doubts have been raised as to whether the Act may not become the fifth wheel of India's industrial cart. We have today a plethora of controls which regulate corporate sector. The number of such controls is almost infinite. They cover evey segment of corporate activity from the very point of conception of a project. The Monopolies and Restrictive Trade Practices Act is the latest in the armoury of the State to regulate the corporate sector. Main criticism against this legislation are discussed below.

1. The serious lacuna in the Act is that it mixes up considerations about concentration of economic power and monopoly. The provisions of the Act dealing with concentration of economic power seek to regulate expansions, mergers, amalgamations and take overs, and appointment of directors in respect of *(a)* dominant undertakings have assets of Rs 1 crore and more; and *(b)* undertakings which by themselves or together with inter-connected undertakings have assets of not less than Rs. 20 crores in value. It also seeks to regulate starting of new undertakings which would become inter-connected undertakings of such existing undertakings, the total assets of which exceed Rs. 20 crores.

The restrictions are merely in the form of securing approval of the Union, Government. In actual practice, the delay they will involve if past experience is any guide, will seriously handicap the growth of the so-called dominant undertakings or industrial groups. This would postpone and delay development and the bais objective of the Act will not be attained.

2. Monopoly in economic terms implies an industrial unit which can so control production in the industry as to restrict competitive forces in the market and have a price structure based on various non-competitive considerations and devices like manipulation of production. In India, there does not seem to be a place for monopoly of this kinds because our industrial development is expected to take palce on planned lines. Merely because some individuals or companies are able to do better than this, there should be no room for us to condemn them as monopolists or monopolies. Already industry has to contend with a variety of controls such as industrial licensing, import control, clearance for capital issues and so on.

3. If we take cognizance of the international trends we may find ourselves going in the reverse direction. The world trend is towards larger companies, amalgamations, and mergers of units.

They are aimed at improving competitive strength and technical efficiency.

4. The provisions of MRTP Act relating to diversification and expansion of large undertakings are difficult to harmonise with anti-monopoly legislation are world over. Nowehere else has monopoly legislation taken assets into account for the purpose of restriction and control on companies regarding their expansion or diversification. This is so, because assets *per se* are not considered a sound criterion for determining monopoly power. The only valid consideration is the functioning of big companies against the interest of the consumers.

5. All public undertakings controlled, managed or sponsored by Government and the trade practices in which they participate as parties are exempt from the provisions of the Act. It is undersirable to exempt all public undertakings not only from the control against concentration of economic power but also from the provisions on restrictive trade practices and on the behaviour of dominant firms. Many public undertakings compete with private firms in the same product and many of them enjoy dominant positions in their respective markets. The profit motive is very much a part of their operation. It cannot be assmed that just because they are owned by Government they will not take advantage of their dominant market position to adopt discriminatory and restrictive pratices unfair to customers and/or competitors. They are subject to the same danger of losing the urge for improving efficiency and productivity that private enterprises in monopolistic situations are subject to. In fact, all public industrial and commercial undertakings should be on part with private undertakings and they should been brought within the scope of a least the provisions regarding the investigation and control of monopolistic and restrictive trade practices.

6. Sufficient thought has been given by the Government to the need to reconcile the provision of this legislation with Governments other economic policies. It will not be surprising, therefore, if enforcement of this law lands Government in embarrasing situations. For instance, how will it reconcile the provisions of this legislation with the policy of enforced voluntary price fixing through producers'

associations (in case of vanaspati) or with the working of Joint Plants Committee in steel? Or, for that matter, how will it reconcile the provision for curbing concentration with, the need for achieving investment targets particularly in industries which may call for allowing big business house to expand existing units or set up new units? For this very reason Government has been considering the amendment of Section 27 of the Act to delink some of the units belonging to larger house with a view to allowing the expansion of such concerns.

7. The fundamenal difficulty of administering this Act is that we have hardly any knowledge of economics of business concentration. As the intention behind the Act is not to control concentration *per se* but to control it only to the extent that its effects are detrimental to the public interest, some rudimentary information and analysis of the economic effects of concentration of economic power are absolutely essential. The debate on concentration has been extremely vague on the basic economic issues involved. No attempt has been made to answer the question; assuming that a sbstantial portion of private industry and trade is concentrated is increasing, what is wrong with such concentration? In what way does this tendency harm or help the economic interests of the community? Hazari's "Structure of the Corporate Private Sector" also did not analyse the economies of concentration. No information is available regarding the effects of concentration on the incentive from growth of enterpreneurial talent and specialised managerial known-how on the rate of incentive for technological development on the growth and pattern of private industrial investment, on the productivity of such investment on the market performance of industries in which such groups have predominant interest, on the development of bank credit. There are no hypotheses on the basis of which workable critieria can be set up for judging whether any development that has the effect of increasing concentration of economic power is or is not against the public interest.

8. The policy envisaged in the Act is fashioned on British model and has very little in common with American anti-trust laws. It goes

by the abuse principle', *i.e.* it strikes not at the position of acquisition of monopoly power but at the abuse of such power. The American approach, generally described as the *per se* approach, identifies public interest with the maintenance of free or unrestricted competition. Its primary emphasis is more on market structure than on market performance. Broadly speaking, under United States anti-trust laws, any action (individual or collective) that results or is likey to results in diminution of competition is considered *per se* detrimental to the public interest and is, therefore, un-lawful. The British (or abuse) approach is by contrast neutral between the intrinsic superiority of free competition or monopoly. This type of anti-monopoly policy requires individual investigation of each situation of monopoly or restricted competition in order to assess its effects on the public interest. The public interest is broadly defined in terms of performance variables like the reasonableness of prices, costs and profits, output and investment growth, quality of products, innovation and technical efficiency, exports, etc., Under the abuse principle, therefore, the law requires not only proof of the fact of monopoly or restriction of competition, but also proof of pubic deteriment resulting therefrom.

9. The references made to the Monopolies Commission so far show that the Commission is going to be tied down to investigation proposals for expansion, mergers, and new undertaking from the stand point of concentration of economic power. The Government is inclined to refer almost every proposal which technically comes within the purview of the Act. Given the number of applications for industrial licences for exampsion or new units pending. Licensing Committee will have to clear them at the rate of more than 100 applications a month. Of these, if 50 per cent are sponsored by large houses or dominant companies and if Government refers even 120 per cent of these to the Commission, it seems the Commission will have its hands more than full with just concentration enquiry. It appears from the cases which have been referred to the Commission that the Government finds the Commission as a useful device for shrugging its responsibility to take decisions. A cursory reading of the public notices issued in connection with these references suggests

that many of the proposals are really insignificant from the point of view of concentration of economic power to the common deteriment.

10. Examining licence applications from the concentration angle is, however, something which can be done better at licensing stage. As the cases referred to the Commission so far illustrate, all that the Commission will do is to duplicate the work done by the Licensing Committee or in the case of margers, by the Company Law Board. The Commission's investigations and recommendations can be useful only if it is called upon to investigate proposals before the Licensing Committee has taken its decisions on them. Only then the commission can examine a particular proposal in relation to the rival claims for licence. Otherwise, the Commission might be put in a awkward position of having to suggest reversal of a Government decision already taken. Surely it cannot be the Government's intention to keep the Commission busy but not ineffective.

11. The present activity of the Commissions gives an impression that it is going to be bogged down in concentration enquiries and may never find time to work on the other two and no less important objectives of the Act-control of the working of existing monopolies and of restrictive trade practices. Actually, for the point of view of safeguarding the interest of the public as consmers and as small traders and producers, these on two objectives are far more important.

WORKING AND ADMINISTRATION OF THE MRTP ACT

In the four years from 1970 to 1973 a total of 12,086 applications for industrial licences were received by the Government. Of these, those falling within the purview of Sections 21 (substantial expansion) and 22 (establishment of new undertaking) of the MRTP Act numbered on more than about 400, from the enforcement of the Act in June 1970 to November 1973. These 400 applications pertained to 917 undertakings registered with the Government 803 as inter-connected undertaking having assets worth Rs. 20 crores or more and 114 as dominant undertakings having singly or jointly assets of the value of not less than Rs 1 crore. The figure of 400 applications from large house and dominant undertaking out of total of 12,000 applications is small. The reason for this is obvious. The provisions of the MRTP

Act with regard to registration have been applied legalistically and restrictively that a large number of inter-connected undertakings have evaded registration. For instance Birlas as a large industrial house had a total of 276 concerns under them according to the Dutt Committee Report in 1966. Against this, as revealed in the Government's reply to a question in Parliament, only 45 undertakings belonging to Birlas have been registered as inter-connected undertakings. With so many undertakings belonging to the large house registered with the Government it is not surprising that the number of applications for industrial licences falling within the MRTP should bear little relationship to the actual number of a applications made by the large houses.

Out of these 400 applications, only 32 were referred to the Monopolies Commission for detailed inquiry. The rest have been disposed of by the government without reference to the Commission. There is no apparent logic behind the government's decision to refer to not to refer to the Monopolies Commission perticular cases pertaining to the large houses. The Commission itself complains in its annual report for the year 1972. That as against 72 references received in 1971 only 10 references were received in 1972. A number of cases of large magnitude and importance to the economy were decided by the Central Government without reference of the Commission. The Commission is not able to understand the policy which is being pursued in this respect. The Commission cannot help feeling that there is some incongruity in that sometimes cases not involving any major issues are referred to the Commission while other, which would *prima facie* involve important considerations, are not referred. The present chariman of the Commission Justice J.L. Nain confirmed the general compression about the irrelevance of the Commission when he was rebutting the criticism that the MRTP Act had impeded industrial growth. He stated that "the Commission plays even a less important role than what the act envisages." One of the members of the Commission has observed that" people give us too much credit. We are not that effective because the number of cases covered by the MRTP constitutes a very small part of total industrial growth."

The position at present seems that only 4 per cent of the industrial licence applications come under the provisions of the MRTP Act as restrictively interpreted by the Goverment. Of these 4 per cent, less than 10 per cent are referred to the Monopolies Commission. Of the number of proposals referred to the commission, those rejected from less than 10 per cent. In the circumstances, even a cursory cost-benefit study of the Monopolies Commission and the attendant paraphernalia can lead to only one conclusion; disband the Commission and Scrap the Act. As things are, the existence of the Act and the Commission only serve to create a false impression that the government is concerned about checking the growth of the large business houses and the concentration of economic power.

Proposed Reorganisation. In March 1973, it was reported in the Press that a major decision had been taken by the Government to break up monopoly industrial houses. Section 27 of the MRTP Act was proposed to be amended to provide for the dilution of control of business groups on companies and to break up big conglomerates into functional units. This decision had been taken as part of the new industrial policy aimed at the twin objectives of preventing concentration of economic power and at the same time allowing the expansion of industrial units in priority sectors. These twin objectives were proposed to be harmonised by assuming powers to break inter-connections where necessary and promote mergers and amalgamations where needed so that these unit were allowed to expand without inhibition to achieve economies of scale.

An official committee set up by the Ministery of Industrial Development also endorsed the above suggestion after gaining experience in clearing applications of larger industrial houses, particularly the difficulties faced in reconciling the conflicting aims of prevention of conentration of economic power and increasing the production capacity.

It was in March 1973 that the Union Law Minister has announced that he would soon introduce a bill to amend the MRTP Act. The amendment bill, again an indication was given in March 1975, would be introduced in the budget session. But it had not been introduced.

This delay is being attributed to the failure to come to an agreed draft to amend the MRTP Act to empower the Union Government to de-link such undertaking having regard to the primary object of increasing industrial porduction.

The Monopolies Commission is being restructured and broken up into two wings. There will be a tribunal for restrictive trade practices and a monopolies commission to check concetration of economic power. The tribunal will be basically a judicial body which will deal with all problems relating to monopolistic and restrictive trade practices. At present more than 9,000 restrictive trade agreements have already been registered with the Registrar Trade Agreements. Even a small proportion thereof would burden the work of the Commission to an extent that would leave no time for it to handle the work visualised under the proposed break-up of conglomerates. The MRTP Commission combines economics power and monopolistic trade practices as also independent disposal of cases concerning restrictive trade practices. This combination of functions owes itself to the recommendations of the Monopolies Inquiry Commission which had in mind very limited role for the MRTP Commission.

The Government wants to break up the conglomeretes because it has come to the conclusion that the fundamental source of concentration of economic power is the existing conglomerate which operates either as a single unit with several activities or in the shape of family control over the entire business. There has been a feeling that some of the industrial houses are unwilling to effect expansion because they do not want any diluation of their control. It has been felt that some of these houses try to prevent the entry of professional management so that they may retain their family control. There have been cases where larger business houses have tried to enter fields reserved for small and medium entrepreneurs.

The Monopolies Commission, as now envisage, will be expected to go into the entire question of inter-connection between various undertakings and also adivse the Government on product classification. It is officially agrued that this has become all the more necessary as substantial number of large undertakings have not got themselves registered under Section 26 of the MRTP Act and thus avoided the regulatory provision of the Act Secondly, the Ministry has received more than 120 applications for deregistration of the ground that the undertakings are inter-connected with such undertakings whose assets when added to their own assets amount to not less than Rs. 20 crores. Thirdly, some undertakings have advanced the argument that according to the product classification prescribed by the Government, they are not dominant.

REVERSAL OF POLICIES TOWARDS MRTP

As a first step towards reversal of policy the Government has announced that large industrial houses will be allowed to set up industries in 90" zero indusry" districts in the country—districts rich in reasources but without any industry whatsoever big business houses will not attract the provisions of MRTP Act. To help the big business houses to set up units in backward districts, infrastructual facilities are being provided on a top priority basis. The Government is also considering an increase in transport subsidy to make the scheme more cost compenstory and to mitigate the logistical handicaps in the far flung areas.

Further, under the proposed amendments of the Industrial (Development and Regulation) Act, the Government plans to remove restrictions on MRTP companies to bring them into key sector areas to boost production. The Government also intends to encourage MRTP companies in core sector where high capital and sophisticated technology are involved. It also intends to facilitate investment by such companies in areas where small-scale entrepreneurs are not in a position to meet the growing needs of the economy for specific items, which sometimes are in short supply. For instance, it has been suggested that the areas where private investment could flow into area two-wheeler scooter, heavy automobile sector and manufacture of trucks.

A major decision announced by the then Union Finance Minister Mr. Vishwanth Pratap Singh while presenting the 1985-86 budget related to raising the limit of assets for MRTP companies from Rs. 20

crores to Rs. 100 crores. Even the monopolies did not expect that the Government will, in one single jump raise the ceiling of assets for MRTP companies to five time the existing limit. The immediate impact of raising the assets limit was the delinking of almost 49 out of 101 large industrial houses from the provision of the (Section 26) MRTP Act. Obviously the aim is not have a pattern of growth in which investment is judiciously allocated between large, medium and small sectors. but to have excessive dependence on large, corporate sector.

MRTP Amendment Act, 1984. The MRTP (Amendment) Act 1984 introduced certain changes in the MRTP Act on the basis of the experience gained and the recommendations made by Sanchar Committee. The main thrust of the amendment was to clarify certain definitions so as to include certain categories which were hitherto left uncovered. Some of the important definitional changes were:

> ***Definition of Goods.*** Goods have now the same definition as in the sale of Goods Act 1930 and include shares and stocks. Thus a major deficiency in the existing provision of the MRTP Act has been removed and investment companies have been brought within its ambit.
>
> ***Group and Inter-connected Undertakings.*** Another important change introduced is the concept of Group to include enterprises under the same management, Sachar Committee recognised the existence of the concept in the Companies Act of 1974 and recommended its transference to MRTP Act since it had a special importance in this context. The MRTP (Amendment) Act 1984 has incorporated it.
>
> The (Amendment) Act 1984 has redefined interconnected undertakings. Under the existing provision in the MRTP Act, not less than 1/3rd control over voting power or positions of the Board is required for establishing inter-connection. The (Amendment) Act 1984 has reduced this proportion to 25 per cent.

Definition of Undertaking. The (Amendment) Act of 1984 has made the definition of 'undertaking' exhaustive so as to widen the scope of the MRTP Act. The earlier definition of undertaking covered enterprises engaged in production, sale distribution or control of goods etc. The Supreme Court criticising the lacunae in this regard pointed "out the word undertaking is a coat of many colours as it has been used in different sections of the act to convey different ideas. In some of these sections it has been used to denote enterprise itself while in many other section it has been used to denote a person who owns it "There was therefore, an urgent need to bring about consistency in the various sections of the act so as to make its coverage wide so that mergers which went unchecked could be controlled. The revised definition of 'undertaking' covers enterprises engaged or proposed to be engaged in the production, storage, supply, distribution, acquisition or control of articles or goods or the provisions of any services either directly or through one or more of its units or divisions whether located at the same place or at different places. Thus any branch or office established for the provision of any service is also coverd. Besides this a body corporate which is, or has been, enaged only in the business of acquiring, underwriting or dealing with shares, debentures or other securities of any other body corporate shall be deemed to be an undertaking. Thus the definition of undertaking becomes comprehensive to include companies dealing in goods and services, stoks and shares as well as investment companies. This is a welcome rationalisation.

Limits to Capacity Expansion. The (Amendment) Act of 1984 has tried to limit the misuse of the provision by taking recourse to expansion of capacity to an unlimited extent under the garb of modernisation. As rcommended by the Sachar Committee, the Amendment provides that exemption of these lines would be permitted only to the extent of 25 per cent of the licensed capacity. However, it has been clarified that this is in addition to the normal expansion upto 25 per cent of licensed capacity which does not require approval under the Act.

The Amendment Act has removed the concept of monopolistic undertaking since it served no useful purpose because monopolistic practices can exist even without "monopolistic undertaking" and what is relevant in this context is the dominant undertaking. This has been incorporated in the Amendment Act.

Severance of Interconnection. A very important provision introduced in the Amendment Act 1984 is the power given to the Central Government regarding severance of interconnection, if the Government forms an opinion that such interconnection "is deterimental to the interests of the principal undertaking, or the steady growth of the industry to which the principal undertaking pertains or the public interest." The Central government can refer the matter for inquiry by the MRTP Commission. The merit of this new provision 27-A of the Amendment Act lies in the fact that it binds the Government to the scheme suggested by the MRTP Commission once the Central Government has decided to act on the report of the Commission on the lines recommended by it. However, it is left open to the Central Government to reject the report as a whole.

Unfair Trade Practices. On the lines suggested by Sachar Committee, the MRTP (Amendment) Act 1984 has brought within the purview of the Act certain unfair trade practices like mis-leading advertisements, bargain selling etc. Although the Commission held the view that such unfair practices were automatically covered under the Act, the Supreme Court held in the case of TELCO *vs.* RRTA in 1977 that the practices enumerated in section 33 do not provide statutory illustrations of restrictive trade practices, but merely of trade practices, which required registration. In order to get over this difficulty created as a result of the judgement, the

Amendment Act 1984 provides that every agreement falling within one or more of the categories specified there in shall be deemed to be an agreement relating to restrictive trade practices.

But under Section 38, The Government has justified the provision of certain restrictions to meet the requirements of the defence of India or the Security of the State, or where the restrictions are necessary to ensure the maintenance of supply of goods and services essential to the community. Criticising this provision, MR. H. K. Parnjape writes "Section 38 of the original Act provided what has been called gateways" through which restrictive trade practices can pass so as not to be deemed prejudicial to public interest. The Amendment Bill proposes more gateways namely in cases where the restrictions have been expressly authorised and approved by the Central Government."

CHANGES IN MRTP ACT IN 1990S

In response to the demands of big business the government in its Industrial policy of 1991 decided to abolish MRTP asset limit altogether. The industrial policy (1991) states the following with regard to MRTP Act." The interference of the government through the MRTP Act in investment decisions of large companies has become deleterious in its effects on Indian industrial growth. The pre-entry secruity of investment decision by so-called MRTP companies will no longer be required. Instead emphasis will be on controlling and regulating monopolistic, restrictive and unfair trade practices rather than making it necessary for the monopoly houses to obtain prior approval of central government for expansion, estabiishment of new undertakings, merger, amalgamation and takeover and appointment of certain directors. The thrust of policy will be more on controlling unfair or resrictive business practices.

The new Industrial Policy announced in July 1991 scrapped the assets limit for MRTP companies altogether. The MRTP Act was amended and Chapter III on monopolies dropped so that now a company no longer need prior permission of the Commission for investment decisions (pertaining either to establishment of new undertakings, capacity expansion or diversification.) The government hopes that this will enable Indian firms to become large enough to compete effectively in global markets. The MRTP Act as amended now will give more emphasis to the prevention and control of monopolistic, restrictive and unfair trade practices so that consumers are adequately protected from such practices.

NEW LICENSING POLICY AND PROCEDURES 1970

In February, 1970 the Government announced its new industrial licensing policy. It accepted the recommendation of the Industrial Licensing Policy Inquiry Committee that there should be a list of core industries in the economy. The core sector would consist of:

A. Agricultural inputs. *(a)* fertilisers: *(i)* Nitrogenous, *(ii)* Phosphatic, *(b)* Pesiticides; *(c)* Tractors and power tillers; *(d)* Rock-phosphate and pyrit;

B. Iron and Steep : *(a)* Iron Ore; *(b)* Pig iron and steel; *(c)* Alloy and special steel;

C. Non-terrous metals;

D. Petroleum *(a)* Oil exploration and production; *(b)* Petroleum refining; *(c)* Selected petro-chemical such as integrated petro-chemical complexes, D.M.T. Caprolactum Acryonitrile and Synthetic rubber;

E. Coking Coal;

F. Heavy Industrial mechinery;

G. Ship-building;

H. News-print an Electronics.

Such of the industries in the 'core' list as are included in Schedule 'A' of the Industrial Policy Resolution, 1956 (as amended from time to time) are reserved for the public sector.

Apart from this, all new investment propositions of over Rs. 5 crores were deemed to be in the 'heavy investment' sector. Except for industries reserved for the public sector under the Industrial Policy Resolution (1956), larger industrial houses, foreign companies, subsidiaries or branches of foreign companies, were allowed to participate in the core and heavy investment sector, leaving the opportunities in the remaining sectors primarily to other class of entrepreneurs.

In the joint sector, involving investment ranging from Rs. 1 crore to Rs. 5 crores, licence applications of parties other than undertakings belonging to the larger industrial houses were to be given special consideration. Licence applications from undertakings belonging to or controlled by the larger industrial groups and foreign branches/subsidiaries, were to be considered for normal expansion where such expansion was necessary to develop to a minimum economic level or which would ensure greater cost efficiency.

The existing policy of reservation for the small-scale sector was to be continued and the area of such reservation was to be extended in the future.

The exemption limit from licensing provisions including licensing of new undertakings and substantial expansion of existing units was to be raise from Rs. 25 lakhs to Rs. 1 crore (by way of fixed assets in land, of building and machinery) in the cases of undertakings which had existing assets of less than Rs. 5 crores and which *(i)* did not belong to the larger indsutrial houses, as classified by the Industrial Licensing Policy Inquiry Committee; *(ii)* did not require more than Rs. 10 lakh or more than 10 per cent by way of foreign exchange for import of machinery and equipment and did not also require foreign exchange, except marginally, for import of raw materials, components and the like, and *(iii)* were not included in the category of 'dominant undertakings' as defined in the Monopolies Act.

The Industrial Policy Statement of Feburary, 1973 modified the licensing policy and procedures further. Import modifications were:

(a) In the list of core industries, such Industries as were included in schedule A of the industrial policy were reserved for the public sector. Larger houses (with assets of not less than Rs. 20 crores) were made eligible to participate in the contribute to the establishment of such industries along with other applicants, provided that the item was not one that was reserved for production in the public sector or in the small sector.

(b) The Government (both Centre and state) would develop joint sector as a promotional instrument in priority areas.

(c) Foreign concerns and subsidiaries and branches of foreign companies were also made eligible to participate in these industries.

(d) Cooperatives and small and medium enterpreneur were to be encouraged to participate in the production of mass consumption goods with the public sector also taking an increasing role.

In October 1975, the Government announced major changes liberalising industrial licensing policy. It delicensed 21 industries and permitted unlimited expansion, beyond the licensed capacities to foreign companies and monopoly houses in 30 other important industries.

Subsequently, on November 5, 1975, the Government announced that 25 per cent of excess unauthorised capacity was declared legal on the basis of normal expansion, another 25 per cent was sought to be covered in five years by automatic licensing. Although in the large-scale sector, industrial licensing has not been formally withdrawn, but in actual practice the industrial houses create unauthorised capacities which have later ractified by the government. The principal objective of the Government was to raise production and the objective of checking concentration of economic power was relegated to the background.

LIBERALISATION MEASURES 1985

Soon after resumption of power in 1984, the then Prime Minister Rajiv Gandhi's Government brought about a sea-change in terms of liberalisation of licensing policy in favour of large business houses, particularly in terms of making them free from the provisions of MRTP Act and FERA. The major changes introduced were as under:

1. Liberalisation of Licensed Capacity in the Name of Economies of Scale and Modernisation. The policy changes of 1985 envisaged the need for the industry to grow at a rapid pace, achieve economies of scale and undertake modernisation which signified the introduction of latest technology. With this end in view, the scheme for re-endorsement of capacity was liberalised automatic increase was granted to units wanting to achieve economies of scale and a 49 per cent rise in capacity due to modernisation was allowed. The Government decided to delicense 23 industries for MRTP and FERA companies provided the industrial undertaking is located in any of the Centrally-declared backward areas in 1986.

2. Concept of Broad-banding Introduced. To encourage production and to provide flexibility to the manufacturers to adjust their product-mix depending on the market demand, the concpet of broad-banding was introduced in a large number of items. Some of these are machine tools, motorised two wheelers, motorised four wheeler, paper and paper pulp, chemical, pharmaceutical, petro-chemical and fertilizer machinery industry and entertainment electronics.

3. Raising the Asset Limit of MRTP Companies. The threshold asset limit for companies under MRTP Act was raised from Rs. 20 crores to Rs. 100 croes. As a consequence, 112 companies came out of the purview of the MRTP Act leaving 379 units still under MRTP Act. Besides, the Government announced in May 1985, its decision to exempt 27 industries from the Section 22A of the MRTP Act and in December 1984 again, 22 of these industries were delicensed for MRTP and FERA Companies. These two measures together virutally abolished all controls on MRTP and FERA companies in respect of the 22 industries.

4. Attitude Towards Small-scale Sector Units. Some scopes were provided for the small-sector. The limit on investment by small-scale units and ancillaries was enhanced from Rs. 20 lakh and Rs. 25 lakh to Rs. 35 lakh and Rs. 45 lakh respoectively. However nearly

200 times which were on the reservation list were de-reserved and made open for the medium and lrge-scale sector.

INDUSTRIAL LICENSING POLICY, 1988

The Union Government announced on June 3, 1988 further liberalisation of the industrial licensing system and also provide incentives to give a stimulus to industrialisation of backward areas.

Non-MRTP and Non-FERA companies will not be required to obtain industrial licences under IDRA for project involving investment in fixed assets upto Rs. 50 crores if they are located in Centrally declared backward areas and upto Rs. 15 crores if they are located in non-backward areas. The number of industries requiring compulsory licensing has been reduced from 56 to 26. The delicensed sector under the new dispensation has been extended to units importing upto 30 per cent of their input needs against 15 per cent in the past. This is a case where import liberalisation has been combined with industrial liberalisation to good effect.

For the development of backward areas, the Government intends to establish 100 growth centres throughout the country over the next five years. Each growth centre will be provided with funds of the order of Rs. 25 crores to Rs. 30 crores for creating infrastructural facilities particularly in respect of power, water, telecommunications and banking.

To promote industrialisation in backward areas new industrial undertakings established in declared backward areas, are entitled to the income tax relief under Section 80 HH of the Income Tax Act by way of deduction of 20% of the profits available for a period of 10 years. Furthermore, under section 80-I of the I.T. Act, all new undertakings are entitled to an income tax relief by way of deduction of 25% of the profits for the period of 8 years. The benefits of both these sections are available cumulatively to industrial undertakings established in notified backward districts.

There is no doubt that there was justification for revision of asset limits of large business houses in view of the sharp escalation of prices that had taken place earlier, but it was no expected that the

Government would take a quantum jump and raise it 5 times. Considerations of liberalising investment with the objective of raising production have been paramount with the Government. Moreover, the Government is dead set to promote computerisation and electronics along with expansion of communications. Any obstacles in this regard in the form of MRTP and FERA regulations are sought to be removed. But in this process, the Government is making the small-scale industry a victim of its programme of modernisation. The de-reservation of about 200 items will hit small-scale sector. The abnormal benefits provided to the large corporate sector to compete with the small-scale sector will hit it further. As a consequence, the objective of promoting full employment via encouragement to small sector will be jeopardized.

NEW INDUSTRIAL POLICY (1990)

The Janata Dal Government announced its new Indsutrial Policy on May 31, 1990. The sailent features of third policy are the following:

The Pormotion of Small-scale and Agro-based Industries. In pursuance of our policy to reorient industrial growth to serve the objective of employment generation, dispersal of industry in the rural areas, and to enhance the contribution of small-scale industries to exports it has been decided to take the measures enumerated below.

1. The investment ceilling in plant and machinery for small-scale industries (fixed in 1985) was raised from the present Rs. 35 lakhs to Rs. 60 lakhs and correspondingly, for ancillary units from Rs. 45 lakhs, to 75 lakhs. In order to enable small-scale industries to play an important role in the total export, such of the small-scale units which undertake to export at least 30 per cent of the anual production by the third year would be permitted to step up their investment in plant and machinery to Rs. 75 lakhs.
2. Investment ceilling in respect of tiny units would also be increased from the present Rs. 2 lakhs to Rs. 5 lakhs.

3. (i) Presently, 836 items have been reserved for exclusive manufactures in the small-scale sector. Efforts would be made to identify more items amenable to similar reservation.

   (ii) A new Scheme of Central Investment Subsidy exclusively for the small-scale sector in rural and backward areas capable of generating higher level of employment at lower capital cost would be implemented.

   (iii) With a view to improving the competitiveness of the products manufactures in the small-scale sector, programmes for modernisation and upgradation of technology would be implemented. A number of technology centres, tool rooms, process and product development centres, testing centres, etc. will be setup under the umbrella of an apex Technology Development Centre in Small Industries Development Organisation.

   (iv) The existing regime of fiscal concessions would be reviewed both to provide sustained support to the units in the small-scale sector and to remove the disincentives for their graduation and further growth.

   (v) An exercise will be undertaken to identify locations in rural areas endowed with adequate power supply and intensive compaigns would be launched to attract suitable entrepreneurs, provide all other inputs foster small-scale and tiny industries. Similary, industries which are not energy intensive will be identified for proliferation in rural areas where power supply is presently a constraint.

   (vi) To ensure adequate and timely flow of credit for the small-scale industries, a new apex bank known as SIDBI and other commercial bank/financial institutions would be to channelise need based, higher flow of credit, both by way of term loan and working capital, to the tiny and rural industries.

(vii) One of the persistent complaints of the small-scale units is their being subjected to a large number of Acts/ Laws, being required to maintain a number of registers, submit plethora of returns and face an army of inspectors, particularly in the field of labour legislations. These bureaucratic conrols will be reduced so that unnecessary interference is eliminated.

4. In order to assist the large number of aritsans engaged in the rural and cottage industries, the activities of the KVIC and KVI boards would be expanded, and these organisation, would be strengthened to discharge the responsibility more effectively. Special marketing their products and also in supply of raw materials. Besides, providing concessional credit, training facilities and free consultancy to group of artisans will also be provided.

5. Agro processing industry would receive high priority in credit allocation from the financial institutions.

6. In sector where units require licensing, the policy would also encourage location of processing units in rural areas where growers are concentrated. Apart from economic benefits of proximity to raw materials it would help in dispersal of industry and increasing employment in rural areas.

7. In agro-processing indsutries greater success has been achieved where growers and processors have been integrted, as in the case of sugar. For the successs of other agro based industries also, close links must be forged between the growers and processor units. Industrial Policy would therefore, specially promote projects which are organised in close co-operation on the basis of joint ownership. Growers will be encouraged to set up processing units within the framework of co-operative societies or similar institutional framework. This will also ensure the transmission of better technology for enhanced agricultural production.

8. Import of Raw Materials and Components. From imports of raw materials and components imports would be permissible upto a landed value of 30 per cent of the ex-factory value of annual production. The ex-factory value of production will exclude the excise duty on the item of production. Raw materials and components on OGL will not be included within this 30 per cent limits.

9. **Import of Capital Goods.** For the import of capital goods, the entrepreneur would have entitlement to import upto a landed value of 230 per cent of the total value of plant and machinery required for the unit.

10. **Delicensing.** All units up to an investment of Rs. crores on fixed assets in non-backward area and Rs. 75 crores in Centrally notified backward areas would be exempted from requirement of obtaining licence/registration.

11. **Foreign Collaboration.** In respct of transfer of technology, if import of tecnology is considered by the entrepreneur, he can conclude an agreement with the collaborator, without obtaining any clearance from the Governments, provided that royalty payment does not exceed five per cent on domestic sales and eight per cent on exports.

12. **Foreign Investment.** It may be clarified that in the application of the proposals listed above, 836 items which are reserved for production in the small scale sector will continue to be excluded.

13. **Export-oriented Units.** 100 per cent export oriented units (EOUs) and units to be set up in export processing zones (EPZs) are also being delicensed under the scheme up to a investment limit of Rs 75 crores.

Units set up by MRTP/FERA companies will be covered by the procedures set out above, but they will continue to need clearances under the provision and regulations of these two Acts.

Abolition on Industrial Licensing

The Government of India announced a New Industrial Policy on July 24, 1991. This policy aimed at liberalising the industrial economy considrably and, with this end in view, announced a series of initiatives in respect of industrial licensing, foreign investment and technology agreements, public sector, and MRTP Act. As far as industrial licensing is concerned, the new industrial policy abolished all industrial licensing, irrespective of the level of investment, except for certain industries related to security and strategy concerns, social reasons, concerns related to safety and overriding environmental issues, manufacture of product of hazardous nature and articles of elitist consumption. The 1991 industrial policy listed 18 industries for which industrial licensing would remain compulsory. These industries were as under—coal and lignite; petroleum (other than crude) and its distillation products; distillation and brewing of alcoholic drinks; sugar; animal fats and oils; cigars and cigarettes; asbestos and asbestos-based products; plywood and other wood based products; raw hides and skins, and leather; tanned or dressed furskin; motor cars; paper and newsprint; electronic aeroscape and defence equiment; industrial explosives; hazardous chemicals; drugs and pharmaceuticals; entertainment electronics; and white goods (domestic refrigerators, washing machines, air conditioners, etc.). However, of these 18 industries, three industries were delicensed in April 1993. In later years more industries were delicensed. Thus at present only 6 items of health, strategic and secuirity considerations remains under the purview of industrial licensing. These are alcohol, cigarettes, hazardous chemicals, electronic aerospace and defence equipment, industrial explosives and dogs and pharmaceuticals (excepting bulk dry industry which has been delicensed.

FOREIGN EXCHANGE REGULATION ACT, 1973

The Foreign Exchange Regulation Act, 1973, serves as tool for implementing the national policy investment in India. Sections 28, 29, 30 and 31 of the Act empower the Reserve Bank of Inida to regulate or exercise direct control over the activities of foreign companies and foreign nationals in India.

In this section the term *foreign companies* means companies (other than banking companies) which are not incorporated in India or in which the non-resident interest is more than 40 per cent, or any branch of such company.

Under Section 28 of the FERA non-residents (including Indian citizens), foreign citizens resident in India and foreign companies require the permission of the Reserve Bank to accept appointment as agents or technical management advisers in India of any person or company, or permit the use of their trademarks by any person or company, for direct or indirect consideration.

The trading, commercial and indsutrial activites in India of persons resident abroad, foreign citizens resident abroad, foreign companies are sought to be regulated under section 29 of the Act. They have to obtain the prior permission of the RBI for:

(i) Carrying on in India any activity of a trading, commercial or industrial nature:

(ii) Opening branches/offices or other places of business in India;

(iii) Acquiring any business undertaking in India; and

(iv) Purchasing share of Indian companies.

Correspondingly, under Section 19, the transfer or issue of any security, including shares, to a non-resident requires the prior permission of the RBI.

Those persons and companies already functioning on the date of coming into force of the Act, had to seek the RBI's permission to continue their activities in the country or to hold the share already acquired. Repatriation of investments made in India with the approval of the Central Government or the Reserve Bank is permissible, provided that the disinvestment has also been made with the approval of the RBI.

Section 30 of the Act prohibits foreign nationals from taking up any profesion, etc., without the permission of the Reserve Bank, if they wish to have remittance facilities for transfer of their earnings outside India. Section 31 regulation the acquisition, holding, transfer and disposal of immovable property in India by foreign citizens and foreign companies. General permission has been granted by the RBI to foreign companies (other than those established purely as liasion offices) to acquire or hold any immovable property in India which is necessary for, or incidental to any activity undertaken by them with the permission of the Reserve Bank under Section 28 or Section 29 of the Act.

Foreign Exchange Regulation Act (FERA) was promulgated in 1973 and it came into force on January 1,1974. Section 20 of this Act referred directly to the operations of MNCs in India. According to the Section, all non-banking foreign branches and subsidiaries with foreign equity exceeding 40 per cent had to obtain permission to establish new undertakings to purchase shares in existing companies, or to acquire wholly or partly any other company. Guidelines for administering this Section FERA were announced in 1973 and later amended in 1976.

According to these guidelines, the principal rule was that all branches of foreign companies operating in India should convert themsevles in India companies with at least 60 per cent local equity participator Furthermore, all subsidiaries of foreign companies should bring down the foreign equity share to 40 per cent or less. The 1976 guidelines provide for three levels of foreign equity: 74 per cent, 51 per cent, and 40 per cent Companies were allowed to retain foreign equity holdings above 40 per cent and upto 74 per cent, on condition that they were enagaged in *(i)* core industries; *(ii)* predominantly export oriented production; *(iii)* activities requiring sophisticated technology or specialised skills; or *(iv)* the plantation activities.

If the turnover from any or all of these activities combined exceed 75 per cent of the total turnover of the company, it was entitled to retain up to 74 per cent foreign equity. The same level applied to companies exporting more than 40 per cent of their own production or the equivalent of at least 60 per cent of their total turnover.

Implementation of FERA. There were substantial delays in implementing FERA. A large number of companies which were issues directions for dilution, did not carry out the directions. Some did not even initiate the process of dilution. The Government itself exempted a number of units. Martinussen's study shows that of the 895 companies 249 companies were exempted from the general rule stipulating a maximum of 40 per cent non resident interest 132 companies were allowed to continue with more than 40 per cent foreign equity, 116 with more than 51 per cent or upto 74 per cent foreign equity and one company was given permission to hold 100 per cent foreign equity.

In regard to the companies that did not comply with FERA regulations Martinussen observe a certain pattern. For instance, he found that almost all these companies belonged to only three groups. They were either engaged in tea plantation activites or in the manufacture of drugs and pharmaceuticals or they were affiliated with particularly large TNCs. The special treatment to tea companies was due to the importance of tea in India's foreign trade. As far as the drugs and pharmaceutical industry is concerned, India's heavy dependence on MNCs for bulk durgs came in the way of compliance of FERA regulations. As far as the third category of powerful MNCs is concerned, Martinussen gives in detail the experience with regard to Hindustan Lever Ltd. This company managed to secure concessions from the government on flimsy grounds. For instance, it succeeded in getting 60 per cent of its toiletries manufacturing classified by government as high technology activity as it helped in 'import substitutions'.

NEW CONCESSION FOR FERA COMPANIES

In line with the liberalisation measures announced in the New Industrial Policy, July 1991, and subsequent period the government announced major concessions to FERA companies in November 1991 and January 1992. On January 8, 1993 the government promulgated an Odinance to amend FERA with immediate effect. The ordinance has removed a large number of restriction on companies with more than 40 per cent non-resident equity, removed FERA controls on Indian firms setting up joint ventures abroad and allowed Indians to hold imovable property abroad, subject to certain conditions stipulated by the Reserve Bank of India. Important concessions announced in November 1991, January 1992, and January 1993 are as follows:

Companies with foreign share holding can increase foreign equity to 51 per cent by remittances in foreign in the 34 high priority industries.

Section 26(7), 28, 29 and 31 of the FERA which were considered to be restrictive by the FERA companies have been revoked, Section 26, sub-section 7, required the FERA companies to get Reserve Bank's permissions before raising working capital or even deposits. Now with it revoking, FERA companies (other than banking companies) wanting to borrow money or accept deposits will not require the permission of the Reserve Bank.

Sections 28 and 29 stand revoked. The implication of this is that the Reserve Bank will now allow the FERA companies to use their trade marks in India and permit them to act on behalf of or advise any Indian person or company. FERA companies can now carry on the India any activity of a trading, commercial or industrial nature. FERA companies so far had a Rs. 5 crore limit on trading which has now been completely relaxed.

Section 31 stands revoked, implying that FERA companies can now deal in immovable property in India.

Section 27 which restricted Indian companies setting up joint ventures abroad and resident Indians associating themselves with or taking part in overseas concerns has been scrapped. This has allowed Indian firms to set up joint ventures abroad and Indians to take up directorship of foreign firms without needing FERA approval.

Restrictions regarding assets held in India by non-residents have been removed. Under Section 11 it was provided that Reserve Bank would block securities and bank accounts of persons migrating abroad or planning to migrate, by way of a statutory backing. Now,

Reserve Bank will not block such accounts and these accounts will be treated as non-resident accounts on their becoming non-residents.

A FERA provision under Section 12 which provided that the government could direct certain payments to be made by FERA companies in a special account, has been deleted.

Indians have now been allowed to keep foreign currency upto 500 or Rs. 15,000.

Import and export in gold silver has been exempted from FERA. These commodities would be overned by EXIM policy. Only trade in gold or silver coins, foreign exchange and Indian currency will continue to be regulated under FERA. Section 17 conferring on government power to regulate uses of imported gold and silver has been deleted.

Section 15, which conferred on government powers to direct payment in foreign currency in certain cases, has also been deleted, since the Reserve Bank has already granted general permission to firms and companies to offer hospitality to non-residents on visits to India.

A New section has been introduced which permits taking goods on rental, lease, hire or on any other arrangement, which does not amount to disposal of such goods. This will greatly benefit exporters.

Restrictions on transfers of any security from a regiser in India to a register outside India have been removed, as these were intended to take care of erestwhile sterling companies, which had dual registers.

Restrictions on transfer of shares by a non-resident to another non-resident have been removed. But such controls on transfer by a non-resident to a resident and by a foreign national resident in India to another resident have been retained because the questions of valuations of shares and permission for remittances outside India arise.

The Provision allowing the government to acquire foreign securities for purposes of strengthening foreign exchange position has never been invoked and is unlikely to be invoked. Since this could cause avoidable misapprehensions and fears in foreign investors, this provision has been deleted.

Prior permission by foreign nationals before taking up employent in India will not be required under FERA. The home ministry will continue its control through grant of visas.

In March 1993, government of India passed a bill. The main highlight of this bill are the following:

(i) 100 per cent foreign equity participation.

(ii) Foreign investors espcially non-resident Indians can invest in the form of shares in India without any prior approval/ permission from the government.

(iii) Full convertibility of rupee.

The above list of concessions shows that FERA has now been rendered almost redundant. The FERA companies can now use their trademark, accept appointment as agent or technical or management advisors, borrow and accept deposits from the public, open branches and liastions offices, acquire and sell immovable property provided the proceedings are not remitted abroad, and export goods on rental, hire or lease basis. According to the Reserve Bank by virtue of these general permissions, FERA companies would, in their operations, be placed on par with Indian Companies and would not be subjected to any special restrictions under FERA."Some critics have expressed serious reservations regarding foriegn investment and technology. For instance, H.K. Paranjape argues that highly optimistic expectations regarding what MNCs can achieve for us, is misplaced. The past record of these companies in India does not warrant much enthusiasm. None of the MNCs operating in India has tried to build up the R and D base in this country effectively and none has tried to expand export markets substantially (in fact MNCs undertook export activities only to the extent that they were compelled, to do so under export obligations). Moreover, the large number of foreign collaborations entered into during the last few years have only led to repetitive agreements for similar kinds of goods and high import dependence resulting in rapid escalation in the balance of payments deficit and in India's foreign indebtedness.

FOREIGN EXCHANGE MANAGEMENT ACT (FEMA)

The Foreign Management Management (FEMA) Bill was introduced by the Government of India in Parliament on August 4, 1998. It was adopted by the Parliament in 1999 and is known as the Foreign Exchange Management Act, 1999. This Act extends to the whole of India and shall also apply to all branches, officers and agencies outside India owned or controlled by a person resident in India.

1. Definition of 'Resident'. Section 2 (sub-section V) defines 'person resident in India' as *(i)* a person residing in India for more than 182 days during the course of the preceding financial year; *(ii)* any person or body corporate registered or incorporated in India, *(iii)* an office, branch or agency in India owned or controlled by a person resident outside India; *(iv)* an office, branch or agency outside India owned or controlled by a person resident in India.

2. Regulation and Management of Foreign Exchange. Chapter II of the Act deals with the regulation and management of foreign exchange. Section 3 states that except as otherwise provided in this Act, no person shall in any manner deal in or transfer any foreign exchange or foreign security to any person not being an authorised person. Section 4 states that except as otherwise provided in this Act, no person resident in India shall acquire, hold, own, possess or transfer any foreign exchange, foreign security or any immovable property situated outside India.

3. Current Account and Capital Account Transactions. According to Section 5, any person may sell or draw foreign exchange to or from an authorised person if such sale or drawal is a current account transaction. According to Sub-section 1 of Section 6, any person may sell or draw foreign exchange to or from an authorised person for a capital account transaction subject to provisions of Sub-section 2. Sub-section 2 states that Reserve Bank may, in consultation with the Central Government, specify: *(a)* any class or classes of capital account transactions which are permissible; *(b)* the limit up to which foreign exchange shall be admissible for such transactions. However, the Reserve Bank shall not impose any restriction on the drawal of foreign exchange for payments due on account of amortization of loans or for depreciation of direct investments in the ordinary course of business.

Sub-section 4 of Section 6 states that a person resident in India may hold, own, transfer or invest in foreign currency, foreign security or any immovable property situated outside India if such currency, security or property was acquired, held or owned by such person when he was resident outside India or inherited from a person who was resident outside India. Sub-section 5 states that a person resident outside India may hold, own, transfer of invest in Indian currency, security of any immovable property situated in India if such currency, security or property was acquired, held or owned by such person when he was resident in India or inherited from a person who was resident in India.

According to Sub-section 6 of Section 6, without prejudice to the provisions of this Section, the Reserve Bank may be regulation prohibit, restrict, or regulate establishment in India of a branch, office or other place of business by a person resident outside India, for carrying on any activity relating to such branch, office or other place of business.

(i) Export of Goods and Services. Sub-section 1 of Section 7 of the Act lays down that every exporter of goods shall—

(a) furnish to the Reserve Bank or to such other authority a declaration in such form and in such manner as may be specified, containing true and correct material particulars, including the amount representing the full export value (or if the full value in not ascertainable at the time of export, the value which the exporter expects to receive);

(b) furnish to the Reserve Bank such other information as may be required by the Reserve Bank for the purpose of ensuring the realisation of export proceeds by such exporter.

(ii) Realisation and Repatriation of Foreign Exchange. Section 8 lays down that save as otherwise provided in the Act, where any amount of foreign exchange is due or has accrued to any person resident in India such person shall take all reasonable steps to realise and repatriate to India such foreign exchange within such period and in such manner as may be specified by the Reserve Bank.

Section 9 provides the following exemptions from realisation and repatriation of foreign exchange: *(a)* possession of foreign currency of foreign coins by any person upto such limit as the Reserve Bank may specify; *(b)* foreign currency account held or operated by such person or class of persons and the limit up to which the Reserve Bank may specify; *(c)* foreign exchange acquired or received before the 8th day of July, 1947 or any income arising or accruing thereon which is held outside India by any person in pursuance of permission granted by the Reserve Bank; *(d)* foreign exchange held by a person resident in India upto such limit as the Reserve Bank may specify, if such foreign exchange was acquired by way of gift or inheritance from a person referred to in clause (c) including any income arising therefrom; *(e)* foreign exchange acquired from employment, business, trade, vocation, services, Honorarium, gifts, inheritance or any other legitimate means upto such limit as the Reserve Bank may specify; and *(f)* such other receipts in foreign exchange as the Reserve Bank may specify.

4. Authorised Person. Chapter III of the Act relates to the authorisation of a person by the Reserve Bank to deal in foreign exchange, Reserve Bank's powers to issue directions to authorised person and the power of Reserve Bank to inspect authories person. Section 10 of the act says that the Reserve Bank may authorise any person to deal in foreign exchange or in foreign securities, as an authorised dealer, money changer or of-shore banking unit or in any other manner as it deems fit. The authorisation shall be in writing and shall be subject to the condition laid down therein. Section 11 empowers the Reserve Bank to give directions to the authorised person in regard to making of payment or the doing or desisting from doing any act relating to foreign exchange or foreign security to ensure compliance with the provisions of the Act Section 12 empowers the Reserve Bank to inspect the business of any authorised persons for the purpose of:

(a) varifying the correctness of any statement, information or particulars furnished to the Reserve Bank;

(b) obtaining any information or particulars which such authorised person has failed to furnish on being called upon to do so;

(c) securing compliance with the provisions of the Act or any rules, regulations, directions or orders made thereunder.

5. Contravention of Penalties. Chapter IV deals with the issue of contravention and penalties. Section 13 says that if any persons contravenes any provisions of this Act, he shall, upon adjudication, be liable to a penalty upto thrice the sum involved in such conravention where such amount is quantifiable, or upto two lakh rupees where the amount is not quantificable, and where such contravention is a continuing one, further penalty which may extend to five thousand rupees for every day after the first day during which the contravention continues. Section 14 says that if the person concerned fails to make full payment of the penalty imposed on him within a period of ninety days, he shall be liable to civil imprisonment. According to Sub-section 1 of Section 15, any contravention under Section 13 may, on an application made by the person committing such contravention, be compounded by the Director of Enforcement or such other officers as may be pescribed by the Central Government Sub-section 2 of section 15 says that where a contravention has been compounded under Sub-section 1, no proceeding or further proceeding, as case may be, shall be initiated or continued as the case may be, against the person committing such contravention under that section, in resepct of the contravention so compounded.

6. Adjudication and Appeal. Chapter V deals with the issue of adjudication and appeal. Section 16 states that the Central Government may appoint Adjudicating authorities for holding an inquiry in the manner prescribed after giving the accused person a reasonable opportunity of being heard for the purpose of imposing any penalty.

The Adjudicating Authority shall have the same powers of a civil court which are conferred on the Appellate Tribunal under Sub-section (2) of Section 28 (discused later). Section 17 provides for the appointment of one or more Sepcial Directors (Appeals) to hear appeals against the orders of the Adjudicating Authorities. Section 18 says that the Central Government shall, by notification, establish an Appellate Tribunal to be known as the Appellate Tribunal for Foreign exchange to hear appeals against the order of the Adjudicating Authorities and the Special Director (Appeals) under this Act. The Appellate Tribunal shall consist of chairperson and such number of Members as the Central Government may deem fit. Section 21 state that a person shall not be qualified for appointment as the chairperson or a Member unless he—*(a)* is or has been or is qualified to be a judge of a High Court; and *(b)* in the case of a Member is or has been or is qualified to be a Judge of a District Court. A person shall not be qualified for appointment as a Special Director (Appeals) unless he—*(a)* has been a member of the Indian Legal Service and has held a post in grade I of that service; or *(b)* has been a member of the Indian Revenue Service and has held a post equivalent to a joint Secretary to the Government of India.

Section 34 of the Act states that no civil court shall have jurisdiction to entertain any suit or proceedings in respect of any matter which an Adjudicating Authority or the Appellate Tribunal or the Special Directors (Appeals) is empowered by or under this Act to determine and no injuction shall be granted by any court or other authority in respect of any action taken or to be taken in pursuance of any power conferred by or under this Act. Section 35 lays down that any person agrieved by any decision or order of the Appellate Tribunal may file an appeal to the High Court within sixty days from the date of communication of the decision or order of the Appellate Tribunal to him on any question of law arising out of such order.

7. Directorate of Enforcement. Chapter VI deals with the establishment of the Directorate of Enforcement and its powers, etc. Sub-section 1 of Section 36 states that the Central Government shall establish a Dirctorate of Enforcement with a Director and such other officers or class of officers as it thinks fit, who shall be called

Officers of Enforcement, for the purpose of this Act. Sub-section 1 of Secton 37 lays down that the Director of Enforcement and other officers of Enforcement not below the rank of an Assitant Director, shall take up for investigation the contravention referred to in Section 13. Section 38 empowers the Central Government to authorise any officer of customs or any central excise or any police officer or any other officer of the Central Government or a State Government to exercise such of the powers and discharge such of the duties of the Director of Enforcement or any other office of Enforcement under this Act as may be stated in the order.

8. Miscellaneous. The last chapter, chapter VII consisting of Section 39 to 49 deals with micellaneous issues. Sub-section 1 of Section 40 empowers the Central Government in the public interest and by notification to suspend or relax the provisions of the Act in certain circumstances. Section 41 empowers the Central Government to give general or special directions to the Reserve Bank. Section 42 provides that where conravention of any of the provisions of this Act is committed by a company, the person responsible for the conduct of its business shall be deemed to be guilty of the contravention. Section 44 bars the prosecution of legal proceedings against the officers of the Central Government or the Reserve bank or any other persons exercise any powers or discharging any functions or performing any duties under the provisions of this Act for anything done in good faith. Section 45 empowers the Central Government to remove the difficulties in giving effect to the provisions of the Act. Section 46 empowers the Central Government to frame the rules and section 47 empowers the Reserve Bank to make regulations to carry out the provisions of this Act and the rules made thereunder. Section 48 provides for laying before parliament the rules and regulations made under this Section 49 provides for repeal of the Foreign Regulation Act, 1973 and for dissolution of the Appelate Board Constituted under Section 52 of the said Act.

FEMA : A MAJOR DEPARTURE FROM FERA

As is clear from the name of the Act itself, the emphasis under FEMA is on 'exchange control. Under FERA it was necessary to obtain Reserve Bank's permission, either special or general, in respect of most of the regulations thereunder. FEMA has brought about a sea change in this regard and except for Secton 3, which relates to dealing in foreign exchange, etc., no other provisions of FEMA stipulate obtaining Reserve Bank's permission. The demand for new legislation was basically on the following counts: *(i)* FERA was introduced in 1974 when India's foreign exchange reserve position was no satisfactory. Accordingly, stringent controls were requird on the use of foreign exchange. With improvement in foreign exchange position, it is argued that such stringent control are not now required; *(ii)* India had given notice to the IMF in August 1994 that it has attained Article VIII status. This notice meant that no restrictions will the imposed on remittances of foreign exchange on account of current account transaction; and *(iii)* the private corporate sector had been complaining for long against, what in termed, the 'draconian provisions' of FERA to arrest any person, search any premises, seize documents and start proceedings against any person for contravention of FERA. The conravention under FERA was treated as a criminal offence and the burden of proof was on the guilty.

FEMA has changed all this. The purpose of FEMA is to facilitate external trade and payments' and 'promote the orderly development and maintenance of foreign exchange market in India.' As far as facilitating external trade is concerned, Sections 5 of the Act removes restriction on drawal of foreign for the purpose of current account transactions. As external trade, involves transactions on curent account, there will be no need for seeking the permission of Reserve Bank of India in connection with remittances involving external trade. As far as the 'draconian provisions' are concerned, FEMA has reduced their rigour significantly. For instance, unlike in the case of FERA, violations of FEMA will not attract criminal proceedings. The contravention will not be trated as a civil offence. Thus FEMA removes the "threat of imprisonment" which businessmen abhor. Now they will either compound their illegal acts by paying a fine if it is not too high, otherwise they will pay lawyers to engage in lengthy (and mostly inconclusive) litigation with the government.

FEMA represents major departure from the past policies in two important respect: "First, it can be seen as an initial step towards capital account convertibility. Secondly by removing the FERA from the statute book and replacing it with the FEMA, the government seems to have finally decided to give up even the bare intention of regulating foreign capital in the economy. As far as the issue of capital account convertibility is concerned, Section 6 of FEMA introduces some elements in this respect. The section state that "RBI shall not impose and restrictions on the drawal of foreign exchange for payments due on account of amountization of loan or for depreciation of direct investments in the ordinary course of business." This leaves out an important set of capital account transactions outside the RBI's ambit.

CONSUMER PROTECTION

In India consumers spread over the entire length and breadth of the country are unorganised. Many of them are also illiterate poor and backward. As against this, the producers are relatively much more organised. They have huge resources at their disposal and can decive and explit consumers in a number of ways. In a bid to beat competition, increase their market share and maximuse their profits, they at times adopt dubious means to push up sales of their market share and maximise their profits, they at tmes adopt dubious means to push up sales of their products.

STEPS REQUIRED FOR CONSUMER PROTECTION

On account of the these factors, a strong public opinion has built up over the years demanding protection to consumers. Protection to consumers requires the recognition of the following rights of the consumers by the business and the government :

1. The Right to Safety. Consumers should have the right to protection of health and life against goods which are hazardous to health and life.

2. The Right to Choose. Consumers should be given the right to choose from a variety of goods. This will give them an opportunity to select goods of their choice. In addition, because of competition, the prices charged would also be reasonable.

3. The Right to be Informed. Consumers should be given proper information about the goods that they intend purchasing. They should be protected against wrong and misleading advertisement.

4. The Right to Get Redress. It is not enough to hear the complaints of the consumers. It is also necessary to take action on these complaints as early as possible. For this purpose an appropriate redressed machinery must be in place.

5. The Right to be Heard. Consumers should be given a 'sympathetic ear' by the government. Their complaints and grievances should be properly looked into.

According to *Human Development Report*, 1998, consumer rights must be defended through *(i)* Strict standard for consumer health and safety; *(ii)* Product labelling about the content and proper use of products and their environmental and social impact; *(iii)* Information and awareness campaigns about potential health hazards, such as smoking tobacco and the improper use of feeding formula for infants.

Consumer Protection : How ?

The most important methods for consumer protection are as follows:

1. Imposition of self-regulation and discipline on themselves by the manufacturing and trading community.
2. Voluntary organisation of consumer to safeguared their interests.
3. Spreading information and awareness regarding different products.
4. Government legislation to stop the malpractices resorted to be the traders and manufactures.

Here we shall confined our analysis only to government legislation to stop the malpractices resorted to by the traders and manufactures. This government legislation is known as Consumer Protection Act.

CONSUMER PROTECTION ACT (1986)

Enactment of Consumer Protection Act, 1986 was one of the most important steps taken to protect the interest of the consumers. All the provisions of the Act came into force with effect from July 1, 1987. The Act was thoroughly amended in 1993 to make it more purposeful and it increase the powers of Consumer Disputes Redressal Agencies. The objective of the Consumer Protection Act is "to provide for the better protection of the interest of consumers and for that purpose to make provision for the establishment of consumer councils and other authorities for the settlement of consumers' disputes and for matter connected therewith." The Act applies to all goods and services unless especially exempted by the Central Government. It covers all the sectors whether private, public or cooperative. The provisions of the Act are compensatory in nature.

Section 6 (of Chapter II) of the Act enshrines the following rights of the Consumers:

(a) the right to be protection against the marketing of goods (and services) which are hazardous to life and property;

(b) the right to be assured, wherever possible access to a variety of goods (and services) at competitive prices;

(c) the right to be heard and to be asssured consumer' interests will receive due consideration at appropriate forums;

(d) the right to the informed about the quality, quantity, potency, purity, standard and price of goods (or services, as the case may be) so as to protect the consumer against unfair trade practice;

(e) the right to seek redressal against unfair trade practies (or restrictive trade practices) or unscrupulous exploitation of consumers; and

(f) the right to consumer education.

CONSUMER PROTECTION COUNCILS

The act provides for the establishment of a Central Consumer Protection Council by the Central Government and State Consumer

Protection Councils by the respective State governments. The Central Council shall consist of the following members, namely: *(a)* the Minister incharge of consumer affairs in the Central Government, who shall be the chairman, and *(b)* such number of other official or non-official members representing such interests as may be prescribed. The Central Council shall meet as and when necessary, but at least one meeting of the council shall be held every year. The objects of the Central Council are to promote and protect the right of consmers noted above [clauses (a) to (f) of Section 6].

The State Council shall be established by the State Government in question and shall consist of the following members; *(a)* the Minister incharge of consumer affairs in the State Government who shall be the chairman; and *(b)* such number of other official or non-official members representing such interests as may be prescribed by the State government. The State Council shall meet as and when necessary but not less than two meetings shall be held every year. The objects of every State Council shall be to promote and protect within the State the rights of the counsmers laid down in clauses (a) to (f) of Section 6.

CONSUMER DISPUTES REDRESSAL AGENCIES

Section 9 of the Consumer Protection Act provides for the establishment of a three-tier consumer disputes redessal system at the District, State and national level. The three redressal agencies are as follows:

1. A Consumer Disputes Redressal Forum at the District level known as the 'District Forum'.
2. A Consumer Disputes Redressal Commission at the State level known as the 'State Commission.
3. A National Consumer Disputes Redressal Commission established by the Central Government.

Composition. Section 10 of the Act is concerned with the composition of the District Forum. Sub-section (1) of this Section states that each District Forum shall consist of *(a)* a person who is, or has been, or is qualified to be a District Judge, who shall be its

President; and *(b)* two other members, who shall be persons of ability, intergrity and standing, and have adquate knowledge or experience of, or have shown capacity in dealing with problems relating to economics, law, commerce, accountancy, industry, public affairs or administration one of whom shall be a woman.

Section 16 relates to the compositon of the State Commission According to sub-section (1) of this Section, each State Commission shall consist of *(a)* a person who is or has been a Judge of a High Court, appointed by the state government, who shall be its president (the appointment is to be made after consultation with the Chief Justice of the High Court), and *(b)* two other members, who shall be persons of ability, integrity and standing and have adequate knowledge or experience of, or have shown capacity in dealing with, problems relating to economics, law, commerce, accountancy, industry, public affairs or administration, one of whom shall be a woman.

Section 20 relates to the composition of the National Commission. According to Sub-section (1) of this Section, the National Commission shall consist of *(a)* a person who is or has been a Judge of the Supreme Court, to be appointed by the Central Government, who shall be its President (the appointment is to be made after consultations with the Chief Justie of India), and *(b)* four other members who shall be persons of ability, integrity and standing and have adequate knowledge or experience of, or have shown capacity in dealing with, problems relating to economics, law, commerce, accountancy, industry, public affairs or administration, one of whom shall be a woman.

Jurisdiction. Section 11 relates to the jurisdiction of the District Forum. According to this Section, subject to the other provisions of this Act, the District Forum shall have jurisdiction to entertain complaints where the value of the goods or services and the compensation, if any, claimed does not exceed rupees five lakhs. A complaint shall be instituted in a District Forum within the local limits of whose jurisdiction *(i)* the opposite party or each of the opposite parties, at the time of the institution of the complaint, actually residies or carries on business; or *(ii)* any of the opposite parties, where there are more than one, at the time of the institution of the complaint, actually resides or carries on business, provided that in such case either the permission of the District Forum is given, or the opposite parties who do not reside, or carry on business, acquiesce in such institution; or *(iii)* the cause of action, wholly or in part, arises.

Section 17 relates to the jurisdiction of the State Commission. According to this Section, subject to the other provisions of this Act, the State Commission shall have jurisdiction:

(a) to entertain:

 (i) complaints where the value of the goods or services and compensation, if any, claimed exceeds rupees five lakhs but does not exceed rupees twently lakhs; and

 (ii) appeals against the orders of any District Forums with the State; and

(b) to call for the records and pass appropriate orders in any consumer dispute which is pending before or has been decided by any District Forum within the State, where it appears to the State Commission that such Forum has exercised a jurisdiction not vested in it by law, or has failed to exercise a jurisdiction so vested, or has acted in exercise of its jurisdiction illegally or with material irregularity.

Section 21 relates to the jurisdiction of the National Commission. According to this Section, subject to the other provisions of this Act, the National Commission shall have jurisdiction:

(a) to entertain:

 (i) complaints where the value of the goods or services and compensation, if any, claimed exceeds rupees twenty lakhs; and

 (ii) appeal against the orders of any State Commission; and

(b) to call for the records and pass appropriate orders in any consumer dispute which is pending before or has been decided by any State Commission where it appears to the National Commission that such State Commission has exercised a jurisdiction not vested in it by law, or has failed to exercise a jurisdiction so vested, or has acted in the exercise of its jurisdiction illegally or with material irregularity.

Complaints. According to Section 12 of the Act, a complaint in relation to any goods sold or delivered or any service provided may be filed with a District Forum by:

(a) the consmer to whom such goods are sold or delivered or to whom such service is provdied;

(b) any recognised Consumer association whether the aggrieved consumer is it member or not;

(c) the Central or the State Government.

Section 13 lists the procedure to be followed by the District Forum on receipt of a complaint. The District Forum, on receipt of the complaint, shall refer a copy of the complaint to the opposite party directing him to give him version of the case within a period of 30 days (extendable by another 15 days). If the opposite party denies or disputes the allegations contained in the complaint, or fails to take any action within the prescribed time period, the District Forum an obtain a sample of the goods from the complainant and send it for testing to an appropriate laboratory. One receipt of the report from the laboratory, the District Forum shall send a copy of the report to the opoosite parties and given them reasonable time to submit their objections to the report. If this procedure cannot be followed, or if the complaint relates to any services, the District Forum shall refer a copy of such complaint be followed, or if the complaint to the opposite directing him to give his version of the case within a period of 30 days (extendablc by another 15 days). Where the opposite party denties the allegations contained in the complaint or fails to take any action on the complaint, the District Forum shall proceed to settle the consumer dispute:

(a) on the basis of evidence brough to its notice by the complaint and the opposite party, where the opposite party denies or disputes the allegations contained in the complaint, or

(b) on the basis of evidence brought to its notice by the complaint where the opposite party units or fails to take any action to represent his case within the time given by the Forum.

REMEDIAL ACTION

If any of the consumer dispute redressal agencies is satisfied that the goods complained against suffer from any of the defects specified in the complaint or that any of the allegations contained in the complaint about the services and provided, it shall issue an order to the opposite party to do one or more of the following things namely:

(a) to remove the defect pointed out by the appropriate laboratory from goods in question;

(b) to replace the goods with new goods of similar deciption which shall be free from any defects;

(c) to return to the complainant the price or, as the case may be, the charges paid by the complainant;

(d) to discontinue the unfair trade pratice or the restrictive trade practice or not to repeat them;

(e) not to offer the hazardous goods for sale;

(f) to pay such amount as may be awarded by it as compensation to the consumer for any loss or injury suffered by the consumer, due to the negligence of the opposite party.

(g) to remove the defects or deficiences in the services in question;

(h) to withdraw the hazardous goods from being offered for sale;

(i) to provide for adequate costs to parties.

Appeal. According to Secton 15, any person agrieved by an order made by the District Forum may prefer an appeal against such order to the State Commission within a period of 30 days from the date of the order, in such form and manner as may be prescribed. Any person aggrieved by a order of the State Commission may prefer an appeal against such order to the National Commission with a period of 30 days (Section 19). In case a person is aggrieved by the order made by the National Commission, he may prefer an appeal against such order the Supreme Court within a period of 30 days from the date of the order (Section 23). [In all cases, the appeal can be entertained even after the expiry of 30 days provided that the authority (redressal agency) to whom such appeal is being made is satisfied that there was sufficient. cause for not filling it within that period.]

Penalties. Section 27 pertains to the issue of penaltie. According to this Section, where a trader or a person against whom a complaint is made or the complainant fails or omits to comply with any order made by the redressal agency, he shall be punishable with imprisonment for a term which shall not be less than one month but which may extend to three years, or with fine which shall not be less than Rs. 2,000 but may extend to Rs. 10,000, or with both.

Dismissal of Frivolous or Vexatious Complaints. Where a complaint instituted before any redressal agency is found to be frivolous or vexatious, the redressal agency shall dismiss the complaint and make an order that the complaint shall pay to the opposite party such cost, not exceeeding Rs.10,000 as may be specified in the order.

❐

7

Technology Environment in India

Technology plays important role in the economic development of accounting. It is an essential tool to get rid of socio-political and economic backwardness. It is mainly essential for the developing and less developed countries. The fate of nation and of civilization has often been determined by a different in the technology of production and warfare for which the inferior side was unable to compensate in other ways. Power of a nation dependence very much on the modern technology it possess. The quality and productive capacity of the industrial plant, the know-how of the working man, the skill of the engineer, the inventive ganius of the scientists, the managerial organization—all these are the factors upon which the industrial capacity of a nation depends. Therefore, a technological prerequisite is needed which could lead a country to establish itself in international community.

PATTERN OF SOCIO-ECONOMIC CONDITIONS IN THE DEVELOPING COUNTRIES

Most of the underdeveloped countries in Latin America, Asia and Africa have already set in motion a process of growth along the classical path of capitalist development. Their growth exercise is very much similar to the process of industrialisation in the West particularly in terms of output and mechanical technology and human skills used. The developing countries force the socio-economic backwardness and could not fulfil their pressing social and public needs. The masses in these countries are below poverty line. They are illiterate and uneducated. Unemployment is the common phenomenon in these countries which gives birth of disgrumble elements. The society is divided due to caste, creed or colour differences.

This type of social set up, when adopts a capitalist system of economy, there are less chances of solution of any socio-economic problems. These countries became independent from colonial rule in forties fifties or early sixties. But till today, they are not able to over come these socio-economic problems. They still remain backward group of countries.

Need of Technology. The developing countries need modern technologyto get rid of their backwardness. They need new industrial ventures and managerial experience. The adoption of modern means and new technology can only help them in getting rid of illiteracy and poverty. It could improve the agriculture sector to make them self-sufficient in food. The establishment of new industries may provide job opportunities to the unemployed youths. The technology could innovate new systems of education which can be job oriented. The people in the developing countries are very much influenced by the development of the west and inspired by its economic success. Therefore, they felt a need to import technology of the West.

The modern technology of today the monopoly of the Multi-national Corporations. They have the know-how and capability to run new projects in the developing countries. But there are a few countries which suspected the aims and objectives of MNCs in their land. It is true that the MNCs generally transfer an inappropriate technology to the developing countries. Their technologies were developed according to the needs of west which is capital intensive technology, while the developing countries are labour surplus countries and they need a technology which could fulfil the local aspirations. Moreover the high technology of west creates many socio-economic problems in the developing countries. It leads to destruction of capital goods industry of the developing countries and produce over-sophisticated items which could not fulfil the needs of masses.

The Governments in the developing countries is also fearful of the MNCs as those may encroach their sovereignty and independence by imposing terms and conditions. But inspite of the fear and doubts, the developing countries are dependent on the developed countries and multinational corporations for the import of technology which in turn would bring socio-economic development in their country.

Technology According to Local Needs. Technology must suit local needs and fulfil the aspirations of the people. The absolute technology is of no use, rather it creates problems in society. The highly westernize technology is unless for the developing countries as the later is a labour-surplus country and need employment for them. But the imported technology would need only a small groups of skilled labour. Moreover, the products of the MNCs and their venture should also be according to the needs of the larger part of the backward society of developing countries.

The above discussion shows that, in fact, the developing countries do not need highly westernize technology for their own socio-economic development.

Need to Develop Indigenous Technology. It has been already admitted that technology is essential for the economic development of a country and as the economy is very much related with the society, technology is essential for socio-economic development, Therefore the policy makers of the developing countries put stress on the development of the indigenous technology. The attempt should be made to modernise and upgrade the indigenous methods which could remilalise economic growth. The leadership of the country should not be ignorant of the new technology and carefully judge and decide the need of the nation and its people. The economic and the industrial policies of the country should be carefully formulated to promote, regulate and direct economic activities of the country. The Government should accelerate industrial and economic development by expanding large scale industries in the core sector.

Need to Encourage Research and Development. Instead of importing and buying technology, the governments, in the developing countries should stress on research and development regarding science and technology. The institutions and the researcher should be encouraged to find out innovation technologies which could make the country self-relevant and reduce vulnerability making the maximum use of indigeneous resources. It should arrange for modernization for both equipment and technology. The government should sponsor the Researchers, students and managerial staff to visit abroad and get training, because it will help in bringing the foreign technology at home. It should ensure acccssibility of technology to all segments of the society. The Research and Development wing should be established by the government as it could provide vital inputs to both large scale and small scale industry. This wing could help in developing new intermediate technologies according to the nations specific conditions. There is a strong case for developing labour intensive technologies in all labour surplus backward economies.

It can be said that in this age of rapid scientific and technological development technology has a large impact on economic growth. but in the technological race between different countries, the developing countries lag far behind, consequently they are dependent on the developed industrial world for technology required to accelerate their development process. The international technology market is highly imperfect and is dominated by a few multi-national corporations. They follow various discriminatory trade practices to maximise profits and to perpetuate their monopolistic or oligopolistic positions. Therefore, the use and the development of technology must relate to the people's aspirations. Our own immediate needs in India are the attainment of technological self-reliance, as swift and tangible improvement in the conditions of the weaker sections and speedy development of backward regions. Technology must suit local needs and to make an impact on the lives of ordinary citizens, must give constant thought to even small improvements which could made better and more cost effective use of existing materials and methods of work. Our future depends on our ability to resist the imposition of technology which is obsolete or unrelated to our specific requirement and of policies which tie us to systems which serve the purpose of their rather than out own. Thus the developing countries which having a large reservoir of human and manufacturing capacity can meet parts of requirements for aid, investment and technology through mutual exchange. the harmonization of policies and preferences of third world countries in the sphere of technology can bring about significant revolutionary developments in the economic growth of these countries.

MODES AND INSTRUMENTS OF TECHNOLOGY TRANSFER

Technology is an essential mode for socio-economic development of a country. But as it is well known, the modern know-how and technology is today monopolicy of the Multinational Corporations (MNs). The less developing countries are lacking it and are totally dependent on MNCs for borrowing has sophisticated and costly technology. This recent practics the made essential to throughly study the problems and prospects of transfer to technology.

Modes of technology transfer can be broadly classified in two ways: *(1)* According to the nature of the technology transfer, and *(2)* According to the nature of the instrument used. As far as classification according to the nature of the technology transfer is concerned, Cooper and Hoffman have presented a three-fold categorisation of technology transfer:

(a) 'simple direct' sales of technology, which consist of outright sales of embodied (machinery) or disembodied (specific consulting services) technology by unrelated firms for prices which are more or less competitive;

(b) 'process packaged' sales of technology, where a complete industrial process or plant is supplied by machinery manufacturers, independent engineering firms or final manufacturers of products; and

(c) 'project packaged' sales of technology, where the technology is accompanied by other requirements for the commercial operation of a project— *i.e.*, management, capital, brand names, etc.,—and by some element of continuous link or control by the seller."

The second method of classifying technology transaction is by the nature of the instrument used, *i.e.*, whether technology is sold in the form of equipment, designing of plant, commissioning, supervision, management, licences, direct investment, etc.

Transfer of technology between countries can take place in a number of ways:

(i) by the flow of books, journals and other published information;

(ii) by foriegn investment and the accociated transfer of know-how and equipment;

(iii) by the movement of people between countries, including immigration, return of emigrants, study visits, and other travel;

(iv) by the import of machinery and equipment;

(v) by technical cooperation programmes, multilateral and bilateral, official and private;

(vi) by licensing patent and know-how agreements.

Most developing countries employ all these methods simultaneously. The first method is more important for transfer of fundamental scientific knowledge rather than industrial technology. All other methods are directly relevant for the transfer of industrial technology.

Through technical cooperation programmes with other countries, governments of the developing countries have sought to introduce latest technology in their industrial sector. For this purpose, they send their missions abroad or invite technical missions from abroad. Through the establishment of a network of technical training and research institutions, they have tried to improve the supply of technical services.

However, the chief instruments of the transfer of technology from developed to the developing countries are the multinational corporations (MNCs). MNCs are huge industrial organisations which extend their industrial and marketing operations in a number of countries through a network of their branches or subsidiaries. They bring with them technical knowledge and equipment and also participate in the industrial development programmes of the developing countries by licensing, patent and know-how agreements. MNCs organise their operations in different countries through any of the following five alternatives:

Branches. The simplest form of extending business operations is to set up branches in the developing countries, which bring with them the technology of the parent company and are linked up with it.

Subsidiaries. MNCs also operate by setting up national affiliates as subsidiary companies. A subsidiary in a particular country is established under the laws of the country.

Frnachise Holders. This is a special kind of arrangement by which an affiliate firm produces or markets the produce of a multinational firm after obtaining a licence from that firm.

Joint Venture Company. At time, MNCs enter into a joint venture with an indigenous firm or agency. Under this arrangement the MNC makes available machinery, capital goods and technological expertise to the indigenous firm.

Turn-Key Pojects. Under this orgnisational form, the multinational undertakes to complete the project from scratch to the operational stage. When the project is ready it is handed over to the host country.

Throguh these various methods of operations, MNCs carry their technology to the developing countries. If MNCs set up a branch on a subsidiary company, it is claimed that there is a direct injection of foreign experience and expertise in the developing country. The branch or the subsidiary company can provide a channel for the transmission of the latest improvements from the developed to the underdeveloped countries. However, success on this front depends crucially on how far the recipient countries are able to regulate the activities of MNCs keeping the local interests in view.

Basic Characteristics of Technology Transfer. Technology is transferred by the advanced capitalist countries to the developing countries. There are the two basic characteristics of technology transfer. First the principal instrument of technology transfer are MNCs which either through their subsidiaries or through the contractual transactions made with developing countries bring mechanised processes and equipments not locally available. Very often the terms and conditions are arbitrarily settled under high imperfect market conditions by the technology supplying MNCs. The monopolistic strength of the technology suppliers emanates from the patents protection for differentiated products and processes.

The second basic characteristic of technology transfer is that the large part of the influx of technology in developing countries is in response to the policy of industrialisation through import substitution. In developing countries, due to structural factors and their consequential effects on terms of trade much reliance cannot be placed on exports to transform savings into current investment goods. Naturally a deliberate strategy of creating a tariff wall to overcome the foreign exchange difficulties has to be followed, and this provides an incentive to MNCs to move to developing countries with their unaltered plants and technical know-how to manufacture import restricted goods for sale in local elite markets.

Transfer of Inappropriate Technology. Conditions in developed countries are vastly different from conditions in developing countries. The first important difference is with regard to the relative factor prices. The wage levels in the developing countries are considerably lower than in the developed countries primarily because of their general poverty the relative abundance of labour and scarcity of capital. The conditions in the development countries are just the opposite, this raises the question of the 'appropriateness' of the technology transferred. The technology that is made available by the developed to the developing countries is capital-intensive in nature by the developed to the developing countries is capital-intensive in nature and accordingly, not suitable to the factor endowments of the latter.

Destructions of Indigenous Capital-Goods Industry. Not only is the technology transferred inappropriate, the operations of the MNCs retard the development of an indigenous capital-goods industry.

As noted Multinations may stifle the growth of indigenous enterpreneurship, so that the net addition to capital accumulated is such less than the investment provided by the multinationals themselves.

PRODUCTION OF OTHER SOPHISTICATED PRODUCTS

The technology transferred by MNCs is inappropriate also in the sense that it produces commodities which are unnecessary or over-sophisticated in relation to the needs of the developing countries. Moreover, MNCs encourage forms of consumption among the broad mass of the people, particularly in the urban areas, which are inappropriate in the stage of development and often nuritionally damaging. Important examples here are powder, baby-milk and Coca Cola.

These tendencies distort economic structure of the under-developed countries, are wasteful in nature, encourage acquisitiveness, reduce domestic saving and can worsen balance-of-payments by encouraging expensive tastes.

MNCs and Employment Creation. Because of the capital-intensive nature of their technology the employment effect of the operations of MNCs in the host countries is negligible. Moreover, such technology transfer is likely to increase income inequalities. When a multinational corporation sets up a unit in a developing country, it concentrates on employing a few highly skilled labour force of that country. These people are offered higher wages than the incomes of the unskilled domestic labour force. Thus technology transfer fails in increase employment opportunities in the developing countries on the one hand, and promotes inequalities in income and wealth on the other hand.

Some supporters of MNCs have argued that the impact of technology transfer by MNCs on employment position in development countries is positive. However, they take only a partial view of the reality. Almost all developing countries of Asia, Africa and Latin America and labour abundant economies. The transfer of highly sophisticated technology to these countries by the MNCs leads to greater unemployment. The incapability of this technology to absorb labour is simply due to the fact that "it was designed to do the opposite, *i.e.*, to be labour saving and capital using."

Impact on Industrial Concentration in Developing Countries. The penetration of MNCs in underdeveloped countries leads to higher concentration in the long run to the following reasons: *First*, due to their competitive strength the MNCs may force local firms out a business. This may simply by due to the fact that market forces reduce the profitability of marginal suppliers and force them to leave the industry. *Secondly*, a multinational corporation may buy out its local rivals through acquisition. *Thirdly*, the conduct of foreign firms may have an indirect effect on concentration by stimulating defensive amalgamation among local firms. *Finally*, through skillful negotiations with the host government, the MNCs may bargain for themselves secure and influential positions in their industries.

The net effect of these tendencies of concentration promoted by the activities of MNCs is very damaging for the small scale industrialists who find it more and more difficult to exist in the face of increasing penetration by MNCs.

Capital Flows and Balance of Payments. The developing countries are often required to pay high direct costs for technology transfer in the form of profits by many MNCs have been substantial and many more times than their total investment in India.

On account of the above factors, some critics argue that the operations of the MNCs 'decapitalize' developing countries—that is leave them with less capital than they would have had in the absence of MNCs. A related criticism is that outflows of imcome lead to a futher deterioration in the already weak balance of payments positions of the underdeveloped countries and lead to erosin of their foreign exchange reserves. While a loan creates obligations for only a certain number of years, private investment may involve an unending commitment.

The behaviour pattern of MNCs reveals that they do not engage in R and D activities within the development countries. Their R and D efforts are concentrated in laboratories in the home country or in other industrialized countries. However, the developing countries are forced to bear the cost of the R and D activities as the affiliates of the MNCs remit payments on this account also.

Restrictive Practices of MNCs. MNCs impose a number of restrictions in their technology transfer agreements with the developing countries. One of the most common restrictive clauses in contracts of technology transfer is that of export prohibition. In other words, foreign technology using national firms and subsidiaries of MNCs obtain capital equipment and technical know-how on the specific condition that the production will be done only for domestic market. In rare cases MNCs grant freedom to technology consumers in respect of exports. The implications of these restrictive clauses in backward economies are serious. First, by virtue of these restrictive provisions technology supplier MNCs exercise control over the business decisions of the technology buyers in respect of output, market prices, and often this results in creation of excess capacity. Secondly, restrictions forbidding sales in third markets inhibit host country's export promotion drive and thereby prove to be serious obstacle to development.

A large number of technology transfer contracts include obligatory conditions with regard to purchase of equipment and intermediate goods from the same sources as that of technical know-how. For technology supplying MNCs such tie-in arrangements serve an important purpose. They ensure a secure market for their capital equipment and intermediates and facilitate earning of monopoly profits. Tie-in restrictive arrangements in technology transfer contracts take several forms. The most common form is to explicitly forbid the purchase of capital goods and intermediate inputs from other sources. Sometimes in addition to this, use of local material is either limited or even completely prohibited.

International Institutional Structure Biased in Favour of MNCs. The international institutional structure also has a distinct bias in favour of MNCs and against the developing countries. As far as technological transfer is concerned, this bias is reflected at four different levels: *(1)* Institutional arrangements such as international patent system have a negative effect for the interests of the developing countries; *(2)* International mechanisms such as international insurance scheme to cover properties of MNCs facilitate existing relations of MNCs with host governments; *(3)* International efforts as the preparation of codes of conduct has limited effects in favour of developing countries interests; *(4)* Thus, there is an absence of internationally agreed provisions for the disclosure of information and accountability with respect to the activities of the MNCs.

Technological Dependence and Threat to National Sovereignty. Last but not the least is the 'technological dependence' that technological transfer at times introduces in the recipient country. Many developing countries have not paid sufficient attention to the programmes of research and development within their own national boundaries and have continued to depend on the import of technology from abroad. From a long term point of view, the costs of such a policy are colossal as the country becomes more and more passive to the needs of educational, scientific and technical development. Thus the basic infrastructure of 'learning' fails to evolve in the country. However, even more risky than this is the power that such technological dependence confers on the MNCs to dictate terms to the recipient country. As the technological dependence of the developing country increase on the MNCs, the ability of the latter to dictate economic and political terms to be former also increases. At times, the powerful MNCs gain control over local assets and jobs and then exert considerable influence on the political decision-making process at all levels. They may even subvert the very political process in small countries and jeopardize their economic and political freedom.

SCIENCE AND TECHNOLOGY POLICY

India became independent in 1947 after about 200 years of colonial rule. The Government of India from the very beginning adopted a policy regarding the scientific and technological development of the country. In fact, the new leadership of India was very much aware of the national conditions and capacity along with the international condition and the superiority of the west on the fields of science and technology particularly. Hence, with the desire to make India a modern country and a big regional power with an international role, the leadership put more emphasis on the development of science and technology. particularly, Prime Minister, Jawaharlal Nehru realised that to get rid of backwardness, science and technology would be most helpful.

Jawaharlal Nehru was instrumental for the adoption of Scientific Policy Resolution (SPR) by Government of India on 4th March 1958. It recognised science and technology as the key to national prosperity. India is scarce in capital and initial materials. It has to heavily depend on modern technology to overcome such limitations. The aims and objectives of SPR are:

(i) To promote, foster, cultivate and sustain science and scientific research-basic and applied;

(ii) To ensure adequate supply of highly trained and qualified research personnel by recognising their work as an important component of nation's strength; and

(iii) To secure the benefit of science and technology to all the people in the country.

Thus, the SPR acknowledges the cardinal importance of cultivating science and scientific thinking on mass scale by the masses by building large number of scientific institutions, training large number of scientific manpower and applying the science and technology results to the economic cultural development of all the people.

In response to the need for guidance on a wide ranging and complex set of inter-related areas of science and technology industry, economy and trade, the Government of India had announced the Technology Policy Statement (TPS) in January 1983. Its main objectives are to develop indigenous technologies help absorption of the improved ones. Accordingly its main aims are:

(1) To attain technological conscience and self reliance;

(2) To blend a correct mix of technologies of mass production by the masses and for the masses;

(3) To upgrade both technologies and equipment on continuous basis;

(4) To develop essential technologies in the critical areas which are nationally relevant and internationally competitive;

(5) To promote economic efficiency and quality in production; and

(6) To Ensure harmony with environment, ecology and habitant and so on.

Historical Background. The Industrial Policy Resolution (IPR) of 1948 and 1956 was one of the first policy options of Government of India. It aimed at promotion, directional and regulative aspects of economic activity of country. The aim of IPR was to accelerate industrial and economic development by expanding large scale industries in the core sectors through public and co-operative sectors. It emphasized the need for equitable distribution of wealth among the population by the state by promoting basic and strategic industires. Massive import of both capital and technology was considered essential for the industrial development of the country. The Industrial Development and Regulation (IDR) Act of 1951 was considered as an instrument of achieving the objectives of IPR. It allowed grant of licences to select and thrust areas which are considered essential for Economic Development.

Later Developments. The Monopolies Restrictive Trade Practices (MRTP) Act of 1969. extended its scope mostly to private sector industries whose main objectives were, prevention of concentration of wealth, direction of flow of investment and business operations towards select industries needing advanced technologies, and promotion of regional development.

Foreign Exchange Regulation Act (FERA), 1974 extended its scope and covered private sector firms whose foreign equity was more than 40 per cent. Its main objectives were similar to that of MRTP Act. Higher rate of foreign equity was allowed, provided the firms operated in the high technology areas, exported all their manufactured goods and shouldered the responsibility of developing backward areas.

The government provided certain incentives to promote R and D by industries. The Department of Science and Technology (DST) formulated and implemented a scheme in 1973 to recognise in house Research and Development centres of industries by registration. Such centres are eligible for certain fiscal benefits including import of critical materials and equipment under open General Licence (OGL). They are also entitled for a grant of foreign exchange for deputation of experts abroad, allocation of special controlled materials, exemption of excise duties, Income Tax (IT) exemption upto 100 per cent of expenditure incurred on R and D, preferential treatment in licensing for utilization of indigenously developed technologies.

Industries sponsoring research projects with national laboratories under C.S.R.I. are eligible to Income Tax deduction, subject to proper approval of competent authority. There is a provisions of Income Tax deduction on the amount spent on a pilot or semi-commercial plant based on C.S.I.R. technologies and on expenditure incurred as enhanced capacity in the form of plant and machinery.

Depreciation rate higher than 50 per cent is allowed to users of indigenously developed technologies. Central and State Financial Corporation operate several incentive schemes such as interest subsidies to encourage industries who venture to commercialize newly developed indigenous technologies. The subsidy varies between Rs. 20,000/- for small units and Rs. 4 lacs for large scale units. Interest free personal loans, under Risk Capital Foundation Scheme, limited to 50 per cent of equity share in the project, is available for setting up of medium and large scale projects.

The IDBI, operates a Venture Capital fund created by Government of India 1986-87 budget by imposing 95 per cent cess on all imported technologies Finance Corporation Limited RCTC assistance is available in three forms., *viz. (1)* Conditional loans as an instrument of profit and risk sharing without any interetst bearing; *(2)* conventional loan carrying progressive interest ranging 6—15 per cent per annum; and *(3)* direct equity participation in the company.

A look at the trends in the growth of annual expenditure on Science and technology activities and per cent share in GNP (Gross

National Product) shows that though Science and technology expenditure in absolute terms made a 742 fold increase, its relative share in the GNP increased only 50 times. It is obseved world-wide that many developed countries spend 2 per cent of GNP or more on indigenous Science and technology efforts.

However, inadeqate it might be, India's consistent efforts to raise Reserch and development expenditure have created a wide ranging network of Science and Technology agencies and institutions.

Due to inter-institutional competition and changing socio-economic priorities a readily altered pattern of distribution of Research and Development expenditure is seen now. Today Defence related Science and Technology activitives share the bulk of Research and Development expenditure.

Distribution of expenditure by nature of research is experimental development 30 per cent, applied research 30 per cent basic research 14% and other 24 per cent. Likewise, discipline 49 per cent natural science 31 per cent, agricultural sciences 15 per cent and medical sciences 5 per cent.

Development of Science and Technology infrastruture in India has 3-tier activity: *(1)* Agencies for policy promotion and planning; *(2)* Agencies under ministries and departments to implement the policy formulations; and *(3)* Institutions undertaking Research and Development projects and programmes. The Ministry of Science and Technology is the nodal wing of the government. Individual powers are delegated to DST, DSIR and DBT. Besides, there are many state councils for Science and Technology programmes. The chronology of individual Science and Technology agencies set up by government are: CSIR (1942); ICAR (1947); ICMR (1949); DAE (1954); UGC (1956); DRDO (1958); DST (1971); DOE (1971); DOS (1972); DOEN (1980); DOD (1981) and DNES (1982).

Over 100 professional bodies like National Science Academy. Indian Academy of Sciences, National Academy of Sciences, Institution of Engineers. All India Management Association, Institution of Costs and Works Accountans, National Productivity Council,

State Productivity Councils. etc. are functioning in the country to promote professional excellence in their respective disciplines.

TECHNOLOGY POLICY STATEMENT OF 1983

Technology Policy statement was issued in 1983 for the development of indigenous technology and efficient absorption of imported technology according to the national priorities and resources its aims to:

(a) Attain technological comeptence and self-reliance, to reduce vulnerability, particularly in strategic and critical areas, making the maximum uses of indigenous resources.

(b) Use traditional skills and capabilities making them commercially competitive.

(c) Provide the maximum gainful and satisfying employment to all strata of society with emphasis on the employment of women and weaker sections of seciety.

(d) Ensure a correct mix between mass production technologies and production by the masses.

(e) Identify obsolescnce of technology in use and arrange for modernization of both enquipment and technology.

(f) Develop tecnhologies which are internationally competitive partcularly those with export potential.

(g) Ensure maximum development with minimum capital outlay.

(h) Reduce demands of energy, particularly energy from non-renewable sources.

(i) Improve production speedily through greater efficiency and fuller utilztion of existing capabilities and enhance the quality and reliability of performance and output.

(j) Ensure harmony with the environment preserve the ecological balance and improve the quality of the habitat; and

(k) Recycle waste material and make full utilization of by prodcuts.

The statement mentioned that in technology development, special emphasis will be focused on food, health, housing, energy and industry with particular importance on agriculture including dry land farming. It mentioned:

1. Optimum use of water resources, increased production of pulses and oilseeds,
2. Provision of drinking water in rural areas, improvement of nutrition, rapid reduction in incidence of blindness, eradication of major communicable diseases and population stabilisation,
3. Development of use of renewable non-conventional sources of energy, and
4. Low cost housing,
5. Industrial development. The Government of India decide to give full attention to the development of indigenous technology to achieve technological self-reliance and reduce dependence on foreign inputs, particularly in critical and vulnerable areas and in high value added items, in which the domestic base is strong. The technological potential inherent in this system of interliked capabilities must be fully utilized and in turn provide fill up for further development from within the system. Therefore, incentives will be provided to users of indigenous developed technology and for products and processes resulting from such use.

The technnology policy mentioned about environment too. It referred that:

> To facilitate utilization of natural resources for ensuring a sustainable benefit stream for a better quality of life, it is essential that the technology conversion process must be made as efficient as possible, as this will provide a much higher output of the productive goods and services from the same material inputs. The policy therefore aims at:
>
> — adoption, adaption and promotion of state of the art technologies for waste prevention and reduction by

lesser consumption of raw material with special emphasis on indigenous efforts;

— modification of upgradation of the process technologies for optional utilisation of natural resources;

— adoption of preventive approach for pollution control;

— promotion and use of cleaner technologies;

— ensuring access to cleaner technologies available abroad.

The policy mentions a few thrust areas:

(1) Energy related technology including those for alternative fuel, renewable non-conventional source and energy consevation technologies with due weightage to domestic local availability base.

(2) Indigenous industries like those in the small scale sector or based on traditional and household skills.

(3) Technologies for conservation of land, water and energy resources and their integrated management for sustainable development.

(4) Extensive and intensive mapping and exploration of natural resource as well as estimation of reserves.

(5) Agriculture, allied services and agro-based industries including development of non-hazardous pesticides, herbicides and fungicides.

(6) The necessity of protecting vast sections of people against natural hazards like earthquakes, cyclones, droughts and floods.

(7) Technologies to betterment of infrastructural facilities such as transport, communication and housing.

(8) Technologies for provision and maintenance of health services, as well as leading to developing of new drugs/ medical devices and instrumentation, vaccines and their delivery systems.

The tecnology policy statement of 1983 is directed to:

— achieve a greater spread in the use of technological developments;

— ensure accessibility of technological devices to all segements of the society with a speical emphasis on remote and rural communities in order to improve their quality of life;

— enahance infrastructural facilities;

— upgrade traditional skills and reduce drudgery keeping in view the special needs of women and weaker section of society;

— encourage industries for enahancing human skills and upgrade existing technology to comparable international levels as well as to attain such levels for newer and emerging technologies.

Policy has also mentioned about the role of Research, Development and Engineering. It stated as below:

(1) Association of the relevant R and D Elabouratory systems for technology acquisition.

(2) Institution of measures to upgrade the efficiency and productivity of technologies for ensuring quality and enhancing competitiveness.

(3) Enlarged role of R and D E in our economy.

(4) Providing technology support and services for major export oriented areas like leather, textiles, jute, jewellery, handicrafts and agro-products.

(5) Providing support for substantive value addition for export in areas which may emerge due to rapidly changing global mix of technologies and

(6) Development of indigenous clean technoloies which are urgently needed to preserve the environment and ensure the health and safety of our people.

It is also noted that Rand D E could provide vital inputs of enabling small scale industry to grow and successfully compete with large scale industry.

Due to its policy towards science and technology India has made quite a good development in its socio-economic conditions. It is today a recognizable fore in the world and particularly in South Asia. Its leadership and bureaucrats realised that in this age of rapid growth science and technology are important tools. But international technology market is highly imperfect and dominated by a few multinational corporations. They follow various discriminatory trade practices for their own benefit. It was also realised that the developing country depend on them to borrow technology. Hence, Indian government followed a dual policy *(1)* to borrows developed and costly technology; and *(2)* to develop indigenous science and technology for the betterment of society and the nation.

❐

8

India's Fiscal and Monetary Policies

Is it necessary that government should interfere in economic activities? It is impossible for industry and trade to grow without intervention of state? What will be the condition of trade and industry in absence of government interference? To discuss these issues it is reqired to understand the subject in right perspectives. We shall therefore discuss the reasons for state intervention.

REASONS FOR STATE INTERVENTION

1. Socialistic Pattern of Pociety. In July 1954, the all India Congress Committee promised for the establishment of socialistic pattern of society. The same year, the parliament also passed a resolution regarding the expansion of public sector and government ownership. The ideology of socialistic society gave a new direction to it. After taking the decision of establishment of socialistic pattern of society, it is necessary for the government to take the active participation in the growth of trade and industry.

2. Public Utility Services. The availability of a few services is considered essential for the economy and the citizen of a country. The interest of private sector sometimes put obstacles and creats dangers in the development of these public utility services. Posts & Telegraph, Railways, transport, defence equipment, water, electricity, gas etc. are a few of examples of public utility services.

3. Planned Economy. Though the process of planning had been introduced even before independence but in order of five year plans the first five year plan (FYP) started after independence in 1951. This process is still in continuation. After introducing planning process in India the participation and supervision contive of state becomes necessary. National planning is the activity which cannot be performed by any other organisation in a better way other than government. In a planned economy like India, the government not only control trade and industry but also actively participate in economic activitives. The importance and role of government and expansion of public sector were emphasized even in first FYP.

4. Balanced Economic Growth. It is essential to eliminate regional and industrial disparties for the overall development of a nation. The private sector generally establishes and develops the industries near available markets and developed regions. Private sector mostly ignores the backward regions and this sector directly and indirectly has increased backwardness of the backward regions. Keeping the interest of these regions in consideration, the balanced regional development is necessary.

5. Creation of Infra-structure. The industrial development of country basically depends upon the availability of infrastructual facilities. No country can make progress in absence of infrastructural facilities. These facilities can be created without developing electricity, water, irrigation, education health facilities etc. The government of India has given a more attention on the growth of these facilities after third five year plan.

6. Less Profitable and Highly Risky Industries. Heavy and basic industries are considered the backbone of industrial development of a country. These industries have long gestation period and required capital investment in hang quantity. Though these industries are very important formal nation's point of view, but their operation and establishment becomes very risky. Private sector generally do not want investment in these industries because of the factors involved. Therefore the state intervention becomes necessary. The government has done a commendable job in their growth of oil and naturalgas electricity, house building, air and water transport, newspaper, cement medicine, engineering industries etc.

7. Establishment of Defence Industries. The arms and ammunition industry must be established in the ownership government so that security and secracy can be preserved. If these industries are established in private sector then it can pose a threat to the security and secracy of a nation.

The main forms of State intervention are the following :

1. Fiscal and Monetary Policies.

2. Union Budget.

3. Development Banking.

4. Industrial Policy Resolutions.

5. Exim Policy.

6. Public Sector.

8. Foreign Competition and Protection. The domestic industry in the primary stage of its development, faces many difficulties due to the competition, from foreign industries. The domestic industry can not develop in absence of adequate protection.

OBJECTIVES OF FISCAL POLICY

Fiscal policy is that part of government policy which is concerned with raising revenue through taxation and other means and deciding on the level and pattern of expenditure. The nature of fiscal policy in an underdeveloped economy is bound to be different from that of a developed country. In a developed economy, the problem is not so much that of achieving economic stability on account of business fluctuations caused by the trade cycle. The compensatory fiscal policy is eminently suited to achieve a high degree of economic stabilization in a developed economy. But the problem in an underdeveloped economy is not so much that of economic instability as that of promoting rapid cconomic growth in the country. The fiscal policy, as such, much not only be that of compensatory spending as in a developed economy, but also one capable of promoting rapid economic growth in the country. The following could be the major objectives of fiscal policy in an underdeveloped country:

(i) The first objective of fiscal policy in an underdeveloped country should be to maximize the level of aggregate saving by applying a cut to the actual and potential consumption of the public at large.

(ii) The second objective of fiscal policy should be to divert capital resources from less productive to more productive, and from socially less desirable to socially more desirable uses. This objective is implicit in planned economic development.

(iii) The third objective should be to maximize the rate of capital formation to break down economic stagnation and to lead the country on the path of rapid economic progress.

(iv) The forth objective of fiscal policy should be to protect the economy of an underdeveloped country from the demon of inflation. Inflation can prove ruinous to an underdeveloped economy. It can undermine the very process of economic growth. As such, the fiscal policy of an underdeveloped country should be designed in such a manner as to curb inflationary forces arising during the process of economic growth.

(v) The fifth objective of fiscal policy should be to eliminate, as far as possible, the glaring economy inequalities bedevilling the economy and to bring about an equitable distribution of income and wealth in society. The objective, however, clashes with the first objective, namely, that of rapid economic growth throgh maximization of the rate of capital formation. Rapid economic growth is not possible without maximization of aggregate saving in the economy. And aggregate savings cannot be increased unless there are wide disparities in income and wealth distribution. A wise, prudent government should attempt through appropriate measures to reconcile the two conflicting objectives of rapid growth and social justice in a judicious manner.

(vi) The sixth objective of fiscal policy should be to eliminate, as far as possible, sectoral imbalances arising in the economy from time to time. Though the fiscal policy as visualized above, will help to maintain price stability in the economy as a whole by curbing inflationary forces, there may arise sectoral price fluctuations in certain sectors of the economy on account of the existence of certain bottlenecks. Toward off that possibility, fiscal policy must be attumed to correct such imbalances in time before they could inflict any damage on the economy.

ROLE OF FISCAL POLICY

Fiscal policy influances growth performance of an economy in two ways. In the first place, it affects growth by influencing the mobilisation of resources for development. Secondly, if exercises its influence by improving the efficiency of resource allocation and thirdly it influences social equity through fixation and expenditure policies.

1. Fiscal Policy and Resource Mobilisation. During the planning period the fiscal policy has done externally well on this account. In 1950-51 the tax-GDP ratio was just 5.9 per cent. Since then it is rising and stood at 15.7 per cent in 1991-92. During the 1905 the tax-GDP ratio registered a decline and was 14.6 per cent in 2000-01. In India all the major taxes, except personal income tax and land revenue, have recorded buoyancy greater than unity. In recent years the bouyancy of Union excise duty and sales tax has been very high. Obviously this has enabled far greater mobilisation of resources through taxation than what would normally expect in the conditions prevailing in India. But there is still same scope for a raising additional tax revenue in the country.

Apart from tax revenue, other important aspects of resource mobilisation and generation of non-tax revenue, restructuring of government expenditure and raising of surplus of public sector enterprises. The first two have very little impact on resource mobilisation. Hence we shall focus are attention on public savings. The realisation of public sawings has always been less than the targets fixed it. In 1976-77, the rate of public swing relative to GDP was 4.9 per cent and it came down to zero in 1998-99. The real problem for Government saving has been the rapid growth of revenue expenditures which outpaced the revenue receipts of the government. Revenue expenditures of the government which were 13.1 per cent of GDP in 1970-71 rose to 18.5 per cent of GDP in 1980-81 and further to 28.8 per cent in 1997-98. The main factors which led to the growth of revenue expenditures were subsidies and interest payments. Another factor which explains the lacklustre public savings performance is failure of public sector enterprises to generate adequate surpluses. At the central level the net after-tax profits of public enterprises showed a return of around 5.7 per cent of the capital invested in them in 1995-96 which was much below the potential. At the Central level, in 1994-95 there were 241 enterprise out of which only 120 were profitable. The overall rate of return over capital employed in all the Central public undertakings was as low as 2.75 per cent during 1994-95. At the State level, the performance of the public sector enterprises is far more disappointing. Both the State Electricity Boards and the State Road Transport Undertakings have been incurring heavy losses for quite some time.

In India, fiscal policy has been used for providing both special incentives for private savings and encouraging investment in specified areas like housing. As a result of these policies in case of the last three Five Year Plans, the actual private savings rate has exceeded the Plan target. The failure of the fiscal policy in India is perhaps the most conspicuous in it inability to prevent the growth of black economy. Which the government. On heavy losses to resulted in account of tax evasion. This revenue loss to the government has reduced the built-in elasticity of the tax system. The black economy has also constrained the resource mobilization effort through larget scale leakages of funds from development projects and other programmes. This black income has a general tendency to lower down the savings propensity as its common outlet is consumption expenditure on "luxary service". The use of black income for accumulation of real or financial assets is often avoided because it carries far greater risks of detection and penalty.

2. Fiscal Policy and Allocational Efficiency. Fiscal Policy also influences growth performance of an economy through its effects on the allocation of resources. An efficient and rational allocation of resources will obviously be helpful in raising the rate of economic growth. Therefore, if fiscal policy favourably affects the efficiency of resource allocation, then in the process growth performance of the economy is bound to improve. An indifferent fiscal policy adversely the efficiency of resource allocation on the contrary retards the productive activity and thereby results in lower rate of economic growth.

Among the various instruments of fiscal policy perhaps tax policy is the most important deteriminant of the efficiency of resource use. During four and a half decades of economic planning the reliance on commodity taxation has increased and now it accounts for around 76 per cent of the tax revenue. Among the indirect taxes, the prepondent role has been played by customs and excise duties at the Central government level and the sales tax at the State government level. These tax have been generally levied mainly on revenue-raising considerations and have sometimes resulted losses. The case of customs duties is particularly mentioned to prove this point. In recent years a number of studies have revealed that the structure of customs duties along with restrictive controls have provided effective protection to a number of industries and as a result there has been unnecessary loss of efficiency in resource use. The policy of levying taxes on inputs has led to the problem of "cascading" of tax and interest costs and distorted the incentive structure for investment. It has also adversely affected the international competitiveness of exports.

In India, a sizeable black economy exists which poses serious problems for the allocative dimensions of fiscal policy leakages from government expenditure programmes adversely affect the efficiency of public expenditure which mans that in practice the actual return from public expediture is far less than the anticiptated return.

3. Fiscal Policy and Equity. It is often doubted that India's fiscal policy conforms to the principle of equity. During the four and a half decades of economic planning the share of direct taxes in total tax revenue has fallen from 40 per cent to 25 per cent. In the same period the share of income tax on personal incomes has dropped from 21 per cent to 7.6 per cent. H.H. Hinrichs has pointed out that in the course of development in most countries the share of direct taxes in the total tax revenue has shown a tendency to increase. It is thus surprising that the trends in India are just opposite to the trends witnessed in other countries. In India, in spite of all its pretensions, the government has been reluctant to put the major burden of economic development on the relatively rich. In fact, it is this reason why over the years the share of direct tax has steadily declined in the total tax revenue. Apart from the various exemptions provided, the government has willfully tolerated large scale tax evasion.

In terms of nominal rates personal income tax is certainly progresssive. But who can deny that there is large undisclosed income in the country on which no tax is paid. This income is mostly in the hands of industrialists, traders, professionals, bureaucrats and politicians. Therefore, the sharpness of progression in nominal rates does not guarantee that the principle of equity in personal income taxation will not be violated. Indirect taxes are generally believed to be regressive. Ahmad and Stern found that certain indirect taxes are progressive but this is not true of all taxes. Moreover, for urban areas the burdens of most of the taxes were found to be proportionate to expenditure levels.

For assessing the equity implications of the fiscal policy it is also necessary to analyse as to who benefits from public expenditure. The fact of the matter is that the benefit of most of the government expenditure has hardly reached the poorest of the poor. After all who does not know that poor rarely benefit from expenditures on defence, public administration higher education and urban based medical facilities. Even the benefit of most development rarely trickles down to reach the poorest of the poor. Therefore, the equity implications of the public expenditure are clear; the poor have benefits the least from them.

Fiscal Policy and Business Firm. In the broad framework of the economic liberalisation approach of the recent years, the major themes of the fiscal policy have been concertised. Now the emphasis is on reasonable tax rate with better administration and enforcement so that the compliance can be improved and more revenue can be raised. There is broad agreement on these themes and they can be summarised as follows:

1. A systematic effort to simplify both the tax structure and the tax laws;
2. A deliberate shift to a regime of reasonable dirct tax rates, combined with better administration and enforcement, to improve compliance and raise revenue;
3. More reliance on non discretionary fiscal and financial instruments in managing the economy as compared to adhoc; discretionary physical controls;
4. The fostering of a stable and predictable tax policy environment;
5. Greater recognition and weight given to the resource allocation and equity consequences of taxation;
6. Concerted efforts to improve tax administration and reduce the scope for arbitrary harassment;
7. Growing appreciations of the links between fiscal and monetary policy;
8. Fresh initiative to strengthen of expenditure control.

These new fiscal measures will significantly affect a business firm directly and indirectly both. If tax rates are reasonable and stable for a long duration, a business firm can envisage its expansion plan and boost the industrial growth rate in the country.

DEFICIT FINANCING

In ordinary language when the income of a country is less than the expenditure it has to incur on different heads, to make up for this deficit the government adopts a new policy for mobilisation additional resources. This policy is known as the deficit financing. Deficit financing is usually used according to two different views. In America and Western countries where the expenditure of the government is more than is income the government makes up for this deficit by public borrowings. It is called deficit financing. But in India the term is used in a different sense. When the deficit is made up by issuing new currency notes, withdrawal of past accumulated cast balances by the government and getting loans from the Central Bank instead of public debt, it is called deficit financing. Whatever may be the method of deficit financing it is sure that there is expansion in the supply of money. But it is different to guess what would be its impact on the price level.

Objectives of Deficit Financing

There are various objectives for deficit financing and to achieve them every government of sometimes or other resort to this method. Some of the chief objectives are—*(i)* To check the depression. *(ii)* To meet the expenditure on war, *(iii)* To make up for the deficit of private investments, *(iv)* To accelerate the pace of economic development.

Deficit financing in India has served only three objectives. Deficit financing has been mostly used to accelerate the economic development. At the same time it has helped in increasing the rate of private investment. It has helped in creating social overhead facilities and has encouraged private investment.

Does Deficit Financing Always Lead to Inflation. Deficit financing and inflation are understood as synonymous. It is because deficit financing surely increases price level. The reasons that through deficit financing public expenditure increases and additional money comes into circulation. It provides additional purchasing power with hands of the people in society and therefore demand for goods and services increases. If the supply of these goods and services cannot increase proportionately so price level rises. But this fear cannot be taken up to neglect the objective of deficit financing. If deficit financing is made use of for economic development, the future increase in production will bring down the price. In this way price level and the objective of deficit financing are also affected by the condition of the economy. Deficit financing will not produe any increase in price level when *(i)* the production of the country has been constantly increasing, *(ii)* with the economic development monetary sector also develops, *(iii)* as a result of economic development income increases and demand for cost money also rises, *(iv)* import increase on account of foreign aid. Thus the secret of deficit financing can be expressed relatively.

Though there are certain evils associated with deficit financing yet it is necessary for accelerating the role of economic development. Where other sources of financing projects are limited.

TABLE : EXTENT OF DEFICIT FINANCING IN FYPS

Plans	*Amount (Rs. crores)*	*Per centage of total outlay*
First Five Year Plan (1951-56)	333	17.0
Second Five Year Plan (1956-61)	954	20.4
Third Five Year Plan (1961-66)	1,133	13.2
Annual Five Year Plan (1966-69)	676	10.2
Fourth Five Year Plan (1969-74)	2,060	12.8
Fifth Five Year Plan (1974-78)	3,560	8.8
Sixth Five Year Plan (1980-85)	15,684	14.2
Seventh Five Year Plan (1985-90)	34,669	15.4
Eighth Five Year Plan (1992-97)	33,037	8.6
Ninth Five Year Plan (1997-2002) (Target)	0	0.0

In the Third Plan the total volume of deficit financing was about Rs. 1133 crores. The Plan proposed a basic volume of deficit financing in order to keep prices low. But, the total amount of deficit financing during the Third Plan turned out to be of Rs. 1006 crores.

Deficit financing in the Fourth Plan (1969-74) was of the order Rs. 2060 and in Fifth Five Year Plan (1974-78) of Rs. 3560 crores and in the Sixth Plan (1980-85) of Rs. 15684 crores. The deficit financing for Seventh and Eighth plan was Rs. 34,669 crore and Rs. 33,037 crore respectively. The Ninth plan envisaged to zero amount but it will not met.

MONETARY POLICY OF R.B.I.

The monetary policy of the Reserve Bank of India seeks to help in achieving the national objectives of economic growth with equity and price stability. Since development requires finance which the banking system provides through credit or bank money, the monetary policy is designed to make available adequate supply of credit for investment in diverse fields of economic activity. It also seeks to reduce the cost of credit as an incentive for great use of bank finance in developmental process. But since the excess supply of credit (money) can cause inflation, the RBI is also concerned with control of inflation and ensure a reasonable degree on price stability. Since inflation affects adversely and severely the weaker sections of society, a monetary policy which seeks to achieve price stability is also one which serves to achieve the objective of equity.

The monetary policy of the RBI thus seeks to promote economic development through expansion of credit and its availability at low cost on the one side; it seeks to achieve price stablity and ensure equity by using instruments of credit control that can prevent excess liquidity and unreasonable rise in price level. The main instruments of credit control used by the RBI are:

(i) Variations in reserve requirements *i.e.*, cash reserves and statutory liquidity ratio;

(ii) Variation in the cost and availability of Reserve Bank's accommodation to banks;

(iii) Changes in the deposit and lending rates of the banks;

(iv) Selective credit controls; and

(v) Quantitative guidelines on credit expansion.

Monetary policy of the RBI has, by and large, ensured that adequate credit support is available to various sections of the economy. In the absence of such support, healthy growth of the economy would not have been possible. The pursuit of socio-economic objectives by the RBI's monetary policy has enabled large sections of people, who were in the past virtually bypassed by the banking system' to acquire considerable access to the bank credit. Now we shall discuss monetary policy in details.

A REVIEW OF MONEARY CONTROLS

1. The Period 1951-60. Since the establishment of the Reserve Bank in 1935, monetary policy was quite passive until 1951. This was the trend in many countries of the world. Monetary policy was not given adequate importance probably under the influence of Keynes' thinking during the great depression and due to compulsions of financing defence expenditure during the World War II. Along with the Central Banks of other countries, such as the US, the UK, etc. The Reserve Bank of India also activated monetary policy in 1951. Bank rate was raised for the first time from 3% to 5%. Open market sale policy was followed which resulted in a fall in the prices of gilt-edged securities and a rise in their yields. This led to a monetary contraction and decline in the general price level. The wholesale price index declined by 12.8% in four years partly due to good harvests. To reverse this trend, easy money policy was followed for a year or two. But when the price level increased by 14% in 1956-57, the RBI raised the Bank rate from 3½% to 4%. By and large, the monetary policy had remained independent during the 1950s. The Reserve Bank's policies were not constrained by the commitment to support the giltedged market. This decade witnessed some price stability on account of reasonable growth of real income, restrictive monetary policies, moderate does of deficit financing and a comfortable situation of foregin exchange (sterling balances).

2. The Period 1961-70. The planning effort was designed to gather momentum during the Third Plan period (1961-66). Out of the total resources of Rs. 8,577 crores for the public sector plan Rs. 1,133 crores (13.2%) were to be generated by deficit financing. Perhaps the Reserve Bank had to resume its support to the government bond market resulting in open market purchases. During 1961-65, the Bank's holding of government securities (excluding treasury bills) increased by Rs. 1,820 crores. The wholesale price index startred rising after 1963. The average rise in the general price level during the period 1963-68 was about 10 per cent per year. This was partly during two consecutive drought years, 1965-66 and 1966-67 and partly owing to the Indo-Pakistan war. The Bank resumed its tight policies. The bank rate was raised on four occasions during the decade.

Date	*Bank Rate*
23 January 1963	4.5
26 September 1963	5.0
17 February 1965	6.0
4 March 1968	5.0

The Reserve Bank reduced its holding of government securities (excluding treasursy bills) by Rs. 4,143 crores during the period 1965-68. This may imply open market sales. The price situation was under control during last two years of decade. This may be due to restrictive monetary policies of the precding years and good agricultural production during 1968-70.

3. The Period 1971-81. As far as the price situation is concerned this decade can be divided into three phases. During 1971-75, the first phase of the period, there was severe inflation. The wholesale price index increased by 75% during these four years. Then came a turning point. Emergency was declared in India. Drastic economic and political measures were taken. Even during the period of political changes and the Janata Party rule prices remained stable until 1978-79. During the third phase of the period 1979-81 the average price rise was of the order of 17 per cent (1979-80 was a drought year).

During the inflationary phase (1971-75) the Reserve Bank tried to follows restrictive policies in vain. The bank rate was raised three times during this period. The bank rates was probaby following the money market rather than leading it.

Date	*Bank Rate*
8 January 1971	6.0
30 May 1973	7.0
23 July 1974	9.0
23 July 1981	10.0

The cash reserve ratio which had prevailed at 3% of demand as well as time liabilities was increased to 7% during the year 1973. It is surprising why the Bank decided to reduce this ratio to 4% in 1974. This expansionary measure is just not explanable particularly when the inflation rate was around 20 to 25% per year. Excessive expansion of money and credit completed the RBI to raise again the statutory reserve ratio of banks to 6% in 1976. From 14 January 1977 the banks were further required to deposit with the Reserve Bank 10% of their incremental demand and time liabilities.

The Reserve Bank has followed open market sale policy throughout this period.

It is however, strange that open market sales were moderate during the inflationary years 1971-75. The magnitude of sales picked up after the inflation was brought under control by the Emergency measures. As it was pointed out earlier, it is difficult to interpret the data of Table because of the mix nature of RBI's operation of debt management on behalf of the government and open market operations as such.

THE RESERVE BANK'S OPEN MARKET OPERATIONS

(Rs. Crores)

Year	*Net Sale*
1971-72	56.2
1972-73	142.6
1973-74	79.4
1974-75	274.2
1975-76	506.3
1976-77	530.6
1977-78	630.7
1978-79	673.8
1979-80	343.3
1980-81	341.8

As a part of the anti-inflationary policy, the Reserve Bank has recently raised the bank rate to 10% on 12 July 1981, the Reserve ratio was also raised from 6 to 7%.

4. The Period 1981-1991. The bank rate remained at 10 per cent throughout the period. The cash reserve ratio also raised up to 15% of net demand and time liabilities. Now this has been brought down to 11 per cent in 1993. As far as statutory liquidity ratio is concerned it was 38.5 per cent of total demand and time deposits liabilities. The RBI also used selective and direct credit controls to curb the rate of inflation from time to time. During this period RBI fixed minimum margins for all foodgrains, oilseeds, vegetable oils ect. Many other direct controls had also been imposed by RBI on the nationalised banks.

5. The Period 1991 Onwards. The government of India introduced economic reforms in the early 1990s. Since then the RBI has taken steps to strengthen the bank rate as a policy instrument for transmitting signals of monetary and credit policy. It now serves as a reference rate for other rates in the financial markets. With this new role assigned to the bank rate it has been brought down and the bank rate pervailing in July 2002 was 6.5 per cent per annum.

The RBI has changed cash Reserve Ratio (CRR) from time to time for controlling inflation. The Narsimham Committee which submitted its report in 1991 did not favour use of CRR to combat inflationary pressures. In its opinion a high CRR adversely offects the bank profitability and pressures banks to change high rates of interest. This government decided to reduce the CRR from 15 per cent to 14 per cent in two phases. Later on CRR was reduced to 8.5 per cent effective from April 8, 2002 and to 8 per cent effective from April 22, 2000. The final reduction of CRR was made to 5.0 per cent effective from June 1, 2002. All these reductions of CRR freed cash balances and the lendable resources of the commercial banks.

The Statutory Liquidity Ratio (SLR) has been varied from time to time. Effective from September 22, 1990, SLR was made as high as 38.5 per cent of the commercial banks net demand and time liabilities. The Narsimham Committee, suggested to reduce SLR in phases to 25 per cent. The SLR was lowered down to 25 per cent effective from October 10, 1997 and is presently at this level (Till July 2002).

Selective Credit Controls

The Reserve Bank attempts to regulate credit supply for the genuine needs of the trading activity as reflected in market arrivals of paddy and rice, wheat, groundnut, cotton, etc. The Bank also attempts to see that undue credit expansion does not take place for financing hoarding of these senstive commodities. Thus price stability of essential commodities appears to be the main objective of selective controls. However, it must be noted that price variations are caused mainly by variations in production and market arrivals. As far as credit is concerned, speculators and hoarders have many other dependable sources of finance. Therefore regulation of bank credit can have only a limited success. The RBI pursure other objectives also. Certain exemptions are granted from credit controls to develop branch banking. Moreover development of warehouses, co-operatives, etc., are some other objectives of selective controls. The RBI also attempts to assist the operations of Food Corporation of India (FCI). Advances to FCI for food distribution programme have been fully insulted from the control frame. It appears that the RBI is aiming at too many objectives with too few instruments of policy. All types of exemptions given from credit control conflict with the main objective of price stability of essential commodities.

Margin and ceiling regulations regarding credit against paddy and rice and wheat where put on a regular footing for the first time in 1956. In order to see that the genuine trading activity is not hampered, demand documentary bills were given exemptions. The margin requirements (effective from July 1981) against stocks of paddy, pulses and other foodgrains is 45% for processing units and mills and 60% for others. Similar requirements against wherehouse receipts is 50%. The margin requirements for gur and khandsari is 65% against stocks and 55% against ware-house receipts. In 1996-97 the selective credit controls were liberalised on bank advances against a large number of price sensitive commodities such as pulses, coarse, oilseeds, oils including vanaspati, sugar, khandsari and cotton. They have now been dispensed with.

AN EVALUATION OF MONETARY POLICY

The objective of monetary policy was at one time characterised by RBI itself as 'controlled expansion'. On the one hand, RBI was taking steps such as the bill market scheme to expand bank credit to industry and trade and thus help in economic development. On the other hand RBI was using both quantitative (general credit restraint) and selective credit controls so that the deployment of loans and advances by the commercial banks for speculative purposes was under control. This was necessary to keep the rising price under check.

Thus, the monetary policy had twin aims-expansion of the economy and control of inflationary pressure. Monetary policy RBI has certain inherent onstrints and is obviously limited in its usefulness.

The Chakraverty Committee recognised the existene of violent fluctuations in agricultural production in India caused by weather conditions and the consequent difficulty of controlling inflationary pressures. Accordingly, the Committee recommended strong supply management measures. At the same time, demand management is equally important, that is, the demand for goods and services based on the volume of money and credit in the country. Thus, to achieve the objective of controlling inflation and stablise the price level, the Comittee suggested a two-pronged strategy: *(a)* the Government should aim at raising output levels; and *(b)* RBI should control the expansion in reserve money and money supply.

In this connection, it is important to realise the inter-relationship between money supply, output and prices. In the last two decades, the increase in reserve money and in money supply has been largely due to a rise in the level of RBI credit to Government which reflects a significant monetisation of debt. In this connection, the Chakraverty Committee has made two related recommendations. First, the target for increase in money supply in the broad sense (M_3) during a year should be announced in advance. The target should be in term of range, based on anticipated growth input and in the light of the price situation. The target range can be modified but the circumstances under which the modification is being made should also be announced in advance. This policy of monetary targeting will help RBI in the use of its monetary policy instruments.

Secondly, the Government should restrict it recourse to RBI at predetermined levels so as to restrict monetisation of debt. Towards this end, the yeild rate and dated Government securities and Treasury bills should be made more attractive.

Finally, the weapons and the powers available to RBI are such that they cover only organised banking sector *viz.*, commercial banks and cooperative banks. To the extent inflationary pressure is the result of bank finance, the RBI's general and selective controls will have positive effect. But if inflationary pressure occurs due to deficit financing and shortage of goods, RBI's control may not have any effect at all. This is what is probably happening in India in recent years. Besides, it should always be help in mind that RBI has no power over non-banking financial institutions as well as indigenous bankers who play such a major role in financing trade and industry.

According to Partha Sen, monetary policy has a limited role in the Indian context. Montary policy in India is functioning in an environment where it can be expected to deliver very little if any thing at all. At the best of times, monetary policy can ensure a smooth functioning of an economy if a number of pre-conditions are met. Put differently, monetary policy in India can do a lot of damage but its single handedly do good in limited.

UNIONS BUDGET

In simple words, the budget is a document which contains estimates of the government revenue and expenditure for a year. According to the Indian constitution, "Budget means the annual financial statement containing an estimate of all anticipated revenue and expenditure of the government for the coming financial year." Besides, the budget also contains a review of the financial position of the last year, the proposals for financing revenue and capital expenditure for the coming year. The union budget can be balanced or unbalanced.

Balanced Budget Approach

According to the classical economists, fiscal policy should have the minimum range of operations and the budget should be balanced annual. They firmly struck to the doctrine of laissez fair and Say's law of markets. According to Adam Smith, economic eqilibrium and progress are attained through inherent and self-oriented indegenous forces of the economic system. In classical opinion, thus, when full employment is supposed to reach automatically, productivity of government services in the economic field is nill. And since government services are rendered at the cost of the national product. Thus, when government's productivity is zero in a free enterprise economy, it is desirable that government confines itself only to its primary functions of protection and security of life and property and does not interfere with the free working of the economic system. Even if government efforts are productive, it cannot increase national income and level of economic activity above the level reached without its intervention. Thus, when full employment, optimal allocation of resources and equitable distribution can be achieved automatially through the operation of free economic forces, fiscal operations have to be a non-regulatory, non-interfering nature. As such, the smallest budget was considered to be the best in the classical era. As such, classicists firmly advocated a balanced budet, in the sense that current annual revenue and expenses of the government must be equal. It, thus, does not provide for borrowings. The balanced budget principle was thus recognised as a principle of sound finance in orthodox economics.

Under the theory of sound finance, classicists favoured a balanced budget criterion for the following reasons:

(i) Unbalanced budgets may generate inflation on account of large and unproductive public expenditure.

(ii) Unbalanced budgets imply a wide extension of state functions beyond the capacity of the government, which may invite irresponsible governmental action.

(iii) A series of unbalance budgets imply an increase in the burdern of pubilic debt.

(iv) If the budget is unbalanced, the government has to borrow. The government's market borrowing cause reduction in loanable funds available to private productive employment and investment activities.

(v) Economic stability is secured by the adoption of a balanced budget policy. Unbalanced budgets, on the other hand, causes economic uncertainty and promote instability.

(vi) A balanced budget, on the other hand, is a limited budget designed in a rational way.

Furthermore, when the public debts mature, the government will have to impose additional taxes to obtain resoruces for their repayment. Thus, additional taxation would again tend to have an adverse effect on the incentive to work and save. It would also cause the accentuation of income distribution. Moreover, government borrowings cause the rate of interest in the money market to rise, as the demand for loanable funds rises. A rise in the rate of interest adversely affects investment activity in the private sector.

In short, according to the principlies of sound finance, a budget must be balanced annually and the gap between revenue and expenditure should be minimum. Thus, classical economists firmly advocated a laissez-faire policy and were confident of the unhampered optimum operations of the free enterprise economic system. Neoclassical economists, however realised the socially undesirable effects of unregulated free enterprise on the economic system. It was argued by them that careful state action for raising income and public spending was essential to attain maximum social welfare under the concept to welfare state development in the neoclassical era.

The concept of fiscal policy, however, received a new vista with the inception of "new economics" (Keynesian economics) in modern times. Keynesian theory shattered the basic foundation of the classical doctrine when the former asserted that the competitive process of free enterprise economy does not necessarily ensure an effective demand such as to absorb all productive resources at full employment supply does not create its own demand and the economy may attain equilibrium at under-employment level. Unemployment may persist due to secular forces causing underconsumption and oversaving in an advanced economy, thereby creating a condition of plenty in the midst of poverty on account of deficiency of aggregate demand. He therefore, regarded the inevitability of a positive fiscal policy as follows. At a level of income corresponding to full employment, the gap between total income and total consumption is so high in a mature economy that private investment is inadequate to fill it. If unemploment is to be avoided, the gap must be filled either by government expenditure or by increasing the propensity to consume. But, in a capitalist economy, which is characterised by wide inequalities in the distribution of income and other institutional factor which make for a high propensity to save, the propensity to consume cannot easily be raised enough to have a significant effect on employment. Therefore, the chief responsibility for maintaining high levels falls on the public sector expenditure, designed to narrow the gap between income and consumption at full employment. Further, in Keynes's view, a depression in an advanced industrial economy occurs due to the deficiency of aggregate demand. Thus, during a depression, when the aggregate spending is inadequate to achieve full employment, the government must increase spending directly by undertaking public workers programmes on a large scale and indirectly by inducing people to spend more.

In short, the Keynesian fiscal policy for attaining full employment implies a technique by which total outlay is manipulated, *i.e.*, when private outlays are deficient, public outlays should be increased which ensures the full use of economic resources available in the country.

Unbalanced Budget Approach

Keynesian revolution in economic thinking reconstituted the whole basis of public finance and affirmed functional finance as a fiscal norm in modern times. Though the lead in the development of "functional finance" concept was taken by Keynes, credit goes to Prof. A.P. Lerner for coining this concept. Lerner puts that : "The principle of judging fiscal measures by the way they work or function in the economy, we may call "functional finance". He contends that the fiscal operation of the government—taxing, borrowing, public spending, management of public debt, etc., deficit financing etc.—should be designed with the objective of fulfilling certain functions which have an immediate bearing and far-reaching effects on the economic system as a whole. In economic philosophy, the term "functional finance" embraces public expenditure public revenue and debt management which are regarded as fiscal instruments effectively used to achieve objectives like attainment and maintenance of full employment with economic stability.

As Prof Chelliah points out, the functional concept of fiscal policy, thus, implies that: *(i)* the fiscal operations of government should be conducted on a functional basis, and public finance should not be considered as being induced solely by the need for securing social goods meant for collective consumption, and *(ii)* the budget need not always be balanced. As a matter of fact, the fiscal norm of functional finance is the complete antithesis of the orthodox rule of balanced budget. The functional finance norms suggests the formation of large budgets with a wider functional coverage of government spending to promote basic economic goals, *e.g.* *(a)* to obtain optimal allocation and efficient use of scarce resource at full-employment level, *(b)* to achieve economic stability and bring about an equitable distribution of income and wealth in the best possible manner.

Quite contrary to the classical notion, the concept of functional fiscal policy suggest that the state need not and should not assume a passive role in the economic affairs of the country. It implies that public spending may be incurred not merely for the sake of its direct benefits, but for the sake of indirect effect it produces in raising the level of income, output employment; and the public revenue may be raised not to meet an anticipated expenditure, but to curtail excessive demand and curb inflationary potentials in the economy. Taxation is, thus, regarded as an important and effective weapon in the hands of government to promote economic progress with stability.

Lerner suggest the following rules for government's responsibility and activity under functional finance.

(i) The government should incur public debt by borrowing money from the private sector only during inflation when it is absolutely essential to mop up the excessive purchasing power from the public, thereby reducing the pressure of excess monetary demand.

(ii) The government budget should be directed towards the achievement of full employment and price stability. For this purpose, the government budget need not necessarily be balanced.

(iii) During depression only, public expenditure in excess of current public revenue may be met by deficit financing. *i.e.*, printing additional currency notes.

In short the main tenet of functional finance is the formation of unbalanced budget from time to time for perfecting the countercyclical goal of fiscal policy. A surplus budget is recommended during inflation and a deficit budget for recovery public spending during a deflation or depression.

Functional finance, thus, deliberately aims at unbalancing the budgets with a view to attaining and maintaining full employment level in a developed economy. In an underdeveloped economy, however, the main problem is not one of full employement but that of rapid economic growth. In a developing economy, thus the functional aspect of fiscal policy is to be conceived in the context of a planned process of economic development.

Budget Tool of Control. The budget is a government document which present a report of the actuals of the revenue and expenditure of the previous year and the estimates of the proposals for the coming year. The budget provides necessary information regarding government debt.

The Union Budget affects and controls economic activities directly and indirectly both. It is through the budget that the legislature exercises an effective control over the executive. In the absence of budget, every ministry and department will collect and spend money in a arbitrary manner. As the functions of various departments are interconnected and develop with each other, there is likely to be dyarchy and wastage of funds. When the budget allocates separate funds to each department according to that department's proposals, there is proper allocation of public money. Thus the budget not only allocate public money among various ministries and departments but also put effective control over the executive.

The Union Budget affects economic activities by following balanced budget stratgey and unbalanced strategy. In case of former, the government's interference with the working of economic system is lowest. On the other if government adopts latter, the interference is much more. The unbalance budget strategy can be of two types—surplus budget strategy and deficit budget strategy. In case of surplus budget government collect more revenue than the expenditure, the economic activities are at the minimum. If government follows the policy of deficit budget (expenditure is more than the revenue), economic activities are at their peak.

The government affects and control economic activities through its socio-economic policies. The budget of a country is prepared keeping these socio-economic policies in mind. For example if objective is to achieve higher rate of growth the tax rates will be regressive. A reduction in tax rates with increase in personal income increase disposable income more which will encouraged consumption and savings both. Increase in the demand for consumer goods will encourage the production of these goods. Similarly reduction in corporate tax rates encourages production. If government spends more expenditure on particular types of industrial and capital goods, the demand for these goods increase, thereby encouraging their production.

Thus the Union Budget affects and control economic activities effectively.

❐

9

Industrial Growth and Policy

INDUSTRIAL GROWTH

At the time of independence, India was industrially and economically backward. In 1951-52, the share of agriculture was 56.5 per cent of GDP while the share of industry was just 13.3 per cent. Due to the programme of industrialisation, the share of industrial sector has gone up to 25.0 per cent in 2000-01. The industrial sector has become well diversified. The structure of industrial growth in India during the five decades of planning can be more easily examined and analysed under two broad heads *viz.*, *(I)* Industrial growth and *(II)* Pattern of industrialisation.

I. INDUSTRIAL GROWTH

India's industrial growth can be looked from three different aspects:

(i) Growth rate in industrial output.

(ii) Industry's contribution in national income, and

(iii) Industry's contribution to employment.

(i) Growth Rate in Industrial Output. The compound rate of growth was quite impressive during the first three plans. The industrial growth rate in first plan was 5.7 per cent and it rose to 7.2 per cent in second plan and further to 9.0 per cent in third plan. During the eleven year period (1996 to 1976) growth rate declined to 4.1 per cent per annum. The position did not improve even after.

Industrial Growth Rate

Period	*Annual growth Rate (per cent)*	*Period*	*Annual Growth Rate (per cent)*
1951-1956	5.7	1985-90	8.5
1956-1961	7.2	1990-91	9.0
1961-1966	9.0	1991-92	0.8
1966-1976	4.1	1992-94	0
1976-1980	3.8	1994-97	8.6
1980-1985	6.4	1997-2002	4.9

1975-76 as the annual rate of industrial growth during the four period (1976-80) remained very low *i.e.* 3.3 per cent per annum. During sixth plan *i.e.* 1980-85 the industrial activities picked up and achieved the growth rate of 6.4 per cent per annum. The industrial growth rate during 1985-90 (Seventh plan) was satisfactory *i.e.* 8.5 per cent per annum. Industrial sector requested a robust growth of 9.0 per cent in 1990-91. However, industries suffered a serious set-back in 1991-92 and production declined by 0.8 per cent. In the following year there was near stagnation. The industrial recovery started in 1993-94 and in two four period from 1993-94 to 1996-97 the industrial production increased at the annual rate of 8.6 per cent which is quite encouraging. But the indstrial growth declined again during the Ninth Five Year Plan (1997-2002) and it has been 4.9 per cent per annum. In the terminal year of this plan the rate of industrial growth registered a further decline and was low as 2.7 per cent.

(ii) Industry's Contribution to National Income. During the first three plans, similar trends relating to the distribution of NDP by different sectors were aslo observed in India. The share of the secondary sector to the NDP went up from a meager 13.3 per cent in 1950-51 to about 17.0 per cent in 1960-61; correspondingly, the share of the primary sector declined from 59.2 per cent in 1950-51 to 50.1 per cent in 1960-61. The fact that during this period, the national income has recorded a sizable increase would prove the fact that industrial production was increasing at a faster rate than agricultural production. In the subsequent decade, however, this trend could not be maintined but the share of the scondary sector, was still rising and it reached at 19.7 per cent in 1970-71. Over the seventies no change worth mentioning occurred in the structure of national output, except during 1967-77 when industrial production had shown a remarkable recovery. Eighties, however, brought a welcome change, as borne out by the recent CSO data. Based on the 1980-81 prices (the new base year now being used by the CSO), industry share in NDP which is reported as 23.3 per cent in 1981-82 went up to 25.9 per cent in 1991-92. However during the 1990s the share of industrial sector declined and it was just 21.7 per cent in 1999-2000. But during the year 2000-01, it has increased to 23.0 per cent.

(iii) Industry's Contribution to Employment. The contribution of industrial sector in providing employment is not encouraging. During 1951 to 1969, factory production rose at an annual compound rate of 7 per cent per annum, while employment rose at less than 3 per cent per annum. Recent estimates of employment elasticity with reference to the growth of manufacturing sectors shows that employment elasticity India is falling. The employment elasticity in manufacturing sector during 1972-73 to 1977-78 was 1.0 and it declined to 0.67 in 1977-78 to 1983 and further to 0.33 during 1983 to 1993-94.

If we look at the absolute number of workers employed in manufacturing sector, we find that it has increased from 34.03 million in 1983 to 42.50 million in 1933-94 and further to 48.01 million in 1999-2000. In absolute terms it looks quite impressive however in per centage terms, the importance of manufacturing as a provider of employment has not changed significantly. The per centage of workers employed in manufacturing sector has marginally increased from 11.3 per cent during 1983 to 1993-94 to 12.1 per cent in 1999-2000.

II. PATTERN OF INDUSTRIALISATION

The second important aspect of industrial growth relates to the pattern of industrialisation that has been followed since Independence. The pattern of industrialisation can be studied under two heads: *(a)* Functional Pattern of Industries, and *(b)* Ownership Pattern of Industries.

A. Functional Pattern of Industries

The pattern of industrialisation can be studies with the help of the following three criteria.

(i) compound rates of growth in different industries;

(ii) change in weights assigned to different industries;

(iii) contribution to the value-added.

(i) Compound Rate of Growth in Different Industries. Four distinct phases relating to the compond rates of growth in different industries can be observed, *viz. (a)* the first phase till mid-sixties, *(b)* the second phase of 1965-80, *(c)* the third phase of 1981-91, and *(d)* the fourth phase since 1991-92 onwards. In the earlier phase, the rate of growth of industries, in general, had picked up very fast. A major contribution in this direction was made by the basic and capital goods industries. The annual rate of growth in basic industries had gone up from 4.7% during 1051-55, to 10% during 1955-60: similarly, the annual rate of growth in capital goods industries had gone up from 9.8% during 1951-55 to 13.3% during 1955-60, and further to 19.6 during 1960-65. On the contrary, consumer goods industries recorded only a marginal growth. The annual rate of growth in these industries was only 4.8 during 1955-55 which came down to 4.4% during 1955-60, and recorded a little improvement to go up 4.9% during 1960-65. In short, the pattern of industrilisation that evolved during the first fifteen years had shown two features: one, a rapid growth of basic and capital goods industries, and two, a slow growth of consumer good industries. This pattern was in consonance with the strategy of growth evoloved during the Second Plan and followed during the subsequent Plan.

In the next phase, beginning with the mid-sixties the rate of industrial growth, as already seen, began to trigger off. The growth of basic and capital goods industries has been slower than in the past and also slower than even the meagre average growth in industrial output; where growth has been moderately high, a majority of the industries belonged either directly or indirectly to elite-oriented consumption goods' sector, like consumer durables. In the third phase, as would be seen from table below, basic goods industries picked up fast and their rate of growth accelarated between the Fifth and Sixth Plan periods, intermediate goods industries and consumer goods industries slowed down. In the first half of the Seveth Plan it was the capital goods industries sector that recorded the stupendous growth as also the basic goods industries. Intermediate goods and consumer goods industries picked up well during the First year of the Plan, but subsequently lost momentum. Over all, the growth momentum in the industrial sector during these two plans, as also during the first three years of the Seventh Plan, was maintained largely by growth in basic goods industries.

Table : Annual Average Growth Rates (Per cent)

Industry	*1974-79*	*1980-81 to 1991-92*	*1992-93 to 2000-01*
Basic Goods Ind.	8.4	7.4	5.9
Capital Goods Ind.	5.7	9.4	5.4
Intermediate Goods Ind.	4.3	4.9	8.6
Consumer Goods Ind.	5.50	6.0	6.5
All Industries	6.10	7.8	6.6

The table reveals that the industrial growth rate during 1980-81 to 1991-92 (Sixth and Seventh Plan) was 7.8 per cent and it reduced to 6.6 per cent during 1992-93 to 2000-01 (post-reform decade). This poor performance is basically due to a steep fall in the rate of growth of capital goods sector. On the other hand, the intermediate goods sector and consumers goods sector put up a better performance during 1992-93 to 2000-01. The main causes for poor performance of industrial sector are exposure to external competition, slowdown in investment, the infrastuctual constraints, lack of funds for expansion, sluggish growth in exports, anomalies in tariff structure and contraction in consumer demand.

(ii) Changes in Weighs Assigned to Different Industries. The pattern of industrialisation can also be studied with the help of changes in weight assigned to different industries. These weights are generally expressed in proportion to their share in value added in the organised manufacturing sector. The weight of capital goods industries expanded from 4.21 per centages points in 1956 to 11.76 per centage points in 1960 and further to 18.66% in 1965; subsequently, the weight of consumer goods industries declined from 48.37 in 1956 to 37.25 in 1960, and further to 30.89 in 1965. It, however, increased to 31.03 in 1970. During the seventies, the weight of basic and capital goods industries kept on falling down, while that of consumer goods industries moved up. The following table revals the weights in index of industrial production.

Weights in Index of Industrial Production

	1951	*1960*	*1970*	*1980*	*1990*
Basic Goods	19.8	25.1	32.3	39.4	38.4
Capital Goods	3.5	11.8	15.3	16.4	23.7
Intermediate Goods	29.0	25.9	21.0	20.5	17.5
Consumer Goods	47.6	37.3	31.5	23.7	20.4
Denable Goods	–	5.7	3.4	2.6	–
Non-durable Goods	–	31.6	28.1	21.1	–

(iii) Contribution to the Value added. The industrial sector growth rate in post-reform decade has declined in comparison to the pre-reform decade. Similarly the compound annual rate of growth of manufacturing sector during the 1990-91 to 1998-99 has also fell in comparison to pre-reform decade.

Table : Compound Annual Rate of Growth of Manufacturing

(Per cent)

Year	*Combined Rate of Growth of Gross value added of Registered Manufacturing Sector at Constant Prices*
1950-51 to 1965-66	7.03
1955-56 to 1965-66	7.47
1980-81 to 1990-91	7.66
1990-91 to 1998-99	5.91

This table reveals that the rate of growth of growth value added in industry during pre-reform period was highest *i.e.* more than 7.0 per cent per annum. But the gross value added in industry during the eight year period of 1990s (1990-91 to 1998-99) was just 5.91 per cent per annum. It was lowest. This shows that economic reforms and 'opening up' of the inudstrial economy in 1990s did not accelerate industrial growth as expected but slowed it down. Moreover, as the above table shows the growth record during the reforms of 1990s has been worse than the during 1980s.

B. Ownership Pattern of Industries

On the basis of the type of ownership, the industrial units can be divided into the following categories: *(i)* public sector, *(ii)* joint sector and *(iii)* private sector. Table presents information on the structure of Indian industrial sector by type of ownership for the year 1996-97.

This table reveals the following factors regarding the structure of Indian industries by type of ownership:

1. The total number of factories in 1996-97 was 1,34,556 of which as many as 1,22,772 (*i.e.* 91.2 per cent) were in the

private sector. Only 8,825 units (6.6 per cent) were in the public sector.

2. Of the total fixed capital of Rs. 3,84,560 crore in the industrial sector in 1996-97, as much as Rs. 1,42,156 crore (*i.e.* 36.9 per cent) was in the public sector. The share of the private sector was Rs. 2,12,920 crore (*i.e.* 55.4 per cent). Thus with only 6.6 per cent of the factories, the public sector had 36.9 per cent of fixed capital. This shows that the public sector units are much more capital intensive as compared with the private sector units.

Table : Structure of Indian Industry of Ownership 1996-97

	Factories Number	*Employment '000s*	*Fixed capital*	*Gross output*	*Value added*
			Rs. crore		
Public Sector	8,825 (6.6)	2,285 (23.5)	1,42,156 (36.9)	1,51,174 (21.8)	36,915 (25.8)
Joint Sector	2,899 (2.2)	524 (5.5)	29,416 (7.6)	59,882 (8.7)	11,458 (8.0)
Private Sector	1,22,772 (91.2)	6,891 (71.0)	2,12,920 (55.4)	4,81,218 (69.5)	94,664 (66.2)
Unspecified	60 (...)	7 (...)	68 (...)	246 (...)	39 (...)
Total	1,34,556 (100.0)	9,707 (100.0)	3,84,560 (100.0)	6,92,520 (100.0)	1,43,076 (100.0)

3. Out of the gross output of Rs. 6,92,520 crore, the private sector units contributed Rs. 4,81,218 crore (or 69.5 per cent). As against this, the public sector units contributed Rs. 1,51,174 crore of gross output which is 21.8 per cent of the total.

4. Total employment in the industrial sector was 9,707 thousand in 1996-97. Of this, 71.0 per cent were employed in the private sector and 23.5 per cent in the public sector.

5. The Industrial Policy Enquiry Committee which was constituted by the Government of India in July 1967 under the chairmanship of Dr. Subimal Dutt had strongly recommended the setting up of the joint sector. However, the concept proved to be a still born child. As is clear from table only 2.2 per cent indusrial units were in the joint sector in 1996-97 and they possessed only 7.6 per cent of fixed capital and provided employment to only 5.5 per cent industrial labour. Their share in gross output was 8.7 per cent and in value added, 8.0 per cent in 1996-97.
6. The total value added in the industrial sector in 1996-97 was Rs. 1,43,076 crore. Of this, private sector contributed Rs. 94,664 crore (66.2 per cent) and the public sector contributed Rs. 36,915 crore (25.8 per cent).

FEATURES OF INDUSTRIAL GROWTH

Some distinguishing, but disturbing, features of the industrial development process in India can be indentified as follows:

Firstly, along with external financial assistance, technological dependence on MNCs increased. The old private foreign capital, which had operated in the colonial period, worked mainly through branches in India or through managing agency house. It was organised in pools which were small by the standard of metropolitan countries and operated in areas like trade, finance and export oriented activites. A goods part of this capital either left the country in the wake of independence or clung on in a stagnant or precarious state. The new private foreign capital which entered particularly during the Second and Third Plans went into technologically intensive areas and produced mainly for the domestic market which was cordoned off by high protective barriers.

Secondly, industrial growth was accompanied by a considerable increase in the country's indebtedness. The share of foreign aid, as a proportion of gross investment, of Plan outlay and of national income increased dramatically during the decade 1955-65. The entire industrialisation drive, however, impressive, was indeed far from being financially self-reliant.

Thirdly, industrialisation in India had virtually a negligible impact on either unemployment or the sectoral distribution of the work-force. The employment-creating capacity of industrialisation was not enough either to make a dent in the backlog of urban unemployment which also experienced a natural growth over time or to absorb immigrants from rural areas. The economic stagnation since the mid-sixties worsened the unemployment situation.

Fourthly, inudstrial growth in India has been accompanied by a virtual stagnation in real wages. This is not to say that with changing industrial composition and the creation of many more skilled job, opportunities have not been opened up or utilised but the picture of stagnation remains roughly valid for any particular category of workers, especially unskilled workers.

Fifthly, although the share of agro-based industries has dclined over the years the impact of agricultural growth on industrial growth does not seem to have weakened. This is borne out by the fact that as Prof. K.N. Raj has noted the fluctuations in indusrial production are preceded by fluctuation in agricultural production.

Finally, few of the industrial groups appear to have bccn interested in providing for systematic reasearch. In this respect, the Indian experience has been contrary to the Japanese and this lacuna, to be traced historically perhaps to the dominance of trading and money lending communities in industrial entrepreneurship in India and an explicit state policy for import-substitution in an attentuated from through the planning period for different reasons arising primarily from the operation of industrial and trade policies.

PROBLEMS OF INDUSTRIAL GROWTH

(i) Growth of Big Industrial Houses. Despite the various policy measures taken by the Government such as the MRTP Act and the licensing policy, the share of the large industrial house in the total assests of the private corporate sector has increased. According to Prof. S.K. Goyal, "during the period 1964 and 1976, the number of Big Houses in India rose from 33 to 75; and the number of large independent undertakings increased from 8 to 26. The combined assets of the big houses and the large independent undertakings expanding from Rs. 2,412.04 crore to Rs. 8,955.70 crore in 1979, *i.e.*, an increase of 271.3% in 13 years". And, similarly, a recent study by the Economics Times Research Bureau has brought out that as on March 31, 1990, the 20 large industrial houses had assets worth Rs. 33, 919 crore constituting 68.9 per cent of the assets of 78 large industrial houses. The top 10 houses, have total assets worth Rs. 1,53,091 crore in the year 1998-99. The largest house in terms of assets and not sales in Tata. This industrial house had assets worth Rs. 47,446 were in 1998-99. This shows that large indusrial houses worth most in the post liberalisation phase.

(ii) Increase in Regional Imbalances. Another unfavourable aspect of the industrial science is the imbalance that exists in the industrial development of different regions. Massive investment in the Central sector projects in the expectation that this would have a wide ranging 'ripple effect' in stimulating small and ancillary industries have not succeed in many states such as Bihar, Orissa and Madhya Pradesh. The natural tendency of enterpreneurs to go where the infrastructure is strong, markets are close and various services are readily available cannot be ignored.

(iii) Higher Cost of Industrial Product. Another weakness of the industrial scene is the high cost of some of its products as compared to international prices. *(a)* This has partly arisen out of the absence of healthy competition, a situation which industrial licensing tends to foster. High tarriff barriers and tight controls on imports have tended to shield these units from international competition and projected them from the consequences of the relatively low rate of inflation in India as compared to other countries. Non-competitiveness, in general, has resulted in the slowing down of growth through a pervasive waste in the utilisation of scarce capital resources or a parts of the economy. Dealing with it is, therefore, important not only for the export effort but more fundamentally to bring about an acceleration in the rate of economic growth in the country. *(b)* High costs have sometimes been a direct outcome of the Government's licensing policy. Where the demand was large enough to sustain only one plant of an economic size, several plants with suboptimal capacity were licensed in the name of diffusing ownership and preventing monopolies. *(c)* In the policy of import substitution also insufficient attention has been paid to costs and a few industries have been set up whose cost of production is not low according to international standards. While this may be necessary in certain strategic areas, it was not essential in many other.

(iv) Industry's Dependence on the Government. A consequences of a regime of government-imposed constraints has been that the industry has become heavily dependent upon the government. Hence the contradictory demands that the government should reduce this tax or duty (to protect an importer), raise that duty (to protect a local manufacturer), make imports easier or more difficult, allow the expansion of capacity (to achieve economies of scale) or prevent new capacity from coming up (to protect existing producers), etc. If an individual unit or an industry faces a problem and a simple, adaptive answer is elusive, the tendency is to run to the government for help without making a thorough search for self-relient solution. This habit has become widespread and even those without fewer controls often fall a prey to the soft option of appealing to the government for an instant solution usually with a penalty to offers or to the economy as a whole.

(v) Lack of Proper Employment Planning. Perhaps the most serious lacuna in our industrial planning has been the lack of attention paid to the employment implications in choosing technologies. The main victim of this policy has been the cottage sector where the growth of industries like textiles, oil crushing, shop making, matches, leather and leather goods has been stifled. Another area in which industrial development could have been directed better both from the point of view of cost reduction and employment generation is the development of ancillaries particularly by way of off-loading existing low technology activities to the small-scale and ancillary industry. While there have been areas and industries which have done well in this field, the rate of growth of ancillaries suggests that inadequate attention has been paid to this problem.

(vi) Sickness in Industry. The incidence of sickness in large and medium-scale industries has increased in recent year; and in the case of some of the traditional industries like cotton textiles, jute textiles and sugar, the economic viability of a large number of units has been seriously eroded. The phenomenon of industrial sickness not only tends to aggravate the problem of unemployment, but also renders infructuous capital investment any generally creates an adverse climate for further industrial growth. While in advanced countries, where there are adequate social security benefits, this is accepted as a normal features of the industrial scene, such sickness has much more serious economic consequences in a country where unemployment is a major problem and resources are scarce.

(vii) Growing Dependence of the Organised Private Sector on Financial Institutions. The growing capital-intensive nature of industry and relatively high corporate tax rates have increased the dependence of the organised private sector on financial institutions. This has meant that the role of financial institutions in financing new ventures has grown substantially. Increasingly, therefore, the agencies which determine the pattern and structure of industrial growth are the term lending institutions rather than the Industrial Licensing Committee which at best can play a negative role. Since this is not the purpose for which these institutions were set up, some new mechanism would have to be devised to ensure that the flow of funds from financial institutions is in accordance with national priorities.

(viii) Poor Productivity Performance. Dr. Hollis Chenery in a recent study covering 40 countries has found India at the bottom of the list in terms of productivity growth. Productivity growth has been a major contributing factor, in the economic growth of many industrial countries. Productivity can be measured either in the form of a partial productivity like labour productivity, capital productivity and material productivity, or as total factor productivity (TFP). Labour productivity can be defined as the output per unit of labour. Other partial productivities are also similarly defined. TFP is defined as the ratio between real product or output and real factor input (a weighted sum of the different inputs). TFP is a better measure of productivity as it relates output to all the conventional inputs simultaneously.

(ix) Underutilisation of Industrial Capacity. Another major problem of industrial development in India has been the underutilisation of industrial capacity. Some of the important industries have been reporting utilisation rates of only 50 to 60 per cent. Underutilisation poses serious problems to the process of growth. All out efforts have to be made to create conditions conductive to optimm utilisation of capacity.

INDUSTRIAL POLICY

At the time of independence, there was no well coordinated industrial policy of India. The Government of India along with investors and entrepreneurs felt the need of a well coordinated industrial policy because rapid growth of industries was almost impossible in the absence of such an industrial policy. Consequently within less than one year after independent the Government of India announced the Industrial policy Resolution on 6th April 1948.

INDUSTRIAL POLICY RESOLUTION 1948

The Government of India evolved its first new Industrial policy after independence which envisaged a mixed economy with overall responsibility of the government to secure planned development of industries and their regulation. The government also acknowledged the valuable role of the private entreprise properly directed and regulated. The main features of this industrial are the following:

(i) Acceptance of the importance of both private and public sectors.

(ii) **Division of the Industrial Sector.** The Resolution divided industries in four categories namely—*(a)* industries where state has the monopoly (3 industries); *(b)* mixed sector (6 industries); (c) the field of government control (18 industries); and (d) the field of private enterprise (all other industries not included in the above three categories.

(iii) Role of small and cottage industries.

(iv) Other important features (less importance to foreign investment, harmonious relations between management and labour force).

Indian capitalists were satisfied with the Industiral Policy Resolution of 1948 since the role assigned to the public sector in that policy was, on the whole, acceptable to them. However, there were certain weakness and gaps in the 1948 policy and it was subjected to a number of criticisms.

INDUSTRIAL POLICY RESOLUTION OF 1956

In 1956 came the second Industrial policy Resolution of the Government of India which sought to start an era of stabilisation against the background of the declared goal of a socialist pattern of society.

The 1956 Resolution laid down the following objectives for the industrial policy: *(i)* to accelerate the rate of growth and to speed up industrialization; *(ii)* to develop heavy industries and machine making industries; *(iii)* to expand public sector; *(iv)* to reduce disparities in income and wealth; *(v)* to build up a large and growing cooperative sector; and *(vi)* to prevent monopolies and the concentration of wealth and income in the hands of a small number of individuals. The main features of this Resolutions are the following:

1. **Division of the Industrial Sector.** As against four categories in the 1948 Resolution, the 1956 Resolution divided industries into the following three categories:

   (a) Monopoly of the State. In the first category, those industries were included whose future development would be the exclusive responsibility of the State.

Seventeen industries were included in this category and were listed in Schedule A. Of these, four industries—arms and amunition, atomic energy, railways and air transport, were to be governement monopolies. In the remaining 13 industries, all new units were to be established by the State. However, existing units in the private sector were allowed to subsist and expand.

(b) ***Mixed Sector of Public and Private Enterprise.*** In this section 12 industries listed in Schedule B (appended to the Resolution) were included. In these industries, State would increasingly establish new units and increase its participation but would not deny the private sector opportunities to set up units or expand existing units.

(c) ***Industries Left for Private Sector.*** All industries not listed in schedules 'A' or 'B' were included in the third category. The main role of the state in this category was to provide facilities to the private sector to develop itself.

2. **Assistance and Control of Private Sector.** According to the 1956 Resolution, the government could assist expansion and development of private sector through participation in its risk capital and share capital and by providing other types of services, fiscal incentive etc. However, the private sector was also to fit into the "framework of the economic and social policy of the State". Thus, the private sector was to remain subject to various government regulations and controls. Such regulation and control was to be exercised by the government through the Industries (Development and Regulation) Act, 1951, and other related legislations.

3. **Mutual Dependence of Public and Private Sectors.** The only four industries in which private sector was not allowed to function were arms and ammunition, atomic energy, railway and air transport. In all other industries either to private sector was allowed to operate freely or its help

could be obtained if the government deemed fit. Accordingly, the 1956 Resolution emphasized not only the mutual coexistence of private and public sectors but also provided for their mutual cooperation and help.

4. **Importance of Small-scale and Cottage Industries.** The 1956 Resolution recognized the importance of small-scale and cottage industries just as the 1948 Resolution had done. Such industries could create large scale employment opportunities, ensure a more equitable distribution of income and wealth, and help in effective mobilization of human and physical capital. Assistance to this sector was to be provided either through direct means or through indirect means.

5. **Technical and Managerial Personnel.** Shortage of technical and managerial personnel to carry out the programmes of industrial development in the economy has been accepted and emphasized by the government right from the beginning of the planning era. According, the 1956 Resolution advocated the establishment of proper technical and managerial cadres through the organisation of apprenticeship schemes of training on a large scale, establishment of technical institutions, etc.

6. **Reduction of Regional Inequalities.** The 1956 Resolution called for reduction in regional imbalances and inequalities. For this purpose it was advocated that transport facilities, power and other facilities should be provided in the backward regions. Stress on balanced development of agriculture and industry in each region was also laid.

An Appraisal of the Industrial Policy of 1956. The industrial policy of 1956 contemplated a mixed or controlled economy in which public and private enterprises work hand in hand so as to make the development plan a success. The industrial policy of 1956 has been appreciated for bringing about an excellent synchronisation between government's industrial policy and industrial development programmes included in the plan. The 1956 industrial Policy was a positive Policy improvement over the 1948 industrial policy since it was broader and more liberal. The 1956 industrial policy has held good till today even though some changes have been made in it in the last few years.

Cooperative Sector. In respect of agro-industries specially industries processing sugarcane, jute and other agricultural commodities, preference in licensing will be given to applicants from cooperative sector.

INDUSTRIAL POLICY RESOLUTION OF 1980

The 1980 industrial policy is based on 1956 Industrial policy. As a matter of fact it is a supplement to it. The new Industrial production through optimum utilisation of the installed capacity and expansion of industries. The policy emphasises on rapid and Balanced industrialisation of the country with a view to benefitting the common man by increasing availability of goods at reasonable prices, larger employment and higher per capita income. The new policy aims at the revival of the economy by solving the problems of shortages of major industrial inputs like energy, transport and coal. This industrial policy has been formulated to achieve these objectives-modernisation, expansion and development to backward areas or regions.

The 1980 industrial policy also emphasise the need to make available the benefits of industrialisation to all the sectors of the society by extending preferential treatment to agro-based industries, by promoting the development of small, medium, and large enterprises, by promoting the dispersal of industries in backward rural and urban areas and protecting consumers against high prices and bad quality of goods.

Chief Objectives and Features. The 1980 industrial policy envisages the following objectives:

(i) Maximum use of the existing production capacity;

(ii) to obtain the highest level of production;

(iii) to give priority to agro based industries and there by strengthen the agricultural base;

(iv) to remove regional imbalance by giving priority to development of industrially backward areas;

(v) to create more employment opportunities;

(vi) to accelerate the development of export oriented and import substitution industries;

(vii) to protect consumers against high prices and bad quality goods;

(viii) to encourage economic federation through coordinate development of small medium and large enterprises.

Growth of Cottage, Village and Small Industries. The limits of Industries were enhanced as follows:

(i) tiny units-from one lakh rupees to two lakh rupees.

(ii) small scale units-from ten lakh rupees to twenty lakh rupees.

(iii) ancillary units-from fifteen lakh rupees to 25 lakh rupees.

Sectors where efficient production can be secured on a small scale would continue to be reserved for future expansion only by the small scale units.

3. Public Sector. The policy statement reiterates that public confidence in the public sector would be restored and the public sector would continue to occupy a vital position in the country's economic structure.

4. Private Sector. The private sector industries would also be allowed to develop in accordance with the objectives and targets of national plans and policies. However, the government would not allow monopolistic tendencies to grow in the private sector units.

5. Removal of Regional Imbalances. To achieve this end the policy encourages the establishment of new industrial units in industrially backward areas. Further, for securing greater regional balance the policy emphasises the dispersal of those industries in which economics of scale are not important. This would be economically and socially desirable. Special concession and government aids would be made available in industrially backward areas.

6. Export Production. This industrial policy statement also emphasises on increasing export production. To achieve this end 100 per cent export oriented units would be set up the existing units would be expanded exclusively for purpose of export.

7. Technological Self Reliance. The industrial policy statement lay adequate stress on keeping the technology in use up to date. To achieve this end import of technology particularly for export oriented and key industries may be liberalised.

8. Sick Units. The industrial policy statement reiterates that strict action would be taken against those industrial units which are sick by their own mismanagement and financial misappropriation. Government would determine such sick units which are found in critical condition. The government would make effort to revive such sick units by encouraging them to merge into healthy units who are in a position to revive them.

NEW INDUSTRIAL POLICY 1991

The Congress (I) Government led by Mr. Narasimha Rao has announced the new industrial policy on July 24, 1991. The main aim of the new industrial policy is to unshackle the Indian industrial economy from the cobwebs of unnecessary bureaucratic control, to introduce liberalisation with a view of integrate the Indian economy with the world economy, to remove restrictions on direct foreign investment as also to free the domestic entrepreneur from the restrictions of MRTP Act. All these reforms of industrial policy have led the government to take a series of initiatives in respect of policies in the following areas:

1. Industrial Licensing. In the sphere of industrial licensing, the role of the government was to be changed from that of only exercising control to one of providing help and guidance by making essential procedures fully transparent and by eliminating delays. This calls for bold and imaginative decisions designed to remove restraints on capacity creation, which at the same time, ensure that over-riding national interests are not jeopardised. The industrial licensing will henceforth be abolished for all industries, except those specified, irrespective of levels of investment. These specified industries will continue to be subject to compulsory licensing for reasons related to security and strategic concerns, social reasons, problems related to safety and overriding environmental issues, manufacture of products of hazardous nature and arcticles of elitist consumption.

2. Foreign Investment. In order to invite foreign investment in high priority industries, requiring large investment and advanced technology, it has been decided to provide approval for direct foreign investment upto 51 per cent foreign equity in such industries. For the promotion of exports of Indian products in world markets, the government will encourage foreign trading companies to assist Indian exporters in export activities. Besides this, the government will appoint a special board to negotiate with such firms so that purposive negotiations can be carried out with such large firms which provide the avenues for large investment in the development of industries and technology in the national interest.

3. Public Sector Policy. Public enterprises have shown a very low rate to return on the capital invested. This has inhibited their ability to regenerate themselves in terms of new investments as well as in technology development. The result is that many of the public enterprises have become a burden rather than being an asset to the Government. The original concept of the public sector has also undergone considerable dilution. The most striking example is the take over of sick units from the private sector. The category of public sector units accounts for almost one-third of the total losses of central public enterprises. Another category of public enterprises, which does not fit into the original idea of the public sector being at the commanding heights of the economy, is the plethora of public enterprises which are in the consumer goods and services sectors.

It is time therefore that the Government adopt a new approach to public enterprises. Units which may be faltering at present but are potentially viable must be restructured and given a new lease of life. The priority areas for growth of public enterprises in the future will be the following:

(a) Essential infrastructure goods and services.

(b) Exploration and exploitation of oil and mineral resources.

(c) Technology development and building of manufacturing capabilities in areas which are crucial in the long term development of the economy and where private sector invesment is inadequate.

(d) Manufacture of products where strategic considerations predominate such as defence equipment.

Government will strengthen those public enterprises which fall in the reserved areas of operation or are in high priority areas or are generating good or reasonable profits. Such enterprises will be provided a much greater degree of management autonomy through the system of memoranda of understanding. Competition will also be induced in these areas by inviting private sector participation. In the case of selected enterprises, part of Government holdings in the equity share capital of these enterprises will be disinvested in order to provide further market discipline to the performance of public enterprises. There are a large number of chronically sick public enterprises incurring heavy losses, operating a competitive market and serve little or not public purpose. These need to be attended to.

4. Foreign Technology. With a view to injecting the desired level of technological dynamism in Indian industry, government will provide automatic approval for technology agreements related to high priority industries within specified parameters.

Similar facilities will be available for other industries as well if such agreements do not require the expenditure of free foriegn exchange. Indian companies will be free to negotiate the terms of technology transfer with their foreign conterparts according to their own commerical judgement.

5. Industrial Location Policy Liberalilsed. In a departure from the earlier locational policy for industries, the new industrial policy stated that in locations other than cities of more than 1 million population, there will be no requirement of obtaining industrial approvals from the Centre, except for industries subject to compulsory licensing. In cities with a population of more than 1 million, industries other than those of a non-polluting nautre, were required to be located outside 25 kms of the priphery. Major amendments in the industrial location policy were effected during 1997-98. Now notified industries of a non-polluting nature such as electronics, computer softwer and printing, may be located within 25 kms of the periphery of cities with more than 1 million population. Other industries are permitted only if they are located in designated industrial areas set up prior to July 25, 1991. Zoning and Land Use Regulation as well as Environment Legislation continue to regulate industrial locations.

6. Monoplies and Restrictive Trade Practices Act (MRTP) Act. With the growing complexity of industrial structure and the need for achieving economies of scale for ensuring higher productivity and competitive advantage in the international market, the interference of the Government through the MRTP Act in investment decision of large companies has become deleterious in its effects on Indian industrial growth. The pre-entry scrutiny of investment decisions by so-called MRTP companies will no longer be required. Instead, emphasis will be on controlling and regulating monopolistic, restrictive and unfair trade practices rather than making it necessary for the monopoly houses to obtain prior approval of Central Government for expansion, establishment of new undertakings, mergers, amalgamation and takeover and appointment of certain directors. The trust policy will be more on controlling unfair or restrictive business practices.

7. Removal of Mandatory Convertibility Clause. A lare part of industrial investment in India is financed by loans from banks and financial institutions. These institutions have followed a mandatory practice of including a convertibility clause in their loans into equity if felt necessary by their management. Although this option has not generally been exercised, it has often been interpreted as an unwarranted threat to private firms of takeover by financial institutions. The new industrial policy has provided that henceforth financial institutions will not impose this mandatory convertibility clause.

8. Abolition of Phased Manufacturing Programmes for New Projects. To force the pace of indigenisation in manufacturing, Phased Manufacturing Programmes have been in force in a number of engineering and electronic industries. The new industrial policy has abolished such programmes in future as the government feels that due to substantial reforms made in the trade policy and the devaluation of the rupee, there is no longer any need for enforcing the local content requirements on a case-by-case, administrative basis. Various incentives that are currently available to manufacturing units with existing Phased Manufacturing Programmes will continue.

According to J.C. Sandesara, the new indutrial policy seeks to raise efficiency and accelerate industrial production in five different ways.

(1) The changes in repsect of foreign investment and foreign technology agreements are also designed to attract capital, technology and managerial expertise from abroad. This will raise the availability of such scarce resources in the country on the one hand, and will improve the level of efficiency of production on the other hand.

(2) Some changes as regards public sector may enhance the 'allocative efficiency'. Opening up to eleven areas (so far reserved for the public sector) to the private sector implies an opening for the sector which has, by the large, given a better account of itself. Closure, liquidation or rehabilitation etc. of sick/weak public sector units will free resources for more productive use. Similarly, privatisation may make for improved efficiency of the public sector, through its being subjected to the stock market discipline.

(3) A number of changes in industrial licensing policy, foreign investment, foreign technology agreements and MRTP Act are such as to do away with the prior clearance of the government. In such cases, project time and 'getting things done' will be reduced. Material and human resources engaged in cultivating contacts and 'getting things done' will be released for more productive uses. Thus efficiency will improve.

(4) Greater emphasis in controlling and regulating monopolistic, restrictive and unfair trade practices and the strengthening of powers of the MRTP Commission will curb anti-competitive behaviour of firms in the monopolistic,

oligopolistic and ineffectively competitive markets and thus promote competition and efficiency.

(5) Other measure in this area such as purposeful formulation and implementation of Memorandum of Understanding and its monitoring, professionalisation and greater autonomy may be expected to improve the performance of the enterprises that will remain in the public sector.

Critics of the new industrial policy, however, point to the dangers of 'opening up' the economy to too much foreign influence. For instance, H.K. Paranjape argues that the list of high priority industries (in which direct foreign investment up to 51 per cent will now be freely permitted) includes industries which have been well established in the country for long and where technological development with indigenous R and D should not prove difficult. Invitation to foreign investors in these industries "would make it possible for large transnationals to dominate certain growing areas of our economy and push to the wall any Indian concerns which attempt to stand out on their own. Indigenous R and D will be doomed." Moreover, as correctly pointed out by Parajape, the past record of the multinationals operating in the country does not warrant much enthusiasm. None of the multinationals operating in this country has attempted to develop India as an important base for a significant part of its world-wide research and development work. Despite various tax concessions and incentives none of the multinationals tried to expand export markets. They undertook export activities only to the extent they were compelled to do so under export obligations, or when it was found necessary to do so in order to be able to earn foreign exchange for importing some of their essential requirements. In fact, instead of developing India as a major production and export base, many multinationals have only attempted to use their international trade capacities and contacts mainly for exporting goods manufactured by other—usually small scale—units. Thus they have operated more as trading than as manufacturing and exporting concerns.

Moreover, despite talks of globalisation, many rich countries are reluctant to permit unrestricted export of technologies as, in many areas, technologies are common for civilian and defence-related items. Multinationals which make a technological breakthrough are also usually reluctant to permit the use of their up-to-date technologies even by their subsidiaries unless these are located in politically 'safe' countries. India obviously does not satisfy this criterion from the viewpoint of these multinational companies, or the defence authorities of the USA and other rich countries. Coming to the import of foreign technology, Paranjape again expresses some reservations. According to him, in the whole eagerness to import foreign technology, little attention seems to have been paid to the possibility that production and managerial technologies found more suitable in other countries may not necessarily prove to be the best in our circumstances. As correctly pointed out by him, one of the very purposes of India's industrialisation is to ensure that our very large manpower resources are effectively utilised. This implies the adoption of labour-intensive and capital saving technologies in whichever areas it is feasible to do so. This may imply major readjustments in technologies that have developed in the labour scarce and capital abundant rich countries. This will not be an easy task.

❐

10

Foreign Trade Policies

IMPORT-EXPORT ACT, 1947

Economic development is characterised by the growth of the foreign trade sector and the structural changes in the economy are usually reflected in the changes in the direction and composition of foreign trade. Government of India earlier imposed many types of restrictions has relaxed its export and import policy recently. The objective of commercial policy of India is to transform the business sector according to the Objectives of national development.

In India, the trade is required because of following reasons:

1. To have favourable balance of payments and increase in foreign exchange reserves.
2. To protect domestic industries from the competition from rest of the world.
3. To encourage import substitution.
4. The encourage exports and for export promotion.
5. To keep foreign exchange reserves upto a reasonable extent.
6. To develop economy of India.

The role of foreign trade has become very important in India. The value of foreign trade has been increased many folds since the introduction of first five year plan. The value of foreign trade Rs. 1972 crores in 1950-51 increased to Rs. 75,698 crores in 1990-91. If we look at data of foreign trade, then we find that the gap between export and import value is continuously increasing like Import and Export control Act. 1947 etc. steps to reduce the gap between export value took many steps like import and export control Act, 1947 etc. to reduce the gap between export value and import value. Now we shall discuss import and Export act, 1947 in detail.

IMPORTS AND EXPORTS (CONTROL) ACT

The Imports and Exports (control) Act 1947, amended from time to time empowers the central government to prohibit or control certain imports and exports in the public interest.

The act enables the Central Government to make provisions for prohibiting, restricting or otherwise controlling:

(a) The import, export, carriage, stores of goods of any specified desription; and

(b) The bringing into any part or place in India of goods of specified description intended to be taken out of India without being removed from ship or conveyance in which they are being carried.

The Government can also prohibit, restrict or impose conditions on the clearance, whether for homes consumption or for shipment abroad, of any goods or class of goods imported into India.

There are provision in the Act according to which imported goods or materials can be confiscated in certain cases. An authorised person, as specified in the Act, may enter, at any reasonable time, any premises in which any imported goods or materials which are liable to confiscation under this Act are suspected to have been kept or concealed, and inspect such imported goods or materials as he may think fit. Such kinds of inspections may be made by the authorised person of any books of account or other documents of things which, in his opinion, will be useful for, or relevant to, any proceeding under this Act. If the authorised person has any reason to believe that any such imported goods or materials or documents are secreted in any place, he may enter into the search such place or premises for them. If the authorised person has any reason to believe that any imported goods or materials are liable to confiscation under this Act, he may seize them. Where it is not practicable to seize andy such goods or materials, the authorised person any serve on the owner of the goods or materials an order that he shall not remove, part with or otherwise deal with, the goods or materials, except with the previous permission of such authorised person.

Any imported goods or materials in respect of which:

(a) any condition of the licence of letter of authority, under which they were imported, relating to the utilisation or distribution of such goods or materials, or

(b) any condition relating to the utilisation or distribution of such goods or materials subject to which they were received from, or through, a recognised agency, or

(c) any direction given under the control order with regard to the sale of such goods or materials, has been, is being or is attempted to be, contravened shall, together with any package, covering or receptacle in which such goods are found, be liable to confiscation and, where such goods or materials are so mixed with any other goods or materials that they cannot be readily separated, such other goods or materials shall also be liable to confiscation.

It has been laid down in the act that any authorised person may stop, or compel to land, as the case may be, any conveyance or animal which is suspected to be used or is about to be used for the transport of any imported goods of materials liable to confiscation under this Act, and search/examine the conveyance and the goods or materials in the conveyance or on the animal.

Any means of transport which has been is being or is attempted to be, used for the transport of any imported goods or materials which are liable to confiscation under this act, shall be liable to confiscation unless the owner of the means of transport proves that it was, is being or is about to be, so used without the knowledge or connivance of the owner himself, his agent, if any, and the person in change of the conveyance or animal, and that each of them has taken all reasonable precautions against such use.

IMPORTS (CONTROL) ORDER

In exercise of the powers conferred by the impors and exports control Act 1947, the central government made on 7th December,

1955, an order namely, the Imports (Control) Order, 1955. This Order has been amended from time to time.

This Imports (Control) order prohibits the import of any goods of the description specified on schedule I of the order except under, and in accordance with, a licence or a customs permit granted by the central government or by any officer specified in schedule II of the order.

The order lays down that it, in any case, it is found that the goods imported under licence do not conform in every respect *(i)* to the description or value of the goods as contained in the licence, or *(ii)* to the other conditions relating to such goods, contained in, or applicable to the licence, the Import of Such Goods shall be deemed to be Prohibited.

The order states that the licensing authority issuing a Licence under this order may issue the same subject to one or more of the conditions stated below:

(i) That the goods converted by the licence shall not be disposed of except in the manner prescribed the licensing authority or otherwise dealt with without the written permission of the licensing authority or any peron duly authorised by it;

(ii) That the goods coverd by the licence on importation shall not be sold or distributed at a price exceeding that which may be specified in any direction attached to the licence;

(iii) That the applicant for a licence shall excute a bond for complying with the terms subject to which a licence may be granted.

A licence granted under the order shall also be subject to the conditions contained in schedule *V*, which deals with certain payment conditions, "Actual user" conditions applicable to import licences issued to "Actual User", and conditions applicable to licences issued for the import of capital goods.

It has also been laid down that it shall be deemed to be a condition of every such licence that:

(i) No person shall transfer and so person shall acquire by transfer any licence issued by the licensing authority except under, and in accordance with, the written permission of the authority which ranted the licence or any person empowered in this behalf by such authority;

(ii) The goods for the import of which a licence is granted shall be the property of the licences at the time of import and thereafter up to the time of clearance through the customs. (There two conditions, however, shall not apply to licences issued to the State Trading Corporation of India, the Minerals and Metals Trading Corporation of India and other similar institutions or agencies owned or controlled by the central overnment and which are entrusted with the canalisation of imports. The above two conditions shall also not apply to the licences issued to eligible Export Houses for the import of goods meant for disposal to actual users under the import policy for registered exporters);

(iii) The goods for the import of which a licence has been granted shall be new goods, other than disposal goods, unless otherwise stated in the licence.

A licence granted under this order may contain such other conditions, not inconsistent with the Act or this order, as the licensing authority may deem fit.

A licence shall comply with all the conditions imposed or deemed to be imposed under the order.

The Order also deals with the details of matters like refusal of licence; amendement of licence; power to debar from importing goods or from receiving licences or allotment of imported goods; power to suspend importation of goods; grant of licences or allotments of imported goods power to keep in abeyance applications for licences or allotments or imported goods. Cancellation of licences; declaration as to the value, sort, quality etc. of imported goods; uilistion of imported goods; power to make directions for the sale of imported goods in certain cases; exceptions from this order, etc.

EXPORT CONTROL ORDER

In exercise of the powers conferred by the imports and exports (control) Act, 1947, the central government on 24th March, 1977, made an order called the Exports (control) order, 1977.

The exports control order restricts the export of certain goods. Accordingly, no person shall accordingly, no person shall export any goods of the description specified granted by the central government or by an officer specified in schedule II of the order {clause 3(1)}. The same rule is applicable to exports to Pakistan {Clause 3(2)}.

Notwithstanding anything contained in sub-clauses (1) and (2) mentioned above, goods specified in schedule III of the order may be exported on fulfilment of the terms and conditions specified therein.

The order states that if, in any case, it is found that the value, sort, specification, quality and description of the goods to the exported are not in conformity with the declaration of exporter in those respects, or if the quality and specification of such goods are not in accordance with terms of the export contract, the export of such goods shall be deemed to be prohibited.

It has been laid down in the exports (control) order that a licence granted under this order may contain such condition, not inconsistent with the Imports and Exports (Control) Act, 1947, or this order, as the licensing authority may deem fit.

It shall be deemed to be a condition of every licence that:

(i) No person shall transfer and no person shall acquire by transfer any licence issued by the licensing authority except under, and in accordance with, the written permission of the authority which granted the licence or of any other person empowered in this helf by such authority,

(ii) The goods for the export of which the licences has been granted shall be the property of the licence at the time of the export.

The licence shall comply with all the conditions imposed or deemed to be imposed under the relevant clause of the order.

The order also deals with the details of matters like refusal of licences amendment of licences, power to debar from receiving licences of exporting goods, power to suspend grant of licences or permission to export goods, cancellation of licences, declaration as to value, sort, quality, etc., of exported goods, prohibition regarding making, signing, etc., of any documentation, statement of document, exemptions from the order, etc.

FOREIGN TRADE ACT, 1992

Foreign Trade (Development and Regulation) Act, 1992 replaced the Imports and Exports (Control) Act, 1947. The objective of the Act is to provide for the development and regulation of foreign trade by facilitating imports into and augmenting exports from, India and for matters connected therewith or incidental thereto.

The main provision of the Act are as follows:

1. Power to Make Provisions Relating to Imports and Exports. Section 3 of the Act deals with the powers to make provisions relating to imports and exports. According to this Section, the Central Government may by order published in the official gazette, make provision for *(i)* the development and regulation of foreign trade by facilitating imports and increasing exports, and *(ii)* prohibiting, restricting or otherwise regulating the import or export of goods. Section 5 authorises the Central Government to formulate and announce, by notification in the Official Gazette, the export and import policy and also, in like maner, to amend that policy.

2. Importer-Exporter Code Number. According to Section 7, no person shall make any import or export except under an Importer-Exporter Code Number granted by the Director General or the officer authorised by the Director General in this behalf , in accordance with the procedure specified in this behalf by the Director General. Section 8 states that if any person has contravened by law relating the Central Excise or Customs of Foreign Exchange or has committed any economic offence under any other law in force at that time, or the Director General has reason to believe that person has made any export or import in a manner gravely prejudicial to the trade relations with other countries, the Importer-Exporter Code Number given to him can be cancelled. In such circumstances, the person whose code number has been cancelled or suspended will not be entitled to import or export goods except under a special licence granted.

3. Issue, Suspension and Cancellation of Licence. According to Section 9, the Director General or an officer authorised by him may, after making an enquiry, grant or renew or refuse to grant or renew a licence to import or export goods. In the event of suspension or cancellation of the licence of any person to import or export goods. he shall be provided a reasonable opportunity of being heard.

4. Director General of Foreign Trade. Section 6 provides for the appointment of Director General of Foreign Trade by the Central Government for the purposes of this Act. The Director General replaces the Chief Controller of Imports and Exports under the Imports and Exports (Control) Act, 1947. His job is to advise the Central Government in the formulation of the export and import policy and he shall be responsible for carrying out that policy.

5. Power Relating to Search and Seizure. According to Section 10, the Central Government may authorise any person for the purpose of exercising such powers with respect to entering such premises and searching. inspecting and seizing of such goods, documents, things and conveyance, subject to such requirements and conditions, as may be prescribed.

6. Penalty for Contravention. According to Section 11, no export or import shall be made by any person except in accordance with the provisions of this Act, the rules that orders made thereunder and the export and import policy for the time being in force. Any contravention to this provision will invite a penalty not exceeding one thousand rupees or five time the value of the goods in respect of which any contravention is made or attempted to be made, whichever is more. Failure to pay the penalty could lead to the suspension of the Importer-Exporter Code Number of the person. Section 11 further state that where any contravention of any provision of this Act or any rules or orders made thereunder or the export and import policy has been is being, or is attempted to be made, the goods shall be liable to confiscation by the Adjudicating Authority. Section 14 provides that before imposing any penalty or confiscating goods. the person concerned would be given a proper notice in writing and would also be given an opportunity of being heard.

7. Appeal and Revision. Section 15 lays down that any person aggrieved by any decision or order made by the Adjudicating Authority may appeal against any such decision or order within a period of fortyfive days from the date on which the decision or order was served on him. The Appellate Authority can, if it so wishes, futher extend the period by thirty days, and can, at its discretion, dispense with the penalty to be deposited by the appellant either unconditionally or subject to such conditions as it may impose. The Appellant Authority may, after giving to the appellant a reasonable opportunity of being heard, confirm, modify or reverse the decision or order appealed against. The order made in appeal by the Appellant Authority shall be final. Section 16 confers the power on the Central Government to examine the records of any proceeding in which a decision or an order imposing a penalty or redemption charge or adjudicating confiscation has been made and against which no appeal has been preferred, for the purpose of satisfying itself as to the correctness, legality or propriety of such decision or order and make such orders thereon as may be deemed fit.

COMPOSITION OF FOREIGN TRADE

In order to study the composition or structure of India's foreign trade, it is necessary to analyse the changing pattern of imports and exports.

Pattern of Imports. Inputs have been classified into Bulk imports and non-bulk imports. Bulk imports are further subdivided into petroleum, oil and lubricants (PoL) and non-PoL items such as consumptions goods, fertilizers and iron and steel. Non-bulk items such as consumption goods (which include electrical and non-electrical machinery), pearls, precious and semi precious strong and other items.

The structural changes in imports since 1951 show:

(a) rapid growth of industrialisation necessitating imports of capital goods and raw materials.

(b) growing imports of raw materials on the basis of liberalisation of imports for export promotion; and

(c) declining imports of foodgrains and consumer goods due to the country becoming selfsufficient in food gains and other consumer goods through agricultural and Industrial growth.

TREND OF PRINCIPAL IMPORTS

Foodgrains. The imports of food grains were necessitated by the partition of the country and the growing demand for food for the rising population. The average annual imports of food grains which were about Rs. 200 crores during the first plan rose to Rs. 161 crores during the second plan, further increased to an average rate of Rs. 241crores during the third plan. The drought of 1965-66 further worsened the situation and consequently, foodgrains imports worth Rs. 1,201 crores were made during the three years *i.e.* 1966-67 to 1968-69. During the 5-years period (1980-81-1984-85) food grains worth Rs. 66 crores were imported a negligible figure indeed. But during 1991-1992, they again rose to Rs. 395 crores. In later years the share of foodgrains fill almost to zero. The import of foodgrains during the year 1999-2000 was of Rs. 222 crore and it declaimed sharply to Rs. 20 crore in 2000-2001. This has happened mainly because of continuance rise in the production of food grains in the country.

Mineral Oils. Imports of mineral oils are also on the increase. India is short in the supply of mineral oils, especially petroleum. Annual import of mineral oil during 1969-70 to 1973-74 averaged Rs. 226 crores. On account of the sharp increase in the prices of crude announced by the organisation of petroleum exporting countries, during 1973-74 alone, petroleum imports were of the order of Rs. 569 crores. Their annual average during 1974-75 to 1979-80 was of the order of Rs. 2,063 crores. Though the share of mineral oils in imports has declimed from 45.1 per cent in 1990-91 to 39.6 per cent in 1999-2000 but it has increased from Rs. 10,816 crore to Rs. 54,649 crore during the period in abosolute terms.

Machinery. This item includes electrical and non-electrical equipment. In a country which is rapidly industrialising her economy imports of machinery are bound to increase. Compared to the average annual import of machinery which was about Rs. 1991 crores during the 1951-61, the annual average during the third plan rose to Rs. 472 crore. During the fourth plan, they were of order to Rs. 484 crore. Machinery imports during Seventh Plan jumped to Rs. 6,415 crore annually and further to Rs. 11,895 crore during the year 1999-2000.

Metals. India imports iron and steel and also some non-ferrous metals. The annual average imports of ferrous and non-ferrous metals which were about Rs. 54 crores during the first plan have gone up steadily with every plan and are about Rs. 2,450 croes during 1985-86 and 1989-90 Import of metals on such a large scale is necessitated by the vast programmes of industrial expansion, development of railways and hydro-electric projects. With improvement in capacity utilisation of our steel plants, imports of iron and steel should be cut down. During 1990-91 metals worth Rs. 1,528 crore were imported which futher increased to Rs. 3,789 crore in 1999-2000.

Chemicals Drugs and Medicines. There has been an increase in the imports of chemicals, drugs and medicines. The anual average of these items was about Rs. 55 crores during the third plan. Imports of chemicals, drugs and medicines rose to Rs. 113 crores per annum on the average during the Fourth plan. During 1980-81 and 1984-85 annual average imports of this item rose to Rs. 660 crores. They further rose to Rs. Rs. 2,289 crore in 1990-91 and to Rs. 12,420 crore in 1999-2000.

Pearls and Precious Stones. The imports of pearls and precious stones averaged Rs. 223 crores during 1974-79 and they have further increased to Rs. 2,405 crores per annum for the period 1985-86 to 1989-90. Part of these imports is meant to satisfy the demand of the afluent sections and part of these imports serve as raw material for the handicrafts export industry. It may be noted that the India imported pearls and precious stones worth of Rs. 3,738 crore in 1990-91 and it further·increased to 23,556 crore in 1999-2000.

Fertilisers. Following the adoption of the new strategy in Indian agriculture, the imports of fertilizers were stepped up. The average annual imports of fertilizers which stood at Rs. 28 crores during 1966-67 to 1968-69. During 1980-81 to 1984-85 the annual imports of fertilizers were of the order of Rs. 698 crores. As a consequence of liberalisation, fertilizer imports jumped to Rs. 1,436 crores in 1985-86 and were of the Rs. 1,114 crores per annum on an average during 1985-86 to 1989-90. Imports of fertilizers touched a level of Rs. 1,765 crore in 1990-91 and Rs. 6,063 crore in 1999-2000.

The data related to average annual principal imports is shown in the following table.

Average Annual Imports of Principal Commodities

Items	*1951-52 to 1960-61*	*1980-81 to 1984-85*	*1985-86 to 1989-90*	*1990-91 to 1999-2000*
1. Foodgrains	141	374	516	624
2. Machinery	191	2,515	6,415	14,976
3. Mineral Oils	77	5,264	4,498	27,469
4. Metals	93	1,448	2,450	7,003
5. Chemicals	44	660	1,868	1,921
6. Fertilisers	–	698	1,114	4,707
7. Pearls and Precious Stones	–	730	2,405	9,993

PATTERN OF EXPORT

Exports of India are broadly classified into four categories: *(i)* Agriculture and allied products which include coffee, tea, oil cakes, tobacco, cashew kernels, spices, sugar, raw cotton, rise fish and fish preparations, meat and meat preparations, vegetable oils, fruits, vegatables and pulses; *(ii)* ores and minerals include manganese ore, mica and iron ore; *(iii)* Manufactured goods include textiles and ready-made garments, jute manufactures, leather and footwear handicrafts including pearls and precious stones, chemicals, engineering goods and iron steel; and *(iv)* mineral fuels and lubricants.

Table : Classification Indian Exports

(Rs. crore)

	1970-71	*1980-81*	*1991-92*	*1999-2000*
1. Agriculture and Allied Products	487 (31.7)	2,057 (30.6)	7,638 (17.3)	24,301 (15.2)
2. Ores and Mineral 164	413 (10.7)	2,281 (6.2)	2,643 (5.2)	3,970 (2.5)
3. Manufactured Goods	772 (50.3)	3,747 (55.8)	32,384 (73.5)	1,28,761 (80.6)
4. Petoleum Products	13.28 (0.8)	102.2 (0.4)	905.2 (.23)	168 (0.1)
5. Others	99.0 (6.5)	465 (6.9)	717 (1.6)	2,361 (1.5)
Total	1,535 (100.0)	6,710 (100.0)	44,042 (100.0)	1,59,561 (100.0)

Data given in table reveal that traditional exports dependent upon agriculture and mineral wealth accounted for 42 per cent of total exports in 1970-71, their share has, however, declined to about 18 per cent in 1999-2000 in 1970-71 to about 80.6 per cent in 1999-2000. An interesting feature of the changing pattern of exports is the sharp increase in the share of manufactured products. Obviously, the structure of Indian exports is changing in favour of manfactured goods and petroleum products whose combined share has gone up from about 51 per cent in 1970-71 to about 81 per cent in 1999-2000.

Exports of Principal Commodities

Tea. Tea is one of the most important items of Indian exports. It had the first position in our exports in certain years. The average annual exports of tea were Rs. 106 crores during the first plan period. Tea exports further picked up to touch Rs. 195 crores in 1960-61. But later they declined. Tea exports earned Rs. 1,985 crores during 1999-2000.

Cotton Yarn and Manufactures. During the first plan period, the average annual exports of cotton yarn and manufactures touched Rs. 81 crores, but they declained to a small figure of Rs. 55 crores during the Third plan. On account of relatively high cost in Indian textile industry, Indian found it diffcult to capture the international market. In fact high costs were due to rising labour cost and use of old and worn-out machiner. In the post-devaluation period exports of cotton textiles have increased on account of their competitiveness in the international market. During 1970-71 and 1991-2000 exports of cotton (yarn and manufactures) improved from Rs. 75 crores to Rs. 18,151 crores.

Engineering Goods. In 1970-71 exports of engineering goods were of the order of Rs. 130 crores, During the 1970's engineering exports surged forward. In 1976-77, they exceded Rs. 500 crores and in 1999-2000 they were of the order of Rs. 22,325 crores, this is really creditworthy.

Readymade Garments. In recent years, the exports of cotton apparel or ready-made garments have shown significant improvement. These exports were just Rs. 9 crores in 1970-71. They jumped to Rs. 196 crores in 1974-75. During 1999-2000 cotton apparel exports touched a record of Rs. 20,649 crores. This indicates the increasing importance of this item in our exports.

Leather and Leather Manufacturers. Onc of the traditional items of Indian exports is raw hides and skins. But recently, in the exports of this item, the proportion for leather and leather manufactures to raw hides and skins is on the increase. This is really a healthy development. India earned about Rs. 39 crores in 1960-61 from this item. It touched Rs. 486 crores in 1979-80 and rose further to Rs. 6,891 crores during 1999-2000.

Handicrafts. The exports of Indian handicrafts assumed great importance in the 1970s. From a low level of Rs. 70 crores in

1970-71 they increased to Rs. 120 crores in 1972-73 and stood at Rs. 6,285 crores in 1989-90. The most important item among the handicrafts was pearls and precious stones which averaged Rs. 3,177 crores during 1985-86 to 1989-90. At present, the single largest item of export in handicrafts. During 1999-2000 handicrafts exported were of the order or Rs. 37,568 crores.

Iron ore. Indian exports iron ore. India earned about Rs. 30 crores per year from iron ore during the first first plan. During 1970-71 exports of iron ore rose to Rs. 117 crores and touched Rs. 1,175 crores during 1999-2000. This is an unhealthy development. India should increase the share of steel in exports by utilising iron ore in her own steel plants.

Changing Structure of Exports

The structure of Indian exports is typical of a developing economy. India has traditionally been an exporter of agricultural raw materials and manufactures based on agricultural raw materials. There has been a continuous decline in the share of agricultural raw materials and allied products. One reason for the relative decline of food, beverages and tabacco in the total exports is the increase in population and consequent increase in domestic consumption of these goods, Accordingly, the export surplus in many traditional commodities like tea has not been increasing as much as the Government would have wished. In this connection, the growing importance of certain products in this category should be noted, *i.e.*, fish and fish products, cashew kernels and coffee.

We should not, however, conclude that only non-traditional items are to the fore and the traditional items have suffered are treat. Exports of traditional items are also expanding, though probably not to the extent desired. Examples are the respectable growth in cotton fabrics, tea, leather and leather manufactures etc.

Thus the pattern of India's exports indicates that:

(a) The Indian economy is being diversified and both traditional and non-traditional items of exports are growing in importance.

(b) India is now in a position to take advantage of both favourable demand situation and attractive price assituation in international markets and this explains the expansion in the exports of many traditional and non-traditional items.

(c) The large expansion of engineering goods is partly the result of pick-up in demand in industrial countries and also from the Middle east countries which have undertaken infra-structural projects like roads, ports and rail construction, tele-communication and civil construction.

(d) While some commodities have tremendous exports poetential (*e.g.* handicrafts, engineering goods and readymades), others (like sugar, jute, yarn and manufactures, iron and steel) have fluctuated hopelessy.

DIRECTION OF INDIA'S FOREIGN TRADE

Our trade with East European socialist countries *viz.*, U.S.S.R. Poland, Romania, Bulgaria, Hungary, East Germany, Czechosolovakia and Yugoslavia has developed in recent years. The main items of imports from these countries are iron and steel, non-ferrous metals, chemicals, capital equipment, railway stores, paper, medicines and pharmaceuticals and petrolium products. The imports of most of these commodities are of crucial help for our core projects and several industries of strategic kernels, tobacco, oil seeds, leather, metallic ores, jute manufactures etc.—the traditional items of Indian exports. The composition of imports from these countries suggests the significance of the trade from the viewpoint of economic development. In 1960-61 India imported 4 per cent of her total imports from this region and exported about 8 per cent of her total exports to this region. But soon after the Indo Chinese conflict in 1962 and Indo-Pak war in 1965 our trade relations with the East European Socialist countries improved remarakably. In 1969-79 this group of countries accounted for 18 per cent of total imports and about 22 per cent of our exports. U.S.S.R. the chief contributor and accounted for nearly 84 per cent of trade with this region. By 2000-2001 India's imports from East European countries declined to about 1 per cent and our exports to these countries which declined to 14 per cent in 1979-80 further fell to about 2 per cent in 2000-2001 with the disintegration of the soviet Union into common wealth of independent states (CIS) Trade relations with these countries are undergoing a change.

Our trade with the countries in Asia and oceania has been of great significance. Our exports of these countries which were about 28 per cent of total import in 1951-52 increased to 32 per cent in 1969-70. As against it, imports from these countries declined from about 23 per cent in 1951-52 to 19 per cent in 1969-70 (Refer table 13) the ECAFE* region was of great significance and four countries, viz, Japan, Austalia, Iran and iraq were very important.

Table—Direction of India's Foreign Trade

Region/Country	1980-81		2000-2001	
	Exports	Imports	Exports	Imports
1. OECD of which	3,126 (46.6)	5,747 (45.8)	1,07,238 (52.6)	92,090 (39.9)
(a) European Union	1,447 (21.6)	2,639 (21.0)	47,561 (23.4)	48,015 (20.8)
(i) Belgium	144 (2.2)	296 (2.4)	6,718 (3.3)	13,112 (5.7)
(ii) U.K.	395 (5.9)	731 (5.8)	10,512 (5.2)	14,472 (6.3)
(b) North America	806 (12.0)	1,851 (14.8)	45,509 (22.4)	15,588 (6.7)
(i) Canada	62 (0.9)	332 (2.6)	2,999 (1.5)	1,814 (0.8)
(ii) U.S.A.	744 (11.1)	1,519 (12.1)	42,570 (20.9)	13,774 (6.0)
(c) Other OECD	708 (10.5)	932 (7.4)	14,168 (6.9)	28,487 (12.3)
(i) Japan	598 (8.9)	749 (6.0)	8,198 (4.0)	8,416 (3.6)
2. OPEC	745 (11.1)	3,490 (27.8)	22,223 (10.9)	12,358 (5.4)
3. Eastern Europe	1,486 (22.2)	1,296 (10.3)	6,020 (2.9)	3,884 (1.7)
USSR/CIS	1,226 (18.3)	1,014 (8.1)	4,061 (2.0)	2,365 (1.0)
4. Developing Countries	1,266 (18.9)	1,971 (15.7)	59,381 (29.2)	50,865 (22.0)
(i) Asia	880 (13.1)	1,428 (11.4)	45,858 (22.5)	38,647 (16.7)
5. Others	65 (0.9)	45 (0.4)	350 (0.2)	8 –
Total 1 to 5	6,711 (100.0)	12,549 (100.0)	2,03,571 (100.0)	2,30,873 (100.0)

However, due to increasing importance acquired by the import of Crude oil, OPEC countries have assumed very great significance in our import. These countries acounted for barely 8 per cent in our total imports in 1970-71 but as against it their share in 1980-81 has jamped upto about 27.8 per cent. Much of the increase is due to the sharp hike in the price of oil and does not indicate a corresponding increase in the quanitity index, of imports. On the export front also our exports to OPEC countries have also increased from 6.4 per cent in 1971-72 to about 11 per cent in 2000-2001 with a fall in the international price of oil, the share of OPEC countries in our imports declined to 5.4 per cent in 2000-2001.

The share of Japan in our export which was about 8.9 per cent in 1980-81 has come down to 4.0 per cent in 2000-2001. As against it, the share in our imports from these two countries has also declined from 6.0 per cent to about 3.6 per cent during the same period.

India has a great potential for increasing her foreign trade with Asian countries, because the Indian manufactures can be readily acceptable in these countries. Similarly, India can import raw materials for her growing industries from these relatively more under-developed regions. This is evidenced by the fact that during 2000-2001, imports from this region accounted for 16.7 per cent of our total imports whereas they were in the range of 11.4 per cent in 1970-71 to. On the export side, there has been a gradual and steady improvement and exports to this region increased from 13.1 per cent during 1980-81 to a level of nearly 22.5 per cent in 2000-2001.

It would be of interest to examine the direction of trade with reference to some important countries. U.S.A. U.K. west Germany U.S.S.R. Japan, Saudi Arabia, Australia and Canada were the 8 countries of significance in our trade. The share of these 8 countries in our exports has ranged between 54.7 and 41.6 per cent during 1980-81 to 2000-2001. As against it, their share in our imports has ranged between 46 and 24.5 per cent during this period.

Although U.K. was of prime importance in our foreign trade before independence, U.S.A. was growing in importance up to 1970. During the Seventies, especially after the Indo-Pak war of 1971,

U.S.S.R. has grown in significance in our foreign trade. On the import side, the share of U.K. was the highest in 2000-2001 followed by USA, Belgium, Germany, Japan, Saudi Arabia and Switzerland. On the export side, Indian exports to U.K. were always higher than the exports to U.K. and subsequently exports to U.S.A. but during the Third Plan, the exports of U.S.A. levelled off with exports of U.K. and subsequently exports to U.K. fell futher to an abnormally low level of about 5 per cent. Our imports from West Germany were on the increase till 1965-66, but have declined since then. As against it, our exports to this country have been of the order of 2-3 per cent of total exports in the past but have risen to about 2 per cent in 2000-2001. Japan and U.S.S.R. are both growing in importance in our foreign trade. We had trade relations with Japan in the pre-war period, but trade was cut off during the war. It has been revived again. With U.S.S.R. Although our foreign trade is of recent origin, the share of imports was 1.0 per cent in 2000-2001 as against 8.1 per cent in 1980-81. Similarly the share of exports of USSR has risen from 1.0 per cent in 1951-52 to 18 per cent in 1980-81 but declined to 2.0 per cent in 2000-2001. Iraq and Iran also became important especially for oil imports, but due to continued Iran-Iraq was imports from these two countries became negligible but imports from Saudi Arabia rose to 1.3 per cent and from Indonesia to 1.8 per cent in 2000-2001. With the distintegration of Soviet Union our trade with this retio has suffered a serious setback.

Some salient features of the changes in the direction of trade in the post-independence period may be noted here.

(i) **New Trading Partners.** Before Independence, U.K. was the principal trading partner for India, accounting for 34 per cent of India's exports and 30 per cent India's imports. After Independence, even though India has continued to be a member of the British commonwealth, she has succeeded in getting new trading partners. Besides U.K. other countries of importance are U.S.A. U.S.S.R. West Germany, Japan and members of OPEC. Thus an important future of the new direction of trade since 1951 is the increasing in the number of trading partners for India. This spatial or geographical diversification has helped India to go for diversification of industries along with specialisation in certain goods, and secure new markets for her products.

(ii) Larger and More Attractive Outlets for Exports. India has been diversifying her exports to match her imports. Naturally, she has to search for new countries to sell her goods. Even though U.K. continues to buy a larger volume of goods from India, it has been relegated to second and even third place. U.S.A. has become the biggest buyer of Indian goods. Likewise, UAR, Honkong and Japan along with U.S.A. and UK constitute the first five leading countries absorbing 42 per cent of India's exports. These are rich countries with high national and per capita income and they manufactures, specially carpet backing, leather manufacturers and non-traditional items such as marine products, pearls and precius stones, etc. Middle East countries offer a good market for Indian exports.

(iii) Larger Sources of Imports. The increase in the number of countries from whom we by has been necessitated by many factors peculiar to the post-World War II. For one thing, the planned economic development and the tremendous increase in the requirements for machinery, equipment, industrial raw material, etc. could not be met by U.K. alone, or even by USA. For another reason, grant of aid and other assistance by international institutions like the World Bank allowed India to by from the cheapest sources (through global tenders). Thirdly, tied aid and grants from some countries willing to help India in per planning effort necessitated India to import from particular countries. Fourthly, foreign exchange shortage with reference to some capitalist countries induced India to make bilateral rupee arrangements with U.S.S.R. and other socialist countries. Finally, since the hike in the price of oil in 1973 India's imports from Iran, Iraq, Kuwait, Saudi Arbia and other members of the OPEC have gone up.

Scope for Direction. The share of Africa and South America is only marginal. These are rich continents with very bright future. India should cultivate trade relations with these countries-they could offer huge markets for India's exports. Likewise, the scope of India's exports to the development countries of the Middle East Asia is vast and in recent years, India is increasingly cultivating these markets. The Composition of imports by source reveals that OECD countries as a group accounted for the largest share in India's imports accounting for 40 per cent in 2000-2001. This was followed by the developing countries (excluding members of the OPEC) whose share was about 22 per cent. OPEC and East European countries accounted for 5.4 per cent and 1.7 per cent respectively in India's imports in 1991-92.

The destination-wise share of India's exports shows sufficient diversification. In 2000-2001, the share of exports going to industrial market economies as represented by OECD group was 52.6 per cent, while developing countries accounted for 29.2 per cent. The countries of OPEC accounted for 10.9 per cent of our total exports. During recent years, the share of countries of Asia and Pacific region in particular has been increasing in our exports. The economic survey reviewing the position mentions: "There has been a high growth in exports/imports to/from India to developing countries of Asia (excluding members of the OPEC). Some of these economic (Korea, Singapore, Malaysia, Hong Kong and Taiwan) have withnessed continued economic growth along with significant trade liberalisation and economic deregulation. Therefore, these economies provide excellent opportunities for export thrust. On the other hand, India's exports may have to contend with uncertainty in East European market arising out of proposed economic reforms underway. Exports from India will now have to face increasing competition in view of switch over by these economies to trading based on world prices and convertible currencies."

INDIA'S TRADE POLICY

The trade policy played an important role in the development of advanced countries like U.S.A., U.K., Germany, France, Japan etc. It restricted their imports and provided a sheltered market for their own industries so that could develop rapidly and promoted their exports so that expanding industries could secure foreign markets. India, however, did not have a clear trade policy before independence, though some type of import restrictions-known as discriminating protection was adopted since 1923 to protect a few domestic industries against foreign competition. It was only after independence that a trade policy as a part of the general economic policy of development was formulated by India. The time period of India's Trade Policy can be divided into five different phases:

1. First Phase (1947-48 to 1951-52)
2. Second Phase (1952-53 to 1956-57)
3. Third Phase (1956-57 to June 1966)
4. Fourth Phase (1966-67 to 1977-78)
5. Fifth Phase (1978-79 to 1990-91)
6. Sixth Phase (1991-92 and onwords)

First Phase. During the first phase up to 1951-52. India could have liberalised imports but on account of the restrictions placed by the U.K. on the utilisation of the sterling balances, she had to continue wartime controls. Since our balance of payments with the dollar area was heavily adverse, an effort was made to screen imports from hard currency areas and boost up exports to this area so as to bridge the gap. This also necessitated India to devalue her currency in 1949. By and large, the Import policy continued to be restrictive during this period. Besides this, restrictions were also placed on exports in view of the domestic shortages.

Second Phase. During the second phase (1952-53 to 1956-57) liberalisation of foreign trade policy. Import licences were granted in a liberal manner. An effort was also made to encourage export by relaxing export controls, reducing export duties, abolishing export-quotas and providing incentives to exports. Liberalisation led to a tremendous increase in our imports but exports did not rise appreciably. Consequently, here was fast deterioration in our foreign exchange reserves.

Third Phase. During the third phase which began in 1956-57; the trade policy was re-oriented to meet the requirements of planned economic development. A very restrictive import policy was adopted and the import controls further screened the list of imported goods. On the other hand, a vigorous export promotion drive was launched. The trade policy assumed that a lasting solution to be balance of payments problem lies in the promotion and diversification of our export trade. Not only should the export of traditional items be expanded, but export of newer items should also be encouraged. Similarly, import substitution industries should also be encouraged so that dependence of foreign countries should also be encouraged so that dependence on foreign countries be lessened. It was in this period that India's trade policy was thoroughly reviewed by the Mudaliar Committee (1962).

Fourth Phase. The fourth phase stated after the devaluation of the rupee in June, 1966. During this period trade policy attempted to expand exports and strangely liberalised imports too. Actually, export promotion was given a big boost through the acceptance and implementation of the recommendations of the Mudaliar committee (1962). The major recommendations included increased allocation of raw materials to export-oriented industries, income tax relief on export earnings, export promotion through import entitlement, removal of disincentives, and setting up of Export Promotion Advisory Council, a ministry of International trade, etc. When these export promotion measures did not succeed and adverse balance of payments persisted, the government of India undertook devaluation on the rupees in 1966 as a major step to check imports and boost exports. Initially devaluation was not successful and the adverse balance of payments worsened during the annual plans. But during the Fourth plan, the trade policy was quite successful in restricting imports and promoting exports. This period continued till 1977-78.

Fifth Phase. During the last phase (1978-79 onwards), the Government adopted a policy of import liberalisation, with a view to encourage export promotion. During Janata rule import liberalisation was also adopted to augment domestic supply of essential goods and to check rise in price level. Import-export policy of the Indian government attempted to achieve such objectives as: *(i)* to provide further impetus to exports; *(ii)* to provide support to the growth of indigenous industry; *(iii)* to provide for optimum utilisation of the country's resource endowments, especially in man power and agriculture; *(iv)* to facilitate technology up-gradation with special emphasis on export promotion and energy conservation; *(v)* to provide a stimulus to those engaged in exports and in particular, to manufacturing units contributing substantially to the export efforts; and *(vi)* to effect all possible savings in imports. Thus it is clear that the present trade policy has been to stimulate economic growth and export promotion via import liberalisation.

Import liberalisation along with export promotion at a time when *(a)* prices of imported goods were rising such faster, and *(b)* foreign markets for Indian goods were depressed, resulting in huge adverse balance of trade and payments from 1979-80 onwards. Instead of curtailing imports, the Tandon Committee (1981) recommended a policy of vigorous export promotion and further import liberalisation as a means of export promotion. The IMF loan (1981) had also stipulated that India should use export promotion and not import restriction as the strategy for controlling adverse balance of payments. Such a trade policy has forced India almost into a debt trap and the Indian bureaucrats are knocking at the doors of Aid India consortium and other advanced countries to bail India out.

While framing the export-import policy (1985) the Government was guided by the recommendations of Abid Hussain Committee. Whereas the committee emphasized the need for striking a balance between export promotion and import substitution, the Government in its wave of import liberalisation permitted a much greater quantum of imports in the name of export promotion and capital goods imports for technological upgradation. Thus, grave distortions have appeared in the process of implementation of the recommendations of the committee's report which need to be rectified.

Sixth Phase (New Trade Policy and Trade Liberalisation). The massive trade liberalisation measure adopted since 1991-92 to mark a major departure from the relatively protectionistic trade policies pursed in earlier years. The main features of the new trade policy since 1991 are as follows:

1. ***Free Imports and Exports.*** In the pre-reform period, India's trade policy regime was complex and combersome. There were different categories of importers, different types of import licences, alternate ways of importing etc. Substantial simplication and liberalisation in all these respects has been carried out in the reform period. Under its commitment to the World Trade Organisation (WTO) India, in November 1997, agreed to phase out all curbs on 2,714 tariff lines over a six year phase out period starting April 1, 1997. However, USA did not agree to this schedule and appealed to the WTO which ruled against India. As a result, India has to remove all quantitative restrictions by April 1, 2001. After the announcement of Exim Policy, 2000-2001 the number of items on which quantitative restrictions remain in 715 and exim policy 2001-02 removed quantitative restrictions on the balance 715 items. Thus in line with India's commitment to the WTO quantitative restrictions on all import items have been withdrawn.
2. ***More Facilities to EOUs and EPZs.*** The 1992-97 policy conferred higher benefit to 100 per cent export oriented units (EOUs) and units in export processing zones (EPZs) over those exporting from the domestic tariff area (DTA). The EOU and the EPZ schemes have now been extended to newer activities and services. By a separate notification, such units dealing with broad agro-based products can sell 50 per cent (twice the normal) output in the DTA. This can prove to be a powerful initiative for boosting exports.

3. ***Decanalisation.*** A large number of export and imports used to be canalised through the public sector agencies in India. The supplementary trade policy announced on August 13, 1991 reviewed these canalised items and decanalised 16 export items and 20 import items. The 1992-97 policy decanalised imports of a number of items including newsprint, non-ferrous metals, natural rubber, intermediates and raw materials for fertilisers. However, 8 items (petroleum products, fertilisers, edible oils, cereals, etc.) were to remain canalised. Large scale decanalisation is an important step towards opening up more areas of the economy to the private sector. The Exim policy 2001-02 put 6 items under special list. These itmes would be allowed though state trading agencies.

4. ***Trading Houses.*** The 1991 policy allowed export houses and trading houses to import a wide range of items. The government also permitted the setting up of trading houses with 51 per cent foreign equity for the purposes of promoting exports. Under the 1992-97 trade policy, export houses and trading houses were provided the benefit of self certification under the advance licence system, which permits duty free imports for exports.

   The 1994-95 policy introduced a new category of trading houses to be called Super Star Trading Houses. To attain the status of a Super Star Trading House, an exporter must have registered an average FOB value of exports of Rs. 925 crore during the preceding three years or Rs. 1,387.50 crore during the preceeding year. On the basis of NFE criterion, an exporter must have registered an average net foreign exchange (NFE) value of exports of Rs. 740 crore during the preceding three years or Rs. 1,100 crore during the preceding year. These houses will be entitled to membership of apex consultative bodies concerned with trade policy and promotion, representation in important business delegations, special permission for overseas trading and special import licences at enhanced rate.

5. ***Export Scheme for the Services Sector.*** Since trade in services is becoming increasingly important for our country a new scheme called the "Export Scheme for the Services Sector" has been introduced. Under the scheme, person who render professional services have been allowed to import capital equipment at a concessional rate of duty of 15 per cent. The export obligation to be achieved by them will be in the form of the foreign exchange earned by them, regardless of whether the services are rendered in India or abroad.

6. ***Export Promotion Capital Goods Scheme.*** The Export Promotion Capital Goods (EPCG) scheme has been revamped by having only one window with a concessional customs duty rate of 15 per cent with export obligation (earlier there were two windows—15 per cent and 25 per cent). The 1994-95 policy simplified the EPCG scheme and third party exports were permitted for purposes of fulfilment of export obligations. The 1995-96 policy placed the services sector at par with the supply of goods under the Export Promotion Capital Goods (EPCG) scheme. This ensures rich dividends for several companies in wide ranging sectors like financial services, banking, hotels and airlines, advertising, software and legal firms. In March 1996, the EPCG scheme was enhanced by inclusion of 'mining' in the definition of manufacture for the purpose of export-import policy.

7. ***Export Promotion Industrial Parks.*** A centrally sponsored Export Promotion Industrial Parks scheme was introduced in Aug. 1994 with a view to involving the State governments in the creation of infrastructural facilities for export-oriented production. It provides for 75 per cent of capital expenditure towards creation of infrastructural

facilities limited to Rs. 10 crore of grant to the State government. So far 11 parks have been completed.

8. ***Duty Exemption Scheme Enlarged.*** The duty exemption scheme has been strengthened under which imports are provided at two concessional rates of 15 per cent and 25 per cent subject to appropriate export obligations. The exporters have been given a choice to opt for advance import licences under the duty exemption scheme either under quantity based or (for the first time introduced) value based norms. This will given greater flexibility to the exporter to import and export goods within the overall value limits and without any quantitative restrictions except in the case of sensitive goods.

9. ***Rationalisation of Tariff Structure.*** In its Final Report published in January 1993, Chelliah Committee had advocated drastic reductions in import duties. The committee expressed the opinion that the rupee had depreciated considerably in the eighties and the early nineties, pushing up the level of protection to Indian industries considerably. For instance, the committee pointed out that in the seven year period 1985-86 to 1992-93, the real exchange rate of the rupee has depreciated by 57.45 per cent. This had pushed up the cost of the imports considerably leading to very high levels of protection to the Indian industry. The Committee, therefore, recommended that the prevailing import duties be rationalised and drastically lowered by 1997-98 so that parity in prices of goods produced domestically and internationally can be established. Action on the recommendations of the Committee, the Finance Minister announced substantial cuts in import duties in the 1993-94, the 1994-95 and the 1995-96 Budgets. The 1993-94 Budget reduced the maximum rate of duty on all goods from 110 per cent to 85 per cent except for a few items including passenger luggage and alcoholic beverages. The 1994-95 Budget further brought down the maximum rate

of duty from 85 per cent to 65 per cent. This was brought down to 50 per cent in the 1995-96 Budget, to 40 per cent in the 1997-98 Budget and further to 35 per cent in the 2000-2001 Budget. In the budget 2002-03, the Finance Minister announced that by the year 2004-05, there would be only two basic rates of custom duties, namely 10 per cent and 20 per cent. For the year 2002-03, the peak custom duty rate has been reduced from 35 per cent to 30 per cent.

Rupee Depreciation and Convertibility. Prior to the devaluation of 1966, one US dollar was equal to Rs. 4.76. After the devaluation in 1966, one U.S. dollar became equal to Rs. 7.50. The system of fixed exchange rates was abandoned by most countries in 1973. The Government of India also abandoned it and pegged Indian rupee to a basket of currencies of the countries which are her major trading partners. This floating exchange rate system has been in operation since September 1975. Under the new system, the rupee started to slide against the dollar and other major currencies of the OECD countries. By the end of 1990, one US dollar had become equal to Rs. 18.07. The rate, Rs. per SDR, was 7.58 in 1970 and reached Rs. 25.71 by the end of 1990. The Government devalued the rupee in early July 1991 which led to a depreciation in the value of the rupee against the five major international currencies by roughly 22 per cent.

(i) ***Partial Convertibility of Rupee.*** The Finance Minister announced the liberalised exchange rate mechanism system (LERMS) in the Budget for 1992-93. Under this system a dual exchange rate was fixed under which 40 per cent of foreign exchange earnings were to be surrendered at the official exchange rate while the remaining 60 per cent were to be converted at a market determined rate. The foreign exchange surrendered at official rate was to be used for the import of essential items (like crude oil, petroleum products, fertilisers, life saving drugs, etc.) and the foreign exchange converted at the market rate was to be used to finance all

other imports. Since the official exchange rate was lower than the market rate, this system meant taxing the exporters to subsidize the government's bulk imports. The implicit export tax was between 8-12 per cent and was highly resented by exporters.

(ii) ***Full Convertibility on Trade Account.*** The 1993-94 Budget introduced full convertibility of the rupee on trade account. Side by side, the official RBI rate also stayed on for the conversion of items not permitted under the unified markets rate, *i.e.*, more than half a dozen of invisible items of current account as well as capital account. In addition, various exchange control norms of the Reserve Bank remained in operation all along, albeit with some relaxation of provisions.

(iii) ***Full Convertibility on Current Account.*** In February 1994, the Reserve Bank undertook several steps towards achieving current account convertibility when it announced relaxation in payment restrictions for a number of invisible transactions and liberalisation of exchange control regulations upto a specified limit relating to *(a)* Exchange Earners' Foreign Currency (EEFC) Account; *(b)* basic travel quota; *(c)* studies abroad; *(d)* gift remittances; *(e)* donations; and *(f)* payments of certain services rendered by foreign parties. India achieved full convertibility on current account on August 19, 1994 when the Reserve Bank further liberalised invisible payments and accepted obligations under Article VIII of the IMF, under which India is committed to foresake the use of exchange restrictions on current international transactions as an instrument in managing the balance of payments. Many other relaxations of restrictions on current transactions were announced in later years.

After the country moved to a single market-determined exchange rate system in March 1993, the rupee exhibited goods stability and for over two years after March 1993, the rupee-dollar exchange rate remained steady at about Rs. 31.6. After reasonable stability the Indian rupee, in August 1997, experienced a mild attack on contagion emanating from currency turmoil in East Asia. Beginning in the second week of November, 1997, the exchange rate of the rupee against the dollar came under renewed downward pressure. The rupee depreciated to a low of Rs. 40.36 per dollar by January 16, 1998. and fell further to Rs. 48.58 per dollar at the end of January 2002.

The Government of India has introduced convatibility on capital account in stages. For this the Union Budget, 2002-03, announced following measures:

1. There will be full convertibility of deposit scheme for Non-Resident Indians.
2. The schemes which do not offer full convertibility to NRIs will be discontinued from April 1, 2002.
3. NRIs will be free to repatriate in foreign currency their current earnings in India such as rent dividend, pension, interest and the like based on appropriate certification.
4. Indian mutual funds will now be allwed to invest in rated securities in countries with fully convertible currencies, within the existing limits.
5. With a view to liberalising the capital account transactions it is proposed to put foreign currency Convertible Bond (FCCB) scheme under the automatic route upto $ 50 million.
6. Indian companies wishing to invest abroad may now invest upto US $ 100 million on an annual basis through the automatic route, up from the existing limit of US $ 50 million.
7. Corporates with proven records can set up educational chairs in educational institutions abroad from their foreign exchange earnings.

The Government of India announced the new Exim policy for the 5 year period (2002-07) on March 31, 2002. The highlights of this new policy are the following:

1. Indian banks have been allowed to set up offshore banking units in special Economic Zones to attract foreign direct investment.
2. The promote the export Hardware and Software industry, the government modified Electronic Hardware Technology Park (EHTP) scheme. Now this sector will face zero duty regime under information Technology Agreement. The government has allowed free import of equipment and other goods used aborad for more than one year.
3. Exim policy has initiated a member of measures in the field of agriculture, cottage sector and handicrafts, small scale sector etc. Exim policy has removed all quantitative restrictions on all agricultural products excepts jute and onion. The Govt. has earmarked Rs. 5 crores for the promotion of exports of cottage sector and handicrafts. Three towns namely Tirpur, Panipat and Ludhiana have been granted special status for their export excellence. The Government has allowed the import of rough diamonds on zero custom duty basis.
4. Like focus LAC (Latin Americam Countries) launched in 1977, the government had been launching focus Africa since April 2002. In the first phase 7 countries will be focus. Links with CIS (Commonwealth of Independent States) to be revived. To cncourage relocation of industries in India plant and machineries would be permitted to be imported without a licence, where the depreciated value of such relocated plants exceeds Rs. 50 crore.
5. With a view to reducing transaction cost, govt. has introduced various procedural simplifications. For example a new 8 digit commodity classification for inputs has been introduced. It will help to eliminate the classification disputs and hence transaction costs and time.

6. To make the system, trust based, the following measures have been taken:
   - (i) Penal interest rate for bonafide defaults to be brought down from 24 per cent to 15 per cent.
   - (ii) No seizure of stocks in trade so as to disrupt the manufactuing process affecting delivery schedule of exports.
7. The Government has decided to abolish Duty Exmption Entitlement Certificate (DEEC) book. The govt has withdrawn annual advance licence requriement. Now the exporters can avail of advance licence for any value. The government granted to continue value cap exemption on 429 items.

The Government hopes that as result of the Exim Policy (2002-07) India will be able to capture 1 per cent of global share of trade by 2007, up from the present level of 0.67.

Critical Evaluation of the New Trade Policy. The trade policy reforms initiated in 1991 have shifted its eruphasis from inward-oriented to an outward-oriented policy. Due to liberalisation, the level of protection of Indian industry has declined significantly. Many people view the foreign trade sectors as the leading sector of the economy—a sector will change the face of the economy. But economists have raised serious doubts against it because of the relative importance of home market, the nature or the degree of State intervention, and the acquisition or development of the technology. Hence it will be very difficult to capture 1 per cent of global share of trade by 2007.

DEVALUATION OF RUPEE

Devaluation of a currency means lowering of the value of a currency in terms of gold or in terms of other currencies. The difference between devaluation and depreciation is that while develuation is the reduction of the value of a currency by the government, depreciation stands for automatic in the value of a currency by market forces. But in substance, both mean the same thing-lower value for a currency in terms of foreign currencies and both have similar effects. When the local currency depreciates in value and the foreign currency appreciates in value, the foreign commodities are made costly and hence imports are checked while the local commodities are made cheap and hence exports are promoted. Thus, a tendency towards a favourable balance of payments is created.

Conditions for the Success of Devaluation. The immediate effect of devaluation of a currency will be reflected in the increase in exports and decrease in imports. This is to be expected since, by devaluation the domestic currency will become cheap and, therefore, the domestic goods will also become cheap to foreigners, while the foreign currency will become costly and, therefore, foreign goods will become costly to consumers of the devalued currency. But curtailing imports and by expanding exports, devaluation creates favourable balance of payments and removes the chronic adverse balance of payments which had existed earlier. It will, however, the successful only under the following favourable circumstances:

(a) ***Cost-price Structure.*** There should be no change in the cost price structure in the devaluaing country. Only the external value of the currency unit has been reduced through devaluation. But it is possible for costs and prices within a country to change for two reasons : First, the merchants and speculators may raise the prices of those goods whose imports have been cut off or reduced owing to devaluation. Seconldy, imports which have now become costly because of devaluation may form a significant part of the consumption of the working and middle classes, in which case, the cost of living will rise, necessitating higher wages and higher prices. As a result of these reasons, the cost-price structure in the devaluing country may change and thus may prevent the favourable effects of devaluation to come into existence.

(b) ***Elasticity of Demand.*** The demand for imports and exports should be elastic. If Indian demand for foreign goods is inelastic, that is, whatever be the price of the foreign commodities, India will buy more or less the same amount; the total value of imports will increase as a result of devaluation. At the same time, if foreign demand for Indian goods is inelastic, India will not gain anything by lowering its price level through devaluation, for the same amount will be sold whatever be the price and, therefore, as a result of devaluation the total value of exports will fall. Thus, if the demand for imports and exports is inelastic, devaluation will worsen the balance of payments situation by increasing the total value of exports. It can be successful only if demand is elastic on both sides—that is, demand for imports is elastic, and as a result when the prices of foreign goods are high due to devaluation, imports will be curtailed; likewise, demand for exports by the foreigners is also elastic and as a result, when the local goods are cheap, exports will be stimulated.

(c) ***Co-operation of Other Countries.*** The efficacy of devalution of a currency by a country will depend upon the co-operation of foreign country or countries whose currencies have appreciated as a result of devaluation. Foreign countries will experience contraction of demand for their exports from the devaluing country, while their own demand for the goods of the devaluing country will expand due to lower exchange rate of the latter's currency. The natural tendency under the circumstances is to retaliate. This may take the form of high tariffs to prevent imports from the devaluing country or grant of subsidies to push up exports of devaluation of their currencies too.

India devalued its currency for the first time in 1966. Prior to the devaluation of 1966, one US dollar was equal to Rs. 4.76. After the devaluation in 1966, one U.S. dollar became equal to Rs. 7.50. The system of fixed exchange rates was abandoned by most countries including India and government pegged Indian rupee to a basket of currencies of major trading partner countries. Now government adopted floating exchange rate system, which resulted into the depreciation of the rupee against dollar and major currencies of the OECD countries. The government again devalued rupee in July 1991 which led to a depreciation in the value of the rupee against the five major international currencies by roughly 22 per cent. The purpose of this devaluatin was to boost the exports of goods and contain imports by making them cheaper and costlier respectively.

After the devaluation of currency the exports and imports both have gone in absolute terms. The value for exports gone up from U.S. $ 17,865 million in 1991-92 to U.S. $ 44,560 million in 2000-2001. Similar by the imports have also gone up from $ 19,411 million to $ 5,05,036 million during the same period. Hence the trade balance has increased from $ 1,546 million to $ 5,976 million during 1991-92 to 2000-2001. This shows that devaluation did not help in narrowing the trade deficit.

If we compare the growth rate of foreign trade pre-devaluation period with post-devaluation period, we find that devaluation has not made any significant impact on foreign trade.

During 1980-81 to 1989-90 the Growth Rate of Exports was 8.1 and Imports was 7.2. During 1990-91 to 1999-2000 it was 8.6 (Exports) and 9.6 (Imports).

This trade reveals that growth rates of exports has increased marginally and growth rates of imports has increased significantly. The main cause for high increase in imports is their inelastic demand trade liberalisation policies the Govt. Near stable export growth rate and higher import growth rate has widen the deficit in trade balance. Thus devaluation has not affected foreign trade sector significantly and India is still facing deficit it its trade balance.

❐

11

Development Banking in India

Development banks are those banks which are established mainly to provide long-term capital for industry and agriculture. It has been formed that commercial banks, by the short term nature of their deposits which they mobilise are in a position to grant only short-term credit to industry and agriculture to meet their working capital requirements.

The Government of India started a series of institutions since Independence to handle the problem of term financing of industry. These institutions are broadly known as developed banks. There is one basic difference between development banks and financial corporations. The former are interested in granting term loans (medium and long-term loans) to industry or agriculture; the latter are interested not only granting term loans but also in subscribing to equity capital of industrial enterprises and in certain cases may take up their management as well. But fundamentally, both are intersted in granting long-term loans for fixed capital formation, set up by the Government or by the Reserve Bank of India to promote economic development.

There are a few financial institutions namely IFCI, SFCs ICICI, IDBI, IRBI, UTI, LIC, GIC which promote industrial finance. We have the export Import Bank known as the EXIM Bank which specialises in international trade. We have also development banks to promote the growth of agriculture; we call them land development banks (LDBs) NABARD. Here we shall describe the development banks specialising in industrial finance. The important development banks are the following:

1. Industrial Finance Corporation of India Ltd. (IFCI)
2. Industrial Credit and Investment Corporation of India Ltd. (ICICI)
3. Industrial Development Bank of India (IDBI)
4. Small Industries Development Bank of India (SIDBI) and
5. Industrial Investment Bank of India (IIBI).

The development banks are playing an important role in the industrial development of the country by providing medium and long term loan. All Financial Institutions distribused Rs. 19,422 crores in 1990-91 an assistance and it rose to Rs. 1,04,766 crores in 1999-2000. Out of this the share of development banks was Rs. 84,657 crore which comes to 80.0 per cent. This shows that how much important role are development banks playing in sanctioning and disbursing the medium and long term assistance to the industrial sector of the country. Now we shall describe in brief the working of important development banks.

1. Industrial Finance Corporation of India (IFCI)

The industrial finance Corporation of India (IFCI) was the first to be established among the existing chain of development banks in India. It was set up in July 1948 with objective of providing medium and long-term credit to the indsutry. The IFCI seeks to fill up the gap in the capital market by making available to the large industrial concerns, cheap, adeqate and timely credit facilities to the public limited companies for renovation and expansion of their plants and for setting up new industrial ventures. Small-scale industries are not financed by the IFCI.

The IFCI provides medium and long-term finance to large-scale industrial units organised as public limited companies. The assistance provided by the IFCI is in the following forms:

(i) Grant of loans and advances, both in rupees and in foreign currencies, repayable within 25 years.

(ii) Gauranteeing deferred payments in respect of purchase and/or import of machinery by the individual concerns.

(iii) Guaranteeing loans raised by industrial concerns which are repayable within a period of 25 years and are floated in the pulic market.

(iv) Subscribing to debentures of the industrial conerns.

(v) Underwriting the issue of stock, shares or debentures of industrial concerns. Any share or debenture acquired in this process must be disposed of within seven years :

The paid-up capital of the IFCI, as on the 21st March 2001, was Rs. 1,088 crores. The major part of this capital is held by the IDBI. Before the setting up of the IDBI, the major share of capital of the IFCI was held by the RBI and the Central Government, who transferred their shares to the IDBI. Now, the IFCI is a fifty per cent subsidiary of the IDBI. The other subscribers to the share capital of the IFCI are Scheduled Commercial Banks; Co-opoerative Banks, Life Insurance Corporation of India etc. No private individual or company holds the shares of the IFCI. The IFCI has also built up substaintial reserves over the years of its operations. To augment its resources, the IFCI borrows from the Government, the RBI the IDBI and also raises foreign currency loans. The borrowings of the IFCI amounted to Rs. 1043.30 crores on the last Friday of March 1990. Of these borrowings from the IDBI amounted to Rs. 162.63 crores and foreign currency borrowings of Rs. 880.14 crores. For foreign currency loans, the IFCI is authorised to borrow from foreign agencies and international institutions.

The Industrial Finance Corporation of India gives long-term and medium-term loans to the extent of Rs. 1 crores to an industrial unit. During 2000-01, the IFCI sanctioned financial assistance of Rs. 1,858 crores. Of the total financial assistance of Rs. 1,858 crore sanctioned in 2000-01, Rs. 1,207 crore (65.0%) was in the form of rupee loans, Rs. 146 crore (7.9%) in the form of foreign currency loans, Rs. 390 crore (21.0%) in the form of underwriting and direct subscription and Rs. 116 crore (6.2%) in the form of guarntee. The criticism levied against the working of IFCI are the following:

(i) The lending operations of IFCI has encouraged concentration of wealth and capital.

(ii) IFCI did nothing to remove regional disparities.

(iii) IFCI did not take care of national priorities while santioning loans to private sector.

2. Industrial Credit and Investment Corporation India (ICICI)

The Industrial Credit and Investment Corporation of India (ICICI) was set up in January 1955 as a private sector joint stock company with the aim of stimulating and promoting new industries, expanding and modernising existing industries and furnishing technical and managerial assistance to industries to increase production and expand employment opportunities in India. The ICICI is, thus, a privately owned and managed industrial bank unlike the IFCI and IDBI which are the public sector development banks. It was sponsored by the World Bank who has played a key role in its inception, organisation, functioning and raising resources for it. The ICICI is essentially designed to mobilise internationl finance to develop and extend private enterprises in India.

The main functions of the Corporation are as follows:

(a) to help promotion, expansion and modernisation of privately owned industrial enterprises;

(b) to help expansion of the investment market;

(c) to encourage and extend participation of private capital, both India and foreign enterprise.

The paid-up capital of the ICICI, which was a mere Rs. 5 crores in 1955, has gone up to Rs. 91.56 crores by the end of March 1990. The share capital of the ICICI is held by the *(i)* Indian banks, insurance companies and corporation as well as individuals, *(ii)* the banks in UK, an (iii) the US national and companies. Besides paid-up capital, the ICICI has built up substantial reserves which amounted to Rs. 385.52 crores in March 1990.

The ICICI was set up to provide finance to large industries in the private sector, but the scope of its coverage was gradually extended to projects in the joint sector and the cooperative enterprises. However, even now the private sector large industrial ventures account for bulk of assistance provide by the ICICI. The assistance is provided in the form of Rupee loans, foreign currency loans, underwriting of shares and debentures, direct subscription to shares and debentures and guranteeing of loans and deferred payments. During 1990-91, the ICICI sanctioned assistance worth Rs. 3744.0 crores while it disbursed assistance worth Rs. 1967.6 crores. From its inception in 1955, up to the end of March 2001 the industrial Credit and Investment Corporation of India has sanctioned as aggregate assistance of Rs. 56,092 crores. The ICICI has played an important role in providing financial assistance to private sector. Its pioneer work as the undrwriting institution in this country has been widely acclaimed. The ICICI also provide foreign curency loans. It has given a helping hand to a number of industries.

The working of ICICI is criticised on the ground that provides assistance mainly to large units. It has done nothing of promoting backward regions of the country.

3. Industrial Development Bank of India (IDBI)

The IDBI was established as a wholly owned subsidiary of the RBI 1964. However, February 1976, the IDBI was made an autonomous institution and was thus delinked from the RBI. It is now an in dependent public sector financial institution whose ownership vests in the Government of India.

The paid-up capital of the IDBI, which was merely Rs. 50 crores in June 1976, when it was delinked from the RBI and made an autonomous institution, had gone up to Rs. 637 crores in March 1990. Its resources too increased to Rs. 71,383 crores in 2001-01. However, paid-up capital and reserve form only an insignificant proportion of the IDBI's resources. Largest share of its resources has been raised through issue of bounds and debentures whch amounted to Rs. 43,351 crores in 2001-01 Next in significance are the deposits from the companies which amounted Rs. 10,359 crores in 2001 Borrowings from the Government in 2001-01 stood at Rs. 2,669 crores.

The function of the IDBI can be broadly grouped into three categories, *viz.*, *(i)* direct assistance to industrial units in the form of loans and advances; *(ii)* indirect assistance through refinancing of the loans and advance given by other financial institution and (iii) promotional activites in respect of industrialisation of backward areas, small industrial etc.

(1) Direct Financial Assistance. The industral development bank of India Provides direct assistance to industrial units in the form of loans and advances. Besides, it also subscribes to their shares and debentures thereby giving them strong financial support. The Bank can guarantee the loans and advances raised by the industrial concerns from the scheduled banks. IFCI and other notified sources. It can also underwrite the shares and debentures issued by the industrial concerns.

(2) Promotional Activities. The promotional activities of the Industrial Development Bank of India include; *(i)* special assistance for industrial development in the backward areas; *(ii)* assistance to small-scale industries and *(iii)* special assistance by way of Soft Loan Scheme.

With a view to promoting the industrial development of the backward areas the IDBI provides concessional financial assistance to the small and medium projects in these areas. This concession assistance is availablc upto an amount of Rs. 2 crores and has a longer repayment period.

(3) Indirect Financial Assistance. The Industrial Development Bank of India provides indirect assistance by refinancing the loans and advances given to the industry by other agencies, such as IFCI, SFC's Scheduled Commercial Banks and State Co-operative Banks. In brief, the IDBI can refinance the term loans given to the industrial concerns by the IFCI, SFC's and other financial institution, repayable within 25 years; it can refinance loans given to industry by the scheduled banks and the State co-operative Bank, payable within 10 years and it refinances the export given by the scheduled banks and the State Co-operative Banks. In fact, a major part of the assistance by the IDBI is in the form of this refinancing activity. Besides refinancing the loans, the IDBI can subscribe to the shares, bonds and debentures of the ICI, SFC's and other notified financial institutions, thereby argumenting their resources and thus enabling them to increase the financial assistance they are providing to the industry.

The IDBI is the leading Development Bank in India. It has sanctioned comulative assistance to the tune of Rs. 2,72,078 crore till the end of March 2001. The amount of assistance disbursed by IDBI till the end of March 2001 totalled Rs. 1,73,350 crore. During 2000-01, assistance sanctioned and disbused by IDBI stood at Rs. 28,711 crore and Rs. 17,498 crore respectively. Industry wise analysis of IDBI's financial assistance reveals that core and other manufacturing sectors accounted for bulk of the assistance sanctioned and disbursed.

If we judge the performance of IDBI in quantitative terms, its performance is quite impressive. Over the years not only the amount but also the range and pettern of assistance have grown. However, it has failed to develop itself as a true development bank. Its accent on providing loans and treating underwriting of shares and debentures of industrial concerns as a secondary activity is not very appropriate.

Though the IDBI is providing assistance to small scale industries and backward areas but big industrial units are still getting more loans from it. IDBI only provides financial assistance. The promotional and consultancy works are also of equal importance and IDBI is not paying one attention towards these functions. Over a period of time the financial performance of IDBI has been declining moreover the ratio of its non-performing assets to net assets rose to 13.40 per cent in 1990-2000. Hence there is need to give an immediate attention to IDBI's strartegy.

4. Small Industries Development Bank of India (SIDBI)

With a view to ensuring flow of financial and non-financial assistance to the small-scale sector the government of India announced in the budget for 1988-89, its decision to establish small Industries. Development Bank of India (SIDBI) as a subsidiary of IDBI. The SIDBI Act was passed by the Parliament in October 1989 and the Bank commenced its operations from April 2, 1990. To equip SIDBI to play its apex role in SSI credit provision more effectively, the Union Budget 1998-99 proposed the delinking of SIDBI from IDBI and transferring of IDBI shareholding of SFCs to SIDBI. The SIDBI commenced its operations with an initial paid-up capital of Rs. 250 crore and by taking over the outstanding portfolio of IBDI relating to small-scale sector held under Small Industries Development Fund as on March 31, 1990 amounting to Rs. 4,200 crore. The financial resources of SIDBI aggregated to Rs. 17,090 crore in 2000-01.

With a view to ensuring larger flow of assistance to the small-scale units, the immediate thrust of SIDBI was on *(i)* initiating steps for technological upgradation and modernisation of existing units; *(ii)* expanding the channels for marketing the products of the small-scale sector; and *(iii)* promotion of employment-oriented industries especially in semi-urban areas to create more employment opportunities and thereby checking migration of population to urban areas. SIDBI provides assistance to the small-scale units through the existing credit delivery system comprising State Financial Corporation, Co-operative Banks, State Industrial Development Corporations, Commercial Banks and regional Rural Banks. The major activities of SIDBI are: *(i)* refinance of loans and advances; *(ii)* discounting and re-discounting of bills; *(iii)* extension of seed apital/soft loans; *(iv)* granting direct assistance and refinancing of loans; *(v)* providing services like factoring, leasing etc; and *(vi)* extending financial support to State Small Industries Development Corporations. During 2001-01 SIDBI sanctioned assistance worth Rs. 10,821 crore of which assistance worth Rs 6,441 crore was disbursed. Till end March 2001, cumulative Sactions and disbursements by SIDBI were of the order of Rs. 66.227 crore and Rs. 46,461 crore respectively.

5. The Industrial Investment Bank of India (IIBI)

There are a number of industries having sick industrial units. These units possess obsolescent machinery and poor management. The economic position of some units has deteriorated because the managers of these units have paid more attention to distribution of dividends rather than reinvestment (or ploughing back) of profits. The Government does not want these units to shut down because this would lead to retrenchment of employees and large-scale unemployment of industrial workers. Accordingly, it established the Industrial Reconstruction Corporation of India (IRCI) in 1971 to provide financial assistance to industrially sick units and, if necessary, to provide managerial and technical assistance as well.

By a notification issued on March 20,1985, the Government converted the IRCI (which was a company registered under the Companies Act) into a statutory corporation to be called the Industrial Reconstruction Bank of India (IRBI) with a view to overcoming the inherent difficulties which had been faced by the IRCI in its efforts to rehabilitate sick industrial units. IRBI was reconstituted into a new full-fledged all purpose development financial institution under the Companies Act, 1956 in March 1997 with adeqate operational flexibility and functional autnomy. The entire assets and liabilities of IRBI have been transferred to this new company which is known as industrial Bank of India (IIBI).

Sanctions and disbursements by IIBI during 1997-98 stood at Rs. 1,446 crore and R. 1,556 crore respectively. The cumulative assistance sanctioned by IIBI as at end-March 2001 was Rs. 12,358 crore. The performance of IIBI is worrisome. The proportion of non-performing assets to net asset is increasing which has affected the working of IIBI adversely.

NEED OF BUSINESS FINANCE

Finance is a pre-requisite for the mobilisation of real resources to organise production and market, therefore it is described as the "life-blood" of industry. Depending upon the nature of the activity to be financed, business requires short-term, medium term and long term finances. The sources of finance are presented in the table given below.

Source of Finance

Short-term	*Medium-Term*	*Long-Term*
(i) Bankcredit	(i) Issue of shares	(i) Issue of shares
(ii) Trade credit	(ii) Issue of debentures	(ii) Issue of Debentures
(iii) Instalments credit	(iii) Loan from banks and other financial institutions	(iii) Loans from financial institutions
(iv) Customer advances	(iv) Public Deposits	(iv) Ploughing back of profits
	(v) Ploughing back of profit	(v) others
	(vi) others	

The detail discussion of sources of business finance is given below:

1. Shares. The shares of a company may be broadly divided into:

(a) Preference Shares, and

(b) Equity Shares.

Preference Shares. Preference shares are those which have preferential right to the payment of dividend during the life-time of the company, and a preferential right to the return of capital when the company is would up.

Preference shares have the following characteristics:

(i) Preference shareholders get their fixed rate of dividend before any dividend is distributed among the other class of share holders;

(ii) At the time of winding up the company, the preference shareholders must be paid back their capital before anything is paid to ordinary shareholders;

(iii) The dividend on them is fixed by the Articles of the company.

Kinds of Preference Shares

(i) Cumulative Preference Shares. The cumulative preference shares are entitled to fixed dividends whether there are profits or no profits. If profits are not sufficient to pay dividends in a particular year, the dividends are accumulated and paid in the succeeding year (s) as profits become available for distribution.

(ii) Non-Cumulative Preference Shares. Unlike the cumulative preference shares. these shares cannot claim arrears of dividends of any year out of the profits of subsequent years.

(iii) Participating Preference Shares. In the case of the participating preference shares, shareholders receive a fixed rate of dividend in priority to ordinary share and, further the right to participate in the balance of profit in an agreed proportion together with ordinary shareholders.

(iv) Non-Participating Preference Shares. These shares are entitled to only a fixed rate of dividend; they have no claim in the surplus profit which belongs to ordinary shareholders.

(v) Redeemable Preference Shares. These are shares which can be purchased back by the company. The company reserves its right to call back or purchase these shares at any time, subject to the provision of its Articles.

(vi) Irredeemable Preference Shares. These are shares that cannot be pruchased back by the company.

Equity Shares. A shares which are not preference shares are equity shares, also called ordinatry shares. Unlike the preference share, quity shares do not have a fixed rate of dividend. Equity shareholders are entitled to dividends only after the dividend claims of the preference shareholders have been met. Similarly at the time of the winding up the company, equity shareholders get back their capital only after the capital of the preference shareholder has been paid back equity shares are always irredeemable and their holders have normal voting rights.

Alteration of Share Capital

Section 94 of the companies Act provides that a limited company can if permitted by its Articles of Association, alter its share capital in any of the following ways:

(i) It may increase its share capital by the issue of new shares;

(ii) It may convert all or any of its fully paid-up shares into stock or reconvert that stock into fully paid-up shares;

(iii) It may consolidate and divide all or any part of its share capital into shares of a larger amount;

(iv) It may subdivide the existing shares into shares of lower denomination; and

(v) It may cancel those shares which have not been taken up and reduce its capital accordingly.

Any of the above alternations can be effected by passing a resolution in the general meeting of the company and requires no confirmation by the court. However, the company shall give notice of any such alternations to the Registrar within thirty days after doing so.

2. Creditorship Securities. Creditorship securities which consist of debentures and bonds, are credit instruments which are widely used by companies to raise funds. The capital raised through creditorship securities is known as borrowed capital or debt capital.

The term *debenture* is defined as "a document under the company's seal which provides for the payment of a principal sum and interest thereon at regular intervals which is usually secured by a fixed or flouting charge on the company's property or undertaking which acknowledge a loan to the company".

Classes of Debentures

(i) Redeemable and Irredeemable. From the point of view of redemption, debentures are classified into redeemable and irredeemable. Redeemable debentures are those that will be repaid by the company at the end of a specified peirod, or on demand, or by instalments. Irredeemable debentures are those that are not repayable during the life-time of the company. Irredeemable debenture are also called perpetual debentures.

(ii) Mortgage and Simple. From the point of view of security, debentures are classified into mortagage and simple or naked debentures. Mortgage debentures, also called secured debentures, are those which are secured by a charge on the assests or property of the company, where as simple debentures are those that are not secured of the company, where as simple debentures are those that are not secured by any charge on the assests of the company.

(iii) Registered and Bearer. From the point of view of records, debentures may be classified into registered and bearer debentures. Registered debentures are those in respect of which the names, addresses and particularly of the holdings of debenture-holders are entered in the Register of Debenture-holders. The transfer of a registered debentures cannot be effected without the execution of a regular transfer deed. As against this, the company keeps no records of bearer debenture-holders. Bearer debentures are negotiable by mere delivery of the document.

(iv) Convertible and Unconvertible. In case of convertible debentures, the holder have the option to convert their debenture holdings into equity shares of the company at a specified rate after a sepcified period.

3. Internal Financing. An important source for fixed and working capital requirement of established companies is the savings generated internally in the form of retained earnings by the process of ploughing back of profits. A profitable company may retain with it a part of the net profit as undistributed profits to strengthen its financial position, or to meet some of the present or future financial requirements. The reserves thus built up over the years by ploughing back profit may be utilised for the following purposes:

(i) Expansion of undertaking;

(ii) Meeting permanent (regular) or special working capital requirements;

(iii) Replacement of obsolete assets and modernisation;

(iv) Redemption of old debts.

The ploughing back of profits benefits the company, shareholders and society.

Dangers of Ploughing Bank Profits

Some dangers are associated with the indiscriminate policy of plouging back profits. Some of the possible dangers are:

(i) It may lead to concentration of economic power because large retained earning enable companies to enlarge their business easily by a continual reinvestment of the profits.

(ii) It gives scope for manipulation. The controlling powers of the company may depress share prices by keeping the devidend rate very low by ploughing back a substantial part of the profit so that they might purchase the shares at low prices and later benefit from a fighter dividend and appreciation of the share value due to the rise in the rate of dividends.

(iii) It may lead to over-capitalisation if the reserves are capitalised by issuing bonus shares or bonus issues.

(iv) The top brass of the management may misuse the funds by locking them up in their pet concerns or companies under the same management against the overall interest of the shareholders.

(v) The ploughing back of profits interests with the rights and freedom of shareholders. If shareholders get higher dividends, they will be at liberty to distribute their investments as they like, whereas they, especially the small shareholders, do not have any significant say in the investment or utilisation or retained earnings.

(vi) From the above point of view, it follows that excessive ploughing back of profits may higher the natural growth of the capital market.

Determinants of Retained Earnings

The following are the three important determinants of retained earnings:

(i) Profits. Obviously, the question of the ploughing back of profits does not arise if a company does not earn profits. Normally, a company has to declare a reasonable rate of dividend to satisfy the shareholders and to prevent a depreciation of share values. Hence, only what is left over after paying a resonable dividend can be ploughed back. Thus, the amount of net profits is an important determinant of internal savings.

(ii) Dividend Policy. The dividend policy is an important determinant of retained profits. A conservative dividend policy is rearded as necessary to build up internal savings. Some people advocate a statutory ceiling on dividends to facilitate a greater ploughing back of profits. At times, the Government has imposed ceilings on dividends.

(iii) Taxation. The rate of corporation taxation is an important determinate of "net profits". A high rate of corporate tax imposes limitations on the building up of internal savings.

4. Public Deposits. Recent years have witnessed a significant increase in public deposits with companies (here the reference is to deposits with non-financial joint stock companies). Public deposits played an important role in industrial fiance in the past as well. For instance, the 1930s, it was an important source for the textile mills of Ahmedabad, Bombay, Sholapur, Bengal and Punjab. The tea gardens of Bengal and Assam also depended on this sources of finance.

The statistics released by the Government of India show that the total number of companies accepting deposits and the total amount of deposits have increased considerably.

Advantages. The increasing popularity of public deposits has been mainly due to the following reasons:

(i) As the rate of interest offered by the companies have been significantly higher than the rates offered by banks for the same periods, there has been a good public response.

(ii) The rate of interest the companies have to pay on deposits from the public is lower than the interest on bank loans.

(iii) Public deposit has been an easier method of mobilising funds than from banks, epecially during periods of credit squeeze.

(iv) To obtain credit from a commercial bank, the company has to satisfy the credit-worthiness of the purpose for which the loan is sought; but in the case of public deposits, there is no such need.

(v) It follows from this that public deposits form a source to finance business activities for which bank finance is not available.

(vi) A further attractiveness of public deposits from the point of view of the companies is that they are unsecured.

(vii) Some public sector undertakings have also been drawing upon this source of finance.

Limitations. Public deposits, however, have demerits from the point of view of society.

(i) As public deposits are unsecured, depositors bear the risks of loss of money in the event of the failure of the company.

(ii) Public deposits with companies may cause of diversion of resources into non-priority and undesirable areas.

(iii) Public deposits tend to defeat the objectives of monetary policy, espeially a dear money policy. They also distort the planned interest rate structure in the economy.

(iv) It has been argued by some people that public deposits adversely affect back deposits. But this argument has been countered by pointing out that if public deposits activate the idle resources in the economy, they would help increase the deposits with commercial banks.

Regulation of Public Deposits

The Government has realised the need for the regulation of the acceptance of public deposits by companies in the interest of the depositing public, the efficancy of the monetary policy and resource utilisation. From time to time, the Reserve Bank has issued directives regulating public deposits.

The salient feature of the regulation are:

(i) Deposits shall not exceed 25 per cent of the paid-up capital and free reserves.

(ii) The maximum period of deposits is 36 months.

(iii) Every company shall invest not less than 10 per cent of its deposits maturing during the year ending 31st March in a current or other account with a scheduled bank free from any charge or lien, or in approved securities. The amount deposited shall be used only for the repayment of deposits maturing during the year referred to under the rules.

(iv) Every company accepting deposits shall file periodical returns with the RBI, giving the required information about public deposits/loans.

(v) While issuing advertisements and application forms soliciting deposits, the company should furnish certain specified information on its financial position and its working.

Until recently, leasing as a method of industrial financing was not popular in India. But now there is such a spurt in the number of leasing companies that one observe comments: "Leasing companies are springing up faster than mushrooms"

5. Commercial Bank. Commercial Banks form another important source of finance to large scale industries but they supply short term loans. Their role in the provision of long term loan has been almost insignificant. They are always hesitant in providing long or medium term finance to industries. There is some justification in their not giving long term credit to industries. We know that the liabilities of these banks are mostly of short term nature and so there is risk in lending for long terms.

6. Investment Trust. In recent years investment trusts have assumed importance in the field of industrial finance in India. Investment trusts are public limited companies. They have large resources. An investment trust raises the capital through the sale of securities to the public. The capital thus raised is invested by the trust in shares and debentures of the industrial concerns. An investment trust does not invest all its funds in one industry but funds are widely diffused on various industries so that the risk should be minimised. A few investment trusts do underwriting business as well. At present there are 620 investment trusts in India.

7. Other Investment Institutions. Life Insurance Corporation and other insurance companies are another source of finance available to industries. They have large funds for investment. They finance these industries through the purchase of their shares and debentures. Life Insurance Corporation is the most important source of long term industrial finance. Its annual premium income in 1964 was Rs. 146 crores. Thus if Life Insurance Corporation takes interest in the field of industrial finance, the problem of long term finance for industries will be over.

8. Special Institutions for Industrial Finance. The sources of industrial finance as discussed above were inadequate to meet the ever increasing demand of finance by old as well as new industrial concerns. The Government have set up many new financial institutions for industrial finance. These institutions are Industrial Finance Corporation, State Finance Corporations, Industrial credit and Investment Corporation, National Industrial Development Corporation. Industrial Development Bank, Unit Trust of India etc.

❐

12

Exim Policy

IMPORT POLICY

Import Policy Before Eighties. The import policy of the government of India prior to the eighties had two important constituents: *(i)* import restrictions and *(ii)* import substitution. The reasons behind this import policy were limited foreign exchange reservers of the country, shortages of essential consumer goods in the economy, requirements of capital goods, machinery, spare-parts and components for the building up of heavy, basic industries, and the role and scope of import substitution in the country. Now we shall discuss two constituents of import policy in detail.

(i) Important Restrictions. Due to the large scale industrialisation of the country from Second plan, the government imported capital equipment, mechinery, industrial raw materials, spare - parts etc. in large quantities resulted into substantial increase in foreign exchange expenditure. On the other hand, constant export earnings and import of foodgrains forced government to restrict the imports of non essential items. The government classifed imports under the categories of banned items, restricted items, cavalised items and items under Open General Licence (OGL). The policy of import restriction was rigorously pursued by government right up to 1977-78.

(ii) Import Substitution. The two broad objectives of the programme of import substitution of India were: *(a)* to save scarce foreign exchange for the import of more important goods, and *(b)* to achieve self-reliance in the production of as many goods a possible. Due to this policy, the structure of imports has undergone significant changes. The country has been able to increase the production of many industrial products like iron and steel, automobiles, railway wagons etc. Though the immediate aim of import substitution was the conservation of foreign exchanges its long term objective was to initiate structural changes in the economy. As a consequence of this, the industrial structure has achieved diversification and depth. Import substitution has helped not only in sawing of foreign exchange but also in accelerating the process of economic growth.

Import Liberalisation in the Eighties. Since 1977-78, the government of India has been following a liberalised import policy with the objective of increasing production, especially export production. There has been an increased emphasis on enhancing maintenance imports in order to promote capacity utilisation. The Government of India has announced three long term import policies at different periods. The broad details of the import liberalisation measures enunciated are outlined below:

(i) A large number of raw materials, components and consumables are put in the Open General Licence, (OGL) list. In 1977-78 there were as many as 570 items and every year a few items are added and some are deleted. In the 1984-85 Export-Import policy, as many as 159 new items of industrial machinery were included for import under OGL. The items allowed under OGL are only those wherein sufficient indigenous capacity does not exist. In 1984-85 policy, as many as 53 items were excluded from OGL which indicates that either the country is now self-sufficient in them and, therefore, no imports were necessary, or the Government wanted to support the indigenous industry to produce these goods and satisfy the local market. In the 1990-92 policy, imports of 1,343 thus were kept free.

(ii) Under OGL, approved 100 per cent export oriented units can import capital goods, raw materials and components. From 1983-84 the OGL was substantially enlarged for the above export-oriented units to include second hand capital goods, diesel generating sets, consumables and packing materials. The import policy of 1990-92 put 870 raw material items under OGL.

(iii) In order to promote capacity utilisation, the import policy had a scheme of automatic licensing for timely arrangement of imports of machinery, machine, tools, spare parts and raw materials. All manufacturing units which export a certain proportion of their production (presently 25 per cent) were eligible to get automatic licences on the basis of the value of consumption of imported raw materials. Actual users who have automatic licences were not required to obtain their licences on a repeat basis for the next 12 months.

(a) REP licensing scheme has been expanded and simplifed.

(b) Registered Manufacturers-Exporters who have been exporting regularly for a periods of three years are permitted to import capital goods upto a maximum value of Rs. 10 crores at a concessional customs duty of 25 per cent. This in subject to an import obligation equivalent to three times the value of imports within 4 year of the date of import.

(c) Export services like computer software, overseas management and cosultancy service constracts as well as advertising jobs will qualify for import replacements at the rate of 10 per cent of net foreign exchange earned.

(d) Under the Duty examption Scheme, Blanket Advance Licensing has been introduced for manufacturer exporters having a minimum net foreign exchange earnings of Rs. 10 crores during the preceeding 3 years.

(e) Under the scheme of registration of Export Houses and Trading Houses, for determining eligibility, the annual averge of net foreign exchange earnings in the base period should not be less than Rs. 5 crores for an Export House and Rs. 20 crores for a Trading House. These houses will be eligible for additional licences for import of raw materials, components, consumables and tools and capital goods allowed under OGL, besides other limited permissible items and canalised items.

(f) Exporters who fulfil certain minimum export requirements for a specified period of time are granted the status of Export House, Trading House, Start Trading House or Super Star Trading House. These are defined on the basis of two criteria the FOB critierion and the NFE criterion. These export houses provited a number of benefits.

Exporters	*FOB Criterion*	
	(for last there years) (increase of Rs.)	*(for preceeding year) (increase of Rs.)*
Export House	12.5	18.75
Trading House	62.5	93.75
Star Trading House	312.50	468.75
Super Star Trading House	925.00	1387.50

Exporters	*NFE Criterion*	
	(for last there years) (in Rs. crores)	*(for preceeding year) (in Rs. crores)*
Export House	10	15
Trading House	50	75
Star Trading House	250	375
Super Star Trading House	740	1100

(g) The government has allowed liberal import of technology to encourage export promotion and technological advancement. However, imported technology.

EVALUATION OF IMPORT POLICY

The main points of critical evaluation are the following:

1. Adverse Effect on the Growth of Capital Goods Industry in India. The most serious liberalisation has been attempted in the

Exim policy 1985-86 in the capital goods list bearining 208 items under the OGL list. Among the additions are mocroprocessor based equipment, machine tools, spinning machines, jute machineary etc. The impact of this ware of liberalisation is bould to be adverse. Given the limited size of the market and the problems of technology transfer and the procedural bottlnecks created by licensing, the development of capital goods industry which was never a very lucrative proposition for Indian industrialists, has been made much more frightening in the wake of liberal imports of customs duty concessions. This is evidence in the case of garment industry. Through the industry exports readymade garments worth Rs 2,100 crores, in the sphere of manufacture of machinery, the country has reached sewing machine type machinery only.

2. Import Liberalisation as a Damper on Indigenous Production. The liberalisation of imports for automatic and electronics industry is being carried out by governments to encourage these industries through concessions in import licensing and custom tariff with a view to achieve modernisation and cost reduction. But as a consequence of this policy, indigenous production is not being promoted, nor is technology being absorbed. Rather the policy has led to imports for assembly into finished goods. This trend of increasing dependence on foreign goods, needs to be reserved. The Government should, therefore, excerise greater vigilance and promote import substitution.

3. Import Policy Likely to Hit Small-scale Industries. Although the statement of objectives specifically mentions encouragement of the small-scale sector, but the measures suggested do not match with the professed aims. Rather the Government in the name of modernisation is helping but business to import labour saving machinery. Economic and political weekly exposing double talk of the Government mentions: "the government's pretensions of encouraging the handloom sector by controlling the textile inudustry are exposed by the fact that latest in the labour-saving the textile industry are exposed by the fact that the latest in the labour-saving textile machinery, air jet and water jet looms (including shuttleless looms) have been placed under OGL on the plea of modernisation.

4. Import of Consumables Under OGL. One may be inclined to agree with a larger import of capital goods (though one may not justify import of every item), but a screeting of the import brought under OGL bings to the foresome shocking revelations. For instance, it passes one's comprehension why billiard cloth, rubber cushions for billiard tables and billard balls have been brought under OGL. Similarly, the elitist bias is reflected in the inclusion of video-cassettes, manmade fibres and yarns, PVC resin, woollen rags, rubber blankets, polystyrene films, etc. Are these essential items of imports?

5. Adverse Effect on Indigenous. The new import policy is trying to over-reach its objectives of liberalisation and under pressure from multi-nationals has opened areas in which indigenous industry has adequate capacity. There are certainly far reaching implications of such sweeping relaxations in imports. The Gujarat state Fertiliser Corporation (GSFC) and the Soda Ash Industry have been continuously pleading before the Government to restrict imports of caprolactum and soda ash since it would hit their interest adversely but the powerful multi-nationals have forced the government dump these raw materials in India. This poses a problem of survival for the indigenous industry.

6. Technological Dumping in the Name of Technology Upgrading. The import Policy of 1984-85 only carries forward the trend set in the import polices announed during the last fiew years regarding liberal import of capital goods in the name of technological upgarding of industry. According to RBI Report on currency and finance (1989-90) capital goods imports increased from Rs. 3,168 crores in 1984-85 to Rs. 8,831 crores in 1989-90 *i.e.*, they have grown at an annual growth rate of 22.8 per cent during the 5 year period. There is, therefore, a relentless drive for unfettered import of capital goods, design and drawings and technology. This is a dangerous trend from the country's point of view. Criticising this approach, the Economic and political weekly mentions: "What is missed in the line of reasoning is that production capacities once built on imported technologies and imported capital goods have to be sustained by imported raw materials, spares and parts. The so-called inflexible imports" are therefore, destined to grow constantly and relentlessly.

Secondly, experience has also shown that the multinationals are hardly interested in technology transfer. Rather they in the name technological upgarding, carry on 'technological upgrading carry on technological- dmping', of such technologies which have been supersened in the developed countries. This, the critics argue, is far more deleterious than dumping of goods-including capital goods.

From the foregoing analysis it becomes evident that opening the door of imports much wider result in increasing the trade gap. The Government under pressure from IMF and powerful multinationals has been permitting a much greater quantum of imports in the name of export promotion. Such indiscriminate liberalisation would create more dependence in terms of foreign exchange and widen the grade gap. A much more prudent course would be to screen imports so as to discriminate between essential and non-essential imports.

EXPORT POLICY

Realising the country's potential for achieving a rising level of export and recognising the need for the adoption of appropriate policies and measure designed to promote investment in the development of the promising sectors to generate exportable surplus and the need to provide adequate facilities and incentives to promote the growth of export trade, the export policy resolutions were announced by the Government of India from time to time. Bimal Jalan classifies export policy of India into three distinct phases.

Important export promotion measures undertaken by the Government of India during the planning period (more specifically, prior to 1991) were as follows:

1. **Custom Duty Concession.** Certain terms of import used in export production enjoy import duty exemptions. The import policy boost contains a list of items for which exporters can obtain advance licences and import them without paying customs duty.
2. **Drawback of Duties.** Under the scheme of drawback of duties, a refund of excise and customs duties paid on the materials used in the manufactures of exported goods can

be availed of. To obtain a refound of the duties, the exporter should file the "Drawback shipping bill." The filling of the shipping bill is itself an application for the grant of drawbacks. If the rate of drawback is fixed, the Drawback Department will make the payment to the claimant. Where the drawback rates are not fixed, the exporter will have to claim drawbacks provisionally, and the final settlement will be made on the fixation of rates.

The rates of drawback are of two types-one, known as brand Rates, is fixed manufacture-wise on the basis of the data furnished, and the other, an All-Industry rate, is applicable to all exporters alike.

3. **Cash Assistance.** The scheme of cash assitance is intended to improve the competitiveness of the Indian exporters in the foreign market. Under this scheme, cash assistance is offered to exporters of selected non-traditional industrial products, such as engineering goods, chemicals and allied products, plastics, leather and leater goods and other animal products, products, sport goods, processed foods, woollen carpets, rugs, natural silk fabrics and garments, etc. The extent of assistance is periodically reviewed by the government. It varies from 5 per cent to 25 per cent of the f.o.b. value. No cash assistance, however, is available for exports to Afghanistan, Bhutan, Bangladesh (except in cases when payment is in free foreign exchange), Nepal and Tibet.

   Only registered exporters are eligible for cash assistance, subject to their registration continuing to be valid.

4. **REP/Exim scrip.** The replenishment licence (Rep) was a facility available to registered exporters to import specified items where the domestic substitutes were not adequate in terms of price, quality or availability. The REP licences which were related to f.o.b value of the exports to sell the REP at a premium because of the great demand domestically for the items which could be imported under these licences.

The trade policy announced on July 5, 1991 significantly modified the REP scheme and renamed it as Exim Scrip.

The exim scrip scheme was abolished with the introduction of the partial convertibility of the Rupee by the union budget announced on Feb 29,1992. According to the Liberalised Exchange Rate Management System (LERMS), 60 per cent of foreign exchange by exports convered into rupee at the market determined rates. This increases the profitability of the export business when the market rate is higher than the official exchange rate.

5. **100 Per cent Export-Oriented Units.** Hundered per cent export-oriented units (EOUs) have been encouraged to help boost India's exports. The term hundred per cent export-oriented unit refers to an industrial unit offering for exports its entire production, excluding the permitted levels of rejects. On December 30, 1980, the Ministry of commerce announced various incentives and facilities for the EOUs.

   Hundred per cent export-oriented units are allowed in industries whose export potential and export targets have been considered by the relevant export promotion council. EOUs are not normally encouraged for products subject to export control quota ceilings which can be reached by the existing units in the industry. The scheme of 100 per cent export-oriented units has been designed to create additional export capacity; units which result in more substitution for the existing units's production are not permitted.

6. **Tax Concessions.** Certain categories of exporters are granted tax exemptions and concessions. For instance, under section 35 B of the Income Tax Act, 1961, specified exporters can avail of export markets development allowance. The assistance is given in the form of weighted deduction from the taxable income. The quantum of deduction is equal to one and one-third times the amount of expenditure incurred directly or in association with any

other person during the previous year. The expenditres that qualify for such deductions are:

(i) Obtaining information on makets outside India for such goods, services or facilities;

(ii) Advertisement or publicity outside India of the goods, services or facilities which the assesse deals in or provides in the course of his business;

(iii) Maintenance outside India of a branch office or agency for the promotion of the sale of goods, services or facilities;

(iv) Distribution, supply or provision outside India of such goods, services of facilities not being expenditure incured in India in connection therewith or expenditure (whenever incurred) on the carriage of such goods to destinations outside India or on the insurance of goods while in transit;

Exporters are also offered some other tax incentives. Companies are granted tax exemption on the whole of their dividend, income loyalties, know-how fees, etc. received from abroad for service rendered.

7. **Finance Facilities.** The export sector, being a priority sector is, offered liberal credit facilities. Interest rate concessions are also offered for export finance. Commercial banks play a very important role in providing pre-shipment (known as packing credit) and post-shipment credit. Pre-shimpment credit, as the name indicates, refers to the credit extended to eligible exporters for providing working capital for the purchase of raw materials, production, packing, transporting goods meant for export, were housing, etc. Post-shipment finance refers to the credit for the actual shipment of goods in order to bridge the period between the shipment of the goods and the receipt of the sale proceeds from abroad.

Exporters can also obtain credit against certain export incentives to be realised from the government on the condition that it will be repaid as soon as the incentive is realised. The IDBI plays an important role in the provision of long-term export credit.

8. **Subsides on Domestic Raw Materials.** The most important scheme in this category is the International Price Reimbursement Scheme (IPRS) for steel, which equalzies the difference between international and dometistic sources.

9. **Advance Licences.** Advance liences facilitate imports of specified raw materials without payment of any customs duty. Such licences are available only against confirmed export orders and/or letters of credit. Under the Intermediate Advance Licensing Scheme, duty free advance licences are granted to Registered Manufacturer Exporters for the supply of intermediate product to an exporter holding a duty-free advance licence.

10. **Blanket Exchange Permit Scheme.** A new Blanket Exchange permit Scheme was introduced by the government in June 1987. The scheme aims to give a major thrust to the country's export promotion drive. The new scheme is more broad based and flexible both as to the eligibility of exporters and the purpose for which exchange can be drawn by holders against their blanket permits. Under the scheme exporters are allowed, barring a few products, to utilise 5-10 per cent of their foreign exchange earnings for undertaking export promotion activities.

11. **Origanisational Structure for Promotion of Exports.** The organisational structure for pormotion of exports includes a number of councils and organisations set up during the post-Independence period. These include:

    (i) Export Promotion Councils,

    (ii) Commodity Boards,

    (iii) Export Houses,

(iv) Agricultural and Processed Food Products Export Development Authority,

(v) The Central Advisory Council on Trade,

(vi) The Federation of India Export Organisations,

(vii) The Federation of Indian Export Organisations,

(viii) The Trade Development Authority,

(ix) The Indian Institute of Packaging,

(x) Export Credit and Gurantee Corporation of India,

(xi) The Export Inspection Council,

(xii) Trade Fair Authority of India,

(xiii) Public sector agencies like State Trading Corporation of India, Minerals and Metals Trading Corporation, Handicrafts and Handloom Export Corporation, Indian Motion Pictures Export Corporation etc., and

(xiii) The Indian Institute of Foreign Trade.

At present 5 Commodity Boards (dealing with tea, coffee, rubber, spices and tobacco) and 19 Export Promotion Councils are functioning. Export Houses specialise in export trade. In additions there are Trading Houses, Star Trading Houses and Super Star Trading Houses. Trade Fair Authority of India is engaged in the organisation of international fairs and exhibitions to project Indian exports. The Federation of India Export Organisations coordinates and supplements the export promotional activiteis of various organisations and institutions. State Trading Corporation (STC) was set up primarily to deal in trade with socialist countries. It export a wide range of products such as sugar, rice, tobacco, coffee, castor oil, etc. and bulk commodities like cement and salt, textiles and manufactured products. Minerals and Matals Trading Corporation (MMTC) was set up specifically for dealing with exports of mineral oils and metals from the country. The Central Advisory Coucil on Trade advises the government on matter relating to export and import policy and programmes, operations of import and export controls etc. Trade Development Authority helps Indian manufacturers and exporters in displaying their products in overseas trade fairs and exhibitions. The Indian Institute of Packaging undertakes research on raw materials for the packaging industry. Proper packaging of export goods is necessary to protect the products and attract the consumers. The primary objectives of the Export Credit and Guarantee Corporation of India is to promote exports from India by providing export credit insurance and guarantee facilities to Indian exporters and commercial bankers. The purpose of Export Inspection Council is to enforce quality control and comulsory pre-shipment inspection of various commodities.

A CRITICAL EVALUATION OF EXPORT POLICY

1. **Absence of a Long Term Export Strategy.** Phase I of export strategy was characterised by export pessimism. There were no concrete efforts to promote exports during this phase. In Second Phase more attention was paid to the export sector as it was realised that import substitution, in itself, would not be able to bring about a viability in India's balance of payments. Accordingly, a number of steps (outlined earlier) were adopted in increase exports. Even then, the criticism remains that we lacked a long term export strategy. In most of the crucial areas affecting the export sector ad-hocism persisted. In the third phase, there has been a new emphasis on exports and many steps have been initiated to increase them. However, the 'linkages' of the exports of different industries to the domestic economy have not been explored. Accordingly, the task of 'integrating' export planning with the overall planning has yet to be accomplished.
2. **Problems Confronting Primary Exports.** Increasing exports of primary commodities was limited on account of a number of external and internal factors. The external

factors included *(i)* steady deterioration in the terms of trade for primary products in the international market; *(ii)* severe fluctuations in international product prices; *(iii)* growth of synthetic substitutes; *(iv)* changes in technology which have reduced the amount of material used in manufacturing; *(v)* pattern of consumption in developed countries which makes for a low propensity to consume such products; and *(vi)* tariffs and other restrictions imposed by industrial countries on some primary products.

Among internal features the most important factor is the rising domestic consumption of exportables either as raw materials for the domestic industry (for example, raw cotton, raw tobacco, raw hides and skins, etc.) or as final goods (like cotton textiles, tea, coffee, vegetable oils, etc.) To meet domestic demand of oilseeds and vegetable oil in the economy, the government banned the exports of most oilseeds in 1952 and the ban has continued since then (this has to be seen in the light of the fact that in pre-war days, India used to supply 40-50 per cent of world exports of groundnuts and groundnut oil). Because of the serious inflationary pressures operating in the economy, profit margins on domestic sales have risen considerably in relation to export sales and this has worked as a disincentive to export primary products. In addition to this export controls and export duties levied on primary exports have also contributed to a fall in India's share of world exports of primary products.

3. **Problems Confronting Non-Traditional Exports.** India's domestic policies have played a crucial role in increasing export earning from non-traditional products. Various export subsidization policies helped in increasing exports of manufactured products. The share of engineering goods exports in total exports rose from 2.1 per cent in 1960-61 to 13.0 per cent in 1998-99. However, exports of manufactured products have also suffered on account of

serious trading and production problems, faulty dometic policies and insufficient efforts.

(i) ***Tradition Problems.*** Among the 'trading problems' one can mention external impediments which pose a problem of "entry" for the Indian manufactures (and manufactures of other developing countries) in makets of industrialised countries. The most important factor is the system of tariffs adopted by the developed countries. The characteristics features of this system is that tariff rates become increasingly higher as one moves from raw material to manufactured product. For example as one moves from iron ore to raw steel and then to machine goods, the tariff rates in industrialized countries frequently increase. Such tariff system makes it difficult for less developed countries to compete in the world market for manufactures. This discriminatory tariff system is accompained by a plethora of quota restrictions and other non-tariff barriers. Another external impediment is that the process of import substitution in other countries encompasses virtually the same range of goods which India is trying to export. The most glaring example in this context is the cotton textile industry which many less developed countries have developed countries have developed successfully in the post war period.

During recent years, international agencies like the IMF and World Bank have been pressurising the developing countries to open up their economies. In fact, such 'opening up' has been made a pre-condition for granting economic assistance under the structural adjustment programme. The IMF - World Bank conditionalities have obviously been dictated by the developed countries who are interested in finding new markets in the devloping countries for their ever increasing range of products. However, they themselves continue to impose restrictions on imports from the developing countries.

(ii) ***Production Problems.*** The most serious problems in this field is the lack of 'technological dynamism' in Indian industry. In spite of changes in the inudstrial and trade policies, most Indian firms continue to produce outdated product with inefficient production technologies. The continued tecnological stagnation of industry is shown by its low expenditure on technology acquisition activities. Not only this, a very large number of firms continue to use plants which are more than 20 years old. These plants suffer from frequent breakdowns, poor and uneven product quality, and high rejection rates. They have also become inefficient users of energy. Furthermore these plants embody obsolete production technologies which have been replaced by more advanced and efficient technologies in the developed countries. Since the advanced process and plants of the developed countries are highly computerised the production quality is far superior and uniform. In this global competitive environment, India is to increase its earnings from manufactured exports, it will have to update its technological capabilities continuously. This calls for massive investment in R&D and plant modernisation.

NEW EXIM POLICY

The Government of India announced its New Exim Policy on 31st March, 2002 for the period of new five years. The main features of this new policy are the following:

1. **Removal of Restrictions.** Exim policy has removed quantitative restrictions on all imports. This policy has also removed quantitative restrictions on exports except jute and onion which will be exported through the state trading enterprises.

2. **Thurst on Agri-exports.** To boost the exports of agro-products, the policy moots transport assistance for fresh and processed fruits, vegetables, floriculture, poultry, dairy products and products of wheat and rice. Here the emphasis is for the divesification of the agricultural sector by diverting farmers from foodgrains to horticulture, of floriculture etc.
3. **Special Status to Sepcial Economic Zones (SEZ).** To achieve export growth of 11.9 per cent per annum, the EXIM policy has trid to make SEZs as the nodal agency. These zones will get a number of tax concessions and examptions. The Indian banks can now open their overseas banking units (OBU) in SEZs in India almost without any restruction from RBI. Hence these banks will provide credit at chapter rate of interest.
4. **Participation of States.** The centre has increased allocation to ensure greater participation. The government has approved Rs. 330 areas for the year 2002-03 for this purpose. States can use these funds for the development of roads connecting production centres with ports, inland container depots etc.
5. **Identification of Towns.** The new Exim policy has identified three towns for encouraging exports of hosiery at Thirupur, woollen balnkets at Panipat and woollen knitwear at Ludhiana. The government will provide special incentives these areas.
6. **Focus on Small Scale Sector.** The small-scale sector accounts for 50 per cent of India's exports. Hence Exim policy has allocated Rs. 5 crore for promoting cottage sector exports comming under the Khadi and Village Industries Commission. Any unit of small sector exports goods worth of Rs. 5 crore will get the status of export house as agaisnt Rs. 15 crore for others.
7. **Identification of More Items.** The government would focus on the exports of 106 items identified in the medium

term export startegy. These items are footwear, watches, marine and poultry items, engineering electrical goods etc.

8. **Special Status for Status Houses.** The statues holders export houses, trading houses and star trading houses - have been granted special benefits. They will be eligible for 100 per cent retention of foreign exchange in external acconts, exemption from comuplsory negotiation of documents through banks, customs clearance for both inports and exports on self-declaration basis.

9. **Duty on Diamonds.** The customs duty on rough diamonds has been reduced from 5 per cent to zero and the licensing regime for rough diamonds has also been abolished.

10. **Capital Goods.** To promote the export of capital goods, certain changes have been made in Export Promotion Capital Goods (EPCG) scheme to help exporters. EPCG licences of Rs. 100 crore or more will now have 12 year export obligation period except of 8 years with five year moratorium.

11. **Foreign Direct Investment (FDI).** In a move to attract FDI, the Exim policy has permitted relocation of industrial requirement of a licence. The depreciated value of such plants should, however, exceed Rs. 50 crore.

EVALUATION OF EXIM POLICY

The purpose of all these measures and other measures is to raise the share of India in global trade from 0.67 per cent in Jan 2002 to 1 per cent by 2007. The trade policy reforms initiated in 1991 have drastically changed the foreign trade scenario and have resulted in the shift from inward-orientation to an outward-oriented policy. Because of these changes foreign trade sector in India is being considered the leading sector of the economy. The Exim policy is being criticised on ignoring the following three issues:

(i) **Ignorance of Home Market.** Economists says that in a country like India domestic market is very important for its industrial growth. In the ultimate analysis, large economies must endeavour to internalise external markets. Therefore industrialisation may stress manufacturing for the domestic market through import substitution or manufacturing for export to external markets. An environments that produces a spectacular export performance is also conducive to efficient import substitution and rapid economic growth.

(ii) Ignorance of State Intervention. According to Deepak Nayyar, in terms of State intervention, there is not much difference important substitution and export promotion. In the former, the state protects the domestic capitalists from foreign competition in the home market while in the latter, the State protects the domestic capitalists from foreign competition in the world market. It is the nature of state intervention that matters which is totally ignored in the Exim policy.

(iii) No Policy Technology Development. The role of government is very important for the development of technology. This requires the formulation of a policy regime for the import of technology, allocating reseaces for reasarch and development and evolving State procurement policies. The Exim policy lacks this.

❐

13

Business Theory

The importance of multinational corporations and the globalisation of production are now well recognised. Since supranational business enterprises conduct inter-nation transactions in many new forms other than traditional importing and exporting international trade theory has proved to be too limited for explaining the current liabilities to international business.

INTERNATIONAL TRADE THEORY

The main questions on which international trade theory focus are why do countries export and import the sort of products they do and and at what relative prices or terms of trade? How are these trade flows related to the characteristics of a country and how do they effect domestic factor prices? What are the gains from trade and how are they divided among trading countries?

Basis for Trade

Differences in prices are the basic cause of trade and reflect international differences in costs. But why should costs differ from country to country? How can a country produce cameras, sewing machines, and cotton shirts more cheaply than the other country? Many people would reply that a country has lower costs because it has lower wages, and wages are important costs. This explanation seems plausible enough; it is firmly based on fact. But it is not adequate. If wage rates were decisive for cost differences and trade, then should undersell the other with higher wages in every product line and every market. Yet a country with lower wages imports labour intensive products from the other country having high wages, and other low-wage countries buy from goods in great variety and enormous quantities. As a matter of fact, the high wage country might be selling more to other countries than it buys abroad, despite its high wages. Differences in wage rates, then, cannot explain trade patterns, and one must look elsewhere for the basis of trade.

An enduring two-way flow of goods must be traced to systematic international differences in the structure of costs and prices: some things must be cheaper to produce at home and will be exported to other countries; some things must be cheaper to produce abroad and will be imported from other countries. This generalisation is basic to the theory of foreign trade, and is known as the principle of comparative advantage. Stated most precisely, it asserts that a country will export the products which it can produce at the lowest relative cost. China, it contends, can export cameras and textiles because it can produce those goods with the least sacrifice of alternative production. The United States can export machinery and aircrafts because it can produce those goods with the smallest sacrifice. Cameras may be cheaper than machines in both countries, but the cost difference is far from uniform, thus creating opportunities for profitable trade.

Sources of Comparative Advantage

A nation's comparative advantage and trade pattern are heavily affected by its resource endowment—both natural and man-made. Nature has decreed important and enduring differences between countries. Some of them are rich in copper, others in petroleum; some have huge waterfalls, others have fertile plains. Some countries have just enough rainfall for rice or cotton cultivation, while some have too much, and others have next to none. Furthermore, some countries have the resource combinations required for the performance of certain vital tasks: one may have the plains and rainfall needed to grow wheat; another may have a rich deposit of iron ore next to a waterway that can carry ore to coal. Finally, some countries have populations large enough to man and support great, complex industries, but others are so very underpopulated that their land cannot even be worked or their ores extracted. In one sense, people are a natural resource; in another they are a major man-made resource. Mere numbers are the gift of nature. But the skills and attitudes of a population are the work of man and strongly influence a country's comparative advantage. A nation rich in people but poor in skills may be suited to certain tasks, but not to the production and export of manufactured goods. A nation that has very few persons per square mile but has lavished its energies on technical training is likely to enjoy a comparative advantage in the production of precision goods.

Going one step further, we must distinguish between types of skill. Some nations have large numbers of factory workers adept at handling modern machinery. Others have an abundance of engineers and scientists and specialise in new research-laden products. It has been said, for example, that the United States enjoys a comparative advantage in research and innovation, but that it loses out to its competitors as each of its new products ages, the market for it grows, and the knowledge required to manufacture it is diffused among other countries.

One part of a nation's capital stock is embodied in its labour force as agricultural and scientific skill. Another part is embodied in physical equipment: roads, airports, harbours, and dams trucks, aircraft, ships and turbines; factories and office buildings; tractors, lathes, conveyers, and typewriters. These represent the portion of past output that was reserved for investment rather than consumption.

Notice that natural and man-made resources can interact powerfully. Bauxite was not valued as a natural resource until the development of the electrolytic process for extracting aluminum, and of the cheap electric power required to fuel that process. Aluminum itself was not very valuable until the metalworking industries found ways to use it. Pitchblende was a geological curiosity until man's skill and malevolence found a use for uranium, and ways to separate one isotope from others. Population also interacts with technology. Modern mass-production methods need mass markets and are apt to take root first in regions of dense settlement that provide outlets for large lots of standardised products. In consequence, such regions are apt to enjoy a comarative advantage in the export of mass-product articles, and they may well retain their advantage *vis-a-vis* regions that start later or on a smaller scale. Notice, too, that comparative advantage always has a time dimension. It depends on the state of technology at a given moment and on its subsequent diffusion. It also depends on the history of capital accumulation and therefore, on the rate of economic growth.

Mercantilism

The economic doctrine that prevailed during the first two centuries of the development of the modern national state - the seventeenth and eighteenth centuries - was mercantilism. The doctrine of mercantilism has many modern features: it was highly nationalistic, it viewed the well-being of the own nation to be of prime importance, it favoured the regulation and planning of economic activity as an efficient means of fostering the goals of the nation, and it generally viewed foreign trade with suspicion.

The most important way in which a country could grow rich, according to the doctrine of mercantilism, was by acquiring precious metals, especially gold. Single individuals, however, were not to be trusted: they might also like gold, but perhaps they liked other things even more. Left to themselves, they might exchange gold for satin and linen, spices from India, or sugar from Cuba, or indulge in whatever private pleasures they preferred, to the detriment of the stock of precious metals stored in the nation. To prevent such undertakings, the nation had to control foreign trade. Exports were viewed favourably as long as they brought in good, solid gold, but imports were viewed with apprehension as depriving the country of its true source of richness precious metals. Therefore, trade had to be regulated, controlled and restricted, no specific virtue being being in having a large volume of trade.

It was against this background that English classical economics developed, for mercantilism was the credo that Adam Smith Ricardo rebelled against. English classical economics was an offspring of liberalism and the Enlightenment of a general philosophy that stressed the importance of the individual and viewed the nation as nothing more than the sum of its inhabitants.

Absolute Advantage

Adam Smith saw clearly that a country could gain by trading. The tailor does not make his own shoes; he exchanges a suit for shoes. Thereby both the shoemaker and the tailor gain. In the same manner, Smith argued, a whole country can gain by trading with other countries.

It takes 10 labour units to manufacture 1 unit of A in country I but 20 labour units in country II, and if it takes 20 units of labour to manufacture 1 unit of good B in country I but only 10 labour units in country II, then both countries can gain by trading.

If the two countries exchanged the 2 goods at a ratio of 1 to 1, so that 1 units of good A is exchanged for 1 unit of good B, country I could get 1 unit of good B by sacrificing only 10 units of labour, whereas it would have to give up 20 units of labour if it produced the good itself. Likewise, country II would have to sacrifice only 10 units of labour to get 1 unit of good A, whereas it would have to give up 20 units of labour if it produced it itself. The implication of this is clearly that both countries could have more of both goods with a given effort, by trading.

This was a simple and powerful illustration of the benefits of trade, and on it Adam Smith rested his plea for non-interference for free trade as the best policy for trade between nations. Smith's argument seems convincing, but it is not very deep. It was left to Torrens and Ricardo to produce the stronger and more subtle argument for the benefits of trade contained in the theory of comparative advantage.

Comparative Advantage

Ricardo did not object to Smith's analysis. It is obvious that if one country has an absolute advantage over the other country in one line of production in a second line of production, both countries can gain by trading. A great deal of trade, perhaps most trade, is governed by such differences.

But what if one country is more productive than nother country in all lines of production? Of country I can produce all goods with less labour cost than country II, does it still benefit the countries to trade? Ricardo's answer was yes. So long as country II is not equally less productive in all lines of production, it still pays both countries to trade.

We will spend some time elucidating this principle, as it is basic importance to the theory of trade. We may as well start with Ricardo's own model before going on to more modern means of demonstration.

Ricardo used England and Portugal as examples in his demonstration, the two goods they produced being wine and cloth. Being a courteous Englishman, and living in an era when no one had heard about 'under-developed countries', Ricardo assumed that Portugal was more efficient in making both cloth and wine. Table-l shows how Ricardo summed up the cost conditions in the two countries.

TABLE-1

Cost Comparisons

	Labour cost of production (in hours)	
	1 unit of wine	*1 unit of cloth*
Portugal	80	90
England	120	100

According to this model, Portugal has an absolute advantage in the production of wine as well as in the production of cloth, because the labour cost of production for each unit of the two commodities is less in Portugal than in England. To demonstrate that trade between England and Portugal will, even in this case, lead to gains for both countries, it is useful to introduce the concept of opportunity cost. The opportunity cost for a good X is the amount of other goods which have to be given up in order to produce one (additional) unit of X. Table-2 gives the opportunity costs for producing wine and cloth in Portugal and England. These costs have been constructed on the basis of the information given in Table-l.

TABLE-2

Opportunity Costs

	Opportunity costs for	
	wine	*cloth*
Protual	80190 = 8/9	90/80 = 9/8
England	120/100 = 12/10	100/120 = 10/12

A country has a comparative advantage in producing a good if the opportunity cost for producing the good is lower at home than in the other country. Table-2 shows that Portugal has the lower opportunity cost of the two countries in producing wine, while England has the lower opportunity cost in producing cloth. Thus Portugal has a comparative advantage in the production of wine and England has a comparative advantage in the production of cloth.

We should now further clarify the meaning of the term 'comparative advantage'.

In order to speak about comparative advantage there must be at least two countries and two goods. We compare the opportunity costs of the production of each good in both countries. As long as the two countries' opportunity costs for one good differ, one country has a comparative advantage in the production of one of the two goods, while the other country has a comparative advantage in the production of the other good. As long as this is the case, both countries will gain from trade, regardless of the fact that one of the countries might have an absolute disadvantage in both lines of production.

To illustrate the gains from trade, let us assume that Portugal and England do not trade but produce and consume in isolation. The prices of cloth and wine in the two countries are then determined by their respective costs of production.

In England it takes 120 hours of labour to make 1 unit of wine, while it takes only 100 hours to make 1 unit of cloth, clearly wine must then be more expensive per unit than cloth-1 unit of wine will cost 120/100, or 1.2 units of cloth. If in Portugal it takes 80 hours of labour to make 1 unit of wine and 90 hours to make 1 unit of cloth, cloth will be more expensive than wine-1 unit of wine will cost 80/90, or 0.89 units of cloth.

Let us now open the possibility of trade. If England could import 1 unit of wine at a price less than 1.2 units of cloth, she would gain by doing so. If Portugal could import more than 0.89 units of cloth for 1 unit of wine, she, too, would gain. Therefore, if the international price of 1 unit of wine is somewhere between 1.2 and 0.89 units of cloth, both countries will gain by trading.

Let us assume further that in the international market, 1 unit of wine exchanges for 1 unit of cloth. It is then advantageous for England to export cloth and import wine, because in the absence of trade England would have to give up 120 hours of labour for every unit of wine she wants. By trading she can, instead with 100 hours of effort, produce 1 unit of cloth and then exchange this unit of cloth for 1 unit of wine. Under autarky—*i.e.*, a country producing and consuming in isolation—she would have to give up 120 hours of labour for every unit of wine she wanted, whereas with trade she only needs to give up 100 hours. With each 20 hours left over she can produce more cloth and enjoy a higher level of consumption—or the workers can rest, and trade will make possible more leisure with a given amount of consumption. Portugal will also gain from trading. In isolation she would have to give up 90 hours of labour to get 1 unit of cloth. Now she can make 1 unit of wine with the effort of 80 hours of labour and exchange this unit of wine for 1 unit of cloth in the international market. Every 10 hours of labour freed by this process can then be used for either increased production or increased leisure.

Thus trade offers each country the possibility of specialising in the line of its comparative advantage and then exchanging these products for those in which she has a comparative disadvantage. Both countries can reallocate their factors of production to the line where their comparative advantage lies and then export this product and import the other product. In short, with a given amount of resources, each country can consume more by trading than in isolation.

A Simple Model

To show how a difference in resource endowments can call forth foreign trade, consider two countries, America and Britain, which are identical in all ways but one. Both of them have 120 man-days of labour available. Both use 2 man-days of labour to grow a ton of potatoes and have enough arable land to employ all their workers in potato-farming. But America's coal deposits are very near to the surface and only 1 man-day of labour is required to dig out a ton, while Britain's deposits are much farther down and 4 man-days of labour are required to dig out a ton. If its whole labour force were employed growing potatoes, America could produce 60 tons per day; 2 man-days of labour can grow a single ton and 120 man-days of labour are available. If, instead, the whole labour force were employed digging coal, America could produce 120 tonnes per day; 1 man-day of labour can dig out a single ton and 120 man-days are available. If, finally, America wished to produce some potatoes and some coal, it could secure anyone of several combinations. To produce a single ton of coal, it would have to divert 1 man-day of labour from its potato fields, reducing potato output by half a ton. To produce 2 tons of coal, it would have to divert 2 man-days from the potato fields, reducing potato output by 1 ton.

America's production possibilities are summarised by the line AB in Figure-l. The distance OA measures the output of coal that would be obtained if the entire labour force worked in the coal mines (120 tons); the distance OB measures the output of potatoes that would be obtained if the entire labour force worked in in the potato fields (60 tons). Points along the line AB describe the combinations of coal and potatoes that could be produced simultaneously. At point P, for example, America would be producing Oc coal and Od potatoes. It would obtain Oc coal by foregoing Bd potatoes.

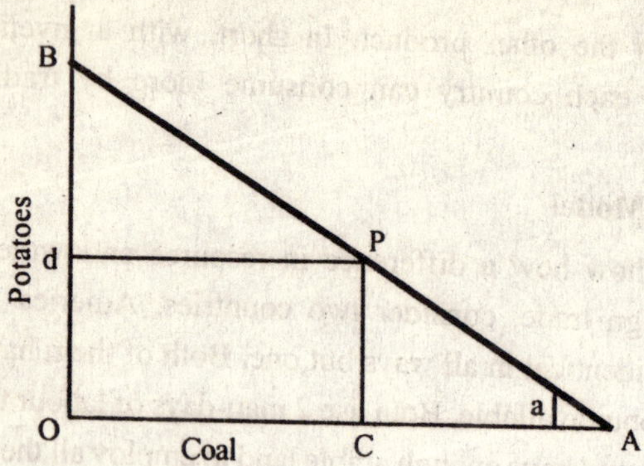

Figure-1

If Americans were not allowed to trade with outsiders, their pattern of consumption would have to coincide with one of the coal and potato combination lying on AB. The output mix prevailing at a particular time would, of course, depend on consumer preferences - demand conditions - and on the price of coal in terms of potatoes. That price ratio, in turn, would be given by the comparative labour costs of coal and potato production. Labour is the only variable input (factor of production) used in this very simple economy, and a single man-day of labour can mine a whole ton of coal but can only grow half a ton of potatoes will cost 2 man-days' wages. A ton of coal will be half as expensive as a ton of potatoes, and it will exchange for half a ton of potatoes in America's markets. This same price relationship appears in Figure-1; it is represented by the slope (steepness) of AB, the production possibilities frontier. The distance OB is half the distance OA, indicating that a ton of coal will sell for half a ton of potatoes.

One can arrive at this same result by examining marginal costs. If product markets are perfectly competitive, prices must equal marginal costs. If labour is the only variable input and labour requirements are constant for all output levels, marginal costs must equal labour requirements per unit of extra output multiplied by the wage rate. Hence:

Price of Coal = Marginal Cost of Coal = Wage Rate × Man-days of Labour Needed to Produce a Ton of Coal

Price of Potatoes = Marginal Cost of Potatoes = Wage Rate × Man-days of Labour Needed to Produce a Ton of Potatoes

Therefore:

$$\frac{\text{Price of Coal}}{\text{Price of Potatoes}} = \frac{\text{Man - days Needed to Produce a Ton of Coal}}{\text{Man - days Needed to Produce a Ton of Potatoes}}$$

The wage rate cancels out in this calculation, for it must be the same in both industries.

Britain also needs 2 man-days of labour to produce a ton of potatoes, and consequently could grow 60 tons if it used all its labour in its potato patches. But it needs 4 man-days of labour to dig out a ton of coal, and could mine only 30 tons if it used all its labour in its coal mines. By implication, Britain could produce a single ton of coal by diverting 4 man-days of labour from potato-growing, thereby giving up 2 tons of potatoes. Britain's production possibilities are described by the line A'B' in Figure 2. Maximum potato output, OB', is the same as in America, because the two countries are endowed with the same amounts of labour and are equally efficient in potato growing. But maximum coal output, OA' is smaller in Britain than in America, for Britain's coal lies somewhat deeper in the ground.

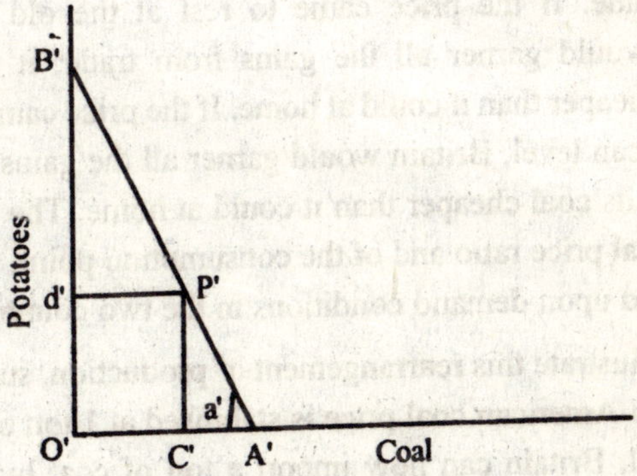

Figure-2

The line A'B' in Figure 2 is much steeper than the line AB in Figure-l. This difference is explained by the difference in mining costs and implies a difference in relative prices. British coal must be twice as expensive as British potatoes, for labour costs are twice as high. Isolated from the outside world, Britain would produce and consume some combination of coal and potatoes lying on A'B' and a ton of coal would be worth 2 tons of potatoes.

But now allow America and Britain to trade and suppose that goods can move between them without transport costs. The opportunity for trade will create a single Anglo-American market and, therefore, a single price for coal in terms of potatoes.

This new common price will lie between the national extremes less than the prior British price (2 tons of potatoes per ton of coal) and higher than the prior American price (half a ton of potatoes per ton of coal). Britain can now obtain a ton of coal without surrendering as many potatoes as it had to sacrifice to furnish its own coal. It will tend to specialise in potato-growing and will use its potatoes to buy American coal. America is able to obtain more potatoes for its coal. It will tend to specialise in coal-mining and to use its coal to buy British potatoes.

The new common price for coal could also settle at one of the national extremes. In that case, one country would capture all the gains from trade, but the other would be no worse off than it was without trade. If the price came to rest at the old British level, America would garner all the gains from trade; it would get its potatoes cheaper than it could at home. If the price came to rest at the old American level, Britain would garner all the gains from trade; it would get its coal cheaper than it could at home. The determination of the actual price ratio and of the consumption point, Q in Figure 3, will depend upon demand conditions in the two countries.

To illustrate this rearrangement of production, suppose that the new Anglo-American coal price is stabilised at 1 ton of potatoes per ton of coal. Britain can now import a ton of coal by growing and exporting a single ton of potatoes. Without trade, by contrast, it had to sacrifice 2 tons of potatoes to produce a ton of coal. In effect, Britain saves 2 man-days of labour on each ton of coal consumed. For its part, America can import a ton of potatoes by mining and exporting a single ton of coal. Without trade, it had to sacrifice 2 tons of coal to produce a ton of potatoes. America saves 1 man-day of labour on each ton of potatoes consumed.

Figure 3 restates these results with greater generality. There, the left hand triangle, OAB, is the American production-possibilities frontier, just as it appeared in Figure-1. The right hand triangle O'A'B' is Britain's production-possibilities frontier, taken from Figure-2 but flipped outside-down. If America and Britain could not trade, each would be confined to its own frontier, America at P and Britain at P'. When they are allowed to trade, they can rearrange production and consumption to mutual advantage. America can specialise in coal-mining, using all its labour to produce OA tons. Britain can specialise in potato-farming, using all its labour to produce O'B' tons. America can then consume Oe tons of coal and export eA tons of coal and export eA tons to pay for potatoes. Britain can consume O[1]F[1] tons of potatoes and exports F[1]B[1] tons to pay for coal. America can buy OF tons of potatoes (equal to PBI Britain will export), and Britain can buy O[1]F[1] tons of coal (equal to the P to Q, and British consumption can move from p[1] to Q. Which country can consume more of both goods than it did before.

The situation described in Figure 3 is not the only possibility. The point Q could settle down anywhere within the unshaded part of the diagram, depending on demand conditions. Furthermore, Q could

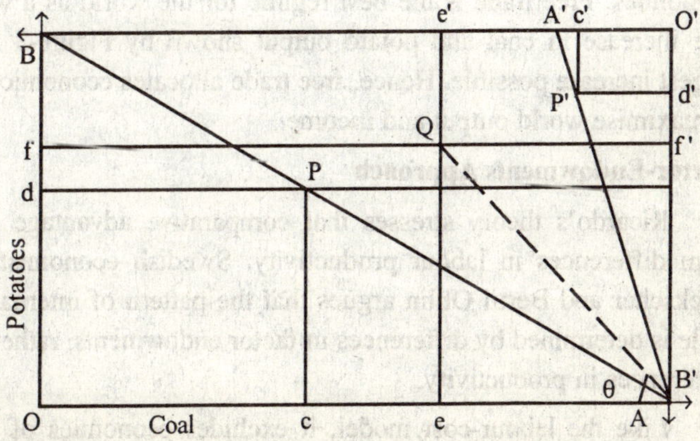

Figure-3

come to rest on AB or A'B', the extreme cases. If Q came to rest on AB, Britian would specialise completely and take all the gains from trade. America would tend to specialise in coal, but would also grow potatoes. If Q came to rest on A[1]B[1], America would specialise completely and take all the gains from trade. Britain would tend to specialise in potatoes but would also mine coal.

Figure-3 describes two ways to view the gains from trade. First, it shows that every country can escape the confines of its own resource endowment. Before trade, each country had to consume a combination of coal and potatoes lying on its own production-possibilities frontier. Its choice was restricted by its resource endowment. But trade allows every country to reshuffle output and to consume a combination of commodities it could never produce by itself. In consequence, the individual consumer enjoys a wider range of choice. Figure-3 also shows that trade enlarges global output by allowing every country to specialise in those tasks it does best. Before trade, total coal output was Oc plus c'O'. With trade it rises to OA (an increase of ce plus e'c'). Before trade, total potato output was Od plus d'O'. With trade it rises to O'B' (an increase of df plus *f'd'*). This increase in output was required for each country to increase its consumption of both commodities in the fashion described in Figure-3. It also leads to a basic proposition in international economics: Free trade is the best regime for the world as a whole. The increase in coal and potato output shown by Figure-3 is the largest increase possible. Hence, free trade allocates economic tasks to maximise world output and income.

Factor-Endowments Approach

Ricardo's theory stresses that comparative advantage arises from differences in labour productivity. Swedish economists, Eli Heckscher and Bertil Ohlin argues that the pattern of international trade is determined by differences in factor endowments, rather than differences in productivity.

Like the labour-cost model, it excludes economies of scale, takes no account of transport costs, and assumes that tastes are the same everywhere. But unlike the labour-cost model, it goes on to assume that each country has access to the same technology, and would employ the same methods of production if confronted with identical factor prices. It thereby rules out the differences in relative efficiency that served as the basis for foreign trade in the labour-cost model.

The Heckscher-Ohlin or factor-endowments approach to trade theory proceeds from two suppositions:

1. Products differ in factor requirements—cars require more machine-time (capital) per worker than, say, cotton cloth or furniture, and aircraft require more machine-time than either cars or cotton cloth.
2. Countries differ in factor endowments—some have large amounts of capital per worker (the capital-abundant countries) and some have very little (the labour-abundant countries).

One could, of course, make cars by several methods, differing in capital-intensities. One could use a small machine-shop or an automated plant. One could also weave cloth by many methods, some of them quite highly mechanised. The choice of technique will depend on the prices of the factors of production-the wages paid to workers and the rental prices of machinery (the interest cost of capital and allowances for repair and depreciation). But the factor-endowments model assumes that the product which is most capital-intensive at one set of factor prices is also most capital-intensive at every other set.

The theory then argues that capital-abundant countries will tend to specialise in capital-intensive goods like cars and aircraft, and will export some of their specialities in order to import labour-intensive goods. Similarly, labour-abundant countries will specialise in labour-intensive goods and will export their own specialities in order to import capital-intensive goods. To put the proposition in general terms: Trade will be based on differences in factor endowments and will serve to relieve each country's factor shortages.

A numerical example will illustrate this proposition. Suppose that the production of a thousand cars requires the employment of 90 machines and 300 man-years of labour, while the production of a million yards of cloth requires the employment of 30 machines and 600 man-years of labour. If a country's entire stock of machinery and its whole labour force are used in these two industries, one can assert that:

Machines in Use = 90 × Thousand Cars + 30 × Million Yards of cloth

Labour Employed = 300 × Thousand Cars + 600 × Million Yards of cloth

If, next, we know how much machinery and labour is on hand, we can solve these two identities as simultaneous equations, and can thereby obtain a country's full-employment car-and-cloth combination. Consider two countries—a labour-abundant country called Manymen, and a capital-abundant country called Fewmen—with the fixed endowments of machinery and labour shown in Table-3. Replacing "machines in use" and "labour employed" with Manymen's stock of capital (600 machines) and labour supply (6,000 man-years), then solving for cars and cloth, we ascertain that Manymen can produce ,OOO cars and 8,000,000 yards of cloth. Repeating this procedure with Fewmen's endowment, we ascertain that Fewmen can produce 9,000 cars and 3,000,000 yards of cloth. As one would expect, Manymen's output combination is heavily weighted with cloth (the labour-intensive product), and Fewmen's output combination is heavily weighted with cars (the capital-intensive product).

TABLE-3

Factor Endowments and Output Combinations

Factors and Products	*Manymen*	*Fewmen*
Factor supplies:		
Machines (number)	600	900
Labour (man-years)	6,000	4,500
Machines per man-year	0.1	0.2
Full-employment output combination:		
Cars (number)	4,000	9,000
Cloth (yards)	8,00,000	3,00,000
Cars per thousand yards of cloth	0.5	3.0

Clearly, these two countries could gain from trade and would, indeed, be led to trade when brought into contact with each other. Having identical tastes and different output combinations, they would have different price ratios in the absence of trade. Cloth, the labour-intensive good, would be cheap in Manymen, the labour-abundant country, while cars, the capital-intensive good, would be cheap in Fewmen, the capital-abundant country. With the opening of trade and the establishment of common prices, Manymen would specialise in cloth production and would export its speciality in exchange for cars, while Fewemen would specialise in cars and would export its speciality in exchange for cloth. Trade would allow each country to obtain the product it is ill-equipped to manufacture for itself—the one that makes the heaviest demands on its scarce factors of production.

Once again, a free-trade regime is best for the two countries taken together. As in the labour-cost model studied earlier, it works to maximise global output by fostering the most efficient patterns of specialisation.

Factor Substitution and Specialisation

The numerical example we have been examining can be recast geometrically and can then be made somewhat more general. To do so, let us rearrange the "machines-in-use" identity so as to show how much cloth could be produced if the supply of machinery were the only effective constraint on a country's production:

$$\text{Million of Yards of both} = \left(\frac{\text{Machines in Use}}{30}\right) - \left(\frac{90}{30}\right)$$

This capital constraint is represented by the line MM' in Figure-4. Next, let us rearrange the "labour-employed" identity to show how much cloth could be produced if the supply of labour were the only effective constraint:

$$\text{Million of Yards of Cloth} = \left(\frac{\text{Labour Employed}}{600}\right) - \left(\frac{300}{600}\right)$$

This labour constraint is represented LL] in. Figure-4.

These two constraints, taken together, define a production-possibilities frontier for a two-product, two-factor country. That frontier is L'FM, and the full-employment point occurs at the kink, F.

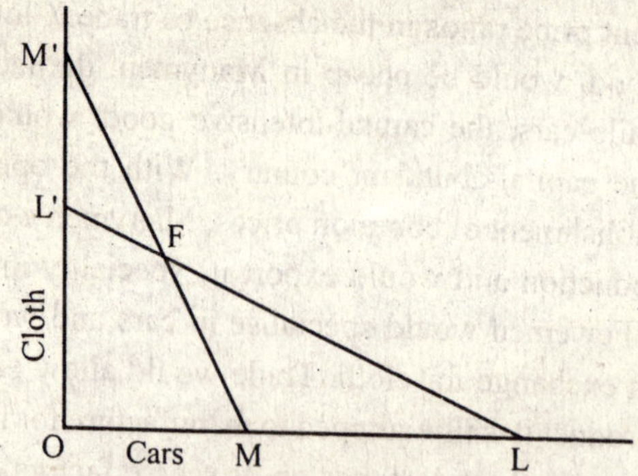

Figure-4

To the left of the kink, production is constrained by the country's limited supply of labour; to the right of the kink, it is constrained by the limited supply of machines. Were such a country unable to engage in trade, its car and cloth consumption would be confined to a combination on or inside L'FM. But were it allowed to trade, it could consume a combination of cars and cloth lying outside L'FM. If, for instance, world prices permitted the exchange of a single car

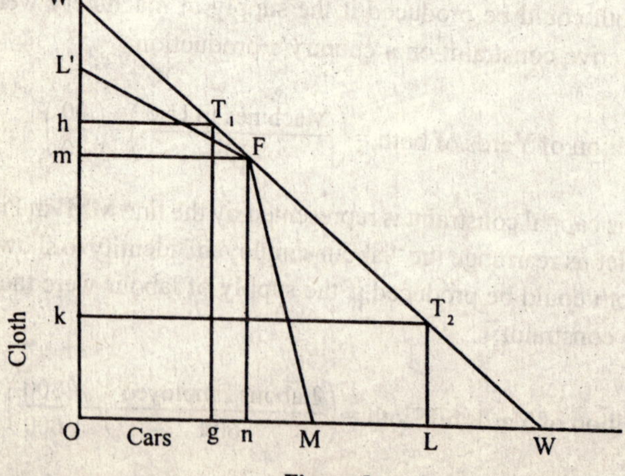

Figure-5

for a thousand yards of cloth, that country would consume any combination of cars and cloth lying on WW' in Figure-5, and it could escape the limitations imposed by its factor endowment: it could consume Og cars and O*h* cloth by exporting gn cars in exchange mh cloth; it could consume OL cars and OK cloth by exporting K*m* cloth in exchange for *n*L cars.

Notice, however, that the country portrayed by Figures 4 and 5 has one and only one full-employment point F. Were it to respond to consumer demand or to opportunities for trade by producing more than O*m* cloth and less than O*n* cars, some of its machines would stand idle and their owners would suffer financial losses. This result derives from an unrealistic assumption regarding technology: that the labour and capital requirements of car and cloth production are entirely rigid. Such a result would not occur at all if manufacturers were able to alter their methods of production. In such circumstances, the owners of idle machines would cut back their rental rates, so as to secure jobs for their machines, and the manufacturers of cars and cloth would respond by choosing more capital-intensive methods of production: they would substitute machinery for labour.

When this sort of factor-substitution is possible, the factor-endowments model changes in two ways. First, the production-

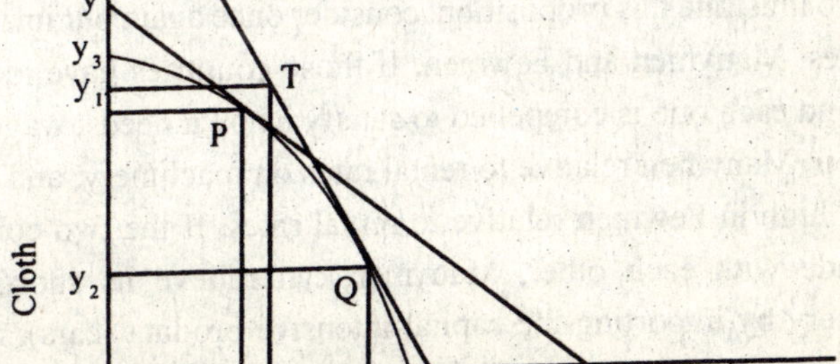

Figure-6

possibilities frontier becomes a smooth curve like XQPY in Figure 6.Second, the domestic price of cars expressed in terms of cloth comes to depend on the output mix, and will equal the slope of XQPY at the point of actual production. If, for example, production were at P, involving Ox_1 cars and Oy_1 cloth, the price of cars in terms of cloth would equal the slope of XQPY at P. If, instead, production were at Q, involving Ox_2 cars and Oy_2 cloth, the price of cars would equal the slope of XQPY at Q.

The curve XQPY is steeper at Q than at P, implying a higher price for cars, and more cars are made at Q. The price of cars must rise to stimulate production. This link between prices and the product mix arises from the difference in capital-intensities between the two industries. Cars are more capital-intensive than cloth at all sets of factor prices, so that a switch from cloth to car production will augment the demand for machines relative to the demand for labour. An increase in demand for machinery will bid up rental charges relative to wage rates, and this increase in rental charges will raise the price of cars more than it raises the price of cloth - precisely because car production uses more machinery than cloth production.

Trade and Factor Prices

There is, in fact, a strong connection between prevailing product prices (cars and cloth) and prevailing factor prices (labour and machines), and this connection has an intriguing corollary: Free trade will tend to euqlise factor prices across the participating countries.

To illustrate this proposition, consider once again our imaginary countries, Manymen and Fewmen. If those countries have identical tastes and each one is compelled to satisfy its own needs, wages will be low in Manymen relative to rental rates on machinery, and wages will be high in Fewmen relative to rental rates. If the two countries can trade with each other, Manymen can relieve its shortage of machinery by importing the capital-intensive product (cars), and its wages will rise relative to rental rates. Fewmen can likewise relieve its shortage of labour by importing the labour-intensive product (cloth) and its wages will fall relative to rental rates.

That is what free trade will do. As wages would be relatively high in Fewmen before trade began, cloth would be expensive compared to cars. With the opening of trade, Fewmen will therefore export cars and import cloth. To do so, it will increase its car production and cut back its cloth production. These shifts in the pattern of production will, in turn, augment Fewmen's demand for machines and will reduce its demand for labour. Manymen, by contrast will increase its cloth production and cut back its car production, and these shifts will augment its demand for labour and will reduce its demand for machines. If there are no transport costs between the two countries, free trade will equalise product prices in Fewmen and Manymen. It will thereby equalise the two countries factor prices. In actual practice, of course, factor prices are not equal around the world and the differences are far too great to be explained by transport costs and trade barriers. Hence, the simple model we have been developing cannot be perfectly applicable to the real world; it may ignore important economies of scale, and the fact that modern technology is not available to every country. Yet the tendency described by the Heckscher Ohlin model—the reduction of factor-price differences through trade—may still be quite important.

Furthermore, available statistics may exaggerate international differences in factor prices. When we compare wage rates around the world, we are comparing rather different things. Some countries' wage statistics are heavily weighted with large returns to skill; others are dominated by the lower wages of unskilled labour. If one were to compare the wage rates of equally skilled workers, of equally fine land, and so on, being sure to match like with like, factor prices might improve to be more nearly equal than they usually appear.

Suppose, again, that cars and cloth cannot move between the countries. Wages would be higher in Fewmen than Manymen, and if there were no travel costs, workers would migrate from Manymen to Fewmen. If, further, this migration were to continue for as long as wage rates differed, it would render the two countries very much alike. Fewmen would wind up with as many machines and very much more labour than it had to start with, but the ratio of man-years to machines would be exactly equalised in the two countries. This is because the wage-rate difference causing migration would persist for as long as the ratio of man-years were lower in Fewmen than in Manymen. It would only vanish when the ratios were equalised.

This example suggests one more way to look at the gains from trade. It argues that free trade can sometimes substitute for international movements of labour and capital. Factor movements and free trade each serve to reduce differences in factor prices. Factor movements do so by erasing differences in national factor endowments. Free trade does so by offsetting those differences. Trade eliminates the need for a redistribution of productive factors by reallocating economic tasks. It allows every country to make the best use of its own factor endowment.

Product Life-Cycle Theory

Raymond Vernon proposed the product life-cycle theory in the mid-1960s. Vernon's theory was based on the observation that for most of the 20th century a very large proportion of the world's new products had been developed by US firms and sold first in the United States (*e.g.*, mass-produced automobiles, televisions, instant cameras, photocopiers, personal computers, and semiconductor chips). Vernon argued that the wealth and size of the market gave US firms a strong incentive to develop new consumer products. In addition, the high cost of labour gave US firms an incentive to develop cost-saving process innovations.

Just because a new product is developed by a US firm and first sold in the US market does not mean-the product must be produced in the United States. It could be produced abroad at some low-cost location and then exported back into the United States. However, Vernon argued that most new products were initially produced in America. The pioneering firms might have believed it was better to keep production facilities close to the market and to the firm's center of decision making, given the uncertainty and risks inherent in product introductions. Also, the demand (or most new products tends not to be based on price. Consequently, firms can charge relatively high prices for new products, which eliminates the need to look follow-cost production sites in other countries.

Vernon went on to say that early in the life cycle of a typical new product, while demand is starting to grow rapidly in the United States, demand in other advanced countries is limited to high-income groups. The limited initial demand in other advanced countries does not make it worthwhile for firms in those countries to produce the new product, but it does necessitate some exports from the United States to those countries.

Over time, however, demand for the new product starts to grow in other advanced countries (*e.g.*, Great Britain, France, Germany, and Japan). As it does, it becomes worthwhile for foreign producers to begin producing for their home markets. In addition, US firms might set up production facilities in those advanced countries where demand' is growing. Consequently, production within other advanced countries begins to limit the potential for exports from the United States.

As the market in the United States and other advanced nations matures, the product becomes more standardized, and price becomes the main competitive weapon. As this occurs, cost considerations start to play a greater role in the competitive process. Producers based in advanced countries where labour costs are lower than in the United States might now be able to export to the United States.

If cost pressures become intense, the process might not stop there. The cycle by which the United States lost its advantage to other advanced countries might be repeated once more, as developing countries begin to acquire a production advantage over advanced countries. Thus, the locus of global production initially switches from the United States to other advanced nations, and then from those nations to developing countries.

Historically, the product life-cycle theory provides an accurate explanation of international trade patterns. Consider photocopiers; the product was developed in the early 1960s by Xerox in the United States and sold initially to US users. Xerox exported photocopiers from the United States, primarily to Japan and the advanced countries of Western Europe. As demand began to grow in those countries, Xerox entered into joint ventures to set up production in Japan (Fuji-Xerox) and Great Britain (Rank-Xerox). In addition, once Xerox's patents on the photocopier process expired, other foreign competitors began to enter the market (*e.g.*, Canon in Japan, Olivetti in Italy). As a consequence, exports.from the United States declined, and US users began to buy some of their photocopiers from lower-cost foreign sources, particularly from Japan. More recently, Japanese companies have found that their own country is too expensive to manufacture photocopiers, so they have begun to switch production to developing countries such as Singapore and Thailand. As a result, initially the United States and now several other advanced countries have switched from being exporters of photocopiers to being importers. This evolution in the pattern of international trade in photocopiers is consistent with the predictions of the product life-cycle theory. The theory clearly explains the migration of mature industries out of the United States and into low-cost assembly locations.

However, the product life-cycle theory is not without weaknesses. Viewed from an Asian or European perspective, Vernon's argument that most new products are developed and introduced in the United States seems ethnocentric. Although it may be true that from 1945 to 1975 most new products were introduced in the United States, there have always been important exceptions. In recent years these exceptions appear to have become more common. Many new products are now introduced in Japan (*e.g.*, high-definition television or digital audio tapes). More importantly, with the increased globalization and integration of the world economy, growing number of new products are now introduced simultaneously in the United States, Japan, and the advanced European nations (*e.g.*, laptop computers, compact disks and electronic cameras). This may be accompanied by globally dispersed production, with particular components of a new product being produced in those locations where the mix of factors costs and skills is most favourable (as predicted by the theory of comparative advantage). In short, although Vernon's theory may be useful for explaining the pattern of international trade during the brief period of American global dominance, its relevance in the modern world is limited.

New Trade Theory

The new trade theory emerged in the 1970s. A number of economists were questioning the assumption of diminishing returns to specialization used in international trade theory. They argued that in many industries, because of the presence of substantial economies of scale, there are increasing returns to specialization. As output expands with specialization, the ability to realize economies of scale increases and so the unit costs of production should decrease. Economies of scale are primarily derived by spreading fixed costs (such as the costs of developing a new product) over a larger output Consider the commercial jet aircraft industry. The fixed costs of developing a new commercial jet airliner are astronomical. For example, Boeing spent an estimated $5 billion to develop its 777. The company will have to sell at least 350 of them to recoup these development costs and break even. Thus, due to the high fixed costs of developing a new jet aircraft, the economies of scale are substantial.

The new trade theorists further argue that because of substantial scale economies, world demand will support only a few firms in many industries. This is the case in the commercial jet aircraft industry, estimates suggest that world demand can profitably support at most three major manufacturers. For example, the total world demand for 300-seater commercial jet ai craft similar to Boeing's 777 model will probably be only 1,500 aircraft over the 10 years between 1995 and 2005. If we assume that firms must sell at least 500 aircraft to get an acceptable return on their investment (which is reasonable, given the breakeven point of 300 aircraft), we can see that the world market can profitably support only three firms!

The new trade theorists go on to argue that in those industries where the existence of substantial economies of scale imply that the world market will profitably support only a few firms, countries may export certain products simply because they have a firm that was an early entrant into that industry. Underpinning this argument is the notion of first-mover advantages, which are the economic and strategic advantages that accrue to early entrants into an industry. Because they are able to gain economies of scale, the early entrants into an industry may get a lock on the world market that discourages subsequent entry. The ability of first movers to reap economies of scale creates a barrier to entry. In the commercial aircraft industry, for example, the fact that Boeing and Airbus are already in the industry discourages new entry.

This theory suggests that a country may dominate in the export of a good simply because it was lucky enough to have one or more firms among the first to produce that good. This is at variance with the Heckscher-Ohlin theory, which suggests that a country will predominate in the export of a product when it is particularly well endowed with those factors used intensively in its manufacture. Thus, the new trade theorists argue that the United States leads in exports of commercial jet air-craft not because it is better endowed with the factors of production required to manufacture aircraft, but because two of the first movers in the industry, Boeing and Mc-Donnell Douglas, were US firms. However, the new trade theory is not at variance with the theory of comparative advantage. Because economies of scale result in an increase in the efficiency of resource utilization, and hence in productivity, the new trade theory identifies an important source of comparative advantage.

How useful is this theory in explaining trade patterns? It is perhaps too early to say, the theory is so new that little supporting empirical work has been done. Consistent with the theory, however, a study by Harvard business historian Alfred Chandler suggests that the existence of first-mover advantages is an important factor in explaining the dominance of firms in certain industries. Also, the number of firms is very limited in many global industries. This is the case with the commercial aircraft industry, the chemical industry, the heavy construction-equipment industry, the heavy truck industry, the tire industry, the consumer electronics industry, and the jet engine industry, to name but a few examples.

Perhaps the most contentious implication of the new trade theory is the argument that it generates for government intervention and strategic trade policy. New trade theorists stress the role of luck, entrepreneurship, and innovation in giving a firm first-mover advantages. According to this argument, the reason Boeing was the first mover in commercial jet aircraft manufacture-rather than firms such as Great Britain's DeHavilland and Hawker Siddely, or Holland's fokker, all of which could have been-was that Boeing was both lucky and innovative. One way Boeing was lucky is that DeHavilland shot itself in the foot when its Comet jet airliner, introduced two years earlier than Boeing's first jet airliner, the 707, was found to be full of serious technological flaws. Had DeHavilland not made some serious technological mistakes, Great Britain might now be the world's leading exporter of commercial jet aircraft!

Boeing's innovativeness was demonstrated by its independent development of the technological know-how required to build a commercial jet airliner. Several new trade theorists have pointed out, however, that Boeing's R&D was largely paid for by the US government; that the 707 was a spin-off from a government-funded military programme. Herein lies a rationale for government intervention. By the sophisticated and judicious use of subsidies, could a government increase the chances of its domestic firms becoming first movers in emerging industries, as the US government apparently did with Boeing? If this is possible, and the new trade theory suggests it might be, then we have an economic rationale for a proactive trade policy that is at variance with the free trade prescriptions of the trade theories.

National Competitive Advantage

In 1990 Michael Porter of Harvard Business School published the results of intensive research to determine why some nations succeed and others fail in international competition. Porter and his team looked at 100 industries in 10 nations. The book that contains the results of this work, The Competitive Advantage of Nations, has made an important contribution to thinking about trade. Like the work of the new trade theorists, Porter's work was driven by a belief that the existing theories of international trade told only part of the story. Porter hoped to explain why a nation achieves international success in a particular industry. Why does Japan do so well in the automobile industry? Why does Switzerland excel in the production and export of precision instruments and pharmaceuticals? Why do Germany and the United States do so well in the chemical industry? These questions cannot be answered easily by the Heckscher-Ohlin theory, and the theory of comparative advantage offers only a partial explanation. The theory of comparative advantage would say that Switzerland excels in the production and export of precision instruments because it uses its resources very efficiently in these industries. Although this may be correct, this does not explain why Switzerland is more productive in this industry than Great Britain, Germany, or Spain. It is this puzzle that Porter tries to solve.

Porter's thesis is that four broad attributes of a nation shape the environment in which local firms compete, and these attributes promote or impede the creation of competition advantage. These attributes are: *(i)* factor endowments; *(ii)* Demand conditions; *(iii)* Relating and supporting industries; *(iv)* Firm strategy, structure, and rivalry.

Porter speaks of these four attributes as constituting the diamond. He argues that firms are most likely to succeed in industries or industry segments where the diamond is most favorable. He also argues that the diamond is a mutually reinforcing system. The effect of one attribute is contingent on the state of others. For example, Porter argues, favourable demand conditions will not result in competitive advantage unless the state of rivalry is sufficient to cause firms to respond to them.

Porter maintains that two additional variables can influence the national diamond in important ways: chance and government. Chance events, such as major innovations, create discontinuities that can reshape industry structure and provide the opportunity for one nation's firms to supplant another's. Government, by its choice of policies, can detract from or improve national advantage. For example, regulation can alter home demand conditions, antitrust policies can influence the intensity of rivalry within an industry, and government investments in education can change factor endowments.

Factor Endowments

Factor endowments lie at the center of the Heckscher-Ohlin theory. While Porter does not propose anything radically new, he does analyse the characteristics of factors of production in some detail. He recognises hierarchies among factors, distinguishing between basic factors (*e.g.*, natural resources, climate, location, and demographics) and advanced factors (*e.g.*, communications infrastructure, sophisticated and skilled labour, research facilities, and technological know-how). He argues that advanced factors are the most significant for competitive advantage. Unlike basic factors (which are naturally endowed), advanced factors are a product of investment by individuals, companies, and governments. Thus, government investments in basic and higher education, by improving the general skill and knowledge level of the population and by stimulating advanced research at higher education institutions, can upgrade a nation's advanced factors.

The relationship between advanced and basic factors is complex. Basic factors can provide an initial advantage that is subsequently reinforced and extended by investment in advanced factors. Disadvantages in basic factors can create pressures to invest in advanced factors. The most obvious example of this phenomenon is Japan, a country that lacks arable land and mineral deposits and yet has built a substantial endowment of advanced factors. Porter notes that Japan's large pool of engineers (reflecting a much higher number of engineering graduates per capita than almost any other nation) has been vital to Japan's success in many manufacturing industries.

Demand Conditions

Porter emphasizes the role home demand plays in providing the impetus for upgrading competitive advantage. Firms are typically most sensitive to the needs of their closest customers. Thus, the characteristics of home demand are important in shaping the attributes of domestically made products and in creating pressures for innovation and quality. Porter argues that a nation's firms gain competitive advantage if their domestic consumers are sophisticated and demanding. Such consumers pressure local firms to meet high standards of product quality and to produce innovative products. Porter notes that Japan's sophisticated and knowledgeable buyers of cameras helped stimulate the Japanese camera industry to improve product quality and to introduce innovative models. A similar example can be found in the cellular phone equipment industry, where sophisticated and demanding local customers in Scandinavia helped push Nokia of Finland and Ericsson of Sweden to invest in cellular phone technology long before demand for cellular phones took off in other developed nations. As a result, Nokia and Ericsson, along with Motorola, are today dominant players in the global cellular telephone equipment industry.

Related and Supporting Industries

The Third broad attribute of national advantage in an industry is the presence of suppliers or related industries that are internationally competitive. The benefits of investments in advanced factors of production by related and supporting industries can spill over into an industry, helping it achieve a strong competitive position internationally. Swedish strength in fabricated steel products (*e.g.*, ball bearings and cutting tools) has drawn on strengths in Sweden's specialty steel industry, Technological leadership in the US semiconductor industry until the mid-1980s provided the basis for US success in personal computers and several other technically advanced electronic products. Similarly, Switzerland's success in pharmaceuticals is closely related to its previous international success in the technologically related dye industry.

One consequence of this is that successful industries within a country tend to be grouped into clusters of related industries. This was one of the most pervasive findings of Porter's study. One such cluster is the German textile and apparel sector, which includes high-quality cotton, wool, synthetic fibers, sewing machine needles, and a wide range of textile machinery.

Firm Strategy, Structure, and Rivalry

The fourth broad attribute of national competitive advantage in Porter's model is the strategy, structure, and rivalry of firms within a nation. Porter makes two important points here. His first is that nations are characterised by different "management ideologies," which either help them or do not help them build national competitive advantage: For example, Porter notes the predominance of engineers on the top-management teams of German and Japanese firms. He attributes this to these firms' emphasis on improving manufacturing processes and product design. In contrast, Porter notes a predominance of people with finance backgrounds on the top-management teams of many US firms. He links this to many US firms' lack of attention to improving manufacturing processes and product design, particularly during the 1970s and 1980s. He also argues that the dominance of finance has led to an overemphasis on maximizing short-term financial returns. According to Porter, one consequence of these different management ideologies has been a relative loss of US competitiveness in those engineering-based industries where manufacturing processes and product design issues are important (*e.g.*, the' automobile industry).

Porter's second point is that there is a strong association between vigorous domestic rivalry and the creation and persistence of competitive advantage in an industry. Vigorous domestic rivalry induces firms to look for ways to improve efficiency, which makes them better international competitors. Domestic rivalry creates pressures to innovate, to improve quality, to reduce costs, and to invest in upgrading advanced factors. All of this helps to create world-class competitors.

Porter's argument is that the degree to which a nation is likely to achieve international success in a certain industry is a function of the combined impact of factor endowments, domestic demand conditions, related and supporting industries, and domestic rivalry. He argues that for this diamond to boost competitive performance usually requires the presence of all four components (although there are some exceptions). Porter also contends that government can influence each of the four components either positively or negatively. Factor endowments can be affected by subsidies, policies toward capital markets, policies toward education, and the like. Government can shape domestic demand through local product standards or with regulations that mandate or influence buyer needs. Government policy can influence supporting and related industries through regulation and influence firm rivalry through such devices as capital market regulation, tax policy, and antitrust laws.

If Porter is correct, we would expect his model to predict the pattern of international trade that we observe in the real world. Countries should be exporting products from those industries where all four components of the diamond are favourable, while importing in those areas where the components are not favourable. Much about the theory rings true, but the same can be said for the new trade theory, the theory of comparative advantage, and the Heckscher-Ohlin theory. In reality it may be that each of these theories explains something about the pattern of international trade. In many respects these theories complement each other.

IMPLICATIONS FOR BUSINESS

There are three main implications of these theories for international businesses: location implications, first-mover implications, and policy implications.

Location Implications

One way in which these theories matters to an international business concerns the link between the theories of international trade and a firm's decision about where to locate its productive activities. Underlying most of the theories is the notion that countries have particular advantages different productive activities. Thus, from a profit perspective, it makes sense for a firm to disperse its various productive activities to those countries where they can be performed most efficiently. If design can be performed most efficiently in France, that is where design facilities should be located; if the manufacture of basic components can be performed most efficiently in Singapore, that is where they should be manufactured; and if final assembly can be performed most efficiently in China, that is where final assembly should be performed. The end result is a global web of productive activities, with different activities being performed in varying locations around the globe depending on considerations of comparative advantage, factor endowments, and the like. If the firm does no do this, it may find itself at a competitive disadvantage relative to firms that do

First-Mover implications

The new trade theory suggests the importance to firms of building and exploiting first-mover advantages. According to the new trade theory, firms that establish a first-mover advantage with regard to the production of a particular new product may subsequently dominate global trade in that product. This is particularly true in those of industries where the global market can profitably support only a limited number of firms, such as the aerospace market, but early commitments also seem to be important in less concentrated industries such as the market for cellular telephone equipment. For the individual firm, it pays to invest substantial financial resources in trying to build a first-mover, or early-mover, advantage, even if that means several years of substantial losses before a new venture becomes profitable. In recent years Japanese firms, rather than their European or North American competitors, have been prepared to undertake the vast investments and bear the years of losses required to build a first-mover advantage. This has been true in the production of liquid crystal display (LCD) screens for laptop computers. While firms such as Toshiba and NEC invested heavily in this technology during the 1980s, many large European and American firms exited the market. As a result, today Japanese firms dominate global trade in LCD screens, even though the technology was invented in the United States.

Policy Implications

The theories of international trade also matter to international businesses because business firms are major players on the international trade scene. Business firms produce exports, and business firms import the products of other countries. Because of their pivotal role in international trade, firms influence government trade policy. By lobbying government, business firms can help promote free trade or trade restrictions. The message for business contained in the theories of international trade is that promoting free trade is generally in the best interests of the home country, although it may not always be in the best interest of an individual firm. Many firms recognise this and lobby for open markets.

Finally, Porter's theory of national competitive advantage also contains policy implications. Porter's theory suggests that it is in a firm's best interest to invest in upgrading advanced factors of production; for example, to invest in better training for its employees and to increase its commitment to research and development It is also in the best interests of business to lobby the government to adopt policies that have a favourable impact on each component of the national "diamond." Thus, according to Porter, businesses should urge government to increase its investment in education, infrastructure, and basic research (because all these enhance advanced factors) and to adopt policies that promote strong competition within domestic markets (because this makes firms stronger international competitors, according to Porter's findings).

❐

14

Global E-Business

The combination of broadband capabilities, connectivity, standard languages, wireless communication and portability have given birth to the digital age and its most pervasive manifestation: the Internet. The Internet is a global network connecting millions of computers across the world, exchanging data, opinions, information and news using a common architecture, the Internet Protocol (IP). The network is also known as the World Wide Web (WWW) or the 'Web'. In essence, the Internet is a global tool since it has abolished physical distance for the transmission of data, images and sounds and it has standardised the transmission protocol as well as the machine software, making it possible for any computer in the world to be part of network and to 'talk' to other computers. Infact, the Internet and its attendant power have made it possible for many companies to conduct global business at a much more discernible and attainable level. New economies and efficiencies of scale have been created. Not too long ago, only a few companies had the resources to compete on a global scale. Now, more than at any time in history, almost any size firm with the vision and ambition to do so can extend its reach globally.

As a result of the Internet and new information technology, many of the myths about globalization can be unmasked. According to one theory, globalization is a conspiracy by big companies against smaller markets. Some companies, of course, are bigger, financially, than others. That's a testimony to the market-based economy that more and more markets are choosing to adopt. But no company or group of companies is calling all the shots. Small and midsize companies are getting in on the act and thriving globally.

What is Global E-Business?

Global e-business is not a simple undertaking. It involves a variety of complex issues. Moreover, failure to adequately address the IT element can alienate entire markets and erode the relationship between a company and the marketplace. A comprehensive global e-business strategy can greatly help to ensure a place in the global economy, thus enabling a business to take advantage of a world of possibilities.

Global e-business strategically uses IT to take apart physical supply chains and reassemble them in better ways, create highly focused communications for specific cultures, and select the parameters needed to support multiple markets.

Global e-business adapts specific IT to a company's products and message to best meet the varied expectations of markets around the world. In addition, global e-business is, in many ways, a complete revolution of how a company perceives distance; time, and location.

Global e-business is the most powerful communications medium the business world has ever known, in large part because of its reach into factories, offices, and homes around the world. The substantially lower cost of communication via the Internet has dramatically lessened the importance of distance: For many products that can be digitized-such as pictures, video, sound, and words-distance will become a nonfactor. The same is true for services. And even for most products, because of the Internet, distance will have much less an effect on overall business costs.

In the physical world, time and season predominate the flow of goods and services around the world. We see this in the hours of operation-activities that occur by time of day and in social and climactic seasons. The virtual marketplace, on the other hand, is always open. The seller need not be awake, or even physically present, for the buyer to be served by the seller. The Internet is independent of season. Time can thus be homogenized-made uniformly consistent for all buyers and for all sellers.

Because any screen-based activity can be operated anywhere on earth, location does not play an important part in most business decisions. Is it even relevant? Does location mean where the firm is officially registered? Is it where most of the people employed by the company work? Or is it where the server is physically located? In most cases, it simply doesn't matter.

Following the recent decade's IT explosion, a world marketplace awaits, with its entire attendant of consumers and competition. An initial presence on the Internet can be relatively easy and inexpensive to establish. And any company that has a presence on the World Wide Web is international by definition, whether it chooses to become a global company or not.

Global e-business exploits the Internet's ability to level the playing field for all participants, regardless of size, especially as it relates to a company's ability to communicate with customers, employers, suppliers, investors, and other targeted groups. No other media can claim this ability. No individual or company has a better right to establish a place on the Web than any other. Mere purchasing of limited physical space in newspapers or magazines, or buying time on radio or TV, cannot achieve such presence. No other medium can even come close to achieving the level of scalability that the Internet can achieve, *i.e.*, the ability to leverage its own power and impact to much higher levels and with a much broader global reach.

Global e-business eliminates the historic rigid hierarchy of business processes. According to leading corporate strategists, individual workers must be given maximum autonomy, and the patterns of communications within a worldwide organization should resemble a knowledge-based ecology more than a flowchart. All of this is irrespective of a company's size and physical location.

The internet would increase the globalisation of markets, reinforce global cost reduction, foster global competition and weaken governments' barriers open trade (See Table-1). The challenge for businesses of all sizes-especially smaller ones-that want to maximize their global presence involves structuring relationships and information flow so that the right parties can obtain the information at the right time. In all these views, IT and e-business initiatives 'play critical roles in the strategy of global competition, especially in regard to their global supply chain application.

TABLE-1

EFFECTS OF THE INTERNET ON GLOBALISA TION

Market globalisation	• Increase global commonality in customer needs and tastes (facilities customised standardisation and strengthen appeal of global brands: Barbie online) • Enables global customers and global channels (facilitates global sourcing) • Supports global marketing (enhances global brands and standardises search) • Makes global products more rapidly visible
Cost reduction	• Exploits differences in country costs and facilitates competition from low-cost small-scale companies from emerging markets • Enhances global sourcing • Speeds up global logistics • Reduces product development costs
Foster global competition	• Makes competitive comparisons easier • Increases the number of potential global suppliers by reverse auctions • Puts new rivals in the global competitive arena
Weaken government barriers to open trade	• Makes it easier for customers to by-pass customs and tax levies • Puts pressures on government to harmonise standards and policies • Gives customers more incentives to lobby their governments to align with more customers • Friendly regulations

Before the advent of the new information and e-business technologies of the past decade and before easy access to global information systems became available to companies, customers and suppliers had to make major decisions with little information on which to base them. With the global e-business solutions, buyers and suppliers of all sizes can now' easily track the status and current location of their orders around the world. Before this proliferation of global e-business capability was available, small and midsize companies, especially, might have found themselves left out of the countless new business opportunities in an exploding global economy.

Obviously, small and midsize companies do not possess the sizable resources usually reserved for the biggest global companies in the world. At the same time, those that will succeed in the future understand that the Internet and e-business technology are invaluable, indispensable business tools that need to be harnessed and crafted into a company's overall strategies. To ensure success on the new global business frontier, business leaders from these companies must do what they've always had to do: formulate and implement ideas, tactics, and strategies. Now, they must do this at a much higher level-at a global level-to enable their companies to survive and prosper in the new global marketplace.

Developing Global E-Business Strategy

The greatest challenge for all businesses that want to truly maximize their global presence centers on structuring relationships and the flow of information so that the right parties-customers, suppliers, employees, etc. can obtain it at the right time and at the right place. In this view, e-business and IT initiatives play critical roles in forging a successful global company. This is especially true for small and midsize businesses.

Many companies, however, large and small, wrongly believe e-business and IT will harvest big rewards by merely overlaying computers on top of traditional work processes. These companies fail to understand that e-business and IT work best when they are used to transform those same traditional processes as well as the entire corporate culture. The most successful companies specifically focus on ways that e-business and IT can add value to existing business systems by gaining improved and increased efficiencies. Such a mind-set and resulting strategy affords a small and midsize company the ability to develop entirely new business capabilities and processes to then forge the company's global presence.

Globally savvy companies and their managers view projects, as well as the business overall, from a global perspective. Striving to overcome cultural challenges, regional, national, and personal differences are subrogated to the overall global good of the company to maximize results for the entire organization. Leaders of these companies realize that success depends on the unrestricted flow of information throughout their global business network, which then comes together in the right place and at the right time. For these companies, this doesn't happen by chance. It's a function of its global company culture, and at its core, it is this culture that drives the global organization and, in turn, its global business success. Now, more than ever, e-business technology is driving culture and this new culture is driving globalization.

E-business Strategy: Manifestly Global

The new digital economy is manifestly global—a global phenomenon, yet truly globalized e-businesses are the exception. Even the largest companies on the planet still have a ways to go before they can claim total globalization. Globalization to a company's e-business processes or its Internet presence is not a simple task. It engages a variety of complex issues, and language translation is just the beginning. Failure to sufficiently tackle e-business globalization can isolate entire markets and jeopardize relationships between a company and the marketplace. Moreover, it has the potential to erode and destroy a company's business on a regional or global scale. A cogent and inclusive e-business globalization strategy can ensure a company's place in the new borderless digital economy, enabling businesses of all sizes to exploit a new world of opportunities.

A global marketplace awaits all business, with all the attendant customers, consumers, competition, and suppliers that this entails. This is an exciting time for business, indeed, but also a potentially dangerous time. Companies of all sizes too often are blinded by the promises of the new global economy. Herein lays the seductive danger of the Internet and its creation of e-business. Harvesting the Internet's potential rewards requires more than just making a company Internet-enabled. Companies that want to offer their products and services to the world and successfully compete in the new global marketplace must fundamentally change the very way they think about doing business. In this new global, digital world, the axiom, "change or die," has never been more appropriate.

Global E-business Strategy: Key Components

Communications. Global business is about adapting a company's products and services to meet the varied expectations of markets around the world. A company must also adapt and customize its communications to customers, consumers, suppliers, and others around the world. There exists no common formula to achieve either of these in business today.

Further complicating matters, developing a successful global e-business strategy demands cautious and thorough consideration of linguistic, cultural, economic, and legislative differences in markets around the world. In the past, only the largest companies attempted to create a truly global presence. Companies incapable of competing at this level simply confined themselves to a domestic market, or to a very limited subset of international markets. The Internet and the advent of e-business fundamentally rewrite the rules by wiping out distance, dramatically reducing the barriers of entry to the electronic marketplace, and inciting an atmosphere of hypercompetition on a global level.

Change or Die. The global companies must discard their previously successful strategies or face real danger. Large and small, new and old businesses similarly must struggle with the challenges of how to best conduct business in the new, global digital world.

In the past, businesses adapted their products simply by translating the language on their packaging and their user instructions or by simply changing electrical connectors and voltage to meet local market requirements. Simple language translation or minimal, basic product modifications are not the solutions today.

Business globalization is likewise not simply including existing local cultural and business nuances into a collective global melting pot. A global e-business strategy with its message streaming along the Internet will have to simultaneously provide localized communications to both internal and external users in dozens of different markets while adhering to exacting performance requirements—all this as it processes real-time content changes. Few companies, if any, have mastered this.

The following information will provide companies of all sizes, and most of all, small and midsize companies, a practical road map or template to use as they develop their own global e-business strategy. This information should serve as a checklist of the most critical activities required to successfully deploy a global e-business strategy for any company. The level and depth to which a company will need to go depends largely on the size of the company, the resources it has available, and its vision and aspirations to become truly global.

Global E-business Strategy and Business Plan Development

Any company's globalization strategy can be tremendously enhanced with an effective e-business strategy. To develop a successful e-business globalization strategy, companies of all sizes must first: clearly articulate their overall business and e-business strategies; Second, possess a keen knowledge of their target markets (countries), considering: geography, demo graphics, economic conditions, internal country politics the political situation between home and target countries, home and target countries legal requirements, and Internet readiness. Third, carefully select target markets (countries), groups of markets, etc. Finally, plan to establish a company and/or brand identity in target markets. Also, regardless of the degree of complexity of the company's global e-business strategy, some common traits typically emerge with most, if not all, e-business sites. Specifically, these include: *(i)* Visitors to multiple-language sites remain on the site almost twice as long as they do with English-only language sites. *(ii)* Business users are three times more likely to buy when the site is in their own local language. *(iii)* Customer service costs decrease when instructions on the site are in the customer's own local language.

Market Selection

A company should prioritize and rank the markets (countries) that may be targeted in its global business strategy. As with all business, developing a global e-business strategy requires that a company know its targeted customer groups very well.

If a company already conducts business in specific markets or if a market is a new high-priority target market; the firm mutest determine if these markets meet a set of strategic screening criteria. Criteria to be considered are as follows:

For Automatic Inclusion:

(i) Markets already accounting for significant company revenue

(ii) Markets where there already is a large e-business presence

(iii) Markets with large physical presences or strategic regional importance (*e.g.*, Brazil in South America, United Kingdom in Europe)

For Automatic Fxclusion:

(i) Markets not a significant source of current revenue

(ii) Markets not a significant source of future revenue

(iii) Markets whose local laws do not support the necessary intellectual property rights or copyrights

(iv) Markets that are subject to trade embargoes or other internationally imposed sanctions

For markets that do not clearly fall into either of the categories of automatic inclusion or exclusion, a more detailed analysis should be conducted. A rating and ranking mechanism should be developed to prioritize these remaining markets. Any mechanism that is developed should rate and rank markets based on key economic, strategic, or business criteria. Criteria for detailed analysis should include: First, economic viability: current market size, potential market size, current market penetration, potential market penetration, current market revenue and profit, potential market revenue and profit, presence or absence of local business and/or brand alliances, and the presence or absence of direct and/ or indirect competition; Second, internet preparedness: current Internet penetration, rate of current and forecasted Internet growth, projected Internet penetration, Internet useage (*e.g.*, willingness to conduct business/purchase online), and, internet infrastructure capabilities; finally, the business capability: size of in market business presence, experience with company/ product brand localization, and the existing language translation capabilities.

Establish Localization/Regionalization Parameters

A company must establish a set of cultural expectations regarding how a local e-business and Internet presence should perform for each market that a company selects. Based on these local expectations, parameters should then be selected for each market.

Sometimes, localization parameters need not apply across all selected markets, but rather they may be applied across a common group of markets in a homogeneous region (*e.g.*, the Middle East). In this case, a regional approach to establishing localization parameters may be more appropriate. Parameters to be considered are: company and/ or product/service brand(s), information architecture, visual design, application functionality, content, and the business processes.

Establish Globalization Parameters

Once a company has set its localization and regionalization parameters it can establish its globalization parameters. The firm must consider relevant factors from each market. To the extent that any localization feature can be applied on a globalized level, localized or regionalized parameters may then influence and otherwise determine specific globalization parameters. Also, not all localization or regionalization parameters may need to be addressed in the final set of globalization parameters. In some cases, it may be more cost-effective to localize or regionalize some systems without globalizing them. Parameters that should be globalized include: languages, writing systems, currencies, weights and measurements, calendars, time zones, time measurements, and postal and telephone systems.

Languages and Phonetic Systems. Language is one of the primary differentiators for many cultures. The importance of language clearly makes language-related functions prime targets in implementing global e-business strategy. This is no simple task, however. Languages are extremely diverse, and they change very rapidly.

There are currently 6,700 living languages in the world, but only 435 of these languages are in commercial use. Of all spoken languages, the top 15 in the world together account for 49.5 percent of all the languages spoken by the world's total population.

Writing and Ideogrammatic Systems. Writing systems have a major impact on the way information is presented. Direction of script varies significantly between writing systems. The direction of Latin script is from left to right, top to bottom. The direction of Japanese scripts is generally from top to bottom, right to left, although there can be a mixture of directions on a single page.

Not only does the direction of script vary between systems, but the method used to sort words differs as well. The Latin writing system sorts words and letters using a process based on a fixed sequence called alphabetical order (A to Z). The Japanese hiragana writing system arranges the syllables in the order they appear in a famous Buddhist poem. The Chinese hanzi writing system orders symbols by the number of brush strokes it takes to draw them.

Currencies. Currency is involved in most commerce, and thus is another prime target of global e-business. Many potential customers in markets around the world expect to purchase goods using their own currencies. While offering them this service is desirable, it can also expose an organization to considerable risk if not handled correctly.

Currency conversion rates fluctuate on a very short time scale because of trading in global currency markets. This fluctuation makes setting fixed prices in different markets difficult to coordinate. The Internet makes this form of arbitrage even easier.

Weights and Measurement Systems. Commerce often involves the exchange of fixed quantities of goods or materials that meet certain dimensional specifications. Thus, it is important to consider internationalizing weights and measures. The International System of Units (SI), more commonly referred to as the metric system, is effectively the global standard for measurement. A few markets still cling to old systems: At this time, only three markets-Myanmar, Liberia, and the United States-have not adopted the SI standard as their official system of weights and measures.

The United States is the only industrialized nation that does not mainly use the metric system in its commercial and standards activities, but acceptance is increasing in science, medicine, government, and many sectors of industry in the United States.

Calender Systems. Calendars, especially in a global e-business context, are useful in determining holidays, shipment dates, or the date on which a transaction took place. Calendars, like writing systems, come in several varieties. Each calendar determines the number and names of days and months in the year, including when leap years occur.

Three calendar types and at least ten calendars are in daily use around the world. Following are the three calendar types with examples of each:

1. Solar-based on the yearly solar cycle. Examples: Gregorian, Julian, Ethiopic, Coptic, Modern Hindu
2. Lunar-based on the cycle of the moon. Example: Islamic
3. Lunisolar-that attempt to reconcile the cycles of both the sun and moon. Examples: Chinese, Hebrew, Old Hindu

These differences can lead to significant confusion when converting from one calendar to another is required. With today's information technology, the task of reconciling the different calendar systems can be made simpler.

Time Zones. Specification of time zones is important for standard time measurement, and could be highly relevant in computer transactions. There are 24 international time zones, and markets set their local time according to the time zone they are in and the time zones adopted by their trading partners and neighbours.

All markets define their own local time in terms of hours ahead or behind Greenwich Mean Time (GMT), up to a maximum of 11 hours ahead or behind. The situation is complicated by the fact that many markets observe daylight saving time, usually hours ahead or behind local time. This is determined at the market level, with different markets beginning and ending daylight saving on different dates (*e.g.*, the U.S. and Canada versus Europe). Individual markets may also vary the start and end dates of daylight saving from year to year, further complicating matters.

Time Measurement Systems. For certain types of e-business systems, the measurement of accurate time is crucial. This is especially true when systems comprise multiple components distributed geographically. The management of time can become a significant hurdle. Coordinating multiple clocks and managing time changes to and from daylight saving time across multiple time zones requires considerable planning. While these problems may be new to many commercial organizations, they have been recognized and solved by scientific and military institutions.

An example illustrating the need for highly accurate time coordination is in the financial and commodities markets. Most financial and commodity market maker systems that provide auctions also require accurate time synchronization so auctions can close exactly when required and bids can be "time-stamped" with the correct time. Time stamps are also very useful in many cryptographic protocols, where time is intimately connected with the exchange of messages.

Postal Systems. The Universal Postal Union (UPU), with headquarters in Bern, Switzerland, is a specialized institution of the United Nations that regulates the postal services of its member countries. The postal addressing systems outline the elements that form the basis for proper postal addressing. These elements ensure the correct wording of addresses and guarantee the quick and efficient handling of letter-post items.

Postcodes can also be used to validate text addresses. Software systems are available that can derive a postcode from a text address and a text address from a postcode. These systems are usually only available with delivery code systems. They require large supporting databases and must be updated frequently to account for new addresses and codes.

Telephone dialing systems. Telephone dialing codes are another means for geographic location; they are quite useful for communication as well. From the standpoint of globalization, it is important to understand the relevant international standards for telecommunications, and also the degree of local variation in the way countries handle telephone numbers.

Key Attributes of A Successful Global E-Business Strategy

Irrespective of any individual company-specific parameters (globalization localization/ regionalization), company size, industry or markets targeted, a successful global e-business strategy should possess three key attributes: flexibility, adaptability and controllability.

Flexibility. Localization/regionalization parameters that may apply in one market may not apply in another. Globalization parameters that are critical to support a single major market may undermine the overall strategy and render it cost-ineffective. Typically, most companies find there is no single, correct solution, and that any global e-business strategy will have its tradeoffs. In the end, any viable globalization strategy chosen must be flexible across targeted markets.

Adaptability. Everything in the world of business and financial markets changes. International and national politics and laws change, sometimes daily. So, too does the Internet; and changes seem to be accelerating each year. Any chosen global e-business strategy must be able to adapt to the many changes that have become part of everyday business life, especially on a global level.

Controllability. To ensure the success of any global e-business strategy, a company must exert a high degree of control to implement a stable and manageable global business organization and its resulting structures. This is especially critical when localizing business processes, for local management will likely be charged with implementing and managing market-specific e-business functions.

Cost-Benefit Analysis

Once a company has determined all the criteria with which to establish its global e-business strategies, it must then conduct a cost-benefit analysis to determine the economic viability of the chosen strategies. When analyzing costs, companies must consider both the implementation costs as well as the costs of re-engineering any business processes, ongoing systems maintenance costs, training costs, etc. Once these costs are determined, they can then be weighed against the strategic and economic benefits offered by extending the company's global reach into targeted markets.

Strategy and Business Plan Optimization

If the cost-benefit analysis reveals anything in the global e-business strategy that may be economically viable, a company should consider either adding or removing markets from the mix, modifying some market-specific localization parameters, or adjusting some of its globalization parameters. For example, the cost of globalizing language and writing systems for the Chinese market may be too high, while localization or regionalization is more viable.

Depending on what parameters will be adjusted, added, or removed, it will likely be necessary to review both sets of localized/ regionalized and globalized parameters. Following each series of adjustments, a new cost-benefit analysis should be conducted and the viability of the global e-business strategy reassessed.

Once optimized, the cost-benefit analysis should yield a global e-business strategy that will include: prioritized list of markets to be targeted; parameters to be localized within the targeted markets; requirements mapping of localization and/or regionalization of selected business processes that may be necessary; parameters to be globalized within various business systems; and estimation of costs and benefits of the global e-business strategy. Table-2 lists the organisational requirement for e-business.

Global E-Business Strategy Implementation

Once a company has successfully developed and optimized its global e-business strategy, it must develop and execute an implementation plan. Key components of any such implementation plan should include the following:

(i) Localization/regionalization of business processes as required

(ii) Globalization of business processes as required

(iii) Globalization of appropriate global parameters as required

(iv) Localize globalized parameters within selected markets

(v) Localize nonglobalized parameters within selected markets

TABLE-2

ORGANISATIONAL REQUIREMENTS FOR E-BUSINESS

Transparency	• Integrity and consistency of information • Clear data and procedures
Sharing Culture	• Horizontal as well as vertical exchange of information • External partners have access to data-bases • No 'silos'
Process Integration	• All management processes are compatible with each other to facilitate information flow
Pooled co-ordination	• Ability to have different department working together instantaneously instead of sequentially • Ability to bundle different parameters in real time • Sequential co-ordination too time-consuming
Real-time commitment	• Ability to make decisions quickly • No time for hierarchical checking
Horizontal processes	• Hierarchical communication and decision processes inefficient

Typically, a phased approach is taken regarding these implementations, with the most strategic markets being implemented first. At the same time, some implementation tasks may be undertaken concurrently with others in selected markets. The ultimate methodology selected by a company will depend on its chosen strategy and the specific challenges presented in each case.

Cultural Adaptability of Global Technology Implementation

Standardized technologies alone won't guarantee successful global e-business operations. The most successful global organizations properly manage multilingual and multicultural implementations of applications and data. Because every successful global e-business implementation must employ components of the technology that require these multilingual and multicultural services and support, companies that specialize in translation, localization, and cultural practices are thriving as part of the global e-business solution. A rudimentary search on the Internet will yield scores of such companies prepared and ready to assist any size company to achieve the desired level of multilingual and multicultural needs that any company may have.

The need to translate and localize foretells that the true challenges in implementing global e-business systems still center on culture, not in the deployment of new technology. In short, everyone can be given the same applications, but ensuring that those applications are used consistently to benefit the company is much more difficult.

By drastically reducing the importance of proximity, the new technologies change people's perceptions of community. The Internet connects people and companies across borders with exponentially growing ease, while separating them from natural and historical associations with nations. Doing business globally filters through many levels of the information technology, local practices, and corporate culture. The more sensitive corporate leadership is toward language and cultural differences, the more an organization is able to improve and add value to its global e-business initiatives. Overall company cultures, particularly in local company offices around the world deeply influenced by their individual market cultures, will need to change their mind sets to make that shift.

Culture-the amalgam of tradition, relationships, and values-shapes business practices and processes in widely varying ways. Cultural differences often make it hard to obtain consensus and collaboration, and not what the "technology of the day" is. The divide between culture, technology, and knowledge can be enormous. To close this divide, successful global organizations of all sizes and cultures realize that a clear understanding of their own company and its home market culture as well as the culture of others is urgently needed.

Cultural Communications in Global E-business Strategy

Cultural differences can make a large impact on the interpretation of tation of visual design. What is considered a cutting-edge design in one culture can appear rude and unprofessional in another. Common interpretations of visual design simply cannot be assumed when working internationally. By their nature, visual messages are often more ambiguous and open to interpretation than is the written word.

Colours. Colours are a part of most people's everyday worlds. We attach a great deal of significance to them, whether we realize it or not. The meanings attached, however, and even the words we use to describe them, vary between cultures. For example, Japanese do not differentiate between green and blue. In the Netherlands, blue connotes quality, and in China, red has negative connotations. Different interpretations of colour abound throughout the world.

Image. Images are also interpreted differently across cultures and locations. It is very difficult for a central organization to make appropriate choices about local imagery. Apart from the obvious case where images include text, images themselves often contain cultural assumptions. Images must be made locally appropriate; what appears as an innocuous pictogram of the thumbs-up signal (representing approval) is, in fact, an offensive gesture in some cultures. A car shown driving down the right side of the road would contradict experience in several markets, thus disrupting the intent of a carefully built design.

Colours, images, and text combine to create a graphical interface, and changes to any one of these elements can impact the entire visual design. Text translation can cause significant expansion in the length of text that, in turn, may create a negative impact on a visual design. Substantial modification of text can disrupt the flow of information and qualitatively change the look and feel of an interface. Careful localization of text helps preserve the original intent and spirit of a visual design.

Cultural assumptions affect function in a way similar to information architecture and visual design. As a result, the function of a system may have to be localized to meet cultural requirements.

For instance, the concept of the shopping cart on a commercial Web site does not translate for all cultures. The supermarket as a standard for a commercial experience is justified only when most customers experience supermarkets as a regular part of their daily life. Only then will they know what to expect when confronted with the Internet shopping cart.

If an application offers a negative or confusing experience to a user with a different set of cultural expectations, it is no longer useful and thus fails in its intent. Before creating any content (words, images, audio, or video), a company with an Internet presence must first develop a content strategy that articulates the voice and tone of its brand. This strategy ensures that the content is consistent and compelling, and that it properly communicates the message of the brand.

As is the case with information architecture and visual design, the local focus of content must account for subtle and not-so-subtle cultural variations. For example, localizing the audio portions of a Web site requires not only translating the audio into the appropriate language, but accounting for dialect and pronunciation differences. The localization of text requires a similar attention-to idiomatic expressions, differences in usage, and culturally specific grammatical conventions.

Language. Language translation is an art, not a science. Literal translation is almost never sufficient. At best, it can produce stilted approximations of the original and, at worst, it can erode a brand's credibility by being unintentionally amusing or even insulting to the target audience and others.

Ensuring text is carefully reviewed by a native speaker is essential even when the text is not ostensibly being translated into another language. In Spain the verb to take is perfectly acceptable, while in Mexico it is considered crude. At first glance, a manufacturer may believe that the American version of a product catalog can be reused in all English-speaking markets. This may be the case; the catalog would probably still be understandable. If local language usage is not taken into account, however, it might also cause serious brand erosion. In effect, this means that language and market are inseparable. For example, American, British, Australian, Canadian, and South African English should be treated as separate languages. Each market has its own language variation that must be handled individually.

Another factor to consider when localizing text is that translation can have a significant, even damaging, effect on visual design and information architectures. When text is translated, the amount of space required to hold that contiguous block of text can change dramatically. On the average, English increases by 30 percent when it is translated to other European languages, and can increase by 400 percent in extreme cases.

Finally, the organisational attributes may sometimes conflict with local cultures. Table-3 contrasts Internet cultural requirements with typical Asian corporate culture. The challenge for the global firm is to overcome these culture differences among their employees, suppliers, customers and partners to make Web transactions effective.

TABLE-3

INTERNET MANAGERIAL CULTURE VERSUS MANAGERIAL CULTURE

Transparency	• Partial, and multiple information • Lack of clear procedures
Sharing culture	• Vertical information sharing • Clannicretention
Process integration	• 'Siloed' processes
Pooled co-ordination	• Top-down processes, otherwise sequential processes
Real-time commitment	• Several checks, vertically organised
Horizontal processes	• Hierarchical

❐

15

Liberalisation and Foreign Investment

Two of the most interesting phenomena in the contemporary world economy are the emergence of new and/or the extension of existing regional trading blocs and the explosive growth of foreign direct investment (FDI). In the 1950s and 1960s. a first phase of regional integration saw the formation of the European Economic Community (EEC) and the European Free Trade Area (EFTA), together with a number of other short-lived trading blocs in Latin America, the Caribbean and Africa. A second phase in the late 1980s and early 1990s has brought initiatives not only in Europe and Latin America, but also in North America, Australasia and South-East Asia. Furthermore, this new phase of 'regionalism' has generated considerable concern about whether the relatively open, multilateral world trading system will be superseded by a small number of large, relatively closed regional blocs.

REGIONAL INTEGRATION AGREEMENT AND TRADE (RIAs)

Regional integration which involves arrangements for preferential trade may take a number of forms. The term trading bloc is usually reserved by economic theorists for arrangements which take the form either of a free trade area or of a customs union. A free trade area involves the elimination of tariffs on trade between the member states, but each member maintains its own national policy towards trade with third countries. Customs inspectors monitor trade at the frontiers between the member states in order to tax trade that might otherwise circumvent high tariff barriers by entering the flea through the member state with the lowest external tariff. In contrast, member states of a customs union adopt a common external tariff. Commodities thus flow freely between member states, and there is no need for customs inspection at national borders.

Trading blocs involve the removal of trade barriers, but stop short of further economic integration. A common market allows not only for the free movement of commodities, but also for the free movement of factors of production. Finally, economic union is used to describe the situation where member states not only participate in a common market, but also promote a high degree of integration in their fiscal, monetary, commercial and welfare policies.

Compared to the ideal of free world trade, RIAs involve discrimination against non-members (they result in preferential liberalization among partner countries only), they are inconsistent with the most-favoured-nation (MFN) rule, the fundamental principle of the WTO. Given the prevalence of regional trade arrangements and the historical importance of trade agreements as instruments of foreign policy and, sometimes, nation-building, the WTO does not prohibit RIAs. Instead, it imposes on members disciplines designed to minimize "opportunistic" behavior that is aimed primarily not at integration but at discrimination against non-members. This is done by requiring that WTO members notify new RIAs to the WTO, that they do not raise barriers to trade against the rest of the world, and, most important, that they eliminate barriers to trade on substantially all intraregional trade in goods. The last requirement is intended to ensure that the RIA has integration as its goal.

BOX-1

Selected Major Regional Integration Agreements and Dates of Formation

Europe

European Union (EU). Formerly European Economic Community (EEC), European Community (EC). 1957, Belgium, France, Germany, Italy, Luxembourg, Netherlands; 1973, Denmark, Ireland, United Kingdom; 1981, Greece; 1986, Portugal, Spain; 1995, Austria, Finland, Sweden.

European Economic Area (EEA). 1994, EU, Iceland, Liechtenstein, Norway.

Euro-Mediterranean Economic Area (Euro-Maghreb). Bilateral agreements: 1995, with Tunisia; 1996, with Morocco.

EU Bilateral Agreements with Eastern Europe. 1994, with Hungary, Poland; 1995, with Bulgaria, Czech Republic, Estonia, Latvia, Lithuania, Romania, Slovak Republic, Slovenia.

North America

Canada-U.S. Free Trade Area (CUSFTA). 1988, Canada, United States.

North American Free Trade Area (NAFTA). 1994, Canada, Mexico, United States.

Latin America and the Caribbean

Andean Pact. 1969 (revived in 1991), Bolivia, Colombia, Ecuador, Peru, the Republica Boliviariana de Venezuela.

Central American Common Market (UACM). 1960 (revived in 1993), El Salvador, Guatemala, Honduras, Nicaragua; 1962, Costa Rica.

Common Market of the South/Mercado Comun del Sur (MERCOSUR). 1991, Argentina, Brazil, Paraguay, Uruguay.

Group of Three (G3). 1995, Colombia, Mexico, Republican Boliviariana de Venezuela.

Latin American Integration Association (LAIA). Formerly Latin American Free Trade Area (LAFT A), 1960 (revived in 1980), Argentina, Bolivia, Brazil, Chile, Colombia, Ecuador, Mexico, Paraguay, Peru, Uruguay, Republica Boliviariana de Venezuela.

Caribbean Community and Common Market (CAR/COM). 1973, Antigua and Barbuda, Barbados, Jamaica, St. Kitts and Nevis, Trinidad and Tobago; 1974, Belize, Dominica, Grenada, Montserrat, St. Lucia, St. Vincent and the Grenadines; 1983, The Bahamas (part of the Caribbean Community but not of the Common Market).

Africa

Cross-Border Initiative (CBI). 1992, Burundi, Comoros, Kenya, Madagascar, Malawi, Mauritius, Namibia, Rwanda, Seychelles, Swaziland, Tanzania, Uganda, Zambia, Zimbabwe.

EastAfrican Cooperation (EA C). 1967 (formerly East African Community, EAC; broke up in 1977 and recently revived), Kenya, Tanzania, Uganda.

Economic and Monetary Community of Central Africa (CEMAC). 1994 (formerly Union Douaniere et Economique de I' Afrique Centrale, UDEAC); 1966, Cameroon, Central African Republic, Chad, Congo, Gabon; 1989, Equatorial Guinea.

Economic Community of West African States (ECOWAS). 1975, Benin, Burkina Faso, Cape Verde, Cote d'Ivoire, The Gambia, Ghana, Guinea, Guinea-Bissau, Liberia, Mali, Mauritania, Niger, Nigeria, Senegal, Sierra Leone, Togo.

Common Market for Eastern and Southern Africa (COMESA). 1993, Angola, Burundi, Comoros, Djibouti, Egypt, Ethiopia, Kenya, Lesotho, Malawi, Mauritius, Mozambique, Rwanda, Somalia, Sudan, Swaziland, Uganda, Zambia, Zimbabwe.

Indian Ocean Commission (IOC). 1984, Comoros, Madagascar, Mauritius, Seychelles.

Southern African Development Community (SADC). 1980 (formerly known as the Southern African Development Coordination Conference, SADCC), Angola, Botswana, Lesotho, Malawi, Mozambique, Swaziland, Tanzania, Zambia, Zimbabwe; 1990, Namibia; 1994, South Africa; 1995, Mauritius; 1998, Democratic Republic of the Congo, Seychelles.

Economic Community of West Africa (CEAO). 1973 (revived in 1994 as UEMOA), Benin, Burkina Faso, Cote d'Ivoire, Mali, Mauritania, Niger, Senegal.

West African Economic and Monetary Union (UEMOA, or WAEMU). 1994, Benin, Burkina Faso, Cote d'Ivoire, Mali, Niger, Senegal, Toga; 1997, Guinea-Bissau.

Southern African Customs Union (SACU). 1910, Botswana, Lesotho, Namibia, South Africa, Swaziland.

Economic Community of the Countries of the Great Lakes (CEPGL). 1976, Burundi, Rwanda, Democratic Republic of the Congo.

Middle East and Asia

Asia-Pacific Economic Cooperation (APEC). 1989, Australia, Brunei Darussalam, Canada, Indonesia, Japan, Republic of Korea, Malaysia, New Zealand, Philippines, Singapore, Thailand, United States; 1991, People's Republic of China, Hong Kong (China), Taiwan (China); 1993, Mexico, Papua New Guinea; 1994, Chile; 1998, Peru, Russian Federation, Vietnam.

Association of Southeast Asian Nations (ASEAN). 1967, Indonesia, Malaysia, Philippines, Singapore, Thailand; 1984, Brunei Darussalam; 1995, Vietnam; 1997, Myanmar, Lao People's Democratic Republic; 1999, Cambodia. (ASEAN members created a free trade area in 1992.)

Greater Arab Free Trade Area (GAFTA). 1998, Bahrain, Egypt, Iraq, Jordan, Kuwait, Lebanon, Libya, Morocco, Oman, Qatar, Saudi Arabia, Sudan, Syria, Tunisia, United Arab Emirates, Yemen.

Gulf Cooperation Council (GCC). 1981, Bahrain, Kuwait, Oman, Qatar, Saudi Arabia, United Arab Emirates.

South Asian Association for Regional Cooperation (SAARC). 1985, Bangladesh, Bhutan, India, Maldives, Nepal, Pakistan, Sri Lanka.

The WTO disciplines can be regarded as rules of thumb intended to minimize the negative implications of regional integration for the multilateral trading system. For historical reasons related to the creation of the European Economic Community in the 1950s,

GATT /WTO rules on regionalism have never been effectively enforced. The Doha Development Agenda of 2001 launched negotiations on the rules applying to regionalism. The issues that arise in this context include technical trade policy measures such as the use of rules of origin and the procedures used to ascertain whether individual RIAs satisfy WTO rules.

Economic Effects of RIAs

The development impacts of RIA membership depend importantly on the countries that are involved, the type of agreement, arid its substantive coverage. Recent research suggests that of particular importance to developing countries are whetherlarge industrial countries are members of the agreement, the extent of sectoral exclusions, and the degree to which the RIAs involve "deeper integration"—that is, extend beyond preferential elimination of barriers to trade in good. In order to understand the economic effects of RIAs, a few definitions are in order.

Trade creation takes place when a member country of the RIA (Country 1) increases its imports from its partner country (Country 2) without a reduction in Country l's imports from the rest of the world (ROW). This occurs because with the removal of tariffs between member countries, Country 2's products become cheaper than those of Country 1. The increase in (cheaper) imports results in an increase in consumption and a reduction in output in Country 1. Trade creation is beneficial.

Trade diversion takes place when imports from the ROW are replaced in Country 1 by more expensive imports from Country 2. Why would Country 1 import more expensive goods from Country 2? Because goods from Country 2 do not pay the import tariff, while ROW goods do. Trade diversion is typically harmful.

Transfers occur between member countries of the trade bloc because removal of tariffs between them means that exports obtain better prices in the partners markets (a positive transfer), while the costs of imports net of tariffs increase (a negative transfer).

Trade Creation and Diversion and the Type of RIA

Assume that Mexico imports either from the United States or from Japan and applies a 20 percent tariff on all imports. For a given product, the United States sells at a price of $100 and Japan sells at a price of $110. With the 20 percent tariff, the cost to the Mexican consumer is $120 for the good from the United States and $132 for the product from Japan. Consumers Import from the cheaper source-from the United States, not Japan. Now assume that Mexico forms an RIA with the United States, along the lines of the North American Free Trade Agreement (NAFTA). Tariffs on imports from the United States fall to zero, and consumers now pay $100. This is a case of trade creation because the United States was already the cheapest source and has become even cheaper, replacing more expensive domestic output and raising consumption I as well. Note that the consumer price must fall for trade creation to take place. Since the United States was the only source of Mexican imports to begin with, having an RIA with the United States is identical to unilateral trade liberalization by Mexico and is beneficial.

Assume now that the good is exported by the United States at $110 and by-Japan at $100. With the 20 percent tariff, the cost to consumers is $120 for the good from Japan and $132 for that from the United States. The good is imported exclusively from Japan at $ 120. After Mexico forms an RIA with the United States, the cost of imports from the United States is $110, which is lower than the $120 consumer cost for imports from Japan. Consumers switch their source of imports from Japan to the United States. But although the United States is the cheapest source for consumers, it is not the cheapest source for Mexico as a whole. The reason is that although the consumer cost or imports from Japan is $120, the true cost for Mexico is only $100. The $ 100 is the cost in scarce foreign exchange that Mexico pays for imports from Japan, while the additional $20 associated with the 20 percent tariff is simply a transfer from consumers to the government and is not a cost to the nation. To put it differently, before entering the RIA, Mexico paid $100 to the foreign supplier, and after entering the RIA, it pays $110.

Thus, Mexico loses $10 per unit of import. This is the cost of trade diversion from a cheaper to a more expensive source. Another way of showing this result is that the consumer price fell by $10 (from $120 to $110), but the government lost $20 in tariff revenue, so the net loss is $10.

Note that trade diversion occurred because the 20 percent tariff is higher than the 10 percent difference in cost between the U.S. and the Japanese good. If the tariff were lower - say, 5 percent - the cost of Japan's imports would be $105, still lower than the D.S. price of $110 free of tariff. Consumers would have continued to import from Japan, the cheapest source, and trade diversion would not have occurred. This example points to an important lesson: RIAs should lower their external trade barriers because that reduces the extent of trade diversion. Another reason for so doing is that reducing external trade barriers makes possible the classical gains from trade. Note also that the welfare impact of an RIA is ambiguous a priod and depends on whether trade creation or trade diversion dominates. Of course, even an RIA that is dominated by trade diversion and has a negative welfare effect can be turned into a beneficial RIA by lowering external trade barriers sufficiently.

In the example above, imports were from either Japan or the United States but not from both. This is relevant for a small country facing imports of a similar good from two large exporters. Countries, however, may import the good from more than one source; this is particularly likely to be the case when a small country imports from another small country and from the ROW. For instance, assume that imports from India and from ROW. Say that the world price for; given product is $100 and Sri Lanka charges an import tariff of 20 percent, or $20. Thus, the import price paid by consumers in (and faced by its producers) is $120. India supply of exports to is not horizontal at $120, as is the case for the ROW. Rather, it is upward sloping: an increase in India supply of exports to Sri Lanka implies a higher (marginal) cost of production because Sri Lanka is a large buyer of India exports (although it is a small buyer of ROW exports). In equilibrium, also sells at $120 because it cannot sell at a price above that of the ROW.

Assume now that Sri Lanka forms an RIA with India. As long as Sri Lanka continues to import from the ROW, the consumer price remains $120. Since the consumer price remains unchanged, no trade creation takes place. Before the RIA, the Sri Lanka government obtained $20 in tariff revenue for each unit imported from India, and exporters obtained $100. After the RIA, Sri Lanka no longer charges a tariff on India imports for its exports. In other words, Sri Lanka now loses tariff revenue and pays $20 more for its imports from India. This amounts to a transfer of income from Sri Lanka, the importing country, to India the exporting country. Note that this occurs even if the quantity of imports from India remains unchanged (that is, even if supply of exports is vertical or perfectly inelastic), in which case there is no trade diversion.

It is likely, however, that India exports to Sri Lanka's will increase after Sri Lanka import tariff is removed. In that case the loss of tariff revenue for Sri Lanka will be larger. The increase in India exports amounts to trade diversion because total imports are not affected by the RIA. Since the consumer price is unchanged, the increase in imports from India comes at the expense of reduced imports from the ROW. The (marginal) production cost of the increased imports from India rises from $100 to $120, which is higher than the $100 price paid for ROW imports. Since there is only trade diversion and no trade creation, forming such an RIA lowers the income of the bloc as a whole. India gains by obtaining a better price in Sri Lanka market, and Sri Lanka loses and it loses more than India gains. The reason is that India additional transfers are obtained by increasing its exports to Sri Lanka, and the increased exports are more expensive to produce than the ROW imports they replace. The difference between India gain and Sri Lanka loss is the net loss) due to trade diversion. It is an inefficiency loss and is not captured by anybody.

To illustrate graphically, assume that a home country and a partner country form an RIA. Both are assumed to be small relative to the rest of the world (ROW), so they take the price of goods from the rest of the world, P_w, as given (Figure-I). D_H represents the home country's demand for imports, S_p represents the partner's supply of exports facing the home country, and S_{ROW} is the supply from the ROW. Under free trade, imports equal Q_4, and home country welfare W_H = triangle ACE. Assume now that the home country imposes an MFN tariff, T. Then the price of imports from the ROW faced by home country producers and consumers rises to Pw'= Pw + T, and SROW shifts to. S'_{ROW}. Similarly, S_p shifts to $S_{1p'}$. Imports from the partner country equal Q_1 ,and imports from the ROW. equal Q_3-Q_1 ,with total imports of Q3' W_H^{MFN} = surplus ABF + tariff revenue BDEF and is lower than W_H under free trade by triangle BCD.

A RIA INVOLVING SMALL COUNTRIES

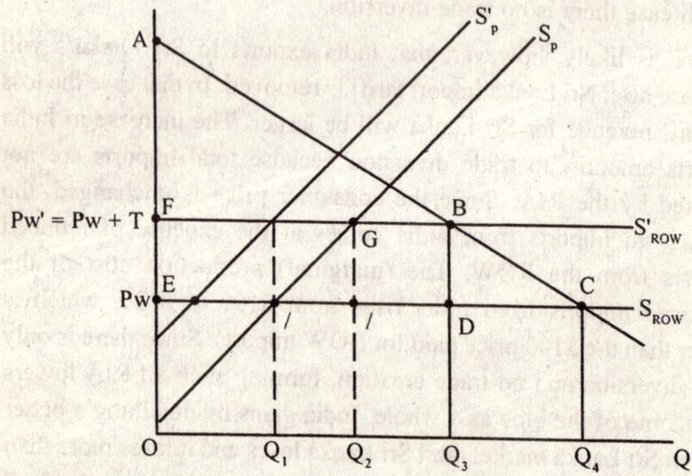

Figure 1

Assume that the home country now forms an RIA with the partner country, As the partner country no longer pays the tariff T, its export supply curve shifts to $S_{p'}$. The ROW still pays the tariff T, so the home country price remains $P_{w'}$, Hence, the partner country imports increase from Q_1 to Q_2, while the imports from the ROW fall from Q_3-Q_1 to Q_3-Q_2. This trade diversion results in a worsening in the home country's terms of trade, Welfare is W_H^{RAI} = ABF + BDIG. In other words, the RIA has no impact on the consumer surplus because the price is not affected (there is no trade creation), but there is a loss of tariff revenue. W_H^{RAI} is lower than W_H^{MFN} by EFGI, the tariff revenue lost on imports from the partner country after forming the RIA, Note that the welfare loss to the home country would occur in the absence of trade diversion as well (for example, the loss would be EFGI if S_p were vertical at level Q_2).

The home country welfare loss from the RIA is proportional to the level of partner country imports. Note also that if the MFN tariff were lower than T, the welfare loss from the RIA would be smaller than area EFGI both because of lower imports from the partner and because of the lower tariff rate. The partner gains EFGJ, which is less than the home country loss of EFGI by the triangle GIf. The reason for the net loss of triangle CIJ for the RIA members as a whole is the trade diversion, Q_2 - Q_1 This amount was previously imported from the ROW at a cost of Pw but is now produced at a higher marginal cost.

Developing countries are more likely to lose by forming a South-South RIA, as opposed to joining a North-South agreement, because the South-South arrangement entails little or no beneficial trade creation. Moreover, there is a high probability that one of the members of a South-South RIA may gain while the other loses. It is the poorest member countries that are likely to lose the most, as the most advanced country will usually have a more developed manufacturing sector. Its manufactures are typically highly protected, and once the RIA is formed, the more advanced country can export them free of tariffs to the poorer member countries. The RIA thus entails an income transfer from the less to the more advanced member countries. Moreover, because the poorer country had more to gain from trading with the North (relative to the more advanced country), it will lose more from creating a South-South RIA. A South-South RIA discriminates against the North and so helps those countries within the bloc that are the closest competitors with the North. Such asymmetric distribution of the gains and losses of integration has led to tensions between members, breakup of RIAs, and even wars. One way to reduce the asymmetry in the distribution of gains and losses, and thus to lessen potential tensions between member countries, is to lower the external trade barriers. The lower the tariff levels with the ROW, the smaller the transfers associated with an RIA.

The foregoing suggests at least three reasons why members of RIAs should lower external trade' barriers: *(a)* to generate classical gains from trade; *(b)* to lessen the chances that trade diversion will occur; and *(c)* to reduce income transfers between member countries resulting from the RIA and the tensions that can arise from such transfers.

Regional Integration Agreements and Foreign Direct Investment

The trade liberalising aspects of regional integration also have repercussions for FDI. To the extent that firms (either domestic or foreign) increase their investment in response to a larger market, or rationalise their production to lower-cost locations within the bloc, then there will be benefits in terms of efficiency and welfare. On the other hand, if trade diversion provides the catalyst for FDI, there will be a loss of economic efficiency and welfare. Other provisions of deeper regional integration will also have an effect on FDI. The removal of restrictions on the movement of factors of production (especially the movement of capital) should facilitate both intra-bloc FDI, and FDI from third countries. And FDI should also be stimulated by the relaxation of ownership and entry requirements, and other liberalising measures to open markets to greater competition.

The liberalisation measures associated with regional integration will, however, typically impact in different ways upon intra-bloc FDI and upon FDI from third countries, and will also have differential effects according to the underlying entrepreneurial motivation of the investing firm. Firms are motivated to invest overseas for a variety of reasons, and six stylised 'types' of FDI may be identified (see Table 1).

(i) The first type of FDI is that undertaken to gain access to specific factors of production (for example, resources, technical knowledge, managerial know-how, patents or brand names) owned by a firm, or firms, in the host country. If such factors of production are not available in the home economy of the foreign firm, and are not transferable at arm's length, then the foreign firm must invest locally in order to secure access. This will typically involve an equity stake in an appropriate host-country firm (if the factor is firm-specific), although the factor in question may take the form of a public good available to all firms in the industry. An example of the latter would be an industry consortium to pool research and development (R&D) resources, and whose results were only available to members.

(ii) The second type of FDI is that identified by Raymond Vernon in his celebrated product cycle hypothesis and considers investment to gain access to cheaper factors of production (for example, low-cost labour). This type of FDI may be encouraged by the government of the host country if it is pursuing an export-oriented development strategy, in which case it may well provide some form of investment in entive (subsidies, grants, tax concessions and so forth) to the foreign firm. If the government is following an import-substitution policy, on the other hand, foreign firms may only be allowed to participate in the host economy to the extent that they possess technical or managerial know-how that is not available to domestic industry. Such know-how may be transferable on an arm's length basis, in which case the foreign involvement may take the form of a licensing arrangement or other form of contractual resource transfer. Or, if the know-how is not transferable in this way, then a foreign minority stake may be encouraged in a joint venture with a local partner.

(iii) The third type of FDI involves international competitors undertaking mutual investment in one another (either through cross-shareholders, or through the establishment of joint ventures), in order to gain access to each other's product ranges. The background to this type of FDI is increased

TABLE 1

A Typology of the Entrepreneurial Motivations for Foreign Direct Investment

Motivation for FDI	*Competitive environment host country government*	*Policy response of*	*Likely characteristics of FDI*
1	*2*	*3*	*4*
Access to factors of production	Host country firm(s) have access to certain factors of production (materials, technology etc.) not available/transferable to foreign firms	Passive (unless deemed against national interest) as host country firms are assumed to hold competitive advantage	Acquisition of host country firms
Access to cheaper factors of production (Product cycle hypothesis)	Shift of comparative advantage from emergence of cheaper factor costs in host country	Conditional upon development strategy and requirements to promote technology transfer. Protection of domestic industry by import quotas/tariffs and controls on foreign equity participation	Contriactual resource transfers and joint ventues with minority equity participation by foreign firms
Access to products	International competition among similar products. Technical change leaves firms in different countries with competitive advantages in different sub-products	Passive, as mutal benefits perceive for foreign and host country firms	Mutual equity participation

1	*2*	*3*	*4*
Access to customers	International trade and competition are limited because of punitive transport costs, because customers require local production/service	Passive, as foeing firms will be operating in the host country on the same basis as domestic firms	Full manufacturing/service operations, together with local design facilities
Access to markets (Tariff-jumping FDI)	International competition among similar products. Technical change shifts comparative advantage in favour of foreign firms. Import penetration in host country increases	Protection of domestic industry through import puotas/tariffs etc.	Assembly operation. Continued parts/components from abroad Investment-shunting. Subsidiaries are wholly-owned or involve majority equity participation by foreign firms
Access to future markets (*Quid pro quo FDI*)	As above	Threat of protection for domestic industry	Full manufacturing operations. together with local sourcing of (parts/ component and local R & I) facilities. Joint ventures/ technical agreements with host country firms.

competition among similar products as a result of R&D induced specialisation. Both firms find it difficult to compete in each others home markets, or in third-country markets for each other's products. If neither product (and hence neither firm) gains the dominant advantage, then the two firms may well invest in each other's area of expertise, and thus promote sub-product specialisation in production.

(iv) The fourth type of FDI relates to that undertaken by firms in order to secure access to customers in the host-country market. No underlying shift in comparative advantage either to or from the host country is observed, but exporting from the firm's home base may be impossible (for example, certain services), punitively expensive because of transport costs (for example, bricks), or unfeasible because customers insist on short supply lines (for example, components) or the capability to request immediate design modifications and/ or amendments. In particular, the limited tradability of many services (for example, banking, other financial services or retail and wholesale distribution) has been an important factor promoting the growth of FDI in these sectors.

(v) The fifth type of FDI relates to the trade diversionary aspect of regional integration. This is commonly known as 'tariff-jumping' FDI and occurs when there are locational advantages for foreign firms in their home country, but the firms are prevented from exporting to the host economy by the existence of tariffs or other barriers to trade. The foreign firms therefore jump the barriers by establishing a local presence within the host economy in order to gain access to the local market. The local manufacturing presence need only be sufficient to circumvent the trade barriers, as the foreign firm will want to maintain as much of the value-added in its home economy, hence simple assembly operations will be the norm.

(vi) The final type of FDI is that undertaken by foreign firms not with the intention of jumping protective barriers, but with a view to defusing the threat of protection itself. As with tariff-jumping FDI, this follows a systemic shift-in comparative advantage in favour of the foreign producers as a result of R&D-induced changes in know-how. The defusion may be achieved either by enhancing directly the benefits (on employment and so on) that FDI confers on the host economy, or by co-opting local firms in joint ventures and thus allocating them a share of the potential benefits. Such *quid pro quo* FDI 1% thus likely to take the form either of full manufacturing operations together with local sourcing of parts and components.

How then are these six types of FDI affected by the various measures which may accompany regional integration? Table-2 provides a summary of the expected effects of the main provisions, upon both intra-bloc FDI and FDI from third countries.

Clearly the relaxation of ownership and entry requirements to restricted industries will stimulate both intra-bloc FDI and FDI from third countries. This will be the case whether the motivation is to gain access to factors of production, products or markets, or whether liberalisation permits foreign firms access to new customers. The liberalisation of intra-bloc labour movement will have little effect on any type of FDI flow, except for intra-bloc FDI which is undertaken to gain access to customers and where the investing firm's competitive advantage lies in the expertise of its workforce. Various service industries (for example, finance, insurance or consulting) would fit this pattern. The liberalisation of intra-bloc capital movements should have little effect upon FDI from third countries, except perhaps through easing the formation of joint ventures with local partners. But freer capital movement will aid all types of intra-bloc investment for obvious reasons.

Of most interest, however, are the differential effects on FDI of the reductions in intra-bloc barriers to trade that accompany regional integration. The reduction of such barriers should have little

TABLE 2

Effects of Liberalisation Measures on Flows of Foreign Direct Investment into a Trading Bloc/common Market

Motivation for FDI	*Source of FDI*	*Relaxation in ownership and entry requirements*	*Liberalisation of intra-bloc labour movements*	*Liberalisation of intra-bloc capital movements*	*Reduction of intra-bloc barriers to trade*
Access to factors of	Within bloc	++	0	+	0
production	Outside bloc	++	0	0	0
Access to cheaper factors	Within bloc	++	0	+	+
of production	Outside bloc	++	0	0	+
Access to products	Within bloc	++	0	+	+
	Outside bloc	++	0	+	+
Access to customers	Within bloc	++	++	+	0
	Outside bloc	++	0	0	0
Access to markets	Within bloc	++	0	+	-
(Tariff-jumping F'QI)	Outside bloc	++	0	0	++
Access to future markets	Within bloc	++	0	+	-
(Quid pro quo FDI)	Outside bloc	++	0	0	++

Notes:

++ inciicate a strong positive effect of the liberalisation measure on foreign direct investment

\+ indicates a weaker positive effect of the liberalisation measure on foreign direct investment

0 indicates little or no significant effect of the liberalisation measure on foreign direct investment

— indicates a negative effect of the liberalisation measure on foreign direct investment

effect on FDI undertaken to gain access to specific factors of production, as the acquisition of know-how, expertise and so on was the primary motivation, not trade. Intra-bloc FDI to gain access to cheaper factors of production will increase as firms within the bloc rationalise their production activities. FDI from third countries may also increase as cheaper locations entice some foreign firms to pursue production within the bloc for export to the higher-cost markets. FDI to gain access to products will also be promoted by reduced barriers to trade as the potential market for the joint venture will be enlarged. In contrast, FDI to gain access to customers should not be significantly affected as, by definition, international trade is either impractical or unfeasible.

The final two types of FDI are both related to the discriminatory aspect of regional integration. Any reduction in intra-bloc barriers to trade will increase the competitive disadvantage (within the bloc) suffered by firms from third countries in relation to firms from within the bloc, and will lead to trade diversion. FDI by the firms from the third countries is therefore a possibility, as they attempt to secure access to the protected market. On the other hand, intra-bloc trade will be stimulated by the reduction in the barriers, and any intra-bloc FDI previously undertaken to secure access to the markets of partner countries may well be reduced.

The various provisions of regional integration agreements thus have quite different effects upon FDI from within the bloc, and from third countries outside the bloc. Furthermore, these effects differ according to the underlying entrepreneurial motivation of the direct investment. Second-round effects may also be identified. For example, much investment in services is linked to investment and/or trade in manufacturing.

THE IMPACT OF REGIONAL INTEGRATION FRAMEWORKS (RIFs) ON FDI DETERMINANTS

(i) The Policy Framework

The majority of RIFs do not explicitly address FDI policy, although there is an increasing tendency for free trade agreements to include investment. Even RIFs postulating a high degree of integration among members, including provisions regarding the movement of capital, may not necessarily contain explicit FDI policy provisions. The overall impact of RIFs on the policy framework for FDI therefore depends on whether a RIF contains provisions liberalising the movement of capital (including FDI capital); on how restrictive the capital movement and investment regimes of the member countries had been prior to the implementation of the RIF; and on other policy liberalisation provisions contained in the RIFs, notably trade policy, Of these conditions, whether or not a RIF contains explicit FDI provisions—for example, on national treatment, most-favoured-nation treatment, rules of origin, performance requirements, dispute settlement—may be the least important for developed countries and most developing countries as far as inward FDI is concerned, because inward investment regimes are typically open even prior to the implementation of RIFs. The OECD member countries, for example, adopted the Code of Liberalisation of Capital Movements in 1961, though capital-movement liberalisation did not accelerate until after the mid-1970s. Even in many developing countries, at least partially open FDI policies have typically been in place prior to the implementation of a RIF, as the example of Mexico prior to joining NAFTA illustrates. So the direct impact of explicit FDI provisions contained in RIFs on FDI policy determinants is likely to be small in many instances, unless they result in a considerable liberalisation of investment regimes.

Other policy provisions contained in RIFs, especially those relevant to trade liberalisation, are likely to be more important in determining FDI. In the overwhelming majority of RIFs, the central elements and the most important factors influencing market- seeking FDI are the liberalisation of trade barriers and the granting of preferential market access to members. Trade liberalisation and trade policy coordination among RIF members contribute to a policy framework conducive to FDI because they create favourable conditions for foreign affiliates within the region to access regional markets for final and intermediate products. They also allow TNCs to establish regionally integrated production networks to enhance their efficiency. In the case of customs unions and free-trade areas, trade discrimination against non-members in the form of tariff barriers makes the size of a regional market more appealing and encourages market-seeking FDI by TNCs not present in the region. The removal of non-tariff barriers, or their harmonization, also exerts a positive influence on market-seeking FDI.

Apart from trade liberalisation, the harmonization of related policies among members can also a role as FDI determinant. The "social charter" of the European Union, for example, seeks to ensure that working conditions, wages, social expenditures, etc. would not differ substantially among members and thus give "unfair" location-specific advantages to some member countries.. Likewise; European Union environmental regulations seeks to ensure that FDI would not be diverted to members with lax environmental regimes. Such policy harmonisation can act as a brake on a "race to the bottom" in competitive policy liberalisation meant to attract FDI.

Finally, RIFs may also influence the speed of FDI (and trade) policy liberalisation. The prospective NAFT A Agreement, for example, prompted Mexico to liberalize its FDI framework even before the Agreement was signed, even though the liberalisation of services and parts of the primary sector accelerated only after Mexico became a signatory. In some cases, however, member countries that are ready to deregulate a particular industry (*e.g.* financial services in the case of the European Union) may be Qbliged to wait until the other members of the RIF have reached a similar point. In the European Union not all countries were ready to deregulate their financial services at the same time, and a tier system was introduced to resolve that. But the reverse may also take place: countries that are lagging behind in terms of deregulation of industries and liberalisation of policies may be pressured to move faster by other RIP members. For example, RIF members may be encouraged to privatise usually with foreign-investor participation, as a means of reducing the share of the public sector in their economies. Even if (as is often the case) pressures to liberalise do not apply to FDI policies *per se*, they can affect the overall policy framework of a member country in a manner that encourages FDI.

More generally, RIFs can reaffirm their members' commitments to adhere to liberal policies and bring about a momentum to continue the liberalisation process in both FDI and trade. To put it differently: unless RIFs substantially alter national FDI policy frameworks, they will not have a major impact on FDI policy determinants from the point of view of individual countries. Their contribution to FDI policy determinants lies in ensuring member countries' commitment to adhere to a liberal existing policy framework, or to liberalise it if is restrictive, to harmonise policies, to lock in liberalising changes, to increase momentum to liberalise further; to strengthen standards of treatment and protection, and to encourage policies that ensure the proper functioning of markets (*e.g.* competition policy).

(ii) Economic Determinants

Market size and growth are the FDI economic determinants that are most affected by the implementation of a RIF. Dynamic effects of RIFs in encouraging higher rates of economic growth can help boost inward FDI. Most importantly, the size of the market is redefined under a RIF as the size of the region's market. The possibility of accessing a market wider than that of a single country for tradable goods and services becomes an inducement to invest in the region. This is exemplified by "United States FDI in the European Union. A part of United States affiliate sales in the European Union are geared to the regional market: their sales in the European Union in countries other than the host country itself accounted for 31 per cent of their total sales in 1995. All this is made possible by the removal of intra-regional trade barriers within the region, which carries the implication that a single host country's market size is no longer as significant a determinant of market-seeking FDI as it used to be before the implementation of the RIP. The redefinition of market size from national to at least regional is encouraged if a common external tariff is imposed. This can induce at least some import-substituting (tariff-jumping) FDI, as firms previously serving the regional market through exports seek to become "insiders" and switch to FDI. The extent to which this takes place depends on how heavily protected the host (regional) market becomes after the implementation of a RIF, and whether TNCs had already invested in the national markets prior to the RIF. In a liberalising world of falling barriers, the location advantage of a large regional market may not be what it used to be, unless the RIF also dictates some protection, say, through a common external tariff. Of course, even in the absence of a common external tariff, the regional market may still be an attractive location as long as the RIF eliminates obstacles beyond tariff barriers or facilitates business transactions. In addition, there may be advantages associated with becoming an "insider" in a regional area, such as benefiting from rules-of-origin regulations.

All this means that regional integration frameworks increase the geographical scope and size of "effective" markets because they increase the ease of access within member markets through the removal of trade and other barriers. However, even if all trade and investment barriers between countries were removed, cultural, linguistic and other less obvious barriers to doing business would remain; as would the importance of proximity to local consumers. So accessing an individual member country's market, although less significant as an FDI determinant under a RIF, cannot be discounted. In this context, it may be observed that access to European Union markets was an important factor but access to the United Kingdom's market was more significant for all types of FDI.

With the implementation of a RIF, the accessibility of a region's market from a given location becomes an important FDI locational determinant. In addition to abolishing customs-clearance procedures that help speed up border crossings, good physical infrastructure, especially in transport and communications, facilitates access to regional markets. The importance of infrastructure as an FDI determinant is therefore enhanced considerably when a RIF comes into effect, for both market-seeking and efficiency-seeking TNCs.

As the importance of market size as an FDI determinant becomes more uniform for all countries that are members of a RIF and as the removal of cross-border barriers within the region increases competitive pressures, determinants related to enhancing efficiency come to play a bigger role for all types of FDI. Increased market size - from national to regional or global—is in itself an efficiency-inducing determinant because it provides the demand dimension that gives rise to the possibility of exploiting economies of scale and scope in production and distribution. Indeed, one of the primary advantages of enlarged markets under RIFs is that they create the demand conditions that allow TNCs to reap economies of scale and scope in all parts of the value chain. On the production side, cost considerations are especially important for efficiency-seeking TNCs. RIFs allow such TNCs to locate each value-added activity of the production process in the most cost-efficient location within the region in order to rationalise operations regionally by taking advantage of productivity-adjusted cost differences in labour, technology, and other resources. In sum, RIFs help to create both the demand conditions and the production conditions needed to improve efficiency in production.

RIFs also influence TNCs' access to resources. In many RIFs, TNCs can access the skills, technologies or other strategic assets available in member countries other than those in which their production operations are located. The European Union, for example, allows all foreign affiliates regardless of their location within the Union to participate in European Union-sponsored R&D projects—subject to certain restrictions on the transfer of technology to non-member countries. When RIFs allow the movement of labour, some labour moves across borders in response to TNC employment opportunities, which may mitigate the importance of the skill-seeking motive for FDI within the region.

Furthermore, RIFs give foreign investors the opportunity to be close to clusters of companies producing similar products or having similar R&O facilities and thus to exploit regional as well as sub-national agglomeration economies and obtain access to created assets. Proximity to a cluster of companies producing similar products or having similar R&D facilities, for example, need not necessarily require that a TNC invests in the same country where these companies or facilities are physically located. It may very well invest in a bordering country in close physical proximity to the cluster of companies or R&D facilities. Thus within regions, a greater concentration of FDI in a few supranational clusters may develop that allows FDI to be more dispersed in terms of country distribution, but more concentrated in terms of geographical space.

Finally, RIFs promote greater competition to capture expanded markets or increase market shares within the region. Firms may respond to the increased competition for markets by establishing a physical presence, especially if arm's-length competition It through trade is hindered by a common external tariff. Increases in intra-regional and n extra-regional cross- border acquisitions designed to access resources or defend if competitive positions often accompany RIFs. About one-quarter of Japanese manufacturing affiliates in Western Europe established during the mid-1990s were; established through acquisitions, compared to 10 per cent of those established in 1990.

(iii) Business Facilitation

The primary effect of RIFs on business facilitation FOI determinants is to reduce intra-regional business transaction costs. Such costs arise directly from inadequacies of information, asymmetries in doing business in different countries, the heterogeneity of administrative procedures, and differences in business support measures. Recognising the importance of business facilitation obstacles, some RIFs seek to harmonise efforts to remove them or replace them with comprehensive region-wide programmes for FDI facilitation. In the case of the European Union, for example, the removal of internal tariff barriers was not sufficient for creating a unified regional market because of other obstacles to intra-regional transactions, especially in services. The. European Economic Community identified 280 barriers to cross-border transactions in 1985, and removed about 90 per cent of them in 1993 as part of the single market programme. APEC has a comprehensive programme to facilitate trade and FDI whose objectives include "smart card" visas for short- term travel; procedures for APEC-wide accreditation of standards; and minimum restrictions on arrival in a member country.

Since RIFs allow a region's market or many of its resources to be more easily accessible by TNCs from any location within the regional bloc, and policy coordination and harmonisation gives rise to a more level playing field, 'business facilitation factors become increasingly important, as they concern matters which individual member countries—and, increasingly, sub-national authorities—can address to distinguish themselves from one another when competing for FDI. Even if some business facilitation measures are harmonised across members, there still remain important differences among members that allow them to compete for FDI. Measures aimed at targeting specific investors, providing social amenities and marketing a country his an investment location usually fall outside the scope of RIFs, and can therefore be used by each RIF member to enhance location-specific advantages. One result is precisely a proliferation of incentives used to attract.

Impact of Regional Integration Framework on FDI Flows

From aggregate FDI data it is difficult to determine the impact of individual FDI determinants on investment flows or stocks received by a region or by specific member countries within a RIF. This is because FDI determinants work together under RIFs as well as in combination with factors unrelated to RIFs, such as certain macroeconomic changes. The evidence presented here relates to the overall impact of RIFs on FDI flows or stocks. Only inferences can be made about the extent to which a particular determinant is responsible for that impact. Furthermore, the evidence presented below is largely static, in the sense that it describes the one-time impact of RIFs on FDI. Dynamic effects of RIFs on FDI deriving from increased growth rates or heightened competition are much more difficult to assess.

Regional Integration and Tnc Production Networks in Asean

ASEAN, through AFTA, provides a regional market with more than 500 million people, a combined GDP of $560 billion in 2001 and an internal tariff rate of no more than 5%. ASEAN is also integrating through the ASEAN Investment Area, the ASEAN Framework Agreement on Services and infrastructure linkages. Regional production networks are not new in the region, but the recent integration is leading more TNCs to explore the creation of more such networks, particularly in the automobile and automotive components industries as well as the electronics industry:

- Japanese and other automakers are consolidating their production in the region and adopting regional production network strategies and plant specialization to service the AFTA market
- Honda Motor Company plans to streamline its production in ASEAN, with some models to be centralized in Thailand.
- Toyota has a network of operations linking different functions—such as regional HQ, assembling facilities financing and training centres and parts suppliers—in different ASEAN countries.
- Nissan is setting up regional network structures in ASEAN to capitalize on the greater production efficiency made possible by AFTA. It plans to build a "Southeast Asian parts sourcing company" in Thailand, to source component parts in ASEAN and decide which models should be built in which plants in the region.
- Ford also has a regional strategy to service the ASEAN market and allow the various plants in the region to specialize. Rather than have two plants producing the same product in the two countries, Ford has its plant for pickup trucks in Thailand and that for passenger cars in the Philippines.
- Isuzu Motors Co. (Thailand), Isuzu Engine Manufacturing (Thailand) and Isuzu Mesin (Indonesia); Volvo (Malaysia) and Volvo (Thailand) are producing and exchanging automotive completely-knocked-down packs through the affiliates in these countries.
- Samsung Coming (Malaysia) provides tube glass as a major input to Samsung Display's Malaysian factory for

colour picture tubes, selling intermediate products to Samsung Electronics (Thailand) and affiliates in Indonesia and Viet Nam for colour televisions and in Malaysia for computer monitors.

- Samsung Electro-Mechanics (Thailand) supplies tuners, deflection yokes, and flyback transformers to affiliates in Malaysia, Thailand and Viet Nam. It also supplies tuners to Indonesian operations for VCRs, oil capacitors to the Malaysian operation for microwave ovens and deflection yokes to Samsung Display Devices (Malaysia) for colour picture tubes.

The ASEAN Industrial Cooperation scheme also encourages TNCs to establish regional production networks. For instance: Denso affiliates in Indonesia, Malaysia and Thailand exchange automotive components; Matsushita affiliates in Indonesia, Malaysia, Philippines and Thailand are part of a production network to exchange electronics parts and components; Nestle's affiliates in Indonesia, Malaysia, Philippines and Thailand are part of a regional production network involving intra-firm trade in food processing; and, finally, Sony Electronics (Singapore) and Sony (Viet Nam) produce and exchange electronics parts and components among themselves. Sony Display Devices (Singapore) and Sony Siam Industries (Thailand) are involved in a similar production arrangement, exchanging electronics parts and components.

Such production networks strengthen regional integration through production and re supply linkages and the intra-firm sourcing of parts and components. Several studies' at the firm level also suggest that the ASEAN Free Trade Agreement (AFTA) has influenced TNCs' decisions to invest in the region, especially in the automotive and electronics industries. But it appears that some rationalization in the automotive industry has occurred as well, with implications for the distribution of flows.

In another econometric study of United States FDI flows to the ASEAN-5 and 26 other countries, market size (GDP) was found to be positively related to FDI flows. And some evidence of a negative relationship between FDI and tariff rates was found over the entire 31-country sample. While the "AFTA effect" was ambiguous, a more integrated market and lower duties on vital imported intermediate goods may have encouraged more market-seeking and efficiency-seeking FDI to the region.

FDI flows to the ASEAN subregion have increased steadily, particularly after the signing of AFTA and until the 1997-1998 Asian financial crisis. In the South Asian Association for Regional Cooperation (SAARC) Preferential Trading Arrangement subregion, FDI has been increasing since the signing of the agreement in 1993.

Although these regional trading arrangements may be stimulating FDI, ASEAN has consistently attracted only about 5% of world FDI over the past 20 years. With so many trading arrangements being signed and at the same time new markets opening up to FDI (such as CEE and China), it is difficult to sift out the effects on FDI flows to the region from those for individual members.

Most of the recent regional arrangements in Asia tend towards free trade areas (AFTA, Singapore-United States, ASEAN-China, Republic of Korea-Chile) and regional investment cooperation (ASEAN Investment Area). These arrangements provide assurances of market access, involve a deeper tariff-cutting programme on a more extensive range of products, address non-tariff barriers, facilitate easier sourcing of production inputs and resources and cover investment matters. The attractiveness of these free trade agreements for FDI is enhanced by these elements, which could affect operations seeking markets, resources and efficiency

NAFTA and FDI

Negotiated by Canada, Mexico and the United States, NAFTA came into force in January 1994, creating the first north-south regional integration agreement in the Western hemisphere. The Agreement opens the three economies to further cross-border trade in goods, services and intellectual property and to investment from one another in almost all industries. The final round of tariff cuts under NAFTA was on 1 January 2003, with some exceptions for agricultural products until 2008.

NAFTA caused a marked jump in intra-regional trade. North American intra-regional exports of goods and services stood at 56% of total exports from North America in 2002, up from 49% in 1996 and 34% in 1980. But the impact has been strongest in Canada and Mexico. In the late 1980s three-quarters of Canadian and Mexican trade was with the United States, and by 2002, more than 85%—with a similar pattern for Canadian and Mexican imports from the United States. But the pattern does not hold for the United States, whose trade with the two other economies over 1996-2001 was remarkably similar to that in 1980.

An increase in FDI flows to the three member countries has also been observed since the late 1980s, but it is unclear to what extent this was due to NAFTA. FDI flows, declining over 1988-1993, rose rapidly after 1994, peaking at $383 billion in 2000, before falling back to $64 billion in 2002. The gains appeared to come primarily from FDI into the United States, not to Canada or Mexico, however. The United States share of North American FDI rose from 71 % in 1994 to a peak at 88% in 1999, before falling back to 47% in 2002. The pattern is similar for North American FDI as a percentage of gross FDI inflows for all aECD countries—and as a percentage of worldwide inflows.

Still, Mexico benefited from increased inflows. But there is no evidence of increased intra-regional FDI intensity, particularly because. Mexico's outward FDI flows to the United States were small over 1980-1998. Intra-NAFTA FDI fell from 30% of the outward FDI stock in 1986 to 18% in 1999. The Canadian share of United States outward stock appears to have been a key factor, down from 17% in 1989 to 10% in 2000. NAFTA appears to have caused United States TNCs to close some plants in Canada and use United States exports to supply the Canadian market. Industries characterized by large economies of scale, low transportation costs and little product differentiation were expected to see such locational shufflings once"tariffs were removed. The most important industry in North America is automobiles and automotive components, accounting for between a third and a half of intra-regional trade, depending on how broadly the industries are defined. The Canadian and United States automobile industries had been integrated since the 1965 Auto Pact. NAFTA thus furthered the integration of the Mexican automobile industry into an already deeply integrated North American automotive industry.

Comparing the position of the United States as an insider in NAFTA and an outsider to MERCOSUR, one study found a significant positive relationship between United States FDI and NAFfA, but no relationship between United States FDI and MERCOSUR. Another study found that Central American countries (except Costa Rica) lagged behind Mexico after 1994. Most affected were textiles and apparel, accounting for most of the FDI flows to El Salvador, Guatemala and Honduras.

The definitive study of NAFTA's impact on FDI has yet to be done. The presumption is that NAFTA benefited its member economies in terms of international trade in goods and services, but less is known about its impact on FDI, for members and non-members. Better linking of micro-level locational strategies of individual firms to macro-level shifts in FDI flows and stocks is probably the key to solving this puzzle.

The Impact of NAFTA on Mexico's Policy on Admission and Establishment

NAFTA membership contributed to Mexico's long-term policy of liberalizing the admission and establishment of FDI in the context of a broader policy to increase the role of FDI in economic development. NAFTA's investment provisions allowed Mexico to retain certain FOI admission and establishment restrictions for economic and non-economic purposes (protecting domestic SMEs and national culture). Because investment was part of a much broader set of issues, agreement on it needs to be seen in this wider context.

Before NAFTA

Mexico started to liberalize its FOI regime prior to NAFTA. But it still restricted foreign entry and foreign equity shares of Mexican companies in some activities for cultural, security and political reasons and for such socioeconomic objectives as the protection of domestic SMEs, income distribution and domestic enterprise development.

The bans and restrictions fell into three categories:

- Activities reserved for the State in whole or in part: petroleum and other hydrocarbons; basic petrochemicals; telegraphic and radio-telegraphic services; radioactive materials; electric power generation; nuclear energy; coinage and printing of money and postal services.
- Activities reserved for Mexican nationals: retail sales of gasoline and liquid petroleum gas; non-cable radio and television services; credit unions, savings and loan institutions; development banks; certain professional and technical services and non-rail land transportation within Mexico of passengers and freight, except for messenger or package delivery services (but foreign majority stakes in companies providing point-to-point-trucking services were permitted).
- Activities with ownership restrictions: the most important among these were airlines (25%) and cable-TV (49%). Approval was needed for foreign ownership to exceed 49% in cellular telephone services, banking, and oil and gas pipelines.

When NAFTA negotiations began, FDI restrictions were scattered through many pieces of legislation. There was nothing mentioned specifically about standards of treatment of foreign investors in the 1989 FDI regulations and little is known about the practice with respect to treatment.

The Free Trade Area of the Americas

By May 2003 the countries participating in the negotiation of a Free Trade Area of the Americas (FTAA) had completed three negotiating phases, with the fourth to be concluded by a meeting of FTAA ministers responsible for trade in November 2003. Two results are important: the preparation of a draft agreement and the launching of market access negotiations.

The single most important achievement is the draft agreement covering the issues addressed by the FTAA negotiating groups, including the Negotiating Group on Investment. The first draft Agreement was prepared for the FT AA Ministerial Meeting held in Buenos Aires on 7 April 2001, the second draft for the Quito Ministerial Meeting on 1 November 2002.

The Negotiating Group on Investment is one of the negotiating groups (market access, agriculture, services, government procurement and investment) instructed by FTAA ministers to initiate market access negotiations on 15 May 2002. As agreed by the FTAA Trade Negotiations Committee, initial offers had to be presented between 15 December 2002 and 15 February 2003, with submissions of requests for improvements of the offers to be made between 16 February 2003 and 15 June 2003. The process for the presentation of revised offers began on 15 July 2003. In the case of the Negotiating Group on Investment the Committee stated that the initial offer had to be comprehensive and in accordance with current laws and regulations. A negative list approach had to be used. The Committee also agreed that investment offers for the supply of services through commercial presence may be submitted and discussed in the Negotiating Group on Services, in the Negotiating Group on Investment or in both. The Negotiating Groups on Services and Investment shall, as general rule, continue to meet separately. However, if deemed necessary, both groups may meet to hold joint discussions on issues in common, particularly commercial presence. At its April 2003 meeting, the Committee instructed the Chairs of these Negotiating Groups on Services and Investment to hold a joint meeting to discuss commercial presence and investment in services.

The 2002 FTAA draft Agreement contains several proposals on the definition of investment, most adopting a broad asset-based definition covering not only FDI but also portfolio and intellectual property, among other elements. As the draft text suggests, the discussion in the Negotiating Group on Investment focuses on whether to adopt a broader definition based on the term "asset" or a narrow "FDI-only" definition, whether to include an illustrative or exhaustive list of elements covered in the definition of investment and whether to include a list that clarifies what should not constitute an investment.

There are two different approaches to national treatment. One implies a market access component with a list of reservations (country-specific exceptions). Some proposals under this approach specify all phases of an investment (establishment, acquisition, expansion, management, conduct, operation, sale or other disposition of investment) and require that national treatment be accorded "in like circumstances". In the other approach, national treatment is granted in accordance with the laws and regulations of the host country. The draft Agreement also includes a provision on national treatment at the subnational level.

On performance requirements, there are two main views in the draft Agreement. One is to adopt a list of prohibited performance requirements (operation and incentives) covering goods and services, the other to favour a much narrower view, not going beyond the WTO TRIMs Agreement. As in NAFTA the issue of investment incentives is addressed under performance requirements only. Some performance requirements, prohibited when mandatory, are allowed when they are combined with an advantage or a subsidy. Examples include requirements to locate production, provide a service, train or employ workers, construct or expand particular facilities or carry out R&D.

The section on expropriation in the second draft of the FTAA Agreement contains language found in many other investment agreements prohibiting a party from directly or indirectly nationalizing or expropriating an investment of an investor of another party-except for a public purpose, on a non-discriminatory basis, in accordance with due process of law and on payment of prompt, adequate and effective compensation. Most relevant here is how the next drafts of the FTAA Agreement take into account the experience of free trade agreements signed in the past decade, such as NAFTA and the Chile-

United States Free Trade Agreement. The same can be said of other issues such as fair and equitable treatment and investor-State dispute settlement.

Potential Impact of a Possible Multilateral Framework on Investment

The development of an MFI, if such a framework were to be negotiated, would represent a change in the policy-framework cluster of determinants. Although such a framework might also affect some elements of business facilitation (such as investment incentives), it would not involve significant and direct changes in the principal economic determinants. Indeed, by making FDI policies potentially more similar, an MFI would underline the importance of economic (and business facilitation) factors in determining FDI flows.

The precise effect of an MFI on the policy-framework cluster of determinants would depend on its content, including definitions, scope and safeguards, Because an MFI is only a hypothesis, three scenarios, based on differing assumptions, are discussed below for purely analytical purposes. The specific implications of each scenario would vary from country to country in accordance with specific economic and developmental conditions and specific national stances *vis-a-vis* FDI.

If there were an MFI, how would it affect the volume and pattern of FDI flows? One conceivable outcome of an MFI is that it would help to increase FDI flows and perhaps affect other features of such flows as well. Such an outcome is based in part on the assumption that a multilateral agreement would not only consolidate recent changes towards more liberal policies by many countries but would incorporate "rollback" provisions—requiring countries to commit themselves to reducing or eliminating existing barriers to FDI and strengthening investment protection and the proper functioning of markets. Even in the absence of further liberalisation, a multilateral framework could facilitate investment by providing stronger assurances—as compared with unilateral or even bilateral measures—when it comes to the protection of FDI and the stability of domestic FDI regimes. The presumably greater stability, predictability and transparency resulting from an MFI would create a generally more favourable climate for investors. The impact on inflows might be greatest for those countries that were not already signatories to bilateral, regional, plurilateral or multilateral investment agreements, and countries whose current policies, even if favourable to FDI, are not considered sufficiently predictable by investors. At the same time, whether or not FDI flows would actually increase—and whether there would be a change in the quality and patterns of flows—would depend on the precise content of an agreement, the nature of national commitments and exceptions to the generalised multilateral rules and, of course, the other FDI determinants that would come into play at that point.

A second conceivable outcome of an MFI is that it could actually reduce the quantity and quality of FDI flows, because the negotiation of an MFI would take several years, creating uncertainties about the investment climate worldwide and thereby discouraging foreign investors. Further, even if negotiations did produce an agreement, the MFI that would result could conceivably enshrine a less liberal multilateral environment than has already evolved unilaterally or regionally. Such an MFI could also alter the patterns of FDI flows across geographic regions and industries. In particular, an MFI might reduce FDI flows to countries that gain from the currently restrictive policies of their competitors for such investment and increase flows to otherwise desirable locations that are receiving little inward FOI because of uncertainties about policies.

A third conceivable outcome of a possible MFI is that it would have little or no impact on the quantity and quality of FDI flows, as it would not materially alter the policy framework for FDI. One reason why this might be the result is that there has already been significant liberalisation in many countries, in particular in many developing countries and countries in transition, during the 1980s and 1990s; and this liberalisation has contributed to a surge of FDI flows that reached a new record in 1997. Therefore, an MFI that contains, for example, standstill provisions—requiring countries to commit themselves not to introduce new barriers to FDI, lower standards of investment treatment or measures likely to impair the proper functioning of markets––would essentially maintain the status quo, as far as the openness of economies to FDI, their treatment of foreign affiliates and the functioning of their markets are concerned. Moreover, the extensive network of bilateral investment treaties, which numbered over 1,500 by the end of 1997, would provide protection for investors and could be easily extended to additional countries. Finally, on this view, there would be no significant effects on the geographic patterns of FDI flows, as they are largely influenced by other FDI determinants.

On balance, these considerations suggest that an MFI would improve the enabling environment for FDI, to the extent that it would contribute to greater security for investors and greater stability, predictability and transparency in investment policies and rules. This, in turn, could encourage higher FDI flows and potentially some redistribution of those flows, particularly to countries whose investment climates would newly reflect the multilateral framework. How much difference an MFI would make, however, in terms of the quantity, quality and patterns of actual FDI flows is difficult to predict because as in the case of BITs, it is precisely the function of an enabling framework to allow other determinants, and especially economic determinants, to assert their influence.

Expectations about the impact of an MFI on FDI flows (if it were indeed to be negotiated) in comparison to the current regulatory framework and the direction in which it is developing should, therefore, not be exaggerated. There are, of course, other issues that need to be considered in connection with a possible MFI especially the possible role of such an agreement in providing a framework for inter governmental cooperation in the area of investment.

Although the most profound shifts among FDI determinants result from integrated international strategies, especially complex strategies, the traditional economic determinants related to large markets, trade barriers and non-tradable services are still at work, and account for a large share of worldwide FDI flows. Data on the distribution of sales of foreign affiliates of United States TNCs in host countries are indicative in this regard: two-thirds of TNC activity is still of this type. These figures are higher in the services sector, including trading affiliates, and lower in manufacturing but they do not change the overall outcome.

Some of the largest national markets remain unmatched in size by the largest regional markets or even by entire continents. For example, the market of the European Union during most of its existence has been smaller that the United States market; the market of the African continent (without South Africa) is smaller than that of the Republic of Korea; and the combined markets of the 14 Central and Eastern European countries are smaller than the market of Brazil. As regards trade barriers, even though the general trend has been towards the reduction or even abolition of tariffs and quotas, they continue to remain in force in several (especially developing) countries and in some industries in a much wider group of countries. These continue to generate import-substituting FDI and discourage efficiency-seeking FDI. In non-tradable services, as well as goods that are perishable or need to be adapted to consumer preferences or local standards, the market-seeking motivation, and the corresponding, locational attractiveness of host countries, remain as strong as ever. In fact, there has been an explosion of FDI in the services sector as a result of the general trend towards the liberalisation of FDI frameworks for services.

Still, although FDI remains strongly driven by its traditional determinants, the relative importance of different locational determinants for competitiveness-enhancing FDI is shifting. For example, again using United States data for foreign affiliates in manufacturing, though it is still true that these affiliates are predominantly oriented towards domestic markets: their domestic sales have dropped from 64 per cent in 1982 to 60 per cent in 1993. A similar trend can be observed in tradable services (*e.g.* computer and data-processing services) in which domestic sales declined from 85 to 81 per cent over the same period. Perhaps more telling are data for United States foreign affiliates in the European Union, as the evolving policy framework there is more indicative of the FDI policy framework emerging globally: sales to local markets in that region declined from 76 per cent to 64 per cent between 1966 and 1993, while exports increased from 24 per cent to 36 per cent.

In their quest for competitiveness, TNCs assign a particularly important role to obtaining access to created (or strategic) assets: the principal wealth-creating assets and a key source of competitiveness for firms. Created assets can be tangible like the stock of financial and physical assets such as the communication infrastructure or marketing networks, or intangible. The list of intangible assets is long, but they have a common denominator: knowledge. They include skills, attitudes (*e.g.* attitudes to wealth creation and business culture), capabilities (technological, innovatory, managerial and leading capabilities), competencies (*e.g.* to organise income-generating assets productively), relationships (such as interpersonal relationships forged by individuals or contacts with governments), as well as the stock of information, trade marks, goodwill and brainpower. These assets can be embodied in both individuals and firms and they can sometimes be enhanced by clusters of firms and economic activities.

The importance of created intangible- assets in production and other economic activities has increased considerably. A large proportion of the costs of many final goods and services, ranging from simple products such as cereals through books and computers to automobiles, consists of the costs of such created assets as R&D, design, advertising, distribution and legal work. Less than 10 per cent of the production cost of automobiles now consists of labour costs; the rest relates to the contributions of various created assets. Moreover, international competition increasingly takes place through new products and processes and these are often knowledge-based. R&D activities leading to new products and processes are costly and risky. At the same time, markets for knowledge-based resources and assets are becoming more open and enterprises-embodying these assets can be bought and sold. The result is that TNCs have taken advantage of these opportunities and used FDI as a major means of acquiring created assets and enhancing corporate competitiveness.

❐

16

Tariff and Non-Tariff

Liberalisation and integration of world markets has been inspired by a combination of hope and necessity. The hope is in the expectation of more efficient allocation of saving and investment, both within national markets and across the world at large. The necessity stems from the macroeconomic and financial instability - the instability engendered Government deficits and external imbalances that required financing on a scale unprecedented in peace time and that exceeded the capacity or willingness of the traditionally fragmented financial markets to cover. These financing needs joined with advances in technology and communications to spawn a host of innovations, ranging from securitisation in place of intermediated bank credit to new derivative instruments.

STATE VERSUS MARKET DEBATE

A fundamental issue which has generated productive debate on the theory, experience and strategies of growth is the one pertaining to the role of the state *vis-a-vis* the market in economic transformation of a country. In the Third World, concerted efforts were made in early 1950s to explain the notion of economic backwardness. Nurkse noted that inducement to invest in these economies is limited by the size of the market. Leibenstein argued that the level of investment is strongly influenced by individual investor's expectation of future rate of growth of the economy. This led Rosenstein-Rodan to make the case for "big push" to encourage simultaneous investment for many consumer goods to enlarge the size of the market. Thus came Rosentein-Rodan's prescription for a coordinated plan of investment by the government and with it the intellectual rationale for planning in development literature.

Much of the distinction on markets and government has been, and continues to be, dominated by the idea of market failure. The economic role of the State in Western economies arises mainly from the realisation that markets fail to provide a Pareto-efficient allocation of resources. A long list of market imperfections emanate from monopoly and monopolistic competition: inadequate knowledge of market options, externalities of different kinds and consequent divergenies between private and social costs and benefits, exposure to risk and uncertainty, decisions between present and future where the response to current prices may be preverse and calculated to have a bearing on future prices. They make any instinct of total reliance on the market forces questionable. In addition, most economists agree that competitive markets cannot solve the problems associated with externalities in production and consumption and with the provision of public goods.

In Western industrial societies, a political consensus emerged after World War II on the responsibility of government to intervene in the economy through short-term demand management. This appeared to work well in the 1950s and 1960s. The 1970s, however, witnessed declining economic growth rates, increase in inflation and unemployment, and growing competition from Japan and the newly industrialised countries (NICs).

This economic malaise gave rise to the widespread view that governments had failed in their macro-economic management. Strong arguments were made that government intervention, undertaken in order to overcome market failure, itself fails mainly by stimulating the excessive growth of public sector activity. This, in turn, leads to the growth and use of political power to benefit politicians, bureaucrats and other rent-seekers who misdirect the use of economic resources. This assessment, coupled with the gains made by the conservative parties in the United States and Western Europe gave rise in the 1970s, and even more in the 1980s, to the spread of the doctrine of economic liberalisation which now dominates professional economic thought.

The doctrine of liberalisation forcefully argues that economic welfare will be improved by freeing private business from regulation by the state. The supporters of the doctrine content that the market serves in various ways to provide incentives to economic growth. They assert that a properly functioning market system would tend to stimulate both economic efficiency and growth. They believe that the market achieves these objectives automatically; it requires no big administrative apparatus, no central decision-making and very little policing other than the provision of a legal system for the enforcement of contracts.

The choice between the state and the market is not simple or clear cut. There are problems and virtues of both state intervention and free market. The problems of the market are particularly severe (relative to those of state intervention) in the area of health, infrastructure, education and social security, while those of planning appear most strongly when government get heavily involved in productive activities outside economic and social infrastructure. The ability of the government to plan comprehensively and effectively is now viewed with much greater scepticism than in the years following the World War. However, one must be careful not to be too sweeping. One should not assume that government intervention in the production process is doomed to fail. As we shall see the South Korean example suggests that careful integration of state intervention with private sector initiative can produce most impressive results.

Attaining some degree of macroeconomic balance through reduction of fiscal deficits (and, when possible, attaining additional resources), moving to a realistic exchange rate, and liberalising the trade and payments regime on clearly necessary first steps. It is to some degree a matter of the circumstances of each individual country as to whether other essential first steps must be taken: removal of food subsidies, or raising the nominal rate of interest to reduce the subsidy component of lending, or reducing the deficit of public enterprises can be crucial in given circumstances. The difficulties are enormous: how to bring about governmental expenditure cuts in a sustainable way that will enhance, rather than impair, the productivity of infrastructure and other essential services; how to reconcile the anti-inflationary objectives with those pertaining to the trade regime; and how to identify those other policies within the economy which must be altered if the realigned incentives and policies are to be felt by decision makers within the economy.

The case for policy reform and liberalisation has chiefly been made by comparing economic development experiences across countries, though sufficient data is now becoming available to enable researchers to examine "before" and" after" examples for individual economies as well. So far the experience has shown the economic conditions in the developing countries and their external creditworthiness are strongly dependent on the external environment, including the strength of demand in the industrial countries, terms of trade developments, the level of world interest rates, and the availability of external financing. At the same time, it has become increasingly evident in recent years that the most decisive determinants of a country's economic performance are its own structural and financial policies. This requires a much deeper understanding of the specific institutions and history of particular countries.

Under orthodox stabilisation, the main tool effecting commodities and service transactions are austerity and devaluation. Auster programme after work in the sense of making the trade balance improve but they succeed by reducing output and capital formation (both with high import contents) rather then by promoting import substitution or export promotion. Devaluation suffers the same drawbacks it helps the trade balance mostly by contraction in the short run. However, exchange rate movements also have longer term effects, some involving improvement in the tradability of domestic products. Experience shows a strong relationship between immediate behaviour of the real exchange rate, following the launching of liberalisation, and the survivability of the experiment; the policy is likely to be sustained when the exchange rate increases, and to collapse when it falls. An increase of the real exchange rate appears to be almost a necessary condition for at least partial survival of a liberalisation policy. The same relationship appears between the behaviour of the real exchange rate during the life of the liberalisation episode and its eventual fate.

This relationship helps to explain the positive association between the strength of a liberalisation policy and its chance of being sustained: in most of the strong episodes, the real exchange rate increased following the launching of liberalisation. In achieving a persistent increase of the real exchange rate, a substantial initial nominal devaluation would make an important contribution. Contradictionary fiscal or monetary policy appears to be important (though not so vital) for achieving a real devaluation. However, the plot of the devaluation story is not easy to unravel.

The first twist is simply the fact that depreciation is unpleasant from the moment it occurs. Avoiding the pain makes appreciation look attractive; it may cut inflation and stimulate production for a time. Unfortunately, other problems arise. An externally strong (or overvalued) currency worsens the trade account, it can put potential export and import substitution activities out of business in short order. Also a strong rate seeds its own destruction. Capital inflow set off by an import led boom can support a trade deficit at first. But as the external gap remains and local tradable goods production falters, pressure for a maxi devaluation—the 'obvious' policy response—intensify. Exchange control cease to determine capital flight in anticipation of the local windfall gain the maxi will bring fall in foreign exchange reserves. The inevitable stabilisation may combine the worst measures that can be imposed: austerity, wage cutting, depreciation etc. The only beneficiaries are exchange rate speculators whose placement of assets abroad is stabilisation's proximate cause.

Second, one has to guide other policies connected with successful exchange rate manoeuvre. If trade gains are linking with devaluation, the capital promotion is necessary for increased production of traded goods. Shifting relative price to 'stimulate' 'tradability' no doubt helped the process along. But whether devaluation or more directed price incentives are essential is another question. Even if they are, overall depreciation is not necessarily the wisest policy choice. Its economy-wide efforts—contraction and inflation—suggest prudence if the exchange rate is roughly on line. They create havoc when it is not.

The moral is that a relatively weak exchange rate is necessary to avoid the perils of devaluation, and may be instrumented (alongwith other facts) in achieving medium term trade improvements without stagflation. These are good reasons not to have the exchange rate 'wrong', but if it is not strongly overvalued there is not much of a case for maxi-devaluation aimed at setting it right. Along with is corollary that extreme appreciation always a risk under inflation should be studiously avoided. A crawling peg roughly indexed to the continuing inflation is a sensible policy for keeping trade relationship on an even keel (although if financial markets are globalised it may feed back into higher local interest rate). The rate of crawl can always be manipulated at the margin to create a list of depreciation or appreciation if real exchange rate connections seem in order.

For some countries undergoing policy reform, devaluation has had yet another effect which has increased the magnitude of the required fiscal adjustment. When the nominal price of foreign exchange is increased, as it must be in the face of a balance-of-payments—inflation crisis, not only do domestic nominal prices of exportable rise, but foreign debt-servicing obligations denominated in domestic currency increases, there by increasing the magnitude of adjustment required in the government fiscal balance. This has provided another basis on which to oppose devaluations or to reduce their magnitude.

Devaluation has other economy wide repercussions depending on institutional circumstances. In primary exporting countries it is tool of fiscal policy—the cash flow of state marketing boards depend on the difference between producers prices and the exchange rate determined border price of export corps. Elsewhere, wealth effects may be important.

In the short run, devaluation tends to be inflationary by driving up intermediate import costs and thereby find goods prices through markups. The higher prices cut real wages while devaluation itself reduces national purchasing power when import initially exceed exports. At the same time, real duplication may stimulate import substitution and an export response. Through the first two channels devaluation will make output contract, especially in a staganationist economy. Better trade performance may make GDP go up. Whether devaluation is contractionary or expensionary (and over what time periods) has been widely debated in developing countries in recent years. If it is contractionary, the current account improvement it induces comes from lower intermediate imports due to the output drop.

Devaluation often does cause stagflation (using prices, falling output), especially in the first year or after it occurs. The Fund/Bank view is that devaluation is expansionary. It may 'rents' an import fustes makeup a subsituated share of insane. The argument is that raising import prices will just wipe the rate out, without effecting the overall price level or aggregate demand.

Besides devaluation, trade liberlisation often shows up in orthodox packages. This moves seen at cross purposes: one is supposed to narrow the trade gap but the other makes it wider. Moreover, the widening can come in socially dubious fashion. A substanatial share of new import after trade barriers are lowered may take the form of consumers goods instead of capital goods or intermediates. Domestic productions activity, except in the import handling service sectors, may not inhance, if a process of income concentration is underway—as is the case in some of the countries that practice liberlisation—letting in more consumers of imports satisfies the changes in demand composition implicit in the distributional shift. But liberalisation does not stimulate domestic production of 'luxuries' so that even the manufacturing thrust that regressive income redistribution can create blunted. From this prospective it has to see what improvements liberalisation may bring.

Trade liberalisation may stimulate output (at least in medium term) by creating neoclassical economic efficiency gains. It may also hold down inflation if the law of one price broadly applies. Such views are typically, of Fund/Bank. By contrast, the libralisation may force de-industrialisation if it draws in imports an not have much effect on inflation if the law of one price is not enforced by a visible presence of price competitive traded goods in the system. Anti-liberal policies such as import quotas and export subsidies have positive effect under these circumstances.

Advocates point to three advantages. The first conjunctured -is that removing trade barriers is anti-inflationary. However, this motion lack decisive empirical support, while theoretical arguments in its foreum are hard to mount with the law of one price in abeyance. The second gain from libralisation is secular: according to numerous theorems of neoclassical economics, production and efficiency rise when distortion are removed. The theory is not supported (uniformly) by evidence, its usefulness in practice depends on the circumstances and surely in the short run, rapid dismantlement of barriers to trade (and capital movements) can create payments problems like a shot. Third, no one doubts that quantitative restriction go hand-in-hand with intrensive bureaucracies, wasteful rent-seeking, and so on. Retaliation on the part of trading partners to import restraints and export subsidies is known to occur. A question of rising sots and decreasing benefits to trade intervention arises, with the slopes and positions of the curves highly dependent on context.

Tariffs

All the theories on trade illustrate the same basic proposition: Free trade maximises world output. Furthermore, these theories show that free trade is beneficial to all of the participating countries. Each country can escape the confines of its own resource endowment to consume a collection of commodities better than the best it can produce. Why, then, do we still hear so much clamor for protective tariffs and other trade barriers? The answer to this question has two parts. Many fallacious arguments against foreign trade are easily refuted but have a peculiar immunity to logic. Economists can demolish the protectionists' arguments, but speeches about "cheap foreign labour" and the "imperatives of national defense" have enormous popular appeal. Furthermore, several of the arguments for tariffs survive rigorous analysis. Free trade may be best for the world as a whole, but it may not be best from a single country's standpoint: tariffs and other trade barriers may sometimes be employed to redistribute the gains from trade in favour of one country, to redistribute income within a single country, to stimulate domestic employment, or to facilitate economic development. Undoubtedly, a country by restricting imports with a tax can sometimes force down the price at which other countries sell it, and thus improve its terms of trade. However, if it carries the process too far, the loss it suffers by foregoing the consumption of imported products will exceed the gain it takes by reducing foreign prices. The monopolist faces as analogous danger: if he cuts back his output too severely, he will lose more on volume than he gain on price. The fact remains, however: a country that enjoys a strategic position in world trade can rearrange the gains from trade in its own favour by a judicious use of import restrictions.

Tariffs and the Distribution of Domestic Income

Tariffs can also be employed to alter the domestic distribution of income. Remember that the product-price differences which give rise to trade have their clear counterparts in factor-price differences. Remember, too, that free trade tends to equalise product prices between the participating countries and, therefore, to equalise those countries' factor prices.

Now let us turn the argument on end. Starting with free trade and equal factor prices in Fewmen and Manymen, let Fewmen impose a tariff on imported cloth. This will raise the price of cloth in Fewmen and lower it in Manymen. It will thereby raise the wage rate in Fewmen and will reduce rental rates on machines. The tariff will encourage Fewmen's cloth production and will discourage its car production, for Fewmen's auto exports will contract with the drop in its cloth imports. In consequence, the tariff will increase Fewmen's demand for labour (the input used intensively in cloth production) and will lower its demand for machines (the input used intensively in car production). It will raise Fewmen's wage rates and reduce. Fewmen's rental rates, redistributing income in favour of labour.

Tariffs and Employment

We have tried to show how tariffs can be used to affect the allocation of resources and the distribution of income. They may also be imposed to affect the utilisation of resources—the levels of employment and production. For instance, when two countries start to trade, they may not strike an equilibrium right away. One country's prices may be higher than the other's when those prices are compared at the prevailing exchange rate, and that country will be compelled to reduce its wage rates. If it fails to do so, its least efficient industries will shrink, yet its more efficient industries will not grow to take up the slack. The country will trade from a point on that frontier, and free trade may be worse than no trade at all. If, then, wage rates and other costs are very rigid, a country may gain by restricting its foreign trade. Tariffs will divert demand from foreign to domestic goods, raising domestic output and employment. This result is most likely to occur if the country's unemployed resources are concentrated in its import-competing industries. Tariffs can also combat unemployment caused by a decline in domestic demand during the business cycle, rather than by wage and price disparities revealed at the opening of trade.

Once again, however, tariffs are inefficient policy instruments. They can only stimulate employment by expanding import-competing industries, not the more efficient export industries. Far better, then, to foster wage-rate flexibility or, what may be simpler, to change the exchange rate until a high cost' country's prices are aligned with those of its competitors. Such a country should devalue its currency, charging its citizens more for a unit of foreign currency and selling its own currency more cheaply to foreigners. A devaluation raises the domestic price of foreign goods (imports), as foreign currency becomes more expensive. To this extent, it is much like a tariff. But a devaluation also lowers the foreign price of domestic goods (exports), as domestic currency becomes cheaper for foreigners. Unlike a tariff, a devaluation stimulates export industries alongwith import-competing industries, and does not distort resource allocation. To put the same point more strongly; tariffs tend to shift one country's unemployment onto its trading partners. One country's import-competing industries (those that benefit from tariff protection) are other countries' export industries (those that make the best use of their resource endowments). Tariffs are a "beggar-my-neighbour" remedy for unemployment.

Tariffs and Economic Transformation

Most of the standard arguments for tariff protection imply a permanent departure from free trade. One group of arguments, however, advocates a temporary deviation. From time to time, it is said, a country must make major changes in its product mix. It must reallocate resources in a large way, not just at the margin, and may find it easier to made the change behind the protection of a tariff wall.

There are two versions of this argument for transitional protection: one of them promises economies of scale, the other promises economies of age. The first version reminds us that production costs may rise quite steeply for a while, but will begin to fall when output has attained a level which justifies the use of modern machinery and mass-production methods. It consequently recommends that tariffs be imposed to stimulate domestic production and that those tariffs be retained until the growth of the internal market has allowed domestic firms to imitate the most efficient methods used in other countries. Once they are "over the hump", it is argued, domestic producers will become fully competitive and may even be able to export, so that they will not need permanent protection, and tariffs can be cut.

The second version of the argument urges protection for an "infant industry", and was given its most famous formulation by Alexander Hamilton in his Report on Manufacturers. A young industry, it argues, may be less efficient than one which has been long established. It may lack seasoned managers, skilled labour, and reliable suppliers of raw materials. Hence, a young industry may warrant protection until it has matured and cut back its unit costs so as to compete with foreign producers. In effect, this version forecasts that temporary tariffs to young industries will actually expand and production-possibilities frontier, and that world output will then be greater because of the transitional departure from free trade.

Both of these versions enjoy widespread respect, for neither has any analytical defect. But enormous problems must be solved in order to apply them correctly. First, one must decide which industries can capture sufficient economies of scale or economies of age to survive after tariffs have been removed. If a country protects all its young industries, it will waste precious resources; almost any industry can grow if given sufficient protection, but some will not endure when their tariffs end. Next, one must determine how large a tariff is required to foster the development of a healthy infant. Too much protection will encourage an excessive expansion, and the protected industries will contract when tariffs are removed. Finally, one must decide if the gains are worth the cost. The use of tariffs, even temporarily, will reduce world output during the transition and may even reduce the real income of the country applying them. These direct and certain losses must be weighed against the distant and uncertain gains offered by protection.

Transitional protection can also pose practical problems. Few industries will readily concede that they have grown up and do not need theirtariffs. During their adolescence, moreover, they will have acquired influential spokesmen in government, having become important to the national or regional economy. It will then be difficult to strip them of their tariffs and expose them of the competition they grow up to face. Finally, some governments seem to believe that tariffs can create new industries; they restrict imports even when skilled labour, raw materials, and capital are too scarce to allow industrial development.

In brief, the occasions which justify transitional protection may be quite rare, and an indiscriminate application of transitional arguments may do great damage. As with most other tariff arguments, there may be better ways to reach an objective ways that do not sacrifice income or invite retaliation. Similarly, the trade-creating regional blocks by generating income and efficiency effects may constitute a step toward global free trade.

NON-TARIFF BARRIERS

Antidumping

Antidumping duties may be levied by an importing country when producers sell their goods in that market at a price below than at what they are sold in the home market (price discrimination), or below the cost of production (normal value). Price discrimination is considered to he unfair and to lead to distortions of trade, which need to be corrected. The duties are designed to offset the injurious effect of the dumping margin in the importing country. When sales are made below cost in the domestic market they are not considered to be sold at no male value, and a calculation is made of what the selling price would normally be in the domestic market based on the producer's costs of production. This is then compared with the export price to determine if there is a dumping margin.

If sellers have no sales or no normal market value sales in their domestic market, a domestic sales price or normal value may be 'constructed', that is, composed according to what the goods would normally cost if they were sold in the domestic market. In these circumstances normal value may also be based on export price to third countries. Again, if the sellers are operating in a non-market economy, for example China, where there are no reliable prices or costs in market terms, analogue prices are used, that is, domestic sales prices in the market economy of another country at a similar level of development.

Sales below cost, or price discrimination, can occur in a number of situations and it is frequently contested that these are 'normal' aspects of competition among firms and not in any sense 'unfair'. This argument tends to ignore the fact that international trade is not taking place in a perfectly free manner, or in one that resembles the normal operation of a single or national market. The international playing field is not level, and this can frequently give rise to distotions and the unfair or unacceptable practice of dumping. The various situations in which this may arise are as follows: First, suppliers may have rational reasons to want to sell below cost. For example, they may have invested at a certain point in time and the prices in the market may have dropped below the original estimate. This is a relatively rare case and the business is unlikely to be sustainable for long. Second, a firm may have a dominant position or monopoly and may wish to undermine its competitors by sales below cost. It can only do this if it has deep pockets. Within national boundaries this practice, which is disallowed by most competition authorities, relates to the situation where a monopolist or a near monopolist is trying either to maintain a monopoly or to establish one. In order to do so the price is reduced to below variable costs in an effort to drive out competitors. When the monopoly has been achieved or reinstated the price is raised again. This practice is known as predatory pricing. Third, the competition rules do not usually address the issue of non-dominant firms using similar tactics. It is assumed that they can not do so and remain viable. If normal profits made on other products made by an industrial group are used to undercut competitors on another product, the whole group will either make a loss or very little profit. It is only the existence of monopoly profits or a dominant position, and the assumption that these profits might be sufficient to eliminate a competitor or frighten off new entrants, that allow a reasonable case to be made for the competition authorities to intervene. Fourth, the argument has also been made that when a single firm sells below costs in order to increase market share, this is reasonable and normal. It will do so if, by increasing production, it can recover its costs through economies of scale. The firm calculates that if it can sell more at a lower price it will ultimately become profitable. A typical example of sales below cost arises where a firm's production at home has reached the point that it has covered its fixed costs. It will then be in a position to sell additional production at a much lower price that covers only its variable costs and a profit.

Whatever the motivation, the key to the ability to dump lies in the level of protection of the home market and the ability to leverage this into a form of subsidy for more aggressive action in a foreign market. These actions may be conscious moves on the part of a state to improve the international position of its industry. A government may use measures to encourage the strategic development of an industry in a way that enables a firm to dump more easily and in a prolonged manner. A typical example, of which the Japanese are frequently accused, is the protection of the home market and the exclusion of foreign competitors by diverse means and its cartelisation in such a way as to permit a firm or a group of firms to sell at high prices domestically. Sales in the home market at a higher profit enable the firms to sell at an unusually low price in export markets. This enables them to build up market share globally, to increase their economies of scale and thus to become real global competitors at the expense of others. Moreover they can achieve this without having a monopoly or dominant position. Protection of the home market, not a monopoly, provides the necessary finance to carry out the operation.

This can make eminent economic sense for the dumper, even if it does not have monopoly power and may have more limited objectives than the elimination of a competitor. It may be carried out in pursuit of more tactical goals, such as gaining a foothold in a new market and offsetting high initial start-up costs, or simply to off-load products that are in excess supply. Price discrimination of this sort has frequently been condemned by competition authorities, though usually the complaints are brought by those who are paying higher rather than lower prices.

While it is difficult to divide national markets, this is not true internationally. A country could have created obstacles to market access that would enable a firm to have one price in its home market and another outside it. Moreover a dumping action could result in losses in the export market, without losses overall, as they could be recouped in the home market. At the same time these losses can be incurred almost indefinitely as long as there is a degree of protection of the home market.

While the rationale for dumping actions is quite clear and has long been recognised by the WTO rules, implementation of the rules has left something to be desired. The main problem with identifying dumping activities is one of measurement. The goods sold for export have a particular price, which must be compared with that of the same product being sold in the producer's home market to see if in fact they are being sold at a lesser price. This seems straightforward enough, but in some cases the producer is not selling in the home market. To find some equivalent measure to the home market price or 'normal value', therefore, it is necessary to know the price of products being sold in third markets. But if this is not happening, the value of the home market price, or 'normal value', has to-be made up or 'constructed' on the basis of production costs. An additional complication is raised by state trading economies, where accounting practices are such that it is impossible to establish or construct a home market price or 'normal value'. In such cases another country is selected and the home market price or 'normal value' is based on prices in that market of producers who manufacture, preferably by the same process, and sell, under competitive conditions, the product concerned on its home market. This is the so-called analogue price.

One can see that in these cases the problem of measurement is considerable and that the method used to arrive at a home market price or 'normal value' is in some ways artificial. In the case of dumping, as ion the case of subsidies, it has to be shown that the behaviour has caused material injury to a domestic industry. The injury test is a fairly strict one that considers all the circumstances of the case, including such matters as loss of market share, price undercutting, loss -of profitability and so on. Above all it has to be demonstrated that it was the dumping that had actually caused the injury and not some other factor, such as the complainant's products going out of fashion (for example a consumer preference for small cars instead of large ones), that the industry as a whole was suffering from a recession, or some other factor that would indicate the operation of greater forces.

It also requires that the margin of dumping be taken into account: if it is small there is less chance of it being the cause of injury. On the other hand it is now possible to cumulate dumped exports from various sources for the purpose of a determination of injury. At the same time it allows exemption for de minimis suppliers (less than 3 per cent of imports, unless suppliers with less than 3 per cent together amount to more than 7 per cent overall). A dumping margin of less than 2 per cent is also considered de minimis. There need not to be an explicit requirement and agreement on to take consumer as opposed to producer interests into account. Such a clause would of course substantially weaken the antidumping remedy, whose main purpose is to protect industry against unfair trade practices. The consumer's interest is nearly always to receive cheaper albeit dumped goods. Nor does it require that a party reserve some discretion allowing it not to impose duties in pursuit of some wider national or economic interest, though some countries do have such a clause in practice.

Two of the most contentious issues in the negotiations covered circumvention and country hopping. Circumvention relates to the practice of firms hit by antidumping duties removing their operation to another country or to the country of export. In either case the firm of frequently use the same inputs and the new operations are mere 'screwdriver' or minimal assembly operations. Both the EU and the United States apply antidumping duties to the imports when this happens. No solution was found to this question during the Uruguay Round: it was not condemned, nor was it condoned. The issue will no doubt be the subject of difficulties in the years ahead. The country hopping is a term used to describe the same circumstances but where a new investigation has taken place. The United States succeeded in having a provision included that would allow retroactive duties when the investigation concluded there was dumping in this situation.

A related issue is the use of rules of origin. If a firm hit by dumping moves to another country but its assembly operations don't qualify it for a new origin, it continues to be subjected to the original antidumping duties. However some countries have continued to apply the anti dumping duties even when a new origin can be established by the degree of assembly in the new country, as the imports were still 'dumped' goods. This was another unresolved issue.

The dispute settlement procedures for antidumping were improved significantly, as they were throughout the WTO. The procedures were also speeded up somewhat and the conciliation steps removed to arrive more rapidly at multilateral resolutions. However resort to the WTO procedures cannot take place until provisional duties are in place; some had wanted to be able to appeal to the WTO when investigations were initiated.

There have been some procedural improvements: *(i)* Provisional duties may only be levied after a preliminary determination of dumping and injury, and not at the start of an investigation as has been the practice of some. Imposition of the provisional duties must not exceed six or, in exceptional cases, nine months. *(ii)* Price undertakings, that is, to raise export prices, are now given somewhat more encouragement, though it is still at governments discretion as to whether to accept them. In the United States, for example, there has always been reluctance to accept undertakings because of their possible anticompetitive effects. *(iii)* There are some new rules on the calculation of duties and retro-activity. *(iv)* There is provision for a 'sunset' clause on duties imposed, unless a review demonstrates the need to continue them. There was no sunset clause before, and duties could continue indefinitely.

The role of panels is substantially restricted in and a new standard of review has been established. If a country's has properly established the facts and evaluation of them is unbiased and objective, a panel cannot overturn them even if it reaches a different conclusion. Nor can new facts be considered. The panel must also accept the interpretation of a provision if it is one of several possible ones. It is clear that this provision is designed to ensure that panels do not easily overturn antidumping decisions; but panels may have their own views of what is unbiased or what interpretations the provisions of the agreement will bear.

While anti dumping activity once tended to be a priestly art practised by a handful of developed countries, now everyone wants to get in on the act, and many more countries are establishing antidumping authorities and legislation, including, for the first time, many developing countries. The number of investigations by developed countries has stabilised and in some cases fallen. However the existence of an investigation can be trade-inhibiting.

To a large extent the increased use of antidumping measures is due to increased liberalisalion around the globe, and countries in the cold wind of competition feel more secure if they have some trade weapons tip their sleeve to be usual as a last resort. In a sense it is the price one has to pay for free trade. However, while there has been an increase in measures taken, these can not be deemed significant or out of control. We do not seem to be on the slippery slope of aggravated protectionism.

What is more difficult is the question of how to treat the old state trading economies, which are now in transition. They bear many of the features of open economies but frequently retain elements of the old. This is true in Eastern Europe, but perhaps more importantly in China. According to the World Bank some 60 per cent of China's economy is liberalised, but the problem is distinguishing those firms that are truly operating according to market principles and those which have some state ownership or subsidy. One way of dealing with this is through individual inspection of firms, but this has certain limits given the bureaucratic burden it can pose. The next round of WTO negotiations, which is likely to deal with competition rules will probably look at the issue of antidumping as well.

Subsidies and Countervailing Duties

The definition of subsidy is broad and covers any financial contribution by a public body whereby a benefit is conferred. It gives some examples, for instance grants, loans, equity infusions, loan guarantees (potential contribution), fiscal expenditure and provision of goods and services (other than infrastructural). It covers price or income supports (which may not involve a direct transfer or contribution). It also covers private bodies acting on behalf of the government. It is also made clear that such contributions as loans, guarantees, equity infusion and provision of goods are only subsidies if they confer a benefit, that is, are provided at rates that are better than those available on the market.

Almost all countries subsidise various sectors of the economy, be these in agriculture, industry or services. They do this through a variety of measures, including direct grants, loans and equity participation through tax expenditure or relief. Many firms that are involved in both military and civilian production receive substantial subsidies on the military side, which then spill over on to the civilian side. Another important source of subsidy can be procurement, in particular in the military field. But the extent of subsidisation varies from economy to economy, but one should be aware that some of the figures on subsidisation do not necessarily reflect the whole picture.

The WTO agreement deals with the issue of subsidies in two ways. A complaining party can take up the matter with the WTO dispute settlement arm as a question of principle, or it can take countervailing measures against such subsidies. The latter course involves the imposition of duties on a subsidised import, to offset or countervail the amount of the subsidy.

The choice between these two approaches is based on different considerations. A government will attack a subsidy as a matter of principle if it wants to have the practice eliminated. If it is a prohibited export subsidy it doesn't have to prove that the practice is causing injury to its domestic industry. If the subsidy is an actionable domestic subsidy it can attack it provided it is causing 'adverse effects'. This can be established by showing, for example, a loss of market share, price under sutting or a nullification of a tariff concession. His equally available whether these adverse effects are in its domestic market or on its exports to third markets, including the market of the subsidising country. If the adverse effects are not eliminated the complaining government can take counter-measures. These procedures are open only to governments, and not individuals.

The second option, countervailing measures, can be taken by governments usually following a complaint from the domestic industry, and requires proof that a like (that is, identical or very similar) product is benefiting from a margin of subsidy that is causing injury to the domestic industry in its home market. The result will be the imposition of a duty to remove the injurious effects of the subsidised imports of that product, but the subsidy or its more general effects are likely to remain in existence in the absence of condemnation by the WTO. The advantage of the procedure is that it does not require a complaint before the WTO: a government may take action autonomously in accordance with WTO rules (if it fails to follow the rules its actions can be challenged in the WTO). On the other hand it only applies in connection with injury in the home market and not in any other.

Safeguards

A sudden surge of imports, whether legitimate or not, and injury to a domestic industry entitles the importing country to introduce temporary controls in accordance with the safeguard procedure of Article XIX of GATT, taken over by the WTO and reinforced by the agreement on safeguards negotiated during the Uruguay Round. The advantage of the safeguard clause is that it makes it easier for parties to the WTO to undertake its obligations. The safeguard clause acts as a sort of safety valve; it also allows time for an industry to adjust and become more competitive.

There are, however, some limitations on the use of the clause. The surge of imports must cause serious injury to the domestic industry or a threat thereon. Serious injury is defined by the WTO and is set at a level higher than material injury, which is the criterion used for unfairly dumped or subsidised goods. The burden of proving injury against the latter is set somewhat lower given that the imports are unfair to begin with. There was no definition, however, of what was meant by a 'temporary' safeguard measure.

Most importing countries only want to control imports that are subject to a sudden surge, and not those coming from all sources. But the WTO requires that the safeguard measure be applied to all such imports from all sources. This may be unfair on other exporters who have not increased their exports to the market in question and may even be losing market share. They nonetheless have to pay for the surge in exports from another country. However this application of the most favoured nation clause to safeguard measures is also an obstacle to its use. Affected countries can retaliate by suspending equivalent concessions and raising tariffs on the exports of the country taking the measure. Most importing countries are reluctant to take such generalised measures and face general retaliation. So the principle of applying the measure to all, in fact works in favour of the exporting countries. This was of course the deliberate intention of the GATT agreement. The idea was to make it difficult, and not easy, for parties to take such measures. The greater the retaliation a country faced, the less likelihood that it would act.

Technical Barriers to Trade

WTO agreement uses the word standard to refer to voluntary standards. Mandatory standards imposed by law are referred to as technical regulations. The agreement covers the standards that are applied to industrial and agricultural products in order to ensure a level of quality or safety for the consumer. It does not cover subjects falling within the new agreement on sanitary and phytosanitary measures. It does however cover standards drafted as processor production methods if product related, unlike the earlier agreement, which only covered standards drafted as product characteristics.

Standards can create major obstacles to trade. A standard that is designed to deal with a locally made product, and incorporates the design of that product in the standard, can effectively exclude imports from other countries where the design is different. In order to comply a foreign producer may have either to change his production line completely or to create a second production line for export to that particular market. In many cases the producer in question will simply decide not to bother exporting to that market.

Mandatory standards clearly oblige producers seeking to sell in a particular market to conform. If they do not they may face sanctions in the form of seizure, fines or even imprisonment. By definition, voluntary standards do not carry the same consequences and in theory at least producers can ignore them. On the other hand, if they do, they may find it very difficult to sell their products to other industrialists or consumers because they may not match commonly used systems, for example light bulbs with the wrong attachment, or because it may be considered that their products are not the best. Moreover insurance companies usually insist that certain voluntary standards are complied with when insurance is being sought.

With tariffs and other forms of protection being lowered to the point where they have become fairly negligible, standards have become the preferred weapon of protection add to this the fact that countries often require that a product not only adhere to a standard, but that it be certified as being in conformity with that standard. This means that the product has to be tested by a recognised laboratory. This procedure is also an attractive way of creating obstacles to trade through administrative delays, refusal of access to a laboratory, the difficulty of carrying out the procedures in a foreign country and so on.

Government Procurement

Government procurement was not covered by the original GATT agreement. Indeed Article iii, which contained the national treatment principle, explicitly stated that procurement was an exception to that principle. In other words a government could discriminate in favour of domestic suppliers against foreign suppliers.

This type of discrimination has been common. One only has to think of the Buy America provisions in federal and state legislation in the United States. Under EU law there is also a degree of discrimination against non-EU suppliers. However in the EU it is sufficient if a product is in free circulation, that is, if it has been imported into the EU, for it to qualify for treatment.

As well as being deeply embedded in legislation, the use of procurement as a form of industrial policy is even more profound. Nearly all governments use their public money to direct and develop industry. This phenomenon is most obvious in defence and research. Governments are strongly committed to promoting their' defence establishments (the so-called military - industrial complex) and nowadays there is even greater pressure to help advance industry's technological base through expenditure on research and development. Add to this the need most governments feel to spend government money to create employment. Domestic employment is not fostered by spending money outside the country on imported goods, however cheap they may be. The instinct to reserve government procurement for domestic purchases, though diminishing in this age of budgetary austerity, is still very deep rooted and strong.

❐

17
Global Competitiveness

With the increasing globalisation of international business, the high technology sector has become a major segment of foreign trade. Such industries as the semi-conductor computer chips, commercial aircraft and engines, and industrial robots have become the battleground where firms fight to increase their market share to survive and prosper in international competition.

The competitive environment that international business face is, to a certain extent a function of the technological environment and the degree of technological innovations attributed to the competitive environment. Technological change and worldwide flow of information are fundamentally reshaping how companies and nations do business. Firms and nations are trying to understand the implications for their competitive strategies. But there is a conflict. The pressures of technological competition increasingly drive corporations towards global strategies while stimulating nationalistic impulses to protect and secure the national technology base from international competition. Misperceived nations, about how governments can promote domestic economic growth are, as a result, complicating the development of an international mind-set needed by both firms and nations to prosper in the emerging technoglobal environment. The costs imposed by tariffs, quotation and other forms of tax discrimination appear on no budget. For this reason, the public loses an important protection against wealth transfers from the less fortunate to the politically well organised, and to an extent undermining the principle of limited government that is the centerpiece of constitutional democracies. Because protections result in an organisation of economic activity through government control rather than markets, it contributes to a system of incentives that promotes the social importance of political power. A significant means of limiting the power of government is to organise economic activity through the voluntary exchange of a free enterprise economy. This separates the computation for control over resources from competition for control over political power.

Although some have tried to point competitiveness as a divisive partisan issue, in reality it enjoys broad support. The debate is not about heavy-handed industrial policy, nor is it about corrosive protectionism. Instead, it is about building partnerships between the public and private sectors that will allows firms and workers to meet global standard. The challenge before policy makers is to formulate constructive policy in such areas as capital formation, human resources, technology and trade; to develop the political consensus necessary for action and to make sure that economic policy is structured so that it enhances the ability of the firms to compete in world markets

What is Competitiveness?

Competitiveness is the contribution of a country's assets, either inherited (*e.g.* natural resources) or created (*e.g.* infrastructure) and the processes (*e.g.* manufacturing) which transform them into economic results, and which meet the test of the international market. A nation's competitiveness is the degree to which it can, under free and fair market conditions, produce goods and services that meet the test of international markets while simultaneously expanding the real income of its citizens. Competitiveness at the national level is based on superior productivity performance and the economy's ability to shift output to high productivity levels which in turn can generate high level of real wages.

For most people, national productivity is an obscure economic term. Simply saying that productivity is key to economic performance does not shed light on how to achieve it. But when the productivity of Indian firms is contrasted to that of foreign firms, and the productivity of the Indian economy to that of their nations, productivity appears in a different light. These comparisons show in stark terms why productivity is so crucial to the standard of living, and more important, what contributes to it. Large trade deficits, high rate of inflation, poor foreign exchange resources, unemployment, poverty etc. are not the sum total of the competitiveness problem, but they signal a need to reconsider such issues as quality, education, innovation, and investment that together point the way towards productivity.

The main factors which can make or break a nation's competitive environment are : *(i)* domestic economic strength: an overall macro-level evaluation; *(ii)* internationalisation: the extent to which the country participates in international trade and investment flows; *(iii)* government: the extent to which government policies are conducive to competitiveness; *(iv)* finance: the performance of capital markets and the quality of financial services; *(v)* infrastructure: how will basic resources and systems serve business needs; *(vi)* management: how will enterprises demonstrate innovative, responsible and profitable management; *(vii)* science and technology: what capacity exists in these areas, and how well the country exploits basic applied research; and finally, *(viii)* people: the quality and availability of human resources. For a nation, a confidence index may be developed to demonstrate the linkage among standard of living, trade, productivity and investment. If a nation wants to have a higher standard of living, it must have a strong performance not only in trade, but also, and especially, in productivity and underlying investments in education, equipment, and technology.

As firms and workers realised the extent of the challenge of international competition, they have reexamined their approval to production, human resource management, and innovation and reached out to embrace new ideas from around the world. Quality is perhaps the most obvious example of his trend. Although an American, Edward Deming, was the father of the modern quality movement, his ideas were not put into practice in the United States until it was clear how successful they had been in Japan. Similarly, new inventory control techniques, known as just-in-time production, that were first developed in Japan have had an extraordinary impart on U.S. industry. Human resource management has also been influenced by methods introduced in other countries. The current emphasis on teams, continuous training, and greater employee involvement in the decision-making process all have their roots overseas. These ideas above have resolutionised much of the industry.

The adoption of these new ideas has not been limited to a new manufacturing firms in the traded goods sector. Total quality management, for example, has imigrated from manufacturing to many other sectors of the economy and today is found in industries as diverse as banking and medicine.

Competitiveness is a term that, for many, captures the challenges facing the Indian economy. Global competition has forced Indian firms to conceive of their business in entirely their ways. It has led them to reassess their products, their customers, their markets, and their rivals. It has prompted them to search out new management ideas around the world and to implement them at home. It has driven them to prove their skills against the most demanding customers worldwide. And it is the major force behind effects to streamline production, improve quality, accelerate cycle-time, and rethink the innovation process.

Export activism is not the sort of reactive protectionism too often embraced in the past. Markets, not bureaucrats, best decide where investments should flow. More market-driven trade is good—it is good for jobs and productivity, for producers who get lower cost inputs, and consumers who reap the benefits. And the trade does for whole to improve living standard then do heavy-handed labour, environmental, or protectionist policies either at home or abroad. But export activism also is not laissez fair. If markets are a fact, it is also a fact that other countries sometimes meddle with them. What export activism is, it is pragmatic. It is a real world approach, one' that recognises the importance of such policies that promote sustained growth in the world economy, multilateral agreements to bring down barriers, regional and bilateral agreements that integrate dynamic reas, and unilateral action to knock down protectionists. Exports must be the top priority. They force a nation to battle with the best firms worldwide. They ensure that Indian business stays nimble, adapting to new challenges. And they provide the kind of jobs that will last, because they require Indian workers be the best in the world. Five steps laying a base for growth, promoting exports, working to bring down barriers globally, pushing regional opportunities, and addressing the problems of free riders on the international trading system - constitute the essence of export activist philosophy.

It is not necessary to equate companies with countries to believe that competitiveness has validity. At bottom it is about much more than the performance of a few sectors or 'exporters; it is about national aspiration and self-discipline in the international economy. The response of India to the challenge this concept off rs will have a decisive impact on the health of its economy and its standard of living. Indians would all be poorer if competitiveness were dismissed as a doyenism irrelevant slogan.

Competitiveness and Changing Corporate Structures

Global aspirations of companies everywhere constitute a major force that is re-shaping the world economy. National economies can no longer be understood or operated within unless they are seen in connection with all other economies. There are no islands any more. No firm can ignore the international dimensions. Even the most domestically oriented business is likely to find that it is operating in somebody else's international market. This inter-linked economy have been so rapid that they have outrun the capacity of many companies and managers to make adjustments both to their organisational structures and to their underlying nationalistic assumptions and outlook.

What kind of changes at the organisational level are required to cope with an increasingly complex and faster moving international environment? Many companies grappling with this question recognise the need to speed up decision-making by reducing bureaucracy and streamlining and flattening the organisation. Some are seeking more flexible structures, experimenting with task forces and project teams. Some are decentralising to focus resources on particular markets, to push "ownership" further down the line and to become generally more responsive to local markets. The nub of the problem is the balance that has to be struck between central authority and local authority. If the pendulum swings too close to the centre, the corporate outposts are left floundering between an inappropriate strategy and local realities; too far in the other direction and the centre may be dragged towards the strongest outposts with no capacity for radical moves when these become necessary. It is the classical dilemma that all global companies experience.

At the same time, however, some firms identify almost the opposite of these trends as necessary to obtain the maximum benefit from global opportunities. Some are seeking to coordinate and structure their activities so that their business work together as appropriate on all major issues such as strategy, products, services and resourcing. Others are focussing on the integration of their worldwide business and acquisition.

A strategic approach to management development requires an organisation to take a worldwide view of its management resources. The main issue here is whether to pursue a centralised or decentralised approach. In decentralised multinational firms, responsibility for the early development of managers has been traditionally desolved to the subsidiaries. The corporate centre usually only becomes involved in the development of individuals when they start to assume more senior jobs or significant international responsibilities. Some firms believe strongly in the merits of decentralisation and aim to respond to local conditions within an overall strategic framework set by head office. Their structure is likely to consist of a corporate centre based in the parent' country and loose connections of scattered subsidiaries in countries abroad. Communication flows up and down the hierarchy through chains of command and the subsidiaries operate very much as separate companies.

Such firms face a particular dilemma. They may wish to respond to local sensibilities by recrimiling local managers and giving the job in subsidiaries to locals. This prevents synergy between the various subsidiaries and leads to the 'power hug' when overall strategy is formulated at the centre of the organisation, much of the information that is needed to monitor and adopt the strategy is situated in the organisation's outposts, Because information is a source of power, the people there naturally try to retain hold of it. This is an increasingly serious handicap as the need to ensure free passage of information and to distribute ownership of strategy across the organisation becomes ever more pressing in an era of fast moving world markets. Breaking down "power hug" is one of the most important tasks facing international firms in the future. The search for right international strategies and structures continues. In this search, models like the transnational corporation and the heterarchy can help to clarify and stimulate thinking about the future of international organisations.

Most of the transnational corporations have traditionally built their international operations around one of three strategies. These trategies are: *(i)* to establish a strong local presence felt through responding to different international market requirements; *(ii)* to operate as global companies, making themselves fiercely competitive by achieving substantial cost advantages from centralised global scale of operations; and, finally, to develop as international companies whose key strategic capability lies in exploiting parent company knowledge through worldwide' diffusion and adaptation. Today, however, no firm can any longer afford to base its strategy one focus. If companies are to cope with the complex international environment, they must have an equally complex and multi-faceted business strategy. Firms operating worldwide must pursue global, multinational and international strategies simultaneously. They must become truly transnational and have an integrated networking structure.

Traditionally, companies have subsidiaries which are either clearly dependent on the corporate centre (as in global companies) or strongly independent (as in multinational firms). Increasingly, however, these relationships are overly simple. International business now demands that every part of an organisation collaborators, shares information, solve problems and collectively implements strategy. An integrated network is needed to share decision-making and enable components, products, resources, information and people to flow freely between the transnational's interdependent units.

A major problem in any worldwide business is that managers in key positions are often limited by narrow perspectives and parochial interests, leading to substandard decision-making. In particularly complex, multi-tiered organisations, this problem is often exacerbated by conflicting interests and overlapping responsibilities. The commitment of every individual employee has to be won to the overall corporate agenda. To develop such a consensus, each individual must understand, share and "internalise" the company's purpose, value and key strategies.

The degree of success that companies achieve in their globalisation policies will depend greatly on their approach to international human resource management (HRM). Major HRM concerns include: identifying and retaining highly qualified people; ensuring sufficient quality and quantity of management at the appropriate time; ensuring management succession; sustaining and improving performance at all levels in all areas of business; increasing the depth of talent in the organisation; making sure that people have the technical and managerial skills to compete; making the management competence and culture that are required sufficiently clear to people; total quality management and changing people's attitudes to quality; establishing training as part et the management culture; gaining top management and line management interest in human resource development; and, finally, linking HRM to strategic objectives. Addressing all these issues is a major challenge in a purely domestic setting. The challenge lies in enstffing that human resource management adequately responds to new international market orientation. International recruitments attracting people with international experience and visions—is accordingly a growing concern.

The transnational organisation makes difficult demands, however. Much more effort has to be put into welding the organisation together. Travel increases exponentially and a high price has to be paid in terms of exhaustion. The transnational is also an 'untidy', multi-dimensional affair; often it is not clear where decisions are made. Nor does it necessarily solve the problem of "power hug". Traditionally companies have controlled their operations through one of the three methods: *(i)* highly formalised and institutionalised control mechanisms; *(ii)* centralised decision-making; and *(iii)* relied on socialisation to instill a common corporate culture and a shared perspective among its managers. Since the very nature of the multi-dimensional transnational results in a dramatic expansion in the number of issues that need to be integrated, a single method of controls is insufficient. All three processes are needed.

For firms entering new markets, a special challenge is to find new business partnerships and build new relationships. Developing joint ventures and close cooperation with companies in other countries means accepting that such cooperation much change the way that a firm looks at its own tasks and activities. Corporate leaders are beginning to learn what the leaders of nations have always known: in a complex, uncertain world filled with dangerous opponents, it is best not to go it alone. Many firms are now forming strategic alliances with companies in other countries to gain access to new markets and technology, to achieve global spread or to share the costs' of research and development. These alliances go beyond the limited scope of the traditional joint venture in that they are central to the fundamental, long-term interests of the partners. Companies may even establish such alliances with firms with whom they are competing in other markets and products. For instance, General Electric deals with companies that are 'competitors in the morning, customers at lunch, and joint venture partners in the afternoon'.

Onc of the most significant factors driving the ever faster rate of changer is the desire of companies to outpace their rivals in developing new products and delivering them to the market place. Under the impact of time-based competition, product life cycles are accelerating and becoming ever shorter. As world economy is becoming more integrated, so too are the internal operations of firms becoming more interdependent. The challenge is to get different of, 'fictions such as research and development, engineering, production, marketing and distribution working much more closely together than in the past, replacing rivalry with collaboration.

Consumers will increasingly demand products that can be delivered in their own time and space. Firms are to consider how they might create "instantaneous" products and services that can be delivered within the blink of an eye of their conception. Few firms may be capable but thinking about how this might be done could speed up even the slowest firms.

Perhaps the most dannting impact of this much increased rate of change is that many firms now" going international" for the first time do not have the option of a slow, cautious "let's test the water gradually" approach. The luxury of a low-risk, slow learning process simply no longer exists. Firms relatively new to the international scene face such problems as lack of detailed market knowledge, unfamiliarity with different distribution channels and having to cope with different product standards.

Many firms are aware of the need to keep pace with faster-moving, often contradictory trends (such a simultaneous globalisation in some market sectors and fragmentation in others), and to identify changing life values, new consumer habits and emerging customer attitude. Some are highly aware of the need to respond positively to growing popular concern about both the global and local environments.

More and more companies realise that service and know-how constitute an increasingly important part of their competitive edge. With products becoming increasingly similar and technological advances offering only fleeting advantage in many industries, service will become ever more important. Maintaining constantly high-quality service is difficult enough in the domestic market, but managers will have to understand how to deliver it in international markets too.

The other major factor that is driving firms to give more attention to international business is the speed of market changes. A number of inter-related forces are propelling this acceleration. Perhaps the most fundamental trend is the globalisation of communications. The allied forces of computers and telecommunications are bringing about the annihilation of space. In telecommunications, companies are moving to a single worldwide information network, just as economicany the world is becoming one global market place. They are moving toward the capability to communicate anything to anyone anywhere, by any form voice, data, text or image at the speed of light. The international currency market has become a largely speculative one whose roller-coaster movements can overnight undermine the best laid plans of any company. The problem of currency management mean a fundamental change of mind-set. They must regard themselves as financial institutions as well as makers of products and services. In other words, the management of currency must move .to the centre of strategy-making and not be left as an afterthought to decision-making.

Like the transnational, the heterarchy uses a wide range of approaches to control and coordinate its operations; it may use arm's-length arrangements such as joint venture for some tasks or it may insist on "managing" by decree in others. Whatever method it uses, the heterarchy always aims to find the best means to achieve the task rather than adhering to a standardised format. Integration occurs through "normative means" such as corporate culture, shared values and managerial style.

The heterarchy describes an organisation that is composed of reciprocally, interdependent and geographically dispersed centres, which are held together by hard strategies, norms and information. The heterarchy has many kinds of centres, allocating head quarters functions to wherever is most appropriate in the world, and allowing overseas "subsidiaries" to undertake strategic and global roles for the whole company. No dimension, whether product, function or country, reigns permanently supreme. The heterarchy is flexible and takes into account shifts in the business environment; at a certain moment, global product management is important; at another perhaps integration of total R&D is paramound.

It is argued that global and multinational companies can stifle the flow of innovation throughout the organisation. On the one hand, independent subsidiaries within multinationals can sometimes block new ideas and innovations developed at the corporate centres. On the other, a centralised global company may be unable to introduce local innovations because of unmotivated or incapable local managers. Instead of encouraging local innovations or imposing ideas from the centre, the transnational allocates worldwide product responsibilities to different national subsidiaries according to their relative skills and strengths. This not only taps the particular expertise of the business unit but also confirms its identity in the company's global operations. This approach constitutes the transnational's most vital strength; its ability to facilitate organisational learning by fostering a flow of intelligence, ideas and knowledge around the organisation. Search for a new business mind-set is one of today's most important challenges. Triumph of process over structure is a key indication of this change. What is important is not how responsibilities are divided but how people can pull together to pursue, new opportunities. In the international arena of the future, it is the ability of people from different countries and cultures to pull together that will be crucial for the success of the international firm.

Internationalisation of business is not merely a challenge waiting around the .corner. It is already here, and any company with ambitions .of global expansion can ill afford to ignore its implications. Internationally advanced companies have recognised for some time that the distances between domestic and export markets are fast crumbling in virtually every part of the world. Almost any kind of domestic business is seeing, or soon will see, its markets invaded by foreign players. These companies may still think of themselves as national operations, yet are nonetheless directly experiencing the impact of internationalisation. They are being forced to learn the lesson that if they will not go to he international market, it will come to them. Those companies that have read the writing on the wall and are making concerted efforts to become truly international do not underestimate the size of the challenge. They are stepping into the unknown.

Boosting Export Competitiveness

Countries engage in international trade for a variety of reasons. Exports, in particular, are a means to generate the foreign exchange required to finance the import of goods and services; to obtain economies of specialisation, scale and scope in production; and to learn from the experience in export markets. In a globalising world, furthermore, export success can serve as a measure for the competitiveness of a country's industries.

Export success among developing countries has been concentrated in a few countries. The comparative advantage of most developing countries lies traditionally in primary commodities and unskilled-labour-intensive manufactures. Over time, as they grow and accumulate capital and skills, and wages rise, their competitive base has to change. They have to upgrade their primary and labour intensive exports into higher value-added items, and they have to move into new, more advanced, export-oriented activities. Both require greater inputs of skill and technology. Countries can attain these objectives in several ways: by improving and deepening the capabilities of domestic enterprises, by tapping into TNC networks as conduits for trade, or by attracting FDI into export activities and upgrading these activities over time. These strategies may be complementary or alternatives. In most cases they are found together, but different countries deploy different combinations of domestic enterprise-led and FDI-led export development. Neither strategy is easy.

The technological context of export competitiveness is changing rapidly. This can be illustrated by changing patterns of world trade. There is a consistent trend for exports of technology-intensive products to grow faster than others. Manufactured exports as a whole expand far more rapidly than primary products. Within manufactured exports, growth rises with technological complexity. As a consequence, there are large changes in trade share by technological category. Complex (high and medium-technology) manufactured products are the most dynamic element in world trade. In the 50 fastest-growing manufactures in world trade, they account for over 60 per cent. The leading four are all high-technology electronics products; together they accounted for one third of the value of dynamic exports in 1995 and for 37 per cent of the growth in value since 1980. High and medium-technology products in the group accounted for three-quarters of the total value of dynamic exports and just under half of all manufactured exports in 1995. This trend has continued beyond 1995.

What does this mean for export competitiveness? Markets for technologically complex products are growing faster than those for other products because of the higher income elasticity of demand and greater scope for product innovation and productivity increases. Thus, it is easier for a country to sustain export growth if it can establish a competitive position in these products rather than in traditional resource-based or simple labour-intensive products. It is still possible to grow rapidly in slow-growing product groups, by specialising in dynamic products or by expanding market shares. Some low-technology products face slow demand growth and technological change, but enjoy rapid trade growth because of rapid relocation of production from high-to low-wage countries. This is the case, for example, with recent growth of exports of clothing and footwear. However, growth is likely to slow as the restructuring process matures. More importantly, a competitive position in such products is vulnerable to easy entry by new, lower-wage competitors. The simultaneous entry of several producers can create a glut and considerably lower prices. It is possible to establish more secure, high-value niches by entering high-quality segments, but this is difficult. It requires advanced technological and marketing capabilities, and until now largely remains the preserve of industrialised countries and established traders. Export sustainability requires that developing countries push into these segments, but also that they diversify into more complex, dynamic products as much as they can. Diversification has another important benefit: low-technology products generally offer limited scope for learning and beneficial technological spillovers in comparison to complex products. Thus, export dynamism has large overlaps with industrial and technological deepening.

Past strategies of protected import substitution have often held developing economies back from exploiting fully their initial endowments or creating new skill or technology-based advantages.

Trade and investment liberalisation can stimulate both. But it may not suffice by itself. Developing countries face pervasive market, structural and institutional deficiencies that can diminish or abort a vigorous response to market signals. It is necessary to calibrate trade liberalisation to the pace at which supply capabilities can develop, and to develop the requisite skill, capital- technology, and other capabilities. Otherwise, a leap into the world of technology-or skill-based competitiveness and growth may prove impossible or exceptionally difficult.

It is not easy for developing countries to launch new exports. They face problems in reaching world levels of productivity and quality. It is costly to collect information about consumer needs and designs or the requirements of industrial firms (where they are exporting intermediate products). Delivery and effective marketing are also difficult. These problems rise with the technical complexity and differentiation of a product. The easiest segments to enter involve simple production processes with low skill needs, no scale economies, undifferentiated products and stable technologies. The most difficult involve complex processes with high learning and skill requirements, rapidly changing technologies, large economies of scale or scope, branded products and after-sale servicing needs.

TNC Strategic Role in World Trade

TNCs are significant actors in world trade. According to the estimate, the TNCs account for two-thirds to three-quarters of world exports, and more than a third of world exports is between affiliated firms. However, the patterns of trade associated with different TNC strategies can be quite complex. They are the outcome of their motivations for FDI (market-efficiency or resource-seeking) and their organisational strategies. In traditional stand-alone strategies, bilateral trade between home and host countries largely consists of the export of headquarter services from the parent firm to an affiliate. Where TNCs adopt simple integration strategies between parent and affiliate firms, the volume of exports from host countries can be significant. The use of more complex integration strategies creates a range of opportunities for developing-country exports in products, resources, information and services, both with unrelated firms in world markets and within TNC networks. These networks provide foreign affiliates, and hence developing host countries, privileged access to internal and external international markets. Domestic firms, in turn, can gain access to these markets by linking themselves to TNC networks through sub-contracting and other arrangements. To the extent that FDI helps build export-oriented capacities in host countries and contributes to industrial restructuring, it can increase host countries competitiveness more generally.

These opportunities may benefit some countries while disadvantaging others, depending on corporate strategies. As trade and investment restrictions decrease, the locational decisions of TNCs on plants or corporate functions (*e.g.* accounting) depend increasingly on economic factors. These include the costs of reaching competitive levels of efficiency as well as transport, marketing and coordination costs. Some activities may be widely dispersed to diversify risk or to be near markets, raw materials or low-cost labour. Others may be more concentrated in a few locations to take advantage of economies of scale in production, innovation or decision-making and agglomeration benefits. In many of the complex and innovation-based industries in which most large TNCs flourish, the forces making for concentration may be stronger.

TNCs themselves are also large markets for internal transactions (intra-firm trade). These markets are, by definition, open only to affiliates and parent firms. Each TNC system comprises a market in which three types of transactions take place: sales by the parent firm to its foreign affiliates; sales by foreign affiliates to their parent firms; and sales between affiliates in different countries. Intra-firm trade provides affiliates access to firm-specific technology and knowledge. The growth of intra-affiliate trade indicates changing industrial structures and consumption patterns in host countries. These changes are also reflected in the export propensities of affiliates. As host developing countries grow, domestic markets become more attractive and domestic costs rise, foreign affiliates tend to export a lower proportion of their output.

There is a close relationship between the intensity of intra-firm trade and the R&D intensity of an activity because rapid technological change involves higher transaction costs. Countries that have or can establish - more complex and technology-intensive industries and activities have significant opportunities for export expansion by integrating more closely into TNC networks. On the other hand, those that can only attract FDI in low-skill manufacturing activities may not be able to access the dynamic internalised markets of TNCs, but can take advantage of the trading networks built up through inter-firm agreements of various kinds.

TNCs also have a role to play in trade in commercial services. In the new context, the potential for exporting services across borders has increased considerably, thanks to technological advances in telecommunications and computer-communication links that enhance the tradability of information-intensive services. While FDI remains one mode of delivery for many services, such as financial services, business services and telecommunications services in which TNCs have strong competitive advantages, there is scope for increasing trade at arm's length. This growth potential can be exploited by developing countries that host TNCs in such services. They may be able to acquire access to the internal and external markets of TNCs as they take advantage of the liberalised trading system.

Role of EDI in Building Export Competitiveness

TNCs impact on export competitiveness in a variety of ways, both positively and negatively. Their greatest potential contribution lies in difficult, technology- and marketing-intensive products, where they have the largest ownership advantages over other firms. There are, of course, different kinds of TNCs. The large globalised firms from industrial countries can promote exports best in complex or branded products. TNCs from developing countries or smaller firms from industrial countries might promote exports of simpler or less marketing-intensive products, or increase regional exports. The pattern of manufacturing export success in the developing world is highly skewed. A small number of countries dominate manufactured export activity with concentration level rising by level of technological sophistication. While there are differences in specialisation, the same economies appear in the list of top exporters of most product categories. If exports are measured on a per capita basis, most leaders remain the same, although large countries like China and India move down the list.

Some small countries a pear unexpectedly high on the list, *e.g.* Trinidad and Tobago and Oman in medium technology and resource-based exports (based on oil production and some assembly) and Mauritius (garment exports).

1. Technology and Trade Patterns

Reflecting TNC strategies and host country conditions, the role of TNCs in manufactured exports, disaggregated by different technological categories, has varied among countries and over time.

Low-technology Activities

TNCs from developed countries played a critical role in the initial stages in stimulating labour-intensive exports from developing countries; TNCs from developing countries become more important in later stages. The evolution differed by host region and country, largely reflecting the growth of local capabilities. International production involving labour-intensive activities led by clothing, started in the 1960s, when developed countries eased their import barriers and facilitated offshore processing by granting tariff privileges. Declining transport costs and the liberalisation of FOI regimes made the process economical. The developing countries that attracted export-oriented FDI had low-cost semiskilled labour. But they also had more attractive fiscal incentives, export-oriented production facilities like export processing zones (EPZs) and infrastructure, and, in the successful cases, a cadre of skilled technicians and managers.

Medium and High-technology Activities

The export role of FDI, particularly by TNCs from developed countries, has understandably been larger in complex industrial activities. Again, this to be has varied by country, and has been especially important in three types of activities: offshore assembly, mature infant industries and large-scale processing of natural resources for exports.

(a) *Offshore assembly* for export is concentrated in electrical and electronic industries, with some activity in automotive and other engineering products. The activity tends to have low local content and take place in EPZs, in relative isolation from the domestic economy of host countries. While its determinants—low labour costs-are similar to those of low—technology export-oriented activities, high-technology activity differs in its 'organisation. It is predominantly a part of integrated TNC systems (making subcontracting to independent local firms difficult); advanced technological functions and processes remain in the home countries. These systems have developed complex specialisation patterns, with assembly facilities being set up in emerging newly industrialising economies, more advanced facilities in mature newly-industrialising economies, and design in home countries.

(b) The second type of complex export-oriented activity involves mature infant industries and is an outgrowth of import substitution, from industries being restructured because of economic liberalisation. In most large import-substituting economies with a large foreign presence, such as Mexico and Argentina, TNCs lead the export surge. The most striking example is the automotive industry, now the single largest manufactured exporter from Latin America.

(c) The third type of TNC activity involves large-scale processing of natural resources for export. Unlike earlier resource-extracting activities that had little local value added, this activity involves large new world-class plants, high levels of local skills and tight integration into international networks.

Given the advanced technological, manufacturing and marketing capabilities required, few developing economies have important local exporters of sophisticated manufactures. The main exceptions are the Republic of Korea and Taiwan Province of China. They pursued relatively autonomous technological strategies and built up the skill base to enable export competitiveness. As local enterprises acquired competence and government policies increasingly favoured national ownership, the direct role of TNCs diminished. Their indirect role, particularly via licensing or original equipment manufacture arrangements, continued. As local firms grew and became international competitors, it became harder for them to obtain technology from TNCs. Independent R&D then became vital in order to copy, absorb and create technology; the leading firms set up large research and design departments and invested heavily in innovation. More recently, they have begun to use strategic alliances with leading foreign TNCs to expand their technology base. Ailing all, the autonomous strategy has given these economies much greater local content in sophisticated manufacturing and industrial depth.

However, this skilful mix of strategy has succeeded in only a few cases most countries have been unable to meet the skill, information and bureaucratic demands of this strategy to mount efficiently the range and depth of policies needed for domestic capacity-building. Furthermore, under the new rules of the game, the scope for industrial policies that favour domestic capacity-building is diminishing. A number of the tools used for example by the Asian newly-industrialising economies are no longer permitted today for advanced developing countries, or are difficult to apply. Technologies are changing much faster and production systems are more integrated, and are raising the barriers of entry into sophisticated markets. In the future, developing countries may well use TNCs more to move into advanced export activity, either through FDI or by tapping into TNC distribution systems.

Indeed, elsewhere in the developing- world, for complex products, an FDI-assisted export strategy has been more common than local enterprise-led export strategies. A substantial proportion of such manufactured exports from developing countries comes from foreign affiliates, and a significant part of this takes the form of intra-firm trade. An FDI assisted export strategy can provide rapid entry into complex activities, along with continuous access to new technologies and close integration into global markets and networks. The result can be impressive export growth; indeed, the relocation of labour-intensive processes in high technology activities has been a major factor in the recent export growth and diversification in the developing world.

However, this strategy is not without costs and risks. Most exports start at the bottom of the skill and technology ladder. The risk is that an erosion of competitiveness (as wages rise or technologies change) follows a burst of exports based on low-wage advantages. Unless the country improves its skill, technology, supplier and infrastructure base, the FDI-assisted route can run out of steam; the creation of backward linkages is particularly important here. As with domestic firm-based strategies, therefore, the upgrading of local factors and institutions becomes vital under FDI-assisted strategies once inherited advantages reach their limit. The only difference may be that the static base of competitive advantage lasts longer under an FDI assisted strategy.

2. Expanding Market Access for Exports

Foreign affiliates have several potential advantages over local firms in developing host countries in accessing and serving foreign markets. Assuming identical production costs, therefore, they can export more from a host economy than their local counterparts in products where such marketing advantages are significant. Affiliates draw an advantage from the very fact of being part of a TNC system and hence being able to use the system's physical distribution network or exploit their parent firms' links with customers. The parent company may have strong links with buyers in importing countries; such links are important in getting orders of customised industrial products or projects (*e.g.* capital goods, specialised components or turnkey plants). Again, these are difficult for new entrants to replicate, Foreign affiliates also face lower transaction costs and have other marketing advantages in exporting than do local firms. They have access to established brand names, warehousing, transport facilities and marketing links, trade finance and channels overseas. Affiliates often can use established brand names which are particularly important in differentiated consumer products, Competing local firms face a severe handicap in having to sell unbranded products, unless they are able to invest the large sum needed to develop independent brands (and the distribution and servicing they require), or a TNC is willing to franchise or license the use of its brand. Both can happen. Some developing country firms have gained the size and spread to build up global brands, but they are few and primarily from advanced newly-industrialising economies. TNCs allow independent firms to sell under their brands, under original equipment manufacture (OEM) arrangements, as in electronics, or under international so contracting, as in clothing.

A number of foreign affiliates are parts of integrated international production systems. Such systems can be of two types (or their combination): different stages of production located in different countries, or different components each sourced from several countries. The first system entails different processes at different levels of technology, spread over countries according to factor costs and capabilities. The second involves distribution of similar production activities across affiliates in countries with similar capabilities. In the latter case, production facilities are distributed geographically to diversify risk, reap scale economies or meet government demands (say, to achieve a rough balance in trade or maintain employment). For instance, automobile firms spread their engine and component manufacture over several countries. While it is possible for non-affiliates to export via such networks, the transaction and coordination costs of participation can be high. The costs rise with the complexity of a network, sophistication and proprietary value of technology, frequency of changes, and speed of response required. Consequently, TNCs are unlikely to involve independent firms deeply in such networks unless the product is simple and standardised, or the independent firm is a specialised supplier of long standing.

Finally, foreign affiliates may have easier access to developed country markets, or face lower tariffs there, because of lobbying by parent companies. One important form of access is favourable treatment of offshore processing (with duties imposed only on value-added overseas). This is favoured by TNCs seeking to relocate labour-intensive processes in low wage areas to maintain competitiveness. The growth of maquiladora exports from Mexico, for instance, owes greatly to such treatment by the Government of the United States.

Being part of TNC systems can also have costs for export competitiveness. Affiliates have to conform to sourcing and location patterns imposed by the parent firm. They are more prone than domestic firms to source inputs as imports from overseas. This may be from other affiliates in the TNC network, or from established suppliers based in the home country or third countries. A high import propensity of affiliates is observed in both low- and high- technological industries - in the former, since affiliates are often limited to processing imported inputs; in the latter, because affiliates' production is capital-intensive or requires sophisticated inputs not available locally. Import intensity can be high in some services industries as well, notably in tourism. Here, one observes problems of leakages, especially in the case of luxury tourism under franchises in low-income developing countries.

Where the parent firm has a regional or global strategy (many do not), affiliates cannot choose whether to export, or, if they do, which markets to serve. TNCs do not encourage competition among affiliates. Where they have affiliates in different markets, they may prohibit competing exports. The process of deep integration then takes a different direction. Infect, there is a possibility that, in a liberalised world, TNCs may centralise production in a few larger-scale facilities. This can boost exports from affiliates that become such bases, but lower or eliminate exports from others, converting them into sale or final-assembly bases. Only to the extent that the process is cumulative, will successful affiliates will deepen their capabilities and pull further ahead of others. In these circumstances, local firms may actually do better than affiliates operating as part of a TNC network because they are not subject to such market access decisions. However, to take advantage of their freedom they must have the technological and marketing capabilities to match TNC competitors.

The role of TNCs in export markets is large and growing. In fact, to support their competitive positions, successful national exporters themselves tend to go transnational, investing in developing as well as developed countries. Firms linked to TNCs tend to follow them overseas with supporting production facilities. With growing liberalisation and globalisation, such trends will intensify. This does not necessarily mean that the same set of TNCs from the same home countries will benefit and increase their dominance of world trade. The identity of competitive firms is constantly changing, and increasing numbers will hail from developing countries. Their market shares are of course, difficult to predict. But a portfolio of locational assets will be increasingly important for their international competitiveness, and hence will lead to the further growth of developing country export-oriented FDI.

3. Building Dynamic Comparative Advantages

Many developing host countries expect TNCs to be agents for the creation of dynamic comparative advantage, particularly in the export of manufactured products. Dynamism can take many different forms, depending on the nature of the host economy and the time-frame considered. In the short term, it can mean moving up to the next level of technological complexity: for a developing country with unprocessed primary exports and endowments of unskilled labour, dynamism means the launching of simple manufactured exports. For countries established in simple exports, it means the shift to higher value added products using relatively simple technologies. For those with a more diverse base of exports, it means entry into high technology products, and so on. In the long term, dynamism means not just the shift up the skill and technology scale in particular activities, but also deepening the content of export activity and building the capacity to sustain such a shift across a range of tradable activities in response to changing world demand and technologies. This means, in turn, that export activity needs to lead to greater local content in terms of labour, resources and intermediate products, more complex technological functions (design and development), and more intense linkages with the local technology system.

There are several reasons why countries may expect TNCs to dynamise their comparative advantage in all these cases. TNCs are considered well placed-relative to local firms-to provide the tangible and intangible assets needed to transform existing resources, skills and technical competence to world levels. They are believed to be better able to overcome the cost of marketing overseas, providing the information, marketing, brand name and other assets needed to generate exports. Over time, they can keep up more readily with changing technologies and shifting demand in different markets. At the same time, developing countries worry that TNCs transfer the technologies and skills that use their existing resources and capabilities, but do not do enough to upgrade or deepen them.

Both perceptions can be valid-the extent depends on the specific country context. TNCs can dynamise comparative advantage, but only where the host economy is able to mount the right policies and improve the base of capabilities that investors draw upon. Or, they also may not provide the dynamic benefits that comparable local firms do the technological deepening of foreign affiliates, their local linkages and their spillover benefits may be less than those of comparable local firms. However, this is only so where comparable local firms exist in activities undertaken by foreign affiliates, or where a country is able to mount the policies needed to enable local firms to develop the necessary capabilities. Generalisations are difficult. What is possible is to review existing, often patchy, data on the contribution of TNCs to export activity and qualitative evidence on .its upgrading in particular countries.

A useful indicator to start with is the share of foreign affiliates in merchandise exports. The evidence shows large differences in these shares across a number of countries, reflecting their locational advantages as export bases. Countries with a low level of FDI (such as Japan) or with low locational advantages have very low shares. Countries with a large FDI presence and strong locational advantages such as close proximity to, and integration with, a large market

(Canada), or input cost advantages (Hungary, Singapore, Malaysia and China), have high shares. The shares of foreign affiliates in exports can also vary greatly by industry, as exemplified by a comparison of the Czech Republic and flungary. Such variations in foreign affiliate shares in national exports are to be expected. They reflect differences in the amount and type of FDI a country receives and the relative export competence of domestic enterprises and foreign affiliates.

Important questions arise relating to the export performance of TNCs in a more dynamic setting. *How do they react as technology changes and wages and other costs rise in a developing host country, making it imeconofnical as an export site? Do they dynamise comparative advantage by upgrading facilities and local capabilities or do they move their facilities to cheaper locations?*

Both outcomes are possible. Which happens depends on the industry, the technology and host-country factors. From the perspective of TNCs, the main considerations are the rate at which costs are rising, the possibility of offsetting this by improved technology and the cost of implementing that technology" weighed against the costs of relocating. Relocation costs depend on the sunk costs. Operations for which sunk costs tend to be low and technical change incremental—simple activities with low costs of training and so on—tend to relocate rather than dynamise capabilities in their original location. This is often (but not always) the case with such activities as clothing and footwear. By contrast, industries with high sunk costs tend to "stick", unless the technological change is so drastic that it either becomes economical (despite sunk costs) to relocate or it is not possible to use new technology at the old location. Apart from that, the capacity of affiliates to absorb new technologies plays a role, as do efforts by governments to retain and upgrade investment. Shifting comparative advantage due to technological upgrading may explain the changing export propensities of United States foreign affiliates. Over time their export propensities have declined in some regions (*e.g.* Asia) and risen in others (*e.g.* Latin America). This may reflect that, in Asia, the rising cost of producing simpler export-oriented products in which most Asian countries had a comparative advantage at an earlier stage has not yet been offset by increased competitiveness in more technology-intensive products.

The upgrading of comparative advantage is not a discrete either "or" decision. There are many possible levels of upgrading, depending on the ability of a host economy to provide the capabilities needed. For instance, TNCs can train employees, but only if the base of formal qualifications needed is present. They can develop the skills for advanced product design locally only if enough design engineers are available. They can import more advanced equipment, but only if local staff can be trained at reasonable cost to use it at world levels of efficiency. Importing skilled personnel can relax the skill constraint temporarily, but this is an expensive solution that can only be used for a small number of high level tasks. Therefore, building up a strong education base that facilitates skills upgrading is indispensable.

FDI can also act as catalyst for the restructuring of domestic firms, directly in those linked to TNCs, or indirectly by intensified competition between domestic firms and foreign affiliates. This is particularly the case in growing industries, *e.g.*, software in India (box-I). But countries cannot rely on TNCs alone to advance restructuring. In the textile and clothing industry, for example, where subcontracting arrangements with TNCs are predominant, the availability of a wide range of potential subcontractors in different host countries means that a subcontractor may be cut out of export markets at short notice. The limited relationships that exists between subcontractors and TNC buyers, and the absence of links with the ultimate clients, make it difficult for domestic firms to build dynamic comparative advantages and restructure their activities. However, firms that develop a sustained relationship with buyers can move up the value chain, even to the point where they can develop their own brand names. In general, judging from the experience of Asian newly-industrialising economies, successful restructuring in the textile and clothing industry in developing countries require substantial effort by local firms, backed by government support, to improve their capabilities (including through outward FDI into low-cost locations), learn (including from TNCs) how to compete in international markets, and develop their own marketing channels.

BOX-1

FDI AND UPGRADING COMPETITIVENESS IN THE INDIAN SOFTWARE EXPORT INDUSTRY

The Indian software export industry, based around Bangalore, Mumbai, Delhi and Madras, had a significant boost in the initial stages from an EPZ. In 1985, Citibank established a wholly-owned, export-oriented, offshore software company in the Santa Cruz Electronics Export Processing Zone in Mumbai. India's attractions were twofold: low-cost English-speaking skilled labour and a time: difference between Europe and North America that allowed for almost 24-hour workdays.

The bulk of the FDI in this industry went into what is known in the software industry low-level data entry work. This refers to contracts in which the client gives software developers exact specifications, and leaves little to the discretion or creativity of the programmers. This form of export activity clid not, however, promise much by way of skill upgrading. An integral part of the restructuring of the industry was the attraction of Texas Instruments (TI) in 1986, which established its first wholly ownedex port oriented subsidiary. In addition to regulatory accommodation, the Government of India developed a Software Technology Parks of India Scheme (1988), where it provided infrastructure, buildings, electricity, telecommunications facilities and high-speed satellite links. In 1989, Hewlett-Packard (HP) set up a 100 per cent owned subsidiary in Bangalore. In 1990-1991 quantitative restrictions on imports of intermediate and capital goods for software exports were abolished.

The TI and HP investments helped the Indian software industry at a critical stage of its development. They demonstrated that India was a viable host for FDI in relatively advanced forms of software writing: Since then, many domestic firms have developed a reputation for reliable, high-quality work at relatively low cost, and have been able to move beyond simple data entry or on-site services. They have won higher value-added work where they and entrusted with a whole project instead of specific components. Others have been able to develop complete software packages, which are rebadged and sold overseas (similar to the OEM relationship in consumer electronics).

The export competitiveness of the Indian software industry is now well established. Exports in 1995 were $485 million, and in 1998 reached $1.75 billion. Until March 1999, exports climbed to $2.65 billion The five largest software companies in India today are domestically owned; two of these are quoted on NASDAQ. TNCs played an important initial role in mobilising domestic capabilities. With government assistance and the removal of import restrictions, domestic companies were then able to supersede foreign affiliates in terms of export competitiveness.

Restructuring by TNCs also implies that small or relatively inefficient import substituting affiliates may have to be wound down, or merged with larger, more viable firms, as affiliates are explosed to world competition. The economic determinants of these processes have been noted: the level of capabilities in existence, the distance from competitive frontiers and the efficacy of policies and institutions to support upgrading. The larger the distance, and the less adequate the policy measures to improve factors or, to provide direct aid to restructuring firms or areas as done extensively in developed countries—the greater the likelihood of there being losers. Strategic factors include a INC's view of a particular location in its global and regional operations, its assessment of country risk, the competitive pressures it faces and its technological strengths and weaknesses.

The interaction of these factors causes continuous changes in the location of activities and sourcing of supplies by TNCs. For instance, in the automobile industry, TNCs are shifting their plants and suppliers across countries in line with changing locational advantages as well as corporate strategies. Corporate strategic differences aside, the response of TNCs is likely to be similar to that of other firms. However, for obvious reasons, it is likely to be more rapid and definitive.

Policy Implications

The trends are clear: there is an increasing liberalisation of trade in a globalising world economy. The impact of liberalisation, globalisation and technological change on trade so far has been highly skewed. Export success is concentrated among a few developing countries, and the level of concentration has risen over time and with the sophistication of the technology involved. Among the successful economies, a few, such as the Republic of Korea and Taiwan Province of China, have been able to establish autonomous competitive positions in complex products. Others have used TNCs to spearhead their export drive. TNCs have generally played a role in promoting export competitiveness, though their role has differed by country. Their potential contribution to strengthening the export competitiveness of developing countries within the existing patterns of comparative advantage and to dynamise this advantage-remains to be exploited fully. Indeed, in many cases it has not even been broached. In the new policy and technological setting, their role in upgrading export competitiveness has considerable potential, if the domestic and international policy environments are supportive.

There are several sets of policy issues related to the role of FOI in boosting export competitiveness in developing countries. Some of the main issues for different groups of developing countries are:

(i) For countries with strong national innovation systems and exports led by national enterprises, the main issues include the following: Can their enterprises and institutions continue to cope with the rapid pace of technical change and keep up with world technology frontiers? *Can they move from imitation and absorption to genuine innovation? Can they keep ahead of emerging competition from cheaper countries and make inroads into markets held by the more advanced industrial countries? What role should inward FDI play in maintaining export competitiveness? How should national enterprises relate to TNCs, both as competitors and as potential collaborators?*

(ii) For countries that have entered areas of dynamic comparative advantage assisted by TNCs, the issues relate to sustainability and upgrading. *Can they continue to attract TNCs that source high-technology products as their wages rise and cheaper competitors appear? How can they induce higher local content and technological depth in local affiliate operations? How can they ensure beneficial spillovers from TNCs to local firms? More generally, how can they strengthen their national innovation systems to ensure that they graduate to sustained growth in sophisticated manufacturing by both TNCs and local firms?*

(iii) For countries that have attracted FDI into low technology export activity but have failed to diversify their export base or to move into higher value products, the main issues concern broadening the competitive base. *How much can they upgrade their exports into less vulnerable, more value-added products within the low technology groups? How can they diversify into more complex activities? How can they attract TNCs into a different set of activities and build more advanced domestic skills and capabilities?*

(iv) For countries that have built up sizeable industries behind protective walls but have not made the transition to dynamic export growth by either foreign or local enterprises, the issues relate to the incentive regime and industrial restructuring. *What is the best way to liberalise in order to build upon the existing base of capabilities and make the FDI regime competitive? How can existing industries be reoriented and upgraded to become export competitive? How can foreign affiliates be induced to integrate their operations better into their parent companies' global operations? How can new export-oriented FDI be attracted, initialy to a range of activities and over time to higher technology activities? What role can TNCs play in restructuring domestic firms? What can be done to re-gear the national technology system to international competitiveness?*

(v) For countries with weak industries, marginalised in export growth and FDI, the issues relate to their ability to attract FDI and to stimulate industrial growth in general. *How can they improve their investment climate and attract manufacturing FDI? What is the best way to create the basic skills and institutions needed to promote learning in simple industrial activities and diversify production from the primary sector? How can they attract investments, as a first step, into the low technology activities becoming uncompetitive in more advanced developing countries? What needs to be done to upgrade traditional SMEs to participate in manufactured export activity?*

In view of the objective of enhancing export competitiveness, a common set of preconditions and issues runs through all of these groups. The preconditions encompass prudent macroeconomic management—especially of the exchange rate and an institutional environment conducive to exporting. The common issues relate to liberalising FDI and trade regimes; attracting export-oriented FDI and upgrading TNC activity; and strengthening domestic skills, capabilities and institutions. Each of these has a vital role to play in realising the role of FDI in generating and upgrading exports. The precise nature of the policy problems differ however, according to the level of national capabilities and development, the nature of the policy regime and the form of participation in TNC networks.

The first set of policy measures relates to liberalisation. The new institutions and rules of international trade and especially the nature of technological change suggest that globalisation will continue. In this new context, the way to raise productivity and living standards lies in greater participation in international investment and trade-albeit with due preparation to ensure that liberalisation does not lead to economic devastation or technological stagnation. The pace of liberalisation has to be calibrated to ensure that domestic capabilities improve and the productive structure is upgraded. The rules of the game may provide sufficient flexibility to developing countries to manage this calibration, but taking advantage of them needs careful preparation and market-friendly strategies. In this situation, governments face several options to increase trade competitiveness.

This liberalisation process has, however, not been uniform. A number of countries have opted to use protection, because full-fledged liberalisation could create problems for the survival of domestic industries. In such policy situations, selective liberalisation might be a way to reconcile efforts to attract export-oriented FDI with the need to protect particular economic activities or industries. Selective liberalisation can take various forms, for example, EPZs - which limit trade and investment liberalisation to a spatially-confined area; bonded-warehouse and duty drawback systems-which exempt export-oriented industries from domestic tariffs; and gradual tariff phase-outs over a period of time which allow an economy to shield selectively certain products or industries considered strategic. Governments might also pursue a policy of "trade neutrality". The objective of this policy is to eliminate any anti-export bias (to the extent that it exists) whereby exporters may be buying inputs at prices above world prices, but can only sell their output at world prices. Trade neutrality might serve to attract export-oriented FDI.

The second policy issue is that of attracting FDI by targeting investment conducive to export competitiveness and upgrading. Again, a variety of measures are available. Where an investment promotion agency exists, it could gear at least part of its activities to this objective. Targeting as a policy instrument may be particularly effective if it has top-level government support and where it is incorporated into a cohesive overall policy framework. The more concrete elements of targeting range from systematically providing comprehensive information on industries with export-potential (*e.g.* databases on local firms and their capabilities, ideally made available through the Internet), to active research and investment promotion.

A special effort, for example, could be made to draw FDI into industries in which the host country has a revealed comparative advantage (RCA), *i.e.* where its exports of a product are growing faster than exports of that product worldwide. If this can be combined with attracting TNCs that have a competitive edge in that product and in world trade, a virtuous cycle could be in the making. Targeting initiatives might also seek out TNCs from developing countries, for example SMEs, that are active in particular export niches or which serve as specialised supplier industries to global exporters.

With the growth of FDI from developing countries, it can become an important reservoir of capital and other assets, and may facilitate access into new markets. This might require Governments to review their FDI regulatory framework to see whether it is not biased against non-traditional TNCs.

The third issue for policy consideration is that of domestic capacity. Strengthening domestic enterprises, as well as the skills, capabilities and institutions on which they rely is probably the single most important long-term element for a successful export-oriented policy. This is so regardless of the role FDI plays in export activity: reliance on TNCs does not eliminate the need to invest in domestic capabilities. The entry of TNCs can complement and catalyse domestic resources; it cannot substitute for them. To foster the creation of backward linkages and to increase the share of value added in the host economy, countries - developed and developing - have used local content requirements. Such requirements are subject to provisions of the Agreement on Trade-Related Investment Measures. Developing countries have also used export performance requirements to encourage the export orientation of foreign affiliates.

Domestic capacity-building also calls for measures to support local export-oriented industries that can serve as a magnet for FDI; nurturing efficient supplier networks is a related measure. Governments can, for example, initiate training programmes for domestic companies to upgrade their product quality and productivity or they can enlist the assistance of the TNCs engaged in the export sector for this training. Indonesia and Malaysia, for example, have had successful programmes in which TNCs in the export sector have conducted training courses for domestic companies in supplier industries. Targeted incentives might include incentives for creating specific skills required by a particular export industry which can yield large dividends in dynamising the export structure. The skilful use of incentives, and investment in skills and supply capabilities, can also induce sequential investment into the upgrading of affiliates.

Strengthening export competitiveness and upgrading is not merely an issue of domestic policy for host developing countries. These countries cannot reach full export competitiveness as long as developed countries restrict access to their markets. Many developed countries have tariff regimes that are characterised by tariff escalation for processed goods looking out potential suppliers - and in the process deterring potential foreign investors in those industries. Similarly, restrictions on certain industries have hampered the development of competitive industries in developing countries that would have a comparative advantage, given their natural resource and labour endowments (*e.g.* the Modifiable Agreement). In other industries such as tropical beverages and some categories of vegetables or fruit tariff peaks make it difficult for developing countries to develop export markets.

In a broader context, an efficient rule-based multilateral trading system is of critical importance to developing countries. WTO membership, and the capacity to follow up on implementation, are important since a number of policy instruments of that Organisation have a direct bearing on the impact of FDI on export competitiveness and upgrading. These concern, in particular, domestic content, and trade-balancing requirements and restrictions on exports: They are contained in the Agreement on Trade-related Investment Measures. It requires WTO members to notify the use of instruments contained in the TRIMs illustrative list. Developing countries can seek extension of these transitional periods, taking into account the individual development, financial and trade needs of the country concerned. Indeed, given that some developing countries have found these measures useful, proposals have been made to extend the transitional period. Active and skilful participation by developing countries can help ensure that the review of the TRIMs Agreement accords with their development interests. As the multilateral trade environment is being developed further, the links between trade and FDI need to be assessed carefully by developing countries as they formulate their agenda. The ability to conduct-complex investment discussions and negotiate international investment agreements is increasingly important for determining the role that FDI can play in boosting the export competitiveness of developing countries. To build a more sustainable and dynamic export base, countries have to use proactive policies. They also need to improve their human capital and capabilities in order to attract higher quality investment. This allows them to attract more sophisticated activities and functions from foreign investors and to strengthen domestic enterprises as direct exporters and as suppliers to TNCs. Only the development of a local capability base will allow countries to plug into the dynamic segments of export activity. TNCs can, in turn, help in the further development of domestic capabilities, leading to a virtuous circle of rising incomes, higher-quality FDI and dynamic competitiveness in trade.

❐

18

Financial Integration

Well-managed international financial integration promises substantial benefits. These benefits accrue on both the production and the consumption side. On the production side, integration permits greater international specialisation and facilitates the allocation of scarce resources to their most productive uses independent of location, thereby accelerating growth. On the consumption side, integration allows individuals (both in the newly integrating and, to a lesser extent, in the already integrated economies) to insure themselves against adverse developments in their home economy both through international portfolio diversification and by tapping global capital markets to smooth temporary declines in income. We look at both benefits in turn.

Iintegration and Growth

Two Engines Drive Economic Growth: Changes in the quantity of inputs-in particular, labour and capital, broadly defined and changes in their quality.

Investment

In a financially closed economy, investment must be funded by domestic savings. The two are matched by movements in the real interest rate-the cost of borrowing and the return to savings. Without international capital flows, there can be no presumption that the returns to investment are equal across countries, resulting in resource misallocation: on the margin, highly profitable investment projects in some countries may not be undertaken for lack of financing, although lower-return projects are funded elsewhere. Financial integration, whether on the national or the international level, severs the link between local savings and local investment, allowing savings to run as surely and instantly where it is most wanted, and where there is most to be made of it, as water runs to find its level. Investors are able to borrow and savers are able to lend internationally, thus the global rather than the national interest rate becomes the relevant cost of capital and return to savings. Of course, savings and investment must still match, but they now do so on a global rather than a national scale. Following integration, investment is, under ideal circumstances, reallocated toward the most rewarding projects (on a risk-adjusted basis), regardless of their location, financed by corresponding capital flows seeking the highest risk-adjusted returns. World production increases, a gain partly accruing to savers in the less productive economies, who now receive higher returns, and partly accruing to firms in the more productive economies, who now enjoy a reduced cost of capital.

The new pattern of capital flows depends on the relative return to investment across countries. Extensive research over the last decade has established a by-now-familiar set of characteristics of successful economies, including (most important) sound macro-economic policies and god microeconomic fundamentals. The point is important: it is the relative return rather than the relative development level that drives capital flows; in consequence, financial integration has primarily resulted in capital flows to countries already enjoying high domestic investment levels. Integration thus raises the payoff for establishing good fundamentals; it does not substitute for fundamentals. In consequence, the trend toward integration may, at least temporarily, widen the gap between the high-and the low-growth developing economies, although in the long term this very widening raises the benefits of improving the fundamentals in low growth group.

For the growing subgroup of developing countries already offering attractive investment opportunities, integration permits an acceleration of investment by argumenting domestic savings with foreign savings. The potential gains vary from country to country, depending on the relative profitability of investment opportunities and on the difference between the domestic cost and the world cost of capital before integration

Can integration permanently raise growth rates in the opening economy, or even in the world economy? Any permanent growth effect must come through an increase in world saving rates or faster productivity growth. There is little reason to believe that integration boosts world saving rates. Indeed, a decline is more likely, since diversification of income risk and access to world capital markets to smooth out temporary income fluctuations reduce the need for precautionary savings. Any permanent gains form integration are thus more likely to come through the quality rather than the quantity of investment.

Productivity

Integration may boost productivity growth by shifting the investment mix toward projects with higher expected returns, a shift brought about by an improved ability to reduce and to diversify the higher risk typically entailed in higher-return projects. The risk of any particular investment can conceptually be divided into four parts: a global component (for instance, a world recession), a national component (for instance, higher profit taxes or political instability), a sector component (for instance à technological advance), and a component specific to the particular investment. The sector and the project-specific risks can be diversified domestically, resulting in sizable benefits from the national financial integration typically preceding international integration. Global risks by their nature cannot be diversified away. This leaves national risk, which cannot be diversified within a country but can be diversified internationally.

If national shocks are a quantitatively important part of the overall risk of investment projects, the diversification benefits obtained by adding another domestic investment project to a portfolio of other domestic projects are lower than the benefits of adding the same project to a portfolio of internationally diversified projects. In consequence, a foreign investor can pursue projects with higher project risks and returns while keeping portfolio risk to an acceptable level. A move form a system of closed national economies to an integrated world economy thus permits a global switch toward projects with higher expected returns, thereby increasing the average world growth rate. The effect is reinforced if integration also permits a reduction in project risk. For instance, if opening is associated with an expansion of the market for domestic production, susceptibility to domestic demand changes declines, enabling a shift to more specialised-and more productive-capital.

The quantitative significance of a switch to higher-return investments in the wake of integration depends on three factors: the technologically of a particular country, risk aversion, and the speed with which existing capital can be reallocated. Very large magnitude of gains reflects the magic of compound interest: even small increases in growth rates have first-order level effects over time. For the economies lagging farthest behind current best practice, the gains comprise both catch-up and the global efficiency gain, while the leading economies benefit from only a latter change. Yet even for these economies the benefits of higher output, and hence consumption growth rates, are very significant: a well-managed integration is a win-win situation.

The equalisation of returns across countries and the higher growth rate resulting from a globally more productive capital stock provide the long-term benefits of integration proper. In addition provides more immediate benefits through knowledge spillovers, particularly in financial markets and via FDI. While these benefits are not strictly dependent on financial integration, integration tends at least to accelerate the knowledge transfer.

Financial System Spillovers

The cost of capital to the end borrower consists of four components: the real interest rate on minimum-risk liquid assets, the risk premium imposed by the financial intermediary for financing particular ventures, the cost structure of the financial system, and the profit margin charged. Integration affects all four components. Integration replaces the local with the world interest rate and reduces the risk premium to the extent that foreign lenders can better diversify the country risk. The other two components-the cost structure of the financial system and the profit margin-are also affected if integration enhances the depth of the financial system (allowing fixed costs to be spread over a broader base) or its competitiveness.

Beyond the effect on the cost of capital, a deepening of the domestic financial system in the wake of integration also aids growth through a more efficient allocation of resources, in turn leading to further financial deepening. This positive feedback lop between financial and real development is well established. International integration is likely to augment the feedback. Foreign financial institutions will introduce or create access to new financial instruments, while participation of foreigners in domestic securities markets enhances liquidity, in turn facilitating long-term maturity transformation.

Equally unambiguously, financial integration is associated with an increase in financial system depth (and hence, indirectly, growth) both in terms of bank lending and in terms of asset market liquidity and turnover. The quantitative benefits of deepening are likely to be augmented by improvements in the quality of financial intermediation. Part of the improvement will come through prerequisites for successful integration, such as improvements in domestic accounting and supervision standards. Another part will come through learning about better practice coupled with the pressures created by greater competition. Most important, however, will be the momentum for additional reforms and development unleashed even by limited first steps toward integration. For example, an initial deepening of the banking system will raise the return to introducing an efficient payment system; the development of domestic equity markets will motivate efforts to improve settlement systems; the potential for issuing securities in foreign markets will enhance incentives to improve settlement systems; the potential for issuing securities in foreign markets will enhance incentives to improve domestic accounting standards; and so forth. Once begun, integration is thus likely to trigger reinforcing dynamics, creating a virtuous cycle of further institutional development that makes possible even more complete integration. Of course, the dynamics thus unleashed also carry significant risks and need to be well managed.

FDI Spillovers

International financial integration also opens the door to both inward and outward FDI, which may influence growth through three channels. First, FDI may increase the total volume of investment in the recipient economy, Second, even if it substitutes for rather than augments domestic investment, it may be more productive than the capital it replaces. Third, it may generate spillover effects that raise the productivity of existing domestic capital.

FDI thus affects growth in two ways: by contributing to the volume of investment and by helping to improve efficiency. The primary growth impact comes through improved efficiency rather than an increased quantity of investment. In this context, however, three caveats must be kept in mind. First, the quality effects are self-eliminating: as domestic practices are adjusted, the scope for additional spillover benefits decreases. Second, the evidence strongly suggests the FDI follows rather than initiates growth. The benefits form FDI, much like the financial market benefits of integration, are thus more likely to buttress existing virtuous cycles that to originate new ones; integration magnifies the benefits of good fundamentals, it does not substitute for them. Third, the net effect of FDI on growth will differ across r cipients. In highly distorted economies, FDI may primarily exploit domestic rent-extracting opportunities; in economies with functioning markets, relative returns are more likely to channel FDI to bottlenecks, with substantially greater benefits.

The production-side benefits of integration find a mirror image on the consumption side. Individuals in the newly integrated economies can stabilise their income and consumption by holding foreign assets (augmenting labour income depending on the domestic economy with capital income depending on foreign economies) and by using international capital markets to buffer consumption against temporary swings in the domestic economy. Integration thus allows individuals to reduce the dependence of their consumption on the fortunes of the domestic economy, which is likely to be the source of most of their labour income.

While residents of already integrated economies benefit from continuing integration by gaining another outlet for their savings, and hence additional diversification, the benefits accrue primarily to the residents of the newly integrating developing economies, for three reasons. First, the starting degree of diversification is likely to be very limited. Second, terms of trade and other shocks tend to have a particularly large impact on poorer economies with less diversified production structures and less effective automatic stabilisers. Third, the welfare cost of reducing consumption in the face of adverse developments is largest for countries with low per capita incomes, and hence so are the gains from reducing consumption volatility through integration.

How large the gains from risk reduction will be depends on how much the volatility of consumption can be reduced, and on the value individuals place on this reduction. If Individuals effectively used capital markets to stabilise consumption, income volatility would significantly exceed consumption volatility. Furthermore, the growth of consumption would be more highly correlated across countries than the growth of income, since consumers in all countries would hold claims on and hence base their consumption choices on-global rather than national production.

Thus, the substantial reductions in the volatility of consumption could be obtained by enhanced use of international financial markets to smooth out temporary domestic income disturbances and to diversify national risks. Whether this potential reduction is a significant benefit depends on the value individuals place on reducing the variability of consumption.

As a result, the financial integration of developing countries is expected to deepen and broaden over the coming decade, against a backdrop of increasing global financial integration. Indeed, given the changes that are taking place at the international level-in particular, the rapid advances in technology, communications, and financial innovation-and the growing economic sophistication in developing countries, the progressive financial integration of the latter in world financial markets appears inevitable.

Gross private capital flows may therefore be expected to rise substantially, with capital flowing not only from industrial to developing countries but, increasingly, among developing countries themselves and from developing to industrial countries.

Aggregate net private capital flows to developing countries are likely to be sustained in the short to medium term because of the continuing decline in creditworthiness risks and other investment risks, the higher expected rates of return in developing countries, and the fact that these countries are underweighted in the portfolios of institutional investors. The rate of growth, though, and eventually, the levels, will inevitably decline. There will probably also be considerable variation among countries, depending on the pace and depth of improvements in macroeconomic performance and creditworthiness. In fact, in countries where economic and policy fundamentals are quite weak, the initial manifestation of growing financial integration may take the form of net outflows of private capital.

With changes in the international financial environment, there are likely to be considerable year-to-year fluctuations in private capital flows to developing countries, even in aggregate. Emerging markets will probably continue to be more susceptible to shocks from the international environment than industrial countries are, a prospect that raises concerns in developing countries because private capital can now respond quite rapidly to actual or perceived changes.

In the international environment, three factors in particular are seen as having the potential for creating significant volatility in private capital flows to developing countries:

(i) Movements in international interest rates and other asset returns-especially movements in industrial country stock markets. Private capital flows to emerging markets are considered to be particularly affected by changes in these factors because investors regard these markets as marginal.

(ii) Investor herding behaviour. The new investor base in developing countries-dominated by institutional investors-is widely thought to be prone to herding behaviour, arising from its incentive structure and the relatively limited information available on developing country investments.

(iii) Contagion or spillover effects, which arise when events in one emerging market cause investors to change their investment decisions in other emerging markets. The likelihood of contagion is also seen to be high in the current international environment, in part because of institutional features in the current investor base.

Structural Forces Driving Private Capital Flows to Developing Countries

The Structural Trends now evident in private capital flows is being driven by two primary forces: higher long-term (as opposed to short-term or cyclical) expected rates of return in developing countries and the opportunity for risk diversification.

Higher Expected Rates of Return

Standard economic theory predicts that if the level of capital stock is relatively low, then, other things being equal, the marginal product of capital will be high. If not constrained by the availability of skilled labour, infrastructure, and other factors that are complements to capital in the production process, therefore, the rate of return to investment will be relatively high in countries with low levels of capital stock.

For the foreign investor, country creditworthiness, or a country's ability to make resources available for external payments, is also a very important determinant of the overall rate of return to investment. In the mid-1980s, the macro-economic performance and creditworthiness of many developing countries started to improve again and this trend accelerated in the early 1990s. Developing countries that have been the major recipients of private capital have seen a decline in inflation, higher growth of output and exports, and higher and more productive investment. The more stable domestic macroeconomic environment has, in turn, improved prospective rates of return to investment in general, while the growth in earning capacity (as manifested in the growth of output and exports), and reduction in the stock of external liabilities in many of the heavily indebted middle-income countries (following the implementation of the Brady Plan), has reduced country risks for the foreign investors. Many of these countries have also seen a significant growth in the skilled labour force and improvements in supporting infrastructure over the past decade,

Underpinning the improvements in economic performance of developing countries has been the systematic adoption of macroeconomic stabilisation programmes and structural reforms by a growing number of countries and a more favourable international environment. A key element of the stabilisation programmes has been sustained fiscal adjustment, with fiscal deficits declining substantially from the high levels reached alter the debt crisis. Trade liberalisation, investment deregulation, and financial sector liberalisation have promoted more private sector and outward-oriented economies. The creditworthiness of these countries we been strengthened by the low international interest rates that have prevailed since the mid-1980s and was further boosted during the cyclical downturn in the early 1990s.

Opportunities for Risk Diversification

The second force behind the structural trend in private capital flows is investors' desire for portfolio risk diversification. Investors can benefit from holding emerging market equities because returns in emerging markets tend to exhibit low correlations with industrial country return-that is, they tend not to move in tandem with those of industrial countries. In general, by holding an asset whose returns are not correlated with the returns of another asset, investors can raise the overall return on their port-folio without a commensurate increase in risk (variance).

The opportunity for portfolio diversification offered by emerging markets is a relatively recent phenomenon, associated with the 1990s that has developed as capital markets in these countries have deepened and broadened.

Changing Enabling Environment in Industrial Countries

The strong response of private capital flows stemmed from changes in the enabling environment in both industrial and developing countries during the 1980s and 1990s. Industrial countries have seen changes in two broad areas. First, in the real sector, increasing competition and rising costs at home, combined with falling transport and communications costs, have heightened firms responsiveness to opportunities to increase efficiency and reduce costs by locating investments abroad. This is leading to the progressive globalisation of production and has spurred the growth of "efficiency-seeking" FDI. Second, in financial markets, a self-reinforcing process of competition, deregulation technological advances, and financial innovations has increased the responsiveness of investors to international investment opportunities. This process is rapidly leading to the linking of domestic markets into one global market.

Changing Enabling Environment in Developing Countries

Changes in the enabling environment of industrial countries have meant that economic agents in these countries-both firms and portfolio investors-have become more responsive to opportunities to earn higher rates of return or diversify risks through international investments. And, developing countries have begun to offer investment opportunities as their creditworthiness and rates of return have improved. Concomitant changes in the enabling environment of developing countries have enabled these forces to be translated into actual investments.

The most important enabling factors are simply whether private capital is permitted to flow into a country and whether the restrictions on the repatriation of profits (income) and capital are prohibitive. Along with the sharp decline in expropriation risks, the 1980s and 1990s have witnessed a progressive dismantling of barriers to capital account mobility in developing countries. Whereas previously most national investment codes and bilateral investment treaties imposed few restrictions on the recipient countries with respect to market entry, recent laws and agreements have emphasised the free flow of investment. Many of the recent laws and agreements also contain provisions for the settlement of disputes, usually providing for several different mechanisms for their resolution-ranging from direct negotiations between the disputing parties to arbitration proceedings in which investors and host states may participate on an equal footing.

In addition to the easing of regulations pertaining to the movement of private capital, structural changes in developing countries have meant a significant expansion of areas for potential foreign investor involvement. In particular, as part of their structural reform programmes, many developing countries have deregulated their investment regimes and reduced the role of the public sector in directly productive sectors, with a view to allowing greater participation of private investors. One manifestation of this has been the gradual reduction of the share of state-owned enterprise investment in total domestic investment.

Finally, trade liberalisations by developing countries have provided an impetus to FDI flows in particular. As a large proportion of FDI flows is being driven by considerations of production efficiency. As a result, trade regimes in developing countries have become more important. Following unilateral and successive rounds of multilateral trade liberalisations since the mid-1990s, three has been a progressive dismantling of trade barriers in developing countries.

Prospects for Private Capital Flows

The structural factors underlying capital flows, too developing countries are still unfolding. The changes taking place at the international level, which are increasing the responsiveness of capital flows to cross-border investment opportunities and leading to progressive global financial integration, can be expected to continue. In particular, all the forces discussed above-deregulation and breakdown of barriers, technological change, and financial innovation-continue to evolve and, as in the past, will keep reinforcing one another, creating pressures for further integration. Internal and external financial deregulation is far from complete in either industrial or developing countries. Although it is difficult to speculate on the nature of future innovation and technological change, competitive pressures and increasing integration have been stimulating investments in technology that are likely to continue to reduce transaction costs and make distant markets more accessible to small as well as large investors. Such innovations will make policy- induced barriers less effective, spurring even more deregulation and competition.

The policy reforms that are being embarked upon- which focus on macroeconomic stability and the promotion of more deregulated, outward-oriented, and market-based economies-are likely to increase/ the productivity of investments in these countries. On the expectation that developing countries will continue to strengthen and deepen their policy reforms, and that the external environment will remain broadly favourable, developing countries are likely to grow at almost double the rate of industrial countries, providing significant opportunities for productive investments.

Developing countries should provide growing opportunities for port- folio investors in particular as their share of world market capitalisation, which is currently around 10 percent, rises further. As financial markets in emerging economies are not fully developed, further financial deepening-including that of capital markets—can be expected. And because developing countries are expected to grow significantly faster than industrial countries, their share of world market capitalisation will rise. Broadening 0.£ the base-as more developing countries undertake reforms and liberalise-will contribute to the rising share of developing countries in world market capitalisation.

Given these trends and the fact that the share of emerging markets in industrial country portfolios remains very small, there is still considerable room for, an expansion of investments by institutional investors in emerging markets.

As a result, the financial integration of developing countries is expected to broaden and deepen over the coming decade. As part of this process, gross private flows are likely to rise significantly, with capital flowing not only from industrial to developing countries, but, increasingly, among developing countries themselves, and from developing to industrial countries.

In the short to medium term, developing countries, in aggregate, are likely to receive net private capital flows because investment risks are declining, expected rates of return are improving, and these countries are underweighted in the portfolios of institutional investors. However, the rate of growth, and eventually the levels, will inevitably decline. Moreover, there is likely to be considerable variation among countries, depending on the pace and depth of Improvements in macroeconomic performance and creditworthiness

Aging in Industrial Countries: A New Force

An important new factor will provide further impetus to these under- lying trends-the demographic shift under way in industrial countries. Industrial countries now have a pronounced bulge in their demographic structure, reflecting the aging of the baby boom generation and declining birthrates. This will lead to a steady rise in the proportion of elderly to active population in all industrial countries, although the pace of this increase will be most pronounced in Japan. This is in sharp contrast to the situation in developing countries, whose demographic structure reflects a much younger population.

There are three broad implications of this difference in demographic patterns. First, the aging of populations in industrial countries could lead to an increase in savings in the short to medium term. Second, aging and the associated slowing of labour force growth is likely to exert downward pressure on the rate of return to capital relative to that of tabour in industrial countries. Given the demographic structure in developing countries, the reverse can be expected there. Thus, differences in demographics are likely to reinforce the differentials in the expected rates of return to capital between industrial and developing countries. Both of these factors should stimulate the flow of capital to emerging markets. Third, the aging of populations in industrial countries is leading to pressures for pension reform. These reforms are likely to result in greater responsiveness on, the part of pension funds to investment opportunities in developing countries.

Demographic patterns, and the attendant slowdown in the growth rate of the labour force, may also affect rates of return to capital in industrial countries. More specifically, because the slower labour force growth implies fewer workers per unit of capital, other things being equal, the returns to capital relative to labour will rend to fall. (Of course, technological innovations that raise the rare of return to capital could mitigate some of the adverse effects of a slowdown in the labour force.) As the reverse is occurring in developing countries, the differences in demographics can be expected to contribute to the differential in the relative rates of return to capital between industrial and developing countries.

Both the developments in industrial country savings as well as the changes in the labour market should provide further stimulus to investments in emerging markets.

Volatility in Various Stages of Financial Integration

Private capital flows and the process of financial integration hold significant potential benefits. Yet the volatility of these flows can have serious repercussions on the domestic economy. These concerns have been heightened in the current international environment in which new types of investor-investing in portfolio flows, which are a new form of investment for emerging markets-can and do respond more quickly to changing conditions.

Two key questions arise with respect to volatility emanating from the international environment. First, what are the main factors that affect the volatility of flows and asset prices in emerging markets? Second, how significant are these factors in terms of their impact? Three factors in the international environment have been identified as having an important bearing on the volatility of flows and asset prices in emerging markets.

Role of International Interest Rates

Private capital flows to emerging markets are as being more susceptible to changes in international interest rates because foreign investors still think of emerging markets as marginal investments. The presumption is that because these investors con-investments in emerging markets as a means of adding higher returns to their portfolios only when their mainstream investment—in industrial countries—are under performing, investments in emerging markets will be very sensitive to changes in industrial countries' interest rates.

However, this presumption seems to be true only for portfolio flows and not for FDI—especially those that occur as part of the globalisation of production-are driven by firms' considerations of long-term profitability. Such flows are therefore much more responsive to changes in the investment environment of the host country than to temporary fluctuations in interest rates. Cyclical changes in interest rates may affect the start of an FDI project. It may also change the form of the financing package but temporary movements in interest rates are unlikely to affect the magnitude of the flows associated with the project.

Investor Herding

A second factor that has recently received a great deal of attention as a cause of volatility in portfolio flows and asset prices is herding on the part of foreign investors. Investor herding is generally attributed to problems of asymmetric information. It has been suggested that the current structure of the investor base—in which the assets of primary investors (retail investors and pension funds) are managed externally by professional fund managers-particularly susceptible to herding behaviour. The essence of this argument is that fund managers will follow the investment decisions of other fund managers in order to show clients that they know what they are doing. If they follow other fund managers decisions and the investment turns out to be unprofitable, they are more likely to be thought of as unlucky than as unskilled, since other fund managers will have made the same mistake. Given that such a high percentage of household savings is now channeled through institutional investors that employ professional funds managers, the potential for such behaviour clearly exists.

Much also depends on how the mandates of fund managers are set: some mandates could reinforce these incentives to herd. Mandates of external fund managers of pension funds in the United Kingdom, for example, often stipulate that the fund manager perform at least as well as the median fund. Consequently, underperformance relative to the median is penalised, while overperformance is not rewarded proportionately. This could arguably provide more of an incentive to herd than if fund managers are evaluated against an index as well as against peers, as is often the case in the United States, or asked to achieve a minimum yield, as in Japan.

Herding behaviour may also be stronger in emerging markets because the investors are less familiar with these markets and will thus be reluctant to rely solely on their own assessment of the fundamental value of an investment. Under these circumstances, investors will at least partly adjust their investment decisions according to those of other investors, behaviour that could lead to herding or trend chasing. A factor that will have some dampening effect on such behaviour, however, is the high transaction costs associated with equity investments, which constitute the bulk of institutional investors' investments in emerging markets. Because of high transaction costs, turnover ratios of equity investments are generally less than one-third that of bonds.

Several other factors also suggest that emerging markets should become less susceptible to volatility related to foreign investor participation as these markets become more integrated:

(i) The conditions under which emerging market investments are undertaken are changing rapidly. In particular, institutional investors are becoming more familiar with emerging markets-as evidenced by the significant increase in both the volume and quality of broker research into emerging markets over the past four to five years. The potential for herding should diminish as better macroeconomic, industry, and company information becomes available to foreign investors—a result of financial integration and capital market development.

(ii) The form of investor participation changes and broadens as countries become more integrated. In the initial, or "pre-emerging," stage of integration, the likelihood of herding is low because investors are specialised and dedicated, Countries in the newly emerging stage are more vulnerable to herding because investments are in a less dedicated form and investors are investing in an environment of possible asymmetric and incomplete information. Finally, as markets become more mature and integrated, the investor base tends to become more heterogeneous and better informed, dampening the potential for excess volatility at the country level.

(iii) As markets become more integrated, another factor comes into play: inefficiencies at the country level will have been exploited, so that excess returns are made not at the country level but at the level of individual stocks. Accordingly, fund managers' investment strategies will tend to move away from top-down allocation and active management at the country level to bottom-up allocation and active management at the stock level. That is, their strategies will combine more passive, indexed-based investment at the country level with the active selection of stocks. The potential for herding at the country level should therefore diminish, even if it remains at the level of individual stocks. Investors at this stage of integration are also likely to be more tactical in the timing of that investments (selecting national markets according to current levels of key benchmark asset returns relative to their long-run equilibrium value). They act, from the country's perspective, in a counter cyclical manner.

In general, therefore, the potential for volatility arising from foreign investor participation can be expected to follow an inverted V-shaped curve countries move from the pre-emerging stage of financial integration to the mature emerging stage. It is likely to be highest when countries are in the newly emerging stage of financial integration.

Cross-Country Contagion

The Mexican crisis highlighted the issue of contagion-spill over effects from one country to another-which can be another source of volatility for emerging markets. Conceptually, two types of contagion can be distinguished. The first is fundamentals contagion, in which a shock in one country can affect investments in other countries because the countries share similar fundamentals or are exposed to common external shocks. Or it is possible that the shocks in one country are transmitted through trade or financial channels and thereby affect the economic fundamentals of other countries. The second type of contagion occurs when shocks in one country affect investments in other countries, even if the economic fundamentals of the latter have not changed. This could be termed "pure" contagion. From the country's perspective, such changes in investments would constitute excess volatility.

A shock in one emerging market may well lead to some volatility in flows and asset prices in other emerging markets. However, experience suggests that such contagion will be short-lived-Lasting only' until investors have reevaluated the prospects in individual emerging markets. Even if investors are becoming more discriminating, however, two factors, "related to the investment strategy (rather than behaviour) of institutional investors and to the structure of the current investor base, have the potential to contribute to contagion.

Capital Inflows and Overheating

The key short-run macroeconomic concern associated with a surge in capital inflows is that of an excessive expansion of aggregate demand-that is, macroeconomic overheating. This outcome can be produced through the following transmission mechanism:

(i) If a country maintains an officially determined exchange rate, the commitment to defend the parity causes the central bank to intervene in the foreign exchange market to purchase the forcign exchange generated by the capital inflow. To do so, the central bank creates high-powered domestic money.

(ii) This expansion of the monetary base creates a corresponding expansion in broader measures of the money supply, lowering domestic interest rates and raising domestic asset prices.

(iii) This action in turn triggers an expansion of aggregate demand. If the economy possesses excess capacity, the short-run implications may be to increase domestic economic activity and cause the current account of the balance of payments to deteriorate. Eventually, however (and perhaps rather quickly if domestic excess capacity is limited), excess capacity will be absorbed and the expansion in demand will trigger an acceleration in domestic inflation.

(iv) If the exchange rate peg is maintained, rising domestic prices will cause the real exchange rate to appreciate, abetting the current account deterioration associated with the expansion in aggregate demand.

Policies to Control Overheating

To avoid potential overheating, developing countries can and have intervened at every step in this transmission process. Policy can attempt to reduce the required scale of intervention in the foreign exchange market, restrict the monetary expansion associated with a given magnitude of intervention, and offset through other means the effects on aggregate demand of a given magnitude of monetary expansion. These policies are not exclusive, and most countries have brought a wide variety of these instruments into play.

Some policies have restricted the required scale of intervention in the foreign exchange market, either through reducing the capital account surplus of the balance of payments or through an offsetting increase in the current account deficit. The main instruments available to the authorities are the following:

(i) The magnitude of gross capital inflows can be reduced by imposing a variety of direct or indirect controls on inflows.

(ii) Even if gross inflows are freely allowed, the liberalisation of capital outflows or the accelerated repayment of public debt can be undertaken to attempt to reduce net inflows.

(iii) The implications of a net capital account surplus on the foreign exchange market can be counteracted by accelerating trade liberalisation to increase the current account deficit.

(iv) The most extreme option in this category would be to eliminate all foreign exchange market intervention by floating the exchange rate. The resulting appreciation of the domestic currency would both reduce net inflows through the capital account and create a current account offset.

There are two policies that restrict the magnitude of the monetary expansion associated with a given amount of intervention in the foreign exchange market:

(i) Expansion of base money associated with a given amount of intervention can be restricted by sterilising the effects of intervention on the monetary base-that is, by contracting domestic credit to offset the expansion of the net foreign assets of the central bank, through mechanisms such as open market operations or transferring public sector deposits from commercial banks to the central bank.

(ii) Increasing reserve requirements on domestic financial institutions reduces the impact of the expansion of the monetary base on the growth of broader monetary aggregates.

Sterilised intervention was the most widely and intensively used policy response to the arrival of capital inflows among the countries. But can, stetilisation be effective? This essentially depends on relative substitutability among assets, both between domestic and foreign interest-bearing assets and among' different types of domestic assets. If domestic interest-bearing assets are perfed substitutes among themselves, then the issue of whether sterilisation can work amounts to whether it is possible to prevent a change in demand for domestic interest-bearing assets from causing a change in their price through a suitable quantity response. Clearly, this will: depend on the degree of substitutability between domestic and foreign interest-bearing assets. If they are close to perfect substitutes, then the quantity response would have to approach infinity to prevent a price response. This is what is typically meant by the impossibility of sterilisation.

However, it is also possible for sterilisation to be ineffective in preventing a change in the price of domestic assets even if foreign and domestic interest- bearing assets are imperfect substitutes. This is the case when domestic assets are imperfect substitutes among themselves and a capital inflow represents an increased demand for a particular type of domestic asset that the central bank cannot provide, either directly or indirectly. In this case, sterilised intervention that keeps the monetary base constant, by issuing an asset other than that demanded by the agents generating the capital inflow, could not prevent relative price adjustments among domestic assets as portfolio equilibrium is restored. If such price adjustments cannot be avoided, then it may not feasible to insulate aggregate demand. For example aggressive sterilisation in Mexico did not prevent the arrival of capital inflows from being associated with a stock market boom. One interpretation of this experience is that external creditors wished to acquire eqllity in Mexican firms, while the sterilisation instrument issued by the central bank consists of claims on the Mexican government. In this case the maintenance of portfolio equilibrium in the wake of increased external demand for Mexican equity would have required higher equity prices in Mexico even if the sterilisation of capital inflows had been complete.

Because sterilisation involves the issuance of additional domestic debt, and because its effectiveness depends on substitutability among domestic assets the form that it takes may matter for both its effectiveness and its desirability. Capital-importing countries have used three alternative sterilisation techniques:

(i) transferring public sector deposits out of the commercial banking system and into the central bank.

(ii) selling public sector bonds in secondary bond markets.

(iii) increasing the reserve requirements on domestic banks.

While these techniques share the common objective of stabilising the domestic money supply, the analysis below suggests that their macroeconomic effects may be quite different.

Sterilisations Through Transfers of Public Sector Deposit

Consider the effects ora capital inflow triggered by a shiftinprivate sector (domestic or foreign) preferences from foreign to domestic interest bearing assets. To effect this portfolio reallocation, the private sector has to sell foreign exchange to the domestic central bank. When the public sector offsets a purchase of foreign exchange by transferring public sector deposits from commercial banks to the central bank, it leaves the stock of base money unchanged but exchanges a claim on the domestic banking system for an external claim. At the same time the private sector changes its portfolio in the opposite direction.

There are two ways that the macroeconomic equilibrium can be affected by this transaction, even if the monetary base is unchanged. First, if interest-bearing deposits in the domestic banking system are imperfect substitutes in private portfolios for other domestic interest-bearing assets, then private portfolio equilibrium will be disturbed unless the domestic asset for which there is increased demand happens to be deposits in the domestic banking system. If that is the case, then the private sector and government simply exchange claims on the banking system and there are no price implications to the transaction. But if it is not the case, then relative domestic asset prices will have to change to maintain portfolio equilibrium. If the initial asset shift was toward domestic securities, for instance, the yield on such securities would presumably have to fall and interest rates on bank assets and liabilities would have to rise.

The second effect is a fiscal one. To the extent that the yield on domestic deposits differs from the yield on foreign exchange reserves, the solvency of the domestic public sector will be affected by the transaction. In the particular case of sterilisation through shifts in public sector deposits, the liquidity services provided by such deposits suggest that the public sector's net interest receipts could rise or fall as a result of the sterilisation operation.

Sterilisation Through Open Market Operations

Open market sterilised intervention requires the central bank to sell enough domestic bonds to purchase the foreign exchange associated with the inflow, thereby leaving the monetary base unchanged but increasing the stock of outstanding domestic public sector debt. The amount of new debt is therefore equal to the increase in demand for interest-bearing claims on the domestic economy. The effect of the transaction on the central bank's balance sheet is to leave its liabilities (the base) unchanged, but to change the composition of its assets, reducing its claims on the domestic government and increasing its international reserves. From the standpoint of the nonfinancial public sector as a whole, sterilised intervention amounts to a portfolio transaction in which the domestic nonfinancial public sector issues interest-bearing debts denominated in domestic currency in order to acquire a foreign interest-bearing claim.

Sterilised intervention through open market operations is not likely to be castles, however. The portfolio reallocation implied for the public sector involves issuing a high-yielding liability (domestic currency debt) in exchange for a lower-yielding asset (international reserves). This interest differential leaves the public sector in a weakened financial position. The net adverse effect of such transactions on the public sector's solvency is overstated by the interest differential, however, because this differential presumably exists in part to compensate creditors for the currency and country risk associated with holding domestic public debt. By issuing such debt in exchange for reserves, the public sector is receiving a benefit that partly offsets the interest penalty—that is, the option to reduce the real value of its obligations by devaluing or defaulting. Nonetheless, these benefits may be worthless to a government that never intends to exercise these options (but is unable to convince its creditors of this fact). In this case, sterilised intervention carries a fiscal burden, the cost of which depends on the ease with which an offsetting fiscal adjustment can be effected.

As in the previous case, the conditions required for sterilisation through open market operations to be effective in insulating the domestic economy are that domestic interest-bearing assets must be perfect substitutes among themselves or, if they are not, that sterilisation operations must be capable of supplying precisely those assets that are in increased demand.

Sterilisation Through Restrictions on Domestic Credit Growth

Sterilised intervention through transfers of public sector deposits and open market bond sales operates by fixing the size of the monetary base. An alternative is to allow the base to expand as a result of central bank intervention in the foreign exchange market, but to restrict expansion of the money supply by raising reserve requirements on banks, thus causing the money multiplier to contract.

Again, the objective is to fix the price of domestic interest-hearing assets in the face of an increase in the demand for such assets. From a portfolio allocation perspective, this policy works, in principle, by having the private sector rather than the central bank issue the domestic interest-bearing assets that are in increased demand. When commercial banks face higher reserve requirements, they are forced to absorb the additional monetary base emitted by the central bank in the course of its foreign exchange operations, rather than acquire domestic interest-bearing assets in the form of credit extended to domestic agents. The contraction of credit on the part of commercial banks causes domestic agents who would otherwise have borrowed from these banks to instead issue securities.

However, bank borrowers squeezed out of credit markets by higher reserve requirements may not have access to securities markets and thus may be unable to supply the assets that are in higher demand. Borrowers with low net worth who lack other forms of collateral are able to obtain credit only from institutions that are highly specialised in evaluating and monitoring loans (banks). Such borrowers cannot securities their liabilities. If this is the case, then there is a prima facie case for imperfect substitutability among the relevant domestic assets when sterilisation is pursued through a policy of altering reserve requirements, suggesting that insulation of the domestic economy is less likely to be achieved under this policy than through open market operations.

An additional difference between sterilisation through restrictions on domestic credit and through open market operations is fiscal cost.

In the case of domestic credit restriction, the public sector still acquires interest-bearing foreign assets but does so by emitting noninterest-bearing liabilities (that is, the monetary base). Thus, the public sector's fiscal situation actually improves when sterilisation is effected by increasing reserve requirements. This approach, however, implicitly taxes private agents. The requirement that banks hold a larger stock of noninterest-hearing reserves imposes an explicit tax on them, which must be apportioned in some way among bank depositors, borrowers, and shareholders. The incidence of the tax will depend on the elasticity of supply of bank deposits, as well as on the demand for bank loans.

Offsetting the Impact of Monetary Expansion on Aggregate Demand

If the arrival of capital inflows is permitted to result in the expansion of broad monetary aggregates, the expansionary effects on aggregate demand can be neutralised through fiscal contraction.

Fiscal adjustment was a key component of the stabilisation and market-oriented reform programmes that many countries undertook prior to receiving capital inflows. Consequently, it is difficult to interpret a tight fiscal stance, or a further tightening of that stance, as a policy response to capital inflows rather than as a continuation of an ongoing adjustment process. Whatever the reason, a tighter fiscal stance during the inflow episocie does help reduce aggregate demand pressures.

How successful are these policies in preventing the overheating associated with a surge in capital inflows? Once again, macroeconomic performance can be understood in terms of the transmission mechanism, that operates during the inflow episodes. According to this mechanism, two conditions are necessary for capital inflows to have an expansionary impact on aggregate demand. First, a change in the net private capital inflow must represent an addition to the country's capital account surplus, rather than merely a change in the identity, whether private or public, of the country's external creditors. Second, the central bank must intervene actively in the foreign exchange market, purchasing the additional foreign exchange generated by the capital inflows.

Macroeconomic Management with Growing Integration

Short of the crisis situation associated with vulnerability, cross-reorder capital flows may exhibit substantial volatility—that is temporary shocks to either capital inflows or out flows caused by changes in world economic conditions or by less extreme changes in portfolio managers' perceptions of domestic creditworthiness. This increased volatility may well be a fact of life for developing countries as they become more integrated with international financial markets, even after stock adjustment inflows associated with the transition have tapered off, and even if severe crises are avoided.

The most direct response to external financial yolatility is to contain its impact by restricting the movement of capital-that is, imposing capital controls. However, economists have long questioned both the effectiveness and the desirability of such restrictions. We take up each of these issues in turn.

Capital Controls are of Questionable Effectiveness

Although, economists tend to have strong views about the effectiveness or ineffectiveness of capital controls, empirical evidence on the issue is ambiguous. Assessing the effectiveness of controls is complicated by a host of factors, including the definition of effectiveness itself (that is, what is the objective to be achieved) and the conditions that determine the effectiveness of different types of controls. It may be argued that the effectiveness of capital controls can only be measured relative to the objective they are designed to achieve. There are three basic types of objectives: to preserve some degree of domestic monetary autonomy over a period of time, to restrict the magnitude of net capital flows Into or not of the country, and to affect the composition of capital flows. However, because monetary autonomy cannot be achieved unless the magnitude of net flows is restricted, these three objectives boil down to two: restricting the size of net capital flows and affecting their composition.

Conditions for Effectiveness of Different Types of Controls

The effectiveness of controls may depend on a variety of factors that not only differ across countries but also change over time as the process of financial integration proceeds. These factors includes:

(i) ***The State of Technology.*** This affects transaction costs in conducting arbitrage among different financial centers. The lower the costs, the more difficult it will be to implement effective controls.

(ii) ***The Extent of International Cooperation in Reporting Cross-border Claims.*** In the case of controls on outflows, for example, host countries may be unwilling to declare the assets of residents from capital-exporting countries, whether or not these residents try to circumvent foreign exchange regulations.

(iii) ***The Size of the Misalignment Motivating Inflows or Outflows.*** If effecting a capital inflow or outflow for an arbitrage operation involves a fixed cost imposed by the control regime, then the deterrent effect of this cost may be nullified if the arbitrage gains promise to exceed the cost.

(iv) ***The Design of the Controls Themselves, in Particular Their Comprehensiveness.*** Controls that are not comprehensive-for example, those that apply to only certain types of flows-can be evaded by changing the composition of flows. While such controls would be ineffective in preserving monetary autonomy (or limiting the total magnitude of flows), they may, however, still be able to alter the composition of flows.

(v) ***The Structure of the Domestic Financial System.*** This may determine the effectiveness of partial controls that leave room for evasion by channeling flows through alternative domestic intermediaries.

(vi) ***The Size of Trade Flows.*** This would determine the scope for under-and overinvolving, as well as for altering leads and for lags on trade credit.

(vii) ***The Type of Cross-border Flows Targeted by the Controls***—that is, controls on capital outflows may differ in effectiveness from controls on inflows, all other things (that is, potential arbitrage margins) being equal. One argument is that the residence of the capital-importing or -exporting agent may matter. Domestic residents may be more prepared than foreign agents to evade restrictions, making controls on outflows less effective than controls on inflows.

Some analysts have argued that controls of any type can be effective under any arbitrary set of circumstances, while others have argued that controls of any type can never be effective. Neither argument is valid. This means, in particular, that the size of capital flows in the presence of controls is not a reliable indicator of the effectiveness of controls, since large flows may simply indicate large arbitrage opportunities.

Are Capital Controls Desirable?

Even if capital controls can be effective, that does not mean they should be used. Since effective controls distort private economic decisions, the benefits of imposing them should outweigh the costs. Arguments for restricting capital movements as a way to control volatility and achieve macroeconomic stabilisation under a high degree of financial integration are:

"Incredible" Reforms. The first argument is that controls may be effective in coping with distortions that arise when the government implements an incredible stabilisation or trade liberalisation (one that observers do not believe it can carry out. Lack of confidence in the government's ability to sustain its announced exchange rate or tariff policies may make external borrowing appear temporarily cheap, with potentially destabilising effects on the domestic economy. The best solution to this problem is for the government to take steps to achieve credibility-most commonly, by getting its fiscal accounts into order-since fiscal problems are often the cause of policy reversal.

Insulation from Shocks Arising in the International Financial Market. The second argument for capital controls on both inflows and out- flows is that they can insulate the domestic economy from identifiable external financial shocks-that is, they can limit the incidence of volatility by preserving some degree of financial autarky. Since controls directly address the source of the shock, they may, it is argued, succeed in stabilising the economy without introducing new distortions. This argument for quantitative controls however, is less persuasive than the first. From the country perspective, fluctuations in world interest rates are just an intertemporal dimension of what terms of trade fluctuations are intra temporally.

Preservation of Short-rule Monetary Autonomy. Under perfect capital mobility, the effectiveness of monetary policy can be preserved only if exchange rate policy is flexible. In this case, however, unpleasant tradeoffs may arise between internal (inflation) and external (current account) balance targets. Tight monetary policy adopted to combat inflation, for example, would increase the domestic real interest rate while causing the real exchange rate to appreciate, possibly resulting in a deterioration of the trade balance. Capital controls would enable the monetary authorities to avoid this tradeoff between targets by making it possible to preserve monetary autonomy with an officially determined exchange rate. Thus controls would, in effect, provide a second independent macroeconomic instrument either monetary policy or the exchange rate-to simultaneously address the two targets of inflation and the external balance of payments. The benefits for macroeconomic management are large, however, only if other stabilisation instruments are not available.

Changing the Composition of Inflows. Finally, there is the argument that controls can be used to alter the composition of capital inflows. Even if controls can be used for this purpose, whether or not they should be depends on whether the composition of inflows matters. Unfortunately, there is currently no consensus on this issue.

A separate argument for being concerned with the composition of flows is that certain types of inflows maybe driven by implicit government guarantees (for example, external borrowing by domestic financial institutions) and thus may not be welfare enhancing. But even if such flows could be discouraged by capital controls, it is not clear that the same implicit guarantees do not also apply to other types of flows (such as direct lending to domestic firms) through less direct means. If they do, then the case for altering the composition of flows would have to rely on the differential welfare effects of direct government guarantees extended to financial institutions for different types of flows. This case seems plausible a period.

Although many developing countries that maintained controls during the initial period of financial integration seem to have preserved a meaningful degree of monetary autonomy, the effectiveness of controls is likely to decrease as these countries become more integrated. As condition change in these countries, the evidence from industrial countries may become more relevant for them, and controls will be able to preserve a degree of monetary autonomy for only a limited period of time. In addition, controls have not been able to prevent large capital outflows and inflows in response to large prospective arbitrage profits. Finally, the controls can be effective in altering the composition of flows.

Exchange Rate Policy

Different exchange rate systems can be and have been used by countries while becoming integrated with the rest of the world—in particular, pure floating; managed, or dirty, floating; fixed exchange rate; or a currency (or quasi-currency) board. Each system has consequences for the effectiveness of monetary and fiscal policy. Thus, while in a pure floating system fiscal policy is less effective and monetary policy more effective, in a fixed exchange rate system the opposite results. Therefore, the advantages or disadvantages of each system vary from country to country depending on the nature-nominal versus real—of the shocks affecting each country and the ability of the authorities to have a flexible fiscal policy. Countries in which fiscal policy cannot be modified effectively in the short run should not relinquish monetary policy completely by adopting a fixed exchange rate system.

In the recent years, an increasing number of economies have adopted" flexibly managed" exchange rate systems, which give them the option of effectively using monetary policy art the cost of eroding their credibility regarding inflation targets. The few exceptions have been economies where the credibility of the government was extremely low—Hong Kong during the 1980s and Argentina and Estonia during the 1990s-all of whom adopted currency boards because of the need to regain market confidence. The major difficulty facing these economies, however, is to maintain a flexible enough fiscal policy and build cushion—such as a large stock of international reserves—to improve the resilience of the economy to shocks.

In the aftermath of the Mexican crisis, many thought that the days of managed exchange rate systems were over. However, most countries were able to go through the Mexican crisis without modifying their exchange rate systems. The evidence to date shows that international capital markets have been selective since the Mexican episode and that fundamentals matter. Thus, there are indications that officially determined exchange rates can be managed successfully within a consistent macroeconomic policy framework.

Since managing the exchange rate indeed seems to be the preference of most developing countries, the issue of how to manage the rate in a financially integrated world become an important one. One way to approach this problem is to consider the exchange rate regime as consisting of a band around a moving central parity. The decisions that need to be made then consist of how to adjust the parity, how wide to make the band, and how to intervene within the band. The objective of central parity should be to maintain the competitiveness. This means adjusting the parity not only in accordance with the domestic foreign inflation differential but also in accordance with changes in underlying equilibrium real exchange rates, which are given by permanent changes in fundamental factors such as terms of trade, commercial policy, fiscal policy, and condition in external financial market. Since the central parity seeks to track the long-run equilibrium real exchange rate, the desirable width of the band depends on the value to the domestic economy of an independent domestic monetary policy. The larger the scope for the exchange rate to deviate from its central parity—that is, the wider the band-the greater the scope for an independent domestic monetary policy. In turn, the usefulness of an independent monetary policy for reducing volatility depends on the availability of alternative stabilisation instruments (a flexible fiscal policy) and on the sources of shocks to the economy. The traditional analysis of this issue focuses on the implications of shocks in the domestic money (nominal) and goods (real) markets, the standard prescription being that, holding fiscal policy constant, domestic real shocks call for exchange rate flexibility, while domestic nominal shocks call for fixed exchange rates. This suggests that if fiscal policy is not available (or is costly to use) as Clastabilisation instrument, countries in which domestic real shocks predominate should adopt fairly wide bands, while those in which domestic nominal shocks are dominant should keep the exchange rate close to its central parity. With a flexible fiscal policy, however, domestic real shocks can be countered through fiscal adjustments, thereby diminishing the value of independent monetary policy as a stabilisation instrument Thus the adoption of a fairly narrow band is more likely to be consistent with the stabilisation objective if fiscal policy is available as a stabilisation instrument.

Regarding intervention within the band, the logic of this analysis suggests that for a given band width, active intervention should accompany nominal shocks, whereas real shocks instead call for some combination of exchange rate and fiscal adjustment. Consider, however, an alternative source of shock-that is, "pure" external financial shocks, say in the form of fluctuations in world interest rates. In this case, exchange market intervention policy determines the form in which the shock is transmitted to the domestic economy. If world interest rates fall, for example, and active (unsterilised) intervention keeps the exchange rate fixed at its central parity, domestic monetary expansion and lower domestic interest rates will ensure-an expansionary shock. If, on the other hand, the central bank refrains form intervention, the domestic currency will appreciate in real terms and the domestic real interest rate will rise—a contractionary shock. Purely from the perspective of stabilising domestic aggregate demand, the appropriate intervention policy within the band in this case depends on the direction in which it is feasible or desirable to move fiscal policy. If fiscal policy is literally inflexible, then the choice confronting monetary authorities is between real appreciation (tinder no intervention) or overheating (under full unsterilised intervention). To avoid both overheating and real appreciation requires a mix of fiscal contraction and intervention to keep the nominal exchange rate close to its central parity.

Though crawling pegs remain a viable exchange rate option for developing countries that become integrated into world capital markets. However, this reduces the scope for deviating from fundamentals, as well as form commitment to the announced regime. Managed rates are certainly capable of generating macroeconomic volatility in this environment, but they have not generally done so.

The following conclusions can be drawn with regard to exchange rate management:

(i) The central parity should be managed so as to track, to the extent possible, the underlying long-run equilibrium real exchange rate. This means not just offsetting inflation differentials but also adjusting the real exchange rate target to reflect permanent changes in fundamentals. Large and persistent temporary misalignments should be avoided, primarily because they threaten the sustainability of the regime and make speculative attacks more likely.

(ii) Small temporary deviations from the central parity can play a useful stabilising role when fiscal policy is inflexible and either real domestic shocks dominate or exchange rate flexibility is required to ensure that external shocks affect domestic demand in the right direction.

(iii) In general, fiscal flexibility can substitute for exchange rate flexibility as a stabilising device.

Monetary Policy

Fixing an exchange rate target in the face of capital movements implies central bank intervention in the foreign exchange market, which has the effect of altering the stock of base money. Sterilised intervention is the indicated policy for a government attempting to simultaneously run an independent monetary policy (targeting either some monetary aggregate or some domestic interest rate) and fix the nominal exchange rate. However, if capital mobility is high, such an attempt may not be successful in the absence of capital controls.

The purpose of sterilised (as opposed to unsterilised) intervention is to prevent a change in the demand for domestic interest-bearing assets from causing too large a change in the price of those assets, essentially by meeting the demand shift with a supply response. Thus, sterilisation in response to capital inflows involves an increase in the supply of domestic debt in one form or another. As in the case of capital controls, the general issues that arise in this context are not only whether sterilised intervention can work to stabilise domestic aggregate demand but also, if it can, whether it is desirable. Even if sterilisation remains possible for financially integrating developing countries, its effectiveness in insulating domestic demand from external financial shocks is questionable. Sterilisation is most effective where domestic interest-bearing assets are close substitutes among themselves but are poor substitutes for foreign interest-bearing assets. Under these circumstances, sterilised intervention can insulate domestic aggregate demand from transitory portfolio shocks. However, the conditions necessary for sterilised intervention to be effective imply that its effectiveness may depend on how it is attempted. Because bank borrowers may not have access to securities markets, for example, sterilising by raising reserve requirements on banks is likely to be less effective in insulating the domestic economy from portfolio disturbances than is sterilising through open market bond sales.

If sterilisation is possible, when is it beneficial? The answer is that sterilisation is beneficial whenever the prices of domestic assets need to be insulated from shocks; that is, whenever the economy experiences transitory shocks to portfolio preferences-domestic nominal shocks or external financial shocks—or when the authorities seek to accommodate a permanent change in portfolio preferences in a gradual fashion. When this happens, domestic aggregate demand can be stabilised by preventing changes in portfolio preferences from being transmitted to the real sector through changes in exchange rates and asset prices. On the other hand, domestic real shocks do not call for sterilised intervention, since in this case the asset price adjustments triggered by the shock are likely to prove stabilising.

The point for policymakers is that sterilised intervention may be indicated when an economy experiences shocks to portfolio preferences. Even when it is desirable for stabilisation purposes, however, sterilisation may carry a fiscal cost, particularly for governments whose claimed intentions not to devalue or default on debt are not fully credible, resulting in high domestic interest rates. Thus, the use of this tool without impairing the government's solvency requires fiscal flexibility. Countries that lack such flexibility may be tempted to sterilise through changes in reserve requirements, despite the likelihood that the use of this tool will result in imperfect insulation, because the fiscal implications of doing so are less adverse than those of open market operations. This advantage, however, is at the cost of implicit taxation of banks and their customers.

Fiscal Policy

From the standpoint of reducing volatility, the key characteristics of fiscal policy are short-run flexibility, the perceived solvency of the public sector, and its vulnerability to liquidity crises.

Short-run Fiscal Flexibility Plays an Important Role in Neutralising Shocks

The importance of short-run fiscal flexibility can be observed from the reference case of a pure external financial shock for a country with well-integrated financial markets. In this case, sterilised intervention is not an option, and thus the country has only one independent monetary policy instrument. Faced with an external financial shock, the domestic monetary authorities can choose a value for either the exchange rate or the domestic money supply (and thus the domestic interest rate), but not for both. Therefore, when both the level and the composition of aggregate demand are important, the authorities will find themselves one instrument short and may face an unpleasant choice between, say, stabilising domestic demand and safeguarding the competitiveness of exports. This tradeoff suggests an important role for short-run fiscal flexibility. If fiscal policy can be counted upon to sustain the level of aggregate demand at its pre-shock value (by adopting a more or less expansionary stance as needed), then the choice of monetary response can be based on the desired composition of aggregate demand. In the absence of short-run fiscal flexibility, however, the nature of the monetary response may depend on tradeoffs between the level and composition of demand.

How can Fiscal Flexibility be Achieved? There are at least two important constraints tending to limit the flexibility of fiscal policy. The first concerns inflexibility of fiscal instruments arising from inefficient tax systems that associate large excess burdens with policy-induced changes in tax revenues, as well as from political imperatives that tend to drive up the level of public expenditures. Structural measures that remove rigidities on either the expenditure or revenue side of the government's budget-such as privatisation of state enterprises and tax reform designed to widen the tax base and remove egregious distortions in marginal tax rates, as well as to improve the efficiency of tax administration—can thus make an important contribution to enhancing fiscal flexibility. The second restriction on fiscal flexibility arises from the behaviour of creditors. If fiscal profligacy during good times causes creditors to question fiscal solvency during bad times, then countercyclical fiscal measures will be ruled out by an inability to finance deficits during downturns. The upshot is that overly expansionary fiscal policy in response to positive shocks is likely to make fiscal policy procyclical in both directions by constraining fiscal flexibility when the economy is hit by adverse shocks. Thus a key step in achieving symmetric fiscal flexibility is the implementation of mechanisms that permit the fiscal authorities to restrain spending when times appear to be good.

Beyond the role of short-run stabilisation in response to external financial shocks, fiscal policy plays a more fundamental role in the context of increased financial integration, when both the direction and the magnitude of capital flows are likely to become very sensitive to perceptions of domestic public sector solvency. Potential insolvency can generate large capital outflows and large interest rate premiums, as creditors try to avoid taxation of domestic assets while demanding compensation for exposing themselves to the risk of taxation they face by continuing to lend in the domestic economy. This situation is aggravated when the government makes explicit guarantees to creditors, however, since the value of the guarantees will fluctuate with the government's perceived financial ability to back them. The key point is that in the context of high financial integration, the stock dimension of fiscal policy, in the form of changes in the government's perceived net worth, may itself represent an important source of shocks to the domestic, economy, transmitted through the terms on which both domestic and foreign creditors are willing to hold claims on the domestic economy.

The stock and flow dimensions of fiscal policy are not independent. A critical link between them is created by the fact that what matters for creditors is the perceived solvency of the public sector. For a government whose long-run fiscal stance is uncertain, short-run policy changes will be scrutinised for information about the government's longer-run intentions. Knowing this, governments may be reluctant to act in ways may be perceived as sending the wrong signal to creditors, and this reluctance may limit the government's abort-run policy flexibility. Thus, achieving a reputation for fiscal responsibility may maximise the government's short-run policy flexibility.

FINANCIAL INTEGRATION AND INTERNATIONAL BANKING SYSTEM

The Banking System plays a leading role in the process of financial integration and is one of the main channels through which the benefits of integration materialise. This is so because banks dominate financial intermediation in developing countries and therefore they end up directly or indirectly intermediating a large proportion of private flows. Since an increasing share of private flows is being used by the private—as opposed to the public-sector in recipient countries, banks are increasingly responsible for its allocation. In addition, in the medium and long term, banks in developing countries can benefits from financial integration by adopting more advanced financial technologies, achieving greater diversification in their portfolios, having access to a larger supply of funds, and realising efficiency gains derived from economies scale and scope and a higher degree of market competition.

However, the transition toward greater financial integration also involves risks for the economy in general and the banking sector in particular. During the process of financial integration banks will be adversely affected by increased macroeconomic volatility and by structural changes in banking. The main structural changes affecting the banking sector that result from integration are an increase in competition, which can erode banks worth, and exposure to new sources of risk that banks may not be prepared to manage properly. Because conditions can change more swiftly and markets can react faster and with increased amounts of funds, the room for maneuver available to policy-makers is significantly reduced in an integrated environment. The weaker the initial conditions in the banking sector-and in the macroeconomy—are in integrating economies, the greater the challenge for policymakers. One of these challenges arises because during integration banks are given easier access to funds and are therefore able to expand lending much more quickly, so they can finance a longer-lasting boom in expenditures and asset prices. If initial conditions in the banking sector are weak, banks are likely to extend credit in excess and to more risky sectors.

The process of financial integration is usually accompanied in its early stages by a surge in private flows that may increase bank lending and exacerbate macroeconomic and financial sector vulnerability. The surge in private inflows is partly due to improved economic prospects in the recipient country, which, in turn, will increase economic agents expectations. The inflows also often finance a rapid expansion in bank lending and aggregate expenditures, accelerating economic growth and validating agents' expectations, and cause an increase in asset prices. These effects can reinforce one another, leading to additional borrowing, higher expectations and output growth, and increased levels of expenditures and asset prices. In developing countries with weak infrastructure and regulatory institutions in banking—a common condition in many emerging economies—the surge in bank lending and the rise in asset prices will be associated with a deterioration in banks' portfolios. Poorly managed and supervised banks will tend to invest in highly profitable although risky activities. For example, poorly regulated banks may finance consumption booms and speculative activities, such as a boom in construction and real estate, that increase macroeconomic vulnerability. Also, because of poorly diversified portfolios and lack of adequate provisioning, the surge in bank lending usually exacerbates financial sector vulnerable abilities. This Chain of events is potentially costly not only because of resource misallocation but also because in the extreme it can lead to financial distress and crisis.

An integrating economy is more likely than an autarkic one to experience a boom-bust cycle in bank lending, and the potential cost associated with such a course is higher. This is so because, in an integrated environment banks can expand lending more quickly and in larger amounts, circumstances can change more swiftly, and markets react faster. All these factors can lead to swift changes in market sentiment and cause large reversals of flows, creating significant macroeconomic and financial sector distress and carrying high economic and social costs. In addition to the direct costs of bailing out failed banks, the sudden loss of liquidity in the banking sector, which is more difficult to contain in an integrated environment, can amplify economic downturns. Such distress can set back economic reforms severely. An important challenge, therefore, is for a country to maintain or improve the health of the banking system.

Bank Lending and Macroeconomic Vulnerability

Financial intermediaries play a crucial role in the process of economic development and growth by channeling savers money to more productive uses in an economy; they do this by screening and selecting investment projects and transforming assets, usually from short-term deposits to long-term investments, but more generally from illiquid to liquid assets. The fact that banks overcome informational problems between lenders and borrowers and facilitate the creation of liquidity makes them vulnerable to confidence crises and, therefore, susceptible to runs and liquidity crises.

Thus, the banking sector amplifies the magnitude of the business cycle because bank credit behaves pro cyclically. For example, a positive development in the real sector that raises expectations about the future will increase firms' willingness to invest, induce them to borrow more, and cause an expansion in bank credit. This process, if accommodated by the monetary authorities, will lead to a lending boom, which, in turn, will enable market participants to increase their level of expenditure and will accelerate economic growth. The increase in economic growth reinforces the expansion of lending and spending by validating economic agents' expectations about the future. The state of euphoria triggered by the initial increase in spending also leads to an increase in asset prices and financial wealth, which raises the value of loan collateral, increase households' aggregate consumption, and further reinforces the process. At the same time, however, the economy as a whole becomes more vulnerable because of the increase in indebtedness of firms and households and the risk of a collapse in asset prices. A plunge in asset prices would reduce borrowers' financial wealth and thereby affect the financial health of banks. A shock that reduces economic growth, or that leads agents to believe that the current conditions are no longer sustainable, will induce agents to cut their spending on consumption and investment and thereby will slow economic growth. Firms and households will then have difficulty servicing their debts, banks will start calling loans back in and liquidating the assets used as collateral, and asset prices will plunge, all of which will depend the slowdown in economic activity. Because the banking system is vulnerable to confidence crises, this sequence of events may lead to a bank run, further reducing total credit and liquidity and aggravating the slowdown in economic activity.

In addition to amplifying the magnitude of the business cycle, a poorly regulated and supervised banking industry will tend to misallocate resources, increasing the economic cost of the boom-bust cycle in bank lending. Poorly capitalised and regulated banks may, for instance, invest excessively in risky projects, such as real estate, or in other sectors prone to suffer boom-bust cycles. Also, poorly managed banks operating under distorted incentives will not diversify their portfolios adequately, thus exacerbating financial sector vulnerability. These banks will suffer greater losses during the contradictionary phase of the cycle. The weaker initial conditions in the banking sector are, the move vulnerable countries will be large downturns and costly banking crises.

In an integrated environment these effects can become even more pronounced. This is so for several reasons. First, integration gives banks access to a larger supply of funds to intermediate, either directly or indirectly, which allows them to increase credit rapidly. Second, financial integration usually occurs with the implementation of economic reforms-in the financial sector, the real economy (trade, fiscal), or both-that improve the country's economic prospects and raise agents' expectations. Third, integration increase the sources of risk and the speed of market reaction.

The first two reasons above, the implementation of economic reforms and the easier access to funds, create the necessary conditions for a lending boom to start. In particular, the surge in private flows that usually accompanies financial integration provides the additional resources needed to finance an increase in aggregate demand and output, validating agents' expectations. Given the size of the capital inflows for the average recipient country observed in recent years, the potential for experiencing a large increase in asset prices and a lending boom-one lasting several years—is faster in an integrated environment.

The third reason above, the increased sources of risk and speed of market reaction, makes it more likely that a banking industry operating under suboptimal conditions—a common occurrence among developing countries—will misallocate resources, exacerbating the country's macroeconomic and financial sector vulnerabilities. In particular, if an increasing amount of funds flowing into a country is intermediated by an undercapitalised and poorly regulated banking sector, one that is too prone to risk taking, the economy is likely to end up investing either insufficiently or in risky projects. The could be the case if the banking sector finances a consumption and imports boom, which in turn will make the economy more vulnerable to shocks. Because of the additional sources of risks and faster market response, the likelihood and the cost of a banking crisis increase with integration.

Bank Lending and Financial Sector Vulnerability

The surge in private capital flows that accompanies financial integration in developing countries usually leads to an increase in monetisation and to banks intermediating a larger volume of funds, The increased financial intermediation, especially when it occurs over a short period of time, not only can exacerbate macroeconomic vulnerability, but may also exacerbate microeconomic problems, especially when the banking system suffers from initial distortions and weaknesses.

Lending Booms and Banking Sector Vulnerabilities

A fast-growing banking industry will become more vulnerable if it is amenable to evaluate the risks of increased lending (because of lack of regincd personnel), and if its greater risk exposure is not accompanied by an improved ability to absorb negative economic shocks. Two common indicators of banks' ability to absorb shocks are their capitalisation rates, measured as the stock of capital relative to the stock of bank assets, and their level of provisioning, measured as the provisions made for future losses as a share of the stock of total loans. An increase in provisions against future losses reduces the probability that banks could go under if borrowers default on their loans. An increase in the capital-assets ratio reduces the likelihood that banks could default on their own borrowing if investment projects turn out to be unsuccessful. (In addition, because shareholders' potential losses increase with the size of capital-asset ratios, well-capitalised banks are usually better monitored by their shareholders and therefore hold safer portfolios than do poorly capitalised banks.) Two other indicators, related to banks' ability to withstand short-term shocks, are the liquidity of their assets and relative maturity of their assets compared with their liabilities. A lower degree of asset liquidity and a shorter maturity of liabilities. A lower degree of asset liquidity and a shorter maturity of liabilities relative to asserts make banks more vulnerable to liquidity crisis.

A booming banking industry is likely to appear profitable and strong. While increased profitability may indicate improved operating conditions, however, in many instances it may simply be a consequence of the fact-that banks are investing in riskier projects. A fast-growing banking industry has the opportunity to prevent to limit increased financial vulnerability if banks use these additional profits to increase their capitalist on rates and provision against future losses.

The Costs of Banking Crises

Policymakers must be concerned about banking crises because these crises are costly in terms of lower economic growth, and the political consequences of allocating loses among bank stockholders, creditors, depositors, and taxpayers can be significant. It is important to note, however, that the direct economic cost of a banking crisis derives from the decrease in economic activity and growth that results from a reduction in the total volume—or a more inefficient intermediation-of loanable funds, while the allocation of losses has primarily distribution effects (usually very important) but on its own does not imply an economic (dead weight) loss. Nevertheless, the allocation of losses is important because it changes the incentives of the different groups of economic agents and, through this, can lead to lower investment and growth. For example, forcing the corporate sector to repay its past-due loans, although it may be fair practice (depending on the primary cause of the sector's financial difficulties), may be counter productive for the purpose of facilitating the economic recovery. If the ultimate cause of the banking crisis is the implementation of "wrong" economic policies by the authorities, then it can be argued that the corporate sector is not fully responsible for defaulting on its debt. Indeed, in the presence of a debt overhang problem entrepreneurs may decide not to start new—or to discontinue old-investment projects, because from a private point of view it may not be worth investing in projects whose profits will benefit the firm's creditors (banks). Similarly, allowing banks to recover their losses by increasing spreads—thereby taxing depositors and debtors in good standing—will reduce the volume of funds intermediated through the banking system and may lead to lower investment and growth.

Quantifying the economic losses associated with a banking crisis is a cumbersome task, mainly because it is not clear how to separate the decrease in economic activity due to the banking crisis *per se* from that which is due to other exogenous factors (such as a terms of trade shock). In fact, a banking crisis may result a decrease in economic activity caused .by other factors, with the banking sector playing a key role in amplifying the effect of the exogenous shock on aggregate output.

International Banking Developments: Recent Trends

Extending a trend evident since mid-2002, and reflecting subdued economic growth, banks in many developed countries shifted their consolidated loan portfolios away from non-bank private sector borrowers. In addition, many banking systems continued to reduce claims on borrowers in the lower-rated developing countries, as evidenced by gradual improvements in the average credit ratings of their consolidated emerging market portfolios. Overall, emerging markets saw an inflow of funds driven by robust lending to banks, although regional differences remained apparent. The net outflow from Latin America continued, reflecting deposit movements and contractions in claims on non-banks in Mexico, Brazil and Argentina. This was more than offset by net inflows to the Asia-Pacific region, mainly the result of increased claims on the Chinese banking sector. Countries in emerging Europe, particularly those in accession negotiations with the European Union were again recipients of additional bank lending.

❐

19

Globalisation and Investment

Economic development remains an urgent global need. Globalisation which links countries closer than ever before with each other reinforces this need. Although many countries have achieved impressive increases in income, over a billion people in more than a hundred countries still live in poverty. Economic inequalities within countries remain large, and there is little sign of convergence in incomes across countries. In fact, a number of developing countries face increasing marginalisation.

Globalisation accentuates the increasing importance of the international economy for developing countries. Flows of finance, information, skills, technology, goods and services between countries are increasing rapidly. FDI is one of the most dynamic of the increasing international resource flows to developing countries. FDI flows are particularly important because FDI is a package of tangible and intangible assets, and because the firms TNCs deploying them are now important players in the global economy. TNCs can affect development, by complementing domestic investment and by undertaking trade and transfers of knowledge, skills and technology. However, TNCs do not substitute for domestic effort: they can only provide access to tangible and intangible assets and catalysedoinestic investment and capabilities. In a world of intensifying competition and accelerating technological change, this complementary and catalytic role can be very valuable. Since globalisation has Its dangers, countries need to prepare their own capabilities to harness its potential, including through FDI. However, FDl on its own cannot counteract the marginalisation of developing countries.

For developing countries the key issue is whether investment is defined narrowly, focusing on FDI, or broadly, including virtually every asset connected with foreign investors. Developing countries have indicated a preference for a narrow definition in the discussions of the WTO Working Group on the Relationship between Trade and Investment, but the trend in international investment agreements (HAs) has been towards a broad asset-based definition. Even a broad definition can be narrowed, for example, through reservations, affording countries the right to exclude certain types of investment (such as portfolio investment) or by limiting the applicability of specific operational provisions. Another approach is to give each government the choice, when negotiating an HA, to commit to either a narrow or a broad definition.

DEFINITION OF INVESTMENT

Why the Definition of Investment Matters?

The definition of investment on its own has no direct impact on attracting FDI or benefiting more from it. But defining a certain capital flow or asset as "investment" bestows certain rights on foreign investors and thus facilitates foreign investment. The definition also raises concerns. Obligations to meet financial transfer requirements could for many developing countries at times be difficult to fulfil. Possible complications could arise for macroeconomic management of capital flows of a type and magnitude that may be beyond the control of national governments.

Thus, the definition of investment is fundamental to national laws and international agreements pertaining to FDI, since it delineates which assets or investment flows are covered by the operational provisions of those laws and HAs, for example, as they relate to national treatment. The main question is not whether FDI should be defined as investment—it is. The question is what other investment should be granted the same status: portfolio investment (both equity and debt components), other capital flows (bank loans, non-bank loans and other flows) and various investment assets (both tangible and intangible, including intellectual property rights).

"Investment" does not have a generally accepted meaning. The internationally accepted method for classifying and recording cross border foreign investment flows for balance-of-payments statistics divides them into direct investment, portfolio investment, financial derivatives and other investment Nation allows and IIAs also provide definitions of "investment" and "foreign investment", which often differ considerably from the balance-of-payments definition. They can include, in addition to some types of cross-border investment flows, a wide variety of assets, both tangible and intangible. Indeed, the definitions utilized in these laws and agreements vary considerably. Note that the legal interpretation of investment cannot be predicted with certainty in the course of the settlement of disputes.

Different types of capital flows have different implications for a host economy: some are long-term flows not normally prone to quick reversal or to speculative movements, and some are highly liquid flows that can easily be reversed. The policy implications of fully liberalizing highly liquid flows may be far reaching. Indeed, the degree of capital account liberalization that may be required of signatories to a given HA is important for some developing countries.

Developed countries, with relatively well-developed financial markets and regulatory frameworks, relatively stable "macroeconomic conditions and convertible currencies, have moved to full liberalization of their capital accounts, covering all forms of capital flows and other types of investment. In negotiations with developing countries, they often seek a broad definition of investment to protect assets generated by investment and to promote liberalization. Private investors also prefer a broader definition, not necessarily because they wish to hedge or speculate but because they want more, security.

But many governments of host developing countries, at least in multilateral discussions, are wary. They wish to retain policy tools to deal with different types of flows in different ways rather than define them all as investment in a way that constrains their use. Because portfolio investment instruments and derivatives can be used for speculative purposes that destabilize foreign exchange markets or domestic financial markets, a government may prefer to exclude them from the definition. This allows government flexibility to implement policies to maintain financial stability-hence many developing countries prefer to confine the definition of "investment" to long-term flows and exclude potentially volatile capital flows.

The inclusion of non-FDI forms of investment is thus a difficult matter for many countries. Some of these difficulties can be addressed through special provisions, exceptions and safeguards. But the broader the definition, the more complicated it is to do so. Safeguards for traditional balance-of-payments crises, speculative attacks and contagion from crises abroad are important here.

In conceptual terms, FDI and foreign portfolio investment are distinct. Direct investment involves both a long-term interest in, and significant management influence over, a foreign affiliate. Portfolio investment may include a long-term interest, but it seldom involves managerial control. For statistical purposes, a threshold of 10% of share ownership has been established to differentiate equity holdings of direct and portfolio investors.. But in practice, the line between different types of investment is sometimes difficult to draw. In some circumstances, foreign investors may use their assets as collateral to borrow from local capital markets and use the proceeds for hedging or speculation.

Scope of Definitions

The general trend towards a broad definition of investment is not universal, and there are significant differences by level of development. A number of developed countries do not have specific legislation or policies on FDI and so do not need to define it. Developing countries, concerned about the effects of volatile capital flows, have narrow definitions (in practice if not in the legal terminology). The financial rises of the 1990s strengthened the case for adopting definitions with great care.

The definition can magnify or reduce the scope of an IIA. But because it is exercised through the substantive provisions of an IIA, it cannot be considered in isolation. IIs have used-three types of definitions of investment: asset-based, transaction based or enterprise-based:

(i) *Asset-based definitions* are the most common in investment protection agreements. They tend to be broad-including assets and capital flows, movable and immovable property, interests in companies, claims to money, intellectual property rights and concessions. They can, however, be deliberately limited. Governments have, for instance, limited the coverage to investment made in accordance with the laws of the host country or on the basis of previous administrative approval. They have also excluded investment made before the conclusion of the IIA, as well as types of investment, such as portfolio investment.

(ii) *Transaction-based definitions* protect not assets but the financial flows through which foreign investors create or acquire domestic assets. For example, the OECD Code of Liberalisation of Capital Movements does not define investment, but it has a list of capital transactions between residents and non-residents that are subject to liberalization commitments, including inward and outward investment.

(iii) *Enterprise-based definitions* confine liberalization and protection to the enterprises established by foreign investors in a host country. Used in the Canada-United States Free Trade Agreement of 1988, for example, this definition appears to be narrower than an asset-based definition, which includes assets other than companies and capital flows.

The way IIAs deal with the definition of investment depends primarily on the scope md purpose of each instrument. Some IIAs aim at the liberalization of investment 'egimes-and some at protecting investment. In reality the distinction is not always clear-cut. For example, bilateral investment treaties (BITs) generally aim at investment protection, but they may also have a liberalizing effect-say, through their national treatment provision.

IIAs aimed at investment protection, which include BITs but also some regional agreements, tend to use a broad, open-ended, asset-based definition "covering virtually all proprietary rights located in the host State which have a financial asset value" (although it may be qualified, for example, by excluding certain types of investment). The trend has been in this direction.

In particular, most BITs use such an approach. The ASEAN Agreement for the Protection and Promotion of Investments, a regional investment protection treaty (like a BIT in aim and function), has a broad definition covering "every kind of asset".

Other regional agreements have followed a different approach, depending on the purpose of the investment provisions. Some aimed at the liberalization of investment regimes have used a relatively narrow definition. For example, the 1998 Framework Agreement on the ASEAN Investment Area explicitly excludes portfolio investment, as does the 2000 free trade agreement between the Suropean Free Trade Association members and Mexico.

National FDI Policy Framework

National policies are key for attracting FDI, increasing benefits from it and assuaging the concerns about it. Those policies have to be seen in the broader context of the determinants of FDI, among which economic factors predominate. Policies are decisive in preventing FDI from entering a country. But once an enabling FDI regulatory framework is in place, the economic factors become dominant. Even then, the regulatory regime can make a location more or less attractive for foreign investors and for maximizing the positive development effects of FDI, while minimizing negative ones.

Countries seek FDI to protonate their growth and development. With its package of tangible and intangible assets, FDI can contribute directly and indirectly to building national capabilities. The growing appreciation of the benefits of FDI reflects several factors. Concessional aid is declining, and various financial crises have created a preference for long-term and more stable capital inflows. Access to innovative technologies is more important. And some of the earlier fears about FDI may have been exaggerated, given the economic benefits that many developing countries have drawn from FDI. Many governments are now more confident in dealing with TNCs.

The best way of attracting and drawing benefits from FDI is not always passive liberalization (an "open door" policy). Liberalization can help get more FDI, but alone it is not enough. Attracting FDI in a highly competitive market for investment now requires stronger locational advantages and more focused efforts at promotion. Getting FDI in technologically advanced or export-oriented activities is even more demanding.

Having attracted foreign investors into a country, policies are crucial to ensure that FDI brings more benefits. Policies can induce faster upgrading of technologies and skills, raise local procurement, secure more reinvestment of profits, protect the environment and consumers and so on. They can also help counter the potential dangers of FDI—say, by containing anticompetitive practices and preventing foreign affiliates from crowding out viable local firms or acting in ways that upset local sensitivities.

Free markets do not always ensure efficient and equitable outcomes particularly in developing countries with weak markets and institutions. Hence, the need for policy intervention. The groundwork for making markets work well-sound legal systems, clear .and enforceable rules of the game, responsive market institutions, a vibrant domestic enterprise sector and the like-has to be laid down by the host country government. But even then, the strategic objectives ofTNCs may not match the development goals of host governments. Policies need to bring them more in line with those goals.

Developed countries have moved towards "market-friendly" policies-pursuing sound macro management; having stable and non-discriminatory rules on business entry and exit, promoting competition, building human capital, supporting innovation and so on. But even the most market-friendly countries have not given up promotional measures to attract foreign investors. Several use sophisticated promotion techniques as well as large grants and subsidies to target particularly valuable investments.

Developing countries are also trying to attract FDI and increase the benefits from it. And they, too, are moving towards market-friendly policies. But they have to be careful doing so, since their market structures are weaker and their development needs more pressing. That is why they are more concerned about preserving their national policy space for investment, to be able to use the policy instruments that can address their special needs.

The discussion here focuses on three objectives-attracting FDI, benefiting more from it and addressing concerns about TNCs. Some objectives and measures overlap, but they are considered separately for convenience.

Benefiting More From FDI

Attracting FDI may not be enough to ensure that a host country derives its full economic benefits. Free markets may not lead foreign investors to transifer enough new technology or to transfer it effectively and at the depth desired by a host country. But policies can induce investors to act in ways that enhance the development impact-by building local capabilities, using local suppliers and upgrading local skills, technological capabilities and infrastructure. The main policies and measures used for this include:

(i) *Increasing the contribution of foreign affiliates to a host country through mandatory measures.* The objective is to prescribe what foreign affiliates should do to raise exports, train local workers or transfer technology. The key issue here relates to the use of performance requirements.

(ii) *Increasing the contribution of foreign affiliates to a host country by encouraging them to act in a desired way.* The key issue here, as in attracting FDI, is using incentives to influence the behaviour foreign affiliates. (Incentives may be tied to performance requirements). Particularly important there is enticing foreign affiliates to transfer technology to domestic firms and to create local R&O capacity.

Countries are learning that foreign affiliate activity can be influenced to enhance host country benefits only if they strengthen their capabilities. New technologies can be diffused in a host economy only if the skill base is adequate or if domestic suppliers and competitors can meet TNC needs and learn from them. Export activity can grow only if the quality of infrastructure so permits. Governments need to mount policies to build domestic capabilities, drawing on foreign affiliates and their parent firms in this effort. And again home countries can help in various ways through measures of their own. Indeed, even TNCs can try to increase the benefits to host economies.

Addressing Concerns About TNCs

Despite the general shift of attitudes in favour of FDI, significant concerns remain about potential negative effects. Some major areas of concern are: anticompetitive practices by foreign affiliate; volatile flows of investment and related payments deleterious for the balance of payments; tax avoidance and abusive transfer pricing by foreign affiliates; transfers of polluting activities or technologies; crowding out local firms and suppressing domestic entrepreneurial development; crowding out local products, technologies, networks and business practices with harmful sociocultural effects; concessions to TNCs, especially in export processing zones, allowing them to skirt labour and environmental regulations; and, excessive influence on economic affairs and decision-making, with possible negative effects on industrial development and national security.

Voiced in the past by developed and developing countries, these concerns are diminishing in intensity. But they remain strong enough so that many governments feel the need to control inward FDI and the operations of foreign affiliates. Most important are concerns about anticompetitive practices of TNCs, especially restrictive business practices.

Nationalisation And Expropriation

Nationalizations and expropriations are the oldest issue in FDI regulation. Indeed, major takings of foreign-owned property in the 20th century led to rules of customary international law that sought to establish the conditions under which such takings could be lawful. Taking property is lawful if it fulfils three basic criteria: it must be for a public purpose, be non-discriminatory and give rise to the payment of compensation. These basic principles have been universally accepted, and many countries refer to them these days as the legal basis for; their national laws and practices. They are also extensively referred to in the provisions of international investment agreements (IIAs). In addition, some IIAs require that a taking must be in accordance with due process of law.

Until recently, the main controversy was over the precise compensation payable on nationalization or expropriation. This has now been joined by the extent to which indirect takings, including so-called "creeping expropriation" and "regulatory takings", should be covered by protection standards.

Sensitivity of Indirect Takings and National Policy Dilemmas

Direct takings of property, involving the transfer of the physical possession of an asset as well as the legal title; can take various forms, ranging from outright nationalizations in all economic sectors or on an industry-wide basis, to large-scale takings of land by the State, or specific takings (expropriations). Indirect takings include creeping expropriations, involving an incremental but cumulative encroachment on one or more of the range of recognized ownership rights until the measures involved lead to the of effect negation of the owner's interest in the property. They also include regulatory takings, in which the exercise of governmental regulatory power - the power to tax or to control operations for environmental protection - diminishes the economic value of the owners' property without depriving them of formal ownership. Distinguishing between the two types is not always easy.

In addition, the notion of indirect takings is itself problematic, given the ever increasing and changing conception of property rights and, in particular, of the social function of property. Against this background, governments have broad powers of regulatory intervention so as to ensure the subjection of private property to the public interest. These powers are highly complex. In the circumstances, indirect takings may be better understood by looking at the results of a governmental action rather than defining the process by which the result is reached.

It is fairly easy to identify acts of outright nationalization or expropriation. They are normally carried out on a given date and on the basis of an explicit national policy. Not so for creeping expropriations. They are usually carried out under the guise of a policy in which the deprivation of the owner's property is not an explicit purpose, and they do not necessarily have a clear date when it can be said that the owners have been deprived of their title to the expropriated property.

For example, the Iran-United States Claims Tribunal had to assess whether emergency measures taken in 1978-1979 in the wake of the revolution in the Islamic Republic of Iran to preserve United States-owned commercial property, after its United States managers had fled, amounted to an indirect taking by the State. Another example may be the action of a host country to intervene in a failing foreign-owned company to protect various stakeholders against an impending bankruptcy. If this effectively deprives the owners of their ability to control the company can this be said to amount to a "creeping expropriation"?

The major difficulty that such cases create is how to identify the point at which a process of governmental action changes to an incremental deprivation of an owner's rights, such that the deprivation becomes the subject of a duty to compensate that definition is drawn too widely it will catch entirely legitimate regulatory and administrative action.

Regulatory takings are particularly sensitive because many government regulations can have an impact on the value of private property. So an expansive interpretation of "regulatory takings" can limit the national policy space by hindering a government's right to regulate, creating the risk of "regulatory chill", with governments unwilling to undertake legitimate regulation for fear of lawsuits from investors.

The three main criteria of the lawfulness of takings may give rise, in principle, to certain disagreements between investors; both foreign and domestic, and host countries. In some cases, for example, investors challenge the public purpose of a taking before an arbitral tribunal or the courts. In most cases, however, it is difficult to prove a total lack of public purpose. In addition, potential disagreement can arise from the way non-discrimination is interpreted and applied in the case of individual takings.

As for the issue of compensation, a distinction must be made between the standard of compensation on the one hand and the method of calculation on the other. The former issue is practically always addressed in IIAs, whereas the latter issue has received less attention. There is no hard and fast agreement among States as to the appropriate level and method of calculating the compensation payable upon a nationalization or expropriation. The approach taken under national law is within the discretion of the State concerned. However, this can lead to disputes over compensation at the international level where States may differ over the correct approach to compensation.

In relation to regulatory takings, the national practice of countries does not always provide clear answers to the questions raised. Even in a deregulated, liberal market environment, investors need to observe certain basic standards of good market behaviour, as prescribed for example by competition rules, and sound practices in areas of concern to public policy whether these involve the protection of the environment, public health, morals, consumers or the promotion of development.

The major problem today is to distinguish between a legitimate exercise of governmental discretion that interferes with the enjoyment of foreign-owned property and a regulatory taking that requires compensation. This requires a balance to be struck between:

(i) Achieving the public policy goals of a regulatory regime, which could reduce property values or values potentially generated in the absence of regulation by unregulated business entities.

(ii) Preserving the economic value of the productive assets of those entities.

Where the interference with private property rights violates the legitimate rights or expectations of owners, the State may need to provide compensation. But where a measure is undertaken as part of the right to regulate in the public interest compensation may not be due. Similarly, where a measure is penal, confiscation without compensation may be a: part of the sanction to be visited on the owner because they violate required regulatory or criminal standards.

Coverage in IIAs

Most IIAs contain provisions on taking property, generally defining a "taking" as including traditional notions of nationalization or expropriation as well as creeping expropriations and regulatory takings. The indirect taking mayor may not be qualified by a carve-out for normal regulatory powers, as in the areas of taxation, intellectual property rights and public debt. If such a clause is included, it may subject the carve-out to an obligation that the regulatory powers must be non-discriminatory. Furthermore, the majority of such agreements require observance, by the contracting parties, of the principal elements of a lawful taking: public purpose, non-discrimination and compensation. In addition, some agreements refer expressly to the need for observance of due process.

However, there is no uniformity on the standard of compensation to be applied, reflecting an absence of full consensus among States on this issue and, also, the relative bargaining positions of parties to HAs. Some agreements refer to "appropriate" or "just" compensation, while others refer to "prompt, adequate and effective" compensation or similar phrasing. The trend in recent years has moved towards the latter approach, in both bilateral or regional agreements.

From a developmental perspective, recent practice in IIAs suggests that developing countries strive to strike a balance between offering reasonable protection to investors and retaining their right to regulate. The utility of Asian referring to takings of property has usually been judged for the effect on the investment climate in developing countries. Treaty-based controls over the scope and legal requirements of a valid taking of foreign-owned property are assumed to have been good for investment conditions. But international disciplines have sometimes been criticized as imposing too much control over the sovereign discretion to limit the enjoyment of private property in the public interest. Where a host country wishes to preserve discretion to discriminate, this may need to be protected under limited and transparent circumstances. The question remains whether the rules of expropriation or other standards of protection, such as non-discrimination, are the best way to offer some protection to investors while preserving the right to regulate.

The issue of compensation may attract renewed interest in light of the emergence of regulatory takings as an important issue. If regulatory measures give rise to compensation, two questions arise: first, when is compensation due and, secondly, how to measure the right amount? For example, if environmental measures were subject to a duty of compensation, could this not, in effect, insure the investor against compliance costs, or the costs of causing environmental harm, if the regulatory measure in question was seen as a regulatory taking? Equally, such a duty to compensate might inhibit a host country from enforcing its laws or from complying with international environmental agreements. These dilemmas lead governments to protect themselves through interpretative provisions, carve-outs or international review mechanisms: to permit a legitimate exercise of regulatory power. So how will international arbitral tribunals develop the applicable principles in the course of settling disputes brought before them?

Dispute Settlement

The two key issues in dispute settlement concern the role of investor-State procedures in future IIAs and the extent to which the investment dispute settlement process is self-contained. IIAs normally have State-State dispute settlement provisions, but investor-State procedures are now being included more as well. That raises fears of frivolous or vexatious claims that could inhibit legitimate regulatory action by governments. Another issue is balancing national and international methods of dispute settlement. The second key issue concerns the isolation of investment disputes from existing State-State systems of dispute settlement, such as that in the WTO. Questions also arise as regards open and well-functioning procedures that can deal better with the developmental aspects of investment disputes.

National Policies on Dispute Settlement in the Investment Field

The settlement of disputes between investors and host countries is central to national FDI policy. Usually, a host country provides dispute settlement procedures and remedies as a part of the general law of the land. But investors may, in some circumstances, prefer an internationalized approach to dispute settlement, usually arbitration between an investor and a host country. This can be ad hoc, with a panel and procedure agreed between the investor and the host country. Or there may be an institutional system of international arbitration for the dispute in question.

National policies on investor-State dispute settlement differ. Some require the exclusive use of national procedures and remedies. Some require the prior exhaustion of domestic remedies in the host country before recourse to internationalized dispute settlement systems is permitted.

National investment laws often expressly permit such internationalization of investment disputes by enshrining investor choice in a special dispute settlement provision in the FDI legislation. But many FDI laws are silent on this. In such cases, the investor is required, to use the internal legal remedies available to them under host country law. The same is true of countries that have no FDI laws. In these cases international remedies may be available under the international treaty obligations of the host country in HAs.

So a dispute settlement clause in a BIT that allows the investor choice between national and international procedures binds the host country as a matter of international legal obligation. Such an international obligation can also be made enforceable before national tribunals where the investment contract between the investor and host country includes a dispute settlement clause that incorporates the country's international treaty obligations to allow the use of internationalized systems of dispute settlement.

Legal Effectiveness

The effective settlement of any dispute, not just an investment dispute, often requires adopting the most speedy, informal, amicable and inexpensive method available. In recent years the emphasis has been on "alternative dispute resolution" mechanisms-avoiding procedures provided by the public courts of a country or of an international court. They usually include direct methods of settlement through negotiation or informal methods employing a third party, such as the provision of good offices, mediation or conciliation. Arbitration can be an alternative dispute resolution mechanism, but its practical conduct may be only marginally different from that of a court proceeding.

So the first step in the resolution of any investment dispute is to use direct, bilateral, informal and amicable means of settlement. Only where such informal means fail to resolve a dispute should the parties contemplate informal third-party measures, such as good offices, mediation or conciliation. The use of arbitration should be contemplated only where bilateral and third-party informalrneasures have failed to achieve a negotiated result.

The choice of a dispute settlement method is but one choice that the investor and State have to make when seeking to resolve a dispute. Another concerns the forum. Most recent BITs provide for some type of international dispute settlement mechanism to be used in relation to investment disputes. Foreign investors have traditionally maintained that, in developing countries, investor-State disputes should be resolved by internationalized dispute-settlement governed by international standards and procedures. But host countries may perceive such an emphasis on international systems as a sign of low investor confidence, which mayor may not be justifiable.

The willingness of the host country to accept internationalized dispute settlement may be motivated by a desire to show its commitment to creating a good investment climate. This may be of importance where the country has followed a restrictive policy on FDI and wishes to change that policy. In so doing, it should be entitled to expect that the internationalized system is impartial and even-handed.

An institutional system of arbitration may be a more reliable means of resolving a dispute than an ad hoc approach. Once the parties have consented to its use, they have to abide by the system's procedures. These are designed to ensure that, while the parties retain a large measure of control over the arbitration, they are constrained from any attempt to undermine the proceedings. Furthermore, an award made under the auspices of an institutional system is more likely to be consistent with principles of procedural fairness applicable to that system-and so is more likely to be enforceable before municipal courts. Indeed, recognition of awards may be no more than a formality. One system has been developed for investment disputes between a host country and a foreign investor: the conciliation and arbitration procedures available under the auspices of ICSID.

Foreign Portfolio Investment (FPI)

While FPI has traditionally been concentrated in developed markets, new interest has been sparked by the co-called "emerging" capital markets. The emerging markets have at least three attractive qualities, two of which are their high average returns and their low correlations with developed markets. Diversification into these markets in expected to give higher expected returns and lower overall volatility.

Many individual investors, as well as portfolio and pension fund managers, are reexamining their basic investment strategies. The 1990s, fund managers realised that significant performance gains could be obtained by diversifying into high-quality global equity markets. These gains are limited, however, by the fairly high cross-correlations returns in these markets. The resulting investment strategy reflects current information. In terms of portfolio theory, adding low-correlation portfolios to an optimisation enhances the reward-to-risk profile by shifting the mean-variance frontier to the left.

The portfolio optimisation problem requires important inputs-the expected returns and the variance-covariance matrix. In principal, all of these measures should be forward-looking. That is, the returns, volatilities, and correlations should be forecasted.

An upsurge in portfolio investment in developing countries has marked the end of the debt crisis, or perhaps even helped to end it. Using the World Bank's definition of portfolio flows as consisting of bonds, equity (comprising direct stock market purchases, American

Depository Receipts (ADRs), and country funds), and money market instruments (such as certificates of deposits (CDs) and commercial paper). Broadly speaking, there are six groups of investors in the emerging markets, each having a tolerance for different degrees of risks and returns:

(i) Domestic residents of developing countries with overseas holdings and other private foreign investors, who constitute the dominant category of portfolio investors who are currently active in the major emerging markets. These investors keep abreast of developments in their country on a regular basis and monitor change in government policy. Their investments in emerging markets are motivated by expected short-term high yields. Preference is given to instruments that are in bearer form and provide returns in hard currency. These external fund as "Hot Money" which are kept in the "Latin American Bank" which mayor may not be beneficial to the long-term growth prospects of developing country depending on the manner in which they are invested.

(ii) Managed funds (closed-end country funds and mutual funds), whose portfolio managed buy and sell shares and high-yield bonds in one or more of the emerging markets for performance-based trading purposes.

(iii) Foreign banks and brokerage firms, who allocate their portfolio for inventory and trading purposes.

(iv) Retail clients of eurobonds houses who are involved in emerging securities markets due to portfolio diversification motives.

(v) Institutional investors (such as pension funds, life insurance companies), who have a longer time horizon for expected gains from their portfolio and look for stability and long-term growth prospects in the market in which they invest.

(vi) Non resident nationals of developing countries, who could be a potential source of portfolio investment from abroad (as opposed to flight capital).

The first three groups are active in the emerging securities markets primarily because of expectations of short-term returns and have been observed to move funds among different ESMs frequently. Purely speculative traders also continuously move funds between the emerging markets and the developed markets (primarily the United States).

The lower degree of integration of the emerging markets in the global capital markets often makes them better avenues for achieving higher yields relative to the more globally integrated developed securities markets. Since all listed companies in the ESMs are not very well researched by foreign investors and their market information may be limited, there exists the potential for finding undervalued stocks which may yield high returns to potential investors. In general, P/E ratios in several ESMs may be lower than those in developed markets. Therefore, one expects to see larger inflows of portfolio investments into the emerging markets from institutional investors worldwide.

The integration of international equity markets observed in recent years can be attributed to several factors: *(a)* the emergence of international banking syndicates and brokerage houses which have the necessary information technology and communication facilities to be able to place large international equity issues within shorter periods of time at lower syndication and distribution fees than domestic issues; *(b)* the introduction of foreign equity-based instruments, such as ADRs and Rule 144A issues in the United States, which have significantly reduced the regulatory and physical impediments that in the past hind red such investments; and *(c)* and widespread practice of multiple listing of shares across different stock exchange in different countries have become widespread. The globalisation of the international capital markets has resulted in global allocation of portfolios in a relatively inexpensive manner.

It should be understood, however, that at the earlier stages of "openness" of the ESMs, the return of flight capital that is observed is generally motivated by short-term speculative motives. Significant movements of such funds in and out of these markets give rise to increased volatility in stock prices as well as potential problems for domestic monetary management. Rapid increases of international reserves due to these large capital inflows have to be dealt with carefully by policymakers. These rising international reserves will strengthen the domestic currencies of the countries where these large inflows occur and have lowered inflationary expectations. Investors have observed the underutilised capacity, especially in the infrastructure sector of the emerging markets, and expect increased demand for manufactured products as a result of "impending free trade agreements."

It is crucial for developing countries that the experiencing such large capital inflows in the short term to endeavor to continue to attract these private financing flows in the long term. Given the increasing integration of the international financial markets and the incresingly advanced communication and information technology facilities that are emerging today, the task of maintaining "financial competitiveness" in the international capital markets is a challenge that the emerging markets must face. To this end, the role of appropriate market-oriented domestic policy reforms and an endeavour to maintain a sustained growth performance in the developing countries concerned will go a long way in keeping the repatriated capital with their boundaries. From the long-term point of view it has been observed that flight capital is the last to return. This makes the task at hand for the emerging markets very challenging.

If developing countries wish to attract a sustained inflows of portfolio investment from abroad rather than short-term speculative movements of funds in and out of their countries, it is crucial to address some of the major constraints that inhibit such flows. These constraints exist both on the demand as well as the supply side of ESM securities.

On the demand side for emerging market securities, the most important hurdle inhibiting institutional investors abroad from investing in these markets are regulatory impediments imposed by source country governments and restrictions on investment practices imposed by the trustees of these institutions. Some governments have imposed restrictions on foreign investment by their institutional investors because they feel that possible large foreign exchange outflows may have an adverse impact on the country's balance of payments, by institutionalising capital flight. However, institutional investors need to be strictly monitored in the absence of a strong and transparent pension system and when pension fund managers lack a thorough understanding of the complexities of their investment in the international financial markets. The role of the domestic securities and exchange commissions and regulatbry agencies for institutional investors in the emerging markets is crucial in maintaining a steady inflow of foreign capital and ensuring responsible behaviour on the part of domestic institutional investors.

Tight regulation of investment decisions by institutional investors (in both developed and developing countries) is not necessary for ensuring for safety of contractual savings. In the United Kingdom, for example pension funds and life insurance companies are only expected to demonstrate that their portfolio of assets, when prudently valued, meet the requirements for technical reserves and solvency margins. This enables these institutions to appropriately manage their portfolios by ensuring flexibility in matching assets and liabilities. Excessively strict investment limits may undermine the private management of a portfolio and, in effect, result in government-directed investment. Nevertheless, pension funds and insurance companies of most developed countries are still subject to restrictive regulations on their foreign investment. These include Canada, Germany and the Netherlands.

On the supply side of the emerging market securities, institutional fund managers are concerned about the illiquielity of most of the emerging markets due to restrictions on direct entry by foreigners, the small number of players (and therefore inefficient market-making), poor accounting practices, high transaction costs, and unreliable settlement systems. Almost all ESMs suffer from the shortage of good-quality, large capitalisation shares. This results in quick overheating (*i.e.* rapid increases in market capitalisation) once domestic and international interest is generated in these markets due to regulatory changes or other factors. The relatively small turnover of most stock in the emerging markets also makes it difficult for large foreign investors to consider substantial portfolio investment in these markets. In fact, larger institutional investors often prefer that the companies they may invest in have a domestic market turnover of at least $1 million per week. Custodial services in ESMs also continue to be a major constraint to increased participation by large foreign institutional investors.

Another concern among U.S. institutional investors is that the management staff of the newly privatised firms may not be sufficiently concerned about enhancing the value of their company's shares (*i.e.* there appears to be an "agency" problem). This will have adverse implications for attractiveness of these investments from the long-term point of view. Under these circumstances, short-term yields would be high (which may interest a different group of investors-private investors and performance-based traders). Regulatory constraints and the lower level of sophistication of the capital markets in the developing countries were cited by U.S. institutional investors as other impediments to greater portfolio flows to emerging markets. U.S. institutional investors are expected to take advantage of Rule 144A and significantly increase their investment in private equity and debt offerings by non-US. entities.

Portfolio Capital Flows: Hot or Cold?

Much of the literature implicitly presumes that it is possible to distinguish hot from cold capital flows simply by knowing the nature of the financial instrument being traded or the identity of the transactor. Perhaps the most salient example of this is the presumption that short-term flows are hotter than long-term flows. The basic idea in the literature is that a hot money inflow is likely to disappear or even reverse itself in the near future, whereas a cold money inflow is more likely to persist.

The notion that one can make inferences about the characteristics of financial flows by just observing their label is not new in economic. There is much conventional wisdom that show capital flows reflect speculative, unstable behaviour while other flows reflect evaluations of long run profitability and are based on fundamental economic condition. The flows of funds approach used by many central banks and others for an analysis of the domestic economy developments is based on labels which are deemed meaningful.

This view has also been an important part of the traditional analysis of international finance for many years. In fact, the structure of balance of payments accounts reflects an implicit theory that different types of capital flows have different economic implications. For example, the distinction between short-term "hot money" and long-term capital flows undoubtedly reflects the view that short-term capital movements are speculative and reversible while long-term capital flows are based on fundamentals and are reversed only when the fundamentals change. The fact that capital control programmes in many countries distinguish between short-and long-term positions also points to the importance attached to this distinction.

Another important distinction found in balance of payments accounts is between official capital flows, including changes in international reserves, and private capital flows. A common view in the context of current capital inflows into developing countries-which is based on labels—is that such flows are fundamentally different form inflows to these same countries in the 1970s because the current inflows are private-to private transactions not guaranteed by the government of any country.

Finally, it is often argued that direct investment has different implications for the host and recipient countries as compared to other capital flows. For example, direct investment capital flows are often associated with technology transfers and a range of costs and benefits for both countries. An implicit assumption behind these ideas is that the transactions reported in the balance accounts are closely related to the behaviour of interest in the real economy.

This reasoning-based on the label of the flow-at times underlies substantive policy measures. Once a flow is identified as "hot money," it is then seen as requiring some policy response. At various times countries (especially developing countries) have responded with exchange rate management, (sterilised) intervention, fiscal contraction, borrowing taxes, absolute foreign borrowing constraints, and reserve requirements.

There are a number of good reasons to doubt, however, that the micro nature of international capital flows reveals much about the economic importance of such flows. Since many assets are (increasingly becoming) tradable, a distinction between flows based on their terms (for example, short versus long) is (increasingly becoming) less meaningful. A treasury bond with a 30-year maturity can easily be more liquid, and thus lead to a higher volatility of short-term flows than a 30-day time deposit at a commercial bank. And, a short-term asset which is rolled over can in many ways be identical to a long-term asset.

Furthermore, the explicit label given to a flow may not cover its implicit nature. For instance the inflows to developing countries in the 1970s were private capital flows in name, the universal government guarantees of both lenders and borrowers considerably subdued the discipline of the market. In effect the capital flows that helped generate the debt crisis of 1982 should have been considered official capital flows since the private parties undertaking the transactions relied on a government guarantee (and ex post, private claims indeed became the liability of the government).

This experience should act as a warning against evaluating capital flows according to their label (for example, the instrument traded or the transactor recorded in the balance of payments statistics). In the past few years inflows to developing countries have taken the form of non-guaranteed portfolio investments and direct investments. If the behaviour behind such investments is different in some important way, it follows that we may not be inviting another debt crisis even if conditions change as they did in 1982. But if the flows are to a significant extent guaranteed by the government, their label "private" may be meaningless.

The starting point should then also be a clear methodology on how the hypothetical economic implications of different types of capital flows can be identified empirically. If credit markets were perfect and complete, the form of capital flows would not be important. A useful analog here is the Miller-Modigliani theorem from corporate finance. Under a set of strong assumptions, the structure of assets and liabilities among various types of debt and equity have no effect on the value of the firm because investors can offset the structure chosen by the firm in credit markets. If we think of the balance of payments accounts as records of how a country finances its international capital position, it follows that under the Miller-Modigliani assumptions, the structure of capital flows and the structure of the gross international asset and liability positions would be unrelated to the country's net indebtedness.

It might be useful here to look at an analogous issue that has recently been carefully explored in a closed economy context. That issue is whether a "credit crunch" contributed to a downturn in economic activity. This is an interesting hypothesis because it explicitly rests on the view that one type of financial transaction, in this case loans by domestic banks to domestic nonfinancial firms, had important economic effects.

This view is an important part of the (new literature on business cycles, which links financial structures and real activity. This literature provides a useful analytical framework that can be adapted to a discussion of international financial flows. It points out that the importance of changes in bank credit for economic activity, as opposed to bank liabilities or money, is an empirical issue. If good substitutes for bank credit exist in an economy, it follows that a decline in bank credit that is not matched by a decline in money will have no effect on economic activity. Firms would easily substitute other forms of credit, for example commercial paper, to offset the reduction in bank credit. In contrast, if banks have special information about their customers that is not easily transferred to other lenders, a reduction of bank credit will not be easily offset by borrowing from other institutions or markets. In this case an interruption in bank credit could have a depressing effect on expenditures and output.

There are two important lessons from this,. First, meaningful tests of the importance of capital account transactions require a specification of the economic behaviour of interest. Second, a financial transaction is likely to have measurable effects on the specified economic behaviour in cases where the institutional environment, information structures, or other departures from complete markets limit the ability of investors to substitute one type of transaction for another in response to changing incentives.

The view that labels matter can take comfort from the fact that international financial markets are not complete and transactions are subject to a large number of distortions. Many of these are imposed by governments in the form of controls on types of transactions that are considered undesirable. Moreover, subsidies often take the form of a government guarantee of private liabilities, favourable tax treatment on earnings (direct investment), or access to special government facilities (debt equity swaps).

Furthermore, governments also intervene directly in international capital markets. Developing country governments borrow for long-term objectives and, increasingly, in middle-income countries, to offset short-run pressures on exchange rates and domestic interest rates. A difficulty thus arises in interpreting private capital flows that are sterilised by intervention transactions by the central bank as, to some extent, the composition of private capital flows is conditioned by governments' capital transactions. Clearly a country trying to maintain interest rates above its trading partners in some sense generates the private capital inflow by standing ready to match private inflows with official outflows in the form of increases in reserve assets. Such private inflows are "sustainable" as long as the official capital outflows are "sustainable."

In general, if international capital transactions are effectively distorted by taxes, subsidies and direct intervention, the structure of private capital flows might follow predictable patterns as long as the structure of distortions itself is stable. Over a period the financial transactions are motivated by a variety of economic forces. Over time the institutional framework changes, the behaviour of the official sector probably changes, the exchange rate regime changes, capital control programmes come and go, and banking markets (both on and offshore) develop, fail, and are recapitalised.

The final economic behaviour that seems to provide the most appropriate test for the importance of various capital flows is the net intertemporal trade among countries, conventionally measured by the current account. While there are other interesting candidates, for example, the exchange rate, questions about the sustainability of certain type of capital flows are motivated by concern about the sustainability of a path for changes in net indebtedness to the rest of the world, that is, the mirror image of the cumulative current account balance. Policymakers wish to assess the likelihood of sudden and destabilising changes in the total capital account-not just its components.

On a macro level, national accounts identities state that the sum of all capital flows is equal to the difference between savings and investment. For a given savings investment imbalance, capital flows have to satisfy an adding-up constraint. Unless flows influence domestic investment or domestic savings (or a combination of the two), some substitution between the various flows has to occur, for a given current account, the volatility of one flow will on aggregate be canceled out. The extent of interaction between the various components and the possibility of systematic interactions between components thus needs to be addressed before making inferences from the parts to the whole.

A fundamental difficulty this is that the linkage between current account and any of the capital flows data series might be very weak. For one thing we know that gross capital inflows and outflows are several times larger than net capital flows. Yet it is the net flow that we are interested in when considering sustainability of current account position. It seems clear that the motivation for two-way flows of international capital are very different from the general view that developing countries should be net capital importers and that each type of transaction should show a net inflow.

For example, residents of a small open economy might hold most of their financial wealth in the form of foreign clams since this allows them to diversify their income streams and protect themselves from domestic taxation and income shocks. Offsetting this preference would be the tendency for foreign investors to purchase claims on the country again in order to diversify their risk. This diversification motive for international capital movements might account for much of the recorded flows in balance of payments data.

Moreover, it might be the case that residents of wealthy countries prefer long-term investments such as bonds or loans while residents of developing countries prefer short-term investments such as bank deposits. In this case, we would expect to see short-term capital outflow from developing countries matched by long-term loans to residents developing countries. These preferences imply nothing about the desired imbalance in the capital or current account.

In fact, the short-term positions of residents might be quite stable if there are relatively few alternative investments. In contrast, the long-term capital inflow to the developing country might take several alternative forms. In one year foreign investors might prefer equities, in another bank loans, and in another bonds. These preferences might in turn reflect subtle changes in tax rules (in the industrial countries) that the analyst would find difficult to identify. The point is that the pattern of financial intermediation might be quite stable for a while but that small differences in the institutional framework, due to either regulation or innovation in credit markets, might alter the form that the intermediation taken in balance of payments statistics.

In general, direct investment is a difficult capital flow to interpret. Balance of payments data on direct investment include short-and long-term capital transactions of a loosely defined set of reporters who own more than a given percent of the equity in a domestic or foreign chartered firm. Because direct investors hold factories and other assets that are impossible to move, it is sometimes assumed that a direct investment inflow is more stable than other forms of capital flows.

This need not be the case. While a direct investor usually has some immovable assets, there is no reason in principle why these cannot be fully offset by domestic liabilities. Clearly, a direct investor can borrow in order to export capital, and thereby generate rapid capital outflows. In most developing countries, there are laws against this, so it would be surprising to see negative flows for foreign domestic investment in a developing country. There could, however, be offsetting movements in other balance of payments accounts or in errors and omissions.

On a micro level, there is also much (anecdotal) evidence that, from the point of view of foreign direct investors, flows with very different classifications are actually close substitutes. Multinationals often substitute between and among the various forms of intercompany transfers (retained earnings, provision of and repatriation of capital, and intercompany loans) and loans from local or foreign banks-for example, to achieve higher profits net of overall taxes. In other cases, flows maybe complementary, that is foreign investment may take place through a combination of FDI and portfolio equity investment.

❑

20

Globalisation with Social Responsibility

Privatisation, deregulation and liberalisation create more space for firms to pursue their corporate objectives. International agreements give more rights to firms to operate internationally. Should this expansion of action, space and rights be accompanied by an increase in corporate responsibilities? In the international context, this question attracts particular attention because TNCs are one of the principal drivers of globalisatien, They are also seen to be the most important beneficiaries of the liberalisation of investment and trade regimes, with rising influence oh the development of the world economy and its constituent parts. The concept of "social responsibility" captures the search for an answer to this question. It implies that firms have obligations that go beyond what countries require individually, and agreements prescribe internationally. The assumption of greater social responsibility by TNCs would be particularly important in light of the economic and social disruptions that accompany the globalisation process, which if not tackled—could threaten the very framework within which firms build their international production systems.

Social Responsibility of TNC

Corporate social responsibility encompasses an array of meanings and intended applications that have undergone substantial modifications over time. These are important to note and understand because they influence the dialogue between governments, business and other civil society groups. The same term, or its variations may carry different implications among various parties regarding the legitimacy, obligations and impact of corporate social responsibility standards. All societal groups are expected to perform certain roles and functions that can change over time with a society's own evolution. Expectations related to business enterprises, and particularly TNCs, are undergoing unusually rapid change due to the expanded role these enterprises play in a globalising society. Discussions relating to TNC social responsibility standards and performance therefore comprise an important component of efforts to develop a stable, prosperous and just global society.

1. Beyond Compliance with Law

Corporate social responsibility is sometimes mistakenly equated with either corporate philanthropy or simple compliance with law. These two ideas actually stand at opposite extremes to the social responsibility concept whose focus rests centrally on a firm's operational behaviour and its impacts on the surrounding society. Corporate philanthropy involves an activity extraneous to a firm's actual operations: while generally appreciated by social recipients, it does not represent an essential or even necessarily expected business function. By contrast, corporate compliance with law is no more than the mandated minimum necessary to permit the continued existence of any legally-chartered corporate entity.

A confusion between corporate philanthropy and corporate social responsibility can arise from this connection between corporate giving and a firm's business activities. Recipients of corporate gifts are often local communities in which an enterprise maintains its headquarters or significant production sites. Other gifts may seek to improve educational programmes in technical fields connected to corporate operations, or sponsor youth or elderly programmes related to the age groups comprising a firm's main product market. In these cases, philanthropic motivations can blend with marketing or brand-name enhancement objectives, creating a link between "good deeds" and corporate interests. However, such a philanthropic programme is really tangential to how a firm's operational behavior: impacts on society, which is the essence of corporate social responsibility. An external programme of "good deeds" will not protect a firm whose actual operations harm its surrounding society, nor will a society reject productive, well-behaved firms just because they do not engage in philanthropic activities.

Compliance with legal requirements constitutes a mandatory minimum standard for corporate conduct. Corporate entities are legal persons granted the right to exist and operate within a society, subject to the laws of that society. Violations of law subject firms to civil or criminal penalties and can result in revocation of the corporation's licence to operate. Some international instruments include references to a general duty of TNCs to observe the laws of the host country. However, these provisions simply recognise the essential role of national law in setting a mandatory minimum floor for corporate conduct. Corporate social responsibility rises above this required floor to incorporate standards of behaviour that may be expected, but are not required, under a society's legal statutes.

Compliance with law, then, is really nothing more than a minimum standard of conduct legally necessary to the corporation's continued existence. Corporate social responsibility that extends beyond legal mandates can help meet societal expectations in the absence of statutory devices. Such conduct may be particularly important to meeting social needs in developing countries where legal regimes may be absent or underdeveloped in areas related to certain aspects of TNC conduct.

2. Evolving Corporate Social Contracts and Stake Holder Interests

The intellectual foundation for most evolving views of corporate social responsibility lies largely with the notion of a "social contract" between a corporation and its host society. The legal incorporation process results in a formal corporate charter that grants an enterprise the right to operate within the governing society's body of established laws and regulations. From one viewpoint, these legal requirements can be seen to constitute the full extent of a corporation's societal responsibility; for anything else, "the business of business is business". A contrasting philosophy, however, asserts a broader, extra-Legal social contract that encompasses a society's implicit assumptions and expectations regarding the behaviour of corporations to which the society has granted a right of existence. This social contract incorporates a firm's contractual legal obligations but extends beyond them to include additional expectations or responsibilities that are not (currently) mandatory. The contents of a corporation's social contract can evolve more rapidly than its legal charter, reflecting a society's changing social and cultural modes. When governed parties, such as corporations, are slow to comply with new societal values, those norms may then be formulated into legally-binding mandates.

In several respects, social contract theory helps bridge the conceptual gap between the early history of voluntary gifts involving personal or corporate philanthropy and broader, contemporary concepts of corporate social responsibility. The first essential step is to attach a stronger sense of moral duty or obligation to desired corporate activity. If certain norms of behaviour are part of an implicit social contract, then complying corporate actions become a more obligatory response rather than a philanthropic "good deed" whose design and initiation re t entirely unilaterally with the charitable benefactor. A second element arises from the potential relationship between social and legal contracts: to the extent that evolving values encompassed within social contract expectations may become viewed as "moral minimums", the expectation is strong that those norms will be made into legal mandates, unless complied with "voluntarily". This notion corresponds to the implicit (or sometimes explicit) "threat" that some corporations perceive behind "voluntary" codes of conduct, where noncompliance may result in even more restrictive mandatory regulations. The third link ties social responsibility standards more closely to the essential nature of corporate operations. Social contract theory encompasses a broad range of corporate behaviour, certainly including the normal operating standards for a firm's core activities. This operational agenda introduces social responsibility notions into a firm's internal operations whereas self-initiated acts of charitable giving to external constituencies keeps non-legal societal standards at a safe distance from the corporation's inside processes. Hence, corporate social responsibility has come to be associated with standards of performance that are applied to both internal and external corporate activities, addressing societal norms that are not (but may become) legally-required mandates.

Stakeholder analysis represents a companion concept to social contract theory. A stakeholder approach seeks to define corporate social responsibility broadly in relation to the groups or interests that affect, or are affected by, a corporation's actions. A contrasting shareholder view of corporate responsibility focuses more narrowly on an enterprise's need to serve the interests of its owners by pursuing and delivering profitable returns to its investing shareholders. Shareholders are indisputably important stakeholders in business enterptises. But these two concepts carry very different implications about whether shareholder interests should be given exclusive or even relative priority over other stakeholder goals.

No consensus exists on any single list of corporate stakeholders, although most discussions include groups such as shareholders, workers, managers, customers, suppliers, local communities and governments. Affected stakeholder interests can also be conceptualised in such terms as the unknown or as yet unrecognised interests (future generations or unexpected side-effects). To some degree, the number of relevant stakeholders, and the nature of a corporation's social responsibility to them, vary with a corporation's own unique characteristics, including its size, sector, product and operations. In any event, it will comprise all those that for one reason or another—feel that they are affected by a company's operation.

The sizc, scope and impact of modern TNCs extends their potential takeholder groups beyond the realm defined by the normal activities of national corporations. In all societies, some groups affected by corporate activity will lack the economic or political power to ensure that their interests are represented adequately through market mechanisms or governmental regulations. In a global society, however, the under-representation of developing country needs and concerns presents a challenge of far greater magnitude, with considerably broader consequences. Special concerns arise from TNC interactions with developing countries, where FDI can play a large role especially in a relatively small domestic economy. In countries with weak competitive discipline of efficient markets or lacking "good governance" reflected in effective governmental institutions to represent the public interest, TNC social responsibility requires that the corporation pay special attention to the interests of under-represented stakeholders that could be adversely affected by business operations.

3. The Scope and Content of Corporate Social Responsibility

The scope of corporate social responsibility is conceptually quite unbound at the present time. Although the debate between TNCs, civil society and governments often focuses on a few key issues-notably human rights, the environment and workers' rights—this list is by no means exhaustive. In principle, a company is broadly responsible for the consequences of its operations, including direct impacts as well as unintended side-effects or other externalities that affect third parties. In fact, a more expansive definition of the scope of social responsibility would also cover firms linked to another firm by more or less strong business ties (*e.g.* with supplying firms)—what, in the environment discussion is called the "environmental footprint". Calls for greater corporate social responsibility generally arise from incidents involving negative external effects in areas in which legal responsibilities are-not (yet) clarified. These externalities can occur in a wide range of areas involving various stakeholder groups. Negatively affected groups will ask companies causing these impacts to take measures to prevent, reduce or rectify such consequences, or otherwise to internalise the costs resulting from their activities. External effects can, for example, relate to the social changes produced in a community by a TNC's decision to close down large existing operations. Negative externalities involving environmental impacts are well known.

Although the list of issues that can be included under a comprehensive definition of corporate social responsibility is long (and could include, *e.g.* consumer rights, information disclosure and fiscal and commercial probity), very few issues actually receive levels of public attention that might convince TNCs to include them in their responsibilities. Infact many issues, especially ones that may particularly affect people in developing countries, go often unnoticed by the wider public and are not taken up by TNCs as long as they are not associated with sufficiently influential public pressure. A number of development-related issues—such as technology transfer, training of the local workforce, the importance of backward linkages and the promotion of local entrepreneurship—that are of great interest to developing countries are generally not included when TNCs and civil society in the developed countries engage in debates over corporate social responsibility.

4. Business, Civil Society and Government Perceptions of Corporate Social Responsibility

The relationship between standards of corporate social responsibility and potential legal requirements governing corporate operations lies at the heart of the sometimes adversarial relationship between civil society groups and the business community. For many civil society groups, corporate social responsibility signifies conduct that rises above the minimum required by law but still constitutes a corporate duty to act rather than a more optional norm or charitable "good deed". This view—that corporate social responsibility standards are, in fact, normative obligations—is evident when civil society groups implicitly or explicitly threaten to seek legal mandates should business fail to comply with acceptable voluntary guidelines deriving from the social contract. Private enterprises on the other hand generally prefer the flexibility of self-designed voluntary standards. However, when voluntary guidelines are devised as part of a public process involving governments and/or civil society, corporate executives tend to worry that the content and precise wording of voluntary guidelines may become a precedent for subsequent legal requirements.

The business community's aversion to binding international legal standards governing corporate operations contrasts with its strong advocacy of international law commitments applied to the obligations of governments towards foreign investors. This view is advocated on issues such as expropriation and compensation standards, and guarantees of nondiscriminatory national treatment relative to domestic firms. In these cases, governmental responsibilities are seen as normative duties or obligations, based on fair treatment principles, that should be backed by international legal sanctions.

For governments, the relationship between a social contract and legal regulations governing corporate operations assumes new meaning and complexities when the business concerned is transnational. A mismatch exists between the territorially-bounded-authority of national governments and the transnational reach of a TNC's integrated international production system. Although an individual country may seek to extend its law extra-territorially, its reach may infringe on another country's sovereignty, raising the potential for political conflicts and confrontations. The obvious solution is to devise a common foundation of international law whose reach will match the global span of modem corporate activities; but in a world of diverse nation-states with often divergent goals and priorities, this remedy proves difficult, time- consuming and, in many cases, impossible to achieve as a near-term outcome.

Generalisations about national government perspectives on the concept of TNC legal and social contracts can mask important differences both within and between countries. Conflicting domestic pressures exist in many countries that reflect divergent views on whether outward FOI and trade expansion are in the national interest, and how resulting economic and social adjustment costs should be managed, at home and abroad. Perceiving an incipient backlash against globalisation in some home countries, developing countries may fear that proposals for new TNC social responsibility standards can represent a disguised form of protectionism. Thus, proposals that seek improvements in TNC global operating standards can generate mixed reactions within and among countries based on differing views of how national Finterests may be affected.

5. International Guidelines and Codes of Conduct

A consensus on TNC-related issues capable—of supporting international law formulations was unattainable during the turbulent decade of the 1970s when acrimony, over TNC roles and activities was at its zenith, and debates in international organisations split along a widening North-South divide. Faced with the apparent impossibility of generating international standards backed by legal sanctions, some governments initiated discussions aimed at developing nonbinding codes of corporate conduct. These devices developed into new "soft law" alternatives, somewhat akin to a defined social contract, whereby governments would endorse and promote the agreed standards as embodying the type of conduct expected of "good corporate citizens". These soft law standards were achievable precisely because they did not require intergovernmental consensus on the level of detail necessary for legally-enforceable regulations. Instead, differing points of view and emphases could be accommodated through creatively broad and sometimes deliberately ambiguous language that left room for flexible implementation.

Sometimes, voluntary compliance regimes can provide an alternative that permits public action while shifting the burden somewhat onto corporations to discern, apply and monitor the voluntary standards in a way that will be deemed acceptable to that firm's surrounding society (which, in the case of a TNC, actually comprises numerous and diverse societies whose views, expectations and priorities may differ and perhaps conflict). Governments and other constituent groups can then judge corporate performance case-by-case, with wide latitude to interpret the guidelines and respond to corporate actions as they see fit. This aspect might play a particularly important role in countries with deficits of governance, fed where governments lack (the will or) the means to enforce legal standards.

Regardless of the question whether legally binding standards are superior to voluntary regimes or not, voluntary standards appear to be gaining renewed favour among some governments. One reason may be that legally binding standards prove difficult to negotiate internationally. In other instances some governments find voluntary compliance regimes more efficient and cost-effective to address technically complex and rapidly-changing business operations.

6. International Aspects of Corporate Social Responsibility

The concept of corporate social responsibility embraces standards of good business practice that can apply to all firms, whether they are national or international in their scope and orientation. But to devise international legal regulation of TNC operations can be difficult, because of the multiple sovereign governments involved and the great diversity among their respective countries' perspectives, policies and priorities. These same differences also make it difficult, although somewhat more possible, to forge agreement on non-binding corporate guidelines or codes to conduct. For corporations, the task can be equally daunting, for they must strive to meet or exceed these diverse and sometimes conflicting expectations while operating simultaneously in many sovereign countries around the world. Both the greater number of interested governmental and non-governmental' constituencies, as well as the magnitude of differences among them, magnify the challenge of defining and applying corporate social responsibility concepts to TNCs as opposed to national corporations.

Another unique aspect of corporate social responsibility as applied to TNCs arises from activist pressures generated by civil society groups in a TNC's home country (or even a host country) related to the firm's operations in other countries. Although international trading ties may allow groups in one country to bring pressure to bear against interests based in another country, the locally invested presence of a TNC provides an easier channel with a more proximate array of interests and activities to target. From a different perspective, these same TNC interrelationships mean that host governments can face policy pressures generated by non-citizen groups located in foreign countries, channeled through their influence on locally invested TNC operations. Actions by TNCs, whether on their own initiative or impelled by pressures from constituencies in other countries, can be viewed by a host country as unwelcome and unjustified external interference in its internal affairs. Of course, this result may be the explicit intention of external groups, as was the case with opponents of the former apartheid regime in South Africa.

The main point for this analysis is that a TNC's international investments give it a scope and capacity for social responsibility activities in multiple societies and political jurisdictions that broadens the audience of interested external constituencies while increasing the impact of corporate decisions on how to respond to calls for actions based on social responsibility norms.

A TNC's social responsibility may exert a differential impact on developing countries which are most often the target rather than an initiator of such actions. Much of this difference stems from the practical reality that developing countries are more host than home countries for TNCs, meaning that an enterprise will have matured using operating standards developed under a set of foreign legal and social expectations. Although TNCs can and do adjust to their host societies, where significantly different standards are encountered the invested enterprise must decide how to respond, bringing a potential for introducing change within the host society to cl degree that exceeds impacts arising under traditional commercial trading relationships.

The differential impact arising from FDI is reinforced by the earlier emergence and maturation of civil society groups in the developed countries. Developing country organisations that represent various elements of civil society are growing in both number and capabilities, and are expanding their ties with similar organisations in other countries. Still, developed country civil society groups provide the main impetus and follow-through influence for defining social responsibility standards and selecting the issues and business applications to target. Even where internationally—defined standards have been achieved as on certain environmental and human rights, including labour issues the proposition that local applications by TNCs in host developing countries fall unacceptably short of those standards (even though they may be consistent with local law and practice) is often made by groups from outside the country. Affirmative TNC responses to calls for change will then alter local operations and impacts in response to external rather than internal evaluations of "higher" social values and norms. This outcome may be question by developing countries, especially if the evaluation criteria and methodology for social performance measures are designed and implemented developed countries. In reality developing-country standards and practices may differ from those used in developed countries, and differ sometimes from desirable internationally-agreed narrows as well In these cases, however, it is important to assure that evaluation and performance measures derive primarily from international and not solely developed-country normative standards. The powerful influence of TNCs based in developed countries, and the prominent role played by similarly-located NGOs, may sometimes obscure the proper societal reference points for normative standards of corporate social responsibility.

7. Global Corporate Citizenship

The presence of foreign affiliates in many countries also engenders the notion of "global corporate citizenship". This idea can be conceptualised more broadly than the recent usage of corporate social responsibility that may appear one-sided if only the responsibilities or obligations of corporations to their host societies are discussed. Citizenship involves both rights and responsibilities. The "rights" involve the business community's concerns with standards of treatment in host countries for foreign investors become more complicated because TNCs may operate in societies that may well have different norms and expectations.

The citizenship notion also provides a bridge between legal regulations and broader social contract standards, acknowledging that a citizen's responsibilities to society rise beyond a floor of legally-mandated obligations. The addition of "global" to "corporate citizenship" emphasises that, for TNCs, rights and responsibilities must be reconciled within the global arena that constitutes their "society". This concept suggests that TNCs are not just legal citizens in each country in which they do business, responsible to that... society's standards and mores. TNCs are, in fact, "global citizens" whose international span, involvement and capabilities confront them with challenges, as well as opportunities, not encountered by national corporations.

The terminology of global corporate citizenship is naturally employed more by international organisations than by national governments, and by NGOs when they are addressing applications of corporate social responsibility outside a TNC's home country. Corporations themselves tend to use the term in a broadly ambiguous sense that specifies adherence to all host-country legal norms, without much specification of what standards may be global rather than national in character, or ho'" national norms should be dealt with if they conflict with global citizenship responsibilities. On the other hand, TNCs are usually quite clear that international investor rights should be respected if they conflict with national norms (for sample, when seeking the better of national treatment and the international law standard.

Global corporate citizenship has come to emphasise capability as much as causality, with an accompanying shift to notions of "doing good" rather than just "not doing harm". This broadened concept engenders calls on TNCs based in one country to prevent or rectify disagreeable conditions in other countries, because they have the capacity to influence outcomes, even where the firms may be, at most, distantly connected to the problem's origin. This type of challenge arises most obviously in the realm of political issues where TNCs are called upon to influence a host government's policies, or even press fot a change in the regime itself (for example, as occurred in protests against the former apartheid regime in South Africa). Activists in such cases often seek to demonstrate linkages by positing various types of TNC support for, or beneficiary interests in, an objectionable regime's governance. However, the clear trend over the years has been to incorporate as broad an array of TNC actors as possible, despite widely varying degrees of involvement with a country's political situation, in order to maximise potential capacity to alter outcomes. This historical expansion of corporate social responsibility concepts, particularly for TNCs underlines the need to work towards a consensus in the international community regarding how terms such as global corporate citizenship should be understood, defined and applied.

Overall, the idea of global corporate citizenship rests on the linkage between the rights granted in an enabling national and international regulatory framework that permits global business activities, and an accompanying set of social responsibility commitments accepted by TNCs that operate within, and benefit from, an integrating global community. Modern business activities require the certainty and regularisation provided by international agreements and institutions. Much of the expansion of global commerce over the past decade stems from the extension of liberal policy regimes wherein TNCs can organise their operations to seek optimal business efficiencies. However, maintaining the current investment and trade framework and ensuring its implementation—much less formulating new international economic instruments—may well depend on corollary progress towards the achievement of related societal goals that lack so specific an international legal elaboration.

Growing Importance of TNC Social Responsibility

The increased importance of TNC social responsibility corresponds to the growing scope of activities undertaken by these enterprises in the globalising world economy. Another factor that explains the broadened importance of TNCs in the global economy is the conceptual as well as operational expansion in the definition of TNCs, as they are now—in addition to their traditional FDI mode—increasingly defined by a variety of low- or non- equity investments. For example, large retailers, face calls for action against abusive working conditions in foreign plants that produce clothing for them under sub-contracting arrangements, although the retailer has no equity ownership or even foreign presence in the country in which the abusive labour conditions exist. A similarly broadened scope arises with enterprises whose valuable brand-names reflect many years of significant financial investments in building a product's reputation and image. These firms seek to protect their assets from misappropriation or misuse in foreign markets, establishing contractual obligations and accompanying controls that shape related business activities in those markets, with or without an actual presence by the TNC itself. Other low or non-equity TNC investments are reflected in the rapidly expanding range of international strategic alliances and partnerships that blend the comparative and competitive advantages of firms from several different countries in complex sets of evolving TNC linkages.

The changes in the magnitude and nature of TNC activity increase the relevance and importance of social responsibility in o interrelated ways. First, the impact of TNCs on people around the world has grown exponentially as these agents of economic globalisation reach into the life of domestic societies through both equity and non-equity mechanisms. Reflecting their increased global span and scope, TNCs have become more capable, proximate and aware actors whose activities can create causal links to societal outcomes in multiple countries and cultures. This impact can raise particular concerns for governments if the main TNC purveyor of change does not even have an invested local presence that is susceptible to the country's legal jurisdiction. This situation is most likely to occur in smaller developing countries whose societies may already be among the most vulnerable to the impact of external forces. Second, the rate of societal change in all countries has increased exponentially over the past few decades, affecting nearly every segment of the population and fostering noticeable feelings of anxiety and insecurity about the future. Globalisation brings the potential for more dramatic forms of change, derived from foreign influences, than would have developed more naturally and slowly within a country's own society. When channeled through FDI directly into a country's domestic fabric, these external influences can sometimes bypass or overwhelm a society's traditional adjustment mechanisms, thereby causing unexpected disruption or dislocation in social as well as economic processes.

Evidence of a potential backlash against globalisation is now appearing among societal groups most affected by the adjustment costs or other adverse impacts of rapid changes often associated rightly or wrongly with TNC activities. These pressures are most evident in labour and environmental organisations but are also present among domestically-oriented businesses that worry about increased competition and other societal interests that fear a loss of national autonomy or identity. Considered within a global context, social responsibility thereby takes on immediate practical and political importance for an international business community whose operations are conditioned on continued globalisation. In fact, there is a significant recent expansion of attempts to design newly cooperative ways for TNCs to respond, individually and collectively, to the evolving public expectations of a global social contract.

Recent Developments in Corporate Social Responsibility

Recent developments influencing the application of social responsibility concepts to international business derive from many different sources that comprise the stakeholders of TNCs, as well as from the corporations themselves. The major new development, at least in developed countries, is a proliferation of groups representing general public or specific issue interests that utilise a wide array of public pressure tactics, intermingled with instances of more direct dialogue, to promote an activist view of TNC duties towards an expanding agenda of social responsibility objectives. An expanding number of private enterprises are creating and/or revising individual statements of business principles or codes, although this group would still constitute only a small percentage of the total TNC community. Collective business organisations have adopted a mixed approach. Some sectoral groups actively responded to social responsibility pressures with industry-specific initiatives, while most organisations take a more cautionary approach, with the notable exception of a new statement on environmental principles. Governments continue to use international organisations to promote guidelines or codes of conduct on issues or in sectors in which international consensus is insufficient to support more precise legal standards. Only occasionally do national governments individually endeavour to develop TNC social responsibility initiatives.

1. Increased Activities by Civil Society Groups

A major development, particularly evident over the past decade, is the expanding number, range, coordination and activism among parts of civil society on issues relating to TNC social responsibility. Although some groups organise around very specific products, such as tobacco or nuclear energy,' most activism focuses on a relatively small set of major issue themes that are then exemplified and addressed in terms of specific products, companies or events. The issues mostprevalent over the past decade involve labour rights and working conditions, the environment and human rights, reflecting primarily a developed country perspective on TNC social responsibility. Some groups choose to focus principally on one of these areas, such as Greenpeace on the environment to Amnesty International on human rights. Others, such as religious organisations or other socially-directed institutional investors, may be active across a spectrum of social issues. Although most groups originate in the developed countries and draw their most involved membership from that base, an increasing number of organisations is emerging in developing countries as well. Where interests and perspectives are shared, groups may forge ties internationally through affiliated networks, conferences, newsletters and an exponential growth in relatively inexpensive Internet linkages. In fact, the emergence of the Internet is virtually unparall led in its impact, both on increasing international communication among elements of civil society and on facilitating these groups outreach to media channels that can focus instant attention on TNC activities worldwide.

2. Business Responses

The business community remains generally cautious regarding international initiatives that call for expansive new commitments to TNC social responsibility obligations. However, the diverse membership of general business organisations makes it difficult to reach a consensus among various industries on a common position that reflects the interests and needs of the full business community. As with some intergovernmental institutions comprised of diverse country members, organisational dynamics can either stall action or drive it towards a lowest common denominator position.

Many individual companies adopt their own codes of conduct that address social responsibility issues, sometimes drawing on an industry code or a set of international business principles. These codes of conduct have been adopted for a variety of reasons, ranging from the personal interest and beliefs of the chief executive officer to explicit expectations voiced by important governmental or other public interest groups. Often TNC code development is reactive, sparked by instances at perceived misconduct by a firm or others in its industry. Sometimes firms are proactive yet still defensive, formulating codes designed to head off possible public criticism. Among the most common factors that impel TNCs to promulgate individual codes are the following: firms, or their business associates, have received criticism for their practices; the industry is "high risk" in terms of exposure to or involvement with recognised social responsibility issues; the company has a "high-profile" name or product brand whose reputation and image is commercially important; and the firm's sales are vulnerable to organised customer boycotts or other commercial sanctions.

Although most corporate codes appear to be associated with past or potential public criticism, backed by possible commercial sanctions for misdeeds, positive inducements can also play a role. For some corporations, proactive corporate social responsibility is perceived as good business. Individual codes can serve to enhance the corporate image and, quite possibly, bottom-line profitability as well. Corporations may explicitly advertise their compliance with evolving social responsibility standards to gain favourable public recognition, particularly on environmental issues.

The increased activities of civil society groups require changes in the way business responds to the expectations stakeholders put forward regarding the companies' behaviour. In fact, companies see themselves confronted with increasing demands as to their accountability to, and interaction with, groups of civil society. For many years, corporations were generally trusted to be good corporate citizens without any particular activities required to prove this proposition right. Over the past 20 to 30 years however, companies have been increasingly confronted with demands from NGOs in many (especially developed) countries to provide evidence on their activities and impacts in different social responsibility areas. Some companies responded to this charge by drafting codes of conduct, others by preparing special reports on issues pertaining to social responsibility (including environmental or social reports). But this is no longer enough: companies are now more and more asked to establish systematic and independent monitoring and auditing processes to demonstrate how corporate principles and policies are implemented in daily business practices. In a further step, some companies are intensifying their interaction with stakeholders on social responsibility issues by actively soliciting stakeholders views on issues over which conflicts may arise or have already occurred. This process can be encapsulated in a four-step sequence:

(i) the "trust me"—phase, in which companies did not face any expectations going beyond the respect of law and order;

(ii) the "tell me"—phase in which companies were asked to give an account of their companies principles and impacts regarding certain social responsibility issues;

(iii) the" show me"—phase, in which companies are asked by civil society to actually demonstrate that they adhere to their principles and standards; and

(iv) the "join me"—phase, in which companies are asked to involve actively and interact with, stakeholders in the process of solving problems pertaining to social responsibility.

At present, companies can be found at different stages of the model. Many have not paid much attention to social responsibility issues, however. Those that have, do not necessarily respond in the same way to civil society expectations as individual companies find themselves under different pressures and, accordingly, respond differently. Still, there appears to be an overall trend that indicates that companies are putting more resources into responding to social responsibility demands and into interacting with civil society groups on issues pertaining to social responsibility.

3. Government Actions

Recent government actions on TNC social responsibility themes centre around renewed interest and activity on previously formulated international guidelines or codes of conduct. Initiatives in United Nations bodies relating to environment and labour issues, as well as continuing OECD reviews of the 1976 Guidelines for Multinational Enterprises, comprise the primary focus of this activity. The United Nations work on human rights issues is also important and relevant

These developments represent the most active recent government initiatives at the international level that directly address TNC social responsibility issues. Considerably more governmental time and energy has, however, been devoted to formulating legal instruments aimed at improving the international climate for foreign investment. For example, the dramatic proliferation of more than 1,700 bilateral investments treaties creates important rights for TNCs, usually enforceable through binding investment dispute settlement mechanisms. Investment provisions in regional trade arrangements such as NAFTA, which has labour and environmental side agreements, and MERCOSUR—which features a social charter—also aim at complementing the lowering of trade barriers with a parallel liberalisation of regional investment regulations.

Policy Implications

Certain patterns appear to be emerging as a result of these most recent trends in how TNC social responsibility issues are being addressed. First impressions form around the striking growth in both the number of organisations and the proliferation of initiatives that have gained importance in this area. Social responsibility concerns claim increasing attention among both government and business policy-makers, largely due to the stimulus of civil society groups and activities. Although the range of specific issues is quite broad, the vast majority of recent undertakings fall under umbrella categories related to labour, the environment and human rights. Other issues such as technology transfer, competitive practices, consumer protection and community relations have attracted less recent attention or have been addressed in aspects related to the other three categories. However, many of the issues that concern development and, therefore, are of particular interest to developing countries, have attracted little attention. Labour, the environment and human rights also all relate to existing United Nations instruments that furnish some common international ground in identifying core values while providing institutional processes that might help carry forward follow-up activities.

Although efforts continue to elaborate agreed standards to guide TNC social responsibility actions, there is also growing recognition of the importance of designing implementation steps that will give life to the standards' application. Hence, more discussion is occurring related to monitoring mechanisms that might provide for review, evaluation, revision and performance improvements. Crucial monitoring questions regarding "what", "who" and "how" remain unresolved in most cases, although there are clear efforts by civil society groups to encourage the use of management systems techniques and performance measures as well as independent auditors. One difficulty with implementation measures is the large variation among standards in their degree of specificity and applicability to particular industries and business operations. Conversely, the more specifically applicable standards and performance measures are to given products or sectors, the more proliferation occurs among institutional standards and follow-up mechanism, generating attendant time, information and resource demands. Indeed, the growth of activity in this area has been accompanied by an increasing overlap and, at times, seeming competition among proliferating standards arid their sponsoring groups. A plethora of codes may contribute to the risk of inducing a "code fatigue" among corporations, particularly where an enterprise may be engaged in multiple lines of business in countries around the world. TNCs aligned in shifting patterns of multiple international strategic alliances may also find it difficult to meld the various standards and reporting systems adopted by different alliance partners.

A positive pattern emerging from recent social responsibility trends is the increased efforts at improved dialogue between TNCs and social interest groups. Early relationships were often marked by mistrust and misunderstandings that fed a cycle of antagonistic actions and reactions. Harsh public commentaries and revelations of corporate misconduct still serve to focus attention on specific TNCs. While this may be necessary, substantive longer-term improvements often depend on establishing a working dialogue or even partnership with corporate representatives where debates over differences are aimed more at identifying mutually acceptable solutions and practical implementation steps. For their part, TNCs that acknowledge social responsibility commitments in a global context often also recognise that social interest groups can open a window on the world that offers valuable perspectives, insights and access to human resources that can assist an international corporation's search for better operational alternatives. Thus far, this pattern appears to develop more within certain industries and companies than others, often occurring in sectors that have experienced hostile clashes in the past.

A difficulty in this dialogue is to involve the various civil society groups that pursue social responsibility initiatives. Although civil society groups in some areas attempt to forge coalitions, or at least coordinate activities, corporations, business organisations and even governments often confront the task of selecting the most appropriate dialogue partners from among at times overlapping and sometimes competitive civil society groups. Furthermore, the representativeness of a given civil society group in terms of affected TNC constituencies is not always clear, particularly when social activists in developed home countries urge actions on behalf of people and interests located in host countries elsewhere. Although some civil society groups have expanded their international membership and seek to collaborate with local groups in many different countries, the decision-making leadership and institutional resources expended on many TNC social responsibility issues are often still heavily weighted towards the perspectives and priorities of the developed countries, especially institutions based in the United States and Europe. All this not withstanding, civil society groups deserve considerable credit for putting social responsibility on the public agenda.

Trade unions although showing solidarity in the drive to raise labour standards worldwide face a diversity of perspectives and interests among different country organisations, including locations in which effective independent unions do not exist. Human rights organisations pressing TNCs to influence political developments in other countries sometimes confront a particularly complicated challenge to demonstrate that their advocated path towards agreed goals is in line with the preferences and priorities of the most affected foreign population. This dilemma is best exemplified in disputes, even among human rights groups pursuing the same ultimate goal, over whether TNCs should withdraw from a country with significant human rights abuses, or stay and work for change.

An examination of recent TNC social responsibility trends can show where patterns of interaction have emerged, but it can also indicate where they have not developed. The three categories of social responsibility; issues that have in recent years attracted most attention have often been pursued independently of each other in terms of goal priorities. Advocacy groups cooperate and coordinate in efforts to press their agendas with government and business, but the collaboration is sometimes more tactical than substantive, playing off a few readily identifiable areas of overlapping interests, such as trade unions and human rights groups joining forces in supporting freedom of association and collective bargaining. Discussions are important among civil society groups, or with corporations and governments, regarding what trade-offs may exist and where priorities should lie in a practical world where attention, time and resources are allocated among many worthwhile objectives.

Discussion is especially crucial concerning he range of issues that, fall outside the three dominant categories, where desirable goals may go unfulfilled due to lack of attention or devoted resources. Development issues are particularly important here. Also important are potentially detrimental side-effects on other worthy objectives that could result from unforeseen (although potentially discernible) impacts arising from specific actions taken to protect the environment, improve working conditions or alter political circumstances in cm effort to aid human rights. A field in which such trade-offs or impacts may occur relates to a range of development goals, particularly for smaller developing countries and economies in transition.

Placed within the context of development goals and objectives, question regarding TNC social responsibility can involve decisions regarding how the formulation and application of particular standards will affect the distribution of costs and benefits among companies, industries and countries. An illustration of this notion is the differences emerging between developed and developing country 'perspectives on appropriate TNC social responsibility standards relating to employment issues such work hours. Proposals for a minimum "floor" that might substantially narrow the differences between developing and developed countries could significantly affect comparative economic advantages central to a country's development plans, with impacts on inward FOI, export and import levels, and local business development. Many aspects of the demands for improvements may be justified against any cultural background and are believed-unlikely to endanger the comparative advantage of developing countries. Even discrete measures such as the use of certification and labelling methods to signify compliance with labour or environmental standards could unintentionally reinforce the competitive powers of large TNCs, to the detriment of a developing country's smaller national firms that may lack the resources to meet consistently a management system's compliance, reporting and outside auditing requirements.

The fact that a discussion has now begun on some issues related to working conditions may aid in recognising when and which measures may have indirect, unintended, consequences if used to establish globally applied standards without a full prior vetting of interests and impacts on the international level. From the perspective of developing countries, some recent social responsibility initiatives may give the impression that TNCs and civil society groups from developed countries are setting standards that can have major impacts on a country's, development goals, without developing country governments playing a substantial role in determining the standards content, implementation or likely impact. Despite all the best intentions, when backed by the power of consumers in the developed countries, such initiatives could function like non-tariff barriers or significantly raise the cost of competitive entry into global markets. Such fears are exacerbated when standards determined in other countries are transmitted directly through TNC investment channels into the host country. Recent cases show that this influence can even be projected without traditional TNC ownership links through the power wielded by large retailers and other firms that can set contractual conditions all along their global supply chain.

The growing economic interdependence of the world community, to which the liberalisation of international investment and trade regimes has contributed significantly, has great potential for enhancing the living standards of people throughout the world. Greater efforts must be made, however, to manage the adjustment costs and social as well as economic disruption that accompany globalisation. By assuming greater social responsibility, firms can assist in these efforts. This is in their international self-interest. It is precisely the purpose of the global compact to contribute to the emergence of shared values and principles, which will give a human face to the global market, the foundation of a stable global society and economy. Failure to build such a foundation could contribute to a backlash against the liberalisation policies that, in the first place, provide the framework of legal rights within which firms pursue global business strategies. With these expanding global rights, however, come the corresponding responsibilities of "global corporate citizenship", including concern for development, the priority of the vast majority of the world's population. The societal boundaries for TNCs in the twenty-first century will be the global community.

❐

21

Multinational Corporation and Foreign Collaboration

Multination Corporations are gaint firms with their headquarters located in the country and with a variety of business operations in several other countries. They are also sometimes refered to an Transnational Corporations (TNCs) which implies that their operations extends beyond the boundaries of the nation in whch they were originally started. An ILO report says, "The essential nature of the multinational enterprise lies in the fact that its managerial headquarters are located in one country while the enterprise causes out operations in a number of other countries as well."

There are now 40,000 MNCs which have 2,50,000 overseas affiliates. The sales of 2000 top corporations in 1982 was equivalent of 24.2 per cent of the world's GDP and have risen to 28.3 per cent of the world GDP in 1998. The combined sales of these 200 MNCs estimated at $ 7.1 Million in 1998 surpass the combined economics of 182 contries. An idea of the giant size of these MNCs can also be had from the revolution made in study that of the 100 largest economics in the world, 51 are corporations; only 49 are countries. This shows that MNCs have the massive control over the world economy. In fact, because of their huge capital resources, latest technology and worldwide goodwill, MNCs are in a position to sell whetever product they choose to manufacture in different countries.

MULTINATIONAL CORPORATION : TREND PERFORMANCE (1973-74 TO 1978-79)

A. Trends and Performance of Branches of MNCs. Table I reveals that out of 540 branches in the country, 319 (59 per cent) were UK-based. US-based were second largest in number (88). Together UK and US-based companies accounted for as many as 407 branches or 75 per cent of the total in 1973-74. In numerical strength, there was a decline to 253 of UK and US-based companies in 1978-79 (or 71 per cent of total). However the assets of UK and US based companies aggregated to Rs. 1,620 crores in 1973-74 but their asset position improved to Rs. 2,194 crores in 1978-79. In relative terms, it was over 90 per cent of assets. In other words, there is a high degree of concentration of assets of UK and US based companies.

Table 1 reveals the industry-wise distribution of branches of MNCs. The data reveal that assets of branches in commerce, trade and finance aggregated to Rs. 1,231 crores in 1973-74 (*i.e.*, 69 per cent of total). The share of this group in assets was Rs. 1,838 crores in 1978-79 and had improved to 79 per cent in total. In the agricultural sector, all the branches deal with tea only. Obviously, the claims of branches of MNCs in terms of transfer of technology do not bear the test of scrutiny since a large majority of them are engage in commerce, trade an finance or export of tea. The share of processing and manufacture in total assets was 12 per cent in 1973-74 which has declined further to 6 per cent in 1978-79. This indicates that the branches of multinational companies are hardly interested in developing technology in terms of improving processing and manufacturing industries.

Table 1 : Branches of MNCs in India-Industries-wise

Industry	*Number*		*Assests (Rs. crores)*	
	1973-74	*1978-79*	*1973-74*	*1978-79*
(1)	*(2)*		*(3)*	
1. Agriculture and allied activities	115	85	223	227
2. Mining & Quarrying	7	7	37	35
3. Processing & Manufacture	80	47	220	151

Contd.

(1)	*(2)*		*(3)*	
4. Construction & Utilities	32	21	46	102
5. Commerce trade & finance	154	68	1231	1838
6. Transport, communication & storage	39	35	4	6
7. Services	113	95	29	42
Total	540	358	1790	2401

Profit Ratios of Branches of MNCs

An important indicator of profitability is the ratio of profits before tax (PBT) to turnover. This ratio was 5.1 pr cent in 1973-74 but has declined to 3.7 per cent in 1978-79. An industrywise analysis of profits earned revealed that the profit ratios PBT to assets and PBT to turnover in tea plantations were much higher than the overall ratios for all branches. For instance, during 1978-79, PBT to assets for branches of MNCs engaged in tea was 10.7 per cent and PBT to turnover was 12 per cent. In drug industry also, the profit ratios were exceedingly high. In 1978-79, profits before tax as a ratio of asset and turnover of branches in medical and pharmaceutical preparations worked out at 55 per cent and 30 per cent respectively. This indicates the extent of exploitation by MNCs in the drug inudstry and the facile manner in which resources were drained out by the MNCs. However, in the manufacures of metals, chemical products, commerce, trade and finance etc., the profitability ratios were generally lower.

Trend and Performance of Subsidiaries of MNCs

Subsidiaries of MNCs are defined as companies incorporated in India in which a single foreign body corporate, *i.e.*, a multi-national corporation holds more than 50 per cent of the paid-up equity capital.

Despite a decline of their numerical strength, together the UK-US based subsidiaries had increase their assets from Rs. 1,011 crores in 1973-74 to Rs. 1,278 crores in 1979-79. In relative terms, the position remained unaltered and they accounted for about 75 per cent of total assets. (Refer table 3). Besides this, the subsidiairies of five countries, *viz.*, Switzerland, Sweden, West Germany, Canada and the Netherlands accounted for assets amounting to Rs. 318 crores in 1973-74. The assets of the subsidiaries of these countries improved to Rs. 386 crores in 1979-79. However, in relative terms, the position remained more or less the same *i.e.* 23.3 per cent of total assets in 1973-74 and 22.6 per cent in 1978-79.

Subsidiaries of MNCs-Distribution by Percentage of Equity Capital held by Foreign Companies

	1973-74	*1978-79*
1. Over 50% but less than 70%	83	57
	(44.1)	(45.5)
2. Over 70 but less than 100%	33	27
	(17.6)	21.6)
3. 100%	72	41
	(38.3)	(32.8)
	188	125

Note : Figures in brackets are per centage of total in the respective column.

Source : *Company News and Notes, June 1980*

Of the 188 subsidiary companies, 72 were wholly owned. In another, 83 subsidiaries of MNCs, the foreign holdings ranged between 50 to 70 per cent, and for the remaining 33 subsidiaries, the holdings were between 70 to 100 per cent. However, the position underwent a change by 1978-79. The number of wholly owned subsidiaries declined from 72 to 41 *i.e.*, from 38 per cent to about 33 per cent. To conclude, the trends and performance of branches and subsidiaries during the period 1973-74 to 1978-79 reveal that.

(i) The beneficient effect in terms of foreign exchange earnings are too little to merit attention.

(ii) To comouflage their activities, the MNCs are rapidly converting their branches into subsidiaries.

(iii) Majority of branches of MNCs are engaged in commerce, trade and finance and export of tea, there is hardly any evidence of transfer of technology.

BENEFITS OF MNCS

We shall mention the important arguments in favour of and against the MNCs. MNCs, it has been claimed, help the host countries in the following ways:

(i) MNCs help increase the investment level and thereby the income and employment in the host country.

(ii) The transnational corporations have becomes vehicles for the transfer of technology, especially to developing countries.

(iii) They kindle a managerial revolution in the host countries by professional management and the employment of highly sophisticated management techniques.

(iv) The MNCs enable the host countries to increase their exports and decrease their important requirements.

(v) They work to equalise the cost of the factors of production around the world.

(vi) MNCs provide an efficient means of intergating national economics.

(vii) MNCs help increase competition and break domestic monopolies.

(viii) The enormous resource of multinational enterprises enable them to have every efficient research and development systems. Thus, they make a commendable countribution in invention and innovations.

DRAWBACKS OF MNCS

MNCs have, however, been subject to a great deal of criticism.

(i) As Loanard Gomes point out, the MNC's technology is designed for world-wide profit maximisation, not the development needs of poor countries, in particular employment needs and relative factor scarcities in these countries. In general, it has been asserted, imported technologies are not adapted to:

(a) Stage of development of many LDCs;

(b) The consumption needs;

(c) The size of domestic markets; and

(d) Resource availabilities.

(ii) Through their power and flexibility, MNCs can evade or undermine national economic autonomy and conrol, and their activities may be inimical to the national interests of particular countries.

(iii) The tremendous power of global corporations poses the risk that they may threaten the sovereugnty of the nations in which they do business.

(iv) MNCs can have an unfavourable effect on the Balance of Payments of a country. By repatriating profits they may deplete for the foreign exchange resource of a countries. For instance, Coca Cola, until 1978, had remitted abroad nearly Rs. 6 crores on an intial investment of Rs. 6.6 lakhs in India.

(v) MNCs may destroy competition and acquire monopoly powers.

(vi) Transfer pricing enables MNCs to avoid taxes by manipulating prices on intra-company transactions.

(vii) MNCs retard the growth of employment in the home country.

(viii) Transnational corporations cause a rapid depletion of some of the non-renewable natural resources in the home country.

Recent Trends

It appears that receently there has been a change in the attitude to multinations. They are not subject to as severe criticism as they were in the past. Even commnist countries have developed some favourable attitude to them. Countries as diverse as Cuba, China and Portugal have loosened the reins on multinationals. Paul Streeten points out that there are five recent trends that suggest that the role of multinational corporations in development has to be reassessed. First, there has been a shift in bargaining power between multinationals and their host countries; greater restrictions on the inflow of packaged technology; a change in emphasis, from production to research and development and marketing among other factors, that have increased the uncertainties of direct foreign investment. As a result, there is some evidence that it has become the policy of multinational companies to shift from equity investment, ownership of capital, and managerial control of overseas facilities to the sale of technology, management services, and marketing as a means of earning returns on corporate asseets, at least in those countries that have policies against inflows of packaged technology.

Second, not only to host countries deal with a greater variety of foreign companies, comparing their political and economic attractions weighing them against their costs, and playing them off against one another, but the large multinationals are being replaced by smaller and more flexible firms.

Third, many more nations are now competing with U multinationals in setting up foreign activities, which means that the controversy is no longer dominated by nationalistic considerations. Japanese and European firms figure prominently among the new multinationals.

Fourth, developing countries themselves are now establishing multinationals. In addition to companies from the Organisation of Petroleum Exporting Countres (OPEC), and firms established in tax-haven countries, the leading countries where multinationals are being established are Argentina, Brazil, Colombia, Hong Kong, India, the Republic of Korea, Peru, the Philippines, Singapore, and Taiwan.

Fifth, some multinationals from developed countries have accommodated themselves to the needs of the developing country.

MNCS AND INDIAN ECONOMY

MNCs have a strong hold over the Indian economy. In fact even two decades ago, these corporations controlled 53.7 per cent of the assets of the gaint sector in India. According to the Industrial licensing Policy Inquiry Committee there were 112 companies in 1966 with assets worth Rs. 10 crore or more. Of these 48 were either foreign branches or Indian subsidiaries of foreign companies. In addition, 14 Indian companies had extermely heavy loans and equity capital and therefore were virtually foreign countrolled. These 62 companies had Rs. 1,370 core worth of assets which constituted 54 per cent of the total assets of India's giant sector.

The operation of MNCs open up the possibilities of interference in the industrial (and other) activities of the recipient country and are thus resented by the 'nationalist' thinkers. Their arguments against the operations of MNCs can be summed up as follows:

1. Payment of Dividends and Royalty. A large sum of money flows out of the country in terms of payment of dividends, profits, royalties, technical fees and interest to the foreign investors. For instance, remittance made abroad by private sector companies stood at Rs. 72.26 crores in 1969-70. This rose to Rs. 398.9 crores. in 1986-87. A study by N.K. Chandra shows that over three-fifths of private corporate, or about two-fifths of factory sector dividends were paid out by the foreign firms in the mid-1980s.

2. Political Intereference. Because of their immense financial and technical power, the MNCs, have gained the necessary strength to influence the decision making process in underdeveloped countries. Though they do not help in transferring technology to underdeveloped countries, is has been often found that models and patterns of industrial development and technologies transferred are not in harmony with the interests of the host countries. The governments of underdeveloped countries have also felt threatened by the direct and indirect interference of MNCs in their internal affairs. The autonomy and sovereignty of the host countries is in danger. Because of these reasons, the government of varous countries have sought to restrict the activities of MNCs in their economics through a battery of administrative control and legal provisions.

3. Distortion of Economic Structure. MNCs can inflinct heavy damage on the host country in various forms such as suppression of domestic enterpreneurship, extension of oligopolistic practices (such as unnecessary product differentiation, heavy advertising, or excessive profit taking), supplying the economy with unsuitable technology and unsuitable products, worsening of income distribution by distorting the production structure to meet the requirements of high-income elites, etc. Modern Marxist economists (Paul Baran, for example) argue that foreign investment (especially through multinational corporations) opens up the doors of 'neoimperialism' and 'exploitation.

4. Technology Transfer not Necessarily Conductive to Development. As far as transfer of technology to underdeveloped countries is concerned, the behavior pattern of MNCs reveals that they do not enagage in R and D activities within the underdevloped countries. Their R and D efforts are concentrated in laboratories in the home country or in other industrialised countries. Though R and D activities continue to be centralized in the parent country, the host countries have to bear the bulk of their costs since the affiliates of MNCs in these countries remit payment on this account generally in relation on their sales volume. Such payments by the affiliates are generally over and above those remitted in the form of royalties and technical fees to the parent firm. The satisfaction expressed on technology transfer is party misconceived also on account of the fact that MNCs which generally command a semi-monopolistic position in their product lines do not transfer their first-line or most advanced technology until foreign firms compel them to do so. In many cases, the technology transferred is of a capital-intensive nature which is not useful from the point of view of a labour surplus economic. In fact, continued insistence on the import of such technology can have serious consequence for the economy of the host country since unemployment will increase. Also, market will fail to grow and this constraint would suffice to restrian the rate of growth from increasing.

FOREIGN COLLABORATION

It would be worthwhile to examine how far foreign private investment has been beneficial for the growth of our economy. At the time of independence, most of our industries were concerned with consumer goods. Except two steel mines, we have hardly any capital goods or intermediate goods industries. Today Indian industry presents a different picture. Petrolium refining, chemicals and pharmaceuticals, steel, light and heavy engineering man made fibre and several other industries have been established and are working on a profitable basis. These industries would not have come into existence or would have taken many years to expand out for the technical know-how and skill obtained from abroad *i.e.* foreign collaboration.

Foreign Collaboration Policy. The policy of Government of India in regard to foreign private investment to be based on the cardinal principle mentioned in the statement made in April 1949 by the late prime minister Nehru in parliament. The uppermost consideration underlying the policy statement were non-discrimination between and Indian and a foreign enterprise in the larger interests of country. These principles were incorporated in the industrial policy Resolution of 1956.

The underyling principles of the policy are, by and large valid even today. These are:

(i) Foreign capital once admitted will be treated at per with the indigeneous capital.

(ii) Facilities for remittence of profits abroad will continue.

(iii) If and when foreign enterprises are acquired, compensation will be paid on a fair and equitable basis.

(iv) As a rule, the major interest in ownership and effective control of and undertaking should be in Indian hands.

(v) The government would not object to foreign capital of a concern for a limited period if it is found to be in the national interest, and each individual case will be dealt on its merits.

The foreigning principles clearly indicate that the government assured a non-discriminatory treatment to foreign capital as also un-restricted facilities for the repatriation of both capital and profits. An important features of its policy was to lay emphasis on the employment and training of Indians in higher position.

FOREIGN COLLABORATIONS AND TRANSFER OF TECHNOLOGY

P. Mohanan Pillai in his paper on "Foreign collaboration in Public sector" analysed the impact multi-national economy. The following main points emerge from his study:

Firstly, transfer of technology under the aegis of foreign collaborations is an act of "unequal exchange than comparative advantages. "Relative bargaining power settles the terms of technology transfer. The bargain will be struck to the disadvantage of the buyers to whom suppliers transfer technology at onerous cost.

Secondly, it is not correct to assume that effective control is necessarily commensurate with formal capital ownership. The interest of foreign collaboration is fully protection even though it has a minority participation in equity, since tenchnical operation and investments other than equity are controlled primarily by the foreign collaboration.

Thirdly, technology transfer to India Public sector is marked by the predominance of package formula (*i.e.* patents, trade mark, know-how) which implies grater control by technolgy suppliers. Moreover, the restrictive featrues of foreign collaboration in the public sector are in no way, different from those in the private sector. They are rather much worse.

Fourthly, by the various contracts for the supply of equipment, plant, construction and also supply of credit, the foreign collaborators derive excessive benefits using technology transfer a cover. Evidence recent study of engineering industry reveals that even the public sector is notable to resist the pressure-cum-conspiracy tactics of foreign collaborators.

Lastly, the dependence on foreign technicians in the public sector was higher in the private sector. The ratio of foreign technicains per collaboration was 37 for the public sector whereas it was only 22 for subsidiaries, 5 for minority participation and 1 for pure technical collaboration companies during 1964-70.

Dr. S.K. Goyal of the Indian Institute of Public Administration made a study of "the impact of foreign subsidiaries on India's balance of payments" for the year 1975-76 covering 133 companies out of a total of 171 foreign subsidiaries operating in India in 1975-76. The important conclusions of the study were:

(i) An overwhelming number of foreign subsidiaries operating in India originate from U.K. and U.S.A. Out of 171 subsidiaries, 116 had their parent company in the U.K. and 25 in the U.S.A.

(ii) Most of the foreign subsidiaries have raised financial resources from within India and the transfer of capital, by way of contribution to share capital or loans from the parent company, has been marginal.

(iii) Large foreign companies in India are fast acquiring the character of multi-product and multi industry enterprises. For instances, Imperial (now Indian) tobacco company (ITC) recently diversified its activities to hotel industry and is alreay having a chain of luxury hotels in India. The union carbide of India has entered into agricultural and marine products. To demonstrate its respect for the national priorities, the Imperial chemical Industries have taken up rural uplift programme in a village of Uttar Pradesh. On the one hand, diversification helps the foreign subsidiaries to expand in new and more profitable areas, but on the other, they escape any likelihood of attracting anti-monopoly legislation and public resentment. There has been an increasing tendency on the part of foreign companies to diversify their activities into areas like hotels, cosmetics and other industrial products which consitute an important part of the budget of the affluent section of the society.

(iv) Nearly all the branches and subsidiaries of foreign companies have accepted the Indianization scheme and a large number of them have already taken measures to reduce the degree of foreign shareholding. Many of the foreign subsidiaries in India, which have accepted the policy of equity dilution, have, however, succeeded in obtaining the government approval to enter into perpetual legal agreements with their parent companies, under which the management control, even when the parent company held only a minority in the total shares, would continue to rest in foreign hands.

(v) The assets of foreign subsidiaries increased from Rs. 1,129 crores in 1969 to Rs. 1,626—crores in 1976—an increase of 33 per cent during the period 1969-76. The share of the processing and manfacturing category increased from 77 per cent of 1969 to 90 per cent in 1976.

(vi) The assumption that the entry of Transnational Corporations (TNCs) would ensure transfer of sophisticated technology to developing countries has not been found valid in practice. In India, there is sufficient evidence to suggest that the transfer of technology is only from one industrial project in a developed country to another 'project site' but it makes no contribution to the low technology-oriented system of production to the poor country. For instance, a clause included in the collaboration agreement between Phillips India and its parent company reads: "The company undertakes both during continuance of this agreement and thereafter not to copy the machinery, tools and insturments or any parts there of applied by phillips or any subsidiaries of phillips to the company or to cause or permit the same to be copied and not to prepare drawing of such machinery, tools and instruments or parts thereof nor to cause or permit the same to be prepared." In such cases, transfer of technology is a myth and TNCs in practiec do not permit such transfer but keep process and technologies a well-guarded secret.

During 1975-76, total value of foreign exchange earned by 133 foreign subsidiaries was Rs. 120 crores. An overwhelming part of it was earned through export of traditional items from India like tea, tobacco; leather products, processed food etc. Against this, the subsidiaries placed a direct burden on India's foreign exchange resources to the extent of Rs. 220 crores. Since the State Trading Corporation, for accounting practices, treats imported raw material supplied to foreign subsidiaries as 'indigenous raw material', the assessed foreign exchange burdern is an under-estimate. Thus, there was a continued international drain on account of the operations of foreign controlled companies.

A study of foreign collaborations reveals cerain interesting results. Thus, a large number of agreements were concluded for the manufacture of products which were non-essential or which could be produced with the help of local technology. These items included vacuum flasks, lipstick, toothpaste, cosmetics, brassiers, ice-cream, gin, beer, buscuits, dry batteries and readymade garments. Not only were collaborations granted for these products, they were often in multiple numbers and were renewed on expiry. Clearly such collaborations were often directed to serve the needs of high income groups and to take advantage of a foreign brand name.

In addition to this 'orientation of foreign collabortions, they also sufferd from a number of other drawbacks as is clear from the following considerations.

(1) The practice of multiple collaborations led to the introduction of standards of various countries (in raw materials, spare parts, design, specifications, and even terms of measurement) into the Indian industry every for very similar products or within the same firm. This multiplicity led to large inventory accumulation and uneconomic locking up of working capital. It also hindered standardisation and variety reduction which are so essential for raising industrial productivity;

(2) The terms of payment were also drawn up so as to squeeze out the maximum payments under one head or other. Generally 5 per cent of the annual turnover for 10 years as royalty plus 5 per cent of the imorted plant cost as technical fees in the case of royalty-cum-technical fees, or 10 per cent of the issued capital as lumpsum

payment for technical fees alone, were the limits of official policy. However, these tended to become routine;

(3) The government permitted collaborations, *i.e.* repetitive import of the same or similar technology. This resulted in respetive payments without adding to the stock of technical knowledge in the country.

(4) The terms of agreements were mostly weighted in favour of the foreign collaborators and were against India interests. This arose on account of the lack of bargaining power in the Indian side and the government's eagerness to acquire foreign participation in the face of foreign exchange shortage;

(5) Since the responsibility of specification and supply of equipment was entrusted to the foreign collaborators, there was close tie-up between the designers and suppliers resulting not only in price mark-up but also in overimport of equipment. Sometimes equipments were imported even when they were available locallly, sometimes they remained idle for want of spares, and often the processes were more highly mechanised and sophisticated than was desirable or necessary. At times, obsolete tecnology was imported;

(6) Foreign collaborations have helped the growth of monopolies and concentration. They joined hands with the big business houses and the latter were only too eager to enter into understanding with them since the presence of foreign links often conferred certain strategic advanages (patent, resources, foreign exchange, etc.) enabling the big business houses to diversify and expand.

(7) The most important part related to the presence of various restrictive clauses in the agreements. 'Some restrictions imposed were: *(a)* the technology cannot be passed on to any one elase, in some cases even after the expiry of the agreement; *(b)* manufacturing is to be carried out according to the specifications laid down by the collaborator and no local adaptations can be made; *(c)* control over oveseas purchase was exercised through the provision that it had to be made directly or indirectly through the collaborator; *(d)* production was tightly controlled at times through the posting of foreign technicians; *(e)* controls over the pricing and marketing of the

products were exercised by requiring that a part of the production was to be sold to the collaborator's subsidiary in India at a fixed commission or that specified firms were to be made the sole selling agents; and (f) right to export was also restricted by the provision that exports could be done only to specific countries or on certain perconditions.

A large number of Indian industrialists have colleborated through MNCs. Foreign collaboration agreements are made between Indian companies and foreign parties, involving sale of technology, as well use of foreign brand name for the final products. The enormity of foreign collaborations entered into by the Indian companies would be clear from the fact that in nearly all of the new industries in the large or medium size group, privately or publicly owned, set up after Independence, some collaboration agreement was present. Foreign collaboration approvals (1961-91) reveals that during 1961-91 a large number of collaborations were approved. Trends of liberalisation in 1980s gave a substantial spurt to foreign collaboration. This would be clear from the fact that of the total 12,760 foreign collaborations agreements approved in 40 years between 1948 and 1988, as many as 6,165 (*i.e.* 48.3 per cent) were approved during the eight years between 1981 and 1988. As a result of liberalised foreign investment policy announced in July - August 1991, there has been a further spurt of of foreign collaborations. For instance from August 1991 to October 2001, the Government approved 7,116 foreign technology collaborations and 13,640 foreign direct investment proposals. The total amount of foreign investment approved in the process amounted to Rs. 2,70,064 crore. However, the actual inflow was only Rs. 1,05,413 crore.

The government policy in the field of foreign collaboration has been criticised on the following grounds:

1. The terms of agreements were mostly weighted in favour of the foreign collaborators and were against Indian interests.
2. A large number of products produced under foreign collaboration were of non-essential nature. There items

were mainly consumer goods which could be produced with the help of local technology.

3. The government permitted multiple collaborations, *i.e.*, repititive import of the same or similar technology. This resulted in repetitive payments without adding to the stock of technical knowledge in the country.
4. Since the responsibility of specification and supply of equipment was entrusted to the foreign collaboration, there was close tie-up between the designers and suppliers resulting not only in price make up but also in over-import of equipment. Sometimes, obsolete technology was imported.
5. Foreign collaborations have helped the growth of monopolies and concentration. They joined hands with the big business houses and the later were only too eager to enter into understanding with them to diversify and expand their business.
6. The royalty and technical fees changed by foreign collaborators was very high which led to the outflow of foreign currency at a high rate.
7. The foreign collaboration agreements were subject to following restictive clauses:
   (i) The technology cannot be passed on the any one else, in some cases even after the expiry of the agreement;
   (ii) Control very overseas purchase was excerised through the provision that it had to be made directly or indirectly through the collaborator;
   (iii) Manufacturing is to be carried out according to the specifications laid down by the collaborator and no local adaptations can be made;
   (iv) Controls over the pricing and marketing of the products;
   (v) Production was tightly controlled at times through the posting of foreign technicians; and

(vi) Right to export was also restricted by the provision that exports could be done only to specific countries or on certain preconditions.

In brief it can be said that in most of the cases foreign collaborations agreements with local industrialists have not promoted the growth of exports, development of technology and use of local resources effectively. This has resulted into the outflowing of foreign exchange in huge quantity and dependence of foreign technology.

NON-RESIDENT INDIANS

The persons of Indian origin who are not living in India but lives abroad are called non-resident Indians. Non-residents can be further divided in two groups: *(a)* non-residents of Indian nationality or origin (NRI), and *(b)* other-residents. Investments by non-residents belonging to category (b) are subject to the policy guidelines framed by the Government of India from time to time in line with its industrial policy. However, investments by non-residents of Indian nationality or origin are allowed more liberally in order to give them wider investment opportunities.

In India, non-resident deposits is a high cost method to attract foreign exchange and finance the import bill. The share of non-resident deposits has increased from 9.7 per cent in 1980-81 to 38.2 per cent in 1985-86 and stagnted around 30 per cent for the years 1986-89. In the last year of the Seventh Plan (*i.e.* 1989-90) the share of NRI (non-resident Indian) deposits in the total capital flows (net) was 26.7 per cent. In order to bolster foreign exchange in Government of India took the following steps.

(i) The Government of India has liberalised the definition of NRI. Now it has extended to include a foreign born husband of a citizen of India or a person of Indian origin to bring more people under the umbrella.

(ii) The RBI has given a general exemption of NIRs for transfer of shares/bonds and debentures of Indian companies through recognised stock exchanges to residents on non-repatriation as well as repatriation basis.

(iii) An NRI can gift by way of transfer shares/debentures/bonds of Indian companies to their close relatives residing in India.

(iv) The Reserve Bank of India with a view to encourage NRI investment has allowed existing or new companies engaged or proposing to engage in the specified activities relating to housing and real estate developments to issue equity shares/convertible debentures to non-residents of Indian nationality/origin upto 100 per cent of the new issue with repatriation benefits.

(v) Authorised dealers are now permitted by RBI to allow remittance of dividends (including interim dividend) on equity preference shares to non-resident shareholders of Indian companies.

(vi) The NRIs are freely permitted to invest funds in Government securities or units of UTI through authorised dealers. Units can also be purchased directly from UTI.

(vii) All the securities/units etc. are easily transferable/sold through authorised dealers, the funds thus accrued from such sales can be repatriated abroad, in case the purchases have been made out of NRE/FCNR accounts.

(viii) NRIs are permitted to make direct investment in shares/debentures of Indian companies. They are also permitted to make portfolio investment, that is, purchase of shares/debentures of Indian companies through stock exchanges in India. These facilities are granted both on repatriation and non-repatriation basis under the Portfolio Investment Scheme. The NRIs are permitted to acquire shares/debentures of Indian companies through the recognised stock exchanges in India.

In case of shares acquired by NRI individuals, through Stock Exchanges under the Portfolio Investment Scheme, general exemption has been granted for transfer of the same through Stock Exchanges, provided the sale is arranged through the same designated branch through whom they were purchased and the shares were held for a period of one year prior to transfer. In other cases, applications for necessary permission are required to be made to RBI.

A new facility provided is the single window service or NRIs through the India Investment Centre and State Development Corporations. Lobbies for explaining Indian policies are being created. Umbrellas for obtaining all information from one service have been opened. Our embassies have been instructed to keep in constant touch with NRIs and with Indian organisations abroad to help solve their problems.

Magnitude of NRI Funds. As per the available information, the direct NRI investment in industry as at the end of 1993-94 amounted to $ 59.3 million crores, portfolio investment $ 1360.0 million crores and bank deposits Rs. 43,419 crores. Over the year, the government of India has given incentives in form of higher rate of interest on deposit and facility of remittance of deposit in foreign currency at the time of withdrawal to NRI to attract foreign currency deposits of India. In 1999-2000, NRI depostis (not were) $ 1540 million which was 14.2 per cent of total capital flows (net.) In 2000-01, NRI deposits (net) rose to $ 2, 317 million which was 27.6 per cent of total capital flows (net) of $ 8,409 million.

If we take into account the funds available with the NRIs, the total amount shown in the table seems insignificant. It is insignifiant because surplus funds available with NRI being but at over Rs. 120,00 crore. We have clearly failed to harness their full potential although we are in more forfitness situation with most NRIs maintaining close family and cultural links back home. These we should try more vigorously for NRI investment in the country.

❑

14

International Economic Institutions

INTERNATIONAL MONETARY FUND

The International Monetary Fund (IMF), also called the fund, is an international monetary institution established by 44 nations under the Bretton Woods Agreement of July 1944. The principal aim was to avoid the economic mistakes of the 1920. The attempts of many countries to return to the old gold system after the First World War failed miserably. The World Depression of the thirties forced every country to abandon the gold standard. This led to the adoption of purely nationalistic policies whereby almost every country imposed trade restrictions, exchange controls and resorted to exchange depreciation in order to encourage its exports. This further brought a marked decline in world trade and extension of depression. It was against this background that 44 nations assembled at the United Nations Monetary and Financial Conference at Bretton Woods, New Hampshire (USA) from 1 July to 22 July 1944. Thus the IMF was established to promote economic and financial operations among its members in order to facilitate the exapansion and balanced growth of world trade. The IMF started its working from 1 March 1947. At the end of June, 1996, the Fund had 181 members.

Nature of the IMF. The International Monetary Fund (IMF) has a two fold function. In the first place, it is a club which prescribes a high code of conduct for its members and also ensures that members comply with the case. The second aspect of the IMF is that it is a financial institution standing ready to provide loan assistance to member countries for relatively short periods and under proper safeguards to assist the countries to tide over their balance of payments difficulties, pending the formulation of appropriate measures for correcting the disequalibrium in balance of payments.

OBJECTIVES OF THE INTERNATIONAL MONETARY FUND

The objectives of the Fund stated in Article I of the Fund Agreement are as follows:

(1) To promote international monetary cooperation through a permanent institutions which provides the machinery for consultation and collaboration on international monetary problems.

(2) To facilitate the expansion and balanced growth of international trade, and to contribute thereby to the promotion and maintenance of high levels of employment and real income and to the development of productive resources of all members as primary objective of economic policy.

(3) To promote exchange stability to maintain orderly exchange arrangements among members and to avoid competitive exchange depreciation.

(4) To assist in the establishment of a multilateral system of payments in respect of current transactions between members and in the elimination of foreign exchange restrictions.

(5) To give confidence to members by making the Fund's resources temporarily available to them under adequate safeguards.

(6) In accordance with the above, shorten the duration and lessen the degree of disequalibrium in the international balance of payments of members, the fund is guided in all policies and decisions by the purposes set forth in the above Article.

It will be seen from the above that international monetary cooperation as conceived by the IMF has two to three fundamental aspects,—harmonisation of the national economic interests with those of other members of the international community, provision of financial assistance on a temporary basis to enable the countries to restore balance of payments equilibrium and the promotion of economic growth and high level of employment. The cornerstone of the IMF edifice is a fixed par value system, with provision for exchange rate changes to correct a fundamental disequalibrium, not only in consultation with the IMF but with its prior approval. Emphasis is also placed on freedom from exchange control on current transactions. In the IMF system there is also a fairly important role of gold. Under the provisions of the Fund the par of the currencies of member-nations as determined either in terms of Gold or the US dollar.

Structure of International Monetary Fund

Under the Fund structure as adopted at Bretton Woods, there is a Board of governors, there being a Governor (also an Alternate Governor) for every member country, appointed by the Government concerned. The Board of Governors is composed in practice of the Finance Ministers of members countries, who would normally meet only anually and would delegate all but the most important decisions to the Executive Directors. The Managing Director to be selected by but not from among the Executive Directors. The Executive Directors would be appointed by member countries, though only the five countries with the largest voting power would have their own Executive Directors.

The IMF was to be an international organisation. Unlike many such organiations, decisions were to be be made by weighted voting rather than by one country-one vote procedure. Both the U.S. and Britain agreed on this point because weighted voting would assure them jointly a dominating voice in decisions. Voting power on the Board of Governors and the Directorate is according to the size of the member's quota, each member having 250 votes plus one additional vote for each part of its quota equal to $ 1,00,000 (US). When voting is required on the waiving of conditions applicable to the granting of an application by a member for use of the Fund's resources, the voting formula is more complex, being designed to give more voting power to surplus countries. The normal vote of the five principal members was originally as follows:

US: 27,750 (27.93 per cent); UK: 13,250, 13.33 per cent); China: 5,750 (5.79 per cent); France: 5,500 (5.54 per cent); and India: 4,250 (4.28 per cent). If the Article V formula were applied, the voting power of the US would be still greater. Subsquent revisions of quotas have altered the absolute number of votes per member but the relative voting strength of members still favours the large rich countries.

Thus it will be evident that the management of the Fund was to be political rather than technical, that governor and directors were to regard themselves as a pool of technical knowledge and that the largest contributor to the Fund had secured for itself a dominant role in policy and decision-making. Such a set up could scarcely fail to undermine the international character of the Fund and help to make it a sounding board for divergencies of political (rather than economic) opinions upon international economic problem. Added to this the location of the Fund's officers in Washington.

International Monetary Fund as a Finance Institution

The IMF is a financial organisation dealing primarily in short-term and medium-term credit to a large number of member-countries owing allegiance to different types of economic idelogies. The Fund was established at the end of the Second World War and at that time were conflicts on the nature of its operations. The UK represented by Late Lord Keyness. It wanted the organisation to be a sort of international money-creating institution. The US, being basically conservative wanted a more modest, rules-bound role for the organisation. Ultimately when the Fund came into existence, a sort of compromise dollar-based, gold exchange standard came into existence. However, the US gradually started playing the role of a world trustee; its dollar obligations expanded and the slender gold-exchange condition could not be observed. After the sixties, when the Euro-currency markets became very prominent on the maket of international liquidity, the Fund has been reduced to the position of a supplier of 'small change'.

The organisation, has evoloved into an expert store house of financial and monetary information concerning most countries of the world. It's role as supplier of short-term and medium-term liquidity is not very important for developed countries, for whom it is a potential cushion in times of very great need of foriegn exchange. However, for the developing countries, it has emerged as one of the leading sources of exchange lending.

The financial resources for the Fund are obtained partly from all members, but more particularly from those countries which are prepared to lend to the Fund some of their surplus in the form of their own hard currency.

Operations of the International Monetary Fund

As a Financial institution, IMF provides 'loan' assistance to the member-countries for relatively short-period. For this purpose the Fund receives from member-countries in the form of 'gold and specified quantities of the currencies of the individual member countries known as 'quotas'. Quotas constitute subscriptions by member-countries to the capital Fund of the IMF. They define the relative importance of the member-countries in the matter of their rights and obligations. For instance, the higher a country's quota, the larger its capacity to borrow from the IMF. Quotas also determine the voting strength of the member-countries and the distribution of international money, *i.e.*, special drawing rights (SDRs), among member-countries is also done exactly in proportion to the quotas of members.

This came to be known as the Bretton Woods formula. According to this, out of a total of $ 8,800 million for the 44 nations gathered at Bretton Woods, the quota for the US was $ 2,750 million. The quota for India was fixed as $ 400 million, the sixth largest after the USA, UK, USSR, China and France.

Generally speaking, the members have to pay 25 per cent of their quotas in the form of gold and the rest in their own currencies. For the original members, gold subscription were set at either 25% of their quotas or 10 per cent of their net official holdings of gold and US dollars as on 12th September, 1946 whichever was less. This formula has usually been followed for later members. But there is a certain of bargaining in the matter. In cases, where the gold subscription is below 25 per cent the members are under an obligations to reduce their currency subscription. The quotas are adjusted from time to time by the Fund. The significance of the gold subscription is to enable the IMF to acquire those currencies which are needed by members but the holdings of which by the Fund have been run down.

The subscriptions (called by quotas) were not, however, the only source of Fund assests. The fund would derive income from charges on members drawings. These charges (similar) to interest payments were to be imposed on drawings and hence only on deficit countries. In addition to one-time service charge of 3/4 per cent on each transaction the Articles of Agreement provided for a slinding scale of periodic changes based on the relations of the amount of drawings to the drawing country's quota and on the elapsed time from the date of the drawing. The charges were payable in gold, though members were monetary reserves less than 1/2 of quotas were permitted to pay a portion of the charge in local currency.

The Articles of Agreement envisaged two other kinds of transactions designed to increase Fund's assets: borrwing, and replanishment by sale of gold. Investment of Fund assets was a possible third source. A fourth source of assets was implicit in the maintenance-of-value provisions. Although the Fund would have large holdings gold and of member currencies, it was not specifically empowered to increase those holdings by investment.

Exchange Transactions of International Montary Fund

When a member-country acquires currencies from the Fund, it is called an exchange operation, that is to say, the member gives its currency to the IMF in exchange for other currencies it requires. When a member acquires currencies in this manner, it is said to be a 'drawing' from the Fund and when it returns to the Fund the currencies, it had acquired earlier, it is said to be making a 'Repurchase' of its currency.

The statutes of the IMF prescribe broad limits to the quantity of credit with a member-country can receive from the IMF. Ordinarily a member should not borrow more than 25 per cent of its quota in any 12 months period. Borrowing in excess of this limit requires a specific waiver of the Executive Board. Besides, there is also a broad limit to the overall credit which a member can receive from the Fund. This limit is 125 cent of a member's quota. Actually the way the Articile runs, a member's borrowings from the IMF should not go beyond a point when the IMF's holdings of the members currency reaches 200 per cent of the quota.

Thus the Fund has developed a number of outlets for lending. These are known as 'Facilities' and are the following:

(i) Gold Tranche (because it corresponds to the country's subscription in gold);

(ii) First Credit Tranche;

(iii) Second Credit Tanche;

(iv) Third Credit Tranche;

(v) Fourth Credit Tranche;

(vi) Stand-by Arrangements;

(vii) Compensatory Financing facility;

(viii) Buffer Stock-facility;

(ix) Oil Facility;

(x) Extended facility; and

(xi) Trust Fund Loan Facility.

Some of these outlets have become possible because of the resources placed at the disposal of the Fund by some of the oil-exporting countries and others.

The gold tranche is the total of a member's gold subscription and the credit, if any, which the members has extended through the Fund, to other members. For example, if a member has paid 25 per cent of the quota in gold, then the gold tranche for the members is 25 per cent of the quota. If a member, besides paying 25 per cent gold subscription has a credit position in the Fund to the extend of 25 per cent, then its gold tranche is 50 per cent of its quota.

As regard drawings under the Credit Trenches, the IMF's policy is to treat the drawing in the first tranche of 25 per cent of the quota on a liberal basis. However, the requests for drawings beyond the first credit tranche 'require substantial justification' *i.e.*, while approaching the Fund for a drawing in the higher amounts, the member would have to give a programme of actions, in fiscal monetary and exchange fields.

The stand-by arrangements were initiated in 1952 and they involve the advance arrangements of future needs with the IMF for such credit facility. Understand-by arrangement, a member of the IMF is given an assurance that, following a review of the member country's financial and economic policies and its balance of payments position, the member can purchase from the Fund the currencies of other members, upto an agreeed amount and during a stated period. According too some the facility of stand-by arrangements is wholly unnecessary and inconsistent with the IMF policy of liberal credit to member countries upto the limits prescribed in the Articles of Agreement. The IMF itself is a source of stand-by credit and a formal stand-by arrangment does not appear to the necessary.

To meet the growing needs of development financing of the less developed countries of IMF adhered to compensatory financing facility—with special rules for countries suffering from a short-fall in export proceed from primary commodities. This facility was available to all members suffering from this particlar balance of payments problem. The effect of the decisions was thus to permit members to draw even though they had already exhausted their credit tranches by conventional drawings. Morcver, as a result of a floating features introduced in 1966 liberalization a drawing under the compensatory financing facility did not affect a member's trache position. Thus, a member not having drawn previously could drew under the facility while leaving its gold tranche intact and fully available for future drawings.

Besides, the Fund has developed a number of other outlets for lending *e.g.*, buffer stock faclity, oil facility, extended facility and trust fund loan facility. Some of these outlets have become possible because of the resources places at the disposal of the fund by some of the oil-exporting countries and others. Since some of these loans are repayable over a longer term, the Fund has the opportunity to extend the time length of its lending operations. The Trust Fund loans are made by the Fund out of the profits it has made by its gold sale operations. The purpose of Buffer Stock Financing Facility is to assist in the financing of member's contributions to international buffer stocks of primary products. This facility was introduced in 1969.

The drawings for buffer stock financing may be made upto 50 per cent of quota. The Fund has authorized the use of Fund resources for tin, cocoa, and sugar buffer stocks, but, drawings have been made only for tin and sugar. The repurchase provisions are roughly the same as for purchases in the credit tranche.

Besides the Fund has the Supplmentary Financing, the purpose of which is to enable the Fund to provide supplementary financing in conjuction with the use of the Fund's ordinary resources to all the members of the Fund facing serious payments imbalances that are large in relation to their quotas.

Under the Extended Fund Facility, the Fund assists those members whose economies suffer from serious balance of payments difficulties resulting from structural imbalances in production, trade, prices, and an inherently weak balance of payments position.

In 1980, the Fund adopted a policy called 'Enlarged Access'. A member's cumulative drawing under these arrangements is not to exceed 600 per cent of quota. These limits are subject to reveiw in the light of the avalibility of borrowed resources to the Fund, when a member draws on the Fund, it uses its own currency to purchase the currencies of other member countries or special drawing rights (SDRs) held by the General Resource Account.

Usually, repurchases are required to be made within three to five years after the date of purchase; but under the extended facility, the period of repurchases is within 4 - 10 years under the oil facility within 3 - 7 years, and under the supplementary financing facility within 3 - 1/2 to years.

If the Fund' holdings of a member's currency are less than 100 per cent of the members quota, the difference is called the reserve tranche. Purchases in the reserve trenches are not subject to prior challenge, to economic policy conditions, or to repurchase requirement.

Special Drawing Rights (SDRS)

Prior World War II, gold constituted over 90 per cent of international liquidity. The balance consisted of foreign exchange holdings, principally in the form of pound Sterling and US dollars. These two currencies were known as 'Reserve Currencies'. Until a few years ago, gold constituted the largest component of international liquidity. Over the years the importance of pound Sterling has steadily decilined and the role of dollars has increased a great deal. A need was, therefore, felt for a new type of reserve and solution of this problem was provided by Special Drawing Rights (also known as SDRs) which was created in 1968 as a supplement to gold and dollars.

The SDRs defined variously as a legal tender or paper gold in international payments—almost like creation of paper currency in the national economies substituting regular coins in gold and silver. SDRs supplement the traditional reserve assets, namely, gold and foreign exchange. The scheme of SDRs was approved by principle in 1967 but into operation only since January 1970.

With the establishment of the facility of SDRs, the accounts of the IMF are divided into two categories, namely, the General Account and the Special Drawing Account. The ordinary transaction of the IMF relating to subscription towards quota, drawings, repurchases and payment of charges are all conducted through the General Account. The transactions relating to the SDRs are conduced through Special Drawing Account.

Every member of the IMF has a right to be a participant in the SDR facility. But a member of the IMF is not compelled to join the SDR scheme. However, most of the IMF members have become members of the SDR scheme. The allocation of SDRs may be made only to participants but the holding of such rights is not restricted. The Fund, by a special majority (85 per cent of voting power) will be able to permit non-members and members that are not participants to engage in operations and transactions involving SDRs. The SDRs themselves are not international money; they are like coupons which can be exchanged for currencies required by the holder of SDRs, for making international payments.

Allocation of SDRs

The allocation of SDRs is made on the basis of the quotas of IMF of the individual member-countries. If a country' quota in the IMF is 25 per cent, then it will receive 25 per cent of the allocation of SDRs.

The decision to allocate or cancel SDRs may be made only by the Board of Governors on the basis of the proposals from the Administration of the Fund and only by a special majority.

The SDRs can be used by members in three altenrative ways:

(1) to obtain US dollars, French France or pound Sterling from other designated participants to obtain cuurency in exchange;

(2) to use SDRs for obtaining balances of its own currency held by another participant by agreement with that participant: and

(3) to use SDRs to effect repurchases and to pay charges in the Fund's general account. Thus the IMF can hold and use SDRs though no allocations are made to it.

Two important observations are important noticeable with regard to SDRs. The SDRs do not solve or cure the basis problem of international monetary relations such as international movement of funds arising out of the disturbance in international monetary equilibrium. The scheme lacks the prevention of currency—gold switches and SDR—gold switches. Secondly, the distribution of SDRs on the basis of IMF quotas also fails to satisfy the canons of equity because according to the scheme a major part of SDRs has been allocated to the rich nations already having enough liquidity.

International Monetary Fund and the Less Developed Countries

One of the major functions of the IMF is to provide financial assistance to its member-countries. It may further be noticed that the less developed countries which are trying to embark on the path of economic development, trying to achieve self-reliance and self-sustained growth, need more financial assistance than do the developed countries of Europe. But the main problem is that these less deevloped countries are already under heavy debt while at the same time their requirements of developmenal finance are on the increase. In fact, what is needed is that these developing countries should get soft loans involving easy terms and conditions and such loans should enable them to achieve economic autonomy in the long run.

It follows from above that the less developed countries are characterised by low degree of development. But at the same time these countries aspire to develop fast. One of the essential requirements of fast growth of these countries is high rate of investment which could make the developmental projects feasible. But the high rate of investment would be possible only when higher rates of savings are forthcoming domestically. Savings are a direct function of income according to Keynes, but the income levels of these less developed countries are low and, therefore, higher domestic savings are not possible over a short span of time. This creates hindrances in enhacing economic development of the countries.

Therefore, in order to enhance their development efforts, the developing countries need for foreign borrowing. In fact, it imposes a lot of debt-burden in the subsequent years. The interest and amortization payments on the loans are called 'Debt-Servicing Charges' and such heavy charges provide a strain on future balance of payments because the payments in past debt also absorb a high proportion of foreign exchange earnings from exports. According to an estimate in 1971 the value of outstanding debt was $ billion and debt-service payments amounted to nearly $ 7 billion, that is, approximately 40 per cent of new capital inflows.

In the case of many developing countries today, however, there is little evidence that the have the ability to pay of their past indebtedness and cut down on net resource inflows. The need for resources is as acute as ever and their indebtedness is mounting because an export-import gap. These countries find it difficult to translate domestic saving into activities which ease the shortage of foreign exchange because exports are price and income inelastic and imports are income elastic. The developing countries difficulties are the culmination of events dating back a decade or more. They are a consequence partly of conditions in the industrial market economies in the industrial market economies and partly of their own policies.

Developing countries are directly affected by fluctuations in the industrial world. Their overal growth rates have been higher, but even those that have grown fastest have not been able to avoid the cylical influence of industrial countries. They have also been affected by high interest rates as a result, many developing countries have been squeezed between stagnating foreign exchange and soaring interest payments on their debt. Countries like Mexico suffer heavy burden of debt. In 1990s the condition deteriorated. The countries like India, which sustained the pressure of foreign debt of 1970s, are today under heavy debt and facing the problem of debt servicing.

India the IMF

India is one of the founder member of the IMF. It signed the fund agreement on 27 December 1945. Till 1970 India's quota in the found was the fifth. After May 1970, the quota stands at 13th place. However, in absolute terms, India's quota stood at SDR 3.05 in January 1993.

India has been one of the major beneficiaries of the fund assistance. Between 1947 to 1955, India borrowed $ 100 million twice to tide over its balance of payments difficulties India borrowed eight times between 1957 to 1975 a total sum of $ 1764 million. It also received SDR 529.01 million from 1 July 1978 to 21 February 1981 under the IMF Trust Fund. In 1979, India entered into agreements with the IMF for a loan of $ 5.6 billion or Rs. 5,220 crores under the Extended fund facility. Till April 1954, India had drawn $ 3.9 billion only and intimated the fund that it did not be drawing the remaining amount at all. After April 1984, India did not take any recourse to the IMF till December 1990. In January 1991, it approached the IMF under compensatory and contingency Financing Facility (CCFF) to get $ 0.79 billion as the first credit tranche of a stand-by arrangement for three months. On 31 October, the IMF approaved a stand-by credit of $ 2.2 billion to the distrused to India in 8 tranches over a 20 month period from November 1991 to June 1993. India's quota in the fund is $3.01 billion (or SDR 2.2 billion) and its gros drawings from the fund from January 1991 to June 1993 total $ 3.5 billion. This speaks of the Fund's confidence in the Indian economy and India has also gained a lot as a member of the fund.

WORLD BANK

The International Bank for Reconstruction and Development (popularly known as World Bank) was set up by decision taken in Brettonwords Conference, New Hampshire held in July 1944 and attended by 44 nations to solve the monetary and financial problems of the less developed countries likely to be faced in post World War II period. This conference decided to set up two organisations the IMF and the IBRD.

The concept of International Monetary System implies a mechanism of interrelated parts, functioning for some clearly defined end, according to known laws. It implies knowledge, certainty and predictability. All these attributes the International Monetary System in a varying degree. To describe it a system is an oversimplification, permissible in the interests of economic analysis, when moving from the precise formulations and general prescriptions of economic theory to the real world of policy, it is necessary to remember that we have the realm of system and precision for a world of approximation.

The concept of an International Monetary System arises mainly from two sources:

1. Within the structure of wider relationshp, the international monetary system is concerned with flows of current and capital funds, with the relationships between national currencies, monetary systems and central bank. One can speak of International Monetary Community and treat it as a part of the framework through which the international monetary mechanism works.

2. It is the apparent parallelism between money's role in a domestic closed economy and its role in a world of many countries. There is a parallelism both in the institutions and their relations in both national and international systems. The parallelism is however, limited.

The IBRD or World Bank was set up on December 27, 1945 when its articles of agreements was signed by 29 Governments in Washington D.C. It had 181 members in June 1996. If a country resigns its membership, it is required to pay back all loans with interest on due dates. If the bank incurs a financial loss in the years in which a member resigns, it is required to pay its share of the loss on demand.

Functions

1. To Assist in the Reconstruction and Developed of its Member Countries. This is done by facilitating the investment of capital for productive purposes, thereby promoting long range growth of international trade and improvements in standard of living;

2. To Promote Private Foreign Investment. This is done by guarantees of, and participation in loans and other investments made by private investors.

3. To Make Loans for Productive Purposes. When private capital is not available on reasonable terms this is done out of its own resources or the funds borrowed by it.

Financing

1. Direct Lending. IBRD may led funds directly, either its capital funds or form the funds it borrows in private investment markets.

2. Guarantee. IBRD may guarantee loans advanced by others of it may participate in such loans.

3. Loans to Member Countries. Loans may be advanced to member countries directly or to any of their political subdivisions or to private business or agricultural enterprises in the territories of members.

As credit rating of many developing countries is poor, they feel difficulties in raising fund in international capital markets. In its efforts to advance loans for developmental purposes, the Word Bank has provided loans to the developing countries for developmental projects and programmes. It is a vital source of finance to the developing countries. When the member Government, in whose territory the project is located, is not the borrower the World Bank asks the member Government for a gurantee.

The IBRD started with an anthorized capital of $ 10 billion divided into 1,00,000 shares of $ 1,00,000. Of this, $ 9, 400 million was actually subscribed. On 30 June 1985 the authorised capital stock of the IBRD comprised 7, 16, 500 anthorised shares of the per value of SDR 1,00,000 each. In July 1992, the total authorised bank capital was provided to the republics of the former Soviet Union.

(i) **Purpose.** Loans are meant for high priority productive purposes mainly to develop the infrastructure for the development such as generation and distribution of electric power, rail, roads, ports and inland waterways, airlines and airports etc.

(ii) **Use.** Loans must be used to meet only the foreign exchange component of the projecs.

(iii) **Interest.** The interest rate of the Bank is somewhat lower but related to market rate. The lending rate of the Bank is calculated by adding 0.5 per centage points to the cost of lending to the Bank during the preceeding six months of a pool outstanding borrowing made sicne July 1, 1982. On July, 1, 1992 the bank adopted a policy of resetting its lending rates half year. At that time, the lending rate was 11.47 per cent. Since then the Bank has been revising its lending rate every half year. The rate has been revised at 8.50 per cent from January 1, 1986 for the half year ending on 30-6-1986. This is seventh consecutive revision since July 1, 1982.

(iv) **Free Loans.** These are not tied.

SUBSIDIARIES OF THE WORLD BANK

Mainly there are two subsidiaries of the World Bank:

1. International Development Association (IDA). In order to structure the economy of less developed countries, the World Bank set up the International Development Association (IDA) in 1960. It is an aiding centre for several developing countries who look up to it for financial assistance. It is an association of donor countries who have come under the aegies of the World Bank to help the developing or less developed countries whose paying capacity is limited due to their socio-economic problems. As such countries mainly those of South Asia and Africa have low domestic resources and are not in a position to pay high rate interest and ask for short maturity periods, the IDA offers credit to the eligible developing countries on exteremely favourable terms:

(i) ***Criteria.*** The main critierion for the allocation of IDA credit is the per capita income of the recipient country. Countries which have an annual per capita Gross National Product (GNP) of less than $ 681 (in 1979 dollars) are eligible for IDA credits. Other parameters taken into consideration are a country's credit worthiness, its accessibility tc commercial borrowing, its economic performance, the desnity of its population and the existence of viable projects in the borrowing nations.

(ii) ***Terms.*** IDA interest-free credits available to Government only may be obtained on payment of nominal service charges at 0.75% per annum. The period of repayment is 40 years, excluding 10 years for initial grace period. This is in contrast to World Bank loan which carries an interest at 12% per annum and the repayment period is 20 years. Thus less dveloped countries have benefited immensely from IDA. The number of beneficiary till June 1982 was 78.

(iii) ***Purposes.*** The purposes for which the IDA has advanced the credits are agriculture, rural development education, energy, industrial development and finance, industry

population and nutrition, transportation and tourism, telecommuncation etc.

(iv) ***Credit to India.*** As the largest beneficiary from IDA, India's share is 40% of IDA funds. During Third Plan India got aid from IDA $ 578 m (Current). During the fourth plan this was trippled to about $ 1,556m (current). During fifth Plan it touched a new height of nearly $ 5,581m (current). This increasing trend halted during the Sixth Plan as the amount of aid authorised during the plan was about $ 4,568m. However, both because of infrastructural difficulties at home and the adverse conditions imposed by donor countries governing such aid, India has not been able to utilise this aid fully.

IDA credits have helped various sectors of India economy such as agriculture, rural development, construction, irrigation, power, tele-communications, industrial imports, fertiliser production, shipping etc. Some of the important projects financed by IDA credit project, are: Gorakhpur fertilizer expansion projects, Bombay development project, Railway project etc. IDA has also been providing funds to the Industrial Development Bank of India (IDBI) and the Agricultural Refinance and Development Corporation (ARDC) for their developmental activities pertaining to industry, agriculture and rural development.

2. International Finance Corporation (IFC). An affiliate of World Bank it was set up in 1956. It extended credits to private business enterprises. It provided equity and loans capital for private enterprises in association with private investors and managements and encourages the development of local capital. Particularly, it supports joint ventures which provide opportunities to combine domestic knowledge of market and other conditions with the technical and managerial experience available in the industrial nations.

IFC had 124 members as on 30th June 1983. On the date its paidup capital was 544 million dollars and its retained earning were 24m, dollars. It has authority to borrow up to 732m dollars. It has made commitments totalling 5520 m dollars to 711 private enterprises. In the fiscal years 1982, it approved investment totalling 612m dollars for 65 projects. In 1983, the approved investment ammounted to 612 m dollars for 59 projects.

Conditions of Assistance

The project, for which IFC advances assistance, must satisfy the following conditions:

(i) It should have the prospects of earning profits.

(ii) It should boost the economy of the country.

(iii) Local investors should be able to participate in the project in the beginning of the project or later.

(iv) The required funds for the project are not available from private investors at reasonable terms.

(v) The management should be capable and experienced.

(vi) The sponsor of the project has a substantial holding in the enterpises.

INDIA AND THE WORLD BANK GROUP

Until June 1983, cumulative lending by the World Bank to India amounted to 5553 m dollars in 76 loans out of a total of 89.6 billion dollars and by the IDA, the cumulative lending was 11, 529m dollars in 149 loans out of total of 30.1 billion dollars. Till then India received 17083m dollars for 225 projects out of cumulative combined assistance of 119.7 billion dollars from World Bank and IDA taken together so far. The IFC has advance 220m dollars for 22 companies till June 1983.

The World Bank's disbursements to India during the fiscal year 1996 amounted to $ 1,309 million. Against if, India paid the Bank $ 1,149 million for past loans and $ 884 million and interest, making the net receipts as minus $ 723 million from the World Bank. The World Bank has been assisting India in such projects as development of ports, oil exploration including the Bombay high and gas power projects, aircrafts, coal, iron, aluminimum, fertilisers, railways modernisation, technical assistance, industrial development financial corporations etc.

Because of constraint of resources the prospects of getting larger funds from World Bank seem to be bleak, because of the failure of the USA to provide funds for its replenishment. The situation is not much better as regard IDA loans. Due to the entry of China as a member of IDA, India's share of aid has been adversey affected. However, the prospects of getting assistance from IEC have improved substantially due to a positive turn in Government of India policy in this respect.

Thus both International Monetary Fund and the International Bank for Reconstruction and Development (IBRD), popularly known as World Bank are international organisations looking after the interest of the developing countries in the world. Both these institutions played important role in the development of developing countries and in bringing the poeple nearer to each other.

OVERLAPPING ROLES OF IMF AND WORLD BANK

As conceived originally, IMF and World Bank differed in the scope and time span of their programmes. While IMF was concerned with macro-economic management and operated on the demand side, World Bank's concern was micro project based lending. The distinct rols of these institutions in the world's economy are the following:

Distinct Roles of The IMF and the World Bank

International Monetary Fund	*World Bank*
1. Oversees the international monetary system and promotes international monetary cooperation.	1. Seeks to promote the economic development and structural reform in developing countries.
2. Promotes exchange stability and orderly exchange relations among its members.	2. Assists developing countries through long-term financing of development projects and programmes.

Contd.

International Monetary Fund	World Bank
3. Assists members in temporary balance of payments difficulties by providing short to medium-term financing, thus providing them with the opportunity to correct maladjutments in their balance of payments.	3. Provided special financial assistance to the poorest developing countries though the International Development Association (IDA).
4. Supplements the reserves of its members by allocating SDRs if there is a long-term global need.	4. Stimulates private enterprises in developing countries through its affiliate, the International Finance Corporation (IFC).
5. Draws its financial resources principally from the quota subscriptions of its members.	5. Acquires most of its financial resources by borrowing on the international bond market.

***(Source :** A.P. Thrilwall, Growth and Development : With Special Reference to Developing Economies)*

However, over the years, IMF and World Bank have come closer in their mode of functioning. While IMF was initiatlly supposed to be concerned with short-term solutions to the balance of payments difficulties, it started providing 10 year Extended Fund Facilities (EFF) since 1974 and structural Adjustment Facility (SAF) in 1986. World Bank, which started with micro issues like project-based programmes has over the years turned its attention to policy based programmes like Structural Adjustment Lending (SAL). It is also taking a keen interest in the issues concerning macro-economic management, including balance of payments. Over period of time the former distinctions between the roles of the IMF and world Bank—macro vessus micro, demand versus supply, adjustment versus development financial versus real, programme versus project loans, short term versus long term etc.—have been severely eroded. For example, the IMF while sanctioning the economic stabilisation programme for a particular country insists that the country adopt policies to lower inflation, improve the effeciency of internal and institutions, lower government spending, review public investments etc., in addition to reforming its exchange rate regime. Thus, in addition to its traditonal insistence on demand-side policies of devaluation and monetary contraction, the IMF has now started insisting on supply-side policies as well as a condition for assistance, which was previously the prerogative of the World Bank alone. Thus IMF has now extended its activities into areas that have traditionally been under the influence of the World Bank. In a similar way, the structural adjustment programmes of the World Bank have begun to include provisions for enhancing the international competitiveness of domestic products through reforms in the trade policy and exchange rates regimes. According to Todaro, the increasing convergence in the approaches of the IMF and the World Bank that is now being witnessed is on account of the "growing recognition that the successful resolution of both external and internal problems requires the simultaneous coordination of macroeconomic and microeconomic policies."

Since the activities and conditionalists of the two institutions have largely converged, and they work in close cooperation in relation to a given country, many economists have been arguing during the last few years that the two institutions should be merged.

Critical Appraisal

The IBRD has been quite successful in achieving its principal objective of reconstruction and development. It helped not only in the rconstruction of Europe but also the developing countries in the process of growth. Of the total IBRD loans of $ 13.4 billion in the fiscal year 1996, member countries in Latin America and Carribean received 15 per cent in Asia 33 per cent and so on. The marking of IBRD has been criticised on the following grounds:

(i) It is argued that bank changes a very high rate of interest on loans and a front-end fee. Recently the bank has made some changes but it is still high. It is 7.6 per cent now.

(ii) The Bank has also been criticised for its failure to meet the financial needs of the developing countries fully. Its lending operations account for only small proportion of the total net aid to developing countries.

(iii) The Bank's lending procedure in faulty because it lays emphasis on the repaying capacity of the borrowing country before getting loan.

(iv) The Bank has been crticised for being discriminatory in its purpose-wise and region-wise assistance to its members. Since 1990 the Bank has been directing it more towards the developing countries and for the development of agriculture and rural development energy, transportation etc.

(v) The introduction of SAF and ESAF has made IBRD loans terms tighter. The borrowing country is required to follow on action programme set out in a latter of development policies such as open trade reform in public budgeting and debt management, revision of price policies, better planning of public investment and management of public enterprises, etc. The second instalment of SAF is only released after a review of the reform programmes that are data bound.

INTERNATIONAL MONETARY SYSTEM

The concept of the International Monetary system implies a mechanism of interrelated parts, functioning for some clearly defined end, according to known laws. It implies knowledge, certainity and predictability. All these attributes the International Monetary System in a varying degree. To describe it as a system is an oversimplification, permissible only in the interests, of economic analysis, when moving from the precise formulations and general prescriptions of economic theory to the real world of policy, it is necesary to remember that we have the realm of system and precision for a world of approximation.

The concept of an International Monetary System arises mainly from two sources:

(1) Within the structure of wider relationships, the international monetary system is concerned with flows of current and capital funds, with the relationships between national currencies, monetary systems and central bank. One can speak of International Monetary Community and treat it as a part of the framework through which the international monetary mechanism works.

(2) It is the apparent parallelism between money's role in a domestic closed economy and it role is a world of many countries. There is a parallelism both in the institutions and their relations in both national and international systems. The parallelism is however, limited.

Elements of International Monetary System. An international monetary system has four elements:

(1) A form of international money usable for clearing residual payments, balances with other countries and for holding reserves with which to meet external deficits;

(2) A mechanism whereby the distribution of international money can be adjusted by action upon the balance of payments;

(3) Institutional arrangements in the form of international banking systems, money markets, foreign exchange markets and the media through which flows of international money may circulate throughout which flow of international money may circulate throughout the system;

(4) Some central power to control the working of international monetary arrangements.

Looking at the international moneary system in historical perspective, it appears that there are four period that correspond roughly to four different international monetary systems.

I. The beginning of the first period is not agreed by the scholars but it suddenly ended with the beginning of the first World War. It was the period of international gold standard.

II. The scond period covers the twenty years between the two world wars and can be thought of in connection with the gold exchange standard through that system actually operated only from roughly 1925 to 1931.

III. The third period after the Second World War spans the quarter centruy in which the Bretton woods system was in operation.

IV. The fourth period begins from 1973 and usually characterised as a floating exchange rate.

I. International Gold Standard. International gold standard means an international moentary standard where all participating have:

(1) Legally defined unit of account (rupee, dollar etc.) in terms of gold so that the purchasing power of a unit of its currency is kept equal to the purchasing power of a given unit of gold.

(2) Established a mechanims whereby local currencies are left equal in value of gold and to each other.

(3) Monetary authorities of the countries on gold standard are committed to a policy of buying and selling gold at fix price in unlimited amount.

(4) External value of their currencies are fixed through the medium of gold.

Mechanism of Gold Standard. The mechanims of gold standard can be explained in terms of maintenance of Exchange Stability, automatic restoration of balance of payments, equilibrium in a movement of capital and adjustment Parity of price level.

The gold standard was put into operation in Britain in 1821. By 1914 the gold standard was the pre-dominant system all over the world with the exception of China, Mexico and some minor countries. Till 1914, the gold standard had centre in London and London market also played the role of a World Central Bank. When the other countries suffered an adverse balance of payments, the London market advanced short them loans that supplemented their dwindling gold pressure.

With the out break of war in 1914, the gold standard was suspended every where for two reasons: *(1)* to avoid continuous adverse balance of payments; and *(2)* to prevent gold exports from falling with the hands of the enemies.

II. Gold Exchange Standard. More than 40 countries returned to gold standard after the First World War. By the end of 1928 and extensive international currency system based on gold was recreated and it was widely assumed that the world would look forward once more to the attainment of a stable international equilibrium. But the gold standard in 1925-28 defered from that in 1914. To alleviate an impending shortage of gold, its coinage was generally discontinued except in the limited states and assets in the form of balances in gold standard countries were permitted to count as a reserve of country's Central Bank. The new gold standard was less efficient than the old one and the various nations started placing greater importance to employment and price level stability. Added to the structural changes in industry were serious maladjustments in important sectors of organisation. All this weakned the international structure and it ultimately collapsed with the on set of great depression in 1930s. The boom was over in USA, industrial activities virtually ceased. Decline in the US income, outlay, imports and exports, and in addition, sustained in the American tariff adversely affected the world trade. This trend followed in a member of other countries which led to the abandoning of the gold standard by them. It was initiated by Britain Due Depreciation of sterling gold block was affected and this created serious balance of payment difficulties for USA and other countries. All this led to devaluation of gold, which intensified deflation in the remaining gold standard countries. In 1936, France abandoned, the gold standard altogether and was followed by the rest of the countries.

III. Bretton Woods System. With the abandonment of the gold standard in 1930s by the major countries of the world, a vacuum was created in the field of international trade and a general tendency of economic and isolationalism developed. As a result, the world trade and growth suffered a great deal, leaching to stresses and conflicts among nations.

It was then realised that the monetary of the world could be corrected only by natural agreement between nations having international economic relations. As it was no possible to revive the gold standard, a new monetary system had to be demised which could provided sufficient flexibility through international assistance without affecting the internal economic order of the country, as also an efficient payment mechanism, which would permit and foster high and stable level of world trade. Hence exports from the US and UK prepared comprehensive plans for international monetary cooperation. The American proposal was known as 'White Plan' and the British proposal was Keynes Plan in 1944, a conference held at Bretton Woods to discuss a joint plan on the establishment of International Monetary Fund of the US and Assocaited Nations.

Bretton Woods Conference was to work out the statutes for the two institutions—International Monetry Fund (IMF) and the International Bank for Reconstruction and Development (IBRD) or World Bank, the IMF became operational in March 1947. It was to operate by 1952 in the full multi-lateral control free world. But it could come into its full operation only in 1959. During this period new structural changes had manifested themselves, the nature direction and strength of which was obscure. The dollar problem whose early virulance threatened the stability of the world economy in the late 40s and early 50s had waved and was replaced in 1960s by a surfeit of dollars. The great industrial power of the US came to be challenged by a resurgence of industrial growth in Western Europe and by its recorganization through the European Common Market. In the trade field, customs wession and free trade areas threatened to compartmentalise the world economy. In this new and sometimes hostile environment the Bertton Woods system had completed fourteen years of full operation. Since the mid-60s, it had operated with great strain and the recurrent monetary crisis since 1968 had been met by modifications in the system. The Brettom Woods system of international monetary relations ended in August 1971. Though the conditions improved a little in 1973, the confidence problem of dollar continued. Elsewhere, countries pursued their own policies. In 1973, Bretton Woods System almost died.

IV. Floating Exchange Rate. There was not system to formally replace bretton Woods system after 1973. In fact, there was no monetary crisis in the litearry sence of the term *i.e.* it was not a situation in which failure to establish a new 'system' would quickly led to financial disintegration and collapse. Continuation of the current makshift was inable though not a desirable alternation. It was the only practical system. In provided in the IMF a Central oraganization but it was politically important as a centre for the system.

After 1973 when the governments let their currencies float, at first the float was expected to the temporary and an attempt was made to design a new monetary system. In which the exchange rate would be pegged, but more readily adjustable than under Bretton Woods System. But the efforts failed in the wake of first oil shock and the Articles of Agreement of the IMF were amended to 'legalise' floating.

But Government have not allowed exchange rates to float freely, because exchange rate fluctuations affect their economies in larger and different ways. In 1978 the members of the European Community established the European Monetary System to peg the exchange rates connecting their own currencies. The US intervened heavily in 1978 to half a depreciation of the dollar. Under the Plaza and Louvre agreement, it joined with other countries in an effort to reverse an depreciation of the dollar.

Experience with floating rates in hand to evaluate, because the years of floating have been punctuated by large shocks, high inflation rates, and deep recessions that should not be blamed on the exchange rates regime. These disorders have produced new problems, including the debt problems of less developed countries.

WORLD TRADE ORGANISATION

The WTO is the successor to the GATT. The GATT was a forum where the member countries met from time to time to discuss and solve world trade problems. But the WTO is a properly established permanent world trade organisation. It has a legal status and enjoys privileges and immunities on the same footing as the IMF and the World Bank. It includes: *(1)* the GATT, as modified by the Uruguay Round; *(2)* all agreements and arrangements concluded under the GATT; and *(3)* the complete results of the Urugauy Round. An agreement for the setting up of the WTO was signed by 104 members. The WTO agreement came into force from January 1, 1995 and India has become a founder member of the WTO, by ratifying the WTO Agreement on Dec., 30, 1994.

Functions and Organisation of WTO. The purpose of the WTO is spelled out in the Preamble and Article II of the Agreement establishing the WTO. Paragraph 1 of Article II reads: "The WTO shall provide the common institutional framework for the conduct of trade relations among its members in matters related to the agreements and associated legal instruments included in the Annexes to this Agreement". WTO has the following five functions as set out in Article III:

First, the WTO 'shall facilitate the implementation, administration and operation, and further the objectives, of this Agreement and of the Multilateral Trade Agreement, and shall also provide the framework for the implementation, administration and operation of the Plurilateral Trade Agreements.'

Second, the WTO 'shall administer the Understanding on Rules Procedures Govering the Settlement of Disputes.'

Third, the WTO 'shall administer that Trade Policy Review Mechanism.'

Fourth, the WTO 'shall provide the forum for negotiations among its membes cocnerning their multilateral trade relations in matters deal with under the Agreements in the Annexes to ths Agreement.'

Fifth, 'with a view to achieving greater coherence in global economic policy-making, the World Trade Organisation shall cooperate, as appropriate, with the International Monetary Fund and with the International Bank for Reconstruction and Development and its affiliated agencies'.

The organisational structure of WTO is presented in Chart. The highest body will be the Ministerial Conference. This will consist of representatives of all the members and will meet at least once every two years. There will also be a General Council again consisting of representatives of all the members. It is the real engine of the WTO which shall act on behalf of the Ministerial Conference. The General Council itself will meet as the Dispute Settlement Body and the Trade Policy Review Body.

There are three councils working under the General Council: Council for Trade in Goods, Council for Trade in Services and Council for TRIPs.

The Ministerial Conference has the authority to create special committees. Accordingly, a Committee on Trade and Development, a Committee on Balance-of-Payments Restrictions and a Committee on Budget, Finance and Administration were created. In addition, as can be seen from the chart, a Committee on Trade and Economic Environment and a Committee on Trade in Financial Services were also created.

Organisation Structure of WTO

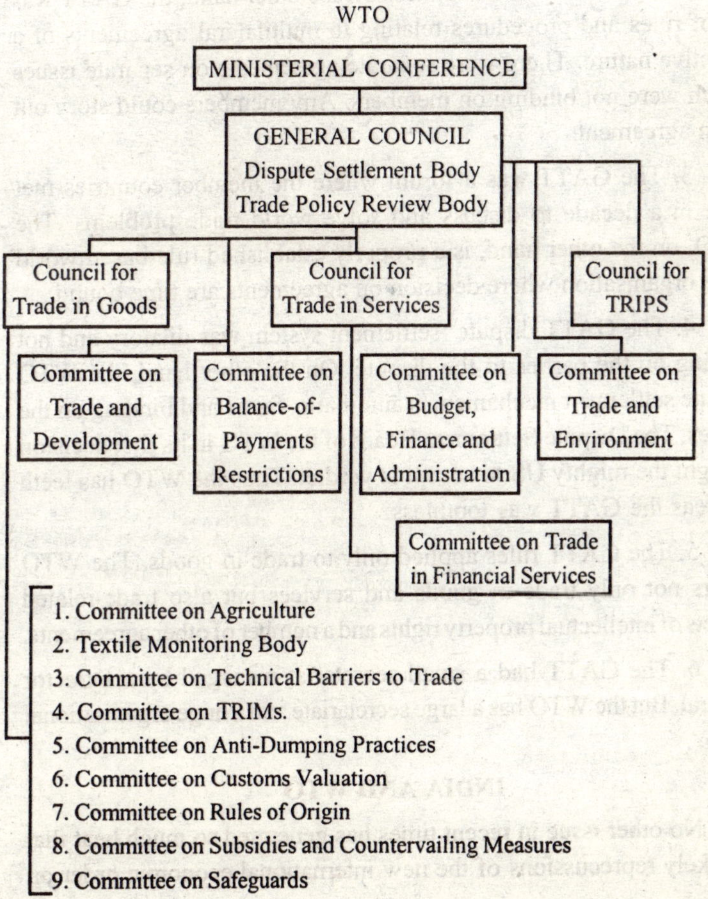

DIFFERENCE BETWEEN GATT AND WTO

The WTO is not an extension of the GATT but successor to the GATT. It completely replaces GATT and has a very different character. The major differences between the two are the following:

1. GATT had no legal status whereas the WTO has a legal status. It has a global status similar to that of the IMF and the World Bank but unlike them, it is not an agency of the UN, although it has a 'cooperative relationship' with the UN.

2. The agreements which form part of the WTO are permanent and binding on all members. Action can be taken against any defaulting member by all the member states. On the other hand, the GATT was set of rules and procedures relating to multilateral agreements of a salective nature. There were separate agreements on separate issues which were not binding on members. Any members could story out of an agreement.

3. The GATT was a forum where the member countries met once in a decade to discuss and solve world trade problems. The WTO, on the other hand, is a properly established rule-based world trade organisation where decision on agreements are time bound.

4. The GATT dispute settlement system was dilatory and not binding on the parties to the dispute. On the other hand, the WTO dispute settlement mechanism is automatic, faster and binding on the parties. The Dispute Settlement Board of the WTO in its first decision brought the mighty US to accept is verdict. Thus the WTO has teeth whereas the GATT was toothless.

5. The GATT rules applied only to trade in goods. The WTO covers not only trade in goods and services but also trade-related aspects of intellectual property rights and a number of other agreements.

6. The GATT had a small secretariat managed by a Director General. But the WTO has a large secretariate and a huge organisational setup.

INDIA AND WTO

No other issue in recent times has generated so much heat that the likely reprecussions of the new international economic order on world economy in general and developing countries in particular. According to the supporters, the Uruguay Round agreement, the Marrakesh Declaration and the ultimate setting up of the WTO, are expected to bring about substantial gains in world trade and increased income from liberalization, improved market access and greater export opportunities, besides greater predictability of the trading environment. The Government of India has also been harping on this tune. However, critics have pointed out the entire negotiation process and ruthlessly domenated by the developed countries and the results that have emerged are highly tilted in their favour. The poor countries operated in the periphery, seldom consulted until the rich ones had completed negotiations amongst themselves.

ADVANTAGES TO INDIA

1. World Bank, OECD and the GATT Secretariat have estimated that the income effects of the implementation of the Uruguay Round package will add between 213 to 274 billion U.S. dollars annually to world income. The GATT Secretariat's estimate of the overall trade impact is that the level of merchandise trade in goods will be higher by 845 billion U.S. dollars in the year 2005, than it would otherwise had been. The GATT Secretariat further projects that the largest increases will be in the areas of clothing (60 per cent), agriculture, forestry and fishery products (20 per cent) and processed food (19 per cent). According to the Government of India, since our country's existing and potential export competitiveness lies in these product groups, it is logical to believe that India will obtain large gains in these sectors. Assuming that India's market share in world exports improves from 0.5 per cent to 1 per cent, and that we are able to take advantage of the opportunities thus created, the government believes that the trade gains may conservatively be placed at 2.7 billion U.S. dollars extra exports per year. A more generous estimate will range from 3.5 to 7 billion U.S. dollars per year.

2. The third benefit that India expects relate to the improved prospects for agricultural exports as a result of likely increase in the world prices of agricultural products due to reduction in domestic subsidies and barriers to trade. While on the one hand earnings from

agricultural exports are likely to increase, on the other hand India has ensured that all major programmes for the development of agriculture will be exempted from the disciplines in the agricultural Agreement. Thus, the operation of the public distribution system will not be affeted by the provisions of the Agreement ; agricultural subsidies granted by developing countries need not be withdrawn till such time they remain within the prescribed limits specified in the Agreement: and protection necessary for developing the agricultural sector in the underdeveloped countries might be continued. In fact, as stated above, India hopes that the reduction of subsidies in the USA and the European Community will enable it increase its earnings from agricultural exports.

3. The phasing out of the MFA (Multi-Fibre Arrangement) by 2005 will benefit India as the export of textiles and clothings will increase. While the developed countries had demanded a 15 years period, the developing countries (including India) had insisted on a 10 year period. Acceptane of the developing countries' demand in the Urguay Round has been enthusiastically received in these countries. However, the catch here is that the phasing out schedule favours the developed countries as a major proportion of quota regime to the extent of 49 per cent cent is going to be removed only during the tenth year, *i.e.* by 2005. Thus the Uruguay Round does not provide an immediate market access for the Third World textile exports. Moreover, as pointed by Bibek Debroy, when quotas are removed, they will be eliminated not only for India, but for everyone else. These will therefore be considerable competition from China, Vietnam, Pakistan, Bangladesh, Indonesia and Malayasia. The question thus basically boils down to evaluating the competitiveness of India's garment exports. In this respect, India not fare well *vis-a-vis* its competitors. There are a number of supply side constraint like higher costs and prices, poor quality and unreliability of the end-product.

4. The Uruguay Round Agreement has strengthened multilateral rules and disciplines. The most important of these relate to anti-dumping, subsidies and countervailing measures, safeguards and disputes settlement. This is likely to ensure greater security and

predictability of the inernational trading system and thus create a more favourable environment of India in the new world economic order.

DISADVANTAGES TO INDIA

1. The most impotant advantage of the new world economic order claimed by its supporters is that it will increase the volume of trade substantially and, as a result, India's export earnings will expand considerably. However, as stated above, the estimates of quantitative gains by India are suspect and the projections may, well prove wrong. Moreover, there will hardy be any liberalization of our textile exports till 2005, with most of the liberalization expected to come at the end of this period. The gains expected by the Government of India on account of tariff reductions on goods may also not materialises the number of goods of export interest to India is very small.

2. TRIPs. Protection of intellectual property rights—patents, copyrights, trademarks etc. has been made more stringent in the Uruguay Round. This has been done to protect the interest of multinational corporations and the developed countries as the Agreement on TRIPs is highly weighted in favour of patent holders. However, as correctly pointed out by Muchkund Debey, IPRs (intellectual property rights) protection is anti-competition and anti-liberalization and goes against the spirit of opening up the world economy and global integration. Thus protection of IPRs is, itself, a barrier to trade. Let us now see how the Agreement on TRIPs is likely to work against India.

(i) The first point to be noted in this context is that the TRIPs Agreement goes against the Patent Act of India, 1970 in almost all important areas as would be clear from the discussion below: *(i)* Under the Indian Patents Act only *process patents* can be granted in food, chemical and medicines. TRIPs Agreement provides for graing *product patents* also in all these areas; *(ii)* Under the TRIPs Agreement methods of agriculture and horticulture and bio-technological process (including living organims like plants and animals) are a patentable, there cannot be any exceptions as under the Indian Act; *(iii)* TRIPs Agreement provides that the general terms of a patent shall be 20 years. The Indian Patents Act provides for a general term of 14 years for both product as well as process patents. In sectors like food, chemicals and medicines, process patents are granted for a duration of 5 to 7 years; *(iv)* Under TRIPs no ceiling can be placed on royalty demanded on patents like in the Indian Patents Act; *(v)* Importation will be treated as working of patent in the TRIPs Agreement, contrary to the patent philosophy in India; and *(vi)* TRIPs also reverses the burden of proof. Under the Indian legal system, the patentee has to establish a *prima facie* case that his patent has been infringed. However, under TRIPs the patentee will just have to accuse a person or a company of patent infringment and the person or company will have to prove that he did not infringe the patent.

(ii) Under the Patents act of 1970 in India, only process patents are granted to drugs and medicines. This means that an Indian company only needs to develop and patent its own process for producing a drug, it is not required to invent the drug itself. The company can then legally manufacture this drug, even if it is protected under a product patent abroad. Finally, Indian drug companies are allowed to obtain what are called 'licences of right' which allow them to produce, regardless of the process used, inventions (again, usually pharmaceuticals) patented abroad. Licences of right can be obtained only 3 year after the original patent is granted.

The effects of these laws have been positive for India. Indian drug prices and considered to be among the lowest has grown rapidly after the passage of the 1970 Act. Not only this, the market share of Indian durg companies in the local drug market has grown from 30 per cent in 1970 to

61 per cent in 1993. Today, India is, in fact, an exporter of drugs to other parts of Asia, Europe, and even USA.

All this will changes in the new order. The granting of product patents will effective place the reins of the Indian pharmaceutical industry in the hands of MNCs who will exploit this advantage to the full by hiking the prices of drugs and medicines considerably. Once product patents are introdcued, generies cannot come to the market until after the expiry of the patent. Thus the introduction of product patents in India is certainly going to affect sections of the poor who will not have the generic option open. In additon, as more and more potential medicines of MNCs are prescribed by the doctors, many Indian drug companies will be forced to shut down. Drug companies' profits start flowing overseas more quickly and skilled labour may face unemployment as production moves overseas.

(iii) The extension of intellectual property rights to agriculture has serious consequences for India, plant breeding and seed production are largely in the public domain. Plant breeding is undertaken by agricultural universities and units of ICAR (Indian Council of Agricultural Research), whereas seed multiplication is in the hands of the National and State Seed Corporations. This is due to the reason that India being a poor country where agriculure is the livelihood of the majority of the population, the government must bear the responsibility of ensuring the supply of adequate quantities of seeds at reasonable prices to the farmer. Patenting of plant varieties will transfer all the gains to the multinational companies. Almost all new varieties will belong to MNCs simply by virtue of their massive financial resources. In fact, the research budgets alone of some of these MNCs are more than the budget of the Indian Union. If Indian research institutions are unable to complete financially and are denied access to patented genetic material the Indian scientists will find it extremely difficult to breed new varieties. This will gradually the sole privilege of the large foreign companies. As a result, the entire Indian food security system will be jeopardised and thrown out of gear.

(iv) Under TRIPs, patenting has been extended not only to plant varieties but to the large area of micro organisms as well. Micro organisms refer to very small forms of life. In this category are included such living creatures as bacteria, virus, fugus, algae small plants and living creatures as bacteria, virus, fungus, algae small plants and animals, and even genes. In the field of agriculture, efforts are on worldwide to develop bio-substitutes (which are based to a large extend on micro organisms) for chemical fertilisers and pesticides as the latter are not ecologically sustainable and will poison our land and water. In the field of pharmacuticals, several kinds of drugs are derived from micro organism. The patenting of life forms will strike at the very roots of indigeneous manufacturing of such drugs. Patents in agriculture, pharmaceuticals and industrial biotechnology linked to micro organisms are either already with the multinational companies or are likely to be acquired at a much faster rate *vis-a-vis* the developing countries. Thsu multinational companies belonging to the developed countries are likely to dominate the 'global' economy that will emerge in the coming years.

3. TRIMs. According to Muchkund Debey, the develop countries achieved almost everything they wanted from the TRIMs Agreement. In order to make the agreement balanced from the point of view of the developing countries, it was necessary to formulate international rules for controlling restrictive business practices of foreign investors. However, the TRIMs Agreement is totally silent on this vital question and is concerned mainly with provisions for elimination of trade related investment measures which are designed to protect the interest of foreign investors in the developing countries.

4. Services. There is a vast level of difference in the development of services like banking, insurance, telecommunications and shipping as between the developed countries and the developing countries. Therefore inclusion of trade in services is bound to benefit developed countries much more than the developing countries like India. In fact, the very inclusion of trade in services in Urugary Round negotiations was on persistent insistence of the developed countries who have all along been arguing that opening up of trade services is an important requirement for globalisation and development of world trade. Data indicate that the size of the world merket for services was $ 1000 billion in 1993 of which the share of the developed countries was as high as $ 950 billion or 95 per cent. Thus developing countries had only a share of 5 per cent in world trade of services in 1993. The principal exporters of services are the USA, France, Japan and Netherlands in that order and together they account for about 60 per cent share of the world trade in services. It is these countries that will benefit most from the new agreement on services as arrived at in the Uruguay Round and the share of the developing countries will decline further. As far as India is concerned, services sector is not as underdeveloped as in many other developing countries. Yet, in terms of the new Agreement, it will be required to denationalise insurance and backing. Thus the banking sector way not be able to play a positive social role as it has been playing since 1969 when 14 major banks were nationalised Foreign firms will now be free to expand their network in the Indian services sector. They will also be free to remit resources to their parent country in the form of profits, interest, royalties etc. All this will involve a foreign exchange burden on India. As far as Indian firms are concerned, they will find it difficult to compete with the firms supplying services in the developed countries. Thus it will not be an easy task for them to penetrate the services sector in developed countries.

5. Most of developed countries impose non-tariff barriers (NTBs) in the form of protectionist policies against Indian exports. Although pressures are being mounting on India by the developed countries via the WTO to dismantle NTBs in view of the improvement in balance of payments and foreign exchange reserves, they themselves continue to impose NTBs on India. The report on NTBs prepared by

the trade policy division of the Union Commerce ministry sometimes ago identifies 13 different non-tariff barriers put up by 16 countries against India. The report finds that as far as textile exports are concerned, the MFA (multi-fibre arrangement) put up by the USA and European Union is a major barrier. As far as agricultural exports are concerned, NTBs in this category include import alert on shirmps by the USA, EU regulations on fish products, Saudi Arabian ban on frozen fish and products, ban on use of pesticides in mangoes, bananas, grapes and potatoes, sales tax discrimination by Austrialia, restrictions on tea by EU and Japan, on sesame, tabocco and cutflowers by use of human rights issues like child labour by US, Canada and EU, constant threat of Special 301 against drugs and pharmaceuticals exports by the US, use of standard specifications and export subsidies as NTBs and stalling movement of personnel from India.

6. The creation of WTO will lead to a substantial and continuous erosion of the authority and jurisdiction of the nation-States. The entire spectrum of intellectual property rights (IPRs) has been lifted out of the national domain and subjected to a rigorous international discipline. The trade in services has been defined in an open-ended manner so as to bring within the ambit of GATS (General Agreement on Trade in Services), any and every possible activity except the essential law making policing and judical functions of the State. The National investment regimes will similarly be subject to the international discipline as land down under TRIMs.

PATENTS LAW IN INDIA

The patent system in India is governed by the Indian Patents Act, 1970. This act which replaced the Indian patents and designs act, 1911, came into force on and from 20th April 1972.

According to this act:

(i) Patents are granted to encourage inventions and to secure that the invention are worked in India on a commercial scale and to the fullest extent that is reasonably practicable without undue delay; and

(ii) patents are not granted merely to enable patentees to enjoy a monopoly for their importation of the patented article.

Under the Indian patents act, the term of a patent has been limited to 14 years from the date of the patent except in cases like food, drug and medicine where the term is seven years from the date of filling the complete specification or 5 years from the date of sealing of a patent, whichever is shorter.

Further, patentability of inventions relating to substances intended for use as food, drug or medicines, or substances by chemcial processes, is limited to the claim for the methods or process of manufacture only. In other words, claims for the substances themselves, such as chemical substances, food drugs, alloys, optical glass, semi-conductors and inermetallic compounds are not allowable in a patent application.

A patent is granted subject to the right of the government to import or make any patented article or use and patented process for the purpose of its own use, or distribution in the prescribed dispensaries, hospitals or other medical institutions.

Further, the patent grant is also subject to the condition that any person may make patented article or use patented process for the purpose merely of experiment or research including the imparting of instructions to pupils.

The patentee is expected to make sufficient availability of the product to the public at reasonable prices. If this requirement is not satisfied, any person interested may apply for compulsory licence after three years from the date of sealing of a patent. The following factors are considered by the controller of patents for grant of such lincence:

(i) the nature of the invention, time elapsed since sealing of patent and measures already taken by the patentee or licensee to make full use of the invention;

(ii) the ability of the applicant to work the invention to the public advantage; and

(iii) the applicant's capacity to undertake risk in providing capital and working the invention.

Section 84 of the act, thus provides for some safeguard against the monopoly abuse of the patent right.

The royalty payable in respect of the compulsory licence will depend upon the nature of the invention and the expenditure incurred by the patentee

It has also been provided that any person interested can have a licence as of right from the patentee on mutually agreed terms.

A patent may be revoked by the controller of patents after the expiry of two years from the date of the grant of the first licence, or from data of the grant of the first licence in respect of a patent endorsed with the words "licences of right", on the request of the central government or any person interested on the ground that reasonable requirement of the public with respect to the patented invention has not been satisfied or that the patented invention is not available to the public at a reasonable price.

The act requires every patentee and licensee to furnish to the controller periodic statements as to the extent to which the patented invention has been worked on a commercial basis in India. Further, the controller is empowered to require as patentee or a licensee to furnish to him information or periodical statements as to the extent of commercial working of the invention in India.

The Indian patents act does not put, in general, any limitations or restrictions on foreigners in the matter of applying or obtaining patents in India. However, for the purpose of international arrangements it is provided that where any country does not accords to the citizens of India the same rights with respect to the grant of patents and protection of patents rights as it accords to its own nationals, no nationals of such country shall be entilled to any privilages under the Indian law.

❑